Principles of European Law
Study Group on a European Civil Code

Mandate Contracts

(PEL MC)

Principles of European Law
Study Group on a European Civil Code

Mandate Contracts
(PEL MC)

prepared by

Marco B.M. Loos
Odavia Bueno Díaz

with advice from the Advisory Council
and the Drafting Committee approved by the
Co-ordinating Group

Volume 10

To be cited as: PEL /*Loos, Bueno Díaz,* Mandate Contracts,
General Introduction, A, I
PEL /*Loos, Bueno Díaz,* Mandate Contracts, Chapter 1,
Article 1:101, Comments, A
PEL /*Loos, Bueno Díaz,* Mandate Contracts, Chapter 2,
Article 2:101, Nat. Notes, 1
PEL /*Loos, Bueno Díaz,* Mandate Contracts, Chapter 2,
Article 2:101, Comp. Notes, 1

OXFORD
UNIVERSITY PRESS

Great Clarendon Street, Oxford, OX2 6DP,
United Kingdom

Oxford University Press is a department of the University of Oxford.
It furthers the University's objective of excellence in research, scholarship,
and education by publishing worldwide. Oxford is a registered trade mark of
Oxford University Press in the UK and in certain other countries

© sellier european law publishers GmbH, Munich together with
Study Group on a European Civil Code 2013

The moral rights of the authors have been asserted

First Edition published in 2013
Impression: 1

Crown copyright material is reproduced under Class Licence
Number C01P0000148 with the permission of OPSI
and the Queen's Printer for Scotland

British Library Cataloguing in Publication Data
Data available

ISBN 978–0–19–956829–1

Printed and bound in Great Britain by
CPI Group (UK) Ltd, Croydon CR0 4YY

Foreword

The Study Group on a European Civil Code has taken upon itself the task of drafting common European principles for the most important aspects of the law of obligations and for certain parts of the law of property in moveables which are especially relevant for the functioning of the common market. It was founded in 1999 as a successor body to the Commission on European Contract Law, on whose work the Study Group has been building.

Both groups have undertaken to ascertain and formulate European standards of 'patrimonial' law for the Member States of the European Union. The Commission on European Contract has achieved this for the field of general contract law *(Lando and Beale* [eds.], Principles of European Contract Law, Parts I and II combined and revised, The Hague, 2000; *Lando/Clive/Prüm/Zimmermann* [eds.], Principles of European Contract Law Part III, The Hague, 2003). These Principles of European Contract Law (PECL) have been adopted with adjustments by the Study Group on a European Civil Code to take account of new developments and input from its research partners. The Study Group has itself dovetailed its principles with those of the PECL, extending their encapsulation of standards of patrimonial law in three directions: (i) by developing rules for specific types of contracts; (ii) by developing rules for extra-contractual obligations, i.e. the law of non-contractual liability arising out of damage caused to another (tort/delict), the law of unjustified enrichment, and the law of benevolent intervention in another's affairs *(negotiorum gestio);* and (iii) by developing rules for fundamental questions in the law on mobile assets – in particular transfer of ownership, security for credit, and trust.

The results of the research conducted by the Study Group on a European Civil Code seek to advance the process of Europeanisation of private law. We have undertaken this endeavour on our own personal initiative and merely present the results of a pan-European research project. It is a study in comparative law in so far as we have always taken care to identify the legal position in the Member States of the European Union and to set out the results of this research in the introductions and notes. That of course does not mean that we have only been concerned with documenting the pool of shared legal values or that we simply adopted the majority position among the legal systems where common ground was missing. Rather we have consistently striven to draw up "sound and fitting" principles, that is to say, we have also recurrently developed proposals and concepts for the further development of private law in Europe.

The working methods of the Commission on European Contract Law and the Study Group on a European Civil Code were likewise quite similar. The Study Group, however, has had the benefit of Working (or Research) Teams – groups of younger legal scholars under the supervision of a senior member of the Group (a Team Leader) which undertook the basic comparative legal research, developed the drafts for discussion and assembled the extensive material required for the notes. Furthermore, to each Working Team was allocated a consultative body – an Advisory Council. These bodies – deliberately kept small in the interests of efficiency – were formed from leading experts in the relevant field of law who are representative of the major European legal systems. The proposals drafted by the Working Teams and critically scrutinised and improved in a series of meetings by the respective Advisory Council were submitted for discussion on a revolving basis to the actual decision-making body of the Study Group on a European Civil Code, the Co-ordinating Group. Until June 2004 the Co-ordinating Group consisted of representatives from all the jurisdictions belonging to the EU immediately prior to its enlargement in Spring 2004 and in addition legal scholars from Estonia, Hungary, Norway, Poland, Slovenia and Switzerland. Representatives from the Czech Republic, Malta, Latvia, Lithuania and Slovakia joined us after the June meeting 2004 in Warsaw.

Besides its permanent members, other participants in the Co-ordinating Group with voting rights included all the Team Leaders and – when the relevant material was up for discussion – the members of the Advisory Council concerned. The results of the deliberations during the week-long sitting of the Co-ordinating Group were incorporated into the text of the Articles and the commentaries which returned to the agenda for the next meeting of the Co-ordinating Group (or the next but one depending on the work load of the Group and the Team affected). Each part of the project was the subject of debate on manifold occasions, some stretching over many years. Where a unanimous opinion could not be achieved, majority votes were taken. As far as possible the Articles drafted in English were translated into the other languages either by members of the Team or third parties commissioned for the purpose. The number of languages into which the Articles could be translated admittedly varies considerably from volume to volume. That is in part a consequence of the fact that not all Working Teams were equipped with the same measure of financial support. We also had to resign ourselves to the absence of a perfectly uniform editorial style. Our editing guidelines provided a common basis for scholarly publication, but at the margin had to accommodate preferences of individual teams. However, this should not cause the reader any problems in comprehension.

Work on this series of Principles of European Law had begun long before the European Commission published its Communication on European Contract Law (in 2001), its Action Plan for a more coherent European contract law (in 2003), and its follow-up Communication "European Contract Law and the revision of the *acquis:* the way forward" (in 2004). These documents for their part were published before we formed the Network of Excellence, together with other European research groups and institutions, which have been collaborating in the preparation of an Academic Common Frame of Reference with the support of funds from the European Community's Sixth Research Framework Programme. This network first published an outline edition of its research results: as a first step, in 2008, an interim outline edition *(von Bar/Clive/Schulte-Nölke et al.* [eds.], Principles, Definitions and Model Rules of European Private Law. Draft Common Frame of Reference (DCFR). Interim Outline Edition, Munich 2008); and, with revisions and additions, a final outline edition in 2009 *(von Bar/Clive/Schulte-Nölke et al.* [eds.], Principles, Definitions and Model Rules of European Private Law. Draft Common Frame of Reference (DCFR). Outline Edition, Munich 2009). A final and full edition was published later in 2009 *(von Bar/Clive,* Principles, Definitions and Model Rules of European Private Law. Draft Common Frame of Reference (DCFR). Full Edition, Munich 2009). The texts laid before the public by the Study Group on a European Civil Code are integrated in these latter texts. However, the extensive comparative law introductions and the translations of the articles of the Book or Part concerned into the other languages of the Member States are only being published in the PEL Series. Moreover, there are occasionally small discrepancies between the model rules published in this series and those of the Draft Common Frame of Reference because each publication within the PEL Series is conceived and prepared as a self-contained treatment of the field while in the consolidated composite DCFR text certain provisions could be trimmed. Repetitions could be avoided. It was also possible to respond to criticism which had been made of the model rules in the PEL Series and which had convinced us of the need to make changes.

In order to leave no room for misunderstanding, it is important to stress that these Principles have been prepared by impartial and independent-minded scholars whose sole interest has been a devotion to the subject-matter. None of us have been rewarded for taking part or mandated to do so. None of us would want to give the impression that we claim any political legitimation for promoting harmonisation of the law. Our legitimation is confined to curiosity and an interest in Europe. In other words, the volumes in this series are to be understood exclusively as the results of scholarly legal research within large international teams. Like every other scholarly legal work, they restate the current law and introduce possible models for its further development; no less, but also no more. We are not a homogenous group whose every member is an advocate of the idea of a European Civil Code. We are, after all, only a *Study* Group. The question whether a European Civil Code is or is not desirable is a political one to which each member can only express an individual view.

Osnabrück, September 2012   *Christian von Bar*

Our Sponsors and Donors

The project of the Study Group on a European Civil Code represents a research endeavour in legal science of extraordinary magnitude. Without the generous financial support of many organisations and individuals its realisation would not have been possible.

Our thanks go first of all to the *Deutsche Forschungsgemeinschaft (DFG)*, which has supplied the lion's share of the financing for the first phase of this project, including the salaries of the Working Teams based in Germany and the direct travel costs for the meetings of the Coordinating Group and the numerous Advisory Councils. The work of the Dutch Working Teams was financed by the *Nederlandse Organisatie voor Wetenschappelijk Onderzoek (NWO)*. Further personnel costs were met by the Flemish *Fonds voor Wetenschappelijk Onderzoek-Vlaanderen (FWO)*, the *Onassis-Foundation*, the Austrian *Fonds zur Förderung der wissenschaftlichen Forschung*, *Norges forskningsråd* (the Research Council of Norway) and the *Fundação Calouste Gulbenkian*. From the middle of 2005 funds were made available to us under the mantle of the 'CoPECL' Network of Excellence established under the European Union's Sixth Framework Programme for Research and Technological Development.

The work of the Austrian working team was financed by the Austrian *Fonds zur Förderung der wissenschaftlichen Forschung* (FWF) and the European Commission's Sixth Framework Program for Research and technological Development.

In addition we have consistently been able to fall back on funds made available to the respective organisers of the eighteen week long sittings of the Coordinating Group by the relevant university or other sources within the country concerned. It is therefore with the deepest gratitude that I must also mention the *Consiglio nazionale forense* (Rome) and the *Istituto di diritto privato* of the *Università di Roma La Sapienza,* which co-financed the meeting in Rome (June 2000), which followed our inaugural meeting in Utrecht (December 1999). The session in Salzburg (December 2000) was supported by the Austrian *Bundesministerium für Bildung, Wissenschaft und Kultur,* the *Universität Salzburg* and the *Institut für Rechtspolitik* of the *Universität Salzburg.* The discussions in Stockholm (June 2001) were assisted by the *Department of Law, Stockholm University,* the *Supreme Court Justice Edward Cassel's Foundation* and *Stiftelsen Juridisk Fakultetslitteratur (SJF).* The meeting in Oxford (December 2001) had the support of *Shearman & Sterling,* the *Hulme Trust, Berwin Leighton Paisner* and the *Oxford University Press (OUP).* The session in Valencia (June 2002) was made possible by the *Asociación Nacional de Registradores de la Propiedad, Mercantil y Bienes Muebles,* the *Universitat de València,* the *Ministerio Español de Ciencia y Tecnología,* the *Facultad de Derecho* of the *Universitat de València,* the *Departamento de Derecho Internacional, Departamento de Derecho Civil* and the *Departamento de Derecho Mercantil "Manuel Broseta Pont"* of the *Universitat de València,* the law firm *Cuatrecasas,* the *Generalitat Valenciana,* the *Corts Valencianes,* the *Diputación Provincial de Valencia,* the *Ayuntamiento de Valencia,* the *Colegio de Abogados de Valencia* and *Aran-*

zadi *Publishing Company*. The subsequent meeting in Oporto (December 2002) was substantially assisted by the *Universidade Católica Portuguesa – Centro Regional do Porto*. For the week long session in Helsinki (June 2003) we were able to rely on funds from *Suomen Kultuurirahasto* (Finnish Cultural Foundation), the *Niilo Helanderin Säätiö* (Niilo Helander Foundation), the *Suomalainen Lakimeisyhdistys* (Finnish Lawyers Association), the *Ministry of Justice* and the *Ministry for Foreign Affairs*, the *Nordea Bank, Roschier Holmberg* Attorneys Ltd., *Hannes Snellman* Attorneys Ltd., the *Department of Private Law* and the *Institute of International Commercial Law (KATTI) of Helsinki University*. The session in Leuven (December 2003) was supported by *Katholieke Universiteit Leuven, Faculteit Rechtsgeleerdheid,* and the *FWO* Vlaanderen Fonds voor Wetenschappelijk Onderzoek (Flanders Scientific Research Fund). The meeting of the Group in Warsaw (June 2004) was substantially assisted by the *Fundacja Fundusz Wspolpracy* (The Cooperation Fund) and the *Faculty of Law and Administration of Warsaw University*. The meeting in Milan (December 2004) was supported by the *Università Bocconi* and its *Istituto di diritto comparato,* by the Milan *Camera di Commercio,* by the *Associazione Civilisti Italiani* and by the *Comune di Milano*. The meeting in Berlin (June 2005) was made possible by *PricewaterhouseCoopers Deutschland AG,* Frankfurt/Berlin; *Sievert AG & Co.,* Osnabrück, and by *Verband deutscher Hypothekenbanken e.V., Berlin*. The meeting in Tartu (December 2005) was supported by the *University of Tartu,* its *Faculty of Law,* its *Institute of Law* and its *Institute of Private Law,* by the *Estonian Supreme Court,* the *Ministry of Justice,* the *Tartu City Government, Iuridicum Foundation,* the Law Offices *Concordia, Lepik & Luhaäär, Luiga Mody Hääl Borenius, Ots & Co, Aivar Pilv, Aare Raig, Raidla & Partners, Sorainen, Tark & Co, Teder Glikman & Partners, Paul Varul, Alvin Rödl & Partner* and *Lextal Law Firm*. The meeting in Oslo (June 2006) was made possible by the *kongelige Justis- og Politidepartement* (The Royal Ministry of Justice), by *Sigvald Bergesen d. y.,* by *hustru Nankis Almennyttige stiftelse, Storebrand* and the law firms *Wiersholm and BA-HR.* The meeting in Lucerne (December 2006) was sponsored by *Schulthess Publishing Company,* by *Schweizerischer Nationalfonds* and by the *Universität Luzern,* the meeting in Budapest (June 2007) by *Eötvös Loránd Tudományegyetem* (Eötvös Loránd University), by *Magyar Tudományos Akadémia* (the Hungarian Academy of Sciences), by *MOL* Magyar Olaj- és Gázipari Nyrt (the Hungarian Oil & Gas Company) and by *Szalma & Partnerei Ügyvédi Iroda* (Szalma & Partners Attorneys at Law), and the meeting in Prague (December 2007) by *Česká advokátní komora* (the Czech Bar Association), *White & Case* Prague, *Squire, Sanders & Dempsey,* Prague, *Ladislav Krym,* Attorney at Law, Prague, *Jan Brož,* Attorney at Law, Prague and the *Representation of the European Commission in Prague*. Our final meeting in Athens (June 2008) had the support of the *Stavros Niarchos Foundation,* the *National and Kapodistrian University of Athens,* the *Union of Greek Civil Law Jurists* and the *Municipality of Athens*. We thank all of these organisations and institutions for the funds which they made available to us and for the extraordinary warmth of hospitality with which our hosts received us.

Osnabrück, September 2012   *Christian von Bar*

Preface to this volume

These Principles were developed to be included in the Draft Common Frame of Reference (DCFR). They were intended to fill a gap that existed in the works of the Working Team on Commercial Agency, Franchising and Distribution Contracts – of which Odavia Bueno Díaz was a member – and those of the Working Team on Service Contracts – of which I was a member, and in the Principles of European Contract Law (PECL). The PECL contain provisions on representation, dealing with the effects of contracts concluded in the name and on behalf of another party, but do not contain any specific rules governing the internal relationship between the party that is being represented (the principal) and the party representing the principal (the agent). Similarly, the Principles on Commercial Agency, Franchising and Distribution Contracts (included in the DCFR as Book IV.E) more or less presuppose specific provisions on mandate contracts. The Principles on Service Contracts (included in the DCFR as Book IV.C) contain some rules that could be applied to the relationship between the principal and the agent, but these Principles were not developed with this relationship in mind. The relation between these Principles on Mandate Contracts and the DCFR is further explained in Section III of the General Introduction of this Book. In the preceding Section II the relation between these Principles and the Principles of European Law on Service Contracts is explained.

The Working Team on Mandate Contracts, consisting only of Odavia and me, started its work in the spring of 2005, when the volumes on Commercial Agency, Franchising and Distribution Contracts and on Service Contracts were still being developed (the first of these was published in 2006, the second in 2007). It soon became clear that the Working Team would be under a lot of pressure to produce results quickly – the Interim Outline Edition of the DCFR ultimately was published already in 2008, which implied that the major part of the work – consisting of the development of the national reports and the construction on the basis thereof of the major policy choices to be taken and the development of the Articles to be included in the DCFR – would have to be finished as early as the end of 2007 (although the final preparation of this volume would take significantly more time).

Given the time pressure, we were very fortunate to receive the help of the national reporters and, at a later stage, the advisors to prepare our drafts. Both the national reporters and the advisors were willing to come to Amsterdam for extensive discussions on these drafts and the policy decisions that needed to be presented to the Coordinating Committee of the Study Group on a European Civil Code. We are indebted to them for their valuable and generous help. Thanks also go out to Kristen Zetzsche of International Writers for checking the English texts (any remaining errors of course are our responsibility), to my (former) assistants Anouk de Morree, Lotte van der Laan, Daniela Baidoo and Esmée Hoogenkamp for their assistance throughout the project, and to Justus Könkkölä, Michel Séjean, Martin Schmidt-Kessel and Christina Dierks, Cecilia Carrara and Adele Pascale, Monika Jurčová and Marianna Novotná, and Jeanette Andersson for the Finnish, French, German, Italian, Slovak, and Swedish translations of the Principles. The Dutch and Spanish translations were obviously prepared by us.

Amsterdam, September 2012   *Marco Loos*

Short Table of Contents

Table of contents

Principles of European Law on
Mandate Contracts

General Introduction

Chapter 1: **General provisions**

Article 1:101: **Scope**

Comments

Comparative Notes

Chapter 2: **Main obligations of the principal**

Article 2:101: **Obligation to co-operate**

Article 2:102: **Price**

Article 2:103: **Expenses incurred by the agent**   218

Chapter 3: **Performance by the agent**

Section 1: **Main obligations of the agent**

Article 3:101: **Obligation to act in accordance with mandate**

Article 3:102: **Obligation to act in interests of the principal**

Article 3:103: **Obligation of skill and care**   256

Section 2: **Consequences of acting beyond mandate**

Article 3:201: **Acting beyond mandate**

Chapter 4: **Directions and changes**

Section 1: **Directions**

Article 4:101: **Directions given by the principal**

Article 4:102: **Request for a direction**

Article 4:103: **Consequences of failure to give a direction**

Chapter 5: **Conflicts of interests**

Article 5:101: **Self-contracting**

Article 5:102: **Double mandate**

Chapter 6: **Termination by notice other than for non-performance**

Article 6:101: **Termination by notice in general**

Article 6:104: **Termination by the agent when relationship is to last for indefinite period or when it is gratuitous**

Chapter 7: **Other grounds for termination**

Article 7:101: **Death of the principal**

Article 7:102: **Death of the agent**

Annexes

Text of Articles

English
Mandate Contracts

Chapter 1:
General provisions

Article 1:101: Scope
(1) These Principles apply to contracts and other juridical acts under which a person, the agent, is authorised and instructed (mandated) by another person, the principal:
  (a) to conclude a contract between the principal and a third party or otherwise directly affect the legal position of the principal in relation to a third party;
  (b) to conclude a contract with a third party, or do another juridical act in relation to a third party, on behalf of the principal but in such a way that the agent and not the principal is a party to the contract or other juridical act; or
  (c) to take steps which are meant to lead to, or facilitate, the conclusion of a contract between the principal and a third party or the doing of another juridical act which would affect the legal position of the principal in relation to a third party.
(2) These Principles apply where the agent undertakes to act on behalf of, and in accordance with the instructions of, the principal and, with appropriate adaptations, where the agent is merely authorised but does not undertake to act, but nevertheless does act.
(3) These Principles apply where the agent is to be paid a price and, with appropriate adaptations, where the agent is not to be paid a price.
(4) These Principles apply only to the internal relationship between the principal and the agent (the mandate relationship). They do not apply to the relationship between the principal and the third party or the relationship (if any) between the agent and the third party.
(5) Contracts to which these Principles apply and to which the Principles of European Law on Service Contracts also apply are to be regarded as falling primarily under these Principles.
(6) These Principles do not apply to contracts pertaining to investment services and activities as defined by Directive 2004/39/EC, OJ L 145/1, as subsequently amended or replaced.

Article 1:102: Definitions
In these Principles;
(a) the 'mandate' of the agent is the authorisation and instruction given by the principal as modified by any subsequent direction;
(b) the 'mandate contract' is the contract under which the agent is authorised and instructed to act, and any reference to the mandate contract includes a reference to any other juridical act by which the agent is authorised and instructed to act;
(c) the 'prospective contract' is the contract the agent is authorised and instructed to conclude, negotiate or facilitate, and any reference to the prospective contract includes a reference to any other juridical act which the agent is authorised and instructed to do, negotiate or facilitate;

(d) a mandate for direct representation is a mandate under which the agent is to act in the name of the principal, or otherwise in such a way as to indicate an intention to affect the principal's legal position;

(e) a mandate for indirect representation is a mandate under which the agent is to act in the agent's own name or otherwise in such a way as not to indicate an intention to affect the principal's legal position;

(f) a 'direction' is a decision by the principal pertaining to the performance of the obligations under the mandate contract or to the contents of the prospective contract that is given at the time the mandate contract is concluded or, in accordance with the mandate, at a later moment;

(g) the 'third party' is the party with whom the prospective contract is to be concluded, negotiated or facilitated by the agent;

(h) the 'revocation' of the mandate of the agent is the recall by the principal of the mandate, so that it no longer has effect.

Article 1:103: Duration of the mandate contract

A mandate contract may be concluded
(a) for an indefinite period of time;
(b) for a fixed period; or
(c) for a particular task.

Article 1:104: Revocation of the mandate

(1) Unless the following Article applies, the mandate of the agent can be revoked by the principal at any time by giving notice to the agent.

(2) The termination of the mandate relationship has the effect of a revocation of the mandate of the agent.

(3) The parties may not, to the detriment of the principal, exclude the application of this Article or derogate from or vary its effects, unless the requirements of the following Article are met.

Article 1:105: Irrevocable mandate

(1) In derogation of the preceding Article, the mandate of the agent cannot be revoked by the principal if the mandate is given:
  (a) in order to safeguard a legitimate interest of the agent other than the interest in the payment of the price; or
  (b) in the common interest of the parties to another legal relationship, whether or not these parties are all parties to the mandate contract, and the irrevocability of the mandate of the agent is meant to properly safeguard the interest of one or more of these parties.

(2) The mandate may nevertheless be revoked if:
  (a) the mandate is irrevocable under paragraph (1)(a) and:
    (i) the contractual relationship from which the legitimate interest of the agent originates is terminated for non-performance by the agent; or
    (ii) there is a fundamental non-performance by the agent of the obligations under the mandate contract; or

      (iii) there is an extraordinary and serious reason for the principal to terminate under Article 6:103 (Termination by the principal for extraordinary and serious reason); or

(b) the mandate is irrevocable under paragraph (1)(b) and:

    (i) the parties in whose interest the mandate is irrevocable have agreed to the revocation of the mandate;

    (ii) the relationship referred to in paragraph (1)(b) is terminated;

    (iii) the agent commits a fundamental non-performance of the obligations under the mandate contract, provided that the agent is replaced without undue delay by another agent in conformity with the terms regulating the legal relationship between the principal and the other party or parties; or

    (iv) there is an extraordinary and serious reason for the principal to terminate under Article 6:103 (Termination by the principal for extraordinary and serious reason), provided that the agent is replaced without undue delay by another agent in conformity with the terms regulating the legal relationship between the principal and the other party or parties.

(3) Where the revocation of the mandate is not allowed under this Article, a notice of revocation is without effect.

(4) This Article does not apply if the mandate relationship is terminated under Chapter 7 of these Principles.

Chapter 2:
Main obligations of the principal

Article 2:101: Obligation to co-operate
The obligation to co-operate under Article 1:202 PECL (Duty to Co-operate) requires the principal in particular to:

(a) answer requests by the agent for information in so far as such information is needed to allow the agent to perform the obligations under the mandate contract;

(b) give a direction regarding the performance of the obligations under the mandate contract in so far as this is required under the mandate contract or follows from a request for a direction under Article 4:102 (Request for direction).

Article 2:102: Price
(1) The principal must pay a price if the agent performs the obligations under the mandate contract in the course of a business, unless the principal expected and could reasonably have expected the agent to perform the obligations otherwise than in exchange for a price.

(2) The price is payable when the mandated task has been completed and the agent has given account of that to the principal.

(3) If the parties had agreed on payment of a price for services rendered, the mandate relationship has terminated and the mandated task has not been completed, the price is payable as of the moment the agent has given account of the performance of the obligations under the mandate contract.

(4) When the mandate is for the conclusion of a prospective contract and the principal has concluded the prospective contract directly or another person appointed by the principal

has concluded the prospective contract on the principal's behalf, the agent is entitled to the price or a proportionate part of it if the conclusion of the prospective contract can be attributed in full or in part to the agent's performance of the obligations under the mandate contract.

(5) When the mandate is for the conclusion of a prospective contract and the prospective contract is concluded after the mandate relationship has terminated, the principal must pay the price if payment of a price based solely on the conclusion of the prospective contract was agreed and
  (a) the conclusion of the prospective contract is mainly the result of the agent's efforts; and
  (b) the prospective contract is concluded within a reasonable period after the mandate relationship has terminated.

Article 2:103: Expenses incurred by the agent
(1) When the agent is entitled to a price, the price is presumed to include the reimbursement of the expenses the agent has incurred in the performance of the obligations under the mandate contract.
(2) When the agent is not entitled to a price or when the parties have agreed that the expenses will be paid separately, the principal must reimburse the agent for the expenses the agent has incurred in the performance of the obligations under the mandate contract, when and in so far as the agent acted reasonably when incurring the expenses.
(3) The agent is entitled to reimbursement of expenses under paragraph (2) as from the time when the expenses are incurred and the agent has given account of the expenses.
(4) If the mandate relationship has terminated and the result on which the agent's remuneration is dependent is not achieved, the agent is entitled to reimbursement of reasonable expenses the agent has incurred in the performance of the obligations under the mandate contract. Paragraph (3) applies accordingly.

Chapter 3:
Performance by the agent
Section 1:
Main obligations of the agent

Article 3:101: Obligation to act in accordance with mandate
At all stages of the mandate relationship the agent must act in accordance with the mandate.

Article 3:102: Obligation to act in interests of the principal
(1) The agent must act in accordance with the interests of the principal, in so far as these have been communicated to the agent or the agent could reasonably be expected to be aware of them.
(2) Where the agent is not sufficiently aware of the principal's interests to enable the agent to properly perform the obligations under the mandate contract, the agent must request information from the principal.

Article 3:103: Obligation of skill and care

(1) The agent has an obligation to perform the obligations under the mandate contract with the care and skill that the principal is entitled to expect under the circumstances.

(2) If the agent professes a higher standard of care and skill the agent has an obligation to exercise that care and skill.

(3) If the agent is, or purports to be, a member of a group of professional agents for which standards exist that have been set by a relevant authority or by that group itself, the agent must exercise the care and skill expressed in these standards.

(4) In determining the care and skill the principal is entitled to expect, regard is to be had, among other things, to:
   (a) the nature, the magnitude, the frequency and the foreseeability of the risks involved in the performance of the obligations;
   (b) whether the obligations are performed by a non-professional or gratuitously;
   (c) the amount of the remuneration for the performance of the obligations; and
   (d) the time reasonably available for the performance of the obligations.

Section 2:
Consequences of acting beyond mandate

Article 3:201: Acting beyond mandate

(1) The agent may act in a way not covered by the mandate if:
   (a) the agent has reasonable ground for so acting on behalf of the principal;
   (b) the agent does not have a reasonable opportunity to discover the principal's wishes in the particular circumstances; and
   (c) the agent does not know and could not reasonably be expected to know that the act in the particular circumstances is against the principal's wishes.

(2) An act within paragraph (1) has the same consequences as between the agent and the principal as an act covered by the mandate.

Article 3:202: Consequences of ratification

Where, in circumstances not covered by the preceding Article, an agent has acted beyond the mandate in concluding a contract on behalf of the principal, ratification of that contract by the principal absolves the agent from liability to the principal, unless the principal without undue delay after ratification notifies the agent that the principal reserves remedies for the non-performance by the agent.

Section 3:
Mandate normally not exclusive

Article 3:301: Exclusivity not presumed

The principal is free to conclude, negotiate or facilitate the prospective contract directly or to appoint another agent to do so.

Article 3:302: Subcontracting

(1) The agent may subcontract or delegate the performance of the obligations under the mandate contract in whole or in part without the principal's consent, unless personal performance is required by the contract.
(2) Any subcontractor so engaged by the agent in the performance of the mandate contract must be of adequate competence.
(3) In accordance with Article 8:107 PECL (Performance entrusted to another) the agent remains responsible for performance.

Section 4:
Obligation to inform principal

Article 3:401: Information about progress of performance

During the performance of the obligations under the mandate contract the agent must in so far as is reasonable under the circumstances inform the principal of the existence of, and the progress in, the negotiations or other steps leading to the possible conclusion or facilitation of the prospective contract.

Article 3:402: Accounting to the principal

(1) The agent must without undue delay inform the principal of the completion of the mandated task.
(2) The agent must give an account to the principal:
    (a) of the manner in which the obligations under the mandate contract have been performed; and
    (b) of money spent or received or expenses incurred by the agent in performing those obligations.
(3) Paragraph (2) applies with appropriate modifications if the mandate relationship is terminated in accordance with Chapters 6 and 7 and the obligations under the mandate contract have not been fully performed.

Article 3:403: Communication of identity of third party

(1) An agent who concludes the prospective contract with a third party must communicate the name and address of the third party to the principal on the principal's demand.
(2) In the case of a mandate for indirect representation paragraph (1) applies only if the agent has become insolvent.

Chapter 4:
Directions and changes
Section 1:
Directions

Article 4:101: Directions given by the principal

(1) The principal is entitled to give directions to the agent.
(2) The agent must follow directions by the principal.

(3) The agent must warn the principal if the direction:
   (a) has the effect that the performance of the obligations under the mandate contract would become significantly more expensive or take significantly more time than agreed upon in the mandate contract; or
   (b) is inconsistent with the purpose of the mandate contract or may otherwise be detrimental to the interests of the principal.
(4) Unless the principal revokes the direction without undue delay after having been so warned by the agent, the direction is to be regarded as a change of the mandate contract under Article 4:201 (Change of mandate contract).

Article 4:102: Request for a direction
(1) The agent must ask for a direction on obtaining information which requires the principal to make a decision pertaining to the performance of the obligations under the mandate contract or the content of the prospective contract.
(2) The agent must ask for a direction if the mandated task is the conclusion of a prospective contract and the mandate contract does not determine whether the mandate is for direct representation or indirect representation.

Article 4:103: Consequences of failure to give a direction
(1) If the principal fails to give a direction when required to do so under the mandate contract or under paragraph (1) of Article 4:102 (Request for a direction), the agent may, in so far as relevant, resort to any of the remedies under Chapters 8 (Non-Performance and Remedies in general) and 9 (Particular Remedies for Non-Performance) PECL; or
   (a) base performance upon the expectations, preferences and priorities a person in the same situation as the principal may reasonably be expected to have, given the information and directions that have been gathered; and
   (b) claim a proportionate adjustment of the price and of the time allowed or required for the conclusion of the prospective contract.
(2) If the principal fails to give a direction under paragraph (2) of Article 4:102 (Request for a direction), the agent may choose direct representation or indirect representation or may withhold performance under Article 9:201 PECL (Right to Withhold Performance).
(3) The adjusted price that is to be paid under paragraph (1)(b) must be reasonable and is to be determined using the same methods of calculation as were used to establish the original price for the performance of the obligations under the mandate contract.

Article 4:104: No time to ask or wait for direction
(1) If the agent is required to ask for a direction under Article 4:102 (Request for a direction) but needs to act before being able to contact the principal and to ask for a direction, or needs to act before the direction is given, the agent may base performance upon the expectations, preferences and priorities the principal may reasonably be expected to have, given the information and directions that have been gathered.
(2) In the situation referred to in paragraph (1), the agent may claim a proportionate adjustment of the price and of the time allowed or required for the performance of the obligations under the mandate contract in so far as such an adjustment is reasonable given the circumstances of the case.

Section 2:
Changes of the mandate contract

Article 4:201: Changes of the mandate contract
(1) The mandate contract is changed if the principal:
    (a) significantly changes the mandate of the agent;
    (b) does not revoke a direction without undue delay after having been warned in accordance with paragraph (3) of Article 4:101 (Directions given by the principal).
(2) In the case of a change of the mandate contract under paragraph (1) the agent is entitled:
    (a) to a proportionate adjustment of the price and of the time allowed or required for the performance of the obligations under the mandate contract; or
    (b) to damages in accordance with Article 9:502 PECL (General Measure of Damages) to put the agent as nearly as possible into the position in which the agent would have been if the mandate contract had not been changed.
(3) In the case of a change of the mandate contract under paragraph (1) the agent may also terminate the mandate relationship by giving notice of termination for an extraordinary and serious reason under Article 6:105 (Termination by the agent for extraordinary and serious reason), unless the change is minor or is to the agent's advantage.
(4) The adjusted price that is to be paid under paragraph (2)(a) must be reasonable and is to be determined using the same methods of calculation as were used to establish the original price for the performance of the obligations under the mandate contract.

Chapter 5:
Conflicts of interests

Article 5:101: Self-contracting
(1) The agent may not become the principal's counterparty to the prospective contract.
(2) The agent may nevertheless become the counterparty if:
    (a) this is agreed by the parties in the mandate contract;
    (b) the agent has disclosed an intention to become the counterparty and
        (i) the principal subsequently expresses consent; or
        (ii) the principal does not object to the agent becoming the counterparty after having been requested to indicate consent or a refusal of consent;
    (c) the principal otherwise knew, or could reasonably be expected to have known, of the agent becoming the counterparty and the principal did not object within a reasonable time; or
    (d) the content of the prospective contract is so precisely determined in the mandate contract that there is no risk that the interests of the principal may be disregarded.
(3) If the principal is a consumer, the agent may only become the counterparty if:
    (a) the agent has disclosed that information and the principal has given express consent to the agent becoming the counterparty to the particular prospective contract; or
    (b) the content of the prospective contract is so precisely determined in the mandate contract that there is no risk that the interests of the principal may be disregarded.

(4) The parties may not, to the detriment of the principal, exclude the application of paragraph (3) or derogate from or vary its effects.

(5) If the agent has become the counterparty, the agent is not entitled to a price for services rendered as an agent.

Article 5:102: Double mandate

(1) The agent may not act as the agent of both the principal and the principal's counterparty to the prospective contract.

(2) The agent may nevertheless act as the agent of both the principal and the counterparty if:

(a) this is agreed by the parties in the mandate contract;

(b) the agent has disclosed an intention to act as the agent of the counterparty and the principal

(i) subsequently expresses consent; or

(ii) does not object to the agent acting as the agent of the counterparty after having been requested to indicate consent or a refusal of consent;

(c) the principal otherwise knew, or could reasonably be expected to have known, of the agent acting as the agent of the counterparty and the principal did not object within a reasonable time; or

(d) the content of the prospective contract is so precisely determined in the mandate contract that there is no risk that the interests of the principal may be disregarded.

(3) If the principal is a consumer, the agent may only act as the agent of both the principal and of the counterparty if:

(a) the agent has disclosed that information and the principal has given express consent to the agent acting also as the agent of the counterparty to the particular prospective contract; or

(b) the content of the prospective contract is so precisely determined in the mandate contract that there is no risk that the interests of the principal may be disregarded.

(4) The parties may not, to the detriment of the principal, exclude the application of paragraph (3) or derogate from or vary its effects.

(5) If and in so far as the agent has acted in accordance with the previous paragraphs, the agent is entitled to the price.

Chapter 6:
Termination by notice other than for non-performance

Article 6:101: Termination by notice in general

(1) Either party may terminate the mandate relationship at any time by giving notice to the other.

(2) For the purposes of paragraph (1), a revocation of the mandate of the agent is treated as termination.

(3) Termination of the mandate relationship is not effective if the mandate of the agent is irrevocable under Article 1:105 (Irrevocable mandate).

(4) The effects of termination are governed by Chapter 9, Section 3 PECL (Termination of the contract).

(5) When the party giving the notice was justified in terminating the relationship no damages are payable for so doing.

(6) When the party giving the notice was not justified in terminating the relationship, the termination is nevertheless effective but the other party is entitled to damages in accordance with the rules in Chapter 9, Section 5 PECL (Damages and interest).

(7) For the purposes of this Article the party giving the notice is justified in terminating the relationship if that party:

  (a) was entitled to terminate the relationship under the express terms of the contract and observed any requirements laid down in the contract for doing so;

  (b) was entitled to terminate the relationship under Chapter 9, Section 3 PECL (Termination of the contract); or

  (c) was entitled to terminate the relationship under any other Article of the present Chapter and observed any requirements laid down in such Article for doing so.

Article 6:102: Termination by the principal when relationship is to last for indefinite period or when mandate is for a particular task

(1) The principal may terminate the mandate relationship at any time by giving notice of reasonable length if the mandate contract has been concluded for an indefinite period or for a particular task.

(2) Paragraph (1) does not apply if the mandate is irrevocable.

(3) The parties may not, to the detriment of the principal, exclude the application of this Article or derogate from or vary its effects, unless the conditions set out under Article 1:105 (Irrevocable mandate) are met.

Article 6:103: Termination by the principal for extraordinary and serious reason

(1) The principal may terminate the mandate relationship by giving notice for extraordinary and serious reason.

(2) No period of notice is required.

(3) For the purposes of this Article, the death or incapacity of the person who, at the time of conclusion of the mandate contract, the parties had intended to perform the agent's obligations under the mandate contract, constitutes an extraordinary and serious reason.

(4) This Article applies with appropriate adaptations if the successors of the principal terminate the mandate relationship in accordance with Article 7:101 (Death of the principal).

(5) The parties may not, to the detriment of the principal or the principal's successors, exclude the application of this Article or derogate from or vary its effects.

Article 6:104: Termination by the agent when relationship is to last for indefinite period or when it is gratuitous

(1) The agent may terminate the mandate relationship at any time by giving notice of reasonable length if the mandate contract has been concluded for an indefinite period.

(2) The agent may terminate the mandate relationship by giving notice of reasonable length if the agent is to represent the principal otherwise than in exchange for a price.

(3) The parties may not, to the detriment of the agent, exclude the application of paragraph (1) of this Article or derogate from or vary its effects.

Article 6:105: Termination by the agent for extraordinary and serious reason

(1) The agent may terminate the mandate relationship by giving notice for extraordinary and serious reason.
(2) No period of notice is required.
(3) For the purposes of this Article an extraordinary and serious reason includes:
    (a) a change of the mandate contract under Article 4:201 (Changes of the mandate contract);
    (b) the death or incapacity of the principal; and
    (c) the death or incapacity of the person who, at the time of conclusion of the mandate contract, the parties had intended to perform the agent's obligations under the mandate contract.
(4) The parties may not, to the detriment of the agent, exclude the application of this Article or derogate from or vary its effects.

Chapter 7:
Other grounds for termination

Article 7:101: Death of the principal

(1) The death of the principal does not end the mandate relationship.
(2) Both the agent and the successors of the principal may terminate the mandate relationship by giving notice of termination for extraordinary and serious reason under Article 6:103 (Termination by the principal for extraordinary and serious reason) or Article 6:105 (Termination by the agent for extraordinary and serious reason).

Article 7:102: Death of the agent

(1) The death of the agent ends the mandate relationship.
(2) The expenses and any other payments due at the time of death remain payable.

Dutch*
Lastgevingsovereenkomsten

Hoofdstuk 1:
Algemene Bepalingen

Artikel 1:101: Toepassingsgebied

(1) Deze Beginselen zijn van toepassing op overeenkomsten en andere rechtshandelingen op grond waarvan een persoon, de lasthebber, bevoegd en verplicht (gemandateerd) is door een andere persoon, de lastgever:

    (a) om een overeenkomst te sluiten tussen de lastgever en een derde of op een andere manier de juridische positie van de lastgever ten opzichte van een derde rechtstreeks te raken;

    (b) om een overeenkomst te sluiten met een derde, of een andere rechtshandeling ten opzichte van een derde te verrichten, ten behoeve van de lastgever maar op zodanige wijze dat de lasthebber en niet de lastgever is partij is bij de overeenkomst of de andere rechtshandeling; of

    (c) om stappen te zetten die bedoeld zijn om te leiden tot de sluiting van een overeenkomst tussen de lastgever en een derde of de sluiting van een dergelijke overeenkomst mogelijk te maken, of het verrichten van een andere rechtshandeling die de juridische situatie van de lastgever ten opzichte van een derde zou raken.

(2) Deze Beginselen zijn van toepassing wanneer de lasthebber de taak op zich neemt om ten behoeve en overeenkomstig de aanwijzingen van de lastgever en, voor zover nodig in aangepaste vorm, wanneer de lasthebber slechts bevoegd maar niet verplicht is om te handelen, maar daar wel toe overgaat.

(3) Deze Beginselen zijn van toepassing wanneer de lasthebber een prijs voor zijn werkzaamheden ontvangt en, voor zover nodig in aangepaste vorm, wanneer de lasthebber om niet handelt.

(4) Deze Beginselen zijn uitsluitend van toepassing op de interne relatie tussen de lastgever en de lasthebber (de lastgevingsrelatie). Zij zijn niet van toepassing op de relatie tussen de lastgever en de derde of de relatie (voor zover deze bestaat) tussen de lasthebber en de derde.

(5) Overeenkomsten waar deze Beginselen op van toepassing zijn en waarop ook de Beginselen van Europees Recht inzake Dienstverleningsovereenkomsten van toepassing zijn, worden beschouwd als voornamelijk onder deze Beginselen vallend.

(6) Deze Beginselen zijn niet van toepassing op overeenkomsten betreffende investeringsdiensten en activiteiten als omschreven in Richtlijn 2004/39/EG, Pub. EG L 145/1, zoals deze sindsdien gewijzigd of vervangen is.

---

* Translated by Prof. Dr. *Marco B.M. Loos*, University of Amsterdam.

Artikel 1:102: Definities

In deze Beginselen betekent:

(a) de 'last van de lasthebber', de bevoegdheid en instructie zoals verleend door de lastgever en gewijzigd bij een volgende aanwijzing;

(b) de 'lastgevingsovereenkomst' de overeenkomst op grond waarvan de lasthebber bevoegd en verplicht is om te handelen, en iedere verwijzing naar de lastgevingsovereenkomst wordt tevens verstaan als een verwijzing naar een andere rechtshandeling op grond waarvan de lasthebber bevoegd en verplicht is tot handelen;

(c) de 'beoogde overeenkomst' is de overeenkomst die de lasthebber bevoegd en verplicht is te sluiten, te onderhandelen of mogelijk te maken, en iedere verwijzing naar de beoogde overeenkomst wordt tevens verstaan als en iedere verwijzing naar een andere rechtshandeling die de lasthebber bevoegd en verplicht is te verrichten, te onderhandelen of mogelijk te maken;

(d) een last tot directe vertegenwoordiging is een last waarbij de lasthebber gehouden is te handelen in naam van de lastgever, of op een andere manier waarbij duidelijk wordt gemaakt dat beoogd wordt de juridische positie van de lastgever te raken;

(e) een last tot middellijke vertegenwoordiging is een last waarbij de lasthebber gehouden is te handelen in eigen naam of op een andere manier warbij duidelijk wordt gemaakt dat beoogd wordt de juridische positie van de lastgever niet te raken;

(f) een 'aanwijzing' is een beslissing van de lastgever betreffende de uitvoering van de verplichtingen op grond van de lastgevingsovereenkomst of met betrekking tot de inhoud van de beoogde overeenkomst welke gegeven is ten tijde van de sluiting van de lastgevingsovereenkomst of, overeenkomstig de overeenkomst, op een later tijdstip;

(g) de 'derde' is de partij met wie de beoogde overeenkomst gesloten of onderhandeld moet worden door de lasthebber of met wie het sluiten van een dergelijke overeenkomst mogelijk gemaakt moet worden door de lasthebber;

(h) de 'herroeping' van de last van de lasthebber is het beëindigen van de last door de lastgever, zodat de last niet langer geldt.

Artikel 1:103: Duur van de lastgevingsovereenkomst

Een lastgevingsovereenkomst kan worden gesloten

(a) voor onbepaalde tijd;

(b) voor bepaalde tijd; of

(c) voor de uitvoering van een bijzondere taak.

Artikel 1:104: Herroeping van de last

(1) Tenzij het hiernavolgende Artikel van toepassing is, kan de last van de lasthebber te allen tijde door de lastgever worden herroepen door daarvan kennisgeving te doen aan de lasthebber.

(2) De opzegging van de lastgevingsrelatie heeft het effect van een herroeping van de last van de lasthebber.

(3) De partijen kunnen niet ten nadele van de lastgever de werking van dit Artikel uitsluiten of afwijken van de gevolgen ervan, tenzij aan de vereisten van het volgende Artikel is voldaan.

Artikel 1:105: Onherroepelijke last

(1) In afwijking van het vorige Artikel kan de last van de lasthebber niet door de lastgever worden herroepen indien de last is gegeven:

    (a) ten einde legitimiem belang van de lasthebber zeker te stellen dat in iets anders bestaat dan zijn belang in de betaling van de prijs; of

    (b) in het gemeenschappelijk belang van de partijen bij een andere juridische relatie, ongeacht of deze partijen alle partij zijn bij de lastgevingsovereenkomst, en de onherroepelijkheid van de last van de lasthebber bedoeld is om het belang van een of meer van deze partijen zeker te stellen.

(2) De last kan desalniettemin worden herroepen indien:

    (a) de last onherroepelijk is op grond van lid (1)(a) en:

        (i) de contractuele relatie waaruit het legitieme belang van de lasthebber voortkomt, ontbonden is wegens wanprestatie door de lasthebber; orf

        (ii) er sprake is van een wezenlijke tekortkoming door de lasthebber in de nakoming van zijn verplichtingen op grond van de lastgevingsovereenkomst; of

        (iii) er sprake is van een buitengewone en ernstige reden voor de lastgever om de overeenkomst op te zeggen op grond van Artikel 6:103 (Opzegging door de lastgever vanwege een buitengewone en ernstige reden); of

    (b) de last onherroepelijk is op grond van lid (1)(b) en:

        (i) de partijen in wier belang de last onherroepelijk is, met de herroeping van de last hebben ingestemd;

        (ii)) de relatie waarnaar in lid (1)(b) wordt verwezen, geëindigd is;

        (iii) de lasthebber een wezenlijke tekortkoming pleegt bij de nakoming van de verplichtingen op grond van de lastgevingsovereenkomst, mits de lasthebber onverwijld vervangen wordt door een andere lasthebber overeenkomstig de voorwaarden die de rechtsverhouding tussen de lastgever en de andere partij of partijen regelt; of

        (iv) er sprake is van een buitengewone en ernstige reden voor de lastgever om de overeenkomst op te zeggen op grond van Artikel 6:103 (Opzegging door de lastgever vanwege een buitengewone en ernstige reden), mits de lasthebber onverwijld vervangen wordt door een andere lasthebber overeenkomstig de voorwaarden die de rechtsverhouding tussen de lastgever en de andere partij of partijen regelt.

(3) Wanneer de herroeping van de last niet op grond van dit Artikel is toegestaan, heeft een kennisgeving van herroeping geen rechtsgevolgen.

(4) Dit Artikel is niet van toepassing indien de lastgevingsrelatie is geëindigd op grond van Hoofdstuk 7 van deze Beginselen.

Hoofdstuk 2:
Hoofdverplichtingen van de Lastgever

Artikel 2:101: Samenwerkingsplicht

De verplichting op grond van Artikel 1:202 (Samenwerkingsplicht) van de Beginselen van Europees Overeenkomstenrecht brengt in het bijzonder met zich dat de lastgever verplicht is om:

(a) verzoeken van de lasthebber om informatie te beantwoorden voor zover als deze informatie nodig is voor de lasthebber om de verplichtingen op grond van de lastgevingsovereenkomst na te komen;

(b) een aanwijzing betreffende de nakoming van de verplichtingen op grond van de lastgevingsovereenkomst te geven voor zover de verplichting daartoe voortvloeit uit de lastgevingsovereenkomst of volgt uit een verzoek tot het geven van een aanwijzing op grond van Artikel 4:102 (Verzoek tot het geven van een aanwijzing).

Artikel 2:102: Prijs

(1) De lastgever moet een prijs betalen indien de lasthebber de verplichtingen op grond van de lastgevingsovereenkomst uitvoert in de uitoefening van een bedrijf, tenzij de lastgever verwachtte en redelijkerwijs mocht verwachten dat de lasthebber zijn verplichtingen anders dan in ruil voor een prijs zou verrichten.

(2) De prijs is opeisbaar wanneer de gemandateerde taak is vervuld en de lasthebber daarover verantwoording heeft afgelegd aan de lastgever.

(3) Wannneer de partijen de betaling van een prijs voor geleverde diensten zijn overeengekomen, de lastgevingsrelatie geëindigd is en de gemandateerde taak niet voltooid is, is de prijs opeisbaar vanaf het moment waarop de lasthebber verantwoording heeft afgelegd over de nakoming van de verplichtingen op grond van de lastgevingsovereenkomst.

(4) Wanneer de last de sluiting van een beoogde overeenkomst betreft en de lastgever zelf, dan wel een door hem aangestelde andere persoon ten behoeve van de lastgever de beoogde overeenkomst heeft gesloten, heeft de lasthebber recht op betaling van de prijs of een evenredig deel daarvan indien de sluiting van de beoogde overeenkomst geheel of ten dele kan worden toegerekend aan de nakoming door de lasthebber van diens verplichtingen op grond van de lastgevingsovereenkomst.

(5) Wanneer de last de sluiting van een beoogde overeenkomst betreft en de beoogde overeenkomst gesloten is nadat de lastgevingsrelatie is geëindigd, is de lastgever de prijs betalen indien partijen overeen gekomen waren dat alleen dan een prijs zou behoeven te worden betaald indien de beoogde overeenkomst zou worden gesloten en

(a) de sluiting van de beoogde overeenkomst hoofdzakelijk het gevolg is van de werkzaamheden van de lasthebber; en

(b) de beoogde overeenkomst gesloten is binnen een redelijke termijn nadat de lastgevingsrelatie geëindigd is.

Artikel 2:103: Door de lasthebber gemaakte kosten

(1) Wanneer de lasthebber gerechtigd is tot betaling van een prijs, wordt de prijs vermoed een vergoeding te vormen voor de kosten die de lasthebber heeft gemaakt bij de nakoming van de verplichtingen op grond van de lastgevingsovereenkomst.

(2) Wanneer de lasthebber geen recht heeft op betaling van een prijs of wanneer de partijen zijn overeengekomen dat de kosten afzonderlijk moeten worden vergoed, is de lastgever gehouden de kosten die de lasthebber voor de nakoming van de verplichtingen op grond van de lastgevingsovereenkomst heeft moeten maken, te vergoeden indien en voor zover de lasthebber redelijk heeft gehandeld bij het maken van de kosten.

(3) De lasthebber heeft recht op vergoeding van de kosten op grond van het bepaalde in lid (2) vanaf het moment dat de kosten zijn gemaakt en de lasthebber over het maken van de kosten verantwoording heeft afgelegd.

(4) Wanneer de lastgevingsrelatie geëindigd is, de beloning van de lasthebber afhankelijk is van het bereiken van een bepaald resultaat en dat resultaat niet bereikt is, heeft de lasthebber recht op vergoeding van de redelijke kosten die de lasthebber heeft gemaakt bij de nakoming van de verplichtingen op grond van de lastgevingsovereenkomst. Lid (3) is van overeenkomstige toepassing.

Hoofdstuk 3:
Nakoming door de lasthebber
Afdeling 1:
Hoofdverplichtingen van de lasthebber

Artikel 3:101: Verplichting om overeenkomstig de last te handelen
Gedurende de gehele duur van de lastgevingsrelatie dient de lasthebber overeenkomstig de last te handelen..

Artikel 3:102: Verplichting om te handelen in het belang van de lastgever
(1) De lasthebber dient overeenkomstig de belangen van de lastgever te handelen voor zover deze belangen bekend zijn gemaakt aan de lasthebber of voor zover de lasthebber redelijkerwijs kan worden geacht bekend te zijn met deze belangen.
(2) Wanneer de lasthebber niet voldoende bekend is met de belangen van de lastgever om de verplichtingen op grond van de lastgevingsovereenkomst te behartigen, dient de lasthebber informatie te vragen aan de lastgever.

Artikel 3:103: Zorgverplichting
(1) De lasthebber is gehouden de verplichtingen op grond van de lastgevingsovereenkomst met de met de zorg en bekwaamheid die de lastgever in de gegeven omstandigheden mocht verwachten.
(2) Wanneer de lasthebber pretendeert te beschikken over een hogere graad van zorg en bekwaamheid, dient hij die zorg en bekwaamheid te betrachten.
(3) Wanneer de lasthebber lid is, of voorgeeft te zijn, van een groep van professionele lasthebber voor welke normen bestaan die zijn vastgesteld door een bevoegde autoriteit of door die groep zelf, dan dient de lasthebber de zorg en bekwaamheid zoals uitgedrukt in die normen te betrachten.
(4) Bij de beoordeling van de zorg en bekwaamheid die de lastgever mag verwachten, wordt onder meer in aanmerking genomen:
  (a) de aard, de omvang, de frequentie en de voorzienbaarheid van de risico's betrokken bij de nakoming van de verplichtingen van de lasthebber;
  (b) of de last wordt uitgevoerd om niet of door een lasthebber die niet handelt in de uitvoering van zijn beroep of bedrijf;
  (c) de hoogte van het loon voor de nakoming van de verplichtingen.

Afdeling 2:
Gevolgen van het overschrijden van de grenzen van de last

Artikel 3:201: Overschrijding van de grenzen van de last
(1) De lasthebber mag de grenzen van de last overschrijden indien:
  (a) de lasthebber een redelijke grond heeft om ten behoeve van de lastgever zo te handelen;
  (b) de lasthebber in de bijzondere omstandigheden van het geval geen redelijke mogelijkheid heeft om op de hoogte te geraken van de wensen van de lastgever; en
  (c) de lasthebber niet weet en redelijkerwijs niet kan worden geacht te hebben geweten dat de overschrijding van de grenzen van de last in de bijzondere omstandigheden van het geval tegen de wensen van de lastgever is.
(2) Een handeling die in overeenstemming met lid (1) is heeft dezelfde gevolgen tussen de lasthebber en de lastgever als een handeling die binnen de grenzen van de last valt.

Artikel 3:202: Gevolgen van bekrachtiging
Wanneer een lastgever de grenzen van de last heeft overschreden bij het sluiten van een overeenkomst ten behoeve van de lastgever en waarbij niet voldaan is aan de vereisten van het vorige artikel, vrijwaart de lastgever de lasthebber van aansprakelijkheid jegens de lastgever wanneer hij de overeenkomst bekrachtigt, tenzij de lastgever de lasthebber onverwijld na bekrachtiging mededeelt dat hij zich het recht voorbehoud om remedies voor de niet-nakoming van de verplichtingen door de lasthebber in te roepen.

Afdeling 3:
Last in beginsel niet exclusief

Artikel 3:301: Exclusiviteit wordt niet verondersteld
De lastgever is vrij om de de beoogde overeenkomst zelf te sluiten, onderhandelingen daarover te voeren of de sluiting van een dergelijke overeenkomst mogelijk te maken, of om een andere lasthebber daartoe aan te stellen.

Artikel 3:302: Onderlastgeving
(1) De lasthebber mag de nakoming van de verplichtingen op grond van de lastgevingsovereenkomst geheel of ten dele uitbesteden of toevertrouwen aan een andere persoon zonder instemming van de lastgever, tenzij persoonlijke uitvoering van de last vereist is op grond van de overeenkomst.
(2) Een door de lasthebber overeenkomstig lid (1) ingeschakelde andere persoon moet voldoende bekwaam zijn.
(3) Overeenkomstig het bepaalde in Artikel 8:107 (Nakoming aan een ander toevertrouwd) van de Beginselen van Europees Overeenkomstenrecht blijft de lasthebber verantwoordelijk voor de nakoming van de verplichtingen op grond van de lastgevingsovereenkomst.

Afdeling 4:
Verplichting om de lastgever te informeren

Artikel 3:401: Informatie over de voortgang van de uitvoering van de last
Gedurende de nakoming van de verplichtingen op grond van de lastgevingsovereenkomst is de lasthebber gehouden, voor zover als in de gegeven omstandigheden geregeld is, de lastgever te informeren over het bestaan van, en de voortgang van de onderhandelingen of andere stappen die kunnen leiden tot de sluiting van de beoogde overeenkomst of het mogelijk maken daarvan.

Artikel 3:402: Verantwoording aan de lastgever
(1) De lasthebber moet onverwijld de lastgever informeren over de voltooiing van de gemandateerde taak.
(2) De lasthebber moet verantwoording aan de lastgever afleggen over:
  (a) de wijze waarop de verplichtingen op grond van de lastgevingsovereenkomst zijn uitgevoerd; en
  (b) de gelden die zijn uitgegeven of ontvangen en de kosten die de lasthebber heeft gemaakt bij de nakoming van die verplichtingen.
(3) Lid (2) is, voor zover nodig in aangepaste vorm, van toepassing wanneer de lastgevingsrelatie is geëindigd op grond van het bepaalde in de Hoofdstukken 6 en 7 en de verplichtingen op grond van de lastgevingsovereenkomst niet volledig zijn uitgevoerd.

Artikel 3:403: Kennisgeving van de identiteit van de derde
(1) Een lasthebber die de beoogde overeenkomst met een derde sluit, moet op verzoek van de lastgever hem de naam en het adres van de derde mededelen.
(2) In het geval van een last tot middellijke vertegenwoordiging is lid (1) slechts van toepassing indien de lasthebber insolvent is geraakt.

Hoofdstuk 4:
Aanwijzingen en Wijzigingen
Afdeling 1:
Aanwijzingen

Artikel 4:101: Aanwijzingen gegeven door de lastgever
(1) De lastgever is gerechtigd om aanwijzingen aan de lasthebber te geven.
(2) De lasthebber moet de aanwijzingen van de lastgever opvolgen.
(3) De lasthebber dient de lastgever te waarschuwen indien de aanwijzing:
  (a) tot gevolg heeft dat de nakoming van de verplichtingen op grond van de lastgevingsovereenkomst significant duurder zou worden of langer zou duren dan overeen was gekomen in de lastgevingsovereenkomst; of
  (b) niet consistent is met het doel van de lastgevingsovereenkomst of anderszins de belangen van de lastgever kan schaden.
(4) Tenzij de lastgever de aanwijzing onverwijld herroept na daartoe te zijn gewaarschuwd door de lasthebber, wordt de aanwijzing aangemerkt als een wijziging van de lastgevingsovereenkomst als bedoeld in Artikel 4:201 (Wijzigingen van de lastgevingsovereenkomst).

Artikel 4:102: Verzoek tot het geven van een aanwijzing

(1) De lasthebber dient de lastgever te vragen om een aanwijzing tot het verstrekken van informatie betreffende de lastgevingsovereenkomst of de inhoud van de beoogde overeenkomst. De lastgever is in een dergelijk geval gehouden de daartoe vereiste beslissing te nemen.

(2) De lasthebber dient een aanwijzing te vragen wanneer de gemandateerde taak bestaat uit de sluiting van een beoogde overeenkomst en de lastgevingsovereenkomst niet duidelijk maakt of de last verplicht tot directe of middellijke vertegenwoordiging.

Artikel 4:103: Gevolgen van het verzaken van de verplichting tot het geven van een aanwijzing

(1) Wanneer de lastgever nalaat een aanwijzing te geven wanneer hij daartoe verplicht is op grond van de lastgevingsovereenkomst of op grond van lid (1) van Artikel 4:102 (Verzoek tot het geven van een aanwijzing), kan de lasthebber, voor zo ver relevant, een beroep doen op elk van de remedies op grond van de Hoofdstukken 8 (Niet-nakoming en rechten bij tekortkoming in het algemeen) en 9 (Afzonderlijke rechten bij tekortkoming) van de Beginselen van Europees Overeenkomstenrecht; of

   (a) nakoming van zijn verplichtingen baseren op de verwachtingen, voorkeuren en prioriteiten van een persoon in dezelfde situatie als de lastgever redelijkerwijs geacht kan worden te hebben, gegeven de informatie en aanwijzingen die zijn verzameld; en

   (b) een evenredige wijziging van de prijs en van de tijd voor nakoming voor de sluiting van de beoogde overeenkomst claimen.

(2) Wanneer de lastgever nalaat een aanwijzing te geven als bedoeld in lid (2) van Artikel 4:102 (Verzoek tot het geven van een aanwijzing) kan de lasthebber kiezen tussen directe of middellijke vertegenwoordiging of nakoming van zijn verplichtingen opschorten overeenkomstig het bepaalde in Artikel 9:201 (Opschortingrecht) van de Beginselen van Europees Overeenkomstenrecht.

(3) De aangepaste prijs die op grond van lid (1)(b) dient te worden betaald, moet redelijk en zijn en te worden bepaald met gebruikmaking van dezelfde rekenmethoden als gebruik zijn bij de bepaling van de oorspronkelijke prijs voor de uitvoering an de verplichtingen op grond van de lastgevingsovereenkomst.

Artikel 4:104: Geen tijd om een aanwijzing te vragen of aft e wachten

(1) Wanneer de lasthebber gehouden is te vragen om een aanwijzing op grond van Artikel 4:102 (Verzoek tot het geven van een aanwijzing) maar dient te handelen voordat hij de lastgever heeft kunnen raadplegen en om een aanwijzing te vragen, of dient te handelen voordat de aanwijzing is gegeven, kan de lasthebber nakoming van zijn verplichtingen baseren op de verwachtingen, voorkeuren en prioriteiten die de lastgever redelijkerwijs geacht kan worden te hebben, gegeven de informatie en aanwijzingen die zijn verzameld.

(2) In de situatie bedoeld in lid (1) kan de lasthebber een evenredige wijziging van de prijs en van de tijd voor nakoming voor de sluiting van de beoogde overeenkomst claimen, voor zover als een dergelijke wijziging in de omstandigheden van het geval redelijk is.

Afdeling 2:
Wijzigingen van de lastgevingsovereenkomst

Artikel 4:201: Wijzigingen van de lastgevingsovereenkomst

(1) De lastgevingsovereenkomst is gewijzigd wanneer de lastgever:
  - (a) op significante wijze de last van de lasthebber wijzigt;
  - (b) een aanwijzing niet onverwijld herroept na te zijn gewaarschuwd overeenkomstig het bepaalde in lid (3) van Artikel 4:101 (Aanwijzingen gegeven door de lastgever).

(2) In het geval van een wijziging van de lastgevingsovereenkomst op grond van lid (1) is de lasthebber gerechtigd:
  - (a) tot een evenredige wijziging van de prijs en van de tijd voor nakoming voor de nakoming van de verplichtingen op grond van de lastgevingsovereenkomst; of
  - (b) tot schadevergoeding overeenkomstig met Artikel 9:502 (Algemene maatstaf voor de vergoeding) van de Beginselen van Europees Overeenkomstenrecht) ten einde de lasthebber zo dicht mogelijk in de toestand te brengen in welke hij had verkeerd indien de lastgevingsovereenkomst niet zou zijn gewijzigd..

(3) In het geval van een wijziging van de lastgevingsovereenkomst op grond van lid (1) kan de lasthebber de lastgevingsrelatie ook beëindigen door het doen van een kennisgeving van opzegging vanwege een buitengewone en ernstige reden op grond van Artikel 6:105 (Opzegging door de lasthebber vanwege een buitengewone en ernstig reden), tenzij de wijziging van geringe aard is of ten voordele van de lasthebber strekt.

(4) De gewijzigde prijs die op grond van lid (2)(a) dient te worden betaald, moet redelijk en zijn en te worden bepaald met gebruikmaking van dezelfde rekenmethoden als gebruik zijn bij de bepaling van de oorspronkelijke prijs voor de uitvoering an de verplichtingen op grond van de lastgevingsovereenkomst.

Hoofdstuk 5:
Belangentegenstellingen

Artikel 5:101: Zelfcontracteren

(1) De lasthebber mag niet de wederpartij van de lastgever bij de beoogde overeenkomst worden.

(2) De lasthebber mag desalniettemin de wederpartij worden indien:
  - (a) dit door de partijen in de lastgevingsovereenkomst is overeengekomen;
  - (b) de lasthebber zijn bedoeling om de wederpartij te worden, kenbaar heeft gemaakt en
    - (i) de lastgever hier vervolgens mee heeft ingestemd; of
    - (ii) de lastgever zich er niet tegen verzet dat de lasthebber de wederpartij wordt nadat hem verzocht is aan te geven of hij hiermee instemt dan wel instemming weigert;
  - (c) de lastgever anderszins wist, of redelijkerwijs geacht kan worden te hebben geweten, dat de lasthebber de wederpartij zou worden en de lastgever zich hier niet binnen een redelijke termijn tegen verzet; of

(d) de inhoud van de beoogde overeenkomst zo precies is bepaald in de lastgevingsovereenkomst dat er geen risico bestaat dat de belangen van de lastgever kunnen worden geschaad.

(3) Wanneer de lastgever is een consument is, kan de lasthebber alleen dan de wederpartij worden indien:

   (a) de lasthebber de informatie kenbaar heeft has gemaakt en de lastgever uitdrukkelijk ermee heeft ingestemd dat de lasthebber de wederpartij bij de specifiek beoogde overeenkomst wordt; of

   (b) de inhoud van de beoogde overeenkomst zo precies is bepaald in de lastgevingsovereenkomst dat er geen risico bestaat dat de belangen van de lastgever kunnen worden geschaad.

(4) De partijen kunnen niet ten nadele van de lastgever de toepassing van lid (3) uitsluiten of of afwijken van de gevolgen ervan.

(5) Wanneer de lasthebber de wederpartij is geworden, heeft hij geen recht op een prijs voor de werkzaamheden die hij verricht heeft als lasthebber.

Artikel 5:102: Dubbele last

(1) De lasthebber mag niet optreden als de lasthebber van zowel de lastgever als de wederpartij van de lastgever bij de beoogde overeenkomst.

(2) De lasthebber mag desalniettemin optreden als de lasthebber van zowel de lastgever als diens wederpartij indien:

   (a) dit door de partijen in de lastgevingsovereenkomst is overeengekomen;

   (b) de lasthebber zijn bedoeling om als de lasthebber van de wederpartij op te treden, kenbaar heeft gemaakt en

      (i) de lastgever hier vervolgens mee heeft ingestemd; of

      (ii) de lastgever zich er niet tegen verzet dat de lasthebber tevens als lasthebber van de de wederpartij optreedt nadat hem verzocht is aan te geven of hij hiermee instemt dan wel instemming weigert;

   (c) de lastgever anderszins wist, of redelijkerwijs geacht kan worden te hebben geweten, dat de lasthebber tevens als lasthebber van de wederpartij zou optreden en de lastgever zich hier niet binnen een redelijke termijn tegen verzet; of

   (d) de inhoud van de beoogde overeenkomst zo precies is bepaald in de lastgevingsovereenkomst dat er geen risico bestaat dat de belangen van de lastgever kunnen worden geschaad.

(3) Wanneer de lastgever is een consument is, kan de lasthebber alleen dan optreden als de lasthebber van de wederpartij indien:

   (a) de lasthebber de informatie kenbaar heeft has gemaakt en de lastgever uitdrukkelijk ermee heeft ingestemd dat de lasthebber als de lasthebber van de wederpartij bij de specifiek beoogde overeenkomst optreedt; of

   (b) de inhoud van de beoogde overeenkomst zo precies is bepaald in de lastgevingsovereenkomst dat er geen risico bestaat dat de belangen van de lastgever kunnen worden geschaad.

(4) De partijen kunnen niet ten nadele van de lastgever de toepassing van lid (3) uitsluiten of of afwijken van de gevolgen ervan.

(5) Wanneer en voor zover de lasthebber overeenkomstige de voorgaande leden heeft gehandeld, heeft hij recht op de prijs voor zijn werkzaamheden.

Hoofdstuk 6:
Beëindiging Door Kennisgeving Op Andere Grond Dan
Wegens Niet-nakoming

Artikel 6:101: Opzegging door kennisgeving in het algemeen

(1) Elke partij kan de lastgevingsrelatie te allen tijde opzeggen door kennisgeving daarvan aan de wederpartij.

(2) Een herroeping van de last van de lasthebber wordt voor de doeleinden van het bepaalde in lid (1) gezien als een opzegging.

(3) Opzegging van de lastgevingsrelatie heeft geen rechtsgevolgen wanneer de last van de lasthebber onherroepelijk is op grond van Artikel 1:105 (Onherroepelijke last).

(4) Op de gevolgen van de opzegging zijn de bepalingen van Hoofdstuk 9, Afdeling 3 (Ontbinding van de overeenkomst) van de Beginselen van Europees Overeenkomstenrecht van toepassing.

(5) Wanneer de partij die de kennisgeving heeft gedaan, gerechtigd was tot opzegging van de lastgevingsrelatie, is hij hiervoor geen schadevergoeding verschuldigd.

(6) Wanneer de partij die de kennisgeving heeft gedaan, niet gerechtigd was tot opzegging van de lastgevingsrelatie, is de opzegging desalniettemin effectief, maar heeft de wederpartij recht op schadevergoeding overeenkomstig de bepalingen van Hoofdstuk 9, Afdeling 5 (Schadevergoeding en rente) van de Beginselen van Europees Overeenkomstenrecht.

(7) Voor de doeleinden van dit Artikel is de partij die de kennisgeving heeft gedaan, gerechtigd tot opzegging van de lastgevingsrelatie indien die partij:

(a) gerechtigd was de relatie op te zeggen op grond van de uitdrukkelijke bepalingen van de overeenkomst en de daarin neergelegde vereisten in acht heeft genomen;

(b) gerechtigd was de overeenkomst te ontbinden op grond van het bepaalde in Hoofdstuk 9, Afdeling 3 (Ontbinding van de overeenkomst); of

(c) gerechtigd was de relatie op te zeggen op grond van een Artikel in dit Hoofdstuk en de daarin neergelegde vereisten in acht heeft genomen.

Artikel 6:102: Opzegging door de lastgever wanneer de relatie voor onbepaalde tijd is gesloten of voor de uitvoering van een bijzondere taak

(1) De lastgever kan de lastgevingsrelatie te allen tijde opzeggen door een kennisgeving met een redelijke opzeggingstermijn indien de lastgevingsovereenkomst is gesloten voor onbepaalde tijd of voor de uitvoering van een bijzondere taak.

(2) Lid (1) is niet van toepassing indien de last onherroepelijk is.

(3) De partijen kunnen niet ten nadele van de lastgever de werking van dit Artikel uitsluiten of afwijken van de gevolgen ervan, tenzij aan de vereisten van het bepaalde in Artikel 1:105 (Onherroepelijke last) is voldaan.

Artikel 6:103: Opzegging door de lastgever wegens een buitengewone en ernstige reden

(1) De lastgever kan de lastgevingsrelatie opzeggen door een kennisgeving wegens een buitengewone en ernstige reden.

(2) De lastgever behoeft geen opzeggingstermijn in acht te nemen.

(3) De dood of handelingsonbekwaamheid van de persoon die, ten tijde van de sluiting van de lastgevingsovereenkomst, overeenkomstig de bedoeling van de partijen de verplichtingen van de lasthebber op grond van de lastgevingsovereenkomst zou uitvoeren, vormt voor de doeleinden van dit Artikel een buitengewone en ernstige reden.

(4) Dit Artikel is, voor zover nodig in aangepaste vorm, van toepassing wanneer de erfgenamen van de lastgevers de lastgevingsrelatie overeenkomstig Artikel 7:101 (Dood van de lastgever) beëindigen.

(5) De partijen kunnen de werking van dit Artikel niet ten nadele van de lastgever of diens erfgenamen uitsluiten of afwijken van de gevolgen ervan.

Artikel 6:104: Opzegging door de lasthebber wanneer de relatie voor onbepaalde tijd is gesloten of de last om niet wordt verricht

(1) De lastgever kan de lastgevingsrelatie te allen tijde opzeggen door een kennisgeving met een redelijke opzeggingstermijn indien de lastgevingsovereenkomst is gesloten voor onbepaalde tijd.

(2) De lastgever kan de lastgevingsrelatie opzeggen door een kennisgeving met een redelijke opzeggingstermijn indien de lastgevingsovereenkomst is gesloten anders dan in ruil voor een prijs.

(3) De partijen kunnen de werking van lid (1) van dit Artikel niet ten nadele van de lasthebber uitsluiten of afwijken van de gevolgen ervan.

Artikel 6:105: Opzegging door de lasthebber wegens een buitengewone en ernstige reden

(1) De lasthebber kan de lastgevingsrelatie opzeggen door een kennisgeving wegens een buitengewone en ernstige reden.

(2) De lasthebber behoeft geen opzeggingstermijn in acht te nemen.

(3) Voor de doeleinden van dit Artikel vormen de volgende situaties een buitengewone en ernstige reden:

   (a) een wijziging van de lastgevingsovereenkomst op grond van Artikel 4:201 (Wijzigingen van de lastgevingsovereenkomst);

   (b) de dood of handelingsonbekwaamheid van de lastgever; en

   (c) dood of handelingsonbekwaamheid van de persoon die, ten tijde van de sluiting van de lastgevingsovereenkomst, overeenkomstig de bedoeling van de partijen de verplichtingen van de lasthebber op grond van de lastgevingsovereenkomst zou uitvoeren.

(5) De partijen kunnen de werking van dit Artikel niet ten nadele van de lasthebber uitsluiten of afwijken van de gevolgen ervan.

Hoofdstuk 7:
andere gronden voor beëindiging

Artikel 7:101: Dood van de lastgever

(1) De dood van de lastgever doet de lastgevingsrelatie niet eindigen.

(2) Zowel de lasthebber als de erfgenamen van de lastgever kunnen de lastgevingsrelatie door kennisgeving wegens een buitengewone en ernstige reden opzeggen op grond van Artikel 6:103 (Opzegging door de lastgever wegens een buitengewone en ernstige reden) of Artikel 6:105 (Opzegging door de lasthebber wegens een buitengewone en ernstige reden).

Artikel 7:102: Dood van de lasthebber

(1) De dood van de lasthebber doet de lastgevingsrelatie eindigen.

(2) De kosten en andere betalingen die opeisbaar waren ten tijde van de dood van de lasthebber blijven verschuldigd.

Finnish*
Toimeksiantosopimukset

Luku 1:
Yleiset Määräykset

Artikkeli 1:101 Soveltamisala

(1) Näitä periaatteita sovelletaan sopimuksiin ja muihin oikeudellisiin toimiin, joilla henkilö, päämies, valtuuttaa ja ohjeistaa toisen henkilön, toimeksisaajan:

    (a) solmimaan sopimuksen päämiehen ja kolmannen välillä tai muuten vaikuttamaan välittömästi päämiehen oikeudelliseen asemaan kolmanteen nähden;

    (b) solmimaan sopimuksen kolmannen kanssa tai ryhtymään muihin oikeudellisiin toimiin kolmanteen nähden päämiehen lukuun, mutta sillä tavoin, että toimeksisaaja tulee sopimuksen tai muun oikeudellisen toimen osapuoleksi päämiehen sijaan; tai

    (c) ryhtymään toimenpiteisiin, jotka tähtäävät sopimuksen solmimiseen tai sen syntymisen edistämiseen päämiehen ja kolmannen välillä tai muun sellaisen oikeudellisen toimen tekemiseen, joka vaikuttaisi päämiehen oikeudelliseen asemaan kolmanteen nähden.

(2) Näitä periaatteita sovelletaan toimeksisaajan sitoutuessa toimimaan päämiehen puolesta ja tämän ohjeidensa mukaisesti sekä, soveltuvin muutoksin, kun valtuutuksen saanut toimeksisaaja toimii valtuutuksen mukaan, vaikka ei ole suoranaisesti sitoutunut näin menettelemään.

(3) Näitä periaatteita sovelletaan sekä silloin, kun toimeksisaajalla on oikeus palkkioon että soveltuvin muutoksin silloin, kun toimeksisaajalla ei ole oikeutta palkkioon.

(4) Näitä periaatteita sovelletaan ainoastaan päämiehen ja toimeksisaajan keskinäiseen suhteeseen (toimeksiantosuhteeseen). Sitä ei sovelleta päämiehen ja kolmannen väliseen suhteeseen, eikä mahdolliseen toimeksisaajan ja kolmannen väliseen suhteeseen.

(5) Sopimuksiin, joihin sekä nämä periaatteet että palvelusopimuksia koskevat periaatteet soveltuvat, on ensisijaisesti sovellettava näitä periaatteita.

(6) Näitä periaatteita ei sovelleta direktiivin 2004/39/EY alaan kuuluviin sijoituspalveluja ja -toimia koskeviin sopimuksiin.

Artikkeli 1:102: Määritelmät

Näissä periaatteissa

(a) toimeksisaajan "toimeksiannolla" tarkoitetaan päämiehen antamaa valtuutusta ja toimintaohjeita myöhempine muutoksineen;

(b) "toimeksiantosopimuksella" tarkoitetaan sopimusta, jolla toimeksisaaja valtuutetaan ja ohjeistetaan toimimaan; viitattaessa toimeksiantosopimukseen tarkoitetaan myös muita oikeudellisia toimia, joihin toimeksisaajan valtuutus perustuu;

(c) "päätettävällä sopimuksella" tarkoitetaan sopimusta, jonka sopimiseen, neuvottelemiseen tai edistämiseen toimeksisaaja on valtuutettu; viitattaessa päätettävään sopimukseen tar-

---

*   Translated by Dr. *Justus Könkkölä*, Aurejärvi Attorneys-at-law Ltd, Helsinki.

koitetaan myös muita oikeudellisia toimia, joiden tekemiseen, neuvottelemiseen tai edistämiseen toimeksisaaja valtuutetaan ja ohjeistetaan;

(d) välittömällä valtuutuksella tarkoitetaan toimeksiantosopimusta, jolla toimeksisaaja valtuutetaan toimimaan päämiehen nimissä tai muuten tavalla, joka ilmentää tarkoitusta vaikuttaa päämiehen oikeudelliseen asemaan;

(e) välillisellä valtuutuksella tarkoitetaan toimeksiantosopimusta, jolla toimeksisaaja valtuutetaan toimimaan omissa nimissään tai muuten tavalla, josta ei ilmene tarkoitus vaikuttaa päämiehen oikeudelliseen asemaan;

(f) "ohjeella" tarkoitetaan päämiehen tekemää toimeksiantosopimuksen mukaisten velvoitteiden täyttämiseen tai aiotun sopimuksen sisältöön liittyvää päätöstä, joka annetaan tiedoksi toimeksiantosopimuksen solmimisajankohtana tai toimeksiantosopimuksen mukaisesti myöhempänä ajankohtana;

(g) "kolmannella" tarkoitetaan osapuolta, jonka kanssa päätettävästä sopimuksesta on tarkoitus sopia tai neuvotella tai jonka kanssa päätettävää sopimusta on tarkoitus edistää;

(h) toimeksisaajan toimeksiantosopimuksen "peruuttamisella" tarkoitetaan päämiehen tekemää valtuutuksen peruutusta.

Artikkeli 1:103: Toimeksiantosopimuksen voimassaoloaika
Toimeksiantosopimus voidaan solmia:
(a) toistaiseksi voimassaolevaksi;
(b) määräaikaiseksi; tai
(c) tiettyä tehtävää varten.

Artikkeli 1:104: Toimeksisaajan valtuutuksen peruuttaminen
(1) Jollei 1:105:stä muuta johdu, päämies voi milloin tahansa peruuttaa toimeksisaajan valtuutuksen ilmoittamalla tästä toimeksisaajalle.
(2) Toimeksiantosuhteen päättäminen johtaa toimeksisaajan valtuutuksen peruuntumiseen.
(3) Osapuolet eivät voi muulloin kuin kohdassa 1:105 esitettyjen edellytysten täyttyessä sopia tästä artiklasta poikkeavasti tai kiertää taikka muuttaa tämän kohdan vaikutuksia.

Artikkeli 1:105: Peruuttamaton valtuutus
(1) Päämiehellä ei ole 1:104 poiketen oikeutta peruuttaa toimeksisaajan valtuutusta, jos tämä on annettu
   (a) toimeksisaajan perusteltujen, muiden kuin palkkion maksuun liittyvien etujen suojaamiseksi; tai
   (b) toisen sopimuksen tai oikeudellisen suhteen osapuolten yhteiseksi eduksi riippumatta siitä, ovatko kaikki näistä henkilöistä toimeksiantosopimuksen osapuolia, ja toimeksisaajan valtuutus on annettu peruuttamattomana yhden tai useamman tällaisen henkilön etujen asianmukaiseksi turvaamiseksi.
(2) Valtuutus saadaan kuitenkin peruuttaa, jos
   (a) valtuutus on kohdan (1)(a) mukaan peruuttamaton ja
      (i) sopimussuhde, johon toimeksisaajan oikeutetut edut perustuvat, lakkautetaan toimeksisaajan velvoitteen täyttämättä jättämisen johdosta; tai
      (ii) toimeksisaaja olennaisesti rikkoo toimeksiantosopimuksen mukaisia suoritusvelvoitteitaan; tai

    (iii) päämiehellä on artiklassa 6:103:ssä (Irtisanominen päämiehen toimesta vakavasta ja erityisestä syystä) tarkoitettu vakava ja erityinen syy irtisanoa toimeksiantosopimus; tai

(b) valtuutus on kohdan (1)(b) mukaan peruuttamaton ja

    (i) osapuolet, joiden eduksi valtuutus on peruuttamaton, sopivat valtuutuksen peruuttamisesta; tai

    (ii) kohdassa (1)(b) tarkoitettu sopimussuhde lakkaa.

    (iii) toimeksisaaja rikkoo olennaisesti toimeksiantosopimuksen mukaisia suoritusvelvoitteitaan, edellyttäen että toimeksisaaja ilman aiheetonta viivytystä korvataan uudella toimeksisaajalla päämiehen ja toisen osapuolen tai toisten osapuolten välistä sopimusta vastaavasti; tai

    (iv) päämiehellä on artiklan 6:103:n (Irtisanominen päämiehen toimesta vakavasta ja erityisestä syystä) tarkoittama vakava ja erityinen syy päättää toimeksiantosopimus, edellyttäen että toimeksisaaja ilman aiheetonta viivytystä korvataan uudella toimeksisaajalla päämiehen ja toisen osapuolen tai toisten osapuolten välistä sopimusta vastaavasti.

(3) Jos tämän artiklan mukaiset edellytykset eivät ole käsillä, ilmoitus valtuutuksen peruuttamisesta on mitätön.

(4) Tätä artiklaa ei sovelleta, mikäli toimeksiantosuhde lakkaa tämän osan 7 luvun mukaisesti.

Luku 2:
Päämiehen Keskeiset Velvollisuudet

Artikkeli 2:101: Myötävaikutusvelvollisuus

Velvollisuus myötävaikuttaa Euroopan sopimusoikeuden periaatteiden ('PECL') artiklan 1:202 mukaisesti edellyttää erityisesti, että päämiehen on

(a) vastattava toimeksisaajaan tiedonantopyyntöihin siinä laajuudessa, kuin tieto on tarpeen toimeksisaajan sopimuksen mukaisten velvoitteiden täyttämiseksi;

(b) annettava toimeksiantosopimuksen mukaisten velvoitteiden täyttämistä koskevia ohjeita, jos toimeksiantosopimus tai artiklan 4:102:n (Ohjeistuspyyntö) mukainen pyyntö ohjeistuksesta niin edellyttää.

Artikkeli 2:102: Palkkio

(1) Päämiehen on maksettava päämiestä osana elinkeinotoimintaansa edustavalle toimeksisaajalle tämän suorituksesta palkkio, jollei päämies ole ollut perustellusti siinä käsityksessä, että toimeksisaaja toimii muutoin kuin palkkiota vastaan.

(2) Palkkio erääntyy maksettavaksi, kun toimeksianto on saatettu päätökseen ja toimeksisaaja on tehnyt tilin toiminnastaan päämiehelle.

(3) Mikäli osapuolet olivat sopineet suoritusperusteisesta palkkiosta, eikä toimeksiantoa ole suoritettu toimeksiantosuhteen päättyessä, palkkio tulee maksettavaksi ajankohtana, jolloin toimeksisaaja tekee tilin toimeksiantosopimuksen mukaisten velvoitteiden suorittamisesta.

(4) Milloin valtuutus on annettu tulevaisuudessa päätettävän sopimuksen solmimiseksi ja päämies solmii tällaisen sopimuksen välittömästi itse tai joku muu päämiehen osoittama hen-

kilö solmii sen päämiehen lukuun, toimeksisaajalla on oikeus palkkioon tai sen kohtuulliseen osaan, mikäli päätettävän sopimuksen solmiminen täysin tai osittain voidaan lukea toimeksisaajan ansioksi.

(5) Milloin valtuutus on annettu sopimuksen solmimiseksi päämiehen lukuun ja tällainen sopimus solmitaan vasta toimeksiantosuhteen päätyttyä, päämiehen tulee maksaa palkkio, mikäli yksinomaan päätettävän sopimuksen solmimiseen perustuvasta palkkiosta oli sovittu ja
  (a) sopimuksen solmiminen on pääasiallisesti seurausta toimeksisaajan ponnisteluista; ja
  (b) sopimus on solmittu kohtuullisessa ajassa toimeksiantosuhteen päättymisestä.

Artikkeli 2:103: Toimeksisaajalle aiheutuneet kulut

(1) Jos toimeksisaaja on oikeutettu palkkioon, palkkion oletetaan sisältävän korvauksen toimeksisaajalle toimeksiantosopimusta täyttäessään aiheutuneista kuluista.

(2) Milloin toimeksisaajalla ei ole oikeutta palkkioon tai milloin osapuolet ovat sopineet kulujen korvaamisesta erikseen, päämiehen tulee hyvittää toimeksisaajalle toimeksiantosopimuksen mukaisia velvoitteita täytettäessä aiheutuneet kulut siltä osin kuin niitä aiheutettaessa on toimittu järkevästi.

(3) Toimeksisaajalla on kohdan (2) mukainen oikeus hyvitykseen kuluistaan, kun kulut ovat aiheutuneet ja toimeksisaaja on tehnyt niistä tilityksen.

(4) Jos toimeksiantosuhde on lakannut, eikä toimeksisaajan palkkion edellytyksenä olevaa tulosta ole saavutettu, toimeksisaajalla on oikeus hyvitykseen hänelle toimeksiantosopimuksen täyttämisestä aiheutuneista kohtuullisista kuluista. Kohtaa (3) sovelletaan vastaavasti näin syntyvään oikeuteen.

Luku 3:
Toimeksisaajan Suoritus
Osa 1:
Toimeksisaajan keskeiset velvollisuudet

Artikkeli 3:101: Velvollisuus toimia valtuutuksen mukaisesti

Toimeksisaajan on toimittava valtuutuksensa mukaisesti kaikissa toimeksiantosopimuksen vaiheissa.

Artikkeli 3:102: Velvollisuus toimia päämiehen edun mukaisesti

(1) Toimeksisaajan on toimittava tiedossaan olevan päämiehen edun mukaisesti tai sen mukaan, mitä hänen kohtuudella voidaan edellyttää tietävän päämiehensä eduista.

(2) Toimeksisaajan on pyydettävä päämieheltään tietoja toimeksiannon hoitamisen kannalta merkityksellisistä päämiehen eduista, jos toimeksisaaja ei ole niistä tietoinen.

3:103: Velvollisuus toimia huolellisesti ja ammattitaitoisesti

(1) Toimeksisaajan on täytettävä toimeksiantosopimuksen mukaiset velvollisuutensa sellaisella ammattitaidolla ja huolellisuudella, jota päämies voi olosuhteiden perusteella edellyttää.

(2) Jos toimeksisaaja esiintyy tavanomaista ammattitaitoisempana, hän on velvollinen toimimaan tätä tasoa vastaavasti ja noudattamaan sen edellyttämää huolellisuutta.

(3) Mikäli toimeksisaaja kuuluu, tai väittää kuuluvansa sellaiseen ammatilliseen ryhmään, jonka toiminnalle asianomainen viranomainen tai ryhmä itse on asettanut tiettyjä standardeja, toimeksisaajan tulee noudattaa näitä standardeja sekä toimia niiden edellyttämällä ammattitaidolla ja huolellisuudella.

(4) Sen huolellisuuden ja ammattitaidon tason määrittämisessä, jota päämiehellä on oikeus edellyttää, merkitystä tulee antaa muun muassa seuraaville seikoille:

(a) velvoitteiden suorittamiseen liittyvien riskien laatu, suuruus, yleisyys ja ennalta-arvattavuus;

(b) velvoitteiden suorittaminen ammattitoimessa tai vastikkeettomasti;

(c) velvoitteiden suorittamisesta maksetun palkkion määrä;

(d) velvoitteiden suorittamiseen kohtuudella käytettävissä oleva aika.

Osa 2:
Toimivallan ylittämisen seuraukset

Artikkeli 3:201: Toimivallan ylittämisen seuraukset

(1) Toimeksisaaja saa ylittää toimivaltansa, jos

(a) toimeksisaajalla on päämiehensä puolesta toimiessaan siihen perusteltu syy;

(b) toimeksisaajalla ei ole olosuhteiden vuoksi riittävää tilaisuutta selvittää päämiehensä toiveita; ja

(c) toimeksisaaja ei tiedä, eikä hänen voida kohtuudella edellyttää tietävän, että hänen toimintansa on näissä olosuhteissa vastoin hänen päämiehensä toiveita

(2) Kohdan (1) mukainen toimenpide vaikuttaa toimeksisaajan ja päämiehen väliseen suhteeseen samalla tavalla kuin valtuutuksen rajoissa tehty toimenpide.

Artikkeli 3:202: Hyväksymisen oikeusvaikutukset
Jos toimeksisaaja muissa kun edellisen artiklan tarkoittamissa olosuhteissa ylittää toimivaltansa solmiessaan päätettävää sopimusta päämiehen lukuun, päämiehen sopimuksen vahvistaminen vapauttaa toimeksisaajan vastuusta päämiestä kohtaan, paitsi milloin päämies ilman kohtuutonta viivästystä vahvistamisen jälkeen ilmoittaa toimeksisaajalle pidättävänsä itsellään oikeuden vedota toimeksisaajan sopimusrikkomukseen.

Osa 3:
Valtuutukseen ei yleensä yksinoikeutta

Artikkeli 3:301: Yksinoikeus ei oletuksena
Päämiehellä on oikeus solmia ja neuvotella päätettävä sopimus itse sekä edistää sen solmimista samoin kuin osoittaa tehtävä toiselle toimeksisaajalle.

Artikkeli 3:302 Alivaltuutus

(1) Toimeksisaajalla on oikeus täyttää toimeksiantosopimuksen mukaiset velvollisuutensa kokonaan tai osittain valtuuttamalla toinen sijaansa ilman päämiehen suostumusta, paitsi milloin henkilökohtaisesta suorituksesta on sovittu.

(2) Jokaisella toimeksisaajan tähän tarkoitukseen valtuuttamalla henkilöllä on oltava tehtävään asianmukainen pätevyys.

(3) Toimeksisaaja pysyy PECL artiklan 8:107 mukaisesti (Toiselle uskottu tehtävän suorittaminen) vastuussa suorituksesta.

Osa 4:
Velvollisuus antaa päämiehelle tietoja

Artikkeli 3:401 Tiedot suorituksen etenemisestä
Toimeksisaaja on tehtäväänsä suorittaessaan ja siltä osin kuin se on olosuhteisiin nähden perusteltua velvollinen antamaan päämiehelle tietoja neuvotteluista ja niiden etenemisestä sekä muista päätettävän sopimuksen solmimiseen tai sen solmimisen edistämiseen mahdollisesti johtavista toimenpiteistä

Artikkeli 3:402: Tilin tekeminen päämiehelle
(1) Toimeksisaaja on velvollinen ilman aiheetonta viivytystä ilmoittamaan päämiehelle toimeksiannon loppuunsaattamisesta.

(2) Toimeksisaajan on tehtävä päämiehelle tili
   (a) tavasta, jolla toimeksiantosopimuksen mukaiset velvoitteet on suoritettu
   (b) kyseisten velvoitteiden suorittamisessa käytetyistä tai sen yhteydessä vastaanotetuista varoista sekä toimeksisaajan tehtäväänsä täyttäessään aiheuttamista kuluista.

(3) Kohtaa (2) sovelletaan vastaavasti, kun toimeksiantosuhde lakkaa lukujen 6 ja 7 mukaisesti, eikä toimeksiantosopimuksen mukaisia velvoitteita ole suoritettu kokonaan.

Artikkeli 3:403: Kolmannen henkilöllisyyden ilmoittaminen
(1) Toimeksisaajan on ilmoitettava kolmannen nimi ja osoite päämiehelle tämän pyynnöstä.

(2) Mikäli kyseessä on välillinen valtuutus, kohta (1) soveltuu ainoastaan toimeksisaajan joutuessa maksukyvyttömäksi.

Luku 4:
Ohjeet Ja Muutokset
Osa 1:
Ohjeet

Artikkeli 4:101: Päämiehen antamat ohjeet
(1) Päämiehellä on oikeus ohjeistaa toimeksisaajaa

(2) Toimeksisaajan on noudatettava päämiehen ohjeita

(3) Toimeksisaajan on varoitettava päämiestä, mikäli ohjeet:

(a) tekevät velvoitteiden täyttämisestä huomattavasti kalliimpaa tai niiden noudattaminen edellyttävää huomattavasti enemmän aikaa kuin mitä toimeksiantosopimuksessa oli sovittu; tai

(b) ovat ristiriidassa toimeksiantosopimuksen tarkoituksen kanssa tai voivat muutoin olla päämiehen edun vastaisia.

(3) Jollei päämies toimeksisaajalta varoituksen saatuaan ilman aiheetonta viivytystä peruuta ohjeistusta, ohjeita on pidettävä toimeksiantosopimuksen artiklan 4:201:n (Toimeksiantosopimuksen muutokset) mukaisena toimeksiantosopimuksen muutoksena.

Artikkeli 4:102: Ohjeistuspyyntö

(1) Jos toimeksisaaja saa tiedon, joka edellyttää päämiehen toimitussopimuksen mukaisten velvoitteiden suorittamiseen tai päätettävän sopimuksen sisältöön liittyvää päätöstä, toimeksisaajan on pyydettävä päämieheltä ohjeita.

(2) Toimeksisaajan on pyydettävä ohjeita, jos toimeksianto koskee sopimuksen solmimista eikä toimeksiantosopimuksessa määritellä, onko valtuutus välitön vai välillinen.

Artikkeli 4:103: Ohjeiden antamatta jättämisen seuraukset

(1) Jos päämies ei ohjeista toimeksiantosopimuksen tai 4:102 kohdan (1) (Ohjeistuspyyntö) mukaisesti toimeksisaajaa, toimeksisaajalla on oikeus turvautua PECL luvun 8 (Suorituksen laiminlyönti ja seuraamukset yleisesti) ja luvun 9 (Erityiset suorituksen laiminlyönnin seuraamukset) tarkoittamiin oikeussuojakeinoihin soveltuvin osin; tai

(a) toimia niiden odotusten, mieltymysten ja sen tärkeysjärjestyksen perusteella, joka päämiehen asemassa olevalla henkilöllä kohtuudella voidaan olettaa olevan, ottaen huomioon jo saadut ohjeet ja tiedot; ja

(b) vaatia, että päätettävän sopimuksen solmimiseksi sallittu tai vaadittava aika ja palkkio muutetaan vastaamaan muuttuneita olosuhteita.

(2) Jos päämies ei ohjeista toimeksisaajaa artiklan 4:102 (2) kohdan (Ohjeistuspyyntö) mukaisesti, toimeksisaaja saa valintansa mukaan toimia joko välittömänä tai välillisenä edustajana tai pidättäytyä suorituksesta PECL artiklan 9:201 (Oikeus pidättäytyä vastavuoroisesta suorituksesta) mukaisesti.

(3) Kohdan (1)(b) mukaisesti maksettavan muutetun palkkion on oltava kohtuullinen ja se on määriteltävä samalla laskumenetelmällä kuin alkuperäinen palkkio.

Artikkeli 4:104: Kiireelliset tilanteet

(1) Mikäli toimeksisaajan on artiklan 4:102 mukaisesti pyydettävä ohjeistusta (Ohjeistuspyyntö), mutta hän joutuu toimimaan ennen kuin hän on ehtinyt pyytää ohjeistusta, tai hänen on toimittava ennen ohjeiden vastaanottamista, toimeksisaajalla on oikeus toimia niiden odotusten, mieltymysten ja sen tärkeysjärjestyksen perusteella, joka päämiehen asemassa olevalla henkilöllä kohtuudella voidaan olettaa olevan, ottaen huomioon jo saadut ohjeet ja tiedot.

(2) Toimeksisaajalla on kohdassa (1) tarkoitetussa tilanteessa oikeus vaatia, että päätettävän sopimuksen solmimiseksi sallittu tai vaadittava aika ja palkkio muutetaan vastaamaan olosuhteita. Muutetun ajan ja palkkion on oltava kohtuullisia.

Osa 2:
Toimeksiantosopimuksen muutokset

Artikkeli 4:201: Toimeksiantosopimuksen muutokset
(1) Toimeksiantosopimus muuttuu, jos päämies:
   (a) muuttaa toimeksisaajan toimeksiantoa olennaisesti;
   (b) ei peruuta ohjeitaan ilman aiheetonta viivytystä saatuaan artiklan 4:101 kohdan (3) (Päämiehen antama ohjeistus) mukaisen varoituksen.
(2) Toimeksiantosopimuksen muuttuessa kohdan (1) mukaisesti toimeksisaajalla on oikeus:
   (a) vaatia, että päätettävän sopimuksen solmimiseksi sallittu tai vaadittava aika ja palkkio muutetaan vastaamaan muuttuneita olosuhteita; tai
   (b) vaatia vahingonkorvausta PECL artiklan 9:502 (Vahingonkorvauksen yleinen määrittäminen) mukaisesti päästäkseen mahdollisimman samaan asemaan kuin missä hän olisi ollut, jos toimeksiantosopimusta ei olisi muutettu.
(2) Mikäli toimeksiantosopimus muuttuu kohdan (1) mukaisesti, toimeksisaaja voi myös irtisanoa toimeksiantosuhteen poikkeuksellisista ja vakavista syistä antamalla artiklan 6:105 (Toimeksisaajan tekemä irtisanominen poikkeuksellisista ja vakavista syistä) mukaisen irtisanomisilmoituksen, paitsi jos muutos on vähäinen tai toimeksisaajan edun mukainen.
(3) Kohdan (2)(a) mukaisesti maksettavan muutetun palkkion on oltava kohtuullinen ja se on määriteltävä samalla laskumenetelmällä kuin alkuperäinen palkkio.

Luku 5:
Eturistiriidat

Artikkeli 5:101: Toimeksisaaja sopimuksen vastapuolena
(1) Toimeksisaaja ei saa ryhtyä päätettävän sopimuksen vastapuoleksi
(2) Toimeksisaaja saa kuitenkin ryhtyä vastapuoleksi, jos
   (a) osapuolet ovat sopineet tästä toimeksiantosopimuksessa
   (b) toimeksisaaja on ilmaissut aikomuksensa ryhtyä vastapuoleksi ja
      (i) päämies antaa tähän hyväksyntänsä, tai
      (ii) päämies ei saatuaan tätä koskevan tiedustelun vastusta toimeksisaajan tulemista sopimuksen vastapuoleksi;
   (c) päämies muutoin tiesi tai hänen voidaan kohtuudella olettaa tienneen toimeksisaajan tulemisesta sopimuksen vastapuoleksi, eikä hän ole kohtuullisessa ajassa vastustanut sitä; tai
   (d) päätettävän sopimuksen sisältö on määritelty toimeksiantosopimuksessa niin tarkasti, etteivät päämiehen edut vaarannu.
(3) Jos päämies on kuluttaja, toimeksisaaja saa ryhtyä vastapuoleksi vain, jos
   (a) toimeksisaaja on saattanut tämän päämiehen tietoon ja päämies on antanut nimenomaisen suostumuksensa toimeksisaajan kyseisen päätettävän sopimuksen vastapuoleksi ryhtymiseen; tai
   (b) päätettävän sopimuksen sisältö on määritelty toimeksiantosopimuksessa niin tarkasti, etteivät päämiehen edut vaarannu.
(4) Osapuolet eivät saa päämiehen etujen vastaisesti jättää kohtaa (3) soveltamatta tai kiertää taikka muuttaa sen vaikutuksia.

(5) Jos toimeksisaaja on tullut sopimuksen vastapuoleksi, toimeksisaajalla ei ole oikeutta palk-kioon toimeksisaajana suorittamistaan palveluista.

Artikkeli 5:102: Kaksoisvaltuutus

(1) Toimeksisaaja ei saa toimia sekä päämiehen että päämiehen päätettävän sopimuksen vas-tapuolen toimeksisaajana.
(2) Toimeksisaaja saa kuitenkin toimia sekä päämiehen että vastapuolen toimeksisaajana mi-käli
   (a) osapuolet ovat sopineet tästä toimeksisantosopimuksessa
   (b) toimeksisaaja on ilmaissut aikomuksensa toimia vastapuolen toimeksisaajaksi ja pää-mies
      (i) antaa tähän suostumuksensa; tai
      (ii) päämies ei saatuaan tätä koskevan tiedustelun vastusta toimeksaajan asemaa vas-tapuolen toimeksisaajana;
   (c) päämies muutoin tiesi tai hänen voidaan kohtuudella olettaa tienneen toimeksisaajan asemasta vastapuolen toimeksisaajana, eikä hän ole kohtuullisessa ajassa vastustanut sitä; tai
   (d) päätettävän sopimuksen sisältö on määritelty toimeksiantosopimuksessa niin tarkasti, etteivät päämiehen edut vaarannu
(3) Jos päämies on kuluttaja, toimeksisaajalla on oikeus toimia sekä päämiehen että vastapuo-len toimeksisaajana vain, jos
   (a) toimeksisaaja saattanut tämän päämiehen tietoon ja päämies on antanut nimenomai-sen suostumuksensa sille, että toimeksisaaja toimii myös määrätyn päätettävän sopi-muksen vastapuolen toimeksisaajana; tai
   (b) päätettävän sopimuksen sisältö on määritelty toimeksiantosopimuksessa niin tarkasti, etteivät päämiehen edut vaarannu.
(4) Osapuolet eivät päämiehen etujen vastaisesti saa jättää kohtaa (3) soveltamatta tai kiertää taikka muuttaa sen vaikutuksia.
(5) Toimeksisaajalla on oikeus palkkioon jos ja siltä osin kuin hän on toiminut edellisten koh-tien mukaisesti.

Luku 6:
Irtisanominen Muun Kuin Suoritusvirheen Perusteella

Artikkeli 6:101: Irtisanomisesta yleisesti

(1) Kumpikin osapuoli voi irtisanoa toimeksiantosuhteen milloin tahansa ilmoittamalla siitä vastapuolelle.
(2) Toimeksisaajan valtuutuksen peruuttaminen merkitsee kohdassa 1 tarkoitettua irtisano-mista.
(3) Toimeksiantosuhteen irtisanominen on tehoton, jos valtuutus on artiklan 1:105 mukaisesti peruuttamaton (Peruuttamaton valtuutus).
(4) Irtisanomisen vaikutukset määräytyvät PECL luvun 9 jakson 3 (Sopimuksen päättäminen) mukaisesti.
(5) Jos toimeksiantosuhteen irtosanoneella osapuolella on oikeus irtisanomiseen, irtisanomi-sen perusteella ei tule maksettavaksi vahingonkorvausta.

(6) Irtisanominen on pätevä siitä huolimatta, että ilmoituksen antavalla osapuolella ei ole ollut oikeutta irtisanoa toimeksiantosuhdetta. Toinen osapuoli on kuitenkin oikeutettu saamaan korvausta PECL luvun 9 jakson 5 (Vahingonkorvaukset ja korko) mukaisesti

(7) Osapuoli on oikeutettu irtisanomaan toimeksiantosuhteen tämän artiklan tarkoittamalla tavalla, jos kyseinen osapuoli:

(a) on oikeutettu irtisanomaan toimeksiantosuhteen nimenomaisten sopimusehtojen perusteella ja toimeksiantosuhdetta irtisanottaessa on noudatettu sopimuksessa irtisanomiselle asetettuja ehtoja;

(b) on oikeutettu irtisanomaan toimeksiantosuhteen PECL luvun 9 jakson 3 säännösten nojalla (Sopimuksen päättäminen); tai

(c) on oikeutettu irtisanomaan toimeksiantosuhteen muun tässä luvussa esitetyn artiklan nojalla ja irtisanomisessa on noudatettu kyseisessä artiklassa irtisanomiselle asetettuja ehtoja.

Artikkeli 6:102: Irtisanominen päämiehen toimesta kohtuullista irtisanomisaikaa noudattaen

(1) Jos toimeksiantosopimus on solmittu toistaiseksi voimassa olevaksi tai tiettyä tehtävää varten, päämiehellä on oikeus milloin tahansa päättää toimeksiantosuhde antamalla irtisanomisilmoitus ja noudattamalla kohtuullista irtisanomisaikaa.

(2) Kohtaa (1) ei sovelleta, jos valtuutus on annettu peruuttamattomana.

(3) Osapuolet eivät saa päämiehen vahingoksi jättää tätä artiklaa soveltamatta tai kiertää taikka muuttaa sen vaikutuksia, paitsi milloin artiklan 1:105:n (Peruuttamaton valtuutus) mukaiset edellytykset täyttyvät.

Artikkeli 6:103: Irtisanominen päämiehen toimesta vakavasta ja erityisestä syystä

(1) Päämiehellä on oikeus päättää toimeksiantosuhde vakavasta ja erityisestä syystä antamalla irtisanomisilmoitus.

(2) Irtisanomisaikaa ei vaadita.

(3) Tämän artiklan merkityksessä poikkeuksellisena ja vakavana syynä pidetään sen henkilön kuolemaa tai edustuskelpoisuuden puuttumista, jonka osapuolet toimeksiantosopimuksen solmimisajankohtana tarkoittivat täyttämään toimeksisaajan toimeksiantosopimuksen mukaiset velvoitteet.

(4) Tätä artiklaa sovelletaan, soveltuvine muutoksineen, mikäli päämiehen oikeudenomistajat artiklan 7:101:n (Päämiehen kuolema) mukaisesti irtisanovat toimeksiantosuhteen.

(5) Osapuolet eivät saa jättää tätä artiklaa soveltamatta tai kiertää taikka muuttaa sen vaikutuksia päämiehen tai päämiehen oikeudenomistajien vahingoksi.

Artikkeli 6:104: Irtisanominen toimeksisaajan toimesta toimeksiantosuhteen ollessa voimassa toistaiseksi tai vastikkeeton

(1) Jos toimeksiantosopimus on sovittu toistaiseksi voimassaolevaksi, toimeksisaajalla on oikeus milloin tahansa irtisanoa toimeksiantosuhde antamalla irtisanomisilmoitus ja noudattamalla kohtuullista irtisanomisaikaa.

(2) Jos toimeksiantosopimus on vastikkeeton, toimeksisaajalla on oikeus irtisanoa toimeksiantosopimus antamalla irtisanomisilmoitus ja noudattaen kohtuullista irtisanomisaikaa.

(3) Osapuolet eivät saa jättää tätä artiklaa soveltamatta tai kiertää taikka muuttaa sen vaikutuksia päämiehen vahingoksi.

Artikkeli 6:105 Irtisanominen toimeksisaajan toimesta vakavasta ja erityisestä syystä

(1) Toimeksisaajalla on oikeus irtisanoa toimeksiantosuhde poikkeuksellisista ja vakavista syistä antamalla irtisanomisilmoitus.
(2) Irtisanomisaikaa ei tällöin vaadita.
(3) Tämän artiklan merkityksessä poikkeuksellisen ja vakavan syyn muodostavat
    (a) artiklan 4:201 (Toimeksiantosopimuksen muutokset) mukainen toimeksiantosopimuksen muuttaminen;
    (b) päämiehen kuolema tai edustuskelpoisuuden puuttuminen; ja
    (c) sen henkilön kuolema tai edustuskelpoisuuden puuttuminen, jonka osapuolet toimeksiantosopimuksen solmimisajankohtana tarkoittivat suorittamaan toimeksisaajan toimeksiantosopimuksen mukaisia velvoitteita.
(4) Osapuolet eivät saa toimeksisaajan vahingoksi jättää tätä artiklaa soveltamatta tai kiertää taikka muuttaa sen vaikutuksia.

Luku 7:
Muut Irtisanomisperusteet

Artikkeli 7:101: Päämiehen kuolema

(1) Päämiehen kuolema ei päätä toimeksiantosuhdetta
(2) Sekä toimeksisaajalla että päämiehen oikeudenomistajilla on oikeus päättää toimeksiantosuhde vakavasta ja erityisestä syystä artiklan 6:103:n (Irtisanominen päämiehen toimesta vakavasta ja erityisestä syystä) tai artiklan 6:105:n (Irtisanominen toimeksisaajan toimesta vakavasta ja erityisestä syystä) nojalla antamalla irtisanomisilmoitus.

Artikkeli 7:102: Toimeksisaajan kuolema

(1) Toimeksisaajan kuolema päättää toimeksiantosuhteen.
(2) Kuoleman hetkellä maksettavaksi erääntyneet kulut ja muut maksuvelvoitteet eivät lakkaa.

French[*]
Contrats de mandat

Chapitre 1:
Dispositions générales

Article 1:101: Champ dapplication

(1) Les présents principes s'appliquent aux contrats et aux autres actes juridiques par lesquels une personne, le mandataire, est autorisée et chargée (mandatée) par une autre personne, le mandant:

    (a) de conclure un contrat entre le mandant et un tiers ou de modifier directement la situation juridique du mandant à l'égard d'un tiers;

    (b) de conclure un contrat avec un tiers, ou d'accomplir un autre acte juridique à l'égard d'un tiers, pour le compte du mandant mais de telle manière que ce soit le mandataire, et non le mandant, qui soit partie au contrat ou à l'autre acte juridique; ou

    (c) de prendre des mesures censées aboutir à, ou faciliter, la conclusion d'un contrat entre le mandant et un tiers ou l'accomplissement d'un autre acte juridique qui modifierait la situation juridique du mandant à l'égard d'un tiers.

(2) Elles s'appliquent lorsque le mandataire s'engage à agir pour le compte, et conformément aux instructions du mandant et, avec les adaptations appropriées, lorsque le mandataire est simplement autorisé mais ne s'engage pas à agir, tout en agissant néanmoins.

(3) Elles s'appliquent lorsque le mandataire doit être rémunéré et, avec les adaptations appropriées, lorsqu'il ne doit pas l'être.

(4) Elles s'appliquent uniquement aux relations internes entre le mandant et le mandataire (la relation de mandat). Elle ne s'applique ni aux relations entre le mandant et le tiers, ni aux relations (s'il en existe) entre le mandataire et le tiers.

(5) Les contrats auxquels s'appliquent les présents principes et également les Principes de droit européen des contrats de service sont considérés comme étant régis à titre principal par les présente principes.

(6) Les présents principes ne s'appliquent pas aux contrats relatifs aux services et activités d'investissement ainsi qu'ils ont été définis par la directive 2004/39/EC, JO L 145/1, telle que cette dernière a été modifiée ou remplacée.

Article 1:102: Définitions

Aux fins des présents principes:

    (a) le «mandat» du mandataire est l'autorisation et la mission données par le mandant, telles qu'elles sont modifiées par toute instruction ultérieure;

    (b) le «contrat de mandat» est le contrat par lequel le mandataire est autorisé et mandaté à agir, et toute référence au contrat de mandat renvoie notamment à tout autre acte juridique aux termes duquel le mandataire est autorisé et mandaté à agir;

---

[*]   Translated by Dr. *Michel Séjean*, Université Panthéon-Assas (Paris II).

(c) le «contrat prospectif» est le contrat que le mandataire est autorisé et mandaté à conclure, négocier ou faciliter, et toute référence au contrat prospectif renvoie notamment à tout autre acte juridique que le mandataire est autorisé et mandaté à accomplir, négocier ou faciliter;

(d) un mandat de représentation directe est un mandat par lequel le mandataire doit agir au nom du mandant, ou de façon à indiquer une intention de modifier la situation juridique du mandant;

(e) un mandat de représentation indirecte est un mandat par lequel le mandataire doit agir en son nom propre, ou de façon à ne pas indiquer une intention de modifier la situation juridique du mandant;

(f) une «instruction» est une décision, prise par le mandant, relative à l'exécution des obligations résultant du contrat de mandat ou relative au contenu du contrat prospectif, et qui est communiquée lors de la conclusion du contrat de mandat, ou ultérieurement mais en conformité avec le mandat;

(g) le «tiers» est la partie avec laquelle le contrat prospectif doit être conclu, négocié ou facilité par le mandataire;

(h) la «révocation» du mandat du mandataire est le retrait, par le mandant, du mandat, de sorte que ce dernier ne produise plus aucun effet.

Article 1:103: Durée du contrat de mandat
Un contrat de mandat peut être conclu
(a) à durée indéterminée;
(b) à durée déterminée; ou
(c) pour une mission particulière.

Article 1:104: Révocation du mandat
(1) Sous réserve de l'application de l'article suivant, le mandat du mandataire peut être révoqué par le mandant à tout moment par notification au mandataire.
(2) La fin de la relation de mandat produit l'effet d'une révocation du mandat du mandataire.
(3) Les parties ne peuvent, au détriment du mandant, exclure l'application du présent article, ni y déroger ou modifier ses effets, à moins qu'il soit satisfait aux exigences de l'article suivant.

Article 1:105: Mandat irrévocable
(1) Par dérogation au précédent article, le mandat du mandataire ne peut pas être révoqué par le mandant si le mandat est donné:
   (a) dans le but de protéger un intérêt légitime du mandataire, autre que l'intérêt à recevoir le versement d'une rémunération; ou
   (b) dans l'intérêt commun des parties à une autre relation juridique, que ces parties soient ou non toutes parties au contrat de mandat, et que l'irrévocabilité du mandat du mandataire soit destinée à protéger correctement les intérêts de l'une ou plusieurs de ces parties.
(2) Néanmoins le mandat peut être révoqué si:
   (a) le mandat est irrévocable conformément à l'alinéa (1)(a) et:

(i) que la relation contractuelle dont est issu l'intérêt légitime du mandataire prend fin pour cause d'inexécution par le mandataire; ou

(ii) qu'il y a une inexécution fondamentale par le mandataire des obligations résultant du contrat de mandat; ou

(iii) que le mandant a un motif extraordinaire et grave pour mettre fin au mandat, conformément à l'article 6:103 (Fin par le mandant pour un motif extraordinaire et grave); ou

(b) le mandat est irrévocable conformément à l'alinéa (1)(b) et:

(i) que les parties pour l'intérêt desquelles le mandat est irrévocable ont consenti à la révocation du mandat;

(ii) qu'il est mis fin à la relation dont il est question à l'alinéa (1)(b);

(iii) que le mandataire commet une inexécution fondamentale des obligations résultant du contrat de mandat, pourvu que le mandataire soit remplacé sans retard excessif par un autre mandataire conformément aux stipulations régissant la relation juridique entre le mandant et l'autre partie ou les autres parties; ou

(iv) que le mandant a un motif extraordinaire et grave pour mettre fin au mandat, conformément à l'article 6:103 (Fin par le mandant pour un motif extraordinaire et grave).

(3) Lorsque la révocation du mandat n'est pas permise par le présent article, la notification de révocation est dépourvue d'effet.

(4) Le présent article n'est pas d'application s'il est mis fin à la relation de mandat conformément au chapitre 7 des présents principes.

Chapitre 2:
Obligations principales du mandant

Article 2:101: Obligation de coopérer

L'obligation de coopérer conformément à l'article 1:202 (Devoir de collaboration) des Principes du Droit Européen des Contrats (PDEC) impose au mandant, notamment, de

(a) répondre aux demandes d'informations formulées par le mandataire dans la mesure où les informations concernées sont nécessaires pour permettre au mandataire d'exécuter les obligations résultant du contrat de mandat;

(b) donner des instructions relatives à l'exécution des obligations résultant du contrat de mandat dans la mesure où cela s'impose au titre du contrat de mandat ou que cela fait suite à une demande d'instructions conformément à l'article 4:102 (Demande d'instructions).

Article 2:102: Rémunération

(1) Le mandant doit verser une rémunération si le mandataire exécute les obligations du contrat de mandat en qualité de professionnel, à moins que le mandant ait espéré et ait raisonnablement pu espérer que le mandataire exécute les obligations autrement qu'en contrepartie d'une rémunération.

(2) La rémunération est exigible lorsque la mission objet du mandat a été accomplie et que le mandataire en a rendu compte au mandant.

(3) Si les parties étaient convenues du versement d'une rémunération pour les services ren- dus, que la relation de mandat a pris fin et que la mission faisant l'objet du mandat n'a pas été accomplie, la rémunération est exigible à partir du moment où le mandataire a rendu compte de l'exécution des obligations résultant du contrat de mandat.

(4) Lorsque le mandat porte sur la conclusion d'un contrat prospectif et que le mandant a directement conclu le contrat prospectif ou qu'une autre personne désignée par le man- dant a conclu le contrat prospectif pour le compte du mandant, le mandataire a droit à la rémunération ou à une portion de celle-ci, si la conclusion du contrat prospectif peut être imputée en tout ou partie à l'exécution, par le mandataire, de ses obligations résultant du contrat de mandat.

(5) Lorsque le mandat porte sur la conclusion d'un contrat prospectif et que le contrat pros- pectif est conclu après la fin de la relation de mandat, le mandant doit verser la rémuné- ration, si le versement d'une rémunération était convenu sur le seul fondement de la conclusion du contrat prospectif et que

    (a) la conclusion du contrat prospectif est principalement le résultat des efforts du man- dataire; et que

    (b) le contrat prospectif est conclu dans un délai raisonnable après la fin de la relation de mandat.

Article 2:103: Frais engagés par le mandataire

(1) Lorsque le mandataire a droit à une rémunération, celle-ci est présumée inclure le rem- boursement des frais que le mandataire a engagés pour l'exécution des obligations résul- tant du contrat de mandat.

(2) Lorsque le mandataire n'a pas droit à une rémunération, ou lorsque les parties sont con- venues que les frais seraient payés séparément, le mandant doit rembourser au manda- taire les frais que ce dernier a engagés pour l'exécution des obligations résultant du con- trat de mandat, lorsque, et dans la mesure où, le mandataire a agi raisonnablement en engageant les frais.

(3) Le mandataire a droit au remboursement des frais au titre de l'alinéa (2) dès lors que les frais sont engagés et que le mandataire a rendu compte des frais.

(4) Si la relation de mandat a pris fin et que le résultat dont dépend la rémunération du mandataire n'est pas atteint, le mandataire a droit au remboursement des frais raisonna- bles qu'il a engagés pour l'exécution des obligations résultant du contrat de mandat. L'a- linéa (3) s'applique par analogie.

Chapitre 3:
Exécution par le mandataire
Section 1:
Obligations principales du mandataire

Article 3:101: Obligation dagir en conformité avec le mandat
À toutes les étapes de la relation de mandat, le mandataire doit agir en conformité avec le mandat.

Article 3:102: Obligation dagir dans lintérêt du mandant

(1) Le mandataire doit agir en conformité avec les intérêts du mandant, dans la mesure où ceux-ci ont été communiqués au mandataire ou dans la mesure où l'on pouvait raisonnablement attendre du mandataire qu'il fût conscient de ces intérêts.

(2) Lorsque le mandataire n'est pas suffisamment conscient des intérêts du mandant pour pouvoir exécuter correctement les obligations qui résultent du contrat de mandat, le mandataire doit demander des informations au mandant.

Article 3:103: Obligation de compétence et de diligence

(1) Le mandataire est tenu d'exécuter les obligations résultant du contrat de mandat avec la compétence et la diligence que le mandant est en droit d'attendre compte tenu des circonstances.

(2) Si le mandataire promet un niveau de diligence et de compétence plus élevé, il y est tenu.

(3) Si le mandataire est, ou prétend être, membre d'un groupe de mandataires professionnels pour lesquels des standards existent, qui ont été posés par une autorité habilitée ou par le groupe lui-même, le mandataire doit mettre en œuvre la compétence et la diligence garanties par ces standards.

(4) Pour déterminer la diligence et la compétence auxquelles le mandant est en droit de s'attendre, il convient de considérer, notamment:
   (a) la nature, l'ampleur, la fréquence et la prévisibilité des risques qu'implique l'exécution des obligations;
   (b) si les obligations sont exécutées par un non-professionnel ou si elles le sont à titre gratuit;
   (c) le montant de la rémunération pour l'exécution des obligations; et
   (d) le temps qu'il faut raisonnablement consacrer à l'exécution des obligations.

Section 2:
Conséquences du dépassement de mandat

Article 3:201: Dépassement de mandat

(1) Le mandataire peut agir en dehors des limites du mandat si:
   (a) le mandataire a un motif raisonnable d'agir ainsi pour le compte du mandataire;
   (b) le mandataire n'a pas une occasion raisonnable de découvrir les souhaits du mandant compte tenu des circonstances; et
   (c) le mandataire ne sait pas, et n'est pas raisonnablement censé savoir que l'acte, compte tenu des circonstances, s'oppose aux souhaits du mandant.

(2) Un acte dans le cadre de l'alinéa (1) emporte les mêmes conséquences entre le mandataire et le mandant qu'un acte couvert par le mandat.

Article 3:202: Conséquences de la ratification

Lorsque, dans des circonstances non couvertes par le précédent article, un mandataire a agi au-delà du mandat en concluant un contrat pour le compte du mandant, la ratification de ce contrat par le mandant exonère le mandataire de sa responsabilité envers le mandant, à moins que le mandant informe le mandataire, sans retard excessif après la ratification, que le mandant se réserve le droit d'introduire une action pour inexécution par le mandataire.

Section 3:
Mandat normalement non exclusif

Article 3:301: Exclusivité non présumée
Le mandant est libre de conclure, négocier ou faciliter le contrat prospectif directement ou de désigner un autre mandataire pour ce faire.

Article 3:302: Sous-traitance
(1) Le mandataire peut sous-traiter l'exécution de ses obligations résultant du contrat de mandat en tout ou partie sans le consentement du mandataire, à moins que soit contractuellement requise une exécution personnelle.
(2) Tout sous-traitant ainsi engagé par le mandataire doit présenter la compétence adéquate.
(3) Conformément à l'article 8:107 PDEC (Exécution confiée à un tiers), le mandataire demeure responsable de l'exécution.

Section 4:
Obligation dinformer le mandant

Article 3:401: Information relative à lexécution
Pendant l'exécution des obligations résultant du contrat de mandat, le mandataire doit, dans la mesure du raisonnable compte tenu des circonstances, informer le mandant de l'existence et du progrès des négociations ou d'autres étapes menant à la conclusion ou à la faciliation éventuelles du contrat prospectif.

Article 3:402: Comptes à rendre au mandant
(1) Le mandataire doit sans délai excessif informer le mandant de l'accomplissement des tâches faisant l'objet du mandat.
(2) Le mandataire doit rendre compte au mandant:
    (a) de la manière dont les obligations résultant du contrat de mandat sont exécutées; et
    (b) de l'argent dépensé ou reçu, ou des frais engagés par le mandataire pour l'exécution de ces obligations.
(3) L'alinéa (2) s'applique avec les modifications appropriées si la relation de mandat prend fin conformément aux chapitres 6 et 7 et que les obligations résultant du contrat de mandat n'ont pas été pleinement exécutées.

Article 3:403: Communication de lidentité dun tiers
(1) Un mandataire qui conclut un contrat prospectif avec un tiers doit communiquer au mandant le nom et l'adresse de ce tiers, à la demande du mandant.
(2) En cas de mandat de représentation indirecte, l'alinéa (1) ne s'applique que si le mandataire est devenu insolvable.

Chapitre 4:
Instructions et modifications
Section 1:
Instructions

Article 4:101: Instructions données par le mandant
(1) Le mandant est en droit de donner des instructions au mandataire.
(2) Le mandataire doit suivre les instructions données par le mandant.
(3) Le mandataire doit avertir le mandant si l'instruction:
  (a) a pour effet de rendre l'exécution des obligations résultant du contrat de mandat considérablement plus onéreuse ou considérablement plus lente à exécuter que ce dont il était convenu dans le contrat de mandat; ou
  (b) est incohérente avec le but poursuivi par le contrat de mandat, ou peut, d'une autre façon, porter atteinte aux intérêts du mandant.
(4) À moins que le mandant révoque l'instruction sans délai excessif après avoir été ainsi averti par le mandataire, l'instruction est considérée comme une modification du contrat de mandat conformément à l'article 4:201 (Modifications du contrat de mandat).

Article 4:102: Demande dinstruction
(1) Le mandataire doit demander que lui soit communiquée une instruction dès la réception d'informations exigeant que le mandant prenne une décision relative à l'exécution des obligations résultant du contrat de mandat ou du contenu du contrat prospectif.
(2) Le mandataire doit demander que lui soit communiquée une instruction si la tâche faisant l'objet du mandat est la conclusion du contrat prospectif et que le contrat de mandat ne précise pas si le mandat est de représentation directe ou de représentation indirecte.

Article 4:103: Conséquences du défaut de communication dune instruction
(1) Si le mandant ne communique pas d'instruction lorsque cela est exigé par le contrat de mandat ou conformément à l'alinéa (1) de l'article 4:102 (Demande d'instruction), le mandataire peut, dans la mesure où cela est pertinent, avoir recours à tout moyen régi par les Chapitres 8 et 9 PDEC, ou fonder l'exécution sur les attentes, préférences et priorités que le mandant serait raisonnablement censé avoir, compte tenu des informations et des instructions qui ont été rassemblées.
(2) Lorsque le mandataire fonde l'exécution sur les attentes, préférences et priorités que le mandant serait raisonnablement censé avoir, le mandataire dispose d'un droit à l'ajustement proportionnel de la rémunération et du temps laissé ou exigé pour la conclusion du contrat prospectif.
(3) À défaut d'instructions par le mandant conformément à l'alinéa (2) de l'article 4:102 (Demande d'instruction), le mandataire peut opter pour la représentation directe ou pour la représentation indirecte ou peut suspendre l'exécution conformément à l'article 9:201 PDEC (Droit de suspendre l'exécution).
(4) Le prix ajusté qui doit être payé conformément à l'alinéa (2) doit être raisonnable et doit être déterminé en utilisant les mêmes méthodes de calcul que celles qui ont été utilisées pour établir la rémunération initiale pour l'exécution des obligations résultant du contrat de mandat.

Article 4:104: Absence de temps pour demander ou attendre la communication dune instruction

(1) Si le mandataire doit demander la communication d'une instruction conformément à l'article 4:102 (Demande d'instruction) mais qu'il a besoin d'agir avant de pouvoir contacter le mandant et demander la communication d'une instruction, ou qu'il a besoin d'agir avant que l'instruction soit donnée, le mandataire peut fonder l'exécution sur les attentes, préférences et priorités que le mandant serait raisonnablement censé avoir, compte tenu des informations et des instructions qui ont été rassemblées.

(2) Dans la situation évoquée à l'alinéa (1), le mandataire dispose d'un droit à l'ajustement proportionnel de la rémunération et du temps laissé ou exigé pour l'exécution des obligations résultant du contrat de mandat dans la mesure où un tel ajustement est raisonnable compte tenu des circonstances.

Section 2:
Modifications du contrat de mandat

Article 4:201: Modifications du contrat de mandat

(1) Le mandat est modifié si le mandant:
  (a) modifie considérablement le mandat du mandataire;
  (b) ne révoque pas une instruction sans délai excessif après avoir été averti conformément à l'alinéa (3) de l'article 4:101 (Instructions données par le mandant).

(2) Dans le cas d'une modification du contrat de mandat conformément à l'alinéa (1), le mandataire a droit:
  (a) à un ajustement proportionnel de la rémunération et du temps laissé ou exigé pour l'exécution des obligations résultant du contrat de mandat; ou
  (b) à des dommages et intérêts conformément à l'article 9:502 PDEC (Mesure des dommages et intérêts en général) pour replacer le mandataire autant que possible dans la situation qui aurait été la sienne si le contrat de mandat n'avait pas été modifié.

(3) Dans le cas d'une modification du contrat de mandat conformément à l'alinéa (1), le mandataire peut également mettre fin à la relation de mandat en notifiant la fin du contrat pour un motif extraordinaire et grave conformément à l'article 6:105 (Fin par le mandataire pour un motif extraordinaire et grave), à moins que la modification soit mineure ou qu'elle soit à l'avantage du mandataire.

(4) La rémunération ajustée qui doit être payée conformément à l'alinéa (2)(a) doit être raisonnable et doit être déterminée en utilisant les mêmes méthodes de calcul que celles qui ont été utilisées pour établir la rémunération initiale pour l'exécution des obligations résultant du contrat de mandat.

Chapitre 5:
Conflits dinterêts

Article 5:101: Contrat avec soi-même
(1) Le mandataire ne peut pas devenir le cocontractant du mandant dans le contrat prospectif.
(2) Néanmoins le mandataire peut devenir le cocontractant si:
    (a) cela est prévu par les parties dans le contrat de mandat;
    (b) le mandataire a déclaré son intention de devenir le cocontractant et
        (i) le mandant exprime son consentement en conséquence; ou
        (ii) le mandant ne s'oppose pas à ce que le mandataire devienne le cocontractant après qu'on lui a demandé d'exprimer son consentement ou son refus de consentir;
    (c) le mandant savait, par d'autres voies, ou était raisonnablement censé savoir, que le mandataire devenait le cocontractant, tandis que le mandant ne s'y est pas opposé dans un délai raisonnable; ou
    (d) le contenu du contrat prospectif est déterminé de façon si précise dans le contrat de mandat qu'il n'existe aucun risque que les intérêts du mandant soient méconnus.
(3) Si le mandant est un consommateur, le mandataire ne peut devenir le cocontractant que si:
    (a) le mandataire a révélé cette information et que le mandant a donné son consentement exprès au fait que le mandataire devienne le cocontractant à ce contrat prospectif en particulier; ou
    (b) le contenu du contrat prospectif est déterminé de façon si précise dans le contrat de mandat qu'il n'existe aucun risque que les intérêts du mandant soient méconnus.
(4) Les parties ne peuvent, au détriment du mandant, exclure l'application de l'alinéa (3), ni y déroger ou modifier ses effets.
(5) Si le mandataire est devenu le cocontractant, il n'a plus droit à la rémunération des services qu'il a rendus en qualité de mandataire.

Article 5:102: Double mandat
(1) Le mandataire ne peut agir en tant que mandataire, à la fois du mandant et du cocontractant de celui-ci au contrat prospectif.
(2) Néanmoins, le mandataire peut agir en tant que mandataire du mandant et du cocontractant de celui-ci, si:
    (a) cela est convenu par les parties aux termes d'une stipulation du contrat de mandat;
    (b) le mandataire a révélé son intention d'agir en tant que mandataire du cocontractant et que le mandant
        (i) exprime son consentement en conséquence; ou
        (ii) ne s'oppose pas à ce que le mandataire agisse en tant que mandataire du cocontractant après qu'on lui a demandé d'exprimer son consentement ou son refus de consentir;
    (c) le mandant savait, par d'autres voies, ou était raisonnablement censé savoir, que le mandataire agissait en tant que mandataire du cocontractant, tandis que le mandant ne s'y est pas opposé dans un délai raisonnable; ou

    (d) le contenu du contrat prospectif est déterminé de façon si précise dans le contrat de mandat qu'il n'existe aucun risque que les intérêts du mandant soient méconnus.

(3) Si le mandant est un consommateur, le mandataire ne peut devenir le mandataire à la fois du mandant et du cocontractant que si:

    (a) le mandataire a révélé cette information et que le mandant a donné son consentement exprès au fait que le mandataire agisse également en tant que mandataire du cocontractant à ce contrat prospectif en particulier; ou,

    (b) le contenu du contrat prospectif est déterminé de façon si précise dans le contrat de mandat qu'il n'existe aucun risque que les intérêts du mandant soient méconnus.

(4) Les parties ne peuvent, au détriment du mandant, exclure l'application de l'alinéa (3), ni y déroger ou modifier ses effets.

(5) Si, et dans la mesure où le mandataire a agi conformément aux alinéas précédents, il a droit à rémunération.

Chapitre 6:
Fin par notification pour des motifs autres que linexécution

Article 6:101: Généralités sur la fin par notification

(1) Chaque partie peut mettre fin à la relation de mandat à tout moment en le notifiant à l'autre.

(2) Aux fins de l'alinéa (1), la révocation du mandat du mandataire est traitée de la même façon que la fin du mandat.

(3) La fin de la relation de mandat ne produit pas d'effet si le mandat du mandataire est irrévocable conformément à l'article 1:105 (Mandat irrévocable).

(4) Les effets de la fin du mandat sont régis par Chapitre 9, Section 3 PDEC.

(5) Lorsque la partie qui notifie pouvait valablement mettre fin à la relation, aucune allocation de dommages et intérêts n'est due de ce fait.

(6) Lorsque la partie qui notifie ne pouvait valablement mettre fin à la relation, la fin est néanmoins effective, mais l'autre partie a droit à des dommages et intérêts conformément aux dispositions du Chapitre 9, Section 5 PDEC.

(7) Aux fins du présent article, la partie qui notifie peut valablement mettre fin à la relation si cette partie:

    (a) était en droit de mettre fin à la relation conformément aux stipulations expresses du contrat et qu'elle a respecté, pour ce faire, toutes les exigences contractuelles;

    (b) était en droit de mettre fin à la relation conformément au Chapitre 9, Section 3 PDEC; ou

    (c) était en droit de mettre fin à la relation conformément à toute autre disposition du présent chapitre et qu'elle a respecté, pour ce faire, toutes les exigences posées par la disposition concernée.

Article 6:102: Fin par le mandant lorsque la relation doit durer de façon indéterminée ou lorsque le mandat est donné pour une mission particulière

(1) Le mandant peut mettre fin à la relation de mandat à tout moment en le notifiant avec un délai raisonnable, si le contrat de mandat a été conclu à durée indéterminée ou pour une mission particulière.

(2) L'alinéa (1) ne s'applique pas si le mandat est irrévocable.

(3) Les parties ne peuvent, au détriment du mandant, exclure l'application du présent article, ni y déroger ou modifier ses effets, à moins que soient remplies les conditions posées par l'article 1:105 (Mandat irrévocable).

Article 6:103: Fin par le mandant pour motif extraordinaire et grave

(1) Le mandant peut mettre fin à la relation de mandat en le notifiant pour un motif extraordinaire et grave.

(2) Aucun préavis n'est exigé.

(3) Constitue un motif extraordinaire et grave, aux fins du présent article, le décès ou l'incapacité de la personne dont, au moment de la conclusion du contrat de mandat, les parties avaient souhaité qu'elle exécute les obligations du mandataire résultant du contrat de mandat.

(4) Le présent article s'applique avec les adaptations appropriées si les successeurs du mandant mettent fin à la relation de mandat conformément à l'article 7:101 (Décès du mandant).

(5) Les parties ne peuvent, au détriment du mandant ou des successeurs du mandant, exclure l'application du présent article, ni y déroger ou modifier ses effets.

Article 6:104: Fin par le mandataire lorsque la relation doit être à durée indéterminée ou lorsquelle est à titre gratuit

(1) Le mandataire peut mettre fin à la relation de mandat à tout moment en le notifiant avec un délai raisonnable, si le contrat de mandat a été conclu à durée indéterminée.

(2) Le mandataire peut mettre fin à la relation de mandat en le notifiant avec un délai raisonnable si le mandataire doit représenter le mandant autrement qu'en contrepartie d'une rémunération.

(3) Les parties ne peuvent, au détriment du mandataire, exclure l'application de l'alinéa (1) du présent article, ni y déroger ou modifier ses effets.

Article 6:105: Fin par le mandataire pour motif extraordinaire et grave

(1) Le mandataire peut mettre fin à la relation de mandat en le notifiant pour un motif extraordinaire ou grave.

(2) Aucun préavis n'est exigé.

(3) Aux fins du présent article, un motif est extraordinaire et grave notamment en cas:
  (a) de modification du contrat de mandat conformément à l'article 4:201 (Modification du contrat de mandat);
  (b) de décès ou d'incapacité du mandant; et
  (c) de décès ou d'incapacité de la personne dont, au moment de la conclusion du contrat, les parties ont souhaité qu'elle exécute les obligations du mandataire résultant du contrat de mandat.

(4) Les parties ne peuvent, au détriment du mandataire, exclure l'application du présent article, ni y déroger ou modifier ses effets.

Chapitre 7:
Autres motifs de fin

Article 7:101: Décès du mandant
(1) Le décès du mandant ne met pas fin à la relation de mandat.
(2) Tant le mandataire que les successeurs du mandant peuvent mettre fin à la relation de mandat en notifiant la fin pour motif extraordinaire et grave conformément à l'article 6:103 (Fin par le mandant pour motif extraordinaire et grave) ou à l'article 6:105 (Fin par le mandataire pour motif extraordinaire et grave).

Article 7:102: Décès du mandataire
(1) Le décès du mandataire met fin à la relation de mandat.
(2) Les frais et toute autre dépense dus au moment du décès demeurent payables.

German[*]
Auftragsverträge

Kapitel 1:
Allgemeine Bestimmungen

Artikel 1:101: Anwendungsbereich

(1) Diese Grundregel finden auf Verträge und sonstige Rechtsgeschäfte Anwendung, durch welche eine Person, der Beauftragte, von einer anderen Person, dem Geschäftsherrn, ermächtigt und angewiesen (beauftragt) wird,

    (a) einen Vertrag zwischen dem Geschäftsherrn und einem Dritten zu schließen oder auf sonstige Weise unmittelbar auf die rechtliche Stellung des Geschäftsherrn gegenüber einem Dritten einzuwirken,

    (b) für den Geschäftsherrn in der Weise einen Vertrag mit einem Dritten abzuschließen oder einem Dritten gegenüber ein sonstiges Rechtsgeschäft vorzunehmen, dass der Beauftragte und nicht der Geschäftsherr Partei des Vertrages oder anderen Rechtsgeschäftes wird, oder

    (c) zu dem Zweck tätig zu werden, den Abschluss eines Vertrages zwischen dem Geschäftsherrn und einem Dritten oder die Vornahme eines sonstigen Rechtsgeschäfts, das auf die rechtliche Stellung des Geschäftsherrn gegenüber einem Dritten einzuwirken würde, herbeizuführen oder zu fördern.

(2) Diese Grundregel finden Anwendung, wenn sich der Beauftragte verpflichtet, für den Geschäftsherrn und nach dessen Anweisungen zu handeln; er findet mit den gebotenen Anpassungen Anwendung, wenn der Beauftragte lediglich zum Handeln ermächtigt aber nicht verpflichtet ist und gleichwohl handelt.

(3) Diese Grundregel finden Anwendung, wenn der Beauftrage ein Entgelt erhalten soll, und ferner mit den gebotenen Anpassungen, wenn der Beauftrage kein Entgelt erhalten soll.

(4) Diese Grundregel finden nur auf das Innenverhältnis zwischen Geschäftsherrn und Beauftragtem (Auftragsverhältnis) Anwendung. Er findet weder auf das Verhältnis zwischen Geschäftsherrn und Drittem noch auf ein etwaiges Verhältnis zwischen Beauftragtem und Drittem Anwendung.

(5) Verträge, auf die sowohl diesen Grundregel als auch die Grundregeln des Europäischen Rechts der Verträge über Dienstleistungen Anwendung finden, sind als Verträge anzusehen, die vorrangig diesen Grundregel unterfallen.

(6) Diese Grundregel finden keine Anwendung auf Verträge, die Wertpapierdienstleistungen und Anlagetätigkeiten im Sinne der Richtlinie 2004/39/EG in der jeweils geltenden Fassung betreffen.

---

[*]   Translated by Prof. Dr. *Martin Schmidt-Kessel*, University of Bayreuth and *Christina Dierks*, University of Osnabrück.

Artikel 1:102: Definitionen

Für diese Grundregel bezeichnet

(a) „Auftrag" die Ermächtigung und Anweisung des Beauftragten durch den Geschäftsherrn einschließlich der Änderungen durch jedwede nachträgliche Weisung,

(b) „Auftragsvertrag" den Vertrag, durch den der Beauftragte zum Handeln ermächtigt und angewiesen wird; jede Bezugnahme auf den Auftragsvertrag schließt die Bezugnahme auf jedwedes sonstiges Rechtsgeschäft ein, durch welches der Beauftragte zum Handeln ermächtigt und angewiesen wird,

(c) „Hauptvertrag" den Vertrag, zu dessen Abschluss, Aushandlung oder Förderung der Beauftragte ermächtigt und angewiesen ist; jede Bezugnahme auf den Hauptvertrag schließt die Bezugnahme auf jedwedes sonstiges Rechtsgeschäft ein, zu dessen Vornahme, Aushandlung oder Förderung der Beauftragte ermächtigt und angewiesen ist,

(d) Auftrag zur unmittelbaren Vertretung einen Auftrag, unter dem der Beauftragte im Namen des Geschäftsherrn handelt oder auf sonstige Weise den Willen kundtut, auf die rechtliche Stellung des Geschäftsherrn einzuwirken,

(e) Auftrag zur mittelbaren Vertretung einen Auftrag, unter dem der Beauftragte im eigenen Namen oder auf sonstige Weise so handelt, dass sein Wille, auf die rechtliche Stellung des Geschäftsherrn einzuwirken, nicht offenkundig wird,

(f) „Weisung" eine Entscheidung des Geschäftsherrn betreffend die Erfüllung der Pflichten aus dem Auftragsvertrag oder den Inhalt des Hauptvertrages, die [dem Beauftragten] bei Abschluss des Auftragsvertrages oder zu einem späteren Zeitpunkt in Übereinstimmung mit dem Auftrag mitgeteilt wird,

(g) „Dritter" diejenige Partei, mit der der Hauptvertrag durch den Beauftragten geschlossen, ausgehandelt oder gefördert werden soll,

(h) „Widerruf" des Auftrages die Rücknahme des Auftrages durch den Geschäftsherrn, so dass dieser keine Wirkungen mehr entfaltet.

Artikel 1:103: Dauer des Auftragsvertrages

Ein Auftragsvertrag kann

(a) auf unbestimmte Zeit,

(b) für eine bestimmte Frist oder

(c) für eine bestimmte Aufgabe

geschlossen werden.

Artikel 1:104: Widerruf des Auftrages

(1) Außer in Fällen des Artikel 1:105 kann der Auftrag durch den Geschäftsherrn jederzeit durch Erklärung gegenüber dem Beauftragten widerrufen werden.

(2) Die Aufhebung des Auftragsverhältnisses hat dieselben Wirkungen wie der Widerruf des Auftrages durch den Geschäftsherrn.

(3) Die Parteien können zum Nachteil des Geschäftsherrn die Anwendbarkeit dieses Artikels nicht ausschließen oder von dessen Wirkungen abweichen, es sei denn, die Voraussetzungen von Artikel 1:105 liegen vor.

Artikel 1:105: Unwiderruflicher Auftrag

(1) Abweichend von Artikel 1:104 kann der Auftrag durch den Geschäftsherrn nicht widerrufen werden, wenn der Auftrag

(a) erteilt worden ist, um ein berechtigtes Interesse des Beauftragten zu schützen, welches nicht das Interesse am Entgelt ist, oder

(b) im gemeinsamen Interesse der Parteien eines anderen Vertrages oder Rechtsverhältnisses erteilt worden ist, unabhängig davon, ob diese auch Parteien des Auftragsvertrages sind, und die Unwiderruflichkeit des Auftrages dazu dient, die Interessen einer oder mehrerer dieser Parteien in geeigneter Weise zu schützen.

(2) Der Auftrag kann gleichwohl widerrufen werden, wenn

(a) der Auftrag nach Absatz 1 Buchstabe a unwiderruflich ist und

(i) das Vertragsverhältnis, auf dem das berechtigte Interesse des Beauftragten beruht, wegen Nichterfüllung des Beauftragten aufgehoben wird,

(ii) eine wesentliche Nichterfüllung der Pflichten des Beauftragten aus dem Auftragsvertrag vorliegt, oder

(iii) ein wichtiger Grund den Geschäftsherrn zur Aufhebung nach Artikel 6:103 berechtigt,

oder

(b) der Auftrag nach Absatz 1 Buchstabe b unwiderruflich ist und

(i) die Parteien, in deren Interesse der Auftrag unwiderruflich ist, dem Widerruf des Auftrages zugestimmt haben,

(ii) das Verhältnis im Sinne von Absatz 1 Buchstabe b aufgehoben wird,

(iii) der Beauftragte eine wesentliche Nichterfüllung seiner Pflichten aus dem Auftragsvertrag begeht und der Beauftragte unverzüglich und in Einklang mit dem Vertrag zwischen dem Geschäftsherrn und der anderen Partei oder den anderen Parteien durch einen anderen Beauftragten ersetzt wird, oder

(iv) der Geschäftsherr einen wichtigen Grund für die Aufhebung nach Artikel 6:103 hat, und der Beauftragte unverzüglich und in Einklang mit dem Vertrag zwischen dem Geschäftsherrn und der anderen Partei oder den anderen Parteien durch einen anderen Beauftragten ersetzt wird.

(3) In Fällen, in denen der Widerruf des Auftrages nach diesem Artikel nicht zulässig ist, hat eine Widerrufserklärung keine Wirkung.

(4) Dieser Artikel findet keine Anwendung, wenn das Auftragsverhältnis nach den Vorschriften des 7. Kapitels diesen Grundregel aufgehoben wird.

Kapitel 2:
Hauptpflichten des Geschäftsherrn

Artikel 2:101: Pflicht zur Zusammenarbeit

Die Pflicht zur Zusammenarbeit nach Artikel 1:202 der Grundregeln des Europäischen Vertragsrechts (PECL) umfasst insbesondere die Pflicht des Geschäftsherrn

(a) Auskunftsverlangen des Beauftragten zu erfüllen, soweit er die Auskunft zur Erfüllung seiner Pflichten aus dem Auftragsvertrag benötigt,

(b) Weisungen bezüglich der Erfüllung der Pflichten aus dem Auftragsvertrag insoweit zu erteilen, als dies nach dem Auftragsvertrag erforderlich ist oder einem Ersuchen um Weisung nach Artikel 4:102 (Ersuchen um Weisung) ergibt.

Artikel 2:102: Entgelt

(1) Der Geschäftsherr ist verpflichtet dem Beauftragten ein Entgelt zu zahlen, wenn der Beauftragte bei der Erfüllung der Pflichten aus dem Auftragsvertrag als Unternehmer handelt, es sei denn, der Geschäftsherr erwartete und durfte vernünftigerweise erwarten, dass der Beauftragte die Pflichten anders als gegen Zahlung eines Entgeltes erfüllen werde.

(2) Das Entgelt wird fällig, wenn der Auftrag erledigt wurde und der Beauftragte dem Geschäftsherrn hierüber Rechenschaft abgelegt hat.

(3) Haben sich die Parteien auf die Zahlung eines Entgeltes für die geleistete Dienste geeinigt und hat das Auftragsverhältnis geendet, ohne dass der Auftrag erledigt worden ist, wird das Entgelt fällig, wenn der Beauftragte Rechenschaft über die Erfüllung der Pflichten aus dem Auftragsvertrag ablegt.

(4) Ist der Auftrag auf den Abschluss eines Hauptvertrages gerichtet und hat der Geschäftsherr den Hauptvertrag selbst abgeschlossen oder durch eine andere Person für den Geschäftsherrn abschließen lassen, hat der Beauftragte Anspruch auf das Entgelt oder einen angemessenen Teil des Entgeltes, soweit der Abschluss des Hauptvertrages der Erfüllung der Pflichten aus dem Auftragsvertrag durch den Beauftragten ganz oder teilweise zugeschrieben werden kann.

(5) Ist der Auftrag auf den Abschluss eines Hauptvertrages gerichtet und wird der Hauptvertrag geschlossen, nachdem das Auftragsverhältnis geendet hat, ist der Geschäftsherr verpflichtet, das Entgelt zu zahlen, sofern vereinbart worden ist, dass die Zahlung des Entgeltes allein an den Abschluss des Hauptvertrages geknüpft ist, und

   (a) der Abschluss des Hauptvertrages im Wesentlichen das Ergebnis der Bemühungen des Beauftragten ist und

   (b) der Hauptvertrag innerhalb einer angemessenen Zeit nachdem das Auftragsverhältnis geendet hat, abgeschlossen wird.

Artikel 2:103: Aufwendungen des Beauftragten

(1) Hat der Beauftragte Anspruch auf ein Entgelt, so gilt der Ersatz der Aufwendungen des Beauftragten, die diesem durch die Erfüllung der Pflichten aus dem Auftragsvertrag entstanden sind, als in dem Entgelt enthalten.

(2) Hat der Beauftragte keinen Anspruch auf ein Entgelt oder haben die Parteien den gesonderten Ersatz der Aufwendungen vereinbart, ist der Geschäftsherr verpflichtet, dem Beauftragten die Aufwendungen, die ihm durch die Erfüllung der Pflichten aus dem Auftragsvertrag entstanden sind, insoweit zu ersetzen, als der Beauftragte bei der Entstehung der Aufwendungen angemessen und vernünftig gehandelt hat.

(3) Der Beauftragte hat Anspruch auf Ersatz seiner Aufwendungen nach Absatz 2 sobald sie entstanden sind und er dem Geschäftsherrn über die Aufwendungen Rechenschaft abgelegt hat.

(4) Hat das Auftragsverhältnis geendet und ist der Erfolg, von dem die Zahlung des Entgelts abhängt, nicht eingetreten, kann der Beauftragte Ersatz der angemessenen und vernünftigen Aufwendungen, die ihm durch die Erfüllung der Pflichten aus dem Auftragsvertrag entstanden sind, verlangen. Absatz 3 findet entsprechende Anwendung.

Kapitel 3:
Leistung durch den Beauftragten
Abschnitt 1:
Hauptpflichten des Beauftragten

Artikel 3:101: Pflicht zu auftragsgemäßem Handeln
Während der gesamten Dauer des Auftragsverhältnisses ist der Beauftrage verpflichtet, gemäß dem Auftrag zu handeln.

Artikel 3:102: Pflicht zur Wahrnehmung der Interessen des Geschäftsherrn
(1) Der Beauftrage ist verpflichtet, die Interessen des Geschäftsherrn wahrzunehmen, soweit ihm diese Interessen mitgeteilt sind oder ihre Kenntnis von ihm vernünftigerweise erwartet werden kann.
(2) Der Beauftrage ist verpflichtet, Auskunft über die Interessen des Geschäftsherrn zu verlangen von denen er keine Kenntnis hat sofern diese Auskunft zur ordnungsgemäßen Leistung [des Auftragsverhältnisses] erforderlich ist.

Artikel 3:103: Pflicht zur Sorgfalt
(1) Der Beauftragte ist verpflichtet, die Pflichten aus dem Auftragsvertrag mit derjenigen Sorgfalt zu erfüllen, die der Geschäftsherr unter den gegebenen Umständen erwarten kann.
(2) Bekennt sich der Beauftragte zu einem höheren Sorgfaltsstandard, ist er verpflichtet, diesen einzuhalten.
(3) Ist der Beauftragte Mitglied einer beruflichen Vereinigung von Auftragnehmern oder behauptet er dies zu sein und bestehen für diese Vereinigung Standards, die von einer zuständigen Stelle oder der Vereinigung selbst aufgestellt wurden, ist der Beauftragte verpflichtet, diejenige Sorgfalt einzuhalten, die sich aus diesen Standards ergibt.
(4) Bei der Bestimmung der Sorgfalt, die der Geschäftsherr erwarten kann, sind unter anderem
    (a) Art, Umfang, Häufigkeit und Vorhersehbarkeit der mit der Erfüllung der Pflichten verbundenen Risiken,
    (b) die Frage, ob die Pflichten von einem Nicht-Unternehmer oder unentgeltlich erfüllt werden,
    (c) die Höhe des Entgeltes für die Erfüllung der Pflichten und
    (d) die für die Erfüllung der Pflichten vernünftigerweise zur Verfügung stehende Zeit
zu berücksichtigen.

Abschnitt 2:
Folgen einer Überschreitung des Auftrages

Artikel 3:201: Überschreitung des Auftrages
(1) Der Beauftragte darf nicht in einer vom Auftrag nicht gedeckten Weise handeln, wenn:
    (a) er hierfür im Interesse des Geschäftsherrn einen angemessenen und vernünftigen Grund hat,

(b) er keine angemessene und vernünftige Möglichkeit hat, den Willen des Geschäftsherrn unter den gegebenen Umständen festzustellen und

(c) er nicht weiß, dass sein Handeln dem Willen des Geschäftsherrn für die gegebenen
Umstände widerspricht und dies von ihm vernünftigerweise auch nicht erwartet werden kann.

(2) Handeln im Sinne von Absatz 1 hat im Verhältnis von Beauftragtem und Geschäftsherrn
dieselben Folgen wie auftragsgemäßes Handeln.

Artikel 3:202: Folgen der Genehmigung

Hat der Beauftragte unter Umständen, die nicht vom vorstehenden Artikel erfasst sind, beim
Abschluss des Hauptvertrages für den Geschäftsherrn seinen Auftrag überschritten, befreit die
Genehmigung des Hauptvertrages durch den Geschäftsherrn den Beauftragten von seiner
Haftung gegenüber dem Geschäftsherrn, es sei denn der Geschäftsherr zeigt dem Beauftrag-
ten unverzüglich nach der Genehmigung an, dass er sich seine Rechtsbehelfe wegen Nicht-
erfüllung durch den Beauftragten vorbehält.

Abschnitt 3:
Abschluss des Hauptvertrages durch eine andere Person

Artikel 3:301: Keine Ausschließlichkeit

Der Geschäftsherr darf den Hauptvertrag selbst schließen, aushandeln oder fördern oder sich
hierzu eines anderen Beauftragten bedienen.

Artikel 3:302: Unterauftrag

(1) Der Beauftragte darf ohne Zustimmung des Geschäftsherrn eine andere Person ganz oder
teilweise mit der Leistung unter dem Auftragsvertrag betrauen, es sei denn der Vertrag
erfordert die persönliche Erfüllung.

(2) Jeder Unterbeauftragte muss über hinreichende Fähigkeiten verfügen.

(3) Entsprechend Artikel 8:107 PECL (Einem anderen anvertraute Leistung) bleibt der Beauftragte für die Leistung verantwortlich.

Abschnitt 4:
Pflicht zur Unterrichtung des Geschäftsherrn

Artikel 3:401: Auskunft über den Leistungsfortschritt

Während der Leistung unter dem Auftragsvertrag muss der Beauftragte dem Geschäftsherrn,
soweit dies nach den Umständen vernünftig und angemessen ist, Auskunft über die Aufnah-
me von Vertragsverhandlungen und den Fortschritt der Vertragsverhandlungen oder andere
Maßnahmen, die dem Abschluss oder der Förderung des Hauptvertrages dienen, erteilen.

Artikel 3:402: Rechenschaftspflicht

(1) Der Beauftragte muss den Geschäftsherrn unverzüglich über die Erledigung des Auftrages
in Kenntnis setzen.

(2) Der Beauftragte muss dem Geschäftsherrn Rechenschaft über

(a) die Art und Weise, in der die Leistungen unter dem Auftragsvertrag erbracht wurden, und

(b) Ausgaben, Einnahmen oder Aufwendungen, die dem Beauftragten durch diese Leistungen entstanden sind,

ablegen.

(3) Absatz 2 findet mit den gebotenen Anpassungen Anwendung, wenn das Auftragsverhältnis nach Kapitel 6 oder 7 aufgehoben wird, bevor die Leistung unter dem Auftragsvertrag vollständig erbracht ist.

Artikel 3:403: Mitteilung der Identität des Dritten

(1) Der Beauftragte muss dem Geschäftsherrn den Namen und die Anschrift des Dritten mitteilen, wenn der Geschäftsherr dies verlangt.

(2) Für Aufträge zur mittelbaren Vertretung gilt Absatz 1 nur, wenn der Beauftragte insolvent wird.

Kapitel 4:
Weisungen und Änderungen
Abschnitt 1:
Weisungen

Artikel 4:101: Weisungen des Geschäftsherrn

(1) Der Geschäftsherr ist berechtigt, dem Beauftragten Weisungen zu erteilen.

(2) Der Beauftragte muss Weisungen des Geschäftsherrn befolgen.

(3) Der Beauftragte muss den Geschäftsherrn darauf hinweisen, dass die Weisung

(a) die Leistung unter dem Auftragsvertrag erheblich verteuern oder erheblich mehr Zeit erfordern würde, als im Auftragsvertrag vereinbart, oder

(b) mit dem Zweck des Auftragsvertrages unvereinbar ist oder in sonstiger Weise den Interessen des Geschäftsherrn abträglich sein könnte.

(4) Widerruft der Geschäftsherr die Weisung nicht unverzüglich, nachdem er den Hinweis des Beauftragten erhalten hat, ist sie als Änderung des Auftragsvertrages nach Artikel 4:201 (Änderungen des Auftragsvertrages) anzusehen.

Artikel 4:102: Ersuchen um Weisung

(1) Der Beauftragte muss um Weisung nachsuchen, wenn er von Umständen erfährt, die eine Entscheidung des Geschäftsherrn bezüglich der Leistung unter dem Auftragsvertrag oder bezüglich des Inhalts des Hauptvertrages erforderlich machen.

(2) Der Beauftragte muss um Weisung nachsuchen, wenn der Auftrag auf den Abschluss eines Hauptvertrages gerichtet ist und der Auftragsvertrag nicht bestimmt, ob der Auftrag auf eine unmittelbare oder eine mittelbare Vertretung gerichtet ist.

Artikel 4:103: Folgen des Ausbleibens von Weisung

(1) Erteilt der Geschäftsherr eine Weisung nicht, die nach dem Auftragsvertrag oder nach Absatz 1 von Artikel 4:102 (Ersuchen um Weisung) erforderlich ist, kann der Beauftragte [soweit einschlägig] die Rechtsbehelfe nach Kapitel 8 und 9 PECL ausüben, oder

(a) unter Berücksichtigung der erteilten Auskünfte und Weisungen seine Leistung an denjenigen Erwartungen, Präferenzen und Prioritäten ausrichten, die von einer Person in derselben Situation wie der Geschäftsherr vernünftigerweise erwartet werden können, und

(b) eine verhältnismäßige Anpassung des Entgeltes und der für den Abschluss des Hauptvertrages eingeräumten oder geforderten Zeit verlangen.

(2) Erteilt der Geschäftsherr eine Weisung nach Absatz 2 nicht, kann der Beauftragte zwischen unmittelbarer und mittelbarer Vertretung wählen oder seine Leistung nach Artikel 9:201 PECL (Zurückbehaltungsrecht) zurückbehalten.

(3) Das nach Absatz 1 Buchstabe b zu zahlende angepasste Entgelt muss angemessen und vernünftig sein und ist in Anwendung derselben Berechnungsmethoden zu ermitteln, die für die Bestimmung des ursprünglichen Entgeltes für die Leistung unter dem Auftragsvertrag angewandt wurden.

Artikel 4:104: Eilbedürftigkeit

(1) Hat der Beauftragte gemäß Artikel 4:102 (Ersuchen um Weisung) um Weisung nachzusuchen, besteht jedoch Handlungsbedarf bevor er beim Geschäftsherrn um Weisung nachsuchen kann oder bevor die Weisung erteilt ist, kann der Beauftragte unter Berücksichtigung der erteilten Auskünfte und Weisungen seine Leistung an denjenigen Erwartungen, Präferenzen und Prioritäten ausrichten, die von dem Geschäftsherrn vernünftigerweise erwartet werden können.

(2) Im Falle von Absatz 1 kann der Beauftragte eine verhältnismäßige Anpassung des Entgeltes und der für die Leistung unter dem Auftragsvertrag eingeräumten oder geforderten Zeit verlangen soweit eine solche Anpassung unter den Umständen des Falles vernünftig und angemessen ist.

Abschnitt 2:
Änderungen des Auftragsvertrages

Artikel 4:201: Änderungen des Auftragsvertrages

(1) Der Auftragsvertrag wird geändert, wenn der Geschäftsherr

(a) den Auftrag des Beauftragten in erheblicher Weise ändert oder

(b) eine Weisung nicht unverzüglich widerruft, nachdem er von dem Beauftragten einen Hinweis im Sinne von Absatz 3 von Artikel 4:101 (Weisungen des Geschäftsherrn) erhalten hat.

(2) Liegt eine Änderung des Auftragsvertrages nach Absatz 1 vor, kann der Beauftragte Anspruch

(a) eine verhältnismäßige Anpassung des Entgeltes und der eingeräumten oder geforderten Zeit für die Leistung unter dem Auftragsvertrag oder

(b) Schadensersatz nach Artikel 9:502 PECL (Allgemeiner Maßstab für den Schadensersatz), um den Beauftragten so weit als möglich so zu stellen wie er gestanden hätte, wenn der Auftragsvertrag nicht geändert worden wäre,

verlangen.

(3) Liegt eine Änderung des Auftragsvertrages nach Absatz 1 vor, kann der Beauftragte das Auftragsverhältnis außerdem nach Artikel 6:105 (Aufhebung aus wichtigem Grund durch

den Beauftragten) aus wichtigem Grund aufheben, es sei denn, die Änderung ist unwesentlich oder zum Vorteil des Beauftragten.

(4) Das nach Absatz 2 Buchstabe a zu zahlende angepasste Entgelt muss vernünftig und angemessen sein und ist in Anwendung derselben Berechnungsmethoden zu ermitteln, die für die Bestimmung des ursprünglichen Entgeltes für die Leistung unter dem Auftragsvertrag angewandt wurden.

Kapitel 5:
Interessenkollisionen

Artikel 5:101: Insichgeschäft

(1) Der Beauftragte darf nicht Partei des Hauptvertrages mit dem Geschäftsherrn werden.

(2) Der Beauftragte darf gleichwohl Partei des Hauptvertrages werden, wenn
   (a) die Parteien dies im Auftragsvertrag vereinbart haben,
   (b) der Beauftragte seine Absicht, Partei des Hauptvertrages zu werden, offengelegt hat und
   (i) der Geschäftsherr anschließend sein Einverständnis erklärt, oder
   (ii) der Geschäftsherr nach Aufforderung, sein Einverständnis oder seine Ablehnung anzuzeigen, nicht widerspricht,
   (c) der Geschäftsherr davon Kenntnis hatte oder Kenntnis von ihm vernünftigerweise erwartet werden konnte, dass der Beauftragte Partei des Hauptvertrages werden würde, und er dem nicht innerhalb angemessener Zeit widersprochen hat, oder
   (d) der Inhalt des Hauptvertrages in dem Auftragsvertrag so genau bestimmt ist, dass keine Gefahr besteht, dass die Interessen des Geschäftsherrn missachtet werden.

(3) Ist der Geschäftsherr Verbraucher, darf der Beauftragte nur dann Partei des Hauptvertrages werden, wenn
   (a) der Beauftragte dies offengelegt und der Geschäftsherr ausdrücklich sein Einverständnis damit erklärt hat, dass der Beauftragte Partei dieses bestimmten Hauptvertrages wird, oder
   (b) der Inhalt des Hauptvertrages in dem Auftragsvertrag so genau bestimmt ist, dass keine Gefahr besteht, dass die Interessen des Geschäftsherrn missachtet werden.

(4) Die Parteien können zum Nachteil des Geschäftsherrn die Anwendbarkeit von Absatz 3 nicht ausschließen oder von dessen Wirkungen abweichen.

(5) Ist der Beauftragte Partei des Hauptvertrages geworden, kann er kein Entgelt für als Beauftragter geleistete Dienste verlangen.

Artikel 5:102: Mehrfachvertretung

(1) Der Beauftragte darf nicht als Beauftragter sowohl des Geschäftsherrn als auch der anderen Partei des Hauptvertrages handeln.

(2) Der Beauftragte darf gleichwohl als Beauftragter des Geschäftsherrn und der anderen Partei handeln, wenn
   (a) die Parteien dies im Auftragsvertrag vereinbart haben,
   (b) der Beauftragte seine Absicht, als Beauftragter des Geschäftsherrn und der anderen Partei zu handeln, offengelegt hat und der Geschäftsherr
   (i) anschließend sein Einverständnis erklärt, oder

(ii) nach Aufforderung, sein Einverständnis oder seine Ablehnung anzuzeigen, nicht widerspricht,

(c) der Geschäftsherr davon Kenntnis hatte oder Kenntnis von ihm vernünftigerweise erwartet werden konnte, dass der Beauftragte als Beauftragter der anderen Partei handelt, und er dem nicht innerhalb einer angemessenen Zeit widersprochen hat, oder

(d) der Inhalt des Hauptvertrages in dem Auftragsvertrag so genau bestimmt ist, dass keine Gefahr besteht, dass die Interessen des Geschäftsherrn missachtet werden.

(3) Ist der Geschäftsherr Verbraucher, darf der Beauftragte nur dann als Beauftragter des Geschäftsherrn und der anderen Partei werden, wenn

(a) der Beauftragte dies offengelegt hat und der Geschäftsherr ausdrücklich sein Einverständnis damit erklärt hat, dass der Beauftragte auch als Beauftragter der anderen Partei dieses bestimmten Hauptvertrages handelt, oder

(b) der Inhalt des Hauptvertrages in dem Auftragsvertrag so genau bestimmt ist, dass keine Gefahr besteht, dass die Interessen des Geschäftsherrn missachtet werden.

(4) Die Parteien können zum Nachteil des Geschäftsherrn die Anwendbarkeit von Absatz 3 nicht ausschließen oder von dessen Wirkungen abweichen.

(5) Wenn und soweit der Beauftragte in Übereinstimmung mit den vorstehenden Absätzen gehandelt hat, kann er das Entgelt verlangen.

Kapitel 6:
Aufhebung durch Erklärung aus anderen Gründen als Nichterfüllung

Artikel 6:101: Aufhebung durch Erklärung im Allgemeinen

(1) Die Aufhebung des Auftragsverhältnisses wird wirksam, wenn die Aufhebungserklärung der anderen Partei zugeht oder eine in der Aufhebungserklärung angegebene Frist abgelaufen ist.

(2) Für Absatz 1 gilt ein Widerruf des Auftrages als Aufhebung.

(3) Eine Aufhebung des Auftragsverhältnisses ist nicht wirksam, wenn der Auftrag des Beauftragten nach Artikel 1:105 unwiderruflich ist.

(4) Kapitel 9, Abteilung 3 PECL findet auf die Wirkungen der Aufhebung Anwendung.

(5) War die Partei, die die Aufhebung erklärt hat, zur Aufhebung des Auftragsverhältnisses nach den Vorschriften dieses Kapitels dazu berechtigt, ist sie nicht verpflichtet zum Schadenersatz

(6) War die Partei, die die Aufhebung erklärt hat, zur Aufhebung des Auftragsverhältnisses nach den Vorschriften dieses Kapitels nicht berechtigt, ist die Aufhebung gleichwohl wirksam, aber kann die von der Nichterfüllung betroffene Partei Schadensersatz nach Artikel 9:502 PECL (Allgemeiner Maßstab für den Schadensersatz) verlangen.

(7) Eine Partei ist im Sinne dieses Artikel berechtigt die Aufhebung des Auftragsverhältnisses zu erklären wann diese Partei

(a) dazu berechtigt war auf Grund einer Bestimmung im Vertrag und sie die Anforderungen dazu beachtet hat;

(b) berechtigt war den Vertrag aufzuheben kraft des Kapitels 9, Abteilung 3 PECL; oder

(c) berechtigt war den Vertrag aufzuheben kraft einer anderen Bestimmung dieses Kapitels und sie die Anforderungen dazu beachtet hat.

Artikel 6:102: Aufhebung durch den Geschäftsherrn unter Einhaltung einer angemessenen Frist

(1) Der Geschäftsherr kann das Auftragsverhältnis jederzeit unter Einhaltung einer angemessenen Frist durch Erklärung aufheben, wenn der Auftragsvertrag für unbestimmte Zeit oder für eine bestimmte Aufgabe geschlossen worden ist.

(2) Absatz 1 findet keine Anwendung, wenn der Auftrag unwiderruflich ist.

(3) Die Parteien können zum Nachteil des Geschäftsherrn die Anwendbarkeit dieses Artikels nicht ausschließen oder von dessen Wirkungen abweichen, es sei denn, die Voraussetzungen von Artikel 1:105 (Unwiderruflicher Auftrag) liegen vor.

Artikel 6:103: Aufhebung durch den Geschäftsherrn aus wichtigem Grund

(1) Der Geschäftsherr kann das Auftragsverhältnis aus wichtigem Grund durch Erklärung aufheben.

(2) Eine Frist für die Aufhebung ist nicht erforderlich.

(3) Der Tod oder die Geschäftsunfähigkeit der Person, die zum Zeitpunkt der Abschlusses des Auftragsvertrages nach dem Willen der Parteien die Pflichten des Beauftragten aus dem Auftragsvertrag hätte erfüllen sollen, ist ein wichtiger Grund im Sinne dieses Artikels.

(4) Dieser Artikel findet mit den gebotenen Anpassungen Anwendung, wenn die Erben des Geschäftsherrn das Auftragsverhältnis nach Artikel 7:101 (Tod des Geschäftsherrn) aufheben.

(5) Die Parteien können zum Nachteil des Geschäftsherrn die Anwendbarkeit dieses Artikels nicht ausschließen oder von dessen Wirkungen abweichen.

Artikel 6:104: Aufhebung durch den Beauftragten bei für unbestimmte Zeit eingegangenen oder unentgeltlichen Verhältnissen

(1) Der Beauftragte kann das Auftragsverhältnis jederzeit unter Einhaltung einer angemessenen Frist durch Erklärung aufheben, wenn der Auftragsvertrag für unbestimmte Zeit geschlossen wurde.

(2) Der Beauftragte kann das Auftragsverhältnis unter Einhaltung einer angemessenen Frist durch Erklärung aufheben, wenn der Auftragsvertrag unentgeltlich ist.

(3) Die Parteien können zum Nachteil des Geschäftsherrn die Anwendbarkeit von Absatz 1 nicht ausschließen oder von dessen Wirkungen abweichen.

Artikel 6:105: Aufhebung aus wichtigem Grund durch den Beauftragten

(1) Der Beauftragte kann das Auftragsverhältnis aus wichtigem Grund durch Erklärung aufheben.

(2) Eine Frist für die Aufhebung ist nicht erforderlich.

(3) Im Sinne dieses Artikels stellen
   (a) die Änderung des Auftragsvertrages nach Artikel 4:201 (Änderungen des Auftragsvertrages),
   (b) der Tod oder die Geschäftsunfähigkeit der Geschäftsherrn, und
   (c) der Tod oder die Geschäftsunfähigkeit der Person, die zum Zeitpunkt der Abschlusses des Auftragsvertrages nach dem Willen der Parteien die Pflichten des Beauftragten aus dem Auftragsvertrag hätte erfüllen sollen,
   einen wichtigen Grund dar.

(4) Die Parteien können zum Nachteil des Geschäftsherrn die Anwendbarkeit dieses Artikels nicht ausschließen oder von dessen Wirkungen abweichen.

Kapitel 7:
Sonstige Fälle der Aufhebung

Artikel 7:101: Tod des Geschäftsherrn
(1) Das Auftragsverhältnis endet nicht durch den Tod des Geschäftsherrn.
(2) Sowohl der Beauftragte als auch die Erben des Geschäftsherrn können das Auftragsver-
    hältnis durch eine Aufhebung aus wichtigem Grund nach Artikel 6:103 (Aufhebung durch
    den Geschäftsherrn aus wichtigem Grund) oder nach Artikel 6:105 (Aufhebung aus wich-
    tigem Grund durch den Beauftragten) aufheben.

Artikel 7:102: Tod des Beauftragten
(1) Das Auftragsverhältnis endet durch den Tod des Beauftragten.
(2) Aufwendungen und jedwede sonstige Zahlungen, die zum Zeitpunkt des Todes fällig sind,
    bleiben zahlbar.

Italian[*]
Il Contratto di Mandato

Parte 1:
Previsioni Generali

Articolo 1:101: Ambito di applicazione

(1) La presente Parte del Libro IV si applica ai contratti e agli altri atti giuridici in cui un soggetto, l'agente, è autorizzato ed istruito (mandato) da un altro soggetto, il mandante:

    (a) a concludere contratti tra il mandante ed un soggetto terzo o da altrimenti produrre in altro modo effetti direttamente nella sfera legale del mandante in relazione ad un terzo soggetto.

    (b) a concludere un contratto con un soggetto terzo, o porre in essere altri atti giuridici con soggetti terzi, per conto del mandante ma in modo tale che l'agente, e non il mandante, sia parte del contratto o degli altri atti giuridici; o

    (c) porre in essere le azioni necessarie per rendere possibile, o facilitare, la conclusione di un contratto tra il mandante e un terzo o a porre in essere altri atti giuridici che possano produrre effetti nella sfera legale del mandante in relazione a soggetti terzi.

(2) La presente disciplina si applica quando l'agente si impegna ad agire per conto di, ed in accordo con le istruzioni del mandante e, con i dovuti adeguamenti, quando l'agente sia semplicemente autorizzato ma non si obblighi ad agire; ma ciò non di meno agisca.

(3) Si applica quando l'agente riceva un compenso e, con i dovuti adeguamenti, quando l'agente non riceva un compenso.

(4) Si applica solo ai rapporti interni tra il mandante e l'agente (rapporto di mandato). Non trova applicazione tra il mandante ed il terzo e al rapporto, se esistente, tra l'agente ed il terzo.

(5) I contratti cui si applica questa Parte e ai quali si applica anche la Parte C (Servizi), devono essere considerati regolati in via principale da questa Parte.

(6) Questa Parte non si applica ai contratti relativi ai servizi ed alle attività di investimento ai sensi della Direttiva 2004/30/CE, e successive modifiche ed integrazioni.

Articolo 1:102: Definizioni

Nella presente Parte;

    (a) il 'mandato' conferito all'agente consiste nell'autorizzazione ed istruzioni date dal mandante e come modificate da successive istruzioni;

    (b) il 'contratto di mandato' è il contratto in base al quale l'agente è autorizzato ed istruito ad agire, e ogni riferimento al contratto di mandato comprende il riferimento ad ogni altro atto giuridico con cui l'agente sia autorizzato o istruito ad agire;

    (c) il 'contratto prospettato' è il contratto che l'agente è autorizzato ed istruito a concludere, negoziare o facilitare, e ogni riferimento al contratto prospettato include il rinvio a ogni

[*]   Translated by Avv. Dr. *Cecilia Carrara*, Legance Studio Legale Associato, Rome and Dott.ssa *Adele Pascale*, Pescarainnova, Pescara.

altro atto giuridico che l'agente è autorizzato ed istruito a compiere, negoziare o facilitare;

(d) il mandato con rappresentanza è il mandato in base al quale l'agente agisce in nome e per conto del mandante, o comunque in modo tale da indicare l'intenzione di incidere sulla sfera giuridica del mandante;

(e) il mandato senza rappresentanza è il mandato in base al quale l'agente agisce in proprio nome o comunque in modo tale da non indicare di incidere sulla sfera giuridica del mandante;

(f) 'direttiva è la decisione del mandante che riguarda l'adempimento delle obbligazioni previste dal contratto di mandato o che riguarda il contenuto del contratto prospettato al tempo del conferimento del contratto di mandato o, conformemente con il mandato, in un momento successivo;

(g) il 'terzo' è il soggetto con cui deve essere concluso, negoziato o facilitato, il contratto prospettato dall'agente;

(h) la 'revoca del mandato all'agente consiste nella revoca del mandante del mandato in modo che questo non produca più effetti.

Articolo 1:103: Durata del contratto di mandato

Il contratto di mandato può essere

(a) a tempo indeterminato;

(b) a tempo determinato; o

(c) per particolari affari.

Articolo 1:104: Revoca del mandato allagente

(1) Fatta eccezione per l'applicazione dell'1:105, il mandato può essere revocato dal mandante in qualsiasi momento previa comunicazione all'agente.

(2) La risoluzione del contratto di mandato comporta la revoca del mandato all'agente.

(3) Le parti non possono in alcun modo, a danno del mandante, escludere l'applicazione del presente Articolo o derogare o modificarne gli effetti, salvo che ricorrano le ipotesi di cui all'1:105.

Articolo 1:105: Mandato irrevocabile

(1) In deroga all'1:104, il mandante non può revocare il mandato all'agente se il mandato è stato conferito

(a) al fine di tutelare un interesse legittimo dell'agente diverso dal proprio interesse al pagamento del prezzo, o

(b) nel comune interesse delle parti di un altro contratto e accordo, siano o meno tali soggetti parte del contratto di mandato, purché l'irrevocabilità del mandato dell'agente sia volta a tutelare adeguatamente l'interesse di uno o più di tali soggetti.

(2) Il mandato potrà essere revocato in ogni caso qualora:

(a) il mandato sia irrevocabile ai sensi del successivo paragrafo (1)(a) e

(i) il rapporto contrattuale da cui deriva l'interesse dell'agente viene risolto per inadempimento dell'agente; o

(ii) si verifichi un inadempimento fondamentale da parte dell'agente delle proprie obbligazioni ai sensi del contratto di mandato; o

       (iii) ci sia una ragione grave e straordinaria che faccia sì che il mandante risolva il contratto ai sensi del seguente 6:103; o

  (b) il mandato sia irrevocabile ai sensi del paragrafo (1)(b) e

      (i) le parti nel cui interesse il mandato è irrevocabile decidano di revocarlo; o

      (ii) il rapporto di cui al paragrafo (1)(b) è risolto; o

      (iii) l'agente ponga in essere un inadempimento di un'obbligazione essenziale del contratto di mandato, a condizione che l'agente sia sostituito senza indebito ritardo da un altro agente in conformità con il contratto tra il mandante e l'altra parte o parti; o

      (iv) sussista una ragione seria e straordinaria da parte del mandante per risolvere il contratto ai sensi del 6:103, a condizione che l'agente sia sostituito senza indebito ritardo da un altro agente in conformità con il contratto tra il mandante e l'altra parte o parti.

(3) Laddove la revoca del mandato non sia consentita ai sensi del presente Articolo 6, la comunicazione di revoca sarà inefficace..

(4) Il presente Articolo non si applica se il rapporto di mandato è risolto ai sensi del successivo Capitolo 7 di questa Parte.

Capitolo 2:
principali obbligazioni del mandante

Articolo 2:101: Obbligo di cooperazione

L'obbligo di cooperazione ai sensi del III. – 1:104 impone al mandante in particolare di:

(a) rispondere alle richieste di informazioni dell'agente nei limiti in cui dette informazioni siano necessarie a consentire all'agente di adempiere le proprie obbligazioni ai sensi del contratto di mandato;

(b) dare direttive per l'adempimento delle obbligazioni di cui al contratto di mandato nei limiti in cui ciò sia richiesto dal contratto di mandato o consegue a una richiesta di direttive ai sensi del 4:102 (Richiesta di direttive).

Articolo 2:102: Corrispettivo

(1) Il mandante è tenuto a pagare un compenso se l'agente adempie le obbligazioni previste dal contratto di mandato nello svolgimento di un'attività professionale, a meno che il mandante si aspetti o possa ragionevolmente aspettarsi che l'agente adempia le obbligazioni non a fronte di un corrispettivo.

(2) Il corrispettivo diviene dovuto quando gli obblighi previsti dal mandato siano stati completati e l'agente ne abbia dato conto al mandante.

(3) Se le parti hanno concordato il pagamento di un corrispettivo in relazione ai servizi resi, il rapporto di mandato è terminato e gli incarichi conferiti col mandato non sono stati portati a termine, il compenso sarà dovuto nel momento in cui l'agente abbia dato conto dell'adempimento delle obbligazioni previste dal contratto di mandato.

(4) Qualora il mandato sia stato concluso per un contratto prospettato e il mandante abbia concluso il contratto prospettato direttamente o un altro soggetto da lui nominato abbia concluso il contratto prospettato per conto del mandante, l'agente avrà diritto di ricevere il corrispettivo o una parte dello stesso se la conclusione del contratto prospettato può es-

sere attribuito in tutto o in parte all'adempimento da parte dell'agente delle obbligazioni previste dal contratto di mandato.

(5) Qualora il mandato venga conferito per la conclusione di un contratto prospettato e il contratto prospettato venga concluso dopo che il contratto di mandato sia terminato, il mandante dovrà pagare il corrispettivo all'agente se è stato concordato che il pagamento del corrispettivo è fondato unicamente sulla conclusione del contratto prospettato e

    (a) la conclusione del contratto prospettato è principalmente il risultato dell'operato dell'agente; e

    (b) il contratto prospettato sia stato concluso entro un lasso di tempo ragionevole dopo la conclusione del contratto di mandato.

Articolo 2:103: Spese sostenute dellagente

(1) Se l'agente ha diritto a ricevere un compenso, il compenso si presume includere il rimborso delle spese sostenute dall'agente nell'adempimento delle obbligazioni previste dal contratto di mandato.

(2) Se l'agente non ha diritto a ricevere un compenso o se le parti hanno concordato che le spese debbano essere pagate separatamente, il mandante dovrà rimborsare l'agente delle spese sostenute nell'adempimento delle obbligazioni previste dal contratto di mandato, se e a condizione che l'agente abbia agito in maniera ragionevole nel sostenere tali spese.

(3) L'agente avrà diritto a ricevere il rimborso delle spese sostenute ai sensi del paragrafo (2), dal momento in cui le spese siano state sostenute e l'agente ne abbia dato conto.

(4) Se il rapporto di mandato si è risolto e il risultato da cui dipende il compenso dell'agente non è stato raggiunto, l'agente avrà comunque titolo a ricevere il rimborso delle spese ragionevoli sostenute nell'adempimento delle obbligazioni previste dal contratto di mandato. Il Paragrafo (3) si applica di conseguenza.

Capitolo 3:
adempimento dellAgente
Sezione 1:
Obbligazioni principali dellAgente

Articolo 3:101: Obbligazione di agire in conformità con il mandato
A ogni fase del rapporto di mandato, l'agente deve agire in conformità con il mandato.

Articolo 3:102: Obbligazione di agire nellinteresse del mandante

(1) L'agente deve agire in conformità con gli interessi del mandante, così come comunicati all'agente o che l'agente debba ragionevolmente conoscere.

(2) L'agente deve richiedere informazioni al mandante sugli interessi dello stesso di cui l'agente non sia a conoscenza quando tali informazioni siano necessarie per consentirgli l'adempimento corretto del rapporto di mandato.

Articolo 3:103: Obbligo di diligenza

(1) L'agente è tenuto ad adempiere le obbligazioni previste dal contratto di mandato con la diligenza che il mandante può aspettarsi in base alle circostanze.

(2) Qualora l'agente professi un più alto standard di diligenza, lo stesso si obbligherà ad adoperare tale grado di diligenza.

(3) Qualora l'agente sia o dichiari di essere membro di un gruppo di agenti professionisti per i quali sono stabiliti standard di diligenza dalle autorità competenti o dal gruppo stesso, l'agente dovrà adempiere il mandato conformemente a tali standard di diligenza.

(4) nel determinare il grado di diligenza che il mandante ha diritto di aspettarsi, bisogna tenere in considerazione tra l'altro:

    (a) la natura, l'importanza, la frequenza e la prevedibilità dei rischi relativi all'esecuzione delle obbligazioni;

    (b) se le obbligazioni sono adempiute da un soggetto non professionista o gratuitamente;

    (c) l'ammontare del compenso dovuto per l'adempimento delle obbligazioni; e

    (d) il tempo ragionevolmente a disposizione per adempiere le obbligazioni.

Sezione 2:
Conseguenze dellagire al di là dei limiti del mandato

Articolo 3:201: Azioni oltre il mandato

(1) L'agente potrà agire in modi non compresi dal mandato se:

    (a) l'agente abbia ragionevole motivo di farlo per conto del mandante:

    (b) L'gante non abbia la ragionevole opportunità di scoprire quale sia la volontà del mandante nelle circostanze particolari; e

    (c) l'agente non conosca e non ci si possa ragionevolmente aspettare che conosca che una data azione nelle circostanze particolari sia contraria ai desideri del mandante.

(2) Un'azione ai sensi del paragrafo (1) produce le medesime conseguenze tra l'agente e il mandante di un'azione compresa nel mandato.

Articolo 3:202: Conseguenze della ratifica

Se, in circostanze non comprese dal precedente Articolo, l'agente abbia agito oltre i limiti del mandato nel concludere il contratto prospettato per conto del mandante, la ratifica di tale contratto da parte del mandante libera l'agente da responsabilità nei confronti del mandante a meno che quest'ultimo senza ingiustificato ritardo dalla ratifica, notifichi all'agente che intende riservarsi ogni azione in relazione all'inadempimento dell'agente.

Sezione 3:
Conclusione del Contratto prospettato da Altre Persone

Articolo 3:301: Mancanza di presunzione del patto di esclusiva

Il mandante è libero di concludere, negoziare o facilitare, direttamente il contratto prospettato o di nominare un altro agente per concluderlo.

Articolo 3:302: Subcontratto

(1) L'agente potrà affidare a terzi l'adempimento delle obbligazioni previste dal contratto di mandato in tutto o in parte senza il consenso del mandante, a meno che gli obblighi assunti dal contratto non siano di natura personale.

(2) Ogni subcontraente così incaricato dall'agente dovrà avere le necessarie competenze.

(3) In accordo con III.–2:106 (Adempimento affidato a terzi) l'agente sarà considerato responsabile dell'adempimento delle obbligazioni.

Sezione 4:
Obbligo di informare il Mandante

Articolo 3:401: Adempimento del mandato

Durante l'adempimento delle obbligazioni previste dal contratto di mandato, l'agente nei limiti in cui sia ragionevole in relazione alla circostanze, deve informare il mandante dell'esistenza, o dello stato, delle negoziazioni o degli altri passi intrapresi per condurre alla possibile conclusione o facilitazione del contratto prospettato.

Articolo 3:402: Rendiconto al mandante

(1) L'agente ha l'obbligo, senza immotivato ritardo, di informare il mandante del completamento degli obblighi del mandato.

(2) L'agente dovrà rendicontare al mandante:
   (a) delle modalità in cui ha adempiuto le obbligazioni previste dal contratto mandato; e
   (b) delle somme spese o ricevute o delle spese in cui l'agente sia incorso nell'adempimento di tali obbligazioni.

(3) Il Paragrafo (2) si applica con i dovuti adeguamenti qualora il rapporto di mandato venga risolto in base ai Capitoli 6 e 7 e le obbligazioni di cui al contratto di mandato non sia state adempiute in pieno.

Articolo 3:403: Comunicazione dellidentità del terzo

(1) L'agente dovrà comunicare, su richiesta del mandante, il nome e l'indirizzo del terzo.

(2) Nel caso di mandato senza rappresentanza, il paragrafo (1) si applica solo nel caso in cui l'agente divenga insolvente.

Capitolo 4:
Direttive e modifiche
Sezione 1:
Direttive

Articolo 4:101: Direttive del mandante

(1) Il mandante ha diritto di impartire delle direttive all'agente.

(2) L'agente ha il dovere di seguire le direttive del mandante.

(3) L'agente deve dare pronta comunicazione al mandante se la direttiva:

(a) produce l'effetto che l'adempimento delle obbligazioni previste dal contratto di mandato divengano significativamente onerose e richiedano significativamente più tempo di quanto concordato nel contratto di mandato; o

(b) sono incongruenti rispetto all'oggetto del mandato o possano altrimenti arrecare danno agli interessi del mandante.

(4) A meno che il mandante revochi le direttive impartite senza ritardo dopo essere stato avvertito dall'agente, le direttive devono essere considerate come modifiche al contratto di mandato ai sensi del 4:201 (Modifiche al contratto di mandato).

Articolo 4:102: Richiesta di direttive

(1) L'agente deve richiedere direttive per ottenere informazioni che richiedono che il mandante assuma una decisione relativa all'adempimento delle obbligazioni previste dal contratto di mandato o al contenuto del contratto prospettato.

(2) L'agente deve richiedere direttive se il compito previsto dal mandato sia la conclusione del contratto prospettato e il contratto di mandato non determini se il mandato conferisca rappresentanza diretta o indiretta.

Articolo 4:103: Conseguenze delle omesse direttive

(1) Se il mandante omette di dare direttive quando richiesto di farlo ai sensi del contratto di mandato o ai sensi del paragrafo (1) di 4:102 (Richiesta di direttive), l'agente potrà, nella misura in cui ciò sia rilevante, ricorrere a uno dei rimedi di cui al Libro III, Capitolo 3 (Rimedi per il mancato adempimento); o

(a) basare l'adempimento sulle aspettative, preferenze e priorità che una persona nella medesima situazione del mandante potrebbe ragionevolmente aspettarsi sulla base delle informazioni e direttive a disposizione; e

(b) richiedere un proporzionato aggiustamento del compenso e del tempo necessario o richiesto per la conclusione del contratto prospettato.

(2) Se il mandante omette di dare direttive ai sensi del paragrafo (2) di 4:102 (Richiesta di direttive), l'agente può scegliere di agire con rappresentanza diretta o indiretta o può sospendere l'adempimento ai sensi del III. – 3:401 (diritto di sospendere l'adempimento di obbligazioni corrispettive).

(3) L'aggiustamento del compenso ai sensi del paragrafo (1)(b) deve essere ragionevole ed è determinato utilizzando gli stessi criteri di calcolo utilizzati per determinare il compenso originario per le obbligazioni previste dal contratto di mandato.

Articolo 4:104: Mancanza di tempo per attendere una direttiva

(1) Se l'agente richiede direttive ai sensi del 4:102 (Richiesta di direttive) ma necessita di agire prima che la direttiva sia impartita, l'agente può fondare l'adempimento sulle aspettative preferenze e priorità che il mandante possa ragionevolmente aspettarsi sulla base delle informazioni e direttive ottenute .

(2) Nell'ipotesi di cui al paragrafo (1)), l'agente può richiedere un adeguamento proporzionato del compenso e del tempo necessario o richiesto per l'adempimento delle obbligazioni previste dal contratto di mandato in modo tale che tale adeguamento sia ragionevole date le circostanze del caso concreto.

Sezione 2:
Modifiche del contratto di mandato

Articolo 4:201: Modifiche del contratto di mandato
(1) Il contratto di mandato si intende modificato se il mandante:
  (a) modifichi significativamente il mandato dell'agente;
  (b) non revochi la direttiva senza ingiustificato ritardo dopo essere stato avvertito ai sensi del paragrafo (3) del 4:101 (Direttive del mandante).
(2) In caso di modifiche nel contratto di mandato ai sensi del paragrafo (1), l'agente avrà diritto:
  (a) ad un aggiustamento proporzionato del compenso, della durata necessario o richiesto per l'adempimento delle obbligazioni previste dal contratto di mandato; o
  (b) al risarcimento del danno ai sensi del III. – 3:702 (Risarcimento del danno) al fine di mettere l'agente quanto più possibile nella posizione in cui sarebbe stato se il contratto di mandato non fosse stato modificato.
(3) In caso di modifiche al contratto di mandato ai sensi del paragrafo (1) l'agente potrà altresì risolvere il rapporto di mandato per ragioni straordinarie e gravi ai sensi del 6:105 (Risoluzione dell'agente per ragioni straordinarie e gravi), a meno che le modifiche siano di lieve entità o vantaggio dell'agente.
(4) L'aggiustamento del compenso dovuto ai sensi del paragrafo (2)(a) deve essere ragionevole e deve essere determinato utilizzando lo stesso metodo di calcolo che era stato applicato per determinare il compenso originale per l'adempimento delle obbligazioni previste dal contratto di mandato.

Capitolo 5:
Conflitto d'interesse

Articolo 5:101: Contratto con se stesso
(1) L'agente non può diventare la controparte del mandante nel contratto prospettato.
(2) L'agente può invece divenire controparte se
  (a) ciò è pattuito dalle parti nel contratto di mandato;
  (b) l'agente ha dichiarato la sua intenzione di divenire controparte e
    (i) il mandante ha espressamente accettato; o
    (ii) il mandante non ha obiettato a che l'agente diventasse controparte dopo essergli stato richiesto di esprimere il proprio consenso o manifestare il proprio dissenso;
  (c) il mandante sia altrimenti a conoscenza, o ci si possa ragionevolmente aspettare che sappia, che l'agente sia diventato controparte e il mandante non abbia a ciò obiettato in un lasso di tempo ragionevole; o
  (d) il consenso al contratto prospettato sia determinato così precisamente nel contratto di mandato che non vi sia alcun rischio che l'interesse del mandante possa essere disatteso.
(3) Se il mandante è un consumatore, l'agente potrà divenire sua controparte solo a condizione che

(a) l'agente abbia reso nota tale informazione e il mandante abbia dato espresso consenso all'agente di diventare controparte del particolare contratto prospettato; o

(b) il contenuto del contratto prospettato è determinato con tale precisione nel contratto di mandato che non vi è alcun rischio che l'interesse del mandante possa essere disatteso.

(4) Le parti non possono, a danno del mandante, escludere l'applicazione del paragrafo (3) o derogarvi o modificarne gli effetti.

(5) Se l'agente è diventato controparte del mandante, l'agente non ha titolo al compenso per i servizi resi come agente.

Articolo 5:102: Doppio mandato

(1) L'agente non potrà agire quale agente sia del mandante che della controparte del mandante nel contratto prospettato.

(2) L'agente potrà agire come agente sia del mandante che della sua controparte se

(a) ciò sia pattuito dalle parti nel contratto di mandato;

(b) l'agente abbia reso nota l'intenzione di agire quale agente della controparte del mandante, e il mandante

(i) accetti espressamente; o

(ii) non obietti che l'agente agisca quale agente della controparte del mandante dopo che gli sia stato richiesto il consenso o il rifiuto del consenso;

(c) il mandante sia altresì a conoscenza, o ci si possa ragionevolmente aspettare che sappia, che l'agente agisca quale agente della controparte del mandante ed il mandante non obietti entro un tempo ragionevole; o

(d) il contenuto del contratto prospettato sia così precisamente determinato nel contratto di mandato che non ci sia alcun rischio che l'interesse del mandante possa essere disatteso.

(3) Se il mandante è un consumatore, l'agente potrà solo agire come agente di entrambi il mandante e la controparte se

(a) l'agente ha rivelato tale informazione e il mandante abbia dato espresso mandato al fine di permettere che l'agente agisca anche come agente della controparte in relazione al particolare contratto prospettato; o

(b) il contenuto del contratto prospettato sia così determinato nel dettaglio che nel contrato di mandato che non ci sia alcun rischio che gli interessi del mandante possano essere disattesi.

(4) Le parti non possono, a danno del mandante, escludere l'applicazione del paragrafo (3) o derogarvi o modificarne gli effetti.

(5) Nei limiti in cui l'agente abbia agito in accordo con il precedente paragrafo, l'agente avrà diritto a ricevere il compenso.

Capitolo 6:
Risoluzione del contratto con preavviso per motivi diversi dal mancato adempimento

Articolo 6:101: Risoluzione mediante preavviso in generale

(1) La risoluzione del contratto di mandato produce i suoi effetti quando la sua notizia giunge a conoscenza dell'altra parte o, se il periodo di preavviso è rispettato, quando il periodo di preavviso previsto sia decorso.

(2) Per i fini di cui al precedente paragrafo (1), la revoca del mandato all'agente è considerata come risoluzione del contratto.

(3) La risoluzione del contratto non produce effetti se il mandato dell'agente è irrevocabile ai sensi dell'1:105.

(4) Il Libro III, Capitolo 3, Sezione 5 si applica per quanto concerne gli effetti della risoluzione.

(5) Quanto la parte che dà il preavviso non ha diritto di risolvere il rapporto di mandato ai sensi del presente Capitolo o le sia stato richiesto di osservare un preavviso di ragionevole durata e non vi adempia, la risoluzione non produce effetti.

(6) Nelle ipotesi di cui al precedente paragrafo (5), la parte danneggiata potrà richedere:
   (a) Il risarcimento dei danni ai sensi del III. – 3:702 (Risarcimento del danno); e
   (b) l'esecuzione in forma specifica delle sole obbligazioni derivanti dalle disposizioni del contratto di mandato per la transazione delle controversie o da altre previsioni applicabili anche dopo la risoluzione.

Articolo 6:102: Risoluzione del mandante mediante ragionevole preavviso

(1) Il mandante può risolvere il rapporto di mandato in qualsiasi momento dando un ragionevole preavviso se il contratto di mandato è stato concluso a tempo indeterminato o per particolari compiti.

(2) Il Paragrafo (1) non si applica se il mandato è irrevocabile.

(3) Le parti non possono, a danno del mandante o dei suoi successori, escludere l'applicazione del presente Articolo o derogarvi o modificarne gli effetti, a meno che la condizione di cui all'1:105 (Mandato Irrevocabile) non sia soddisfatta.

Articolo 6:103: Risoluzione del mandante per ragioni straordinarie e gravi

(1) Il mandante può risolvere il rapporto di mandato per ragioni straordinarie e gravi.

(2) Nessun preavviso è richiesto.

(3) Ai fini del presente Articolo, la morte o l'incapacità della persona che, al tempo della conclusione del contratto di mandato, le parti intendevano eseguisse le obbligazioni dell'agente ai sensi del contratto di mandato, costituisce una ragione straordinaria e grave.

(4) Il presente Articolo si applica con i dovuti adeguamenti se il successore del mandante risolve il rapporto di mandato in accordo con 7:101 (Morte del mandante).

(5) Le parti non possono, a danno del mandante o dei suoi successori, escludere l'applicazione del presente Articolo o derogarvi o modificarne gli effetti.

Articolo 6:104: Risoluzione dellagente quanto il rapporto di mandato è a tempo indeterminato o quando è a titolo gratuito

(1) L'agente può risolvere il rapporto di mandato in qualsiasi momento di ragionevole durata se il contratto di mandato è a tempo indeterminato.

(2) L'agente può risolvere il rapporto di mandato in qualsiasi momento dando un preavviso di ragionevole durata se il contratto di mandato è a titolo gratuito.

(3) Le parti non possono, a danno dell'agente, escludere l'applicazione del paragrafo (1) del presente Articolo o derogarvi o modificarne gli effetti.

Articolo 6:105: Risoluzione dellagente per ragioni straordinarie e gravi motivi

(1) L'agente può risolvere il rapporto di mandato dando un preavviso per ragioni straordinarie e gravi motivi.

(2) Nessun preavviso è richiesto.

(3) Ai fini del presente Articolo costituiscono ragioni straordinarie e gravi motivi:
   (a) una modifica del contratto di mandato ai sensi del 4:201 (Modifiche al contratto di mandato);
   (b) la morte o l'incapacità del mandante;
   (c) la morte o l'incapacità della persona che al tempo della conclusione del contratto di mandato, le parti intendevano eseguisse le obbligazioni dell'agente ai sensi del contratto di mandato;

(4) Le parti non possono, a danno dell'agente, escludere l'applicazione del paragrafo (1) del presente Articolo o derogarvi o modificarne gli effetti.

Capitolo 7:
Aaltre ipotesi di risoluzione

Articolo 7:101: Morte del mandante

(1) La morte del mandante non causa la risoluzione del contratto di mandato.

(2) Sia l'agente che gli eredi del mandante possono risolvere il contratto di mandato per motivi straordinari e gravi ai sensi dell'Articolo 6:103 (Risoluzione del mandante per motivi straordinari e gravi) o 6:105 (Risoluzione da parte dell'agente per motivi straordinari e gravi).

Articolo 7:102: Morte dellagente

(1) La morte dell'agente comporta la risoluzione del contratto di mandato.

(2) Le spese ed ogni altro pagamento dovuto al tempo della sua morte restano altresì dovuti.

Slovak[*]
Príkazné zmluvy

Kapitola 1:
všeobecné ustanovenia

Článok 1:101: Pôsobnost

(1) Tieto Princípy sa použijú na zmluvy a iné právne úkony, na základe ktorých je osoba príkazníka oprávnená a inštruovaná (má mandát) inou osobou, príkazcom:

   (a) uzavrieť zmluvu medzi príkazcom a treťou stranou alebo inak priamo ovplyvniť právne postavenie príkazcu vo vzťahu k tretej strane;

   (b) uzavrieť zmluvu s treťou stranou, alebo vykonať iný právny úkon vo vzťahu k tretej strane v záujme príkazcu, avšak takým spôsobom, že príkazník, a nie príkazca bude stranou zmluvy alebo iného právneho úkonu; alebo

   (c) uskutočniť opatrenia, ktoré majú viesť k uzavretiu alebo k možnosti uzavretia zmluvy medzi príkazcom a treťou stranou, alebo k vykonaniu iného právneho úkonu, ktorý by ovplyvnil právne postavenie príkazcu vo vzťahu k tretej strane.

(2) Tieto Princípy sa použijú, ak sa príkazník zaviaže konať v záujme a v súlade s inštrukciami príkazcu a primerane sa použijú, ak má príkazník iba oprávnenie, nie však povinnosť konať, ale bez ohľadu na to koná.

(3) Tieto Princípy sa použijú, ak má byť príkazníkovi poskytnutá odplata a primerane sa použije, ak mu nemá byť poskytnutá odplata.

(4) Tieto Princípy sa použijú iba na vnútorný vzťah medzi príkazcom a príkazníkom (príkazný vzťah). Nepoužijú sa na vzťah medzi príkazcom a treťou stranou alebo na vzťah (ak takýto vzťah existuje) medzi príkazníkom a treťou stranou.

(5) Zmluvy, na ktoré sa použijú tieto Princípy a zároveň tiež Princípy európskeho práva o zmluvách na vykonanie služieb, sa považujú za prednostne upravené touto časťou.

(6) Tieto Princípy sa nepoužijú na zmluvy týkajúce sa investičných služieb a činností tak, ako sú vymedzené smernicou 2004/39/ES, Ú. v. EÚ L 145/1, v znení jej neskorších zmien a doplnkov.

Článok 1:102: Vymedzenie pojmov

V týchto Princípoch;

(a) „mandát" príkazníka je oprávnenie a inštrukcia daná príkazcom so zohľadnením akéhokoľvek následného pokynu;

(b) „príkazná zmluva" je zmluva, na základe ktorej je príkazník oprávnený a inštruovaný konať a akýkoľvek odkaz na príkaznú zmluvu zahŕňa odkaz na akýkoľvek iný právny úkon, na základe ktorého je príkazník oprávnený a inštruovaný konať;

(c) „cieľová zmluva" je zmluva, ktorú je príkazník oprávnený a inštruovaný uzavrieť, dojednať alebo umožniť jej uzavretie, a akýkoľvek odkaz na cieľovú zmluvu zahŕňa odkaz na aký-

---

*   Translated by Dr. *Monika Jurčová* and Dr. *Marianna Novotná*, University of Trnava, Trnava.

koľvek iný právny úkon, ktorý je príkazník oprávnený a inštruovaný vykonať, dojednať alebo umožniť;

(d) mandát na priame zastúpenie je mandát, na základe ktorého má príkazník konať v mene príkazcu alebo inak spôsobom, ktorý naznačuje vôľu ovplyvniť právne postavenie príkazcu;

(e) mandát na nepriame zastúpenie je mandát, na základe ktorého má príkazník konať vo vlastnom mene alebo inak spôsobom, ktorý nenaznačuje vôľu ovplyvniť právne postavenie príkazcu;

(f) „pokyn" je rozhodnutie príkazcu týkajúce sa plnenia záväzkov z príkaznej zmluvy alebo obsahu cieľovej zmluvy, ktorý je udelený v čase uzavretia príkaznej zmluvy alebo v súlade s mandátom neskôr;

(g) „tretia strana" je strana, s ktorou má byť cieľová zmluva príkazníkom uzavretá, dojednaná alebo má byť ním umožnené jej uzavretie;

(h) „odvolanie" mandátu príkazníka je zrušenie mandátu príkazcom, ktorým mandát stráca účinky.

Článok 1:103: Trvanie príkaznej zmluvy
Príkaznú zmluvu možno uzavrieť
(a) na neurčitú dobu;
(b) na stanovenú dobu; alebo
(c) na stanovenú úlohu.

Článok 1:104: Odvolanie mandátu príkazníka
(1) Ak sa nepoužije nasledujúci článok, mandát príkazníka môže byť kedykoľvek príkazcom odvolaný uskutočnením oznámenia príkazníkovi.
(2) Zánik príkazného vzťahu má rovnaké účinky ako odvolanie mandátu príkazníka.
(3) Strany nesmú na ťarchu príkazcu vylúčiť použitie tohto článku alebo sa od neho odchýliť alebo zmeniť jeho účinky, ibaže sú naplnené požiadavky stanovené v nasledujúcom článku.

Článok 1:105: Neodvolateľný mandát
(1) Odchylne od predchádzajúceho článku, mandát príkazníka nemôže byť odvolaný príkazcom, ak je mandát príkazníka udelený
  (a) za účelom zabezpečenia oprávneného záujmu príkazníka, ktorý spočíva v záujme inom ako na poskytnutí odplaty, alebo
  (b) v spoločnom záujme strán inej zmluvy alebo iného právneho vzťahu, bez ohľadu na to, či tieto strany všetky sú alebo nie sú stranou príkaznej zmluvy, a neodvolateľnosť mandátu príkazníka má náležite chrániť záujem jednej alebo viacerých z týchto strán.
(2) Mandát však možno odvolať, ak
  (a) mandát je neodvolateľný podľa ods. (1) písm. (a) a
    (i) zmluvný vzťah, ktorý zakladá oprávnený záujem príkazníka, bol zrušený pre nesplnenie príkazníka; alebo
    (ii) došlo k podstatnému nesplneniu povinností príkazníka z príkaznej zmluvy; alebo

(iii) je daný závažný a mimoriadny dôvod pre zrušenie príkazného vzťahu príkazcom podľa 6:103 (Zrušenie príkazcom pre mimoriadny a závažný dôvod); alebo

(b) mandát je neodvolateľný podľa ods. (1) písm. (b) a

(i) strany, v záujme ktorých je mandát neodvolateľný, sa dohodli na odvolaní mandátu alebo

(ii) vzťah, na ktorý odkazuje ods. (1) písm. (b) zanikol; alebo

(iii) príkazník sa dopustí podstatného nesplnenia povinností z príkaznej zmluvy, za predpokladu, že príkazník je bez zbytočného odkladu nahradený iným príkazníkom v súlade so zmluvou medzi príkazcom a inou stranou alebo stranami; alebo

(iv) u príkazcu je daný závažný a mimoriadny dôvod na zrušenie príkazného vzťahu podľa 6:103 (Zrušenie príkazcom pre mimoriadny a závažný dôvod), za predpokladu, že príkazník je bez zbytočného odkladu nahradený iným príkazníkom v súlade so zmluvou medzi príkazcom a inou stranou alebo stranami.

(3) Ak nie je odvolanie mandátu podľa tohto článku prípustné, oznámenie o odvolaní nemá žiadne účinky.

(4) Tento článok sa nepoužije, ak príkazný vzťah zanikol podľa kapitoly 7 týchto Princípov.

Kapitola 2:
Základné povinnosti príkazcu.

Článok 2:101: Povinnosť spolupracovať

Povinnosť spolupracovať podľa článku 1:202 (Povinnosť spolupracovať) Princípov európskeho zmluvného práva vyžaduje od príkazcu najmä

(a) poskytnúť informácie požadované príkazníkom v rozsahu potrebnom na splnenie záväzkov príkazníka z príkaznej zmluvy

(b) udeliť pokyn týkajúci sa plnenia záväzkov z príkaznej zmluvy, pokiaľ tak stanoví príkazná zmluva alebo ak tak vyplýva zo žiadosti o pokyn podľa článku 4:102 (Žiadosť o pokyn).

Článok 2:102: Odplata

(1) Príkazca je povinný poskytnúť odplatu, ak príkazník plní záväzky z príkaznej zmluvy v rámci výkonu obchodnej činnosti, ibaže príkazca očakával a mohol odôvodnene očakávať, že príkazník plní záväzky inak ako odplatne.

(2) Odplata je splatná, keď bola prikázaná úloha vykonaná a príkazník o tom podal správu príkazcovi.

(3) Ak sa strany dohodli na poskytnutí odplaty za uskutočnené služby, príkazný vzťah zanikol a prikázaná úloha nebola vykonaná, odplata je splatná okamihom, keď príkazník podá správu o plnení záväzkov z príkaznej zmluvy.

(4) Ak je mandát udelený za účelom uzavretia cieľovej zmluvy a priamo príkazca uzavrel cieľovú zmluvu alebo iná osoba určená príkazcom uzavrela cieľovú zmluvu v záujme príkazcu, príkazník má právo na odplatu alebo jej pomernú časť, ak uzavretie cieľovej zmluvy môže byť úplne alebo čiastočne pričítané príkazníkovmu plneniu záväzkov z príkaznej zmluvy.

(5) Ak je mandát udelený za účelom uzavretia cieľovej zmluvy a cieľová zmluva je uzavretá po zániku príkazného vzťahu, príkazca musí poskytnúť odplatu, ak bolo poskytnutie odplaty dohodnuté výlučne za uzavretie cieľovej zmluvy a

(a) uzavretie cieľovej zmluvy je výsledkom prevažne príkazníkovho úsilia; a

(b) cieľová zmluva bola uzavretá v primeranom čase po zániku príkazného vzťahu.

Článok 2:103: Náklady vynaložené príkazníkom

(1) Ak má príkazník právo na odplatu, predpokladá sa, že v odplate je zahrnutá náhrada nákladov vynaložených príkazníkom pri plnení záväzkov z príkaznej zmluvy.

(2) Ak príkazník nemá právo na odplatu alebo ak sa strany dohodli na osobitnej úhrade nákladov, príkazca je povinný nahradiť príkazníkovi náklady, ktoré príkazník vynaložil pri plnení záväzkov z príkaznej zmluvy v rozsahu, v akom boli príkazníkom odôvodnene vynaložené.

(3) Príkazník má právo na náhradu nákladov podľa ods. (2) od okamihu, keď boli náklady vynaložené a príkazník predložil ich vyúčtovanie.

(4) Ak príkazný vzťah zanikol a výsledok, na ktorom je závislá odplata príkazníka nebol dosiahnutý, príkazník má právo na náhradu primeraných nákladov, ktoré vynaložil pri plnení záväzkov z príkaznej zmluvy. Odsek (3) sa použije primerane.

Kapitola 3:
plnenie príkazníkom
Oddiel 1:
Základné povinnosti príkazníka

Článok 3:101: Povinnosť konať v súlade s mandátom

Vo všetkých štádiách príkazného vzťahu musí príkazník konať v súlade s mandátom.

Článok 3:102: Povinnosť konať v záujme príkazcu

(1) Príkazník je povinný konať v súlade so záujmami príkazcu, v rozsahu v akom boli tieto príkazníkovi oznámené alebo v akom by sa dalo odôvodnene očakávať, že sú príkazníkovi známe.

(2) Príkazník je povinný od príkazcu požadovať informácie o príkazcových záujmoch, ktoré mu nie sú známe, ak sú tieto informácie potrebné na riadne plnenie príkazného vzťahu.

Článok 3:103: Povinnosť schopností a starostlivosti

(1) Príkazník je povinný plniť záväzky z príkaznej zmluvy so starostlivosťou a schopnosťami, aké je príkazca oprávnený podľa okolností očakávať.

(2) Ak príkazník deklaruje vyššiu úroveň starostlivosti a schopností, príkazník je povinný konať s takouto starostlivosťou a schopnosťami.

(3) Ak príkazca je, alebo sa správa akoby bol členom skupiny profesionálnych príkazníkov, pre ktorých sú dané štandardy stanovené príslušnou autoritou alebo skupinou samotnou, príkazník je povinný konať so starostlivosťou a schopnosťami vyjadrenými v týchto štandardoch.

(4) Pri určení starostlivosti a schopností, aké je príkazca oprávnený očakávať, je potrebné zohľadniť okrem iného:

(a) povahu, závažnosť, frekvenciu a predvídateľnosť rizík spojených s plnením záväzkov;

(b) či sú záväzky plnené neprofesionálom alebo bezodplatne;

(c) výšku odplaty za plnenie záväzkov; a

(d) čas primerane potrebný na plnenie záväzkov.

Oddiel 2:
Následky prekročenia príkazu

Článok 3:201: Prekročenie príkazu

(1) Príkazník môže konať spôsobom nekrytým mandátom, ak:

(a) príkazník má rozumný dôvod konať takto v záujme príkazcu;

(b) príkazník nemá primeranú možnosť zistiť za daných okolností príkazcovu vôľu; a

(c) príkazník nevie a ani by nebolo možné od neho odôvodnene očakávať, aby vedel, že konanie je za daných okolností v rozpore s príkazcovou vôľou.

(2) Konanie v rámci ods. (1) má vo vzťahu medzi príkazníkom a príkazcom rovnaké následky ako konanie kryté mandátom.

Článok 3:202: Následky ratifikácie

Ak za okolností nekrytých predchádzajúcim článkom príkazník prekročil mandát pri uzatváraní cieľovej zmluvy v záujme príkazcu, ratifikácia tejto zmluvy príkazcom zbavuje príkazníka zodpovednosti voči príkazcovi, ibaže príkazca bez zbytočného odkladu po ratifikácii oznámi príkazníkovi, že si vyhradzuje uplatnenie nápravných opatrení pre nesplnenie príkazníka.

Oddiel 3:
Mandát obvykle nevýlučný

Článok 3:301: Výlučnosť nepredpokladaná

Príkazca má právo priamo uzavrieť, dojednať alebo umožniť uzavretie cieľovej zmluvy alebo určiť iného príkazníka, aby to vykonal.

Článok 3:302: Subkontrahovanie

(1) Príkazník môže bez súhlasu príkazcu v celom rozsahu alebo čiastočne subkontrahovať plnenie povinností z príkaznej zmluvy, ibaže zmluva vyžaduje osobné plnenie.

(2) Akákoľvek podzmluvná strana zapojená príkazníkom musí mať zodpovedajúce schopnosti.

(3) V súlade s článkom 8:107 (Splnenie zverené inej osobe) Princípov európskeho zmluvného práva zostáva za splnenie zodpovedný príkazník.

Oddiel 4:
Povinnosť informovať príkazcu

Článok 3:401: Povinnosť informovať o postupe plnenia

Počas plnenia záväzkov z príkaznej zmluvy je príkazník povinný, pokiaľ je to primerané za daných okolností, informovať príkazcu o vedení rokovaní, ich postupe a o ďalších krokoch smerujúcich k možnému uzavretiu alebo umožneniu uzavretia cieľovej zmluvy.

Článok 3:402: Správa príkazcovi

(1) Príkazník je povinný bez zbytočného odkladu informovať príkazcu o vykonaní prikázanej úlohy.

(2) Príkazník je povinný podať príkazcovi správu:
   (a) o spôsobe, akým boli splnené záväzky z príkaznej zmluvy; a
   (b) o vydaných alebo prijatých peniazoch alebo príkazníkom vynaložených nákladoch pri plnení týchto záväzkov.

(3) Odsek (2) sa primerane použije, ak príkazný vzťah zanikol v súlade s kapitolami 6 a 7 a záväzky z príkaznej zmluvy neboli splnené v plnom rozsahu.

Článok 3:403: Oznámenie totožnosti tretej strany

(1) Na žiadosť príkazcu je príkazník povinný oznámiť príkazcovi meno a adresu tretej strany.

(2) Odsek (1) sa pre mandát na nepriame zastúpenie použije, len ak sa príkazník stane insolventným.

Kapitola 4:
Pokyny a Zmeny
Oddiel 1:
Pokyny

Článok 4:101: Pokyny príkazcu

(1) Príkazca je oprávnený udeľovať príkazníkovi pokyny.

(2) Príkazník je povinný riadiť sa pokynmi príkazcu.

(3) Príkazník je povinný upozorniť príkazcu, ak pokyn:
   (a) spôsobí, že by sa plnenie povinností z príkaznej zmluvy stalo podstatne nákladnejším alebo by vyžadovalo podstatne viac času ako bolo dohodnuté v príkaznej zmluve; alebo
   (b) je nezlučiteľný s účelom príkaznej zmluvy alebo môže byť inak na ujmu záujmom príkazcu.

(4) Pokiaľ príkazca neodvolá pokyn bez zbytočného odkladu po tom, čo bol príkazníkom takto upozornený, považuje sa pokyn za zmenu príkaznej zmluvy podľa článku 4:201 (Zmeny príkaznej zmluvy).

Článok 4:102: Žiadosť o pokyn

(1) Príkazník je povinný požiadať o pokyn na základe získanej informácie, ktorá vyžaduje, aby príkazca uskutočnil rozhodnutie, týkajúce sa plnenia povinností z príkaznej zmluvy alebo obsahu cieľovej zmluvy.

(2) Príkazník je povinný požiadať o pokyn, ak je prikázanou úlohou uzavretie cieľovej zmluvy a príkazná zmluva neurčuje, či je mandát udelený na priame zastúpenie alebo nepriame zastúpenie.

Článok 4:103: Následky neudelenia pokynu

(1) Ak príkazca neudelí pokyn, hoci sa vyžaduje, aby tak podľa príkaznej zmluvy alebo podľa ods. (1) článku 4:102 (Žiadosť o pokyn) urobil, príkazník môže, pokiaľ je to relevantné,

využiť' akýkoľvek z prostriedkov nápravy podľa kapitoly 8 (Nesplnenie a prostriedky nápravy všeobecne) a kapitoly 9 (Jednotlivé prostriedky nápravy pre nesplnenie) Princípov európskeho zmluvného práva ; alebo

(a) založiť' plnenie na očakávaniach, preferenciách a prioritách, ktoré možno odôvodnene očakávať' u osoby v rovnakej situácii ako príkazca, zohľadniac získané informácie a udelené pokyny; a

(b) požadovať' pomernú úpravu odplaty a času poskytnutého alebo vyžadovaného na uzavretie cieľovej zmluvy.

(2) Ak príkazca neudelí pokyn podľa ods. (2) článku 4:102 (Žiadosť' o pokyn), príkazník si môže zvoliť' priame zastúpenie alebo nepriame zastúpenie alebo sa môže zdržať' plnenia podľa článku 9:201 (Právo zdržať' sa plnenia) Princípov európskeho zmluvného práva .

(3) Upravená odplata, ktorá má byť' poskytnutá podľa ods. (1) písm. (b) musí byť' primeraná a určí sa použitím rovnakých metód výpočtu, aké boli použité pre stanovenie pôvodnej odplaty za splnenie záväzkov z príkaznej zmluvy.

Článok 4:104: Nedostatok času žiadat' pokyn alebo čakat' na pokyn

(1) Ak je príkazník povinný žiadať' o pokyn podľa článku 4:102 (Žiadosť' o pokyn), avšak musí konať' skôr, než je schopný kontaktovať' príkazcu a vyžiadať' si pokyn, alebo musí konať' skôr, než bol pokyn udelený, príkazník môže založiť' plnenie na očakávaniach, preferenciách alebo prioritách, ktoré možno odôvodnene očakávať' u príkazcu, zohľadniac získané informácie a udelené pokyny.

(2) V situácii uvedenej v ods. (1), môže príkazník požadovať' pomernú úpravu odplaty a času poskytnutého alebo vyžadovaného na splnenie záväzkov z príkaznej zmluvy, pokiaľ je takáto úprava primeraná s ohľadom na okolnosti prípadu.

Oddiel 2:
Zmeny príkaznej zmluvy

Článok 4:201: Zmeny príkaznej zmluvy

(1) Príkazná zmluva sa zmení, ak príkazca:

(a) podstatne zmení mandát príkazníka;

(b) neodvolá pokyn bez zbytočného odkladu po tom, čo bol upozornený v súlade s ods. (3) článku 4:101 (Pokyny príkazcu).

(2) V prípade zmeny príkaznej zmluvy podľa ods. (1) je príkazník oprávnený:

(a) na pomernú úpravu odplaty a času poskytnutého alebo vyžadovaného na splnenie záväzkov z príkaznej zmluvy; alebo

(b) na náhradu škody v súlade s článkom 9:502 (Všeobecný rozsah náhrady škody) Princípov európskeho zmluvného práva, ktorá príkazníkovi umožní dosiahnuť' postavenie čo možno najbližšie tomu, v ktorom by sa bol príkazník nachádzal, ak by sa príkazná zmluva nebola zmenila.

(3) V prípade zmeny príkaznej zmluvy podľa ods. (1) môže príkazník tiež zrušiť' príkazný vzťah oznámením o zrušení pre mimoriadny a závažný dôvod podľa 6:105 (Zrušenie príkazníkom pre mimoriadny a závažný dôvod), ibaže ide o zanedbateľnú zmenu alebo zmena je v prospech príkazníka.

(4) Upravená odplata, ktorá sa má poskytnúť podľa ods. (2) písm. (a) musí byť primeraná a určuje sa použitím rovnakých metód výpočtu, aké boli použité pre stanovenie pôvodnej odplaty za splnenie záväzkov z príkaznej zmluvy.

Kapitola 5:
Stret záujmov

Článok 5:101: Samokontraktácia
(1) Príkazník sa nemôže stať protistranou príkazcu v cieľovej zmluve.
(2) Príkazník sa však môže stať protistranou, ak
    (a) je to dohodnuté stranami v príkaznej zmluve;
    (b) príkazník prejavil vôľu stať sa protistranou a
        (i) príkazca následne vyjadril súhlas; alebo
        (ii) príkazca po tom, čo bol požiadaný o prejavenie alebo odmietnutie súhlasu, nenamieta, aby sa príkazník stal protistranou;
    (c) príkazca inak vedel alebo bolo možné od neho odôvodnene očakávať vedomosť o tom, že sa príkazník stal protistranou a príkazca nenamietal v primeranej lehote; alebo
    (d) obsah cieľovej zmluvy je v príkaznej zmluve vymedzený tak presne, že neexistuje riziko možného nezohľadnenia záujmov príkazcu.
(3) Ak je príkazca spotrebiteľom, môže sa príkazník stať protistranou iba ak
    (a) príkazník o tom informoval a príkazca udelil príkazníkovi výslovný súhlas stať sa protistranou určitej cieľovej zmluvy; alebo
    (b) obsah cieľovej zmluvy je v príkaznej zmluve vymedzený tak presne, že neexistuje riziko možného nezohľadnenia záujmov príkazcu.
(4) Strany nemôžu na ťarchu príkazcu vylúčiť použitie ods. (3) alebo sa od neho odchýliť alebo zmeniť jeho účinky.
(5) Ak sa príkazník stal protistranou, nemá príkazník právo na odplatu za služby poskytnuté v postavení príkazníka.

Článok 5:102: Dvojitý mandát
(1) Príkazník nesmie konať ako príkazník oboch strán cieľovej zmluvy – ako príkazník príkazcu aj ako príkazník príkazcovej protistrany.
(2) Príkazník však môže konať ako príkazník príkazcu aj protistrany, ak
    (a) je to dohodnuté stranami v príkaznej zmluve;
    (b) príkazník prejavil vôľu konať ako príkazník protistrany a príkazca
        (i) následne vyjadrí súhlas; alebo
        (ii) nenamieta voči príkazníkovi konajúcemu ako príkazník protistrany po tom, čo bol požiadaný o prejavenie alebo odmietnutie súhlasu;
    (c) príkazca inak vedel alebo bolo možné od neho odôvodnene očakávať vedomosť o príkazníkovi, konajúcom ako príkazník protistrany a príkazca nenamietal v primeranej lehote; alebo
    (d) obsah cieľovej zmluvy je v príkaznej zmluve vymedzený tak presne, že neexistuje riziko možného nezohľadnenia záujmov príkazcu.

(3) Ak je príkazca spotrebiteľom, príkazník môže konať ako príkazník príkazcu aj protistrany iba ak

(a) príkazník o tom informoval a príkazca vyjadril výslovný súhlas s príkazníkom konajúcim tiež ako príkazník protistrany vo vzťahu k určitej cieľovej zmluve; alebo

(b) obsah cieľovej zmluvy je vymedzený v príkaznej zmluve tak presne, že neexistuje riziko možného nezohľadnenia záujmov príkazcu.

(4) Strany nemôžu na ťarchu príkazcu vylúčiť použitie ods. (3) alebo sa od neho odchýliť alebo zmeniť jeho účinky.

(5) Príkazník má právo na odplatu, ak konal a v rozsahu v akom konal v súlade s predchádzajúcimi odsekmi.

Kapitola 6:
Zrušenie oznámením z iného dôvodu ako pre nesplnenie

Článok 6:101: Zrušenie oznámením všeobecne

(1) Každá zo strán príkazného vzťahu môže kedykoľvek zrušiť príkazný vzťah uskutočnením oznámenia druhej strane.

(2) Na účely ods. (1) sa odvolanie mandátu príkazníka považuje za zrušenie.

(3) Zrušenie príkazného vzťahu nie je účinné, ak je mandát príkazníka neodvolateľný podľa článku 1:105 (Neodvolateľný mandát).

(4) Pokiaľ ide o účinky zrušenia, použije sa kapitola 9, oddiel 3 (Zrušenie zmluvy) Princípov európskeho zmluvného práva.

(5) Ak strana uskutočňujúca oznámenie bola oprávnená zrušiť príkazný vzťah, nemožno požadovať náhradu škody.

(6) Ak strana uskutočňujúca oznámenie nebola oprávnená zrušiť príkazný vzťah, zrušenie je napriek tomu účinné, ale druhá strana môže požadovať náhradu škody v súlade s kapitolou 9, oddiel 5 (Náhrada škody a úrok) Princípov európskeho zmluvného práva.

(7) Pre účely tohto článku je strana uskutočňujúca oznámenie oprávnená zrušiť príkazný vzťah v prípadoch, ak táto strana

(a) bola oprávnená zrušiť príkazný vzťah na základe výslovných ustanovení príkaznej zmluvy a vyhovela predpokladom, ktoré pre zrušenie príkazná zmluva vyžaduje; alebo

(b) bola oprávnená zrušiť príkazný vzťah podľa kapitoly 9, oddiel 3 (Zrušenie zmluvy) Princípov európskeho zmluvného práva; alebo

(c) bola oprávnená zrušiť príkazný vzťah podľa iného článku tejto kapitoly a vyhovela predpokladom, ktoré sú v takomto článku ustanovené.

Článok 6:102: Zrušenie príkazcom, ak bol príkazný vztah na dobu neurčitú alebo na stanovenú úlohu

(1) Príkazca môže kedykoľvek zrušiť príkazný vzťah oznámením lehoty zrušenia primeranej dĺžky, ak bola príkazná zmluva uzavretá na dobu neurčitú alebo na stanovenú úlohu.

(2) Odsek (1) sa nepoužije, ak je mandát neodvolateľný.

(3) Strany nemôžu na ťarchu príkazcu vylúčiť použitie tohto článku alebo sa od neho odchýliť alebo zmeniť jeho účinky, ibaže sú splnené podmienky stanovené podľa článku 1:105 (Neodvolateľný príkaz).

Článok 6:103: Zrušenie príkazcom pre mimoriadny a závažný dôvod

(1) Príkazca môže zrušiť príkazný vzťah oznámením pre mimoriadny a závažný dôvod.

(2) Nevyžaduje sa lehota zrušenia.

(3) Na účely tohto článku sa považuje smrť alebo právna nespôsobilosť osoby, ktorú strany v čase uzavretia príkaznej zmluvy určili na splnenie povinností príkazníka z príkaznej zmluvy, za mimoriadny a závažný dôvod.

(4) Tento článok sa primerane použije, ak nástupcovia príkazcu zrušia príkazný vzťah v súlade s článkom 7:101 (Smrť príkazcu).

(5) Strany nemôžu na ťarchu príkazcu alebo príkazcových nástupcov vylúčiť použitie tohto článku alebo sa od neho odchýliť alebo zmeniť jeho účinky.

Článok 6:104: Zrušenie príkazníkom, ak bol príkazný vztah na dobu neurčitú alebo bezodplatný

(1) Príkazník môže kedykoľvek zrušiť príkazný vzťah oznámením lehoty zrušenia primeranej dĺžky, ak bola príkazná zmluva uzavretá na dobu neurčitú.

(2) Príkazník môže zrušiť príkazný vzťah oznámením lehoty zrušenia primeranej dĺžky, ak je príkazná zmluva bezodplatná.

(3) Strany nemôžu na ťarchu príkazníka vylúčiť použitie ods. (1) tohto článku alebo sa od neho odchýliť alebo zmeniť jeho účinky.

Článok 6:105: Zrušenie príkazníkom pre mimoriadny a závažný dôvod

(1) Príkazník môže zrušiť príkazný vzťah oznámením pre mimoriadny a závažný dôvod.

(2) Nevyžaduje sa lehota zrušenia.

(3) Na účely tohto článku sa za mimoriadny a závažný dôvod považuje:
   (a) zmena príkaznej zmluvy podľa článku 4:201 (Zmeny príkaznej zmluvy);
   (b) smrť alebo strata právnej spôsobilosti príkazcu; a
   (c) smrť alebo strata právnej spôsobilosti osoby, ktorú v čase uzavretia príkaznej zmluvy strany určili na vykonanie povinností príkazníka z príkaznej zmluvy.

(4) Strany nemôžu na ťarchu príkazníka vylúčiť použitie tohto článku alebo sa od neho odchýliť alebo zmeniť jeho účinky.

Kapitola 7:
Iné dôvody zániku

Článok 7:101: Smrt príkazcu

(1) Smrť príkazcu nespôsobuje zánik príkazného vzťahu.

(2) Tak príkazník ako aj nástupcovia príkazcu môžu zrušiť príkazný vzťah oznámením o zrušení pre mimoriadny a závažný dôvod podľa článku 6:103 (Zrušenie príkazcom pre mimoriadny a závažný dôvod) alebo článku 6:105 (Zrušenie príkazníkom pre mimoriadny a závažný dôvod).

Článok 7:102: Smrt príkazníka

(1) Smrť príkazníka spôsobuje zánik príkazného vzťahu.

(2) Náklady a akékoľvek iné platby splatné v čase smrti ostávajú zachované.

Spanish[*]
Contratos de Mandato

Capitulo 1:
Disposiciones Generales

Artículo 1:101: Ambito
(1) Estos Principios se aplican a los contratos y demás actos jurídicos por los que una persona, el mandatario, está autorizada e instruida (encargada) por otra persona, el mandante:
- (a) para concluir un contrato entre el mandante y un tercero o para afectar directamente, de otro modo, la posición jurídica del mandante en relación con un tercero;
- (b) para concluir un contrato con un tercero, o realizar otro acto jurídico en relación con un tercero por cuenta del mandante, pero de una manera tal que es el mandatario y no el mandante quien es parte en el contrato o en el otro acto jurídico; o
- (c) para realizar las actuaciones que deberían permitir o facilitar la conclusión de un contrato entre el mandante y un tercero, o la realización de otro acto jurídico que afectaría a la posición jurídica del mandante en relación con un tercero.

(2) Estos Principios se aplican cuando el mandatario se compromete a actuar por cuenta del mandante y de acuerdo con sus instrucciones, y, con las adaptaciones apropiadas, cuando el mandatario está autorizado para actuar, pero no obligado a actuar, y aún así actúa.

(3) Estos Principios se aplican cuando el mandatario tiene derecho a una remuneración y, con las adaptaciones apropiadas, cuando no tiene derecho a la misma.

(4) Estos Principios se aplican sólo a la relación interna entre el mandante y el mandatario (la relación de mandato). No se aplica a la relación entre el mandante y el tercero ni a la relación (si la hubiera) entre el mandatario y el tercero.

(5) Los contratos a los que se aplica tanto Estos Principios como los Principios del Derecho Europeo sobre el contrato de Servicios se rigen principalmente por lo establecido en estos Principios.

(6) Estos Principios no se aplican a los contratos referentes a servicios y actividades de inversión, definidos por la Directiva 2004/39/EC, OJ L 145/1, y sus modificaciones posteriores.

Artículo 1:102: Definiciones
En esta Parte,
- (a) el «mandato» del mandatario es la autorización e instrucciones dadas por el mandante, y las posteriores modificaciones de éstas;
- (b) el «contrato de mandato» es el contrato por el que el mandatario está autorizado e instruido para actuar, y toda referencia al contrato de mandato incluye una referencia a cualquier otro acto jurídico por el que el mandatario está autorizado e instruído para actuar;
- (c) el «contrato proyectado» es el contrato que el mandatario está autorizado e instruído para concluir, negociar o facilitar, y cualquier referencia al «contrato proyectado» incluye refe-

---

*   Translated by Dr. *Odavia Bueno Díaz*, University of Amsterdam.

rencia a cualquier otro acto jurídico que el mandatario está autorizado e instruido para celebrar, negociar o facilitar;

(d) un mandato con representación directa es un mandato en el que el mandatario actúa en nombre del mandante, o bien de manera tal que indique la intención de afectar la posición jurídica de éste;

(e) un mandato con representación indirecta es un mandato en el que el mandatario actúa en su propio nombre, o bien de manera tal que no indique la intención de afectar la posición jurídica del mandante;

(f) una «instrucción» es una decisión del mandante relativa al cumplimiento de las obligaciones del contrato de mandato o al contenido del contrato proyectado, que es dada en el momento en que se celebra el contrato de mandato o, de acuerdo con el mandato, en un momento posterior;

(g) el «tercero» es la parte con la que el mandatario debe concluir, negociar o facilitar el contrato proyectado;

(h) la «revocación» del mandato del mandatario es la retirada del mandato por parte del mandante, de manera que éste ya no produzca efecto.

Artículo 1:103: Duración del contrato de mandato
Un contrato de mandato puede celebrarse:
(a) por un periodo de tiempo indefinido;
(b) por un periodo determinado; o
(c) para una tarea concreta.

Artículo 1:104: Revocación del mandato
(1) Salvo que sea de aplicación lo dispuesto en el Artículo siguiente, el mandato puede ser revocado por el mandante en cualquier momento, mediante una notificación al mandatario.
(2) La extinción de la relación de mandato tiene el efecto de una revocación del mandato del mandatario.
(3) Las partes no pueden, en perjuicio del mandante, excluir la aplicación de este Artículo, o restringir o variar sus efectos, salvo que se den los requisitos del Artículo siguiente.

Artículo 1:105: Mandato irrevocable
(1) No obstante lo dispuesto en el Artículo anterior, el mandante no puede revocar el mandato del mandatario si éste se dio:
   (a) para salvaguardar un interés legítimo del mandatario distinto al interés en el pago de la remuneración; o
   (b) en interés común de las partes en otra relación jurídica, sean o no éstas todas las partes del contrato de mandato y la irrevocabilidad del mandato del mandatario está llamada a salvaguardar debidamente el interés de una o más de las citadas partes.
(2) Sin embargo, el mandato puede ser revocado si:
   (a) el mandato es irrevocable de acuerdo con el apartado (1)(a) y:
      (i) la relación contractual de la que deriva el legítimo interés del mandatario finaliza como consecuencia del incumplimiento del mandatario; o
      (ii) se produce un incumplimiento esencial de las obligaciones derivadas del contrato de mandato por parte del mandatario; o

       (iii) concurre una razón extraordinaria y seria que permite al mandante terminar el mandato de acuerdo con el Articulo 6:103 (Extinción por el mandante, por razón extraordinaria y seria); o

(b) el mandato es irrevocable de acuerdo con el apartado (1)(b) y:

       (i) las partes en cuyo interés el mandato es irrevocable acuerdan la revocación del mismo;

       (ii) termina la relación jurídica a la que ser refiere el apartado (1)(b);

       (iii) el mandatario incurre en un incumplimiento esencial de las obligaciones del contrato de mandato, siempre que sea reemplazado sin demora excesiva por otro mandatario, de acuerdo con los términos de la relación jurídica existente entre el mandante y la otra parte o partes; o

       (iv) concurre una razón extraordinaria y seria que permite al mandante terminar el mandato de acuerdo con el Artículo 6:103 (Extinción por el mandante, por razón extraordinaria y seria), siempre que el mandatario sea reemplazado sin demora excesiva por otro mandatario, de acuerdo con los términos de la relación jurídica existente entre el mandante y la otra parte o partes.

(3) Si la revocación del mandato no está permitida de acuerdo con lo dispuesto en este Artículo, la notificación de revocación no produce efecto.

(4) Este Artículo no se aplica si la relación de mandato termina de acuerdo con lo dispuesto en el Capítulo 7 de estos Principios.

Capitulo 2:
Obligaciones Principales del Mandante

Artículo 2:101: Obligación de cooperar

La obligación de cooperar que establece el Artículo 1:202 de los Principios del Derecho Europeo de Contratos (Obligación de Cooperar) requiere especialmente que el mandante:

(a) conteste a las peticiones de información del mandatario, en tanto que tal información es necesaria para permitir al mandatario cumplir las obligaciones derivadas del contrato de mandato;

(b) dé instrucciones referentes al cumplimiento de las obligaciones derivadas del contrato de mandato, en la medida en que ello es requerido por tal contrato o se sigue de una petición de instrucciones de acuerdo con el Artículo 4:102 (Solicitud de instrucciones).

Artículo 2:102: Remuneración

(1) El mandante debe pagar una retribución si el mandatario cumple las obligaciones derivadas del mandato en el ámbito de su profesión o actividad económica habitual, salvo que el mandante esperase o pudiese razonablemente haber esperado que el mandatario cumpliese sus obligaciones por un motivo distinto al de la remuneración.

(2) La remuneración es exigible cuando la tarea encomendada ha sido completada y el mandatario ha rendido cuentas de la misma al mandante.

(3) Si las partes han acordado el pago de una retribución por los servicios prestados, la relación de mandato ha terminado y la tarea encomendada no ha sido completada, la remuneración es exigible desde el momento en que el mandatario haya rendido cuentas del cumplimiento de las obligaciones derivadas del contrato de mandato.

(4) Cuando el mandato es para la conclusión de un contrato proyectado y el mandante lo ha celebrado él mismo, o a través de otra persona designada por él y que actúa por cuenta de éste, el mandatario tiene derecho a la retribución o a una parte de la misma si la celebración del contrato proyectado puede ser atribuida en todo o en parte al cumplimiento por el mandatario de las obligaciones derivadas del mandato.

(5) Cuando el mandato es para la celebración de un contrato proyectado y éste se concluye después de finalizada la relación de mandato, el mandante debe pagar la remuneración si se acordó que el pago de la misma se basaba únicamente en la conclusión del contrato proyectado y:

    (a) la celebración del contrato proyectado es fundamentalmente el resultado de los esfuerzos del mandatario; y

    (b) el contrato proyectado es concluido en un plazo razonable a partir de la extinción de la relación de mandato.

Artículo 2:103: Gastos contraídos por el mandatario

(1) Cuando el mandatario tiene derecho a una remuneración, se presume que ésta incluye el reembolso de los gastos contraídos por el mandatario en el cumplimiento de las obligaciones derivadas del contrato de mandato.

(2) Cuando el mandatario no tiene derecho a una remuneración o cuando las partes han acordado que los gastos se pagarían separadamente, el mandante debe reembolsar al mandatario los gastos que éste haya contraído en el cumplimiento de las obligaciones derivadas del contrato de mandato, en la medida en que el mandatario actuó razonablemente cuando incurrió en los mismos.

(3) El mandatario tiene derecho al reembolso de los gastos descritos en el apartado (2) desde el momento en que los contrajo y haya dado cuenta de los mismos.

(4) Si la relación de mandato ha terminado y el resultado del que depende la retribución del mandatario no se ha completado, el mandatario tiene derecho al reembolso de los gastos razonables en los que haya incurrido en el cumplimiento de las obligaciones del contrato de mandato. Es también de aplicación el apartado (3).

Capitulo 3:
Cumplimiento del Mandatario
Sección 1:
Obligaciones Principales del Mandatario

Artículo 3:101: Obligación de actuar conforme al mandato
En todas las etapas de la relación de mandato, el mandatario debe actuar conforme al mandato.

3:102: Obligación de actuar en interés del mandante

(1) El mandatario debe actuar de acuerdo con los intereses del mandante, en la medida en que le han sido comunicados, o si podía esperarse razonablemente que el mandatario estuviese enterado de los mismos.

(2) El mandatario ha de requerir información al mandate sobre los intereses del mandante no conocidos por el mandatario cuando esta información sea necesaria para permitir el correcto cumplimiento del mandato.

Artículo 3:103: Obligación de diligencia

(1) El mandatario debe cumplir las obligaciones del contrato de mandato con la diligencia que el mandante tiene derecho a esperar de acuerdo con las circunstancias del mandato.

(2) Si el mandatario es capaz de desarrollar un nivel superior de diligencia, debe hacerlo.

(3) Si el mandatario es, o pretende ser, miembro de un grupo de mandatarios profesionales dotado de reglas de actuación fijados por la autoridad competente o por el propio grupo, debe desarrollar la diligencia expresada en las mismas.

(4) Para determinar la diligencia que el mandante tiene derecho a esperar, debe tenerse en cuenta, entre otras cosas, lo siguiente:
   (a) la naturaleza, la magnitud, la frecuencia y la previsibilidad de los riesgos que entraña el cumplimiento de las obligaciones;
   (b) si las obligaciones son cumplidas por una persona no profesional o de manera gratuita;
   (c) el importe de la remuneración fijada para el cumplimiento de las obligaciones; y
   (d) el tiempo razonablemente disponible para el cumplimiento de las obligaciones.

Sección 2:
Consequences de extralimitarse en el mandato

Artículo 3:201: Extralimitación en el mandato

(1) El mandatario puede actuar de una manera no prevista por el mandato si:
   (a) tiene una base razonable para actuar así en beneficio del mandante;
   (b) no tiene una oportunidad razonable para descubrir cuáles son los deseos del mandante en esas circunstancias concretas; y
   (c) no conoce y no cabe razonablemente esperar que conociese que la actuación en esas circunstancias concretas es contraria a los deseos del mandante.

(2) Un acto realizado al amparo del apartado (1) tiene las mismas consecuencias entre el mandatario y el mandante que un acto previsto por el mandato.

Artículo 3:202: Consecuencias de la ratificación

Si por circunstancias no contempladas en el Artículo anterior, el mandatario, al concluir un contrato por cuenta del mandante, se ha extralimitado en el mandato, la ratificación que el mandante haga de ese contrato exonera al mandatario de responsabilidad para con el mandante, salvo que éste, sin demora excesiva tras la ratificación, notifique al mandatario que se reserva el derecho a ejercer las acciones oportunas derivadas de su incumplimiento.

Sección 3:
Celebración del contrato proyectado por otra persona

Artículo 3:301: La exclusividad no se presume
El mandante es libre de celebrar, negociar o facilitar él mismo el contrato proyectado o de encargar a otro mandatario que lo haga.

Artículo 3:302: Subcontratación
(1) El mandatario puede subcontratar o delegar el cumplimiento de la totalidad o de parte de las obligaciones del contrato de mandato sin necesidad del consentimiento del mandante, salvo que el contrato requiera el cumplimiento personal.
(2) El subcontratista así contratado por el mandatario para el cumplimiento del contrato de mandato debe tener una competencia adecuada.
(3) De acuerdo con el Artículo 8:107 de los Principios del Derecho Europeo de Contratos (Cumplimiento confiado a un tercero), el mandatario sigue siendo responsable del cumplimiento.

Sección 4:
Obligación de informar al mandante

Artículo 3:401: Información sobre el progreso del cumplimiento
Durante el cumplimiento de las obligaciones del contrato de mandato, el mandatario debe, en la medida en que ello sea razonable de acuerdo con las circunstancias, informar al mandante de la existencia de negociaciones y de su avance, o de otras medidas conducentes a la posible conclusión o facilitación del contrato proyectado.

Artículo 3:402: Rendición de cuentas al mandante
(1) El mandatario debe, sin demora excesiva, informar al mandante de la finalización de la tarea encomendada.
(2) El mandatario debe rendir cuentas al mandante:
    (a) de la manera en que han sido cumplidas las obligaciones del mandato; y
    (b) del dinero gastado o recibido, o de los gastos contraídos por el mandatario en el cumplimiento de esas obligaciones.
(3) El apartado (2) se aplica, con las modificaciones pertinentes, si la relación de mandato termina de acuerdo con lo dispuesto en los Capítulos 6 y 7 y las obligaciones del contrato de mandato no han sido cumplidas en su totalidad.

Artículo 3:403: Comunicación de la identidad del tercero
(1) El mandatario que concluye el contrato proyectado con un tercero debe comunicar el nombre y la dirección de éste al mandante, si así lo solicita.
(2) En el caso del mandato con representación indirecta, el apartado (1) sólo se aplica si el mandatario deviene insolvente.

Capitulo 4:
Instrucciones Y Cambios
Sección 1:
Instrucciones

Artículo 4:101: Instrucciones dadas por el mandante
(1) El mandante está legitimado para dar instrucciones al mandatario.
(2) El mandatario debe seguir las instrucciones dadas por el mandante.
(3) El mandatario debe advertir al mandante si las instrucciones:
  (a) hacen que el cumplimiento de las obligaciones del mandato pase a ser considerable-mente más caro o requiera un tiempo sustancialmente mayor que el acordado en el contrato de mandato; o
  (b) es incongruente con la finalidad del contrato de mandato o puede, de otro modo, ser perjudicial para los intereses del mandante.
(4) A no ser que el mandante revoque las instrucciones sin demora excesiva, tras haber sido advertido en este sentido por el mandatario, las instrucciones deben considerarse como un cambio en el contrato de mandato, de acuerdo con el Artículo 4:201 (Cambios en el contrato de mandato).

Artículo 4:102: Solicitud de instrucciones
(1) El mandatario debe solicitar instrucciones si llega a su conocimiento información que re-quiere que el mandante tome una decisión relacionada con el cumplimiento de las obli-gaciones del contrato de mandato o el contenido del contrato proyectado.
(2) El mandatario debe solicitar instrucciones si la tarea encomendada es la conclusión de un contrato proyectado y el contrato de mandato no determina si el mandato es con repre-sentación directa o indirecta.

Artículo 4:103: Consecuencias de la falta de otorgamiento de las instrucciones requeridas
(1) Si el mandante no da instrucciones cuando es requerido para ello de acuerdo con el con-trato de mandato o el apartado (1) del Artículo 4:102 (Solicitud de instrucciones), el man-datario puede, si procede, recurrir a cualquiera de las acciones del Capítulo 8 (Incumpli-miento y Remedios en general) y 9 de los Principios del Derecho Europeo de los Contratos (Remedios específicos por incumplimiento), o
  (a) basar el cumplimiento en las expectativas, preferencias y prioridades que puede razo-nablemente esperarse que tuviese una persona en la misma situación que el mandan-te, dadas la información e instrucciones de que disponía.
  (b) reclamar un ajuste proporcional de la remuneración y del tiempo permitido o reque-rido para la conclusión del contrato proyectado.
(2) Si el mandante no da instrucciones de acuerdo con el apartado (2) del Artículo 4:102 (So-licitud de instrucciones), el mandatario puede escoger la representación directa o la indi-recta o puede suspender el cumplimiento de acuerdo con el Artículo 9:201 de los Princi-pios del Derecho Europeo de los Contratos (Derecho a suspender el cumplimiento).

(3) La retribución ajustada que debe pagarse de acuerdo con el apartado (1)(b) debe ser razonable y ha de determinarse usando los mismos métodos de cálculo que se emplearon para establecer la remuneración original por el cumplimiento de las obligaciones del contrato de mandato.

Artículo 4:104: Falta de tiempo para pedir o esperar instrucciones

(1) Si el mandatario debe solicitar instrucciones de acuerdo con el Artículo 4:102 (Solicitud de instrucciones), pero ha de actuar antes de poder contactar con el mandante y pedir instrucciones, o ha de actuar antes de que las instrucciones sean dadas, el mandatario puede basar el cumplimiento en las expectativas, preferencias y prioridades que podía razonablemente esperarse que el mandante tuviese, dadas la información e instrucciones de que disponía.

(2) En la situación a la que se refiere el apartado (1), el mandatario tiene derecho a un ajuste proporcional de la remuneración y del tiempo permitido o requerido para el cumplimiento de las obligaciones del contrato de mandato, en la medida en que tal ajuste es razonable dadas las circunstancias del caso.

Sección 2:
Cambios en el Contrato de Mandato

Artículo 4:201: Cambios en el contrato de mandato

(1) El contrato de mandato cambia si el mandante:
   (a) varía significativamente el mandato del mandatario;
   (b) no revoca unas instrucciones sin demora excesiva tras haber sido advertido de acuerdo con el apartado (3) del Artículo 4:101 (Instrucciones dadas por el mandante).

(2) En el caso de un cambio en el mandato de acuerdo con el apartado (1), el mandatario tiene derecho:
   (a) a un ajuste proporcional de la remuneración y del tiempo permitido o requerido para el cumplimiento de las obligaciones del contrato de mandato; o
   (b) a la indemnización por daños, de acuerdo con el Artículo 9:502 de los Principios de Derecho Europeo de los Contratos (Cálculo de los daños) para, en la medida de lo posible, dejar al mandatario en la misma posición que tendría de no haberse modificado el contrato de mandato.

(3) En caso de cambio en el contrato de mandato de acuerdo con el apartado (1), el mandatario puede también terminar la relación de mandato mediante notificación de una razón extraordinaria y seria de acuerdo con el Artículo 6:105 (Extinción por el mandatario por razón extraordinaria y seria), salvo que el cambio sea menor o redunde en beneficio del mandatario.

(4) El precio ajustado que debe pagarse de acuerdo con el apartado (2)(a) debe ser razonable y ha de determinarse usando los mismos métodos de cálculo que los empleados para establecer la remuneración original por el cumplimiento de las obligaciones del contrato de mandato.

Capitulo 5:
Conflicto de Intereses

Artículo 5:101: Autocontratación
(1) El mandatario no puede convertirse en la parte contratante del mandante en el contrato proyectado.
(2) Con todo, el mandatario puede convertirse en parte contratante si:
    (a) así lo acordaron las partes en el contrato de mandato;
    (b) el mandatario ha manifestado su intención de convertirse en parte contratante y el mandante:
        (i) posteriormente expresa su consentimiento; o
        (ii) no pone objeción a que el mandatario sea la parte contratante, después de haber sido requerido para que indique su consentimiento o su rechazo;
    (c) el mandante conoció de otro modo, o cabe razonablemente esperar que conociese, que el mandatario se convertía en parte contractual, y no puso objeción a ello en un plazo razonable; o
    (d) el contenido del contrato proyectado está determinado de manera tan precisa en el contrato de mandato que no existe riesgo alguno de que los intereses del mandante sean desatendidos.
(3) Si el mandante es un consumidor, el mandatario sólo puede convertirse en parte contratante si:
    (a) el mandatario ha manifestado esa intención y el mandante ha consentido expresamente que el mandatario pase a ser la parte contratante de ese contrato proyectado; o
    (b) el contenido del contrato proyectado está determinado de manera tan precisa en el contrato de mandato que no existe riesgo alguno de que los intereses del mandante sean desatendidos.
(4) Las partes no pueden, en perjuicio del mandante, excluir la aplicación del apartado (3) ni restringir o variar sus efectos.
(5) Si el mandatario se ha convertido en parte contractual, no tiene derecho a la remuneración de los servicios prestados como mandatario.

Artículo 5:102: Doble mandato
(1) El mandatario no puede serlo tanto del mandante como de la parte contratante de éste en el contrato proyectado.
(2) Sin embargo, el mandatario puede serlo tanto del mandante como de su parte contratante si:
    (a) así se acuerda por las partes en el contrato de mandato;
    (b) el mandatario ha manifestado su intención de actuar como mandatario de la otra parte contratante y el mandante:
        (i) expresa su consentimiento con posterioridad; o
        (ii) no se opone a ello, una vez requerido para que manifieste su consentimiento o su rechazo;
    (c) el mandante conocía de otro modo, o cabe razonablemente esperar que conociese, la actuación del mandatario como mandatario de la otra parte, y no puso objeción en un plazo de tiempo razonable; o

(d) el contenido del contrato proyectado está determinado de manera tan precisa en el contrato de mandato que no existe riesgo alguno de que los intereses del mandante sean desatendidos.

(3) Si el mandante es un consumidor, el mandatario sólo puede actuar como mandatario tanto del mandante como de la parte contratante si:

(a) el mandatario ha manifestado esa intención y el mandante ha consentido expresamente que el mandatario lo sea también de la otra parte en el contrato proyectado; o

(b) el contenido del contrato proyectado está determinado de manera tan precisa en el contrato de mandato que no existe riesgo alguno de que los intereses del mandante sean desatendidos.

(4) Las partes no pueden, en perjuicio del mandante, excluir la aplicación del apartado (3) ni restringir o variar sus efectos.

(5) El mandatario tiene derecho a una remuneración si ha actuado de acuerdo con los apartados anteriores.

Capitulo 6:
Extinción por Notificación, Distinta a la Resolución por incumplimiento

Artículo 6:101: Extinción mediante notificación, en general

(1) Cualquiera de las partes puede extinguir la relación de mandato en cualquier momento, notificándolo a la otra.

(2) A los efectos del apartado (1), la revocación del mandato del mandatario es considerada como extinción.

(3) La extinción de la relación de mandato no es efectiva si el mandato del mandatario es irrevocable, de acuerdo con el Artículo 1:105 (Mandato irrevocable).

(4) Los efectos de la extinción se rigen por el régimen general en el Capítulo 9 Sección 3 de los Principios del Derecho Europeo de los Contratos (Resolución del contrato).

(5) Cuando la parte que notifica tenía una justificación para extinguir la relación, no responde por los daños causados.

(6) Cuando la parte que notifica no tenía una justificación para extinguir la relación, la extinción es, con todo, efectiva, pero la otra parte puede pedir la indemnización por los daños, de conformidad con lo dispuesto en el Capítulo 9 Sección 5 de los Principios del Derecho Europeo de los Contratos (Daños y perjuicios).

(7) A efectos de este Artículo, la parte que notifica tiene una justificación para extinguir la relación si:

(a) tiene derecho a extinguir la relación de acuerdo con los términos expresos del contrato y observó todos los requerimientos establecidos en el contrato para hacerlo así;

(b) tiene derecho a resolver la relación de acuerdo con lo establecido en el Artículo 9:301 de los Principios del Derecho Europeo de los Contratos (Derecho a resolver el contrato); o

(c) tiene derecho a extinguir la relación, de acuerdo con cualquier otro Artículo del presente Capítulo y observó todos los requisitos establecidos en dicho Artículo para hacerlo así.

Artículo 6:102: Extinción por el mandante cuando la relación es por un periodo indefinido o cuando el mandato es para una tarea concreta

(1) Si el mandato fue concluido por un periodo indefinido o para una tarea concreta, el mandante puede extinguir la relación de mandato en cualquier momento, notificándolo con una antelación razonable.

(2) El apartado (1) no se aplica si el mandato es irrevocable.

(3) Las partes no pueden, en perjuicio del mandante, excluir la aplicación de este Artículo, ni restringir o variar sus efectos, salvo que se den las condiciones establecidas en el Artículo 1:105 (Mandato irrevocable).

Artículo 6:103: Extinción por el mandante, por razón extraordinaria y seria

(1) El mandante puede extinguir la relación de mandato notificando la existencia de una razón extraordinaria y seria para ello.

(2) No se requiere un plazo de notificación.

(3) A los efectos de este Artículo, la muerte o la incapacidad de la persona que, al tiempo de la celebración del contrato de mandato, las partes designaron para cumplir las obligaciones del mandatario derivadas del contrato de mandato, constituye una razón extraordinaria y seria.

(4) Este Artículo se aplica, con las adaptaciones apropiadas, si los sucesores del mandante ponen fin a la relación de mandato de acuerdo con el Artículo 7:101 (Muerte del mandante).

(5) Las partes no pueden, en perjuicio del mandante o de sus sucesores, excluir la aplicación de este Artículo, ni restringir o variar sus efectos.

Artículo 6:104: Extinción por el mandatario cuando la relación es por un periodo indefinido o cuando es a título gratuito

(1) Si el contrato de mandato ha sido concluido por un periodo indefinido, el mandatario puede extinguir la relación de mandato en cualquier momento, notificándolo con una antelación razonable.

(2) Si el mandatario representa al mandante por otro motivo distinto del precio, puede extinguir la relación de mandato notificándolo con una antelación razonable.

(3) Las partes no pueden, en detrimento del mandatario, excluir la aplicación del apartado (1) de este Artículo, ni restringir o variar sus efectos.

Artículo 6:105: Extinción por el mandatario, por razón extraordinaria y seria

(1) El mandatario puede extinguir la relación de mandato notificando la existencia de una razón extraordinaria y seria para ello.

(2) No se requiere un plazo de notificación.

(3) A los efectos de este Artículo, una razón extraordinaria y seria incluye:
   (a) un cambio en el contrato de mandato, de acuerdo con el Artículo 4:201 (Cambios en el contrato de mandato);
   (b) la muerte o incapacidad del mandante; y
   (c) la muerte o incapacidad de la persona que, al tiempo de la celebración del contrato de mandato, las partes designaron para cumplir las obligaciones del mandatario derivadas del contrato de mandato.

(4) Las partes no pueden, en perjuicio del mandatario, excluir la aplicación de este Artículo, ni restringir o variar sus efectos.

Capitulo 7:
Otras Razones Para la Extinción

Artículo 7:101: Muerte del mandante
(1) La muerte del mandante no extingue la relación de mandato.
(2) Tanto el mandatario como los sucesores del mandante pueden poner fin a la relación de mandato notificando su extinción por una razón extraordinaria y seria de acuerdo con el Artículo 6:103 (Extinción por el mandante, por razón extraordinaria y seria) o el Artículo 6:105 (Extinción por el mandatario, por razón extraordinaria y seria).

Artículo 7:102: Muerte del mandatario
(1) La muerte del mandatario pone fin a la relación de mandato.
(2) Los gastos y demás pagos debidos al tiempo de la muerte siguen siendo exigibles.

Swedish[*]
Fullmaktsavtal

Kapitel 1:
Allmänna Bestämmelser

Paragraf 1:101: Tillämpningsområde
(1) Dessa Principer är tillämpliga på avtal och andra rättshandlingar enligt vilka en person, fullmäktigen, fått fullmakt och instruktioner av en annan person, huvudmannen:
   - (a) att ingå avtal mellan huvudmannen och tredje man eller på annat sätt rättshandla för huvudmannen i förhållande till tredje man
   - (b) att ingå ett avtal med tredje man, eller att på annat sätt för huvudmannens räkning rättshandla i förhållande till tredje man men på sådant sätt att fullmäktigen och inte huvudmannen blir part i avtalet eller rättshandlingen; eller
   - (c) att vidta åtgärder som är avsedda att leda till eller möjliggöra avtal mellan huvudmannen och tredje man eller rättshandlande för huvudmannen i förhållande till tredje man.
(2) Dessa Principer skall tillämpas när fullmäktigen skall utföra uppdrag för huvudmannens räkning och i enlighet med dennes instruktioner och, med lämpliga justeringar, när fullmäktigen endast har fullmakt men inte åtagit sig att utföra uppdrag, men likväl utför uppdrag.
(3) Dessa Principer skall tillämpas när fullmäktigen är berättigad till ersättning och, med lämpliga justeringar, när fullmäktigen inte har rätt till ersättning.
(4) Dessa Principer är endast tillämplig på det inre förhållandet mellan huvudmannen och fullmäktigen (fullmaktsförhållandet). Den är inte tillämplig på förhållandet mellan huvudmannen och tredje man eller på förhållandet mellan fullmäktigen och tredje man.
(5) Avtal som dessa Principer är tillämpliga på och på vilka the Principles of European Law on Service Contracts också är tillämpliga skall primärt regleras av dessa Principer.
(6) Dessa Principer är inte tillämplig på avtal avseende investeringstjänster och aktiviteter definierade i Direktiv 2004/39/EC, OJ L 145/1 med efterföljande ändringar eller ersättande regleringar.

Paragraf 1:102: Definitioner
I dessa Principer skall;
   - (a) fullmäktigens "fullmaktsuppdrag" utgöras av fullmakten (behörigheten) och uppdraget (befogenheten) från huvudmannen med efterföljande ändringar;
   - (b) "fullmaktsavtalet" avse avtalet enligt vilket fullmäktigen fått fullmakt och uppdrag och varje hänvisning till fullmaktsavtalet inkluderar en hänvisning till samtliga rättshandlingar som fullmäktigen fått fullmakt och uppdrag att utföra;
   - (c) "tilltänkta avtal" avse det avtal som fullmäktigen fått fullmakt och instruktioner att ingå, förhandla, och möjliggöra och varje hänvisning till "tilltänkta avtal" inkluderar en hänvis-

---

*   Translated by *Jeanette Andersson*, University of Gothenburg.

ning till samtliga rättshandlingar som fullmäktigen fått fullmakt och uppdrag att utföra, förhandla eller möjliggöra;

(d) ett fullmaktsuppdrag avseende direkt representation avse ett fullmaktsuppdrag enligt vilket fullmäktigen skall agera i huvudmannens namn, eller på annat sätt som ger uttryck åt en avsikt att rättshandla för huvudmannen;

(e) ett fullmaktsuppdrag avseende indirekt representation avse ett fullmaktsuppdrag enligt vilket fullmäktigen skall agera i eget namn, eller på annat sätt som inte ger uttryck åt en avsikt att rättshandla för huvudmannen;

(f) en "anvisning" avse ett beslut av huvudmannen avseende utförandet av förpliktelserna enligt fullmaktsavtalet eller innehållet i tilltänkta avtal som fattas när fullmaktsavtalet ingås eller, i enlighet med fullmaktsuppdraget, vid en senare tidpunkt;

(g) "tredje man" avse den part med vilken det tilltänkta avtalet skall ingås, förhandlas eller möjliggöras av fullmäktigen;

(h) "återkallelse" av fullmaktsuppdraget avse huvudmannens återkallelse av fullmäktigens behörighet och befogenhet.

Paragraf 1:103: Fullmaktsavtalets varaktighet
Ett fullmaktsavtal kan ingås att gälla
(a) för obestämd tid;
(b) för viss bestämd tid;
(c) för ett specifikt uppdrag.

Paragraf 1:104: Återkallelse av fullmaktsuppdraget
(1) Fullmaktsuppdraget kan, förutom i de fall 1:105 är tillämplig, återkallas av huvudmannen vid varje tidpunkt genom meddelande till fullmäktigen.

(2) Uppsägning av fullmaktsförhållandet innebär en återkallelse av fullmaktsuppdraget för fullmäktigen.

(3) Parterna får inte, till skada för huvudmannen, exkludera tillämplighet av denna Bestämmelse eller avvika från eller förändra dess verkan, om inte villkoren i 1:105 är uppfyllda.

Paragraf 1:105: Oåterkalleligt fullmaktsuppdrag
(1) Oavsett bestämmelserna i 1:104 kan fullmaktsuppdraget inte återkallas av huvudmannen om det har uppdragits åt fullmäktigen
(a) i syfte att säkerställa ett hos fullmäktigen legitimt intresse annat än intresset av betalning av priset, eller
(b) i gemensamt intresse hos parter i ett annat avtal eller annat rättsligt förhållande, oavsett om dessa parter samtliga är part i fullmaktsavtalet, och det oåterkalleliga fullmaktsuppdraget är avsett att säkerställa intresset hos en eller flera av dessa parter.

(2) Fullmaktsuppdraget kan likväl återkallas om
(a) fullmaktsuppdraget är oåterkalleligt enligt (1)(a) och
   (i) det avtal från vilket det legitima intresset härrör är uppsagt på grund av fullmäktigens avtalsbrott; eller
   (ii) fullmäktigen har begått ett väsentligt avtalsbrott; eller
   (iii) det finns ett allvarligt och extraordinärt skäl för huvudmannen att säga upp avtalet i enlighet med 6:103; eller
(b) fullmaktsuppdraget är oåterkalleligt enligt (1)(b) och

(i) parterna i vars intresse fullmaktsuppdraget är oåterkalleligt är överens om en återkallelse av fullmaktsuppdraget; eller

(ii) det i (1)(b) omnämnda rättsliga förhållandet är uppsagt; eller

(iii) fullmäktigen begår ett väsentligt avtalsbrott, under förutsättning att fullmäktigen ersätts utan oskäligt dröjsmål av en annan fullmäktig i enlighet med avtalet mellan huvudmannen och den andra parten eller parterna; eller

(iv) det finns ett allvarligt och extraordinärt skäl för huvudmannen att säga upp avtalet enligt 6:103, under förutsättning att fullmäktigen ersätts utan oskäligt dröjsmål av en annan fullmäktig i enlighet med avtalet mellan huvudmannen och den andra parten eller parterna.

(3) Ett meddelande om återkallelse är utan verkan i de fall återkallelse av fullmaktsuppdraget inte är tillåtet enligt denna Bestämmelse.

(4) Denna Bestämmelse är inte tillämplig om fullmaktsförhållandet sägs upp enligt Kapitel 7 av dessa Principer.

Kapitel 2:
Huvudmannens Huvudförpliktelser

Paragraf 2:101: Samarbetsskyldighet
Den samarbetsskyldighet som följer av III. – 1:104 innebär i synnerhet en skyldighet för huvudmannen att

(a) på fullmäktigens begäran lämna information i den utsträckning sådan information behövs för att fullmäktigen skall kunna prestera enligt fullmaktsavtalet;

(b) ge en anvisning avseende utförandet av fullmaktsavtalet i den utsträckning som detta följer av fullmaktsavtalet eller av en begäran om anvisning enligt 4:102 (Begäran om anvisning).

Paragraf 2:102: Pris
(1) Huvudmannen skall ersätta fullmäktigen om denne utför sina förpliktelser i fullmaktsavtalet i yrkesmässig verksamhet, om inte huvudmannen förväntade sig och skäligen kunde förvänta sig att fullmäktigen skulle utföra sina förpliktelser utan ersättning.

(2) Priset är förfallet till betalning när fullmaktsuppdraget är slutfört och fullmäktigen redovisat detta för huvudmannen.

(3) Om parterna har avtalat om betalning av ett pris för utförda tjänster, fullmaktsavtalet har sagts upp och fullmaktsuppdraget inte slutförts, är priset förfallet till betalning när fullmäktigen har redovisat sina prestationer enligt fullmaktsavtalet.

(4) När fullmaktsuppdraget avser ingående av tilltänkta avtal och huvudmannen själv har ingått det tilltänkta avtalet eller när en annan av huvudmannen utsedd person har ingått det tilltänkta avtalet för huvudmannens räkning är fullmäktigen berättigad till ersättning eller en proportionerlig ersättning om ingåendet av det tilltänkta avtalet kan härledas helt eller delvis till fullmäktigens prestation enligt fullmaktsavtalet.

(5) När fullmaktsuppdraget avser ingående av tilltänkta avtal och det tilltänkta avtalet ingås efter att fullmaktsförhållandet har sagts upp är huvudmannen skyldig att betala ersättning om parterna avtalat att ersättning enbart skulle grundas på ingåendet av det tilltänkta avtalet och

(a) ingåendet av det tilltänkta avtalet huvudsakligen är ett resultat av fullmäktigens upp-offringar; och

(b) det tilltänkta avtalet ingås inom en skälig tid efter att fullmaktsförhållandet sagts upp.

Paragraf 2:103: Fullmäktigens utgifter

(1) När fullmäktigen är berättigad till ersättning presumeras att ersättningen inkluderar er-sättning för utgifter som fullmäktigen haft vid utförandet av sina skyldigheter enligt full-maktsavtalet.

(2) När fullmäktigen inte är berättigad till ersättning eller när parterna har kommit överens om att utgifter skall betalas separat är huvudmannen skyldig att ersätta fullmäktigen för de utgifter som fullmäktigen haft i samband med uppdragets utförande så länge och i den utsträckning fullmäktigen agerat skäligt när han ådragit sig utgifterna.

(3) Fullmäktigen är berättigad till ersättning av utgifter enligt (2) från den tidpunkt utgifterna uppstod och fullmäktigen har redovisat utgifterna.

(4) Om fullmaktsförhållandet sagts upp och det resultat som grundar rätt till ersättning inte har uppnåtts är fullmäktigen berättigad till ersättning för skäliga utgifter som fullmäktigen haft under utförandet av fullmaktsavtalet. Stycke (3) är tillämpligt på sådana utgifter.

Kapitel 3:
Fullmäktigens Prestation
Avsnitt 1:
Fullmäktigens huvudförpliktelser

Paragraf 3:101: Skyldighet att agera i enlighet med fullmaktsuppdraget
Fullmäktigen är skyldig att vid var tid agera i enlighet med fullmaktsuppdraget.

Paragraf 3:102: Skyldighet att agera i huvudmannens intresse

(1) Fullmäktigen är skyldig att agera i enlighet med huvudmannens intressen i den utsträck-ning de har blivit kommunicerade till fullmäktigen eller fullmäktigen skäligen kunde för-väntas ha kännedom om dem.

(2) Fullmäktigen är skyldig att begära information från huvudmannen rörande huvudman-nens intressen som fullmäktigen inte har kännedom om när sådan information behövs för avtalsenligt utförande av fullmaktsförhållandet.

Paragraf 3:103: Omsorgsskyldighet

(1) Fullmäktigen skall utföra sina förpliktelser enligt fullmaktsavtalet med den omsorg och skicklighet som huvudmannen är berättigad att förvänta sig mot bakgrund av omständig-heterna.

(2) Om fullmäktigen utger sig för att tillämpa en högre grad av omsorg och skicklighet skall han tillämpa sådan omsorg och skicklighet.

(3) Om fullmäktigen är, eller utger sig för att vara, medlem i en branschorganisation för vilken ett regelverk har skapats av en berörd myndighet eller av branschorganisationen, skall fullmäktigen tillämpa den grad av omsorg och skicklighet som regelverket föreskriver.

(4) Vid fastställande av den omsorg och skicklighet huvudmannen har rätt att förvänta sig skall hänsyn tas till bland annat;
  (a) naturen, omfattningen, frekvensen och förutsebarheten av de risker som uppdragets utförande innebär;
  (b) om uppdraget utförs av en icke-fackman eller kostnadsfritt;
  (c) storleken på ersättning till fullmäktigen; och
  (d) den tid som skäligen står till förfogande för utförande av uppdraget.

Avsnitt 2:
Verkan av överskridande av fullmaktsuppdraget

Paragraf 3:201: Överskridande av fullmaktsuppdraget
(1) Fullmäktigen får agera på ett sätt som inte omfattas av fullmaktsuppdraget om
  (a) fullmäktigen har skälig anledning att agera på detta sätt för huvudmannens räkning; och
  (b) fullmäktigen inte har någon skälig möjlighet att få kännedom om huvudmannens önskemål med hänsyn till de särskilda omständigheterna; och
  (c) fullmäktigen inte vet och inte skäligen kunde förväntas känna till att agerandet med hänsyn till de särskilda omständigheterna strider mot huvudmannens önskemål.
(2) Ett agerande enligt (1) skall, i förhållandet mellan fullmäktigen och huvudmannen, ha samma rättsverkningar som ett agerande som omfattas av fullmaktsuppdraget.

Paragraf 3:202: Verkan av ratificering
När fullmäktigen vid ingående av tilltänkta avtal för huvudmannens räkning har agerat utanför fullmaktsuppdraget, utan att omfattas av föregående Bestämmelse, är fullmäktigen fri från ansvar om huvudmannen ratificerar avtalet. Detta gäller inte om huvudmannen utan oskäligt dröjsmål efter ratificering meddelar fullmäktigen att huvudmannen förbehåller sig rätten att kräva påföljd för fullmäktigens avtalsbrott.

Avsnitt 3:
Ingående av tilltänkta avtal av annan person

Paragraf 3:301: Exklusivitet ej presumerad
Huvudmannen är fri att utse annan fullmäktig eller att själv ingå, förhandla eller möjliggöra det tilltänkta avtalet.

Paragraf 3:302: Anlitande av underleverantör
(1) Fullmäktigen får anlita underleverantör för att helt eller delvis utföra förpliktelserna enligt fullmaktsavtalet utan huvudmannens tillstånd, om det inte är av avgörande betydelse att fullmäktigen utför uppdraget personligen.
(2) Varje underleverantör som anlitas av fullmäktigen skall ha erforderlig kompetens.
(3) I enlighet med III. – 2:106 (Performance entrusted to another) ansvarar fullmäktigen för underleverantörens prestation.

Avsnitt 4:
Skyldighet att informera huvudmannen

Paragraf 3:401: Information om uppdragets utveckling
Under utförandet av förpliktelserna enligt fullmaktsavtalet skall fullmäktigen i den utsträckning det med hänsyn till omständigheterna är skäligt informera huvudmannen om förekomsten av och framskridandet av förhandlingar eller andra åtgärder som kan leda till eventuellt ingående eller möjliggörande av tilltänkta avtal.

Paragraf 3:402: Redovisningsskyldighet
(1) Fullmäktigen är skyldig att utan oskäligt dröjsmål informera huvudmannen om slutförandet av fullmaktsuppdraget.
(2) Fullmäktigen är skyldig att till huvudmannen redovisa
   (a) på vilket sätt förpliktelserna enligt fullmaktsavtalet har utförts; och
   (b) de medel som spenderats eller mottagits eller utgifter som fullmäktigen haft vid utförandet av dessa förpliktelser.
(3) Stycke (2) är tillämpligt med lämpliga justeringar om fullmaktsavtalet sägs upp i enlighet med Kapitel 6 och 7 och förpliktelserna enligt fullmaktsavtalet inte fullgjorts.

Paragraf 3:403: Uppgift om tredje mans identitet
(1) Fullmäktigen är skyldig att på huvudmannens begäran upplysa huvudmannen om tredje mans namn och adress.
(2) I fall av fullmaktsuppdrag avseende indirekt representation är (1) tillämpligt endast om fullmäktigen blir insolvent.

Kapitel 4:
Anvisningar Och Ändringar
Avsnitt 1:
Anvisningar

Paragraf 4:101: Huvudmannens anvisningar
(1) Huvudmannen får ge anvisningar till fullmäktigen.
(2) Fullmäktigen är skyldig följa huvudmannens anvisningar.
(3) Fullmäktigen är skyldig att varna huvudmannen om anvisningen:
   (a) leder till att fullgörelse av förpliktelserna i fullmaktsavtalet blir betydligt dyrare eller tar betydligt mer tid i anspråk än vad som följer av fullmaktsavtalet; eller
   (b) är oförenlig med fullmaktsavtalets syfte eller annars kan skada huvudmannens intressen.
(4) Om huvudmannen inte återkallar anvisningen utan oskäligt dröjsmål efter fullmäktigens varning skall anvisningen anses utgöra en ändring av fullmaktsavtalet enligt 4:201 (Ändring av fullmaktsavtalet).

Paragraf 4:102: Begäran om anvisning

(1) Fullmäktigen är skyldig att begära en anvisning i de fall han erhållit information som kräver att huvudmannen fattar ett beslut angående utförandet av förpliktelserna enligt fullmaktsavtalet eller innehållet i tilltänkta avtal.

(2) Fullmäktigen är skyldig att begära en anvisning när fullmaktsuppdraget avser ingående av tilltänkta avtal och det inte framgår av fullmaktsavtalet om fullmaktsuppdraget avser direkt eller indirekt representation.

Paragraf 4:103: Följder av utebliven anvisning

(1) Om huvudmannen inte lämnar fullmäktigen en anvisning när han är skyldig att göra detta enligt fullmaktsavtalet eller enligt 4:102 (1) (Begäran om anvisning) får fullmäktigen i den utsträckning det är tillämpligt tillgripa någon av sanktionerna i Kapitel 8 (Non-Performance and Remedies in general) och 9 (Particular Remedies for Non-Performance) PECL; eller

   (a) basera prestationen på de förväntningar, preferenser och prioriteringar som en person i samma situation som huvudmannen skäligen kan anses ha mot bakgrund av den information och de anvisningar som inhämtats; och

   (b) kräva en proportionerlig justering av priset och av den tid som avtalats eller som krävs för ingående av tilltänkta avtal.

(2) Om huvudmannen inte lämnar fullmäktigen anvisning enligt 4:102 (2) (Begäran om anvisning) får fullmäktigen välja mellan direkt eller indirekt representation eller hålla inne prestation enligt Artikel 9:201 (Right to Withhold Performance) PECL.

(3) Det justerade pris som skall betalas enligt (1)(b) skall vara skäligt och skall bestämmas enligt samma beräkningsmetoder som användes vid fastställande av ursprungspriset för utförandet av förpliktelserna enligt fullmaktsavtalet.

Paragraf 4:104: Fullmäktigens rätt att agera utan anvisning

(1) Om fullmäktigen är skyldig att begära en anvisning enligt 4:102 (Begäran om anvisning) men behöver agera innan kontakt med eller begäran om anvisning från huvudmannen är möjlig får fullmäktigen basera prestationen på de förväntningar, preferenser och prioriteringar som huvudmannen skäligen kan anses ha mot bakgrund av den information och de anvisningar som inhämtats.

(2) I den situation som följer av (1) får fullmäktigen, i den utsträckning en sådan justering är skälig mot bakgrund av omständigheterna, kräva en proportionerlig justering av priset och av den tid som avtalats eller som krävs för utförandet av förpliktelserna enligt fullmaktsavtalet.

Avsnitt 2:
Ändring i Fullmaktsavtalet

Paragraf 4:201: Ändring i fullmaktsavtalet

(1) En ändring av fullmaktsavtalet föreligger om huvudmannen

   (a) väsentligen ändrar fullmaktsuppdraget;

   (b) inte återkallar en anvisning utan oskäligt dröjsmål efter att ha blivit varnad enligt 4:101 (3) (Huvudmannens anvisningar).

(2) Vid en ändring av fullmaktsavtalet enligt (1) är fullmäktigen berättigad till

    (a) en proportionerlig justering av priset och av den tid som avtalats eller som krävs för utförandet av förpliktelserna enligt fullmaktsavtalet; eller

    (b) skadestånd enligt Artikel 9:502 PECL (General Measure of Damages) för att, så långt det är möjligt, försätta fulllmäktigen i den situation som han skulle ha befunnit sig i om fullmaktsavtalet inte hade ändrats.

(3) Vid en ändring av fullmaktsavtalet enligt (1) får fullmäktigen också genom meddelande säga upp fullmaktsförhållandet på grund av extraordinära och allvarliga skäl enligt 6:105 (Fullmäktigens uppsägning på grund av extraordinära och allvarliga skäl) om inte ändringen är av mindre betydelse eller till fullmäktigens fördel.

(4) Det justerade pris som skall betalas enligt (2)(a) skall vara skäligt och skall bestämmas enligt samma beräkningsmetoder som användes vid fastställande av ursprungspriset för utförandet av förpliktelserna enligt fullmaktsavtalet.

Kapitel 5:
Intressekonflikter

Paragraf 5:101: Självinträde

(1) Fullmäktigen får inte vara huvudmannens motpart i det tilltänkta avtalet.

(2) Fullmäktigen får likväl vara huvudmannens motpart om

    (a) parterna är överens om detta i fullmaktsavtalet;

    (b) fullmäktigen har tillkännagivit sin avsikt att bli huvudmannens motpart och

        (i) huvudmannen därefter samtycker; eller

        (ii) huvudmannen inte motsätter sig att fullmäktigen blir motpart efter att ha blivit uppmanad att tillkännage eller neka samtycke;

    (c) huvudmannen kände till, eller skäligen kunde antas känna till att fullmäktigen blivit huvudmannens motpart och huvudmannen inte invänder mot detta inom skälig tid; eller

    (d) innehållet i det tilltänkta avtalet är reglerat i fullmaktsavtalet i en sådan utsträckning att det inte föreligger någon risk för att huvudmannens intressen inte beaktas.

(3) Om huvudmannen är konsument får fullmäktigen endast vara dennes motpart om

    (a) fullmäktigen har tillkännagivit denna information och huvudmannen uttryckligen har samtyckt till att fullmäktigen blir motpart i det tilltänkta avtalet; eller

    (b) innehållet i det tilltänkta avtalet är reglerat i fullmaktsavtalet i en sådan utsträckning att det inte föreligger någon risk för att huvudmannens intressen inte beaktas.

(4) Parterna får inte, till skada för huvudmannen, exkludera tillämplighet av (3) eller avvika från eller förändra dess verkan.

(5) Om fullmäktigen blivit huvudmannens motpart är fullmäktigen inte berättigad till ersättning för tjänster han utfört som fullmäktig.

Paragraf 5:102: Dubbelt fullmaktsuppdrag

(1) Fullmäktigen får inte representera både huvudmannen och huvudmannens motpart i det tilltänkta avtalet.

(2) Fullmäktigen får likväl representera både huvudmannen och motparten om

    (a) parterna kommit överens om detta i fullmaktsavtalet

(b) fullmäktigen har tillkännagivit en avsikt att representera motparten och huvudmannen
  (i) därefter samtycker; eller
  (ii) inte motsätter sig att fullmäktigen representerar motparten efter att ha blivit uppmanad att tillkännage eller neka samtycke;
(c) huvudmannen kände till, eller skäligen kunde antas känna till att fullmäktigen representerar motparten och huvudmannen inte invänt mot detta inom skälig tid; eller
(d) innehållet i det tilltänkta avtalet är reglerat i fullmaktsavtalet i en sådan utsträckning att det inte föreligger någon risk för att huvudmannens intressen inte beaktas.
(3) Om huvudmannen är konsument får fullmäktigen endast representera både huvudmannen och huvudmannens motpart om
  (a) fullmäktigen har tillkännagivit denna information och huvudmannen uttryckligen har samtyckt till att fullmäktigen också representerar motparten i det tilltänkta avtalet; eller
  (b) innehållet i det tilltänkta avtalet är reglerat i fullmaktsavtalet i en sådan utsträckning att det inte föreligger någon risk för att huvudmannens intressen inte beaktas.
(4) Parterna får inte, till skada för huvudmannen, exkludera tillämplighet av (3) eller avvika från eller förändra dess verkan.
(5) Om och i den utsträckning fullmäktigen agerat i enlighet med (1)-(4) är fullmäktigen berättigad till ersättning.

Kapitel 6:
Uppsägning I Annat Fall än vid Avtalsbrott

Paragraf 6:101: Uppsägning genom meddelande
(1) Vardera parten kan när som helst säga upp fullmaktsförhållandet genom meddelande till motparten.
(2) Vid tillämpning av (1) skall en återkallelse av fullmaktsuppdraget betraktas som en uppsägning.
(3) Uppsägning av fullmaktsförhållandet träder inte i kraft om fullmaktsuppdraget är oåterkalleligt enligt 1:105.
(4) Verkningarna vid uppsägning regleras i Kapitel 9, Del 3 PECL (Termination of the contract).
(5) När part som säger upp avtalet genom meddelande har rätt till uppsägning utgår inget skadestånd.
(6) En uppsägning är giltig i fall när en part genom meddelande säger upp fullmaktsförhållandet trots att rätt till uppsägning inte föreligger. Motparten är i sådant fall berättigad till skadestånd i enlighet med Kapitel 9, Del 5 PECL (Damages and interest).
(7) En part har enligt denna Artikel rätt att säga upp fullmaktsförhållandet genom meddelande om:
  (a) rätt till uppsägning av fullmaktsförhållandet följer av uttryckliga bestämmelser i avtalet och de uppställda kraven för uppsägning har iakttagits;
  (b) rätt till uppsägning av fullmaktsförhållandet följer av Kapitel 9, Del 3 PECL (Termination of the contract); eller

(c) rätt till uppsägning av fullmaktsförhållandet följer av någon annan Artikel i detta Kapitel och de uppställda kraven för uppsägning i den tillämpliga Artikeln har iakttagits.

Paragraf 6:102: Huvudmannens uppsägning med skälig uppsägningstid

(1) Huvudmannen har rätt säga upp fullmaktsförhållandet när som helst genom ett meddelande med skälig uppsägningstid om fullmaktsavtalet ingicks att gälla för obestämd tid eller för specifikt uppdrag.

(2) Stycke (1) är inte tillämpligt om fullmaktsuppdraget är oåterkalleligt.

(3) Parterna får inte, till skada för huvudmannen, exkludera tillämplighet av denna Bestämmelse eller avvika från eller förändra dess verkan om inte villkoren i 1:105 (Oåterkalleligt fullmaktsuppdrag) är uppfyllda.

Paragraf 6:103: Huvudmannens uppsägning på grund av extraordinära och allvarliga skäl

(1) Huvudmannen får genom meddelande säga upp fullmaktsförhållandet på grund av extraordinära och allvarliga skäl.

(2) Ingen uppsägningstid krävs.

(3) Vid tillämpning av denna Bestämmelse skall viss persons död eller myndighets beslut att viss person saknar rättshandlingsförmåga, i de fall när parterna vid tidpunkten för ingåendet av fullmaktsavtalet avsåg att denna person skulle utföra fullmäktigens förpliktelser enligt fullmaktsavtalet, utgöra extraordinära och allvarliga skäl.

(4) Denna Bestämmelse är tillämplig, med lämpliga justeringar, om huvudmannens arvingar säger upp fullmaktsförhållandet i enlighet med 7:101 (Huvudmannens död).

(5) Parterna får inte, till skada för huvudmannen eller dennes arvingar, exkludera tillämplighet av denna Bestämmelse eller avvika från eller förändra dess verkan.

Paragraf 6:104: Fullmäktigens uppsägning när avtalet gäller för obestämd tid eller är av benefik karaktär

(1) Fullmäktigen har rätt att säga upp fullmaktsförhållandet när som helst genom ett meddelande med skälig uppsägningstid om fullmaktsavtalet ingicks att gälla för obestämd tid.

(2) Fullmäktigen har rätt att säga upp fullmaktsförhållandet genom ett meddelande med skälig uppsägningstid om fullmaktsavtalet är av benefik karaktär.

(3) Parterna får inte, till skada för fullmäktigen, exkludera tillämplighet av (1) eller avvika från eller förändra dess verkan.

Paragraf 6:105: Fullmäktigens uppsägning på grund av extraordinära och allvarliga skäl

(1) Fullmäktigen får genom meddelande säga upp fullmaktsförhållandet på grund av extraordinära och allvarliga skäl.

(2) Ingen uppsägningstid krävs.

(3) Vid tillämpning av denna Bestämmelse skall

    (a) en ändring av fullmaktsavtalet enligt 4:201 (Ändring av fullmaktsavtalet);

    (b) huvudmannens död eller myndighets beslut om att huvudmannen saknar rättshandlingsförmåga; och

(c) viss persons död eller myndighets beslut att viss person saknar rättslig handlingsför-
måga, i de fall när parterna vid tidpunkten för ingåendet av fullmaktsavtalet avsåg att
denna person skulle utföra fullmäktigens förpliktelser enligt fullmaktsavtalet, utgöra
ett extraordinärt och allvarligt skäl.

(4) Parterna får inte, till skada för fullmäktigen, exkludera tillämplighet av denna Bestämmelse
eller avvika från eller förändra dess verkan.

Kapitel 7:
Andra Uppsägningsgrunder

Paragraf 7:101: Huvudmannens död

(1) Fullmaktsförhållandet upphör inte vid huvudmannens död.

(2) Både fullmäktigen och huvudmannens arvingar äger rätt att genom meddelande säga upp
fullmaktsavtalet på grund av extraordinärt och allvarligt skäl enligt 6:103 (Huvudmannens
uppsägning på grund av extraordinära och allvarliga skäl) eller 6:105 (Fullmäktigens uppsägning på grund av extraordinära och allvarliga skäl).

Paragraf 7:102: Fullmäktigens död

(1) Fullmaktsförhållandet upphör vid fullmäktigens död.

(2) Betalning skall ske av utgifter och annan ersättning som förfallit till betalning vid tiden för
fullmäktigens död.

Principles of European Law on
Mandate Contracts

General Introduction

I. General

These Principles deal with contracts where one party (the principal) requests another party to arrange some of his legal affairs, often in exchange for a price. The legal affairs at hand consist of the conclusion of a contract with a third party – in these Principles referred to as 'the prospective contract' – or to perform another juridical act. Where the agent is required to act in the name of the principal, the mandate contract is a contract for direct representation. When performed, a direct contractual relationship is created between the principal and the third party. If, on the other hand, the agent is required to act in his own name, the mandate contract is a contract for indirect representation. In this situation, the contract that is concluded by the agent does not bind the principal but the agent himself. These Principles also apply in cases where the agent is authorised but not required to act on behalf of the principal, e.g. in cases where the parties agree that the agent may conclude a contract on behalf of the principal if he sees an opportunity to do so, but do not want to require the agent to actively look for it.

The powers of the agent may also concern only the preparation of a contract with the third party, without the agent having the power to conclude the contract himself. In this case, the mandate contract takes the form of intermediation. The scope of these Principles, however, is restricted to such cases of intermediation where the services of the agent are aimed at the arrangement of the principal's *legal* affairs. Therefore, its provisions do not apply to contracts whereby two parties are to be brought together for personal reasons, as in the case of marriage brokerage.

II. Relation to General Contract Law (PECL) and the Principles of European Law on Service Contracts (PEL SC)

The Principles of European Contract Law (PECL) provide general rules of contract law. Those rules apply, in principle, to all types of contracts, independent of their object (e.g. sales, insurance, medical treatment, construction, and joint venture) or the status of the parties (consumer, merchant, small business, multinational). As a result, these rules are necessarily rather general and abstract. Although abstract rules certainly have an important function – they warrant normative integrity – practice also needs more specific rules. Therefore, in addition to the general contract law contained in the PECL, the Principles of European Law series, developed within the framework of the Study Group on a European Civil Code, also contain sets of principles specifically relating to sales contracts, service contracts, and long-term commercial contracts, for instance.

These Principles fill a gap left by the Principles of European Law on Service Contracts (PEL SC). Although there is much to be said about looking at mandate contracts as a specific service contract, when developing the rules of the PEL SC no specific attention was paid to this type of contract. The reason for this was of a rather practical nature: the research capacity of the Working Team on Service Contracts was rather limited. The team originally consisted of Maurits Barendrecht, Marco Loos, Andrea Pinna, Rui Cascao, and Roland Lohnert. Lohnert eventually left the Team and was much later replaced by Stéphanie van Gulijk. At an earlier stage, Chris Jansen joined the Team. In addition, the Working Team drew on the help of some of the researchers in the Working Teams that prepared the volumes of the Principles of European Law on Sales (PEL S) (Christoph Jeloschek, Giorgos Arnokouros, Hanna Sivesand, and Aneta Wiewiorowska) and the Principles of European Law on Commercial Agency, Franchising and Distribution Contracts (PEL CAFDC) (Odavia Bueno Díaz and Manola Scotton) for the preparation of national notes. The Working Team further benefitted from discussions with the other members of these Working Teams (Ewoud Hondius, Viola Heutger, Martijn Hesselink, Jacobien Rutgers, and Muriel Veldman). Still, the development of the Principles and Comments mainly depended on the Working Team itself. Not surprisingly, the number of types of service contracts that could be covered was limited, and particular services had to be left out.

This was problematic in particular with regard to mandate contracts. The problem was that the rules on representation in the PELC – which regulate the external relationship between the principal and the third party – basically presuppose a preceding contractual relationship between the client and his agent. That internal relationship requires specific regulation, without which the mandate contract would be governed solely by the general provisions on service contracts, i.e. Chapter 1 (General provisions) of the PEL SC. Upon request by the Study Group on a European Civil Code, however, it was decided that such specific rules should be developed after all for mandate contracts. To that extent, a second small Working Team on mandate contracts was established consisting of the authors of this volume. Both of us thus worked on related aspects – Loos on service contracts and Bueno Díaz on commercial agency.

The Working Team originally preferred to take Chapter 1 (General Provisions) of the Principles of European Law on Service Contracts as a starting point for the development of a specific Chapter on Mandate Contracts. It was thought that these contracts could easily be understood as contracts for specific services. That would mean that in principle, the rules of Chapter 1 PEL SC (General Provisions) would apply. Where the rules of this Chapter provide a proper solution for a topic, these rules would apply directly without any modification or specification. This approach would decrease the risk of discrepancies between these specific services and other service contracts, which could lead to litigation on qualification issues. Where Chapter 1 PEL SC (General Provisions) did not touch upon the matter at hand, a specific rule in a Chapter on Mandate Contracts could be needed. Where Chapter 1 PEL SC (General Provisions) would provide for a solution that is not apt to deal with the specific requirements of a mandate contract, the specific Chapter on Mandate Contracts should then contain a modification of or derogation from Chapter 1 PEL SC (General Provisions). It was thought, however, that derogation from the provision in Chapter 1 PEL SC (General Provisions) would not be needed very often.

Illustration 1

A principal wants to buy a shipment of cocoa beans on the market. As he is too busy to participate on the market himself, he appoints an agent to join in on the bidding on the cocoa beans. The parties do not make specific arrangements as to how the price for the agent's services is to be calculated.

If Chapter 1 PEL SC (General Provisions) applied, Article 1:102 PEL SC (Price) would provide that the agent is entitled to the market price generally charged for services of this kind at the time of the conclusion of the contract.

Illustration 2

A principal wants to buy a painting at an auction. Because the principal prefers to remain anonymous, she orders the curator of an art gallery to buy the painting for her without disclosing the principal's name to the seller. The curator examines the painting before the auction starts and discovers the painting may be a fraud.

If Chapter 1 PEL SC (General Provisions) applied, the curator would be required to warn the principal of his suspicions unless the principal already knew of the risk before the contract with the curator was concluded, as in Article 1:110 PEL SC (Contractual Duty of the Service Provider to Warn).

As in these two Illustrations, the provisions in Chapter 1 PEL SC (General Provisions) seem to provide adequate solutions to the question to what price the agent is entitled and whether the principal is to be informed of the curator's suspicions; the Chapter on Mandate Contracts would not contain a specific provision on these issues. This view was supported by a large minority of the members of the Coordinating Committee of the Study Group on a European Civil Code. These members argued that the rules applicable to mandate contracts belonged most appropriately as an additional Chapter in the Principles of European Law on Service Contracts (PEL SC), because they were essentially concerned with contracts for the provision of representation or intermediation services.

However, a (slight) majority of the members of the Coordinating Committee favoured the development of a self-standing set of rules on mandate contracts. Some members argued that mandate contracts could not be regarded as services as the act of representation leads to contractual ties between the principal and the third party. As such they were sufficiently distinctive to merit separate treatment, as was indeed the case in most legal systems. These members further argued that mandates were very often unilateral acts. The focus of the existing national provisions was more on what the agent was authorised and instructed to do on behalf of the principal than on the obligation that the agent took upon himself. This majority view led to the development of a separate Book IV.D in the Draft Common Frame of Reference and to these Principles of European Law on Mandate Contracts (PEL MC).

Therefore, even though the drafters of the PEL MC were well aware of the content of the PEL SC, the rules on service contracts and mandate contracts nevertheless look very different. These rules ultimately have become the subject of a separate book of the Draft Common Frame of Reference (DCFR). There are several reasons for this. First, when the second

Working Team started its work on mandate contracts, some of the members of the Study Group on a European Civil Code had serious doubts whether the rules on mandate contracts should be included in what is now Book IV of the Draft Common Frame of Reference, or rather should be added to the rules on representation (now included in Book II, Chapter 6 DCFR (Representation). These rules govern the external relation between principal and third party, whereas the rules on mandate contracts pertain to the internal relation between principal and agent. In this respect, it should be noted that in many national codifications, these sets of rules are grouped together. Moreover, there was considerable time pressure from the European Commission, which required the rules on mandate contracts to be ready for publication by the end of 2007, whereas the Working Team had only started its work in 2005 when the comments to the PEL SC and the PEL CAFDC were about to be finalised. There was considerable concern in the Study Group that if the Working Team were to start aligning the rules on mandate contracts to those on service contracts, progress would be too slow for the rules on mandate contracts to be included in the DCFR. As a result, the drafting of Principles on mandate contracts became a much more stand-alone undertaking than was originally envisaged. Ultimately, there was no longer any chance to try to harmonise the rules on mandate contracts with those on service contracts. The consequence is that the general provisions on service contracts may apply to mandate contracts only by way of analogy for those cases where the specific rules of Book IV.D of the DCFR do not provide an answer.

III. Relation to Draft Common Frame of Reference (DCFR)

As indicated, these Principles were developed to be included in the Draft Common Frame of Reference. This explains why these Principles are almost a copy of the provisions of Book IV.D of the DCFR – the numbers of the Articles and their headings are identical (with only the reference to Book IV.D being deleted), and the contents of the provisions are almost identical. Some minor changes have had to be made, however, based on the fact that the Principles of European Law series builds on the PECL rather than on the DCFR. This explains why the text of the Articles occasionally refers to the provisions of the PECL instead of their counterpart in the DCFR.

The DCFR was published earlier than the Principles of European Law on Mandate Contracts. This is caused in part by the fact that the Comments to Book IV.D have had to be much shorter than the Comments that the drafters of the PEL MC deemed necessary for a proper understanding of the provisions. Moreover, the final editing and occasionally also the drafting of the Comments to the DCFR was left to the editors of the full edition of the DCFR, and in our view did not always fully reflect the reasons why a certain provision was included in the text of the DCFR and these Principles, or state the correct intention of the text of these provisions. It should be noted, however, that the cases where this has occurred are few in number. Given the fact that the Comments for these Principles may shed some additional light on the meaning of the provisions of Book IV.D of the DCFR, the Comments and the notes to the PEL MC may be relied on when interpreting the provisions of the DCFR as regards mandate contracts.

Substantively, the Articles of the Principles of European Law on Mandate Contracts correspond to those of Book IV.D of the DCFR. However, references to other provisions of the DCFR have been replaced by references to the provisions of the Principles of European Contract Law. Moreover, one Article in the DCFR has not been taken over in these Principles. This concerns Article IV.D. – 7:101 DCFR (Conclusion of prospective contract by principal or other agent). This Article provides that if the mandate contract was concluded solely for the conclusion of a specific prospective contract, the mandate contract ends when that contract is concluded by the principal himself or on the principal's behalf by another agent. The conclusion of the prospective contract is then treated as a notice of termination. Upon further consideration, it was thought that this Article was superfluous, as the conclusion of the prospective contract may also be seen as a revocation of the agent's authority to represent the agent under Article 1:104 (Revocation of the mandate) of these Principles. Under Article 6:101 paragraph (2) (Termination by notice in general), this revocation is then already treated as a notice under that provision. Consequently, Articles IV.D. – 7:102 (Death of the principal) and IV.D. – 7:103 DCFR (Death of the agent) correspond with Articles 7:101 (Death of the principal) and 7:102 PEL MC (Death of the agent).

IV. Mainly Default Rules: Some Mandatory Protection

These Principles mainly contain default rules, with some exceptions explained at the end of each Comment to the individual Articles.

The general idea behind these Principles is that the mandate contract is concluded primarily in the interests of the principal and that the agent typically is a professional party who is sufficiently capable of taking care of his own interests. The default rules of these Principles set out which rules reasonable parties acting in good faith and with fair dealing would agree on given this starting point. Furthermore, these Principles are meant to foster the communication between the parties. For this reason, Chapters 3 (Performance by the Agent) and 4 (Directions and Changes) contain several specific information obligations requiring the agent to inform or warn the principal, and the principal to respond where necessary. Moreover, Articles 2:102 (Price), 2:103 (Expenses incurred by agent), and 3:402 (Accounting to the principal) provides that payment of the price or reimbursement of the expenses incurred by the agent only becomes due after the agent has given account of his activities in performing the mandate contract. Mandatory rules are deemed necessary only with regard to conflicts of interests that were not properly disclosed to the principal (Articles 5:101 (Self-contracting) and 5:102 (Double mandate)), and with regard to some of the provisions on termination of the mandate contract by notice under Chapter 6 (Termination by notice other than for non-performance).

However, in order to prevent the principal from disregarding the legitimate interests of the agent, specific provisions have been included to safeguard these interests as well. In particular, the right of the agent to terminate the mandate contract for extraordinary and serious reason under Article 6:105 (Termination by agent for extraordinary and serious reason) is mandatory as well. With this provision, the agent is also protected from unilateral changes of the mandate by the principal, or by directions which in the view of the agent compromise the possibilities of concluding the prospective contract and for which the agent has warned the principal to no avail, as such situations are considered to constitute an extraordinary and serious reason to terminate the mandate contract under Article 4:201 paragraph (3) (Changes of the mandate contract). Moreover, in certain situations the parties may agree to the irrevocability of the mandate contract under Article 1:105 (Irrevocability), preventing the principal from terminating the mandate contract himself. These provisions obviously are also mandatory by nature. Finally, Articles 2:102 (Price) and 2:103 (Expenses incurred by agent) include (default) rules dealing with the situation where the principal has terminated the contract and has concluded the prospective contract while benefitting from the previous services of the agent. These provisions then set out that the agent is entitled to a proportionate part of the price and to compensation for expenses. The parties may agree otherwise on this last matter, however.

V. Structure of these Principles

These Principles are divided into seven Chapters.

Chapter 1 (General provisions) opens with general provisions on the scope of these Principles and on the definitions of notions used in these Principles. Article 1:103 (Duration of the mandate contract) indicates that the mandate contracts covered in these Principles may be concluded for an indefinite period of time, for a fixed period, or for the fulfilment of a particular task, which is the most common situation. Articles 1:104 (Revocation of the mandate) and 1:105 (Irrevocable mandate) then deal with the question whether and under which conditions the principal may revoke the agent's mandate.

Chapter 2 (Main obligations of the principal) deals with the main obligations arising from the contract for the principal: an obligation to co-operate with the agent when the latter is performing his obligations under the mandate contract and an obligation to pay the price and to compensate for expenses.

Chapter 3 (Performance by the agent) then continues with the main obligations of the agent. Section 1 (Main obligations of agent) contains the obligation to act in accordance with the mandate provided by the principal, the obligation to act in the principal's interests, and the obligation to execute the mandate contract with the skill and care that the principal may reasonably expect. Together, these obligations aim to ensure that the agent acts at all times with the principal's interests and expressed or presumed wishes and priorities in mind and acts sufficiently carefully when performing the contract. Section 2 of this Chapter (Consequences of acting beyond mandate) sets out the consequences of the agent overstepping the boundaries of his mandate. As explained there, there may be good reasons to do so. This applies in particular when the obligation to act in accordance with the mandate as communicated to him conflicts with the agent's obligation to act in the interests of the principal. Section 3 (Mandate normally not exclusive) indicates that the agent may not rely on his mandate being exclusive, unless the principal has agreed thereto: the principal may very well conclude the prospective contract himself or have a second agent conclude that contract. As this may have important consequences as to the agent's entitlement to payment, this constitutes an important incentive for the agent to clearly regulate his affairs, or to risk having to suffer the consequences. On the other hand, as the following Article indicates, the principal may not rely on the personal performance of the mandate contract by the agent either, unless the agent has agreed thereto. This indicates that when the principal has awarded the mandate because of the specific qualities or capabilities of the agent and for that reason wants personal performance of the mandate contract by the agent (or another person, such as a particular employee of the agent), he had better contract in that sense.

Section 4 of Chapter 3 (Obligation to inform principal) and Section 1 of Chapter 4 (Directions) basically deal with the mutual obligations of parties to properly communicate with one another. Section 4 of Chapter 3 (Obligation to Inform Principal) first requires the agent to inform the principal of the progress of the performance and the success of his efforts, as well as an obligation to give account of the manner in which he has performed his obligations under the contract. When asked, he must also reveal the identity of the third party, but this obligation is largely restricted to cases of direct representation, in which situation the principal is contractually bound towards the third party and is therefore in need of the information. In case of indirect representation, no such relationship arises; consequently, the agent is normally not required to inform the principal hereof.

Chapter 4 (Directions and changes) deals with the important matter of directions and changes of the mandate contract. It basically indicates that the principal is at all times allowed to give directions and that the agent is required to follow these directions. This shows that the principal is 'the master of the contract': the contract is performed primarily in *his* interests, and if in his view his interests change, he must be able to change the agent's instructions. However, where the agent perceives a direction to be contrary to the principal's communicated or presumed interests, he must warn the principal thereof. An obligation to that extent is regulated explicitly in Article 4:101 paragraph (3) (Directions given by the principal), but would otherwise follow from the agent's obligations under Article 3:102 (Obligation to act in interests of the principal). Nevertheless, when the principal holds the mandate to the direction, the agent is bound to follow the direction, or to terminate the contract for extraordinary and serious reason under Article 6:105 (Termination by the agent for extraordinary and serious reason). In such a situation, the mandate contract is deemed to have been changed in accordance with Section 2 of Chapter 4 (Changes of the mandate contract), entitling the agent to an adjustment of the price and of the time allowed for the performance of the mandate contract.

Chapter 5 (Conflicts of interests) deals with two classical cases where a conflict may occur between the principal's interests and those of the agent himself: the case where the agent becomes the principal's counterpart to the prospective contract, and the case where the agent also acts as the third party's agent. In both cases there is a substantive chance that the agent will give priority to his own interests and disregard, at least to a certain extent, the principal's interests. The two provisions of this Chapter intend to set rather classical boundaries to the cases where the agent may act as the principal's counterpart to the prospective contract or as the third party's agent. Less traditional is the fact that specific consumer protection provisions have been introduced here, but these Articles are also intended to be mandatory when included in a contract between two professional parties.

Chapters 6 (Termination by notice other than for non-performance) and 7 (Other grounds for termination) deal with different grounds for the termination of the mandate relationship: cases of termination by notice and death of the agent. Death of the principal does not lead to the automatic termination of the mandate relationship, nor does the death of the person who the parties intended to carry out the obligations under the mandate contract. However, in these cases the principal (or his successors, as the case may be) and the agent may in such a case terminate the mandate contract for extraordinary and serious reason under Articles 6:103 (Termination by the principal for extraordinary and serious reason) and 6:105 (Termination by the agent for extraordinary and serious reason). An essential feature of Chapter 6 (Termination by notice other than for non-performance), which regulates the situation where notice of termination is given, is the fact that the notice leads to the termination of the contract, whether or not the party giving notice was in fact entitled to terminate. This is not to say that the party unlawfully terminating the contract does not have to suffer consequences: the other party may very well be entitled to damages, but a claim for (further) performance of the mandate contract is barred. This is different only when the mandate is irrevocable under Article 1:105 (Irrevocability), as the revocation of the mandate is then without effect and the mandate contract continues to exist. Finally, it is important to realise that one typical situation of termination of the mandate contract is *not* regulated in these Chapters: the situation where either the principal or the agent commits a fundamental non-performance of his obligations under the contract, and where the other party terminates because of that reason. Termination for fundamental non-performance is left to the provisions in the Principles of European Contract Law. However, in a case where the terminating party is not sure whether, for instance, the non-performance is fundamental and thus justifies termination under Chapter 9 PECL (Particular remedies for non-performance), he may also rely on the provisions of Chapter 6 (Termination by notice other than for non-performance) of these Principles. Conversely, Article 6:101 paragraph (7)(b) (Termination by notice in general) sets out that when termination for fundamental non-performance would have been possible, termination by notice under these Principles is in any case justified, which implies that the mandate contract terminates and the terminating party is not liable for damages, even if not all requirements for termination for fundamental non-performance have been met – e.g. the contractually required form for termination for fundamental non-performance has not been met.

VI. External Relationship not Dealt with

These Principles exclusively deal with the internal relationship between the principal and the agent. Therefore, the external relationships with third parties are not dealt with here. These external relationships are regulated by Chapter 3 PECL (Authority of agents). The provisions in that Chapter also deal with the question whether the principal is bound by the prospective contract concluded in his name by the agent in a situation where the agent lacked a proper mandate and whether or not the principal may ratify such a contract. The Principles of European Law on Mandate Contracts, however, do deal with the *internal* dimensions of such cases where the agent has not respected the boundaries of his mandate: in principle, the agent breaches his obligations under the mandate contract unless the agent was justified to exceed his mandate under Article 3:201 (Acting beyond mandate). Moreover, Article 3:202 (Consequences of ratification) indicates that when the principal has ratified the prospective contract, this absolves the agent from liability towards the principal, unless the principal without undue delay after ratification notifies the agent that he reserves his remedies for the non-performance by the agent.

VII. Terminology

In these Principles, the word 'mandate' is used in two different senses. On the one hand, it refers to the power invested in the agent and is therefore equal to the authorisation and instruction given by the principal as modified by any subsequent direction, as defined in Article 1:102 under (a) (Definitions). On the other hand, it may also refer to the relationship or the contract created between the principal and the agent: the mandate contract. In this sense, 'mandate' is used in the same way as the word 'service' is used to classify a contract as a contract for services (or a services contract), and to identify the main obligations of one of the parties, in that case the service provider.

Similarly, the words 'mandate contract' are also used in two different senses: they refer to the contract under which the agent is authorised and instructed to act, as defined in Article 1:102 under (b) (Definitions), and the contractual relationship that is created by that contract between the principal and the agent. In this sense, the term 'mandate contract' and the term 'mandate relationship' are used interchangeably.

Because the scope of the Principles extends beyond direct and indirect representation, it was thought that the word 'representative' would not be appropriate here to designate the party who acts for the principal. The term 'mandataris' could have been used, but as that is sometimes associated exclusively with those acting gratuitously and is, in any event, not a common word in everyday speech, it was not chosen. A compound term such as 'agent or intermediary' or 'agent or broker' could have been used, but that would have been cumbersome. Instead, and following the same terminology as in Chapter 3 PECL (Authority of agents), the party charged under the mandate contract is called 'agent'. In ordinary language the term 'agent' also covers agents who are instructed to do non-juridical acts, such as making enquiries that have nothing to do with the conclusion of contracts. So it is only certain types of agent who are within the scope of these Principles. Essentially these Principles are concerned with mandates for representation, negotiation or intermediation in relation to the conclusion of contracts or the doing of other juridical acts. The contracts with agents providing other services are governed by the Principles of European Law on Service Contracts.

Again, the same terminology as under the Principles of European Contract Law is used to indicate the party who has granted the agent authority to act on his behalf; this party is called the 'principal'.

VIII. Member States Investigated

Not every legal system of the Member States of the European Union is represented in the comparative legal study underlying these Principles. Nevertheless, we have included national notes from Austria, Belgium, Bulgaria, Denmark, England, Estonia, Finland, France, Germany, Greece, Hungary, Ireland, Italy, Malta, the Netherlands, Poland, Portugal, Scotland, Slovakia, Spain, and Sweden, i.e. a total of 21 legal systems. It should be noted, however, that we did not always receive notes from all these legal systems on all matters. This is true in particular for the notes from Austria, Belgium, Denmark, Finland, Greece, Hungary, Malta, and Portugal, whose reporters were not able to provide answers to additional questions after the first extensive set of questions. The names and affiliations of the reporters of the different countries are listed above, directly after the text of the Articles. At that place, the names and affiliations of the persons who have provided the translations of the Articles into Dutch, Finnish, French, German, Italian, Slovak, Spanish and Swedish are listed as well.

A final disclaimer must be made: as indicated earlier, these Principles were prepared for the development of the Draft Common Frame of Reference, and the national notes reflect the situations in the Member States in 2006 and 2007. Later developments, with a few exceptions, are not reflected in these notes.

Chapter 1:
General provisions

Article 1:101: Scope

(1) These Principles apply to contracts and other juridical acts under which a person, the agent, is authorised and instructed (mandated) by another person, the principal:
   (a) to conclude a contract between the principal and a third party or otherwise directly affect the legal position of the principal in relation to a third party;
   (b) to conclude a contract with a third party, or do another juridical act in relation to a third party, on behalf of the principal but in such a way that the agent and not the principal is a party to the contract or other juridical act; or
   (c) to take steps which are meant to lead to, or facilitate, the conclusion of a contract between the principal and a third party or the doing of another juridical act which would affect the legal position of the principal in relation to a third party.
(2) These Principles apply where the agent undertakes to act on behalf of, and in accordance with the instructions of, the principal and, with appropriate adaptations, where the agent is merely authorised but does not undertake to act, but nevertheless does act.
(3) These Principles apply where the agent is to be paid a price and, with appropriate adaptations, where the agent is not to be paid a price.
(4) These Principles apply only to the internal relationship between the principal and the agent (the mandate relationship). They do not apply to the relationship between the principal and the third party or the relationship (if any) between the agent and the third party.
(5) Contracts to which these Principles apply and to which the Principles of European Law on Service Contracts also apply are to be regarded as falling primarily under these Principles.
(6) These Principles do not apply to contracts pertaining to investment services and activities as defined by Directive 2004/39/EC, OJ L 145/1, as subsequently amended or replaced.

Comments

A. General idea

The present Article indicates the scope of the Principles of European Law on Mandate Contracts (PEL MC). The first paragraph makes it clear that the Principles apply to three types of situation. The first such situation (a) is direct representation, where the agent is authorised and instructed to directly affect the legal position of the principal in relation to a third party, typically by concluding a contract between the principal and the third party.

Illustration 1

Andrew is charged by Benjamin to conclude in Benjamin's name a contract for the purchase of 1,000 kilograms of wheat, to be processed at Benjamin's bakery, in exchange for a commission. Andrew buys the wheat in Benjamin's name from Charles; a sales contract between Benjamin and Charles is concluded and Benjamin pays Andrew the promised commission. Andrew and Benjamin have concluded a mandate contract for direct representation, which is covered by these Principles.

The second situation (b) is indirect representation, where the agent is authorised and instructed to conclude a contract with a third party, or do another juridical act in relation to a third party, on behalf of the principal but in such a way that the agent and not the principal is a party to the contract or other juridical act.

Illustration 2

In exchange for a commission, Andrew is charged by Benjamin to purchase 1,000 kilograms of wheat from a third party without indicating to the third party that he is acting on behalf of Benjamin. Andrew buys the wheat from Charles; a sales contract is concluded between Andrew and Charles; Andrew subsequently delivers the wheat to Benjamin, and Benjamin pays Andrew the promised commission. Depending on the contractual relationship between Andrew and Benjamin, either Benjamin also compensates Andrew for paying the sales price, or he directly pays Charles on behalf of Andrew. Andrew and Benjamin have concluded a mandate contract for indirect representation, which is covered by these Principles.

The third situation (c) is brokerage and similar activities, where the agent is authorised and instructed to take steps that are meant to lead to, or facilitate, the conclusion of a contract between the principal and a third party or the doing of another juridical act which would affect the legal position of the principal in relation to a third party, but without actually concluding a contract or doing the other juridical act for the principal.

Illustration 3

In exchange for a commission, Andrew is charged by Benjamin to negotiate the purchase of 1,000 kilograms of wheat from a third party without actually concluding the sales contract. Andrew negotiates the conditions of a sales contract with Charles and informs Benjamin of these conditions. Benjamin concludes the sales contract with Charles and pays Andrew the promised commission. Andrew and Benjamin have concluded a mandate contract for intermediation services, which is covered by these Principles.

Paragraph (2) further extends the scope of these Principles to situations where the agent is not required to act on behalf of the principal, but is authorised to do so and indeed does act on behalf of the principal.

Illustration 4

David asks Eric, an art expert, to bid for him at an auction of paintings and to purchase a painting for the amount of no more than € 10,000. If Eric succeeds in the purchase of a painting, he will receive a commission of € 1,000 for his services. Eric merely promises to see what he can do, but in the end does bid on and purchase a painting on behalf of David for the amount of € 9,500. Eric delivers the painting to David and receives the promised commission. These Principles apply to the relationship between David and Eric; paragraph (2) of this Article reclassifies the relationship as a mandate contract.

Paragraph (3) makes clear that these Principles also apply, with appropriate modifications, to mandate contracts where the agent is not entitled to a price for his services.

Illustration 5
Andrew is charged by Benjamin to conclude in Benjamin's name a contract for the purchase of 1,000 kilograms of wheat, to be processed at Benjamin's bakery, but is not entitled to a commission. Andrew and Benjamin have concluded a mandate contract for direct representation, which is covered by these Principles, even though Andrew is not entitled to a commission for his services.

In the case of direct representation, the services of the agent will have led to a contract between the principal and the third party, in the case of indirect representation to a contract between the agent and the third party. Paragraph (4) clarifies that these Principles do not apply to these negotiated contracts with the third party, but only to the *internal* relationship between the principal and the agent.

The fact that contracts for the provision of representation, negotiation or intermediation services are dealt with in these Principles does not, however, mean that their character changes. They are still (also) contracts for the provision of services to which the rules in the Principles of European Law on Service Contracts (PEL SC) may apply with appropriate adaptations. However, paragraph (5) indicates that in so far as the Principles of European Law on Mandate Contracts conflict with the Principles of European Law on Service Contracts, the Principles of European Law on Mandate Contracts take priority. This is in accordance with the general rules on priority and mixed contracts, as provided for in Article II. – 1:110 paragraphs (3)(a) and (4) of the Draft Common Frame of Reference.

Paragraph (6), finally, excludes mandate contracts pertaining to investments services and activities as defined by Directive 2004/30/EC, OJ L 145/1, as subsequently amended or replaced. Such mandate contracts are regulated by specific legal instruments, which are of a very different nature and to a large extent introduce public law requirements and supervision. These mandate contracts therefore differ so much from ordinary mandate contracts that application of the provisions of these Principles would be restricted to extraordinary situations for which the public law regulation would not provide a solution, which would make the application of these Principles merely accidental. In case there were such a need, however, a court could apply these Principles by way of analogy without being required to do so.

B. Representation and mandate

Modern society cannot operate without some form of representation. Legal persons cannot act for themselves and therefore need to be represented by natural persons. Similarly, minors will often have to be represented by their parents or legal guardians. In the legal systems of all Member States, the law provides for such 'statutory representation'.

However, in practice there is much more need for representation. In many cases, it is impractical for natural or legal persons to act themselves or via their legal agents. Labour law and company law often provide for implicit powers of representation for at least certain employees. Nevertheless, in many cases it is necessary for a party to invite another person to act on his behalf for the conclusion of a contract with a third party. Where such a person is both allowed and required to act on behalf of the first party, a mandate contract is concluded. These Principles deals with the obligations arising out of such mandate contracts.

C. External relationship not covered

Paragraph (4) sets out that these Principles are concerned with the contractual obligations between the principal and the agent only. These Principles do not relate to the question whether this 'prospective' contract with the third party is valid or invalid: that question is governed by Chapter 3 PECL (Authority of agents). That Chapter deals with the relationship between the principal and the third party; they leave the internal relationship between the principal and the agent to these Principles.

D. Authorisation and instruction

The characteristic elements of a mandate contract are that the agent is both allowed (authorised) and required (instructed) to conclude a contract between the principal and a third party or to do any of the other acts covered by the Article. The agent may be authorised (and sometimes even instructed) to act in the principal's name, in which case the mandate contract is a contract for *direct* representation, or to act in his own name *(indirect representation)*

In the case of direct representation (as regulated in paragraph (1)(a) of this Article and as illustrated by Illustration 1, the fact that the agent is *authorised* to act on behalf of the principal implies that the exercise of a mandate and the legal consequences in the external relationship are based on the free will of the principal. By authorising the agent, the principal consents to the agent concluding a contract on the principal's behalf or otherwise affecting the principal's legal position. When the agent subsequently concludes a contract in the name and on behalf of the principal, and in doing so respects the limits indicated in the mandate, the rules of Chapter 3 PECL (Authority of agents) lead to the conclusion that the principal is a party to the contract concluded on his behalf by the agent. Moreover, the authorisation also implies that where the agent respects the limits indicated in the mandate and acts in accordance with the provisions in these Principles, the agent may not be held liable for concluding a contract with the third party if the contract ultimately turns out to be detrimental to the principal: the principal assumes that risk.

The fact that the agent is also *required* to act on behalf of the principal indicates that the agent is under a legal obligation to at least attempt to complete the mandated task. By concluding the mandate contract, the agent therefore undertakes an obligation to act.

In the case of *indirect* representation (as regulated in paragraph (1)(a) of this Article and illustrated by Illustration 2), the agent does not act in the name of the principal but in his own name. As a consequence, the agent becomes a party to the contract with the third party himself. In such a case, however, the agent is required under the mandate contract to ensure that the advantages of the contract are transferred to the principal.

E. Application to certain intermediation contracts

In the case of *intermediation services* (as regulated in paragraph (1)(c) of this Article and as illustrated by Illustration 3 above and Illustration 6 below), the agent is authorised and instructed to take steps which are meant to lead to, or facilitate, the conclusion of a contract between the principal and a third party, *but without actually concluding a contract for the principal.*

One may wonder whether such contracts without obligation to act – *i.e.* contracts that are *intended* to lead to the conclusion of another contract (hereafter: the prospective contract) but by which the agent is *not authorised from the start* to actually conclude that prospective contract – should be governed by these Principles.

Illustration 6
A real estate agent undertakes to attempt to sell a house on behalf of its owner. The agent succeeds in finding a buyer and upon request of the owner successively concludes the sales contract on the owner's behalf.

Under paragraph (1) (a) and (b), the contract between the real estate agent and the owner of the house could only partly be covered by these Principles: only once the real estate agent has found a buyer would he be commissioned to sell it to that buyer. Only that latter transaction could then be seen as a mandate, whereas the former transaction – 'find me a buyer for my house' – would not be covered by these Principles. Most likely, that would then qualify as a service under Article 1:101 (Scope of application) of the Principles of European Law on Service Contracts, rendering the whole contractual relationship between agent and owner to be a mixed contract. However, since the purpose of the whole contract is to bring about a contract between the principal (owner) and the third party, one could also consider the whole contractual relationship to fall under the definition of a mandate contract. Paragraph (1)(c) opts for that solution.

The question whether these Principles should apply multiplies when the prospective contract ultimately is *not* concluded by the agent.

Illustration 7
Andrew is charged by Benjamin to negotiate a contract for the purchase of 1,000 kilograms of wheat, to be processed at Benjamin's bakery, in exchange for a commission. Andrew negotiates the purchase of wheat from Charles and keeps Andrew informed of the progress of the negotiations. Before the contract is concluded, however, Benjamin terminates the contract.

Illustration 8
A real estate agent undertakes to attempt to sell a house on behalf of its owner. The agent finds a buyer for the price indicated by owner, but the owner nevertheless refuses to commission the agent to actually sell the house and sells the house himself.

In these cases, the agent has actually performed most of his obligations under a 'mandate contract', but could not conclude the prospective contract. If this contract could not be classified as a mandate contract, it must be classified as a service contract. The Principles of European Law on Service Contracts, however, do not provide clear rules as to whether the contract is terminated and what should happen with the agent's entitlement to payment. If the present Principles are applied, this is different. The conclusion of the prospective contract by the principal himself is treated as a termination of the mandate contract by the principal under Article 6:101 (Termination by notice in general). Had the parties agreed to payment of a price based solely on the conclusion of the prospective contract – which is not uncommon in the case of real estate agents – the agent would in this particular case be entitled to payment under Article 2:102 paragraph (4) (Price).

Moreover, whereas the present Principles include mandatory rules, in particular regarding termination, the provisions of the Principles of European Law on Service Contracts hardly contain any mandatory rules. It should be noticed that by not including these contracts, there is a substantive risk that the stronger party – be it the agent or the principal – would 'cut the mandate contract in parts' and thus be liberated from the applicability of the agent rules of these Principles – primarily the rules of Chapter 6 (Termination by notice other than for non-performance). In any case, this would invite parties to litigate whether in fact a mandate contract was concluded or whether there really were two separate contracts.

For these reasons, paragraph (1)(c) of this Article qualifies contracts under which a person is authorised and instructed to take steps which are meant to lead to, or facilitate, the conclusion of a contract between the principal and a third party as mandate contracts. This is in conformity with the majority of legal systems where the rules applicable to mandate contracts also apply to intermediation contracts. It should be noted, however, that in many legal systems specific rules on brokerage contracts apply where the intermediation pertains to the purchase or sale of real estate. Such specific rules are not to be found in these Principles, but where appropriate the Principles of European Law on Service Contracts may provide for additional rules.

A different situation arises when the agent is not to prepare the conclusion of a contract, or another juridical act, but to bring two parties together for other reasons.

Illustration 9
Anna has not yet found 'Mr Right'. To enhance her chances of finding a partner, she engages the marital agency Together4Ever Ltd. The agency brings her into contact with Barry, who had given the agency the similar task of finding him a wife.

Whereas the services of the agency are not aimed at the conclusion of a contract, the provisions of these Principles are not sufficiently fit to deal with this type of contract. Such contracts fall under the Principles of European Law on Service Contracts, but in applying those Principles, inspiration may be drawn from these Principles where this is deemed appropriate.

Illustration 9 (continued)
Anna has provided information regarding her requirements as to the personal qualifications of a possible partner. Barry does not exactly fit these qualifications, but his personal situation comes rather close. When interpreting whether the agency has acted in accordance with the service contract by bringing her into contact with Barry, notwithstanding the clear instructions by Anna, the provision of Articles 3:201 (Acting beyond mandate) may help determine whether the agency acted reasonably when overstepping the boundaries of the task entrusted to it.

F. Application to contracts without obligation to act

The rules on mandate normally apply to contracts by which the agent is not only authorised but also required to act on behalf of the principal. Paragraph (2), as illustrated above by Illustration 4, extends the scope of these Principles to contracts in which the agent is authorised but not required to act on behalf of the principal, but only in the case where the agent subsequently acts on behalf of the principal, thus making use of the authorisation by the principal to so act. Obviously, this provision is of relevance when the agent indeed acts on behalf of the principal. These Principles then indicate when the agent would be entitled to remuneration and what may be expected of the agent.

G. Application to remunerated and gratuitous contracts

Paragraph (3) indicates that these Principles apply not only to mandate contracts by which the agent is to be rewarded but also to gratuitous mandate services. Adjustments may be necessary to take into account that the agent was acting gratuitously. For instance, in the case of gratuitous mandate contracts, one could imagine that the standard of care and skill expected under Article 3:103 (Obligation of care and skill) will be lower and the obligation to inform the principal of the progress of the performance of the mandate contract and the obligation to give account will be more restrictive than would be the case for a remunerated mandate contract. Moreover, Article 2:103 paragraph (2) (Expenses incurred by the agent) applies in particular where the parties have agreed upon the mandate contract being performed gratuitously.

H. Prospective contract or other legal effects

These Principles will mostly be applicable in the situation by which the agent is commissioned to conclude another contract on behalf of the principal, the second contract being referred to as 'the prospective contract' (cf. Article 1:102(c) (Scope)). However, occasionally the agent will not be commissioned to conclude a *contract*, but to otherwise affect the legal relations of the principal.

Illustration 10
A lawyer is instructed to file a lawsuit against another party for damages in tort. In this particular situation, when filing the lawsuit, the agent actually does intend to affect the legal relations of the principal with the third party, but not by concluding a contract with that third party. Such mandate contracts are covered by these Principles.

I. Investment services and activities not covered

Paragraph (6) indicates that mandate contracts falling within the scope of paragraph (1) are nevertheless exempted from the application of these Principles if they pertain to investment services and activities. The reason for the limitation of the scope of the Principles in this respect is that these mandate contracts are regulated by specific legal instruments, which are of a very different nature and up to a large extent introduce public law requirements and supervision. These mandate contracts therefore differ so much from 'ordinary' mandate contracts that application of the provisions of these Principles would be restricted to extraordinary situations for which the public law regulation would not provide a solution. This would make the application of these Principles in fact merely accidental. If there were such a need, of course, a court could apply these Principles by way of analogy, but these rules do not claim application by themselves.

J. Contracts for the administration of affairs not covered as such

Traditionally, *contrats d'administration d'affaires* – contracts for the general administration of affairs – are covered by provisions on mandate contracts, as is indicated in the Comparative and National Notes to this Article. However, in the case of these 'general mandate contracts', which may be of an indefinite period but also for a fixed period of time, the agent is not necessarily instructed to conclude, negotiate or facilitate a prospective contract, but merely to administer the affairs of the principal.

Illustration 11
William feels he is no longer competent to oversee all the complications of administering his affairs. He therefore asks Veronica to take care of all his affairs. They agree upon a fee for Veronica's services, to be paid automatically at the end of every month.

The contract between William and Veronica does not allow Veronica to buy or sell goods on behalf of William. It can therefore not be considered a mandate contract in the sense of these Principles. It rather falls within the scope of the Principles of European Law on Service Contracts and may occasionally be governed more specifically by Chapter 4 PEL SC (Storage) on storage contracts and possibly by Chapter 3 PEL SC (Processing) on processing contracts.

However, in the performance of such a contract, the service provider often has to affect the legal relations of the principal, e.g. when property belonging to the principal must be sold to safeguard the principal's interests. Where in the course of a contract of administration the service provider is required to buy or sell goods, or do any other juridical acts on behalf of the principal, these Principles may be applied by virtue of the rules on mixed contracts.

Illustration 11 (continued)
Veronica notices that the exterior of William's house badly needs to be painted. For that reason, she concludes a contract with Adam, a professional house painter. Moreover, she buys a new washing machine from Billy's Domestic Appliances Ltd. to replace the defective old machine in William's house. To be able to pay both Adam and Billy's Domestic Appliances Ltd., she sells one of William's paintings to a museum for the market price.

Whether Veronica is authorised to conclude the contract with Adam, with Billy's Domestic Appliances Ltd. and with the museum depends on the content of the contract between William and Veronica. Where that contract – either explicitly or tacitly – allows her to conclude these contracts, paragraph (2) of this Article indicates that these Principles apply as regards the authority of Veronica to represent William and the consequences of her doing so. It should be noted, however, that in many legal systems William would have to explicitly give his consent to the sale of the painting.

Illustration 13
Martha is leaving on a trip around the world and has leased her house to a tenant. She authorises and instructs her friend Nico to collect the rent for the year that she will be away.

As the contract between Marta and Nico does not pertain to the conclusion of a contract with a third party but to the performance of such a contract, these Principles are not applicable to the contract, whereas the Principles of European Law on Service Contracts are.

K. Terminology

As is indicated in Comment VIII of the General Introduction, the term 'agent' is used to describe the party that is to arrange the legal affairs of the other party, who is called 'principal'. Both of these terms are also used in Chapter 3 PECL (Authority of agents), which is an indication of the close relationship between the provisions of these Principles covering the internal relationship between principal and agent, and Chapter 3 PECL (Authority of agents), which cover the external relationship, i.e. the relationship between the principal and the third party, and occasionally the relationship between the agent and the third party.

In Comment VIII of the General Introduction, the double meaning of the word 'mandate' is also explained, referring on the one hand to the authorisation and instruction given by the principal as modified by any subsequent direction, as defined in Article 1:102 under (a) (Definitions), and on the other hand to the relationship or the contract created between the principal and the agent: the mandate contract. Similarly, the words 'mandate contract' may refer to the contract under which the agent is authorised and instructed to act, as defined in Article 1:102 under (b) (Definitions), and the contractual relationship that is created by that contract between the principal and the agent. In this sense, the terms 'mandate contract' and 'mandate relationship' are used interchangeably.

L. Relation to the Principles of European Law and the Draft Common Frame of Reference

Paragraph (4) indicates that these Principles do not relate to the question whether the contract concluded or to be concluded with the third party is valid or invalid: that question is governed by Chapter 3 PECL (Authority of agents). These Principles are related to the provisions of Book IV.D (Mandate contracts) of the Draft Common Frame of Reference, which in fact are based on the work executed in the preparation of these Principles. This particular Article mirrors Article IV.D. – 1:101 DCFR (Scope).

As explained above, contracts for the provision of representation, negotiation or intermediation services may be covered both by the Principles of European Law on Mandate Contracts and the Principles of European Law on Service Contracts. In principle, both the PEL MC and the PEL SC apply to such contracts, if need be with appropriate adaptations. However, in so far as these provisions conflict with each other, the PEL MC take priority. This is expressed in paragraph (5) of this Article. This is in accordance with the general rules on priority and mixed contracts, as provided for in Article II. – 1:110 paragraphs (3)(a) and (4) of the Draft Common Frame of Reference. This is particularly important where the PEL MC contain mandatory rules – for instance, with regard to the rules on termination – and the PEL SC contain merely default rules.

M. Character of the Rule

This Article contains rules dealing with definition and scope. It is mandatory in the sense that the parties cannot, in their contract, qualify a contract authorising a person to conclude a contract with a third party on behalf of the principal or to otherwise affect the legal position of the principal in relation to a third party or to facilitate the conclusion of such a contract, as another type of contract, if the contract or a part thereof contains the essential elements of a mandate contract as defined in this Article.

N. Remedies

As this Article merely indicates the scope of applicability of the Principles of European Law on Mandate Contracts, it does not impose duties on either of the parties. Therefore, this Article does not provide a party with a remedy.

Comparative Notes

1. Rules applicable to mandate contracts for direct and indirect representation

In some legal systems, general rules of agency apply to all forms of representation. This is the case in PO-LAND, where both the contract for direct representation and the contract for indirect representation are governed by the rules of the contract of mandate; if the parties have not agreed otherwise, the representation is presumed to be direct. In ENGLAND, IRELAND, and SCOTLAND, the common law rules of agency are applicable. These rules apply to estate agents, travel agents, insurance brokers, company directors, etc. The case of indirect representation is referred to as an undisclosed agency; this implies some differences in the consequences and effects of this relationship. Similarly, in DENMARK, Part II of the Contracts Act on Agency, the Factors Act and the Act on Commercial Agents and Travellers contain general rules governing all kinds of civil agency not governed by a special ruling. In BULGARIA, the same rules apply to both direct and indirect representation; however, in addition, some rules concerning indirect representation can be found in the OCA and the CA. The same holds true for AUSTRIA, BELGIUM, and THE NETHERLANDS. In SPAIN, the rules on mandate apply to both direct and indirect representation, albeit that the (commercial) commission contract is regulation in the Commercial Code.

In FRANCE, GREECE, ITALY, and POLAND, only direct representation is dealt with in the CC. In FRANCE, the contract for indirect representation is regulated as the 'commission contract'; in SLOVAKIA, the CC contains specific rules applicable to the mandate contract in general, to the contract for the procurement of a thing, and to the contract for arranging the sale of a thing; the commission agent contract, a form of the contracts for indirect representation, is regulated in the Commercial Code. In PORTUGAL, different rules apply to contracts for direct representation and indirect representation. In GERMAN law, a number of groups of rules are to be applied, depending on the characteristics of the contract at hand (rules on mandate, on agency, and on contracts for services or works). Some specific rules applicable to contracts for indirect representation may be found in the Commercial Code.

In some systems more general rules apply: in HUNGARY the general rules on obligations apply, and in ESTONIA the general rules on contracts for services (mandate) apply; these are divided into the general type of serviced contract and the services of work. Indirect representation is referred to as the 'commissionaire agreement'. The FINNISH Contracts Act (ContrA) contains general rules on mandate contracts in Chapter 2; these apply to contracts for direct representation. Contracts for indirect representation are not regulated in legislation, but general principles of contract law apply; by analogous interpretation the rules governing other types of mandate may be applied. In SWEDEN, in addition to general contract law rules, only a few old and general rules on mandate contracts for direct representation can be found in Chapter 18 of the Swedish Commercial Code (HB). When appropriate, the Act regarding Factors (KommL), the Commercial Agency Act (HaL), the Sale of Goods Act (KöpL), and the Consumer Services Act (KTjL) can be used by way of analogy. More specific rules can be found in e.g. the Estate Agents Act (FmL) and the Financial Advisory Services to Consumers Act. The Act regarding Factors provides a set of rules on commission agents, which is applied by way of analogy more generally in cases of indirect representation.

2. Rules applicable with regard to the performance of other juridical acts and mixed contracts

In all legal systems, the rules on mandate contracts also apply to the contracts requiring the agent to perform other juridical acts on behalf of the principal.

In the case of mixed contracts, in ESTONIA and FINLAND, both the rules on mandate contracts and those applicable to the other service apply. This is also the prevailing opinion in ITALY. In AUSTRIA, the rules governing the underlying contract or the performance of the other service apply. In BELGIUM and THE NETHERLANDS, the rules governing the predominant part of the contract apply to the whole of the contract, implying that when the obligations concerning the performance of non-juridical acts are predominant, the rules on mandate contracts will not apply, whereas the rules on mandate apply with the exclusion of other rules when the performance of juridical acts is predominant. In FRANCE, the rules of mandate will nevertheless apply to that part of the contract which concerns the mandate, particularly for questions of failure of performance, even where the mandate is not the main object of the contract. The same is true in POLAND. In GERMAN law, a number of groups of rules are to be applied, depending on the characteristics of the contract at hand (rules on mandate, on agency and on contracts for services or works). Some specific rules applicable to contracts for indirect representation may be found in the Commercial Code.

3. Application to gratuitous mandate contracts

In AUSTRIA, BULGARIA, DENMARK, ESTONIA, GREECE, MALTA, THE NETHERLANDS, POLAND, PORTUGAL, and SWEDEN, largely the same rules apply to gratuitous and remunerated mandates. The same holds true for BELGIUM, FINLAND, FRANCE, ITALY, and SPAIN; however, in these legal systems, it is generally accepted that the agent's liability is less severe for a non-remunerated agent than for a remunerated agent.

In GERMANY as well, largely the same rules apply to gratuitous and remunerated mandate contracts, but in case of a gratuitous mandate, subcontracting is generally not allowed, whereas the rules on termination of the mandate relationship are easier on the agent than in the case of a remunerated mandate contract, leading to liability for wrongful termination only if the agent has not given the principal a reasonable chance for his business to be taken care of otherwise. The same applies in HUNGARY and SLOVAKIA.

In ENGLAND, when the agency is gratuitous, the agent cannot be liable for failing to do what he undertook under no consideration. However, the agent can still be liable in tort. The standard of care for gratuitous agents, however, is lower than for paid agents since the standard of care is that care that the agent would have taken in his own affairs. The same rules apply in IRELAND. Traditionally, gratuitous agents were held to a *higher* standard of care in SCOTLAND, but this no longer seems to be the case.

4. Application to 'general mandate contracts' or 'contracts for the administration of affairs' and
authority to dispose of the principal's goods in the performance of such contract

In most legal systems, the rules on mandate contracts also apply to contracts by which the agent is required to administer (all of) the principal's affairs. Differences exist, however, regarding whether this means that the agent is also entitled to conclude legal acts on behalf of the principal. In BELGIUM, BULGARIA, FINLAND, FRANCE, ITALY, PORTUGAL, SLOVAKIA, and SPAIN, in such contracts the agent is not allowed to dispose of the principal's goods without explicit consent by the principal. In most of these legal systems, explicit consent cannot be given in the mandate contract itself for all affairs for an indefinite period of time.

On the other hand, in ESTONIA, GERMANY, and GREECE, the agent may dispose of goods entrusted to him if this is necessary for the proper performance of the contract. Similarly, in AUSTRIA, the agent will have such authority if it is considered normal that in the course of the performance of his services he will dispose of goods, as is the case for an auctioneer, a broker or a commission agent. In practice, the same holds true for ENGLAND and SCOTLAND. However, in these legal systems, a general mandate to administer the affairs of the principal is generally not interpreted as conferring a power to dispose.

5. Application to intermediation contracts

The rules on mandate contracts apply to intermediation contracts in DENMARK, ENGLAND, ESTONIA, MALTA, POLAND, PORTUGAL, and SCOTLAND. Specific rules on intermediation contracts may apply in IRELAND and THE NETHERLANDS. Where the contract concerns real estate, specific rules pertaining to brokerage contracts may apply in DENMARK, ESTONIA, FINLAND, FRANCE, GERMANY, GREECE, THE NETHERLANDS, SLOVAKIA, and SWEDEN.

National Notes

1. Rules applicable to mandate contracts for direct representation

AUSTRIA: The Austrian legal system draws a distinction between the two different activities of the direct and the indirect mandate. *Direct* agents have power to bind and entitle their principals contractually. They act 'in the name of' their principal. The mandate contract for direct representation covers cases where the third party knows that his counterparty is dealing as an agent for a named principal. *Indirect* agents deal with the outside world as parties but internally owe the duties of an agent to their (disclosed) principals. Such an arrangement is called 'a mandate for direct representation contract'. The Civil Code only expresses the concept of the mandate for direct representation contract, namely in CC Articles 1002 ff. Where the agent deals with the scope of his express or apparent authority as defined by CC Articles 1027-1029, 1033 and Comm.C Article 56, his acts bind the principal and the third party directly and the agent drops out. The general rules established by the Civil Code are often modified by canons of professional ethics – the conduct rules *(Berufsordnungen)* of solicitors and notaries, e.g. statutory tariffs regulating the remuneration. The commercial regulations of Comm.C Article 383 ff.. and 407 ff. express the concept of the mandate contract for direct representation.

BELGIUM: If the agent's main obligation under the contract concerns the conclusion of a juridical act as agent of the principal, the rules on the mandate contract as governed by CC Articles 1984-2007 apply.

BULGARIA: In the Bulgarian law of obligations, a differentiation is made, on the one hand, between a mandate contract *(Договор за поръчка)* and the unilateral legal act of authorization *(Пълномощно)*, and, on the other hand, between direct representation *(Пряко представителство)* and indirect representation *(Косвено представителство)*. According to some commentators in Bulgarian legal writings, so called 'indirect representation' is not an actual mandate, but it represents a separate legal institute, different from direct representation *(Хорозов, СП, 1996, p. 6, 32; Ставру, ТП, 2006, p. 343)*. The mandate contract is regulated in the Bulgarian Obligations and Contracts Act (OCA), Article 280-292. According to the legal definition in OCA Article 280, a mandate is a contract 'under which the agent *(Довереник)* assumes the obligation to perform, on behalf of the principal *(Доверител)*, the acts for which he is assigned by the latter'. Although in the relevant rules it is not explicitly stated so, it is unanimously considered in Bulgarian legal writings (Любен Василев, Облигационно право, p. 20; Меворах/Лиджи/Фархи, III, p. 17; Божидар Василев, p. 92) and also in Bulgarian case law (Supreme Court, Judgment No. 31, 4 April 1995, Civil Case 2453/1993, V; Supreme Court, Judgment No. 1511, 6 October 1995, Civil Case 2551/1994, V) that by virtue of a mandate contract the agent is mandated only for legal assignments, *i.e.* the conclusion of a contract or the performance of another legal act that affects the legal sphere of the principal. The agent can act either in the name of the principal (direct representation) or in his own name (indirect representation), but in any case he acts on behalf of the principal. The same rules (OCA Article 280-292) are applicable to both direct and indirect representation. In order to act in the name of the principal and to affect directly his legal position, the principal must have given the agent the authority to represent him *(Представителна власт)*. This authority is granted by means of a unilateral legal act of the principal *(Пълномощно)* under which he authorizes the agent with the power to act in his name and to affect his legal sphere (Любен Василев, Гражданско право, p. 368). The legal act of authorization is as well regulated in OCA Article 36-43, which rules are also applicable to direct representation.

DENMARK: The most important Danish statutory rules on agency law are Part II of the Contracts Act on agency, the Factors Act and the Commercial Agents and Travellers Act.

These rules are general rules governing all kind of civil agency not governed by special ruling.

ENGLAND: The relevant rules are the common law rules of agency, which in English law are of a general nature and apply to a wide variety of agents (estate agents, travel agents, insurance brokers, company directors etc). An agency relationship refers to the branch of law underwhich 'one person, the agent, may directly affect the legal relations of another, the principal, as regards yet other persons, called third parties, by acts which the agent is said to have the principal's authority to perform on his behalf, which, when done are in some respects treated as the principal's' (Bowstead & Reynolds on Agency, 18th ed, (2006), paragraph 1-003). Because the agent has the power to affect the principal's legal relations with third parties, the internal agency relationship, i.e. the relationship between the agent and the principal, is regarded as a fiduciary relationship. In addition to normal contractual obligations, the agent is also bound by fiduciary obligations, imposed by equity. An agent who merely negotiates the terms of a contract for a principal, such as a solicitor, is also regarded as an agent and the traditional common law rules will therefore apply.

ESTONIA: Contracts governing the internal relationship between the agent and the principal are regulated by the rules on contracts for services (mandate). The Estonian Law of Obligations Act (LOAEst) contains a separate part on 'Contracts for Provision of Services' (part 8, Articles 619-916 LOAEst). There are two general types of the 'services contracts': the (general) contract for services (sometimes also translated as 'mandate contract' or 'authorisation agreement') and the contract of works. These two main types are distinguished by the nature of the obligations rising under the contract. Under the contract of works, the service provider is under a duty to guarantee the result envisaged by the contract, whereas under the (general) services contract the service provider is only under a duty of care. Any agreement on a provision of services that is not a contract of works (i.e. by which the service provider does not guarantee a specific result) comes under the contract for services. The does not specify which services come under the (general) contract for services. In principle, any agreement by which mandate or intermediation is provided comes under the scope of the general contract for services. Specific forms of mandate or intermediation may, however, come under the scope of a specific services contract such as the contract of agency, brokerage contract or a commissionaire agreement. The general rules of the contract for services apply also for its sub-types as far as their regulation does not contain a more specific provision.

FINLAND: The Contracts Act (ContrA) contains general rules on mandate contracts in Chapter 2. These rules are applicable when the authorization includes a mandate to conclude contracts on behalf of the principal. The Law of Contract applies to all such contracts, unless otherwise provided in another Act. Further, Chapter 18 of the Commercial Code (Comm.C) includes general rules on authorisation concerning the relation between the principal and the agent. These rules, too, are only applicable if not otherwise provided in another Act. The Act of Commercial Agents and Salesmen (ACRS), based on EC Directive (86/653/EEC), is applicable when the agent has undertaken continuously to promote the sale or purchase of goods on behalf of the principal by obtaining offers for the principal or by concluding sales or purchase contracts in the name of the principal. In addition, there are rules on specific types of authorization in legislation, e.g. Chapter 15 of the Code of Judicial Procedure, the Attorneys Act, the Real Estate Agent Act (REstateA) and the Insurance Agent Act. Otherwise the general principles of Contract Law are applicable as well as analogous interpretation of other legislation in the area of Contract Law. Of general importance are, for instance, the Sale of Goods Act and the Consumer Protection Act.

FRANCE: Mandate contracts are governed by CC Articles 1984-2007. Some contracts involving mandate are the subject of special rules, particularly for estate agents (Law of 2 January 1970), commercial agents (Comm.C Articles L. 134-1 ff.), insurance agents (Insurance Code Articles L. 520-1 ff.), barristers and solicitors (Law of 31 December 1971).

GERMANY: German law has a number of sets of rules which are to be applied, depending on the characteristics of the contract at hand. These groups of provisions are: (a) Mandate *(Auftrag,* CC Articles 662-674). By accepting a mandate the agent *(Beauftragter)* enters into an obligation to do something for the principal *(Auftraggeber)* without remuneration (CC Article 662). The provisions on mandate are thus not restricted to constellations in which the task of the agent is to conclude a contract or execute a legal act; the task envisaged can essentially be anything. As a mandate by definition is a contract under which the agent acts without being paid for, the importance of CC Articles 663-674 primarily results from the fact that other provisions in the Civil Code make reference to them. (b) The most important contract in the sense just mentioned is the agency contract *(Geschäftsbesorgungsvertrag,* CC Article 675), i.e. a contract for services by which one party undertakes to look after the interests of the other party for a remuneration. CC Article 675 will thus cover the (practically much more important) contracts in which the agent is paid for his actions taken on behalf of the principal (e.g. lawyer, estate manager, administrator of property etc.). CC Article 675 does not stipulate the specific rules applicable to a *Geschäftsbesorgungsvertrag,* but rather says that CC Articles 663, 665-670, 672-674 and, under certain circumstances, Article 671 paragraph (2) (i.e. rules on mandate) shall apply. In addition, the provisions on either contracts for services (CC Articles 611 ff.) or contracts for works (CC Articles 631 ff.) apply. (c) CC Articles 675a-676h contain specific provisions for special types of banking contracts (largely introduced because of EC directives).

GREECE: Mandate for direct representation (άμεση αντιπροσώπευση, amesi antiprosopeusi) is regulated in CC Articles 211-235. In order for the principal to be bound by the juridical acts of his agent, the latter must have acted in the name of the principal, i.e. to have disclosed to the third party both the existence and the identity of the principal. The disclosure may be express or tacit, i.e. it may be indicated from the surrounding circumstances (tacit mandate) (Supreme Court decision no. 752/1987, NoV, 1426; CA Athens decision no. 9826/1989, EllDni 1991, 1631). That is the situation where the agent reveals the existence but not the identity of the principal (Kerameus/Kozyris 1993, p. 70). The Greek term for 'procuration' or power of attorney *(πληρεξουσιότητα, plirexousiotita)* signifies both the juridical act by which a person confers agent authority to another, and the authority conferred thereby. According to CC Article 216, a mandate shall be conferred by a deed drawn up for this purpose. A mandate shall be given by means of a declaration addressed to the attorney or a third party with whom the deed is concluded (CC Article 217).

HUNGARY: In the CC, the rules of representation (external relationship – authority of agents) can be found among the general rules of obligations Articles 219-225. For this reason, the technique of representation is not bound to any special contract type. If the debtor represents the creditor, the contract's qualification is usually agency (CC Articles 474-483) but employees bound by an employment contract may also represent the employer towards third parties. In this last case, the rules of labour law apply (Act XXII of 1992 on the Code of Labour). The rules of the 'agency' contract type do not focus on services with representation but are modelled to all contracts where the debtor (agent) has the obligation to do something according to the instructions and according to the interests of the creditor (principal) without the duty to "create a result achievable by work". CC Article 474 paragraphs (1)-(2) establish that '[u]pon an agency contract the agent has the obligation to carry out the matters entrusted to him. An agent must fulfil the agency according to the instructions and interests of the principal'. (Supreme Court Pfv. V. 20. 876/1994, in BH1995. 571; Supreme Court Pfv. VIII. 21.147/2006, in BH2007. 86; Supreme Court Mfv. II. 11.035/2001, in BH2003. 386; Supreme Court Mfv. I. 10.945/2001, in BH2003. 213; Supreme Court Legf. Bír. Gfv. X. 32.294/1995, in BH1997. 302; Supreme Court M. törv. II. 10 978/1991, in BH1992. 736; Supreme Court Gf. II. 30 521/1986, in BH1987. 174; CA Csongrád Megyei Bíróság 1. Gf. 40 079/1999/2, in BDT2000. 185; CA Fővárosi Ítélőtábla 5. Pf. 21 230/ 2005/3, in BDT2007. 1598)

IRELAND: The primary rules are to be found in the terms of the agency contract. The normal rules of construction will apply to give effect to the intentions of the parties, when interpreting this contract. Further, at common law, the law of agency imposes various rights and obligations on the parties to the agency contract. In particular, an agent is given three basic rights: to remuneration; to an indemnity and to a lien. The common law traditionally regarded agents as independent businesses and took the view that the agent was in the stronger position than the principal. Hence, the principal was in need of protection. As a result, the common law imposed on agents extensive duties, partly because of the fiduciary nature of the agency relationship. In addition, many representation/agency contracts are also subject to the EC (Commercial Agents) Regulations 1994 (SI No. 33/1994) and 1997 (SI No. 31/1997), which partly codify and partly modify the common law and were passed to implement the EC Directive on commercial agency.

ITALY: If the agent's main obligation under the contract is to represent the principal, the rules governing mandate apply, and in particular CC Articles 1388 ff. The rules governing the contract of mandate *(mandato)* also specifically apply, i.e. CC Articles 1703 ff. See Cass. no. 5582/1993, Foro It. Mass., 1993, 4070, no. 6; Cass no. 1329/1983, Foro It. Mass., 1983, 4070, no. 2.

MALTA: When the agent is required or allowed to conclude the contract in his own name, the principal will not be able to pursue an action against the third parties with whom the agent has contracted and neither may the third parties act against the principal. In such cases the agent is directly responsible of the contract as though it were made in his own name. This rule is set out in CC Article 1871, which states – "(1) When the agent has acted in his own name, the principal cannot maintain an action against those with whom the agent has contracted, nor the latter against the principal. (2) In any such case, however, the agent is directly bound towards the person with whom he has contracted as if the matter were his own." This rule has been sustained by the Maltese Courts in various cases. In CA, *Salvatore Debono vs. Giuseppe Farrugia et.,* the plaintiff had demanded payment of the price of goods sold to the defendant. The defendant had refused to pay since he pleaded that he had acquired the goods on behalf and in the name of other people. However the First Hall of the Civil Court decided that since the defendant (i.e. the agent) at the moment of the conclusion of the contract, did not indicate the name of his principal, the agent had become personally responsible. The agent pleaded that he had acted as a commission agent rather than as a broker, however the Court of Appeal held that even if he had acted as a simple agent, since he had done so in his own name, he had become directly bound towards the third parties. If the agent has a special mandate this would be limited to the performance of one or more specified transactions on behalf of the principal. This distinction between general and special mandate is set out in CC Article 1862 whereby "Mandate is either special, if it is for one matter or for certain matters, only; or general if it is for all the affairs of the principal".

NETHERLANDS: Rules on mandate contracts have been established in CC Articles 7:414-424. According to CC Article 7:414, mandate contracts imply that the agent commits himself to the principal to perform one or more legal acts in the name and account of this principal (Haak/Zwitser, p. 153-154). If no specific rules on certain legal issues that relate to mandate contracts have been established, the general rules that apply to contracts for professional services apply (CC Articles 7:400-413).

POLAND: The internal relationship between the agent and the principal is regulated by rules of the contract of mandate (CC Articles 734-750) while the relationships between the agent and third parties are regulated by CC Articles 95-109. The representation under the contract of mandate may be both direct (the agent acting in the principal's name) or indirect (the agent acting in his own name). If the parties have not agreed otherwise the representation is presumed to be direct, CC Article 734 paragraph (2).

PORTUGAL: Representation *(Representação)* is regulated in CC Articles 258-269. It consists of the execution of a juridical act in the name of another person. The act will produce legal effects in the juridical sphere of that person if the agent has acted within his powers, or if the other party subsequently ratifies the act. There are two types of representation: direct representation *(representação própria)* and indirect representation *(representação imprópria),* when the agent acts in his own name, on behalf of the other party Cf. Mota Pinto, p. 535. The two cardinal rules of direct representation are:
- *Contemplatio domini:* the deal or juridical act is executed in the name of the other party, though the agent has a margin of discretion while negotiating.
- The act must be executed within the limits of the powers vested by the other party, otherwise the act will not be effective *vis-à-vis* the other party.

The most usual instruments of representation are:
- *mandato* (mandate), a services contract by which one party has the obligation to execute one or several juridical acts on account of another party (CC Articles 1157 ff.);
- *procuração,* unilateral act of conferral of agent powers (CC Article 262). Cf. Mota Pinto (1994), 535.

SCOTLAND: The rules of agency are general in nature and apply to a wide range of situations and agents (for example, solicitors, estate agents, directors of companies). An agent has been described as 'a person who has authority to act for and on behalf of another (called the principal) in contracting legal relations with third parties; and the agent representing the principal creates, alters, or discharges legal obligations of a contractual nature between the latter and third parties' (Smith, p. 774). The word 'mandate' is traditionally reserved for a gratuitous contract of agency.

SLOVAKIA: The external relationship is covered by the General Provisions of the Slovak CC (Act 40/1964 Coll. as amended). CC Article 22 paragraph (1) defines: 'An agent is anyone who is authorized to act for another person in the latter's name'. This regulation is applicable both to contractual and legal representation (by law or on the basis of a court decision), and to civil and commercial relations. Regarding the regulation of the internal relationship between the principal and the agent, a distinction should be made between civil and commercial relationships. CC Articles 724-732 provide that the agent undertakes to arrange a certain matter or to perform some other activity for the principal. A subtype, the contract for the procurement of a thing, is regulated in CC Articles 733-736. Under these rules, the agent undertakes to procure a certain thing for the principal. 'Thing' is used here in the meaning of 'matter'. These contracts may cover both direct and indirect representation. Mandate may also come under the scope of Commercial Representation Contract (Comm.C). Comm.C Articles 566-576 provide that the agent undertakes either to arrange a certain business matter by effecting certain legal acts in the name of and at the account of the principal, or to arrange another matter at the principal's request, and the principal undertakes to pay him a remuneration for his services. The rules on mixed contracts are applicable in the case of intermediation (e.g. a brokerage contract mixed with an obligation to represent; see Supreme Court decision, No. 72/2004, legal decisions book 5, 16, 5 Cdo 65/03). The Act on Advocacy (586/2003 Coll as amended) contains rules for advocates.

SPAIN: Mandate is regulated in CC Articles 1709-1739. There is not a substantial distinction between mandate and representation; furthermore, the mandate is 'naturally' a representation contract (CC Article 1717, Diez-Picazo, p. 65 ff), though indirect representation is also allowed as a possible content of the mandate (CC Article 1717 paragraph (2)) and similarly for a commercial mandate (commission) (Comm.C Articles 245-247). The mandate rules serve as a basic model for most of the special regulations concerning the accomplishment of services on another's behalf. The main reason for that is that the mandate contract in Spanish law is not as such a contract with a content limited to the instruction of a third party to do "juridical" acts: the juridical nature of the agent's behaviour is not of the essence of the contract (CC Article 1709). So there exists a wide 'grey area' in which mandate and service contracts overlap with each other (Lacruz, p. 224, 228). Anyway, the mandate rules prevail, because legal provisions on services contracts scarcely exist in Spanish law.

SWEDEN: Swedish law does not distinguish a particular set of contract law rules specifically relevant for the supply of services. In addition to general contract law rules, only a few old and general rules on mandate contracts for direct representation can be found in Comm.C Chapter 18. When appropriate, the Act regarding Factors (KommL), the Commercial Agency Act (HaL), the Sale of Goods Act and the Consumer Services Act can be used by way of analogy. More specific rules can be found in e.g. the Estate Agents Act (FmL) and the Financial Advisory Services to Consumers Act. The external relationship between the agent and the third party is governed by rules in Part II of the Contracts Act.

2. Rules applicable to mandate contracts for indirect representation

AUSTRIA: Comm.C Article 383 ff. (commission agents) and Comm.C Article 407 ff. (forwarder) apply to the contract between the commercial agent or forwarder and the principal. If the internal relationship between the principal and the agent is based on a mandate, the regulations of CC Article 1002 ff. apply for the contract between the agent and the principal (Rummel/Strasser, Article 1002 Rz 8), even though the underlying contract of an indirect representation is not a contract of representation pursuant to CC Article 1002 (*Bevollmächtigungsvertrag*).

BELGIUM: The legal relation between the parties to a mandate contract is governed by the legal rules on mandate (provided some particularities), i.e. the legal relation between the principal and the commission-agent (Samoy, p. 182; Van der Perre & Lejeune, no. 42), between the principal and the *prête nom* (CA Brussels 22 February 1927, Pas. 1928, II, 153; De Page, p. 476; Deckers, p. 13; Paulus & Boes, p. 23; Samoy, p. 94-95) and between the principal and the agent acting in his own name (Cass. 17 April 1848, Pas. 1848, I, 387, B. J. 1848, 758; CA Brussels 10 December 1958, J.T. 1959, 225; CA Brussels 28 January 1820, Pas. 1820-21, II, 30; De Page, p. 436; Laurent, p. 61; Paulus & Boes, p. 134; Samoy, p. 305; Tilleman, p. 277; Van der Perre & Lejeune, no. 166; Wéry, p. 152 and 259).

BULGARIA: In the Bulgarian law of obligations, the same rules (OCA Article 280-292) are applicable to both direct and indirect representation. Apart from these rules, to indirect representation some provisions apply that may be found in the rules on benevolent intervention (OCA Articles 60-62), commercial agency

(CA Articles 32-48), commission contract (CA Articles 348-360) and forwarding contract (CA Articles 361-366) *(Ставру, ТП, 2006, p. 343).*

DENMARK: When the agent is required or allowed to conclude the prospective contract in his own name, the principal will not be bound towards the third party (unless the principal accepts the contract concluded).

ENGLAND: At common law, the agent is not required to disclose to the third party that he is acting *in the name and on behalf of* the principal. When the existence of the principal is not revealed to the third party, it is referred to as an 'undisclosed agency'. In such circumstances, there is nevertheless an agency relationship between the principal and the agent since the principal authorises the agent to act for him on the basis that the agent will act in his own name. The consequences of an undisclosed agency are as follows: the internal aspects of the internal relationship are the same: the principal appoints the agent to represent him; the agent is a fiduciary and the principal owes him commissions and indemnity for expenses etc. There is, *a priori,* no external feature since the agent does not create privity between the principal and the third party since the agent acts in his own name towards the third party. Initially, the contract is therefore between the agent and the third party. The principal still authorises the agent to represent him towards third parties but the principal remains hidden. Providing that the agent has actual authority to act on behalf of the principal towards the third party, the principal can intervene on the contract with the third party *(Siu Yin Kwan v Eastern Insurance Co Ltd* [1994] 1 All ER 213), i.e. he can sue and be sued, but only if the agent acted with the principal's prior authority *(Keighley Maxsted v Durant* [1901] AC 240). The effects of an undisclosed agency are as follows: (a) Because the principal is not disclosed, the agent acts in his own name and he is therefore liable on and can enforce the contract made with the third party. Vice versa, the third party can enforce the contract against the agent. This is so, provided that the principal has not intervened. (b) Technically, the law considers that the agent has contracted with the third party but the principal can also intervene on the contract. However, once the existence of the principal is revealed to the third party, he can choose whom to perform the contract with, between the principal or the agent. The third party must therefore elect who to enforce the contract against. Once a choice has been made, the third party cannot however try to enforce the contract against the other *(Clarkson Booker Ltd v Andjel* [1964] 3 All ER 260). (c) The principal can intervene on and enforce a contract made by his/her undisclosed agent with prior authority of the principal *(Siu Yin Kwan v Eastern Insurance Co Ltd* [1994] 1 All ER 213). The principal's right of intervention is subject to certain restrictions in order to protect the interest of the third party: (i) The principal cannot intervene if the contract expressly *(UK Mutual Steamship Assurance Association v Nevill* (1887) 19 QBD 110) or impliedly excludes his intervention *(Siu Yin Kwan v Eastern Insurance Co Ltd* [1994] 1). The difficulty is to see whether the contract impliedly excludes the intervention of the principal. As the privy council decision in Siu Yin Kwan shows, the fact that the agent signed the contract as the 'insured' does not prevent the principal from intervening in the contract. It seems that if the agent is identified in the contarct as a contracting party, this does not prevent the principal from intervening. (ii) The principal cannot intervene if personal factors are important (e.g. the third party wanted to contract with the agent or would not contract with the principal).

ESTONIA: As a rule, such contract would be a 'commissionaire agreement' *(komisjonileping),* regulated in Articles 692-702 LOAEst. The commissionaire agreement is a specific type of the (general) contract for services; therefore, in addition to specific rules contained in Articles 692-702 LOAEst, the general rules applicable for the (general) contract for services (Articles 619-634 LOAEst) apply to the relationship between the agent and the principal. If the specific rules of the commissionaire agreement do not apply, the contract would be a (general) contract for services, for which the law does not distinguish between acting in one's own name and acting in the name of the principal.

FINLAND: Commission trades and other mandates by which the agent acts in his own name but on behalf of the principal and concludes contracts are not regulated in legislation, but governed merely by general principles of Contract Law and by analogous interpretation of the rules applicable to the other types of mandate contract.

FRANCE: The rules of the 'commission contract' (agent with usually undisclosed principal, who is acting in his own name) will apply. This is regulated by Comm.C Articles L. 132-1 ff. The rules of the 'command contract' (purchase agent acting for an undisclosed principal, specifically in the case of sale of goods) can also apply in this specific case. To simplify, the relations between the principal and the 'commission agent' are mainly regulated by the specific rules of the mandate contract, and the relations between the 'commission agent' and the third party are then governed by the specific rules relating to the contract that they have concluded between them.

GERMANY: Comm.C Articles 383-406 provide a set of rules on commission agents, *i.e.* persons who professionally undertake to buy and sell goods or securities in their own name for the account of another (Comm.C Article 383 paragraph (1)). Apart from Comm.C Articles 383-406, there are no rules specifically tailored to contracts for indirect representation, and thus the rules generally applicable to mandate contracts apply (Häuser, in: Münchener Kommentar zum HGB, 2004, Article 383 no. 28).

GREECE: In Greek civil law the applicable rule of CC Article 212 to mandate contracts for direct representation is a rule of interpretation: if it is impossible to ascertain that a person acted in the name of another it shall be considered that such person has acted in his own name. That rule refers to the external aspects of the relationship *vis-à-vis* third parties, whereas the internal relationship between the principal and his agent may be based on a contract such as mandate (CC Articles 713-729). The notion of contract for indirect representation is in fact no mandate in the meaning of the rules of mandate for direct representation (CC Articles 213 ff.) at all, since the effects of the juridical act of the agent who acts in his own name flow directly to him rather than to his undisclosed principal (Kerameus/Kozyris, 70; Georgiadis/Stathopoulos/Doris I, Article 211 CC no. 24). The agent merely incurs an obligation from the internal relationship based on a contract such as mandate to convey these effects to the principal through a separate juridical act, as in the contract for indirect representation no relation is created between the undisclosed principal and the third party (Supreme Court decision no. 752/2003, NoV 2004, 238; CA Athens decision no. 12756/1987, EllDni 1989, 1195).

HUNGARY: If the agent concludes a contract in his own name but for his principal, the rules of the contract type 'commission agency' apply (CC ArticleS 507-513). CC Article 507 establishes that '[u]nder a commission agency contract the commission agent is obliged to conclude a sales contract in his own name, in favour of the principal in return for a commission'. CC Article 513 paragraph (1) prescribes that '[a] contract in which a commission agent assumes an obligation to conclude a contract other than a sales contract shall also be deemed a commission agency contract'. According to CC Article 513 paragraph (2), '[u] nless otherwise provided by this Chapter, the regulations governing agency must be applied to commission agency'. Cf. Supreme Court Pfv. V. 20. 876/1994, in BH1995. 571.

IRELAND: Where an agent concludes a contract in his own name this is referred to as 'an undisclosed agency' and the principal is described as an undisclosed principal. Alternatively, an agency may be disclosed (i.e. the third party knows that the agent is acting for another, either named or unnamed). At common law, an agent is not required to disclose to the third party that he is acting *in the name and on behalf of* the principal. The distinction between disclosed and undisclosed agencies is important in terms of the legal effects of the agent's actions on his principal and other third parties. But, in terms of the relationship between the agent and the principal, the distinction between disclosed and undisclosed agency is not relevant – i.e. the same law of agency applies. Under the doctrine of undisclosed agency, where an agent contracts with a third party without disclosing that he is acting as an agent, as where he contracts in his own name, the contract is initially between the agent and the third party and each may enforce the contract against the other. However, if the third party discovers the undisclosed principal's existence, the third party may enforce the contract against either the agent or the principal. Moreover, provided that the agent acted with actual authority, the undisclosed principal can intervene and enforce the contract against the third party. This doctrine operates as an important exception to the doctrine of privity of contract. Therefore, where an undisclosed agent buys a painting in his own name, but on the account of his principal, the principal (a complete stranger to the third party) can intervene and enforce the contract with the third party. There are limitations, at common law, to the principal's right of intervention. For example, (i) an undisclosed principal can only intervene if he was in existence and had the legal capacity to make the contract at the time it was made; (ii) an undisclosed principal can only intervene if the agent had *actual* authority to conclude the contract *(Keighley Maxsted & Co v Durant* [1901] AC 240); (iii) an undisclosed principal cannot intervene if such intervention is prohibited by the contract, either expressly or impliedly; (iv) an undisclosed principal may be prevented from intervening if it can be shown that the third party contracted with the agent for personal reasons; (iv) in some cases, it has been said that an undisclosed principal cannot intervene where the third party has personal reasons for not contracting with him (e.g. *Said v Butt* [1920] 3 KB 497).

ITALY: The contract by which the agent is required to represent the principal in his own name but for the principal's account is regulated by CC Article 1705 paragraph (1), according to which 'an agent acting in his own name acquires the rights and assumes the duties arising from transactions made with third persons, even if the latter had knowledge of the mandate'. However, the principal may replace the agent by exercising directly his claims arising from the execution of the contract concluded between the agent and the third party, since these claims are considered as automatically transferred to the principal. A distinction has to be made with respect to real rights (rights *erga omnes):* if the agent acquires a movable good, the agent can take action to demand the property of the good, whereas if the agent acquires in his own name and on the principal's account an immovable good, the latter shall transfer the good's ownership to the principal immediately (CC Article 1707; cf. also Cass. no. 202/1974, Foro It., 1974, I, 2739; Cass. no. 2301/1994, Giust. civ., 1994, I, 1887). Prior to this the principal may not vindicate the asset because he cannot be considered the owner of the immovable good.

NETHERLANDS: A contract according to which the agent commits himself to another party to buy or sell movables, shares, or securities in his own name and at the expense of the principal, is regulated by the general rules on mandate contracts.

POLAND: The representation under the contract of mandate may be both direct (the agent acting in the principal's name) or indirect (the agent acting in his own name).

PORTUGAL: In the case of indirect representation, while the agent is acting in the interest and on behalf of the other party, he is not acting in his name, i.e. the *contemplatio domini* is lacking. In this case, the agent acts in his own name, and is under a duty to transfer to the other party the rights he acquired (and the other party is under a duty to accept them). Cf. CC Article 1180-1182 (civil contracts) and Comm.C Article 266 ff. (commercial contracts). Cf. Mota Pinto, p. 542; Lima/Varela (1987), p. 240.

SCOTLAND: Scots law recognises the concept of the agent who acts for the undisclosed principal (Macgregor, paragraphs 147-163; *Meier v Küchenmeister* (1881) 8R 642 at 646, per Lord Young). This allows an agent to act in his own name and conclude a contract on behalf of his principal without disclosing to the third party either the existence or the identity of the principal. The principal can 'intervene' in that contract at a later stage in order to enforce the contract against the third party (Macgregor, paragraphs 150-151). After the principal has been disclosed, the third party must elect to sue either the principal or the agent – he cannot sue both (Macgregor, paragraphs 155-156). The principal's right to intervene is unlimited, and is not triggered by factors such as non-performance by the agent or the agent's insolvency. The concept is subject to certain limiting factors, for example, the principal's ability to act in this way may be excluded as a matter of interpretation of the contract with the third party (Macgregor, paragraph 153). A more debatable restriction is that which prevents the principal from acting in this way where his concealment is a deception (Macgregor, paragraph 154).

SLOVAKIA: The general regulation of the mandate contract can be found in CC Articles 724-732 and of the contract for procurement of a thing in CC Articles 733-736. The contract for arranging the sale of a thing, under which the agent is bound to take from the principal a certain thing determined for sale and to make the necessary arrangements for its sale, is specifically regulated in CC Articles 737-741. In this case, the agent acts in the agent's own name and on account of the principal. Under the commission agent contract, the commission agent undertakes to conduct in the agent's own name but on account of the principal a certain business affair for the latter, and the principal undertakes to pay the agent a commission. This type of contract is regulated in Comm.C Articles 577-590.

SPAIN: Representation is regulated as a substantial effect of the mandate as such. In fact, the main body of rules as to representation law ought to be drawn from the provisions on mandate. However, indirect representation is also contemplated as a voluntary effect of the mandate. If this is the case, the mandate brings about as a rule no direct relationship between the principal and the third party (CC Article 1717 and Comm. C Articles 245-247).

SWEDEN: The Act regarding Factors provides a set of rules on commission agents, i.e. persons who professionally undertake to buy and sell goods, securities and personal property in their own name for the account of another. The Act regarding Factors is also used by way of analogy in cases of commission in a broad sense. Thus, agents of different kinds and stevedores are inter alia considered to be commissionaires if they act in their own name, see Tiberg/Dotevall, p. 87.

No answer received: MALTA.

3. Rules applicable with regard to the performance of other juridical acts and mixed contracts

AUSTRIA: The same rules apply when the agent is not required to conclude a contract but to execute another juridical act (OGH EvBl 1953/136; OGH GesRZ 1980, 95; CC Article 1002 Rummel/Strasser I³, no. 40). In the case of mixed contracts, the rules governing the underlying contract or the performance of this other service apply.

BELGIUM: The rules on mandate apply as well when the agent is not required to conclude a contract but to execute another juridical act (Tilleman, p. 64; Wéry, p. 81 ff.; in particular for a lawyer who is required to bring a claim into court, see Herbots a.o., no. 884; Tilleman, p. 25). In relation to mixed acts the rules on the qualification of mixed contracts) apply (cf. Claeys, 203; Foriers & Glansdorff, p. 594; Samoy, p. 34-35; Tilleman, p. 14; Wéry, p. 105-107) if the agent's main obligation under the contract concerns the conclusion of a juridical act as agent of the principal and if the obligations concerning the performance of other non-juridical acts are only accessory. The rules of the dominating legal relation (mandate) apply in accordance with the 'absorption theory' (e.g. CA (labour) Antwerp 23 November 1989, Pas. 1990, II, 110). If on the contrary the obligations concerning the performance of non-juridical acts are dominating, the rules on 'hiring of services' *(huur van werk)* apply, also in accordance with the absorption theory (e.g. CA Liège 18 June 1981, RGEN 1982, 286). If neither the juridical acts, nor the non-juridical acts are dominating, the rules of both contracts apply cumulatively, as far as possible, in accordance with the 'cumulative theory' (e.g. the rules on mandate, combined with the rules on a building contract (e.g. CA Mons 22 January 1990, Pas. 1990, II, 145). If a cumulative application is impossible because of contradictory rules, the contract will be qualified as a contract sui generis, to which only the general contract law applies.

BULGARIA: The same rules (OCA Article 280-292) are applicable to both mandate contract for conclusion of prospective contract and for performance of judicial act other than contract.

DENMARK: When the agent's main obligation under the contract is not to represent the principal but to perform another service, the scope of the duties of the agent will be governed by the agreement concluded between the principal and the middleman. If under this representation legal steps are to be taken by the agent, Part II of the Contracts Act on agency will apply.

ENGLAND: Providing that the agent has been authorised by the principal to perform a given task, e.g. an architect representing the principal at the reception of the house, the architect still performs a task on behalf of the principal and is therefore still regarded as an agent and the rules of agency will consequently apply to them.

ESTONIA: In case of the so-called mixed contract, the different parts of the contract may be governed by different sets of rules (Article 1 paragraph (2) LOAEst). As far as the contract contains an obligation to represent the principal, that part of the contract would be governed by the rules of the specific contract of services (e.g. the rules of the contract of works) and also by the rules of the (general) contract of services as far as there is an obligation to represent the principal.

FINLAND: As long as the authorisation contains a mandate to represent the principal, the mentioned rules on mandate contracts are applicable. The rest of the contract between the parties should be governed by separate rules applicable to the specific activity in question.

FRANCE: The rules for the mandate contract cover the conclusion of any legal act in the name and for the account of the principal, whether it is a contract or other legal obligation. Where the mandate is not the main object of the contract, French case law will apply the rules of mandate to that part of the contract which concerns the mandate, particularly for questions of failure of performance (Cass.civ. 3e, 8 February 1978, Bull. civ. 1978 III, no. 74).

GERMANY: The same rules applicable to mandate contracts pertaining to the conclusion of a prospective contract apply to contracts to represent in the conclusion of other juridical acts.

GREECE: The same rules that apply when object of the representation is a contract the same rules are applicable when the agent is required to execute another juridical act. That means that in such cases the rules of representation (CC Article 211-235) apply to the external aspects of the relationship. With regard to the internal relationship the applicable rules depend on the contract, which binds the parties such as mandate (CC Article 713-729). It is accepted that only in case of juridical acts the institution of mandate is required, whereas non-juridical acts are in the rule not subject to mandate. That means that the external relationship created by mandate is only needed when the object of the internal relationship which is based on a contract of mandate (CC Articles 713-729) is a juridical act. If the agent's main obligation is to represent the principal at the moment of the reception of a work which constitutes a juridical act, the rules of mandate apply to the external relationship and the rules of mandate to the internal relationship.

HUNGARY: In general, the same rules apply when the agent is to execute another legal act than the conclusion of a contract (Supreme Court Pfv. V. 20. 876/1994, in BH1995. 571).

IRELAND: Where an agent has authority or power from the principal to affect the principal's legal relations with others, whether in contract or otherwise, the same general law of agency will apply.

ITALY: When the agent is granted the authority to represent the principal in the execution of a juridical act other than a contract, the general rule is that the mandate should have the formal requirements of the act which has to be concluded. According to CC Article 1392 '[a] mandate has no effect unless it is conferred with the formalities prescribed for the contract which is to be made by the agent'. If the agent is required to bring a claim in court, the rules governing legal representation apply (in particular CCP Articles 83 and 84) which consists in the defensive activity carried out by the attorney in court proceedings. According to CCP Article 83 the attorney representing the principal in court must have a power-of-attorney, which may be granted either by means of a public deed or of a private act, provided that the signature is certified by a notary. If a power-of-attorney is granted in the same document of the judicial brief the signature shall be certified by the attorney. According to Article 84 CCP the attorney may perform all acts of the proceeding and receive all the communications pertaining thereto. However, unless specifically authorised by the principal, he cannot dispose of the rights which are subject matter of the litigation. So far as mixed contracts are concerned, according to the principle of party autonomy, under Italian law the parties to a contract may regulate their relationship as they prefer, even by entering into a contract which is not specifically regulated by the law ('unnamed contracts'). Mixed contracts, characterised by the concurring presence of the elements of two or more different types of contracts, may be included among the unnamed contracts above. In this case, according to some scholars, mixed contracts are regulated by the provisions governing the type of contract whose elements are prevalent. According to the prevailing opinion, however, the different sets of rules governing each type of contract involved jointly apply.

MALTA: If the agent is not required to conclude a contract but to execute another juridical act, the agent has still been given a contract in express terms, that is, to execute a specific juridical act. Therefore the contract between the principal and the agent would be terminated only when such a juridical act has been performed. In fact in Maltese law, such a function may be executed by an agent as part of his normal functions as set out in CC Article 1865. However in Maltese law we find an exception in this respect in that the agent may not sue or be sued if the principal is not absent from the place/country in which the action is to be tried, although the principal had given him the authority to sue. This is CC Article 1866: "An agent, however, may not sue or be sued, on behalf of the principal, although the latter shall have given him authority to do so, when the principal himself is not absent from the Island in which the action is to be tried ..." CC Article 1868 specifies that "Where a person has been employed to do something in the ordinary course of his profession or calling, without any express limitation of power, such person shall be presumed to have been given power to do all that which he thinks to be necessary for the carrying out of the mandate, and which, according to the nature of the profession or calling aforesaid, may be done by him."

NETHERLANDS: Services in general are covered by the rules in CC Articles 7:400-413. If the performance of juridical acts is not the main element of the contract, there is no mandate contract. For instance, if an architect occasionally performs juridical acts on behalf of the principal, not the mandate contract but the general contract for professional services applies. This also applies to contracts with lawyers or notaries.

POLAND: The rules on the mandate contract apply to other contracts of service (CC Article 750 unless the parties have decided to exclude them. CC Article 95-109 (regulating relations between the agent and the third parties on issues such as liability etc.) always apply and cannot be excluded by contracting parties.

PORTUGAL: The general rules on representation apply. CC Article 258 mentions expressly the execution of a juridical act *"negócio jurídico"*. This can be an unilateral or a bilateral juridical act, such as a contract. There is *lex specialis* provision for representation by an attorney before a court of law: Article 35 ff CCP. In the specific case of *mandato judicial*, the scope of representation includes all necessary acts and procedures related to the procedure.

SCOTLAND: The rules applying to the conclusion of contracts by an agent apply also to the doing of other juridical acts.

SLOVAKIA: The rules on mandate apply also when the agent is not required to conclude a contract, but to perform another legal act or to arrange other matters. The same applies to commercial contracts.

SPAIN: The wording in CC Article 1709 provides for a broad scope as to the object of mandate relationships. It says that one of the parties undertakes the obligation to perform a service or to do something on behalf of the other party. The TS (STS 27 November 1992) and the literature (Sierra Gil de la Cuesta, p. 905; Lete del Río, p. 401; Lasarte, p. 344) have specified that it refers to juridical acts. The conclusion of a prospective contract is one of the possible juridical acts. Lete del Río indicates that this is the factor that differentiates mandate from other type of services contracts (Lete del Río, p. 401).

SWEDEN: The same set of rules applicable to mandate contracts for direct representation is also applicable, with appropriate adaptations, to contracts to represent in conclusion of a juridical act other than a contract.

4. Application to gratuitous mandate contracts

AUSTRIA: The same rules apply to gratuitous and remunerated mandate for direct representation contract (CC Article 1004). Comm.C Article 396 paragraph (1) and 409, HVertrG Article 8, and Rechtsanwaltstar-ifgesetz (RATG) 1 ff, 19a deal with the question of remuneration. In the absence of agreement, lawyers are entitled to remuneration according to the RATG; commission agents, forwarders and commercial agents are entitled to remuneration in accordance with local custom or, in the absence of such custom, to reasonable remuneration. Their right to commission can only be extinguished in very limited circumstances (e.g. when it is established that the contract between the third party and the principal will not be executed for a reason for which the principal is to blame).

BELGIUM: In general the same rules apply no matter whether the agent is compensated or not, except with regard to the contractual liability of the agent, which is less severe for a non-remunerated agent than for a remunerated agent (CC Article 1992; Wéry, p. 143).

BULGARIA: The general mandate contract is in principle a gratuitous contract, providing that there is no other stipulation between the parties, cf. OCA Article 286 (Любен Василев, Облигационно право, p. 20; Меворах/Лиджи/Фархи, III, p. 51; Божидар Василев, p. 131). The special types of mandate contract, for instance, the commission contract and the forwarding contract, are in any case non-gratuitous contracts, cf. CA Article 348 paragraph (1), Article 361 paragraph (1) (Любен Василев, Облигационно право, 40; Божидар Василев, p. 131). The general non-gratuitous mandate contract is regulated in Bulgarian law by the rules for the general mandate contract, see OCA Article 280-292. For the special non-gratuitous mandate contracts there are distinct provisions, see for the commission contract CA Article 348-360; for the forwarding contract CA Article 361-366; for the commercial agent CA Article 32-48.

DENMARK: As for the 'ordinary agent' no specific rules of remuneration will apply according to the legislation. In contrast the Factors Act and especially the Commercial Agents and Travellers Act contain a detailed non-mandatory regulation of the agent's right to commission. Where a contract for which, in principle, the middleman (factor, commercial agent, broker etc) is entitled to receive commission is not performed, the agent's claim for commission will lapse if the principal can prove that the failure to perform is not due to circumstances within the control of the principal. Most instances of non-performance will naturally be due to the particular third party's incapability to perform his obligations under the contract and thus the risk of the third party's insolvency will be on the agent.

ENGLAND: An agency relationship can be created by agreement, whether it is contractual or not. Even if the agent acts gratuitously, he can still affect the principal's relations with third parties. A gratuitous agent is therefore also subject to fiduciary obligations. However, when the agent is gratuitous, 'the internal position between the agent and the principal is imperfectly enforceable' (Bowstead & Reynolds, paragraph 6.026). Since there is no contractual liability, the agent cannot be liable for failing to do what he undertook under no consideration. However, the agent can still be liable in tort since the gratuitous agent owes a duty of care to the principal. The agent can therefore be liable, in tort, if he fails to do what he set out to do with due care and diligence. The standard of care for gratuitous agents is however lower than that for paid agents since the standard of care is that care that the agent would have done in his own affairs (*Chaudry v Prabhakar* [1988] 3 All ER 718).

ESTONIA: Generally the rules applying to a contract governing the internal relationship between the agent and the principal do not differ according to whether the contract is gratuitous or not. The general assumption is that the professional agent is entitled to a price for his services. Special rules for gratuitous contracts exist only as far as the entitlement of the agent for reimbursement of his expenses is concerned.

FINLAND: There are no specific written rules on gratuitous representation. In principle, the general rules are applicable. The requirements to be met when filling the mandate are, however, generally lower if the representation is gratuitous.

FRANCE: The Civil Code's provisions regarding the mandate contract (CC Articles 1984-2007) apply both to remunerated and gratuitous mandates (CC Article 1986), although the liability of the agent will be diminished if there is no remuneration (CC Article 1992 paragraph (2)).

GERMANY: According to the legal definition in CC Article 662, a 'mandate' is a gratuitous contract, and the general rules on mandates (CC Articles 663-674) are based on this assumption. By way of the reference in CC Article 675 paragraph (1), remunerated contracts are subject to the same rules as gratuitous contracts (mandates), with the following exceptions (i.e. those provisions among CC Articles 663-674 not listed in CC Article 675 paragraph (1)): (a) CC Article 664: Under a remunerated contract, it is generally admissible for the agent to have the representation performed through a third person. Under gratuitous contracts, CC Article 664 declares this to be inadmissible ('when in doubt'), as mandates are often based on a relationship of personal trust between the parties. It has, however, been held that an analogous application of CC Article 664 to remunerated contracts is possible in situations in which a relationship of personal trust exists between the parties. (b) CC Article 671 governs the right to terminate a mandate and gives each party the right to terminate the contract at any time, although the agent has to terminate in a manner that will allow the principal to reasonably arrange for his business to be taken care of otherwise. Should the agent not live up to this obligation by terminating at an inappropriate time, he is liable for damages. (c) CC Article 671 is generally inapplicable to remunerated contracts; the question of termination is governed by the rules on contracts for services or works. CC Article 671 paragraph (2), however, is applicable whenever the remunerated contract allows the agent to terminate the contract at any time (CC Article 675 paragraph (1)).

GREECE: With regard to mandate, the award of a price depends on the internal relationship which binds the agent and the principal. If the internal relationship is based on a contract of mandate, the agent undertakes to conduct without remuneration the affair entrusted to him by the principal (CC Article 713). An exception to the rule of gratuitous mandate is explicitly regulated in the Code of Attorneys, which provides for the obligatory remunerated mandate between the lawyer and the principal. Regarding intermediation, a person who promises a fee for the procurement of a contract or for information of the opportunity of making a contract is bound to pay the fee only if the contract is concluded in consequence of such procurement or indication. If, in consequence of such procurement or indication, an agreement containing a promise of contract was concluded but the final contract is frustrated, only one half of the fee may be demanded (CC Article 703 paragraph (1)). If the contract is concluded subject to a condition, the fee may not be demanded until the condition is fulfilled (CC Article 704).

HUNGARY: In general, the same rules apply no matter whether the agent is awarded a price or not. CC Article 478 paragraph (1) sets forth that '[t]he principal shall pay an appropriate fee, unless the circumstances, or the relationship between the parties suggest that the agent has assumed the agency without any consideration'. However, according CC Article 483 paragraph (3), '[i]f the agency is cancelled without substantial grounds, the damages that are caused shall be indemnified, unless the agency is gratuitous and the period of notice is sufficient for allowing the principal to handle the matter.'

IRELAND: The agency relationship is largely based on agreement, contractual or otherwise. Even if the agent acts gratuitously, he can still affect the principal's relations with third parties. However, when the agency is gratuitous, there is no contractual relationship between principal and agent, and the agent cannot be contractually liable for failing to do what he undertook. However, the agent can still be liable in tort since the gratuitous agent owes a duty of care to the principal. But there is English case law which suggests that a different/lower standard of care *may* be required where the agency is gratuitous *(Chaudrhy v Prabakhar* [1988] 3 All ER 718). This case law has authority also in Ireland.

ITALY: Under Italian law there is a general presumption of onerousness with respect to representation (CC Article 1709). This means that unless otherwise provided by the parties the agent is entitled to a compensation. In general terms, the rules governing representation are the same even if no price is agreed by the agent and the principal. However, in case of remunerated representation the agent's liability for breach of contract is valued more seriously than in case of gratuitousness (CC Article 1710 paragraph (1)), because the economic and financial consequences for the principal are graver when he pays a consideration to the agent and the latter breaches his obligation. See Cass. no. 3233/1982, Foro. It. Mass., 1982, 4, 4070.

MALTA: According to Maltese law one of the main characteristics of the contract of mandate is the gratuitousness of the contract. Maltese law is based on the Roman law notion of mandate *"Mandatum nisi graitum nullum est."* The contract of mandate is considered to be naturally gratuitous, however nowadays this element of gratuitousness is no longer considered to be an essential element of the contract of mandate. Article 1861 CC states "Mandate is gratuitous, unless there is a stipulation to the contrary."

NETHERLANDS: In case of professional mandate contracts, the principal will have to pay wages to the agent. In case of non-professional mandate contracts, for instance in case of occasional, onetime juridical acts (e.g. one agrees with a friend to arrange an appointment with a service station regarding the repair of his car), the agent may not be entitled to wages and the mandate is gratuitous. It will depend on the exact content of the agreement between both parties if the rules on mandate contracts apply. According to CC Article 7:405 it seems that the non-professional agent is only entitled to wages if this has been explicitly established. If the gratuitous mandate may be defined as a mandate contract, the same rules apply as to remunerated mandate contracts.

POLAND: The same rules on mandate contract apply regardless whether the service is provided for remuneration or gratuitously.

PORTUGAL: The mandate is presumed to be gratuitous unless the agent is a professional (CC Article 1158) or in case of commercial mandate (CC Article 232, Comm.C Article 1). This implies that, as a rule, the same legal rules apply to the mandate contract, whether or not the mandate is gratuitous.

SCOTLAND: In Scots law a distinction is made between remunerated representation (agency) and gratuitous representation (mandate.) The rules of mandate were discussed by the Scottish institutional writers Stair (I,12), Erskine (III,3,31-38) and Bell, Principles, paragraphs 216-218). 'Mandatars' (agents who are not remunerated) may previously have been subject to a higher standard of care compared to agents (agents receiving remuneration) but this no longer seems to be the case (Stair, I,12,10; Erskine, III,3,36-37; Bell, Principles, paragraphs 218, 212; Macgregor, paragraph 23; *Stiven v Watson* (1874) 1 R 412; *Copland v Brogan* 1916 SC 277).

SLOVAKIA: A mandate may be gratuitous or remunerated in civil relations, commercial contracts (mandate and commission agency contracts) are always remunerated. Provisions on liability for non-conformity of performance do not apply to gratuitous mandate.

SPAIN: The provisions in the civil code apply, with appropriate modifications, to both gratuitous and remunerated mandate contracts). CC Article 1711 indicates that mandate contracts are presumed to be gratuitous, unless the parties provide otherwise. The difference between the regimes of gratuitous and remunerated contracts is explicitly emphasised in CC Article 1726, which indicates that the responsibility of the agent for fault will be determined by the courts depending on whether the mandate is remunerated or not.

SWEDEN: The same set of rules applicable to mandate contracts for direct representation is also applicable, with appropriate adaptations, to gratuitous mandate contracts.

5. *Application to 'general mandate contracts' or 'contracts for the administration of affairs'*
   and authority to dispose of the principal's goods in the performance of such contract

AUSTRIA: The rules on the mandate for direct representation contract also apply to the situation of a 'general mandate' (CC Article 1006). When the awarded authority is meant for a series of judicial acts (Schwimann/Apathy, Article 1006 Rz 1) Comm.C Article 383 ff. and 407 ff. regulate the rights and obligations of commercial agents and forwarders. The mere entrusting of the possession of goods does not confer apparent authority upon the receiver to dispose of them. There must be something more, e.g. the fact that the agent is a person having a usual authority to dispose of goods (auctioneer or broker), or the transfer of additional indicia of title or mandate to sell. A commission agent, e.g., is an agent entitled with the possession and control of goods and securities to be sold for the principal (Comm.C Article 373-406 ff.; Comm.C Article 383 Straube/Griss I³, no. 4; OGH 6.04.1976 (Tankstellenpächter), Arb 9466).

BELGIUM: CC Article 1987 distinguishes a specific mandate (only concerning a specific affair or a multiplicity of affairs of the principal) on the one hand, and a general mandate (concerning all affairs of the principal) on the other hand (see Herbots et al., TPR 2002, p. 733, no. 882; Tilleman, p. 142-148; Wéry, p. 89-90). The rules on mandate apply to both alternatives. In order to know which acts the agent may perform with respect to the affairs under his care, CC Article 1988 distinguishes a mandate in general terms and an express or explicit mandate (De Page, 388-397; Foriers & Glansdorff, p. 602-603; Herbots a.o., TPR 2002, 733; Tilleman, p. 143 and 151; Wéry, p. 88-97). A mandate in general terms does not specify which acts are entrusted to the agent. In that case, the agent only has authority to perform acts of administration. To have authority to dispose of goods belonging to the principal, an express mandate is necessary, specifying the act(s) of disposing as falling within the authority of the agent.

BULGARIA: In Bulgarian law it is allowed an agent to be authorised and instructed to perform general administration of the principal's affairs, with the exception of the judicial acts that have to be performed personally by the principal (for example, marriage, divorce suit, testament) (Меворах/Лиджи/Фархи, III, p. 20). Different rules are applicable depending on the legal capacity of the principle – whether he is or is not a merchant *(Търговец)*. When the principal is not a merchant, the general mandate contract rules (OCA Article 280-292) are applicable to contracts between him and the agent for general administration of the affairs. Furthermore, in such cases the agent can be granted a general power of attorney to act in the name of and on behalf of the principal. The general power of attorney is regulated by OCA Article 36-43. When the principal is a merchant, there are special rules for regulating both the internal contractual relationship between the agent *(Търговски представител)* and the principal-merchant and the power of attorney of the commercial agent, cf. CA Article 21-48. As far as no specific provisions exist for this internal relationship, the general mandate contract provisions, with appropriate adaptation, are applicable to it. There are three different types of commercial agents that can perform general administration of the principal's business affairs – commercial procurator *(Прокурист)* (CA Article 21-25), commercial agent *(Търговски пълномощник)* (CA Article 26-31), and commercial agent *(Търговски представител)* (CA Article 32-48). A commercial procurator is a natural person commissioned and authorized by a merchant (principal) to manage its enterprise in exchange for remuneration, see CA Article 21 paragraph (1). The law defines the limits of authority of the procurator, see CA Article 22 *(Герджиков,* Коментар на Търговския закон, I, p. 102; *Голева,* Търговско право, I, p. 71; Кацаров, p. 129). According to this rule, he is authorized to perform any acts or transactions related to carrying on of the principal's business activities, to represent the principal, and also to authorize third parties to perform specific acts. The procurator may not alienate or encumber any real property of the principal except when he is expressly authorized by the principal to do so. Only one restriction of the authorization of the commercial procurator is allowed – his authority may be restricted to the business of a single branch. No other restrictions shall have legal effect for third parties, cf. CA Article 22.

Commercial agent can be either a natural person or a legal entity, commissioned and authorized by a merchant to perform, in exchange for remuneration, the acts stipulated in the power of attorney. By contrast with the commercial procurator, the limits of authority of the commercial agent are defined by the principal (*Герджиков*, Коментар на Търговския закон, I, p. 111; *Голева*, Търговско право, I, 78; *Кацаров*, p. 135). Unless otherwise stipulated, the commercial agent is deemed authorized to perform all acts related to the merchant's usual business, cf. CA Article 26. For alienating or encumbering real property of the principal, accepting bills of exchange, obtaining a loan, or for a court representation, the commercial agent needs explicit authorization. Any other restrictions on his power of attorney can have legal effects for a third party only if this party knew or should have been aware of such restrictions – CA Article 26. The internal relationship between the commercial agent and the principal is regulated by a contract, that can be either mandate contract or labour contract (*Герджиков*, Коментар на Търговския закон, I, p. 121). Commercial agent is a merchant – a natural person or a company, who independently and in the course of his own business is assisting the business of another merchant. The commercial agent may be authorized to perform transactions and conclude contracts in the name of the merchant or in his own name but always on behalf of the merchant, cf. CA Article 32.

DENMARK: According to Danish law no specific rules will govern the situation where the agent is given a general mandate.

ENGLAND: The law of agency recognises two categories of agents: general and special agents. The distinction is relevant on the question of the nature and the extent of the authority granted by the principal. A general agent will have authority to act for the principal in a particular trade or class of transactions. A special agent will only have authority to act in one given transaction. The distinction used to be particularly important in relation to apparent authority. Nowadays, it seems less important in relation to the notion of usual/customary authority. In addition to the express actual authority of the agent as defined by the terms of the contract (express actual authority), the agent also has an implied actual authority to bind the principal. One category of implied authority is that of usual or customary authority: an agent appointed to a position will have all the authority which an agent in that position would usually have, unless the principal indicates otherwise, i.e. unless he expressly excludes it from the contract (*Panorama Developments (Guildford) Ltd v Fidelis Furnishing Fabrics Ltd* [1971 2 QB 711). The principal can expressly accept that the agent has the usual authority attached to the job he has been appointed to do. The courts decide what amounts to the usual authority of a particular kind of professional by referring to expert evidence as to the practice of a particular trade or profession. The agency rules also apply to contracts for the administration of the principal's affairs. The principal may authorise the agent to do whatever is necessary for the task at hand, so the rules of representation also apply to services of administration of the principal's affairs. Whether the agent can dispose of the goods belonging to the principal will depend on the extent of the authority granted within the contract. There is no problem if the principal has given the agent express authority to dispose of his goods/property. However, even if the principal has not done so, he can still be bound by the act of the agent under the notion of apparent authority.

ESTONIA: As a rule, a contract by which the agent is not required to to conclude a contract but to execute another juridical act would be the (general) contract for services (the service provided under the contract for services can be the conclusion of the contract or the performance of any other (juridical) act. In the rare cases where the agent is not merely under a duty of care in executing the juridical act but (also) guarantees its proper execution, the contract is a contract of works. Article 635 paragraph (2) LOAEst stipulates that specific rules governing the (general) contract for services are (additionally) applicable to a contract of works where the object of the contract is the execution of a transaction (i.e of a juridical act). The law does not distinguish between a general mandate and contracts where the agent is required to execute a specific juridical act. However, such arrangements could fall under the specific regulation of the contract of agency

(Articles 670-691). If the agent acts in his own name, the contract would be the commissionaire agreement. In addition to the rules contained in Article 692-702, certain specific rules governing the contract of (commercial) agency apply to the relationship between the commissionaire and the principal (Article 692 paragraph (3)). Whether the agent who administers his principal's affairs has the authority to dispose of the principal's goods is a question that has to be answered according to the general rules that govern the authority of agents, i.e. the external relationship between the agent and the third parties (GPCCA Articles 115-131). Here, the Estonian law distinguishes, as the German law, between the mandate (*Vertretungsmacht*) and the right to dispose (*Verfügungsmacht*). In most cases this distinction only has theoretical importance. However, the authority to dispose of goods of the principal may also derive from the contract forming the internal relationship between the agent and the principal.

FINLAND: General mandates are mainly governed by the same legislative basis as mandates intended for single transactions. Nevertheless, it may have interpretative importance in application of general principles if the mandate is general. The ACRS includes specific rules on continuous representation. The agent is, in general, entitled to dispose of goods only if this has been agreed. Such an authorisation is, however, often based on legislation or on a mandate given by a court (e.g. to trustees of bankruptcy estates or administrators of an estate of someone deceased).

FRANCE: The rules on mandate contract apply to general mandate contract, cf. CC Article 1987. The rules on representation also apply to services of administration of the principal's affairs, but where there is a general mandate, the powers of the agent are restricted as to the type of legal acts which may be accomplished. These are only acts necessary for the preservation of the subject matter of the contract or its management (CC Article 1987). On the other hand, the agent with a general mandate may not sell or dispose of the goods belonging to the principal (CC Article 1988). For that purpose, it will be necessary to obtain a specific authority to sell or dispose of the subject matter (even though academic writers do accept certain exceptions, particularly in the case of perishable goods).

GERMANY: The same constellation of rules applicable to mandate contracts pertaining to the conclusion of a prospective contract apply to general mandate contracts and to contracts for the administration of the principal's affairs. If need be, the agent may dispose of goods entrusted to him. Unless there are contractual arrangements, no specific conditions apply. Of course, he has to act without negligence when disposing of the goods (there is no specific provision to this end, but CC Article 662 in conjunction with CC Article 280 apply and may give the principal the right to claim damages).

GREECE: The general mandate to represent the principal for a series of juridical acts can be either explicit or be concluded from the general and abstract formulation of the deed or from the nature of the internal relationship based on a contract such as mandate (Vathrakokilis, Article 216 CC no. 11). By a contract of mandate the agent undertakes to conduct the affair of the principal entrusted to him (CC Article 713), which can require the execution of a series of juridical acts for its performance (Georgiadis/Stathopoulos/Karasis, Article 713 CC no. 15). A mandate can be conferred for the purpose of administration of the principal's affairs if the internal relationship is based on a contract of mandate by which the agent undertakes to conduct the affairs of the principal (Georgiadis/Stathopoulos/Doris, Article 216-217 CC no. 31). In such a case the external aspects of the relationship created by the mandate are regulated by CC Articles 211-235 and the internal relationship is regulated by CC Articles 713-729. Under the notion of administration of the principal's affairs falls also the disposal of goods belonging to the principal such as the sale or renting of a house. The mandate for the purpose of administration of the principal's affairs such as the disposal of goods can be also conferred to a broker, who is not considered to be agent of his principal if no mandate is granted to him (Supreme Court decision no. 58/1975, NoV 1975, 879; Georgiadis/Stathopoulos/Karasis, Article 703 CC no. 12).

HUNGARY: The rules on mandate contract apply to the situation of a general mandate (Supreme Court Pfv. VIII. 21.147/2006, in BH2007. 86; Supreme Court Gf. II. 30 521/1986, in BH1987. 174; CA Fővárosi Ítélőtábla 5. Pf. 21 230/2005/3, in BDT2007. 1598) and to contracts for administration of the principal's affairs.

IRELAND: The law of agency applies to both general mandate contracts or mandates for the administration of a person's affairs. The law of agency recognises two categories of agents: general and special agents. A general agent will have authority to act for the principal in a particular trade or class of transactions. A special agent will only have authority to act in one given transaction. The distinction may be relevant to the question of the nature and the extent of the authority granted by the principal however, this distinction is no longer as significant as it once was. Otherwise, general and special agents are bound by the same general rules of agency.

ITALY: The same rules apply both to a general and to a specific mandate. However, the following distinction may be made: if the agent is granted the authority to conclude specific acts, the authority includes not only those specific acts, but also all the acts necessary to conclude the preceding ones (CC Article 1708). These different acts may consist in factual or juridical activities, if complementary to perform the mandate. When a general mandate is granted, the agent can conclude all the acts of ordinary administration even if not exactly individuated or specified in the contract. In this case, in order to validly conclude acts of extraordinary administration a special mandate granting the authority to the agent is necessary towards third parties. A representation agreement often involves the entitlement of the agent to administrate and manage the principal's affairs in order to better satisfy his expectation on the conclusion of the contract and its execution. However, unless otherwise agreed by the parties, the agent does not have the authority to dispose of goods of the principal. This means that in the case of an estate agent in charge of renting the apartment of a principal, the estate agent cannot put the apartment on sale without the principal's specific mandate.

MALTA: If the agent has a general mandate this would usually concern the administration or execution of the general affairs of his principal. The CC refers to the situation when a contract of mandate is drawn up in general terms, whereby CC Article 1863 sets out that "A mandate made out in general terms applies only to acts of administration. The power to make alienations of property, except such alienations as fall within the limits of the administration, or to hypothecate property or to perform other acts of ownership, must be expressed."

NETHERLANDS: The rules on mandate contracts also apply to general mandates. The mandate may be described as one of more specific juridical acts to be performed by the agent, but the mandate may as well be described in a general way. Therefore, it seems that the rules on mandate also apply to services of administration of the principal's affairs, cf. CFI's-Hertogenbosch 3 July 1987, NJ 1988, 550 (GIM/Lucas c.s.).

POLAND: The rules on the mandate contract apply other contracts of service, CC Article 750 provides, including the contract to manage principal's affairs.

PORTUGAL: Representation can be general (but in this case it only covers acts of administration, not transfer of property) or specific (including expressly the acts that the agent is allowed). Cf. CC Articles 262 and 1159; Mota Pinto, p. 539.

SCOTLAND: Agents providing services of a specific nature are governed by the law of agency. There is a distinction between 'general' agents and 'special' or 'limited' agents (Gloag, p. 150; Macgregor, paragraphs 55-56). General agents (e.g. solicitors) are employed to carry out all the business of the principal, or all the business of the principal of a particular type. Special or limited agents are employed to carry out a particular transaction. The main force of this distinction is that only general agents can operate with apparent or ostensible authority. The specific example of the architect who has a very limited authority simply to represent the principal at the moment of reception of the house is likely to be classed as a special agent. Other than the exclusion of special agents from the category of agents who may act with apparent authority, special agents are bound by the same general rules of agency as apply to any other agent. The general rules of agency apply to the situation of a general mandate. A 'general' agent is authorised to transact all the principal's business of a particular kind (Gloag, p. 150; Macgregor, paragraphs 55-56). He can be contrasted with the 'limited' or 'special' agent employed to complete a particular transaction. The same general rules of agency apply to both types of agents, apart from the fact that the special agent cannot act with apparent or ostensible authority. Whether the agent has authority to dispose of the goods of the principal depends on the extent of the authority granted. A general power to administer would not normally be interpreted as conferring a power to dispose. Mere entrusting of the possession of goods does not confer apparent authority to the receiver to dispose of them.

SLOVAKIA: The rules on mandate contracts apply to general mandates. In the general provisions of the Civil Code regulating the representation under a power of attorney (external effects) is only given the condition under which the power of attorney must always be conferred in writing if it concerns more than one specific act in law. Merely entrusting of the possession of goods does not confer apparent authority upon the receiver to dispose of them.

SPAIN: The Spanish CC refers to general mandate contracts in CC Article 1712 *(mandato general)*. The general mandate comprises all the principal's affairs, as opposed to special mandate contracts *(mandato especial)*, which concern one or more of the affairs of the principal. General mandate contracts in CC Article 1712 are to be differentiated from what the civil code calls *'mandate in general terms'*, regulated in CC Article 1713. A mandate in general terms regards the nature of the acts which are to be concluded, which according to CC Article 1713 are the acts of administration, but not acts which are concerned with the acts to dispose of the goods of the principal. Acts of administration are those which are meant to maintain the quality of the administered assets or to obtain the normal benefits produced by the assets (Hernández Gil, p. 921).

SWEDEN: There are no specific rules concerning contracts for administration of the principal's affairs in the Swedish law of contract. The same set of rules applicable to mandate contracts for direct representation also applies to the situation where the agent has been given a general mandate. If a contract for administration of the principal's affairs is made general and at the same time irrevocable it may not also be exclusive. The reason for this is that it can only be tolerated that a person puts himself under "curatorship" within a determined and limited sector of his sphere of interests, see Grönfors, p. 134.

6. Application to intermediation contracts

AUSTRIA: In case the main obligation of the agent is to bring the principal into contact with a third party the respective provisions of the Austrian Broker Act (Maklergesetz) are not applicable because the activity of the agent as it is provided in Article 1 ABA aims at the conclusion of the main contract. Indeed, it does matter whether the aim of such service is to conclude a main contract with a third party or not. Therefore, these provisions of the civil law referring to concrete mediation contracts not regulated in the ABA are applicable.

BELGIUM: The rules on 'hiring of services' *(huur van werk)* or a building contract, cf. Tilleman, p. 14-17 (and the numerous examples of jurisdiction, quoted by Tilleman); Wéry, p. 119.

DENMARK: The making of contracts through e.g. estate agents and brokers is a good example of the flexibility of the law of agency. In the course of making one single contract such agent may act both as *messenger, ordinary agent* and *factor*. It is rare, however, that a real estate agent or broker will act as a factor despite the popular (legal imprecise) description of real estate agents as agents 'having a house on commission' and where such agent exceptionally acts as a factor he will normally not have access to take the buyer's or the seller's place himself (contracting for own account).

ENGLAND: An agent who merely negotiates the terms of a contract for a principal, such as a solicitor for instance, is also regarded as an agent and the traditional common law rules will also apply to the internal relationship between the agent and the principal. Such relationships are also referred to as 'incomplete agencies'.

ESTONIA: As a rule, such contract would be either the brokerage contract *(maaklerileping)* or the contract of (commercial) agency *(agendileping)*. As far as the specific regulations do not apply, the contract would be the (general) contract for services.

FINLAND: In certain areas these types of mandates are governed by specific legislation. Such Acts are the Act of Commercial Agents and Salesmen, the Real Estate Agent Act and Insurance Agents Act. Other areas of practice are governed by analogous interpretation of the general legislation applicable to authorization together with general principles of contract law, including trade customs.

FRANCE: This is a brokerage contract. The type of contract subject to this question may be treated as a contract for services in the sense of CC Articles 1779-1799), and French case law specifies that it may not be treated as a mandate contract (see Cass.com. 22 May 1991, RTD civ. 1992 p. 86), even though certain laws do refer to the mandate contract in certain cases (for example for estate agents, see Law of 2 January 1970, Article 5; for a commercial agent, see Law of 25 June 1991, Article 1; Comm.C Article L. 134-1). There is, in effect, a service which is rendered, consisting of introducing a business partner for the conclusion of a contract or the negotiation of the contract. However, where the service provider does not have the power to conclude the contract in the name and for the account of the person concerned, there should be no mandate referring to the classical agency contract definition.

GERMANY: This is considered to be a brokerage contract *(Maklervertrag;* the CC uses the old-fashioned term *Mäklervertrag)* governed by CC Article 652-655. CC Article 655a-656 contain additional provisions on specific brokerage contracts (loan brokerage, marriage brokerage). Another (more detailed) set of rules on brokerage contracts is contained in Comm.C Article 93-104, applicable only to commercial brokers. Furthermore, only the solicitation of contains for certain goods and services is covered by these provisions, cf. Comm.C Article 93 paragraph (2), e.g. no real estate transactions – these are subject to CC Article 652-655.

GREECE: If the agent is required to bring the principal into contact with a third party or to negotiate the terms of a contract with a third party the rules of brokerage regulated in CC Article 703-712 are applicable. Intermediation with a view to the conclusion of a contract (μεσιτεία, mesiteia) is regulated in CC Article 703 paragraph (1): "A person who has promised remuneration to somebody for the latter's intervention or for the indication by him of an occasion for the conclusion of a contract shall only be bound to pay the remuneration if the contract was concluded as a result of such intervention or indication." Although intermediation without a view to the conclusion of a contract is excluded from the present questionnaire, it should be noted that such kind of intermediation seems not to be permitted in Greek civil law. CC Article 708 regulates that a promise of brokerage for the conclusion of a marriage is null and void. What has been eventually paid on account of the promise may be reclaimed. Although an analogous application of that regulation in the case of engagement and adoption is not acceptable, it is argued that an intermediation with a promise of a fee in such cases is null and void according to CC Article 178 (act contrary to morality), cf. Georgiadis/Stathopoulos/Karasis, CC Article 708 no. 1.

IRELAND: Where the agent lacks 'authority or power' to bind his principal, but merely provides a service (as an intermediary who negotiates between two parties or introduces two parties) then the law of agency will not apply and instead the applicable rules are to be found in the express and implied terms of any contract (e.g. a contract for the provision of services) between the parties; Part IV of the Sale of Goods and Supply of Services Act 1980, which implies various terms into contracts for the supply of services (as regards the quality of the service provided) and restricts the supplier's ability to limit/exclude his liability for breach of these implied terms; specific legislation that may regulate certain professional activity e.g. the Solicitors Acts 1954-1994; soft law in the form of codes of practice which may also have an impact e.g. Irish Bankers' Federation Code of Ethics and Practice; and finally, other sources such as tort law, and the law of restitution. However, it should be noted that in practice, where an agent is engaged to negotiate a contract (though not conclude it) he frequently will have some authority or power to bind his principal, for instance, he may have authority to describe the property being sold and so may bind his principal to statements made in advance of concluding a contract. In these circumstances the 'law of agency' also would apply to that aspect of his activities.

ITALY: If the agent's main obligation is to bring the principal into contact with a third party or to negotiate the terms of a contract with the third party the rules governing the contract of mediation shall apply. This contract is ruled by CC Articles 1754 ff., according to which a mediator is the person who "places two or more parties in contact for the purpose of bringing about a transaction, without being connected with either of such parties by way of collaboration, employment, or representation". The main purpose of the contract of mediation is to facilitate the conclusion of a contract. Italian scholars and judges hold that the mediation is incompatible with representation, both prior to the conclusion of the contract and in the conclusion of the contract. (cf. Stolfi, p. 42; Cass., 19 August 2003, no. 12106, Mass. Foro Italiano, 2003, 4140, no. 20). The Civil Code specifically admits the granting of authority to a mediator only for the execution of a contract which has already been concluded between the principal and the third party. Indeed, there is a sort of incompatibility between the roles of the mediator and the agent during the phase of the negotiations and of the conclusion of the prospected contract: this is due to the rule of impartiality that is of essence with respect to the mediator. It is only after the conclusion of the contract that the mediator may act in favour of one of the two parties only. Cf. CA Milano, 12-05-2004, I Contratti, no. 8-9, 2005 with comments by Battelli.

MALTA: In this situation the contract between the agent and the principal has been made in express terms, that is, to bring the principal in contact with a third party or to negotiate the terms of a contract with a third party. Thus the agent will not be able to do anything beyond the limits of this mandate. In such a situation Maltese law in order to avoid any doubts that might arise, indicates specifically certain powers that are deemed to fall within the competence of the agent. CC Article 1865 specifies that "For the carrying out of the mandate, the agent may institute legal proceedings"; make and prosecute appeals; make proof by reference to the oath of his adversary; take the oath in litem or the suppletory oath; enforce judgments both on movable and immovable property; make demand for the issue of precautionary acts including those for the issue of which an application or declaration on oath is required; make demand for the personal arrest of the debtor of the principal, where such demand is competent; and do any other thing which the principal might do personally, notwithstanding that such powers have not been expressly given in the mandate.

NETHERLANDS: Intermediation contracts are covered by the specific rules of CC Articles 7:425-427 and the more general rules applicable to contracts of services in general.

POLAND: There are no provisions in Polish civil law that deal with intermediation specifically. In practice the rules applicable to mandate contract are applied.

PORTUGAL: The general rules on mandate contracts apply. However, in some cases, *lex specialis* may apply, like e.g. real estate mediation, regulated by DL no. 77/99, 16 March.

SCOTLAND: Agents employed only to bring the principal into contact with a third party may be referred to as an introduction or introducing agent. An estate agent's role may comprise this limited role only, or may be wider than this. Nevertheless, the situation is governed by the normal rules of agency. A significant body of case law concerning this type of agent exists, normally on the issue of whether that agent did, in fact, introduce the eventual contracting party, and is thus due payment of commission, or whether the agent had no role in finding the contracting party and is not therefore due any commission. See, for example, *Walker, Fraser & Steele v Fraser's Trustees* 1910 SC 222, and Macgregor, paragraph 112. The concept of the agent whose role is negotiation only without the ability to conclude a contract is almost unknown in Scots law. There is no concept of a 'commission agent.' There is nothing in strict theory to prevent an agent having this limited role, and, were that the case, that agent would be governed by the normal rules of agency law. However, the practise seems not to exist.

SLOVAKIA: In civil relations, the provisions of CC Articles 774-777 on brokerage contracts apply to intermediation contracts. Similarly, in commercial contracts the specific rules on brokerage contracts of Comm. C Articles 652-672 apply.

SWEDEN: Specific Acts govern the business of real estate agents and insurance agents (Real Estate Agent Act and the Insurance Agent Act). In other cases of intermediary services there is a lack of legislation. Hence, one has to consider analogies with the specific acts as well as general principles of contract, trade custom, Comm.C Chapter 18, the Commission Act, Sale of Goods Act and to some extent Contracts Act, Chapter 2.

No answer received: SPAIN.

No answer received: MALTA. (2) The mandatary may also, in virtue of the said powers, be a defendant on behalf of the mandator, in any law-suit concerning the matter included in the mandate.

Article 1:102: Definitions

In these Principles;
(a) the 'mandate' of the agent is the authorisation and instruction given by the principal as modified by any subsequent direction;
(b) the 'mandate contract' is the contract under which the agent is authorised and instructed to act, and any reference to the mandate contract includes a reference to any other juridical act by which the agent is authorised and instructed to act;
(c) the 'prospective contract' is the contract the agent is authorised and instructed to conclude, negotiate or facilitate, and any reference to the prospective contract includes a reference to any other juridical act which the agent is authorised and instructed to do, negotiate or facilitate;
(d) a mandate for direct representation is a mandate under which the agent is to act in the name of the principal, or otherwise in such a way as to indicate an intention to affect the principal's legal position;
(e) a mandate for indirect representation is a mandate under which the agent is to act in the agent's own name or otherwise in such a way as not to indicate an intention to affect the principal's legal position;
(f) a 'direction' is a decision by the principal pertaining to the performance of the obligations under the mandate contract or to the contents of the prospective contract that is given at the time the mandate contract is concluded or, in accordance with the mandate, at a later moment;
(g) the 'third party' is the party with whom the prospective contract is to be concluded, negotiated or facilitated by the agent;
(h) the 'revocation' of the mandate of the agent is the recall by the principal of the mandate, so that it no longer has effect.

Comments

A. General idea

As with any set of rules, in these Principles specific legal concepts are used to set out the rules contained in these provisions. The most important concepts used in these Principles are defined in the present Article. The definitions in this Article are, it is hoped, self-explanatory. The Article itself does not contain any substantive rules.

B. No definition of agent

As was already mentioned in Comment K to Article 1:101 (Scope), the term 'agent' was preferred over similar words such as 'representative' or 'mandataris', or compound terms such as 'agent or intermediary' and 'agent or broker'. The word 'agent', however, is not defined here. It is a very general term that embraces anyone who acts for another. These Principles deal with only certain types of agents – namely those acting under mandates for direct representation, those acting under mandates for indirect representation and those acting as brokers or intermediaries. The common factor is that they are engaged in relation to the conclusion of other contracts or the doing of other legal acts.

C. Relation to the Principles of European Law and the Draft Common Frame of Reference

This Article mirrors that of Article IV.D. – 1:102 DCFR (Definitions).

D. Character of the Rule

This Article contains only definitions of some of the terms used in these Principles of European Law on Mandate Contracts. It is mandatory in the sense that the parties cannot, in their contract, qualify a contract differently by avoiding the terminology used in these Principles.

E. Remedies

As this Article merely contains definitions of some of the terms used in these Principles of European Law on Mandate Contracts, it does not impose duties on either of the parties. Therefore, this Article does not provide a party with a remedy.

Notes

1. General remarks

As the National and Comparative Notes throughout these Principles will make clear, the definitions in the present Article correspond to similar techniques and concepts in most national systems.

Article 1:103: Duration of the mandate contract

A mandate contract may be concluded
(a) for an indefinite period of time;
(b) for a fixed period; or
(c) for a particular task.

Comments

A. General idea

This Article provides a classification of mandate contracts from the point of view of their duration. Three types of contracts are distinguished: contracts for an indefinite period, contracts for a fixed period and contracts for a particular task. In the mandate contract it may be indicated that the contractual relationship is to terminate at a specific moment in time irrespective of the individual will of the parties, i.e. a contract for a definite period. That specific moment for termination may be a fixed date agreed upon by the parties (sub-paragraph (b)) but may also be the moment at which the particular task that the agent has to fulfil has been achieved (sub-paragraph (c)). Where no such specification exists, the mandate contract is concluded for an indefinite period of time (sub-paragraph (a)).

B. Relevance of classification

The reason for distinguishing between these three types of mandate contracts is a practical one. Whereas mandate contracts for an indefinite period of time can only be terminated by a decision by one of the parties – i.e. by termination of the mandate relationship – mandates for a fixed period and mandates for a particular task may also be terminated by operation of law, in particular by the elapse of the period for which the authority to represent the principal was given (mandate for a fixed period), and by completion of the particular task for which the agent was authorised and instructed. On the other hand, as they are contracts for a definite period, such contracts may normally not be terminated by one of the parties. Chapter 6 (Termination by notice other than for non-performance) indicates that termination of such a contract will nevertheless terminate the mandate relationship, but may lead to liability for the party wrongfully terminating the relationship. However,

Article 6:102 (Termination by the principal when relationship is to last for indefinite period or when mandate is for a particular task) indicates that the principal may also terminate a mandate contract for a particular task by giving notice of reasonable length without having to pay damages to the agent.

C. Types of mandate contracts

In the mandate contract, it may be indicated that it is destined to terminate at a specific moment in time irrespective of the individual will of the parties. Where no such specification exists, the mandate contract is concluded for an indefinite period of time.

Illustration 1
Lionel is a collector of first editions of books that were published in the 19th century. Marc, on the other hand, makes a living from buying rare books and antiques on behalf of customers. As Lionel is not in a position to stroll through antique bookshops as much as he would like to, he commissions Marc to purchase first editions of 19th-century books that he comes across.

As the parties have neither specified which exact books Marc is to purchase on behalf of Lionel, nor when he must have finished his task, the parties have concluded a mandate for an indefinite period of time. The contract, and therefore Marc's authority to buy the first editions on behalf of Lionel, does not automatically come to an end. In order to end the mandate relationship, either party is required to terminate the contract by giving notice to the other party in accordance with the requirements set out in Chapter 6 (Termination by notice other than for non-performance) of these Principles.

Such mandate contracts are in practice rather scarce: most of the time, an agent will be authorised to conclude a particular contract or to perform a particular other legal act, or be authorised to handle the affairs of the principal during a specified period of time. Where the contract indicates a fixed period for its duration, the mandate relationship terminates when the specified time has elapsed.

Illustration 2
Nigel is away on holiday. However, just before going on holiday he was engaged in negotiations pertaining to the development of a new franchise network. For that reason, he has charged Owen to continue the negotiations during the week in which Nigel is on holiday. When Nigel returns to his work the next week, Owen's authority to re-present Nigel in these negotiations ends.

The mandate contract between Nigel and Owen is a mandate contract for a fixed period of time.

However, the most common feature is a mandate contract for a particular task. Such a mandate normally terminates when the particular task the agent is to fulfil is achieved.

In particular, this is the case when the agent has concluded a prospective contract on behalf of the principal.

Illustration 3
Peter falls in love with a beautiful painting by Degas, which is available for sale at a gallery. As he is not capable of negotiating the contract himself, he commissions Randolph to purchase the painting in his name. Once Randolph has succeeded in buying the painting, the authority to represent Peter ends.

Conclusion of that prospective contract (and giving account of the way the agent has performed the contract in conformity with Article 3:402 (Accounting to the principal)) entitles the agent to payment under Article 2:102 (Price) and brings about the termination of the mandate contract.

However, in contrast to mandate contracts for a fixed period, it may be uncertain when the envisaged result will be achieved or even whether it will be finally achieved. This implies that in the case of a mandate contract for a particular task, the parties may be *de facto* linked to the contract for an indefinite period, in particular in the situation where the agent fails to conclude the prospective contract without breaching his obligations under the mandate contract – in which case, the mandate relationship cannot be terminated for non-performance either.

Illustration 4
As Ulrich has found a new job in Berlin, he wishes to sell his house in Cologne. He charges Sandra with negotiating the sale of his house. Unfortunately, as Ulrich's house is relatively expensive and the market for this type of house has collapsed as a result of the credit crunch, Sandra does not succeed in finding a buyer for the house for quite some time and is not certain whether she will find one in the near future.

This indicates that although the contract is a contract for a definite period of time, there may be good reasons why either the principal or the agent – or even both parties – should be released from his or their contractual obligations towards the other party.

Illustration 4 (continued)
As Ulrich is not able to sell his house and can't afford to own two houses, he is forced to forgo his job opportunity in Berlin and stay in Cologne. He therefore wants to terminate the mandate contract with Sandra.

While such a possibility to unilaterally terminate the contract is not very common for contracts for a definite period of time, it is different for this type of mandate contracts. Article 6:102 (Termination by the principal when relationship is to last for indefinite period or when mandate is for a particular task) of these Principles explicitly allows Ulrich to terminate the contract.

Finally, it does happen that the two types of mandate contracts for a determined period of time are mixed.

Illustration 5
Donald commissions Eva to buy a Dalí sculpture before the end of March 2010.

If the sculpture is bought, Eva is entitled to payment once she has given notice and the mandate relationship terminates. If the sculpture cannot be purchased on time, the mandate relationship would terminate automatically once the fixed period has elapsed.

D. Completion of a mandate contract for a particular task

As indicated in Comment C, the typical mandate contract is a mandate contract for a particular task. When that task is fulfilled – the prospective contract is concluded – the authority granted to the agent comes to an end, and as a result the mandate contract terminates. According to Article 2:102 paragraph (2) (Price), the agent is then entitled to payment of the price as soon as he has given account of how he has performed the task, as required in Article 3:402 paragraph (1) (Accounting to the principal).

E. Conclusion of prospective contract by principal or another agent

If the specific mandated task is the conclusion of the prospective contract and it is not the agent but the principal or another agent appointed by the principal who has concluded the prospective contract, the agent is no longer able to complete the mandated task. This implies that the conclusion of the prospective contract by the principal or another agent in fact implies the revocation of the mandate under Article 1:104 (Revocation of the mandate).

F. Expiry of fixed period

When the mandate contract was concluded for a definite period, the mandate contract ends when the fixed period has elapsed. However, if both parties continue performing the obligations under the mandate contract, then the mandate contract becomes a mandate contract for an indefinite period. From that moment on, both parties may nevertheless terminate the mandate relationship by giving notice of reasonable length (see Articles 6:102 (Termination by principal when relationship is to last for an indefinite period or when mandate is for a particular task) and 6:104 (Termination by agent when relationship is to last for indefinite period or when it is gratuitous)). The parties may, of course, derogate from this rule, e.g. by providing that the mandate relationship is continued for (again) a definite period of time, thus limiting the possibilities for the parties to prematurely terminate the renewed mandate relationship.

Illustration 6
Martha sets off for a trip around the world. Before leaving she authorises and instructs a real estate agent to find a lessee for her apartment and to collect the rent while she is abroad. The real estate agent deducts a small amount for his services and ensures that

Martha receives the remaining amount. The mandate contract is therefore concluded for the time while she is abroad. However, when Martha returns, she finds another place to live and the real estate agent continues collecting the rent. Martha does not ask him to stop his task and allows him to continue collecting the rent and retaining the fee for his services. The mandate contract between Martha and the real estate agent has been tacitly prolonged and has become a contract for an indefinite period.

G. Relation to the Principles of European Law and the Draft Common Frame of Reference

This Article mirrors that of Article IV.D. – 1:103 DCFR (Duration of the mandate contract).

H. Character of the Rule

This Article contains a classification of the three types of mandate contracts that exist from the point of view of their duration. It is mandatory in the sense that the parties cannot, in their contract, classify a mandate contract differently by avoiding or choosing other terminology: whether a mandate contract is qualified as falling within the scope of one of the three types or another is a matter for the courts to decide.

I. Remedies

As this Article merely contains a classification of existing types of mandate contracts, it does not impose duties on either of the parties. Therefore, this Article does not provide a party with a remedy.

Comparative Notes

1. General remarks

As the National and Comparative Notes throughout these Principles will make clear, the classification of a mandate contract as a mandate contract for an indefinite period of time, for a fixed period of time or for a particular task has consequences with regard to specific subjects. The national and comparative information will be dealt with below when dealing with these specific subjects.

2. Completion of the particular task terminates the mandate contract

In all Member States, the mandate of the agent terminates when the agent performs the particular task he was authorised and instructed to conclude. In FRANCE, HUNGARY, and SCOTLAND, the mandate relationship terminates only when accounting and payment obligations by the principal are fulfilled.

3. Termination of a mandate contract for a fixed period

According to general contract law rules in almost all Member States, a contract for a definite period terminates when the agreed period elapses.

4. Tacit prolongation of a mandate contract for a fixed period

None of the systems report specific rules for mandate on the tacit prolongation of the contract. However, in all systems, with the apparent exception of POLAND, general contract law rules and the European rules on commercial agency determine that the mandate contract is tacitly turned into a mandate contract for an indefinite period of time.

National Notes

1. Completion of the particular task terminates the mandate contract

AUSTRIA: The mandate relationship ends automatically with the execution of the act to be done by the agent (Rummel/Strasser, Article 1024 Rz 16; Straube/Griss, Article 383 Rz 13).

BELGIUM: The mandate relationship will end automatically. General rules of contract law apply (De Page, p. 450; Wéry, p. 265).

BULGARIA: The Bulgarian OCA Article 287 prescribes that 'the mandate, in addition to other grounds stated in the law, can be terminated upon the withdrawal of the mandate by the principal, upon the agent's renunciation thereof, and upon the death or juridical incapability of the agent or the principal, as well as with the dissolution of the legal entity if it had been either principal or agent'. The almost unanimous opinion in legal doctrine is that performance of the contract is among the 'other grounds stated in the law' (Любен Василев, Облигационно право, p. 28; Меворах/Лиджи/Фархи, III, p. 162; Божидар Василев, p. 132). The mandate relationship is therefore considered to end when the contractual obligations of the parties have been performed.

DENMARK: The mandate relationship will end automatically. The conclusion of the prospective contract means that the agent has carried out the principal's instructions. Further representation will need further instructions from the principal.

ENGLAND: When the agent was asked to perform a particular task, the authority of the agent immediately ends once this task has been successfully completed (*Blackburn v Scholes* ((1810) 2 Camp 341)).

ESTONIA: The mandate relationship ends automatically when the mandated task has been completed and the agent has notified the principal.

FINLAND: The mandate relationship ends automatically when the prospective contract is concluded or other mandated task is completed.

FRANCE: CC Article 2003, which describes the various situations where an agency will terminate, does not refer to this case. However, it is accepted generally that, on the basis of ordinary rules of contract, completion of the mandate by the agent will result in termination of the mandate relationship. Such termination will occur, subject to the provision of accounts to the principal, when the latter has given a discharge to the agent and has paid all sums due to the agent (Bénabent, no. 675).

GERMANY: The mandate relationship terminates when the mandated task is completed (for example, when the prospective contract is concluded). Although there is no specific provision in the law on mandates etc. to this end, general principles of contract law lead to this result (Palandt/Sprau, Article 671 paragraph 4; BGHZ 41, 23).

GREECE: In case of representation based on a contract of mandate, if the authority has been granted for the conclusion of the prospective contract the mandate ends automatically with the conclusion of that contract.

HUNGARY: The end of the mandate relationship depends exclusively on the content of the mandate contract irrespective of the authority of the agent to represent the principal. Naturally, it is senseless to give authority of representation to the agent without a contract for representation, but the contract for representation can continue to have effect for some purposes after the principal has withdrawn the powers of representation from the agent. Moreover, according to CC Article 479(2), '[a]t the time the contract is extinguished, the agent shall be obliged to settle his accounts and give the principal everything that has been acquired for the purpose of fulfilling his agency or as a result of doing so, except for what he has lawfully used in the course of his agency'. For this reason, even if the prospective contract is concluded and the authority to represent had been granted for the conclusion of the prospective contract only, the contractual obligations are not entirely extinguished until the agent has settled accounts with the principal.

IRELAND: When the agent is to perform a particular task, the authority of the agent immediately ends once this task is successfully completed (*Blackburn v Scholes* [1810] 2 Camp 341).

ITALY: According to CC Article 1722 the mandate relationship ends when the prospective contract is concluded.

MALTA: Once the prospected contract has been concluded the contract for mandate ends automatically.

NETHERLANDS: Full performance of the mandate contract (for example, by the conclusion of the prospective contract) ends the mandate relationship (cf. implicitly CC Article 7:411 and Asser-Kortmann, no. 96). Conclusion of the prospective contract is seen as a case where the mandate ends because of 'its completion' (CC Article 7:408 paragraph (2) in fine).

POLAND: There are no specific Civil Code provisions regulating when the mandate contract ends.

SCOTLAND: It is common for the contract for representation to be set up with a view to achieving one specific purpose. In such cases, the right and the obligation of the agent to represent the principal in that matter will automatically terminate once this purpose has been achieved (*Price & Co v Tennent* (1844) 6 D 659; *Black v Cullen* (1835) 15 D 646). However, that is not to say that the whole relationship arising under the mandate contract will necessarily be at an end. Even after completion of the mandated task there may still be obligations of accounting and payment. Only when all such obligations have been performed will the contractual relationship come completely to an end.

SLOVAKIA: The contract for representation will end automatically (CC Article 33b paragraph (1)(a)).

SPAIN: The mandate relationship terminates with the conclusion of the juridical act which was the object of the contract. This is a ground for termination which applies to every contract (Hernández Gil, p. 512; Lete del Río, p. 413).

SWEDEN: Unless the parties have agreed on a consecutive mandate, the successful conclusion of the prospective contract automatically terminates the mandate relationship.

2. Termination of a mandate contract for a fixed period

BELGIUM: General rules of contract law apply. A contractual relationship ends when the contractually agreed definitive period has elapsed (Wéry, p. 265).

BULGARIA: The expiry of the period for which the mandate contract is concluded is considered one of the 'other grounds stated in the law' that terminate the mandate relationship (see OCA Article 287; Любен Василев, Облигационно право, p. 28; Меворах/Лиджи/Фархи, III, p. 162; Божидар Василев, p. 132).

General contract law rules are applicable. If the period is measured in months, it expires on the respective date of the final month; if that month lacks the respective date, the time period expires on its last day. A time period measured in weeks expires on the respective day of the final week. Where a time period is measured in days, the day when the period of time begins to run is not counted and the time period expires at the end of the final day (OCA Article 72).

ENGLAND: When the agency is entered into for a fixed period, and is not renewed, it will end as soon as the fixed period elapses.

ESTONIA: If the mandate contract was concluded for a definite period and the agreed period has elapsed, the mandate contract ends (Article 186(9) LOAEst).

FRANCE: There is no specific rule on this point. On the basis of ordinary rules of contract, it may be accepted that elapse of the period terminates the mandate relationship.

GERMANY: The mandate relationship ends when it was concluded for a specific time period and that period has elapsed (Palandt/Sprau, Article 671 no. 4).

HUNGARY: When the contractually agreed period for performance has elapsed, the mandate relationship ends.

IRELAND: A fixed term agency automatically terminates when the agreed time passes.

MALTA: The expiry of the period is one of the reasons to terminate the relationship.

NETHERLANDS: If the contractually agreed period for performance has elapsed, the mandate relationship ends. General contract law applies.

POLAND: There are no specific rules, but as with all other contracts concluded for a definite period of time, the contractual relationship ends when the time has elapsed.

SCOTLAND: Where the agent has been given authority for a limited period of time, expiry of the period terminates the relationship (Bell, Commentaries, 7, I,526; Black, paragraph 551; *Price & Co v Tennent* (1844) 6 D 659; *Black v Cullen* (1835) 15 D 646; Macgregor, paragraph 182).

SLOVAKIA: The general law of obligations applies: rights and obligations cease to exist by the elapse of the definite period (CC Article 578). This also applies to commercial relations.

SPAIN: The mandate relationship, as any other contractual relationship, terminates when the contractual period expires (Hernández Gil, p. 512; Article 24 paragraph (1) Agency Law).

SWEDEN: If the parties have agreed on a definite period for performance, the mandate relationship ends when such period has elapsed.

No answer received: AUSTRIA, DENMARK, FINLAND, GREECE, ITALY, PORTUGAL.

3. Tacit prolongation of a mandate contract for a fixed period

BELGIUM: There is no specific rule on tacit prolongation regarding the contract of mandate. General rules of contract law will apply.

BULGARIA: There is no explicit provision stating that continued performance after the elapse of the definite period is considered an implicit extension of the contractual duration. The parties are free to stipulate so in their contract. A special rule is applicable to the commercial agency contract: if, after the elapse of the definite period both parties continue to perform their contractual obligations, the contract is considered concluded for an indefinite period of time (CA Article 47(4); Касабова, ТП, 2006, p. 169-170).

ENGLAND: There does not seem to be any agency case dealing with this specific issue. However, relying on contract law principles, if the parties continue to perform the contract after the period has elapsed, the contract is treated as having tacitly been renewed. It is not clear whether the contract would be deemed to be for a fixed or an indefinite duration. This would depend on the circumstances surrounding the case and its interpretation by the courts.

ESTONIA: If the parties continue performance of the obligations under the mandate contract after the period for which the contract was concluded has elapsed, they may be treated as having tacitly agreed upon the extension of the duration of the mandate relationship. In such cases the mandate contract would be treated to be tacitly agreed to be for an indefinite period.

FRANCE: There is no specific rule regarding the mandate contract on this point; general rules will apply (extension of the duration of the contract if both the principal and the agent act as if the contract had not ended; *gestion d'affaires (negotiorum gestio)* if only the agent does so).

GERMANY: If the law on service contracts is applicable to a remunerated *Geschäftsbesorgungsvertrag* by virtue of CC Article 675(1), CC Article 625 provides that the relationship is considered as extended for an indefinite period of time if performance by the agent continues and the principal knows about it. In other constellations, the parties might be viewed as having tacitly derogated from the contractual time limit.

HUNGARY: If the parties have continued performance of the obligations under the mandate contract after the original period for which the contract was concluded has elapsed, they are treated as having tacitly agreed upon the extension of the duration of the mandate relationship.

IRELAND: Where a fixed term agency has terminated due to the passing of time and performance continues, it is usually treated as an indefinite agency, terminable by notice.

NETHERLANDS: If the contractually agreed period for performance of the obligations under the mandate contract has elapsed, the contracting parties are treated as having concluded a contract for an indefinite period.

POLAND: Continued performance does not lead to automatic prolongation of the agreement.

SCOTLAND: The agency relationship may continue on the tacit agreement of the parties where it was general in nature, in other words where the agent is classed as a general agent. It may not so continue where the original agency relationship was entered into for a specific purpose which has now been achieved (Bell, Commentaries, 7, I, 526; Gow, p. 537).

SLOVAKIA: There is no explicit regulation on this issue. The continued performance may be regarded as an implicit agreement of the parties to extend the contract.

SPAIN: The principle of tacit prolongation has been upheld in Spanish law for agency contracts (Article 24 paragraph (2) Agency Law) and the analogy would seem to hold for other similar cases.

SWEDEN: If the parties continue performance of the obligations under the mandate contract after the definite period of performance has elapsed, they are considered to have tacitly agreed upon an extension of the mandate relationship. If nothing else follows from the contract or from the circumstances, the extension is considered as being for an indefinite period of time.

No answer received: AUSTRIA, DENMARK, FINLAND, GREECE, ITALY, PORTUGAL.

Article 1:104: Revocation of the mandate

(1) Unless the following Article applies, the mandate of the agent can be revoked by the principal at any time by giving notice to the agent.

(2) The termination of the mandate relationship has the effect of a revocation of the mandate of the agent.

(3) The parties may not, to the detriment of the principal, exclude the application of this Article or derogate from or vary its effects, unless the requirements of the following Article are met.

Comments

A. General idea

This Article makes clear that the principal is free to revoke the mandate given to the agent at any time by giving notice of revocation (paragraph (1). Article 6:101 paragraph (2) (Termination by notice in general) indicates that the revocation of the mandate also implies the termination of the mandate contract.

Vice versa, where the mandate contract has been terminated by either party, this also has the effect of termination of the mandate of the agent, implying that the agent is no longer authorised to conclude the prospective contract on behalf of the principal.

Paragraph (3) adds that when the conditions set out in Article 1:105 (Irrevocable mandate) are not met, the parties cannot restrict or exclude the principal's right to revoke the mandate and thus to terminate the mandate contract.

B. Revocability of mandate at will

As a general rule, the principal is free to decide that the agent is no longer authorised to act on the principal's behalf. The principal may revoke the mandate at any time, even if the mandate contract was concluded for a fixed period or a particular task. The principal need not state any reasons for his decision to revoke the agent's authority. This implies that the principal may revoke the agent's mandate at any time and without having an objectively sound reason to do so.

Illustration 1
Alberto charges Billy to exchange his old car for a new convertible. When Billy is on his way to purchase such a car, Alberto's friend Charlene points out that it may not be a good idea to buy a convertible in England, as it rains half the time. Alberto immediately changes his mind and phones Billy that, for the time being, he will continue to drive his old car and does not want Billy to buy him a new car.

Alberto is free to change his mind and revoke Billy's authorisation to represent him. Moreover, although in many cases he will indicate why he has changed his mind, Alberto is not required to explain his reasons for doing so.

The reason why the principal may, in principle, always revoke the mandate is that the mandate relationship is based on the confidence of the principal in the agent, and only the principal may evaluate when this confidence is no longer there. When the principal considers that it is no longer in his interest to be bound by the prospective contract concluded by the agent on his behalf, unless the mandate is irrevocable under Article 1:105 (Irrevocable mandate), he may therefore always revoke the agent's authority to represent him.

C. No form requirement

In most cases, the principal will give explicit notice of revocation to the agent. However, such explicit revocation is not a requirement for a valid revocation. In other words, the revocation may occasionally also be implied from the circumstances.

Illustration 1
Donovan is charged by Evelyne to purchase a specific painting by Renoir. When Donovan informs the seller of his interest in the painting on behalf of Evelyne, the seller informs him that Evelyne has told him directly that she has changed her mind and that Donovan is no longer to buy the painting on her behalf. In this situation, Donovan lacks the authority to conclude the sales contract on Evelyne's behalf.

The fact that the principal has informed the third party that the agent is no longer authorised to conclude the prospective contract may therefore be seen as a revocation of the agent's mandate.

Illustration 2
Donovan is charged by Evelyne to purchase a specific painting by Renoir. When Donovan informs the seller of his interest in the painting on behalf of Evelyne, the seller informs him that Evelyne has contacted him herself and has already bought the painting herself. The conclusion of the prospective contract by Evelyne herself is to be regarded as a revocation of Donovan's mandate.

D. When the revocation becomes effective

The revocation does not take effect until the agent becomes aware of the revocation (or should have been aware thereof).

Illustration 3
Donovan is charged by Evelyne to purchase a specific painting by Renoir. The painting is being sold at a gallery in Paris, whereas both Donovan and Evelyne are located in London. Donovan travels to the gallery. Frederick shows Donovan a letter, signed by Evelyne, awarding Frederick the exclusive authority to represent her in the purchase of the painting. When Donovan reads the letter, he becomes aware of the revocation of the mandate and the revocation becomes effective.

This implies that until the agent is informed of the revocation, he remains entitled to act on behalf of the principal and is entitled to a remuneration for his services and, as the case may be, to reimbursement of expenses.

E. Revocation of mandate of the agent and termination of the mandate contract

Paragraph (2) sets out what the consequences of the termination of the mandate contract are: termination of the mandate contract automatically leads to the revocation of the mandate. Similarly, under Article 6:101 paragraph (2) (Termination by notice in general), the revocation of the mandate of the agent is treated as a termination of the mandate contract. As a result, the termination of the mandate contract and the revocation of the mandate in effect are always combined. This ensures that in whichever way the principal indicates his desire to withdraw his authorisation to the agent for the latter to affect the legal relations of the principal, the communication of this decision leads to the end of the mandate relationship and of the mandate itself.

F. Revocation is not a breach of the principals obligation to co-operate

The revocation of the mandate implies that the principal effectively prevents the agent from performing the obligations under the mandate contract and thereby from earning any stipulated remuneration. As such, this could be considered a non-performance by the principal of the obligation to co-operate (with the possibility of the agent claiming specific performance of the right to continue to affect the legal effects of the principal). However, as paragraph (1) explicitly gives the principal the right to revoke the mandate, from this provision it follows that the revocation is not to be seen as non-performance by the principal. Therefore, the agent is not entitled to a remedy for the mere reason that the principal has hindered him in the performance of his obligations.

G. Conclusion of prospective contract by principal or another agent

If the specific mandated task is the conclusion of the prospective contract, and it is not the agent but the principal or another agent appointed by the principal who has concluded the prospective contract, the agent is no longer able to complete the mandated task. This implies that the conclusion of the prospective contract by the principal or another agent in fact implies the revocation of the mandate, and as such leads to the termination of the mandate contract under Article 6:101 paragraph (2) (Termination by notice in general). In many cases, this will imply that the principal will be liable for damages for non-observance of the reasonable notice period.

Illustration 4
Stephanie and Tony conclude a contract under which Tony is authorised and instructed by Stephanie to sell a Chinese vase from the Ping Dynasty. The mandate contract will terminate once the vase is sold. After some months, Stephanie finds a buyer for the vase herself and concludes the sales contract. The mandate of Tony is deemed to have been revoked under the present Article and the mandate contract comes to an end in accordance with Article 6:101 paragraph (2) (Termination by notice in general).

H. Consequences of revocation of mandate

The revocation of the mandate has as its automatic consequence that the mandate contract itself is terminated (see above, Comment E). This implies also that even though the principal is allowed to revoke the mandate at will, the revocation is not always 'free of charge'. Article 6:101 paragraphs (1) and (2) (Termination by notice in general) indicate that the revocation of the mandate is effective when a notice of the revocation reaches the agent. However, as the revocation is seen as a termination of the mandate relationship under Article 6:101 paragraph (2) (Termination by notice in general), the agent may be entitled to damages under Article 6:101 paragraphs (5) and (6) (Termination by notice in general). An exception to this is when there is an extraordinary and serious reason to revoke the mandate which justifies immediate termination under Article 6:103 (Termination by the principal for extraordinary and serious reason). Moreover, even if the principal observed a reasonable period but subsequently concluded the prospective contract himself, he may even be required to pay the price under Article 2:102 paragraph (5) (Price), provided that the conditions for the applicability of that Article are met.

I. Relation to the Principles of European Law and the Draft Common Frame of Reference

This Article mirrors that of Article IV.D. – 1:104 DCFR (Revocation of the mandate).

J. Character of the rule

Paragraph (3) indicates that this Article is mandatory and therefore cannot be derogated from to the detriment of the principal. This implies that where the parties have excluded or restricted the principal's right to revoke the mandate, this provision would not prevent the principal from revoking the mandate. The only exception to this is where the mandate is irrevocable under Article 1:105 (Irrevocable mandate).

K. Remedies

Unless the conditions of Article 1:105 (Irrevocable mandate) are met, the principal is free to revoke the mandate of the agent. However, unless the principal is justified in terminating the mandate contract in accordance with Article 6:101 paragraph (7) (Termination by notice in general), or he has a serious and extraordinary reason that justifies immediate termination under Article 6:103 (Termination by the principal for extraordinary and serious reason), the principal would be required to pay damages under Article 6:101 paragraphs (5) and (6) (Termination by notice in general) for wrongful termination.

Comparative Notes

1. Revocation of mandate

In almost all legal systems, the principal can revoke the mandate at any time, unless the mandate was irrevocable from the start. This is the case in AUSTRIA, BELGIUM, BULGARIA, ENGLAND, FRANCE, IRELAND, MALTA, THE NETHERLANDS, POLAND, SCOTLAND, SLOVAKIA, SPAIN, and SWEDEN. However, in SCOTLAND, the parties may also contractually exclude the possibility of revocation. By contrast, a mandate cannot be made irrevocable in PORTUGAL.

In GERMANY, a gratuitous mandate may be revoked by the principal at any time, but a remunerated mandate may only be terminated, in which case a notice period is to be observed unless there was a serious and extraordinary reason that justifies the immediate termination of the mandate contract.

In most legal systems, the revocation is effective once the agent takes note of the revocation or ought to have been aware of the revocation, which generally implies that the revocation must be notified to the agent. Generally, this revocation is treated as a termination of the mandate contract, implying that if the principal did not observe a reasonable notice period and could not invoke a serious and extraordinary reason to justify the immediate termination of the mandate contract, he is required to pay damages. However, in BELGIUM, the principal need not observe a period of notice to revoke the mandate.

2. Conclusion of mandate contract by principal or another agent is revocation of mandate

The conclusion of the prospective contract by the principal or by another agent is qualified as an implicit revocation of mandate granted to the agent and leads to termination of the mandate relationships in BELGIUM, BULGARIA (doctrine), ENGLAND (if no exclusivity agreed upon), FRANCE, GERMANY, IRELAND (if no exclusivity agreed upon), SCOTLAND, and SPAIN. This seems not to be the case in SWEDEN, where the principal still has to notify the agent. In ENGLAND, termination depends on whether the agent has been granted exclusivity. If not, the contract terminates.

National Notes

1. Revocation of mandate

AUSTRIA: The principal can revoke the granted authority at any time. It is not relevant whether the agent acted in the principal's name or in his own name if the contractual relationship between indirect agent and principal is that of a mandate in terms of CC Article 1002 ff. If the principal concludes the prospective contract of his own motion, the agent is entitled to a proportional part of the price, to his incurred expenses as well as to suffered losses.

BELGIUM: According to the CC Article 2004, a principal can always revoke the authority to represent ad nutum, i.e. without a motive and without a period of notice (De Page, p. 460-462; Tilleman, p. 301-305; Wéry, p. 267-273). No formal requirements apply. As a unilateral juridical act, the revocation does not have to be accepted by the agent to be effective (De Page, p. 462-463; Tilleman, p. 281 and 290-291). The revocation will only be effective at the moment the (revoked) agent takes note or ought to have taken note of the revocation (see for a specific application: CC Article 2006). According to CC Article 2005, the revocation can only be invoked towards third-parties after they have taken note of it.

BULGARIA: According to BULGARIAN law of obligations, the principal has the right to revoke the mandate contract at any time – OCA Article 288 (Любен Василев, Облигационно право, 1, p. 29). This revocation is followed, as a legal effect, by the end of the contractual relationship (Любен Василев, Облигационно право, 1, p. 29; Голева, Облигационно право, p. 239; Меворах/Лиджи/Фархи, III, p. 170). The contract is considered ended from the moment when the agent gets to know about or could have been aware of the revocation – OCA Article 290 (Любен Василев, Облигационно право, 1, p. 30). The ending of the contract, as a result of unilateral withdrawal from the principal's side, does not deprive the agent of the remuneration (if such has been stipulated) and the reimbursement of the expenses – OCA Article 288 (1).

ENGLAND: The principal can revoke the agent's actual authority at any time regardless of whether the agent was disclosed (acted in the principal's name) or was undisclosed (acted on behalf of principal but in his own name) This is so unless the authority is irrevocable.

ESTONIA: The parties can agree (for their internal relationship) that the mandate relationship cannot be terminated (other than by termination for a fundamental breach). The principal may conclude the prospective contract personally even in the case of an irrevocable mandate, but the parties can agree otherwise. For the external relationship a general rule applies that the parties may exclude revocability of the authority (the power of attorney), but even in such case the law allows for revocation upon an important ground as a mandatory rule (GPCCA Article 126 paragraph (3)).

FRANCE: The Civil Code gives the principal the possibility of terminating the agent *ad nutum,* in other words at any time (there is no need of a notice of reasonable length), without specific reason, without any right to compensation (CC Article 2004). The very moment at witch this termination occurs is not ruled by statutory law, but case law considers that the mandate ends when the agent is aware of his revocation by the principal (Cass.civ. 3e, 28 February 1984, JCP éd. G 1984, IV, 146). The termination may even occur as a result of notice to the agent of the appointment of a new agent for the same transaction (CC Article 2006). The principal does, however, have to inform any possible third party contractors of such revocation in order to give them binding notice (CC Article 2005).

GERMANY: A gratuitous mandate may be revoked by the principal at any time (CC Article 671(1)). The unilateral revocation of a remunerated *Geschäftsbesorgungsvertrag* by the principal is, on the contrary, generally not allowed, as CC Article 675(1) does not refer to CC Article 671(1). Under remunerated mandate contracts, the principal may merely terminate the contract according to the rules provided by the law on contracts for services or contracts for works. The rules on contracts for services allow termination by the principal but provide for a termination period which depends on the time frame according to which the service provider is paid (CC Article 621). Contracts for services under which payment is not made after particular time periods can be terminated anytime. Additionally, the principal has the right to terminate irrespective of any termination period where there is an important reason which makes it unacceptable for him to continue the contract (CC Article 626). Furthermore, termination is possible at any time even without an important reason where the contract calls for services 'of a higher kind which are usually assigned on the basis of particular trust' (CC Article 627(1)). This will often be the case where a mandate contract is concluded.

IRELAND: The principal can revoke the agent's authority and terminate the agency at any time (though this may constitute a breach of contract), unless the agency is irrevocable.

MALTA: A principal is free to revoke his mandate whenever he pleases even if the agent has received remuneration. This was held by CA (Commercial) in *Anastasi et. vs. Guillamier et.* 8th June 1936. The Court continued by quoting Baudry Lacantinerie stating that a mandate with a remuneration may be revoked by the principal arbitrarily. The agent does not, in such a case, have a right for his remuneration even if the revocation is not justified. However in such a case although the agent is not remunerated, he is entitled to be compensated when the revocation of the mandate is made without a just cause. With regards to the requirements needed by the principal to effectuate the cancellation of the contract, under CC Article 1887(1) there are no such requirements, in fact the principal may revoke the contract whenever he chooses. However if the procuration has been made for a determinate time, the principal who revokes the mandate before such time is responsible for damages towards the agent, cf. Comm. Court 12 November 1934, *Salomone* vs *Mifsud Speranza et noe.*

NETHERLANDS: In case of a revocable mandate, the principal is allowed to end or revoke the mandate. See CC Articles 7:408 paragraph (1) and 7:422 paragraph (1). See also CFI 's-Hertogenbosch 3 July 1987, NJ 1988, 550 (GIM/Lucas c.s.) and HR 17 November 1978, NJ 1979, 96 (Slavenburg's Bank/Jurgens).

POLAND: The principal may revoke the mandate contract at any time by giving notice (CC Article 746). The agent is entitled to partial remuneration, the principal should also repay any expenses incurred by the agent. If the contract was revoked without a valid reason the principal is also liable for the losses incurred by the agent. The principal's right to revoke the contract because of valid reasons is a *ius cogentis* provision and the parties may not derogate it, cf. Panowicz-Lipska/L. Ogiegło.

PORTUGAL: An irrevocable grant of authority is not possible under Portuguese law (CC Article 265 paragraph (2) and 1170). If the other party has waived his right to revoke the mandate, he can still revoke it, however is liable to pay compensation for the losses that the agent has incurred (CC Article 1172 lit (b)). Losses covered are only those related to the recuperation of the contractual balance (excluding for instance loss of reputation of the agent). Cf. Lima/Varela (1986), p. 735. CC Article 1171 provides that, if the other party appoints another agent to execute the same acts next to the agent with whom the mandate contract was concluded, the previous contract is deemed revoked *(revogação tácita)*, with effect since the moment that the agent knew of the subsequent appointment. According to Lima/Varela (1986), p. 733, this is only the case if the second appointment is incompatible with the previous representation contract. Cf. also STJ 7 December 1989, BMJ 392, 444.

SCOTLAND: The principal may at any time revoke the agent's authority (Macgregor, paragraph 183; Gow, p. 536). It is not relevant whether the agent acted in his own name or in the name of the principal. The right to revocation may, however, be excluded by the contract (Macgregor, paragraph 183) or because the mandate is irrevocable because both parties have an interest in its performance (Macgregor, paragraph 25).

SLOVAKIA: The principal is always entitled to terminate the mandate contract without any conditions. The authority of the agent ends, if the represented person revokes it. Until the revocation of authority becomes known to the agent, his acts in law have legal consequences as if the authority continued to be effective. A third party who knew or must have known about the revocation of the granted authority, however, may not rely on the agent's authority. If the principal has informed a third party that he has granted authority for specified acts upon a certain agent, the revocation of this authority may be put forward as a defence by the principal only if the principal informed the third party of the revocation before his agent's negotiations with this third party, or if the third party knew of the revocation at the time of such party's negotiations, CC Article 33b paragraphs (4-5). If the mandate has been terminated by revocation, the principal is obliged to compensate the agent for all expenses incurred before revocation and for the damage suffered and if any remuneration is due for work that agent performed, for such work or part thereof. This also applies when the completion of the negotiations was frustrated accidentally through no fault of agent (CC Article 732).

SPAIN: CC Article 1733 states that the principal may revoke the mandate at any time. See also Comm.C Article 279. The rationale is that the mandate relationship is based on the confidence of the principal in the agent, and only the principal may evaluate when this confidence is no longer there (Lete del Río, p. 413; Lasarte, p. 345). Revocation can be explicit or implicit. Implicit revocation implies the carrying out of an act which unambiguously indicates an intention to revoke – for example when the principal concludes the prospective contract personally (STS 4 January 1991) or appoints another agent to carry out the task entrusted to the agent (CC Article 1735). Revocation will be effective from the moment the agent knows about it. This requirement is imposed in CC Article 1735 for implicit revocation and in CC Article 1738 for explicit revocation (Lasarte, 345). Acts concluded by the agent without knowledge of the revocation are valid and have effect regarding third parties who have contracted with the agent in good faith (CC Article 1738). Notice of revocation will lead in any case to the termination of the relationship, but, if the principal abuses the right, that is, when the purpose is to damage the interests of the agent or when the revocation is based on illegal reasons, then the agent can claim an indemnity (Lete del Río, 413). The STS 3 March 1998, RJA 1998, 1129 held that the principal was not entitled to freely terminate the mandate where a price for the services and a definite time have been agreed. In any case, the agent cannot seek specific performance, and damages is the only relief available. See for further discussion Gordillo, p. 1584-1585.

SWEDEN: The principal is free to revoke the granted authority at any time without giving reason for such revocation, see Bengtsson, p. 153. This may be a breach of contract towards the agent.

No answer received: FINLAND, ITALY

2. Conclusion of mandate contract by principal or another agent is revocation of mandate

BELGIUM: The classic example of an implied revocation by the principal is the conclusion of the prospective contract by the principal personally (CA Brussels 26 June 1986, Res.Jur.Imm. 1986, no. 6073; Tilleman, p. 294; Wéry, p. 271). The termination may also occur as a result of notice to the agent of the appointment of a new agent for the same transaction (CC Article 2006).

BULGARIA: There is no explicit rule in the sense that the conclusion of the prospective contract by the principal or by another agent, appointed by the principal, is treated as revocation of the mandate. Nevertheless in legal doctrine such behaviour of the principal is interpreted as a case of revocation (Меворах/Лиджи/Фархи, III, p. 176). This means that the contractual relationship is terminated when the agent gets to know about or could have been aware of either the conclusion of the prospective contract or the authorisation of another agent with the same authority. The contract will keep its legal effect when the principal explicitly states that the previous mandate is not revoked (Меворах/Лиджи/Фархи, III, p. 176).

ENGLAND: The position depends on whether the agent has been granted an exclusivity by the principal or not.

FRANCE: CC Article 2003 describes the various situations where an agency will terminate. This Article does not refer to this case. However, it is accepted generally that, on the basis of ordinary rules of contract, the completion of the mandate by the agent or by the principal will result in the termination of the mandate. The termination may even occur as a result of notice to the agent of the appointment of a new agent for the same transaction (CC Article 2006).

GERMANY: While there is no specific provision to this end, general rules of contract law may lead to a mandate relationship ending once the purpose of the mandate has been fulfilled (Palandt/Sprau, Article 671 no. 4). Case law has confirmed this notion at least for the contractual relationship with an executor of a will (BGHZ 41, 23, 25).

IRELAND: It seems likely that, where the mandate is solely for the conclusion of a particular contract, the conclusion of that contract by someone other than the agent would have to result in the termination of the agency (and perhaps also give rise to liability for breach of contract, depending on the terms of the contract).

MALTA: Due to the general provision found in CC Article 1887 that the principal may revoke the contract whenever he chooses, it can be presumed that the principal may conclude the prospected contract of his own motion. If the principal concludes himself the prospected contract, the agent is still entitled to a compensation for the services rendered in order for the transaction to be finalized.

POLAND: There are no specific rules on this matter in the Polish CC.

SCOTLAND: Where the agency was entered into to achieve a specific purpose, and the principal or another agent achieves that purpose, the agency relationship would be brought to an end on the basis that it is now impossible for the agent to achieve the agreed purpose. The agent might remain entitled to payment where the conclusion of the contract which is the purpose of the agency relationship is attributable in part to the agent's efforts, even if the agent is no longer involved at the moment of conclusion (Macgregor, paragraph 112; *Walker, Fraser & Steele v Fraser's Trustees* 1910 SC 222 at 229, per Lord Dundas; *Walker, Donald & Co v Birrell, Stenhouse & Co* (1883) 11 R 369).

SLOVAKIA: The authority as well as the mandate relationship are terminated if the juridical act for which it has been granted is executed (CC Article 33b paragraph (1)(a)).

SPAIN: The appointment of a new agent for the same matter amounts to termination of the former mandate (CC Article 1735). It is accepted also that the conclusion of the intended contract by the principal personally brings about the tacit revocation of the previous mandate (Gordillo, p. 1589).

SWEDEN: The conclusion of the prospective contract by the principal or by another agent appointed by the principal would not automatically be treated as a revocation of the mandate of the agent. The principal would still be required to revoke the mandate by notice.

No answer received: AUSTRIA, ESTONIA, FINLAND, ITALY, THE NETHERLANDS, PORTUGAL.

Article 1:105: Irrevocable mandate

(1) In derogation of the preceding Article, the mandate of the agent cannot be revoked by the principal if the mandate is given:
  (a) in order to safeguard a legitimate interest of the agent other than the interest in the payment of the price; or
  (b) in the common interest of the parties to another legal relationship, whether or not these parties are all parties to the mandate contract, and the irrevocability of the mandate of the agent is meant to properly safeguard the interest of one or more of these parties.

(2) The mandate may nevertheless be revoked if:
  (a) the mandate is irrevocable under paragraph (1)(a) and:
    (i) the contractual relationship from which the legitimate interest of the agent originates is terminated for non-performance by the agent; or
    (ii) there is a fundamental non-performance by the agent of the obligations under the mandate contract; or
    (iii) there is an extraordinary and serious reason for the principal to terminate under Article 6:103 (Termination by the principal for extraordinary and serious reason); or
  (b) the mandate is irrevocable under paragraph (1)(b) and:
    (i) the parties in whose interest the mandate is irrevocable have agreed to the revocation of the mandate;
    (ii) the relationship referred to in paragraph (1)(b) is terminated;
    (iii) the agent commits a fundamental non-performance of the obligations under the mandate contract, provided that the agent is replaced without undue delay by

another agent in conformity with the terms regulating the legal relationship between the principal and the other party or parties; or

   (iv) there is an extraordinary and serious reason for the principal to terminate under Article 6:103 (Termination by the principal for extraordinary and serious reason), provided that the agent is replaced without undue delay by another agent in conformity with the terms regulating the legal relationship between the principal and the other party or parties.

(3) Where the revocation of the mandate is not allowed under this Article, a notice of revocation is without effect.

(4) This Article does not apply if the mandate relationship is terminated under Chapter 7 of these Principles.

Comments

A. General idea

Under Article 1:104 (Revocation of the mandate), the general rule is that a mandate is freely revocable at any time. However, there may be situations where either the agent or other parties have a legitimate interest in the *irrevocability* of such a mandate. This question is dealt with in the present Article. It sets out the circumstances in which a mandate, in derogation of the normal situation as set out in Article 1:104 (Revocation of the mandate), may be irrevocable. Paragraph (1) indicates that this may be the case in two distinct situations: when the agent has a specific interest in performance of the mandate contract other that the interest of being paid for his services, and when the authorisation of the agent has taken place in the interest of not only the principal, but also in the interest of other parties. Paragraph (2) indicates that notwithstanding the fact that the mandate is, in principle, irrevocable, there are situations in which the mandate may nevertheless be revoked. The most important situations where this may arise are when there is a fundamental non-performance of the agent or when there are other reasons justifying an immediate termination of the mandate contracts.

B. Need for the possibility of irrevocable mandate

The fundamental right to revoke a mandate is based on the right of the principal not to be bound by a prospective contract (or other juridical act) if the principal no longer wishes to become bound. As such, that fundamental right is not disputed. However, there are circumstances in which an agreement on the irrevocability of the mandate of the agent may be justified. Indeed, in most Member States, parties to a mandate contract may agree upon its irrevocability. This entitlement is granted under strict conditions, however. In many Member States, parties are only allowed when they have a legitimate reason for the irrevocability of the mandate. In other Member States, the interests of a third party may be considered a legitimate reason to allow irrevocability. In addition to the existence of a legitimate reason, some systems impose time constraints to the validity of an irrevocable contract.

Irrevocability of an agent is possible only when there are legitimate interests at stake of other parties than the principal. These interests may conflict with the principal's interest not to be bound by a prospective contract or other juridical act. This is typically the case in two distinct situations. First, irrevocability may be needed to safeguard a legitimate interest of the agent. In this case, the irrevocability exists *towards the agent*. In the second case, the mandate is to serve the interests of several 'principals', and irrevocability is needed to safeguard the interests of the principals *towards each other*. These situations have in common that they are the result of an underlying relationship between the principal and the agent or other interested parties.

C. Mandate given in the interest of the other party

In the type of case covered by paragraph (1)(a), the underlying relationship may give rise to an irrevocable mandate where the mandate serves an interest of the agent other than the agent's interest in being paid for his services.

Illustration 1
A bank is willing to award a credit contract to a consumer, provided that it is secured by a mortgage on the house of the consumer. In the credit contract, the consumer agrees to give an irrevocable mandate to the bank to establish the mortgage.

The conclusion of a credit contract that is to be secured by a mortgage is a complicated matter, in particular as in many legal systems a mortgage is established through a notary need and publication thereof in a public register. Only upon registration is the mortgage established and the bank's claim secured. If the mandate is not irrevocable, the bank runs the risk that the consumer may revoke the mandate once he has obtained the credit. Even though this would undoubtedly constitute a non-performance by the consumer of the credit contract, it would cause the bank significant inconvenience if such a revocation takes place, in particular if the revocation of the mandate is followed by bankruptcy or insolvency of the consumer. If the bank is not given an irrevocable mandate to establish the mortgage in this situation, the bank will only agree to conclude the credit contract once the mortgage is established, which would clearly hamper an efficient operation of the financial markets.

D. Mandate given in the interest of several principals

In the situation covered by paragraph (1)(b), several parties agree that in the interest of an efficient and effective representation of their interests or in the interest of solving a common problem, a mandate is to be given to one of them or to a third party to act as an agent on behalf of all of them. In this case, on the basis of their common relationship, the 'principals' are bound towards each other not to revoke the mandate. In the relationship between each principal and the agent, this may lead to the irrevocability of the mandate.

Illustration 2
A group of music composers (the principals) agree that in their common interest an organisation of music composers (the agent) will be mandated to act on their behalf with regard to the exploitation of their intellectual property rights.

In this case, irrevocability does not follow from the contract between the music composers, but may very well be stipulated explicitly between these parties.

Illustration 3
Two co-owners of a car mandate each other to sell the car to an interested third party. Here, both co-owners may act independently on their own behalf and that of their fellow co-owner.

Again, irrevocability does not follow from the relationship between the co-owners. Therefore, the parties must agree upon this.

A second category concerns situations where the common interest of the principals consists of solving their conflicting interests and the solution is to be achieved by a third party. If this is the case, the agent necessarily must be somebody else.

Illustration 4
A buyer and a seller (the principals) disagree as to whether the delivered goods conform to the contract. They appoint an arbitrator (the agent) to decide who is right.

In this illustration, the common interest of the principals consists of solving their conflicting interests, and the solution is to be achieved by a third party. If this is the case, the agent necessarily must be somebody else. It follows from the nature of the relationship between these parties that the mandate of the agent must be irrevocable: a party who is dissatisfied with the intermediate decision of the arbitrator should not be able to revoke the arbitrator's mandate and thus escape from a negative outcome of the dispute. As the arbitrator is 'to affect the legal relations of the principal', the contract between the arbitrator and the two principals falls under the definition of a mandate contract. Article 5:102 (Double mandate) applies with appropriate modifications to this situation.

E. Exceptions to irrevocability

Only when the reason for irrevocability of the mandate under the underlying relationship no longer exists may the principal revoke the mandate of the agent and thus terminate the mandate relationship. In this sense, the 'irrevocability' is relative.

1. Irrevocability in the interest of the agent

Even when the mandate is irrevocable and the period of irrevocability has not yet elapsed, the agent is still required to act in accordance with the mandate, to act in the best interests of the principal and to act in accordance with the standard of care that may be expected.

The irrevocability of the mandate should not go so far as to prevent the principal from terminating the mandate relationship for fundamental non-performance by the agent of the obligations under the mandate contract (paragraph (2)(a)(ii)). The mandate can also be revoked if the relationship from which the legitimate interest originates is terminated for non-performance by the agent (paragraph (2)(a)(i). Finally, the principal may revoke the mandate if there is a serious and extraordinary reason to terminate the mandate relationship (paragraph (2)(a)(iii)).

Illustration 5
(Loss of trust in agent): A bank indicates that it is willing to award a credit contract to a consumer, provided that it is secured by a mortgage on the house of the consumer. In the credit contract, the consumer agrees to give an irrevocable mandate to the bank to establish the mortgage. Before the credit is provided and the mortgage established, the possible collapse of the bank is reported on the front pages of all national newspapers.

The consumer should be able to revoke the mandate for a serious and extraordinary reason (paragraph (2)(a)(iii) if the bank is not yet insolvent, or for non-performance by the bank if it already has become insolvent (paragraph (2)(a)(i). In this situation – which nowadays seems much less unlikely than it was before the credit crunch – it would be unacceptable to require the consumer to tolerate that the trustees of the bank would be able to continue establishing the mortgage if there is a substantial risk that the bank will not be able to provide the credit.

2. Irrevocability in the interests of other principals

As is the case with irrevocability in the interest of the agent, in the case of irrevocability in the interest of other principals the agent also should not receive a license to do as he pleases. For that reason, the irrevocability of the mandate should not go as far as to exclude the possibility of the principal to terminate the mandate relationship for fundamental non-performance. Similarly, if the parties in whose interest the mandate had become irrevocable all agree that the mandate should be revoked, there is no legitimate reason to withhold them from exercising that right. For that reason, paragraph (2) introduces a number of cases where the irrevocable mandate that was given in the interest of several 'principals' – whether they are a party to the mandate contract or not – may nevertheless be terminated.

Illustration 6
The five children of the deceased owner of a house mandate an agent to sell the house to an interested third party. To ensure that the sale is not hampered by the fact that ultimately one of the heirs opposes the sale, they decide to award the agent an irrevocable mandate. When six months later the agent still has not attracted any interest in the house, the heirs agree to revoke the mandate and to terminate the mandate relationship.

As in this case all parties interested in the original irrevocability of the mandate agree to the revocation, the need to protect the other principals against the unilateral revocation of the mandate by one of them is absent. In this case, the mandate may be revoked under (paragraph (2)(b)(i)).

Illustration 7
A buyer and a seller (principals) disagree as to whether the delivered goods conform to the contract. They appoint an arbitrator (agent) to decide who is right and agree that the arbitrator will keep the information that he receives confidential. The arbitrator fails to keep the details of the case to himself.

In this situation, both the seller and the buyer may revoke the arbitrator's mandate and terminate the mandate contract (i.e. the arbitration contract) under paragraph (2) (b)(iii).

F. No maximum period for irrevocability

The irrevocability of the mandate of the agent is an exception to the general rule that the principal may revoke the mandate given to the agent at any time (paragraph (1)). As such, the natural tendency would be to restrict the possibility for allowing the irrevocability. In some Member States, parties may agree upon the irrevocability of their contract only if it has a fixed duration. In some of these legal systems, an irrevocable mandate would otherwise be considered illegal because it would be seen as allowing for perpetual obligations. However, given the fact that the mandate may be revoked in case of an extraordinary and serious reason and, in the case of a mandate that is irrevocable to protect the interests of other 'principals', when these 'principals' all agree, it seems that there is no particular need to require a maximum period for irrevocability.

G. Consequences of irrevocability

To the extent that the mandate is irrevocable, a notice of revocation by the principal remains without effect (paragraph (3)). It does not end the authority of the agent to represent the principal, and therefore the mandate relationship is not terminated. Where the principal tries to terminate the mandate relationship by notice, Article 6:101 paragraph (3) (Termination by notice in general) leads to the same result.

H. Termination under Chapter 7 (Other grounds for termination) leads to revocation of mandate

If the mandate relationship terminates because one of the situations under Chapter 7 (Other grounds for termination) occurs – i.e. the relationship is terminated because the agent dies – the rules on irrevocability no longer have effect. This is also the case when the principal dies and the successors of the principal or the agent terminate the contractual relationship on the basis of an extraordinary and serious reason.

I. Relation to the Principles of European Law and the Draft Common Frame of Reference

This Article mirrors that of Article IV.D. – 1:105 DCFR (Irrevocable mandate).

J. Character of the Rule

Paragraph (3) indicates that when revocation under this Article is not allowed, a revocation of the mandate is considered to be without effect. This implies that the parties cannot derogate from the provisions of this Article in so far as and to the extent that the mandate of the agent is indeed irrevocable.

K. Remedies

From paragraph (3) it follows that where the mandate is irrevocable a revocation is without effect, unless one of the exceptions provided for in paragraph (2) applies. This implies that in such cases, the agent remains to be able to bind the principal towards third parties and does not breach his obligations towards the principal if he does so. This also means that the agent may call for specific performance of the mandate contract.

Comparative Notes

1. Irrevocability of mandate

In BULGARIA, FINLAND, FRANCE, HUNGARY, ITALY, PORTUGAL and SPAIN, an irrevocable mandate does not have the effect that the mandate contract continues to exist irrespective of the revocation of the authority of the agent. In these legal systems, when the parties agreed upon irrevocability, revocation by the principal remains possible but is seen as a breach of contract by the principal, giving rise to a claim for damages. However, in ITALY, the principal is not required to pay damages if he has a just cause for revocation, e.g. because of malicious and negligent behaviour of the agent or if the agent does not respect the instructions received by the principal.

In SLOVAKIA, an irrevocable mandate is sometimes seen as void.

In other legal systems, the parties may, and with effect, agree upon the irrevocability of the mandate. This is generally accepted in BELGIUM, DENMARK, ESTONIA, and MALTA. In ENGLAND, IRELAND, and SCOTLAND, irrevocability is accepted in cases where the mandate in fact operates as a security for the agent to safeguard his interests. More generally, in GERMANY, GREECE, THE NETHERLANDS and SWEDEN, irrevocability is accepted if the mandate was given not only in the interest of the principal, but also in the interest of the agent (other than his monetary interest in being paid for his services under the mandate contract). Similarly, in GREECE and THE NETHERLANDS, irrevocability is also accepted if the mandate was (also) provided in the interest of third parties. In AUSTRIA, the parties may validly agree upon irrevocability if there is an interest in doing so to be found in the underlying relationship, but they may agree upon irrevocability only for a definite period. Despite the irrevocability, revocation remains possible in case of fundamental non-performance of the agent (explicitly accepted in ESTONIA) and in case of extraordinary and serious reasons (explicitly accepted in POLAND).

National Notes

1. Irrevocability of mandate

AUSTRIA: Though an agent's authority is normally revocable at any time (CC Article 1020) without prejudice to his right to damages for breach of contract, there is an exception: if the authority is coupled with an interest outside the contract for mandate and the irrevocability is stipulated for contract for a definite period of time, such an authority is irrevocable (Schwimann/Apathy, Article 1020 Rz 7; Straube/Griss, Article 383 Rz 13).

BELGIUM: The parties can validly agree upon irrevocability of the mandate contract (De Page, p. 463-464; Foriers & Glansdorff, p. 640-641; Wéry, p. 275-283).

BULGARIA: Bulgarian contract law distinguishes the revocation of the mandate contractual relationship between the principal and the agent from the revocation of the power of attorney of the agent. Bulgarian legal doctrine makes a difference between absolute and relative irrevocability of the mandate and the authority (Меворах/Лиджи/Фархи, III, p. 171). In case of absolute irrevocability, the principal's withdrawal from the mandate or the authority does not have any legal effect, whereas, in case of relative irrevocability, the principal can put an end to the mandate and the authority with unilateral notice to the agent. Doing so, the principal is liable for the damages. The general rule in Bulgarian law is that the principal can revoke the mandate of the agent at any time, cf. OCA Article 288(1). This rule is considered facilitative, hence, the parties can explicitly stipulate otherwise, i.e. the irrevocability of the mandate. Furthermore, in some cases the irrevocability of the mandate can be implied, for example, if both the principal and the agent or the principal and a third party have a legitimate interest in the mandate (Меворах/Лиджи/Фархи, III, p. 170). According to Bulgarian legal writings the irrevocability of the mandate contract is always relative. Therefore if the principal withdraws from the irrevocable contract, the contractual relationship terminates anyway, but the principal is liable to the agent for the damages, apart from the obligation to pay remuneration for the performed part of the mandate (Меворах/Лиджи/Фархи, III, p. 171). As a rule, the principal can withdraw the power of attorney at any time – OCA Article 41(1). The irrevocability of the power of attorney is a disputable matter in BulgariaN legal doctrine. The first opinion (the old one) is that the authority of the agent can be absolutely irrevocable when it concerns the interests of the agent or of a third party (Меворах/Лиджи/Фархи, III, 169; Диков, ЮА, p. 19). The opposite and more recent opinion is that the principal can withdraw the authority at any time, even though otherwise is stipulated in either the mandate contract or the act of authorization, i.e. the authority is always revocable (Любен Василев, Гражданско право, p. 375).

DENMARK: According to the Danish law the parties can validly agree that the contract authority cannot be revoked. There are no statutory rules on this matter. According to case law a general mandate (general power of attorney) cannot be irrevocable.

ENGLAND: When the agency is said to be irrevocable, it is because it is used for a different purpose than the normal purpose of an agency relationship since it is used 'to confer a security or other interest on the agent' (Bowstead, paragraph 10.007). In such a case, the agent uses the authority for his own benefit. Agency is therefore used as a 'device for supporting or conferring a property interest' and therefore, 'not really within the bounds of proper agency reasoning' (Bowstead & Reynolds, paragraph 10.007). The agent's authority will be irrevocable in 2 instances: (1) when it is coupled with an interest belonging to the agent i.e. that 'the authority is given for the purpose of being a security' *(Smart v Sandars* (1848) 5 CB 895, 918 per Wilde CJ) so that security and authority are closely connected one with another. However, this is only valid when the interest exists at the time that the principal gives the agent authority; the mere right to earn commission is not regarded as an interest *(Doward, Dickson & Co v Williams & Co* (1890) 6 TLR 316). (2) agency will be irrevocable when a power of attorney is given to secure an interest, or some obligation, to the donee, the consent of the donne is required for the authority to be revoked (Power of Attorney Act 1971, Article 4). An agency will only be truly irrevocable in the 2 above-mentioned circumstances. Failing this, the agency, even if described as irrevocable, will not be truly

ESTONIA: The parties can agree that the mandate contract cannot be terminated (other than termination for a fundamental breach). The principal may conclude the prospective contract himself even in the case of an irrevocable mandate, but the parties can agree otherwise.

FINLAND: In literature it is found that an irrevocable grant of authority would not be possible (Hemmo, Sopimusoikeus I, p. 514).

FRANCE: The rule entitling the parties to freely terminate the mandate or agency is a matter of mandatory public policy and the parties cannot validly agree that the agency is irrevocable. In practice, there are clauses in contracts entitled 'irrevocabilité', but these are interpreted as simply giving rise to compensation for the agent (Cass.civ. 1re, 5 February 2002, Bull. civ. 2002 I, no. 40), and do not prevent the principal from carrying out the transaction himself (Cass.civ. 1re, 16 June 1970, D. 1971, 261).

GERMANY: Under German law, which strictly distinguishes between the authority and the contractual relationship between agent and principal, the law of authority in CC Article 168 implicitly anticipates that the parties may exclude revocability of the authority. The courts have since long upheld this possibility (since RGZ 109, 333), but have also ruled that both the irrevocability of the authority and of the mandate contract are only admissible in cases in which the mandate relationship is not merely established in the interest of the principal, but also in the interest of the agent and those interests are as important *(gleichwertig)* as those of the principal (BGH, WM 1971, 956; Schramm, in: Münchener Kommentar zum BGB, Article 168 no. 21). If, on the contrary, the agent is only acting in the principal's interest, the revocability of the mandate cannot validly be excluded.

GREECE: In case of representation based on a contract of mandate an irrevocable mandate can be agreed on if the mandate also concerns the interest of the agent or of a third party (CC Article 724). According to CC Article 218 an irrevocable grant of a mandate can be agreed only if the mandate also concerns the interest of the agent or of a third party (Georgiadis/Stathopoulos/Doris, CC Article 218-221 no. 9). In such cases of irrevocable mandate a revocation from the part of the person represented is void and the agent is entitled to conclude the prospective contract for which the representation was granted (Supreme Court decision no. 197/1983, EEN 1983, 714). In the area of intellectual property rights there are specific rules with regard to the contracts entrusting the administration of copyright to an 'organisation of collective administration'. In such contracts an analogous application of the principal of free revocation of the mandate (CC Article 724) is not accepted. A free revocation does not comply with the nature of those contracts which require stability and continuance of the contractual relationships between the parties.

HUNGARY: CC Article 223 paragraph (2) establishes that '[a] mandate shall be valid until withdrawn, unless otherwise provided; its withdrawal that concerns a bona fide third person shall be operative only if he has been informed thereof. The right of withdrawal cannot be validly waived'. Concerning the contract of agency, CC Article 483 paragraph (4) establishes that '[a]ny limitation or exclusion of the right of cancellation shall be null and void; however, the parties shall be entitled to agree on the limitation of the right of cancellation with regard to continuous agencies'. In case of commission agency, CC Article 512 paragraph

(2) prescribes that '[a]ny limitation or exclusion of the right of rescission shall be null and void' (CA Pécsi Ítélőtábla Pf. III. 20.333/2004/4, in BDT2006. 1396). In general, the legal successor of the principal cannot terminate unilaterally a mandate post mortem (Supreme Court P. törv. II. 20 877/1982, in BH1983. 279).

IRELAND: An agency may be irrevocable where e.g. (i) the agent is given a 'power with an interest', that is, where an agent is given power and a personal interest, as where the principal owes the agent money, and appoints him act as his agent to sell property and thereby rise funds to pay the debt; or (ii) where a power of attorney is expressed to be 'enduring' or irrevocable under the Powers of Attorney Act 1996. It should be noted that regarding (i) where the agent is given 'power with an interest', that this is not a 'true' agency but agency being used as a device. In these cases it is intended that the agent use the 'power' not for the benefit of his principal but for his own benefit.

ITALY: The parties can validly agree that the contract cannot be cancelled (irrevocable mandate). However, also in this case the principal may revoke the mandate, but, unless there is a just cause, he shall be liable for damages vis-à-vis the agent (CC Article 1723(1)). A just cause for revocation may lie in malicious and negligent behaviour of the agent (CC Article 1218) or the fact that he does not respect the instructions received by the principal (CC Article 1711). Representation contracts which are also in the interest of the agent or of a third party *(in rem propriam)* are considered irrevocable *ex lege* (CC Article 1723 paragraph (2)).

MALTA: Although not specifically stated in Maltese law, there may be situations in which an irrevocable contract of mandate is agreed upon. This can be presumed from Maltese Jurisprudence. In fact for example, in CA (Civil) 29 October 1869, *Messina vs Mamo et.*, the Court stated that an irrevocable mandate in virtue of which the debtor grants his creditor the faculty to sell the former's property on the maturity of the debt, whether extra judicially or by a public auction, voluntarily or judicially, without the need of a judicial recognition, is valid by law and is not extinguished by the death of the debtor (principal). The Court dealt with the contract of mandate as a contractual obligation. Irrevocability ends when the raison d'etre of the contract for mandate has been accomplished. Under Maltese law there is no specific law provision that provides for such a circumstance.

NETHERLANDS: The parties may agree that the agent will act in the agent's own name and with exclusion of the principal's authority to act personally. If this is agreed, even as regards third parties the principal is not entitled to conclude the prospective contract; the exclusion of the principal's power to conclude the prospective contract can however only be invoked if the third party knew or should have known of the exclusion (CC Article 7:423 paragraph (1)). Specific provisions apply if the agent is an organisation which has as its statutory purpose to act on behalf of the joint interests of principals by exercising their rights collectively (CC Article 7:423 paragraph (2)). Such organisations exist specifically in the area of intellectual property rights.

POLAND: The principal's right to revoke the mandate contract may be limited but the principal will always retain the right to revoke the contract due to "important reasons" – CC Article 746 paragraph (3).

PORTUGAL: An irrevocable grant of authority is not possible under Portuguese law (CC Articles 265 paragraph (2) and 1170).

SCOTLAND: Scots law does recognise an irrevocable mandate, known as a procuratory *in rem suam* (e.g. Stair, I,12,8; Macgregor, paragraph 20; *Premier Briquette Co Ltd v Gray* 1922 SC 329). This concept applies where the agent has been granted authority to achieve an outcome in which he has an interest. This concept has benefited from very little analsysis, judicial or otherwise, in Scots law. It is described as 'absolute,' suggesting that it may not be revocable even in cases of material breach by the agent (Black, paragraph 551; Gow, p. 536). In cases where the agent has no interest in performance, there would seem to be nothing to prevent principal and agent from agreeing between themselves that the agency will be irrevocable.

SLOVAKIA: The principal may not validly waive the right to revoke the granted authority (CC paragraph 33b paragraph (3)) nor validly agree that the mandate contract may not be terminated; an irrevocable granting of authority is void.

SPAIN: The parties can validly agree on an irrevocable mandate (CC Article 1733; STS 31 October 1987; STS 11 May 1993, STS 19 November 1994; STS 20 July 1995; see also Hernández Gil, 514; Lete del Río, 414). However, even in this case the principal may revoke the mandate, but, unless there is a just cause, is liable for damages vis-à-vis the agent. Representation contracts which are also in the interest of the agent or of a third party *(in rem propriam)* are considered irrevocable (any purported revocation being ineffective) when the irrevocability serves the underlying protected interest as a device to reach the purpose intended by the parties (STS 20 April 1981, RJA 1981, 1658; STS 3 September 2007, STS RJ 2007/4709; STS 30 January 1999, RJA 1999, 331; Diez-Picazo, p. 305 ff; Gordillo, p. 1585).

SWEDEN: There are no rules on irrevocable grants of authority in Swedish contract law. A mandate contract is considered to be revocable in nature since the commission is a type of contract that rests on personal trust. An irrevocable grant of authority is, however, considered allowed to the extent it is due to another underlying legal relationship between the parties and aims at a determined part of the principal's financial sphere and circumstances, see Bengtsson, p. 154; Grönfors, p. 134. A general mandate can always be revoked.

Chapter 2:
Main obligations of the principal

Article 2:101: Obligation to co-operate

The obligation to co-operate under Article 1:202 PECL (Duty to co-operate) requires the principal in particular to:
(a) answer requests by the agent for information in so far as such information is needed to allow the agent to perform the obligations under the mandate contract;
(b) give a direction regarding the performance of the obligations under the mandate contract in so far as this is required under the mandate contract or follows from a request for a direction under Article 4:102 (Request for direction).

Comments

A. General idea

This provision is a specification of the general rule in Article 1:202 PECL (Duty to co-operate), which imposes on the parties an obligation to co-operate with each other when this can reasonably be expected for the performance of the other party's obligations. Under the present Article, the obligation to co-operate requires the principal, in particular, to provide the agent with information and directions to allow the agent to perform the obligations under the mandate contract.

B. Reasonable requests by agent for information

If the agent is required to negotiate the content of the prospective contract and ultimately to conclude it, he needs to know what the principal's intentions are. At some point, the principal therefore needs to inform the agent about his objectives, desires, and needs as regards the content of the prospective contract. If the principal does not communicate his preferences and priorities, the agent cannot properly perform the mandate contract. One question that arises is who is to take the initiative if the parties do not spontaneously exchange the necessary information. On the one hand, it would seem logical that this is the principal, as he commissions the agent to conclude the prospective contract. On the other hand, the principal may not always know what information the agent is in need of. Moreover, it frequently occurs that the principal is not aware of his preferences and priorities, as he is not aware of the consequences thereof. For these reasons, this Article does not impose on the principal an obligation to voluntarily provide information to the agent, but merely imposes an obligation on the principal to answer requests by the agent for information when it is reasonable to expect that such information will enable the agent to perform the obligations under the mandate contract. When the agent is in need of such information, he is required to request such information under Article 3:102 paragraph (2) (Obligation to act in interests of principal).

Illustration 1

Nigel, a real estate agent, is mandated to sell Marco's house. When inspecting the house with a potential buyer, Nigel notices that the walls appear to have sustained damage as a consequence of leakage. Nigel had not noticed this when he first examined the house, as a wardrobe that was later removed had stood directly in front of the wall. Nigel inquires whether the cause of the leakage has been taken away by Marco. Marco is required to answer, as the information is relevant for Nigel in performing his contract in case a buyer inquires about the leakage.

C. Failure to provide answers to request for information by agent

Under this Article, the principal is required to answer requests by the agent for information that the agent needs to properly perform his obligations under the mandate contract. A question that arises is what the consequences should be if the principal – for whatever reason – fails to answer such reasonable requests for information. If the principal is under a contractual *obligation* to answer the questions, the principal would then be in breach of his obligations and could be required to compensate the agent for any damage sustained as a result thereof (e.g. the loss of the profit of the performance of another contract, as the performance of this particular contract has taken more time than expected). Such an obligation is not recognised in most legal systems. This implies that in most legal systems, the 'duty' imposed on the principal is an *Obliegenheit* rather than an actual obligation. In contrast, a failure to answer reasonable questions for information leads to liability in BELGIUM and GREECE, implying that in these legal systems, the principal is indeed under an *obligation* to properly inform the agent.

In these Principles, the majority approach is followed. This implies that, in principle, the agent could resort to any of the remedies for non-performance, in particular to the right to ask for specific performance of this obligation, to withhold his own performance until he is properly informed, or even to terminate the mandate contract. It should be noted, however, that the mere fact that the principal does not perform his obligation under this Article does not necessarily entitle the agent to damages: under Articles 4:103 paragraph (1) (Consequences of failure to give a direction) and 4:104 paragraph (1) (No time to ask or wait for direction), the agent may be authorised – and, under the second Article, even required – to act. In so far as necessary, paragraphs (2) of both Articles also entitle the agent to a proportionate adjustment of the price and the time for performance of the contract. Rather than acting on the basis of these provisions, if the agent wishes to claim damages, he may be said not to have mitigated the loss, which would imply that (part of) the damage would remain for the account of the agent under Article 9:505 PECL (Reduction of loss).

D. Obligation to give directions

According to the present provision, the principal is obliged to provide directions to the agent as to the performance of the obligations under the mandate contract or the content of the prospective contract in two cases: when such an obligation is imposed in the mandate contract, and when the agent is obliged to ask for direction (as regulated in Article 4:102 paragraph (1) (Request for a direction). If the agent is obliged to ask for direction to find out the position of the principal on the issue pertaining to the performance of the obligations under the mandate contract or the content of the prospective contract, it is a logical consequence that the principal is obliged to answer such requests.

> *Illustration 2*
> Gabriela requests Susan to buy Peruvian artefacts from the Inca era from a particular seller in Madrid whose identity and address she will disclose only when Susan has arrived in Madrid. When Susan arrives at the Madrid airport, Gabriela is required to instruct her to whom she must turn to buy the artefacts.

> *Illustration 3*
> Andrew is charged by Benjamin to purchase 1,000 kilograms of wheat from a third party. At that time, they do not specify whether the wheat is to have quality A or quality B. When Andrew has found a seller of wheat and asks Andrew what quality of wheat he is to buy, Benjamin is required to give direction as to the quality of the wheat.

E. Relation to the Principles of European Law and the Draft Common Frame of Reference

This Article mirrors that of Article IV.D. – 2:101 DCFR (Obligation to co-operate). It builds on the more general rule of Article 1:202 PECL (Duty to co-operate).

F. Character of the Rule

This Article constitutes a default rule from which the parties may derogate.

G. Remedies

If the principal is under a contractual obligation to answer the requests of the agent, the failure to provide such answers would constitute a non-performance of the obligation. The principal could be required to compensate the agent for any damage sustained as a result (e.g. the loss of the profit of the performance of another contract, as the performance of this particular contract has taken more time than expected). However, such damages do not solve the agent's problem completely, as the agent does not know how to further perform the obligations. For this reason, Article 4:103 (Consequences of failure to give a direction) also allow the agent to base performance upon the expectations, preferences, and priorities the principal could reasonably expect to have. In so far as the principal's specific interests deviate from what the agent could otherwise expect, the agent cannot be expected to take them into account. Not taking these interests into account does not lead to non-performance of the obligations under the mandate contract by the agent. This therefore constitutes a defence for the agent.

Comparative Notes

1. Duty to inform agent when asked

In most legal systems it is common that both parties have a general duty to act in good faith or to provide the necessary co-operation to enable the other party to render its performance. In these legal systems, it is generally accepted that from these duties it follows that the principal must provide the agent with information if this information is necessary for the agent to fulfil his task. This is the case in AUSTRIA, BELGIUM, BULGARIA, DENMARK, ENGLAND, FINLAND, GREECE, HUNGARY, IRELAND, ITALY, MALTA, THE NETHERLANDS, PORTUGAL, SCOTLAND, SLOVAKIA, SPAIN, and SWEDEN. However, in most legal systems, the principal is not under a binding legal *obligation* to provide the information – leading to liability for breach of contract if the information is not provided – but (merely) under a duty to do so – leading to the application of the doctrine of *mora creditoris* if the principal fails to provide the information.

In BULGARIA and FINLAND, the principal may even be required to provide the agent with information without being asked. The same may be true for ITALY, but not for a consumer contract.

In FRANCE, an obligation for the principal to provide the information does not exist in 'normal' contracts or in consumer contracts, but such an obligation does exist for commercial mandate contracts. In such commercial mandate contracts, the principal may even be required to volunteer information.

There is no obligation to inform the agent in GERMANY, even upon a request for information, but a failure to answer questions would prevent the agent from taking (some of) the interests of the principal into account. Any claim by the principal for non-performance by the agent because the agent failed to take such interests into account is barred, however. It therefore seems that the difference between the GERMAN law and the law in most other legal systems is not as large as it may at first glance seem to be.

2. Consequences of failure to inform agent

When the principal has not provided the agent with the necessary information for the agent to perform the mandate contract, the principal may not invoke a remedy for non-performance – or such a remedy is at least restricted – in AUSTRIA, BULGARIA, DENMARK, ENGLAND, ESTONIA, FINLAND, FRANCE, GERMANY, GREECE, IRELAND, ITALY, MALTA, THE NETHERLANDS, POLAND, PORTUGAL, SCOTLAND, and SPAIN.

The agent is required to warn the principal of the consequences of a failure to provide him with the necessary information in AUSTRIA, DENMARK, and HUNGARY. Such a duty may also exist in ESTONIA. Such an obligation does not exist in FRANCE and SLOVAKIA. In GREECE, a duty to warn exists only in the case of a remunerated mandate between a lawyer and his principal, but not in other mandate relationships. In ITALY, a general duty to warn the principal does not exist, but such a duty may apply if the principal is a consumer.

In certain cases in BELGIUM, FINLAND, SPAIN, and SWEDEN, the agent may claim damages if the principal fails to provide the necessary information. In GREECE, the agent may withhold performance until the principal provides the necessary information. In SLOVAKIA, the agent may terminate the contract for fundamental non-performance, but he must inform the principal and, as a general rule, award a last chance to provide the information after all.

National Notes

1. Duty to inform agent when asked

AUSTRIA: Each party to the contract for mandate is to act dutifully and in good faith. The principal is to provide the agent (commercial; Griss, Article 384 Rz 5; forwarder: Krejci, 308) with the necessary documentation relating to the goods concerned. He has to inform the agent of the content of the prospective contract to be negotiated and to obtain for the agent any information necessary for the performance of the contract for mandate. The principal is thus required to volunteer information, independent of the principal being a consumer or entrepreneur.

BELGIUM: The principal is required to inform the agent, if this information is necessary to fulfil his mission. Like every other party to a contract, the principal is bound by a duty to execute the contract in good faith (CC Article 1134 paragraph (3)) and more specifically to a duty of collaboration. A specific application of the duty of collaboration is the duty to enable the agent to fulfil his mission. This entails the obligation to hand over all information and all documents necessary to fulfil the mission (Wéry, p. 220).

BULGARIA: According to Bulgarian legal writings, the principal has the right to give directions to the agent for the performance of the mandate contract (Любен Василев, Облигационно право, p. 24; Голева, Облигационно право, p. 237). In the general rules about the mandate contract (OCA Article 280-292), there is no explicit provision imposing on the principal an obligation to give, neither on his own initiative nor under the request of the other party, information or directions to the agent in the course of performing the mandate contract. Hence, the general rules about the performance of the obligations are applicable. Firstly, it is required that each of the parties has to perform its contractual obligations in conformity with good faith and not to obstruct the other party from performing its obligations in the same manner (OCA Article 63 paragraph (1)). As far as information and directions from the principal are necessary for the proper performance of the obligations of the agent, the principal has to give such co-operation. Having failed to provide the necessary assistance without which the agent, as a debtor, is unable to perform his obligations, the principal, as a creditor, breaches his duty to co-operate. This is a case of mora creditoris (Забава на кредитора), cf. OCA Article 95. A duty to give all relevant information regarding the performance of the agent's obligations is explicitly provided only for the principal-merchant towards the agent-commercial agent, cf. CA Article 34 paragraph (1) (Герджиков, Коментар на Търговския закон, I, p. 159; Касабова, ТП, 2006, p. 163). This obligation to give information and directions is imposed on the principal-merchant regardless of the relevant request of the other party.

DENMARK: Under a rule covering all types of civil contracts, the principal, prior to the conclusion of the contract of representation, is required to inform the agent of his interest and needs as regards the proper performance of the contract or the content of the prospective contract to be negotiated or concluded by the agent. If the principal fails to fulfil this basic obligation, the agent will not be liable for damage caused by the negligence on the part of the principal. The principal must spontaneously provide the agent with all necessary information.

ENGLAND: When the principal appoints an agent, the principal wants the agent to perform certain tasks. The needs and the interests of the principal will be apparent from such tasks and the instructions the principal will have given the agent pursuant to the contract (actual express authority). The instructions of the principal must be as precise as possible. There is a distinction between contractual and non-contractual agents. When the agency is contractual, the agent is under an obligation to carry out the instructions that the principal has given him as to the performance of the required tasks. When the principal gives clear and unambiguous instructions, the agent must perform such instructions as defined or be liable for breach of contract *(Turpin v Bilton* (1843) 5 Man & G 455). If the principal fails to give the agent clear and unambiguous instructions, the agent will not be liable if he acts fairly and honestly on a reasonable interpretation of the instructions and the principal will be bound by his interpretation even if such interpretation was not the one the principal envisaged *(Ireland v Livingston* (1872) LR 5 HL 395). However, nowadays, because it is much easier to communicate, there is probably a duty on the agent to obtain clarification of instructions *(Woodhouse AC Israel Cocoa Ltd SA v Nigerian Produce Marketing Co Ltd* ([1972] AC 741). If that is the case, it seems that the principal is not required to volunteer information but must do so when asked by the agent. When the agency is not contractual, the agent is consequently under no duty to act, so he cannot be liable if he does nothing. However, his failure to act may give rise to a liability in tort *(Hedley Byrne & Co Ltd v Heller & Partners Ltd* ([1964] AC 465; *White v Jones* [1995] 2 AC 207; *Henderson v Merrett Syndicates Ltd* [1995] 2 AC 145).

ESTONIA: The law does not contain a specific rule, which stipulates that the principal, prior to the conclusion of the contract, is required to inform the agent of his interests and needs as regards the performance of the contract. The agent is under a general duty to act in the best interest of the principal.

FINLAND: It is a general principle that a party has a duty of disclosure before entering into a contract. The principal ought to give sufficient information to the agent in order to ensure that he is able to complete his contractual performance in the required way (ACRS Article 8). It depends on the circumstances whether the information should be given voluntarily or not (e.g. which of the parties knows the area of activity better). When the principal is a consumer, the agent is generally required to investigate the interests and needs of the principal more on his own initiative than in pure business relations.

FRANCE: There is no specific obligation on the principal to provide information under the law, whether spontaneously or at the request of the agent. The same principles apply under the Civil Code and under consumer law, except with regard to the relationship between the commercial agent and the principal, which is 'subject to an obligation of fair dealing and a reciprocal duty of information. The commercial agent shall perform its mandate as a proper professional, and the principal shall enable the commercial agent to perform its mandate' (Comm.C Article L.134-4). Otherwise, the law contains no specific obligations for the principal to spontaneously provide information.

GERMANY: The principal is not required to inform – either when asked or spontaneously – the agent of his interests and needs as regards the performance of the contract or the content of the prospective contract to be negotiated or concluded by the agent. However, as the agent only has to take into account interests of the principal that he can be aware of, he takes the risk that the contract concluded/arranged will not meet his (hidden) interests. The principal would to that extent be barred from claiming non-performance by the agent. However, the agent can be under an obligation to warn the principal. In German case law, such obligations have been assumed in expertise cases, in particular where relationships between banks and their customers were involved.

GREECE: In case of a contract of mandate, good faith requires that the principal informs the agent of his interests and needs regarding the performance of the mandate. If he fails to do so, the principal cannot claim a deviation from the limits set in the mandate (CC Article 717). The principal can either provide information voluntarily or when he is asked to do so.

HUNGARY: The clear consent of the agent requires that he has the necessary information about the interests and needs as regards the performance of the contract or the content of the prospective contract to be negotiated or concluded. In this sense, CC Article 205 paragraph (2) establishes that '[i]t is fundamental to the validity of a contract that an agreement is reached by the parties concerning all essential issues as well as those deemed essential by either of the parties. The parties need not agree on issues that are regulated by statutory provisions'. Moreover, the parties are under the obligation to cooperate, including the obligation to inform each other of all important circumstances affecting performance of the contract (CC Article 277 paragraphs (4) and (5)). On the basis of CC Article 474 paragraph (2), '[a]n agent must fulfil the agency according to the instructions and interests of the principal'. Naturally, the agent cannot be liable for the failures and damages caused by the lack of information that the principal should have given, but according to CC Article 476, '[i]f the principal issues imprudent or incompetent instructions, the agent shall call the principal's attention to the matter. If the principal insists on the instructions despite the warning, he shall be liable for the damages sustained on account of the instructions'.

IRELAND: At common law, there is no express duty to inform placed on principals however, an agent is required to follow the lawful instructions of his principal. It has been held that where instructions are ambiguous an agent will not be held liable where he acts on a reasonable interpretation of the instructions (*Ireland v Livingstone* (1872) LR 5 HL 395), though an agent should seek clarification, where possible (*Woodhouse AC Israel Cocoa Ltd SA v Nigerian Produce Marketing Co Ltd* [1972] AC 741 at 772 per Lord Salmon; *European Asian Bank AG v Punjab & Sind Bank* [1983] 2 All ER 508 at 517 per Goff LJ).

ITALY: Under the provisions regulating the mandate there are no specific rules governing the principal's duty to inform the agent of his interests and needs, whether he should volunteer information or whether he has a duty to answer when he is asked. However, on the basis of CC Article 1719 ('In the absence of an agreement to the contrary, the principal is bound to furnish the principaly with the means necessary to perform the mandate and to fulfil the obligations which the principaly has undertaken in his own name') it can be argued that the principal has to provide to the agent all relevant information which is necessary for the execution of the mandate. With respect to the more specific issue concerning the existence of a duty of information prior to the conclusion of the contract, it should be noted that the general rules of the Civil Code on precontractual liability apply also to representation agreements. According to CC Article 1337, 'the parties, in the conduct of negotiations and the formation of the contract, shall conduct themselves according to good faith'; in addition, according to the general clause of good faith, '[t]he debtor and the creditor shall behave according to rules of fairness' (CC Article 1175). Furthermore, CC Article 1338 provides that 'a party who knows or should know the existence of a reason for invalidity of the contract and does not give notice to the other party is bound to compensate for the damages suffered by the latter in relying, without fault, on the validity of the contract'. There are no particular rules of consumer protection on this specific issue; however, if the principal is a consumer his position will be evaluated differently by the courts. Since the consumer may not be in a position to establish what information is relevant for the agent (a professional) in order to perform the mandate (information asymmetries), it is mostly the agent who has a duty to inquire as to the exact interests of the principal.

MALTA: Although such a requirement is not amongst the obligations of the principal under Maltese law, it is presumed that the principal is required to answer the requests for information by the agent.

NETHERLANDS: According to literature, the principal may be obliged to provide the agent with information which is necessary to perform the mandate contract. A specific duty of the principal to inform the agent lacks, however. Usually, the contracting parties will agree in the individual mandate contract on the principal's duty to inform the agent. Furthermore, according to reasonableness and fairness, the principal may have certain duties to inform the agent.

POLAND: The Polish CC contains no specific rules on the principal's duty to provide information to the agent.

PORTUGAL: According to CC Article 1167 lit (a), the principal has a duty to supply the agent with the necessary information so that the agent can carry out the mandate, unless the parties stipulated otherwise. The duty of the principal to correctly inform the agent of his interests concerning the mandate is covered by this provision.

SCOTLAND: In Scots law the principal is subject to very few duties towards the agent, in contrast to the numerous duties which the agent must fulfil towards the principal. At common law, there is no general duty on the principal to act towards the agent in good faith (although such a duty will apply in situations of commercial agency governed by the Commercial Agents (Council Directive) Regulations 1993 (SI 1993/3053, regulation 4 paragraph (1)). Whilst no obvious expression of the principal's duties at common law exists, individual duties are identifiable in the case-law concerning the agent's duty of care (Macgregor, paragraph 87). Thus, a delay by the principal in giving instructions, or the giving of defective instructions constitutes a breach of the agent/principal contract which will result in the principal losing the right to damages from the agent for defective performance *(Mackenzie v Blakeney* (1879) 6 R 1329). Looked at from the principal's perspective, this could constitute a duty imposed on him to provide clear instructions.

SLOVAKIA: According to the General Law of obligations, the principal is in default when contrary to the contract he fails to cooperate with the agent to enable the latter's performance. Comm.C Article 568 paragraph (2), which applies to a commercial mandate contract, contains a similar provision.

SPAIN: The principal has to determine how the mandate is to be performed by giving the directions and instructions which the principal deems necessary for the successful performance of the mandate (Lasarte, p. 346). Beyond that there are no rules as to the duty to inform the agent. Properly speaking, the mandate is a unilateral contract and the principal's obligations only arise as indemnity duties when the contract is ended (CC Articles 1728 and 1729). This basic scheme is modified where the agent acts on a commercial basis. In this case, the general rules on bilateral contracts apply. Accordingly, the duty to inform should be deduced from the general duty to act in good faith (CC Article 1258).

SWEDEN: The principal has a duty to be loyal and co-operate with the agent. This includes a duty to answer requests for information in order for the agent to be able to perform according to the contract. The scope of this duty is somewhat uncertain due to lack of precedents (see HaL Article 7; Hesser, p. 64; Ramberg, p. 246; Hellner, p. 114).

2. Consequences of failure to inform agent

AUSTRIA: Due to his duty of care, the principal is to obtain for the agent the information necessary for the performance of the mandate contract. If the principal fails to inform the agent thereof, he cannot argue a non-performance of the agent. The agent is required to warn the principal for such consequence.

BELGIUM: If the agent is not able to fulfil his mission because of a lack of information, he can claim damages (in general: Wéry, p. 224).

BULGARIA: When the agent, in order to perform his contractual obligations, needs information or directions from the principal, the latter has a duty to co-operate. This is not an actual obligation, which can be enforced, but rather a legal burden (Тежест, Obliegenheit) for assistance. Therefore if the principal does not assist, either voluntarily or under the request, there is no breach of contractual obligation, but a case of mora creditoris – OCA Article 95 (Голева, Облигационно право, p. 110; Апостолов, Облигационно право, p. 331). In such a case, the agent can terminate the contract and claim the expenses due to mora creditoris – OCA Article 98 (Голева, Облигационно право, p. 111; Кожухаров, Облигационно право I, p. 352; Supreme Court, Judgment No.209, 4 July 1999).

DENMARK: It is part of the principal's obligation towards the agent to answer a request for information by the agent. In carrying out this obligation the principal must act in accordance with good faith and fair dealing. If non-performance of the contract is due to failure of the principal to provide information, the agent cannot be held responsible. The agent must warn the principal of such consequences. However, the consequences will mostly appear when it comes to an evaluation of the prospective contract.

ENGLAND: The principal must answer the requests for information by the agent. Should the principal fail to answer such queries, then the agent will not be liable for any consequences following such failures, or for the reasonable interpretations the agent has made of the instructions.

ESTONIA: If the principal's failure to answer the request of the agent to give information as to the principal's interests leads to negative consequences for the principal, the principal will most likely not be in a position to argue that the agent is in breach of its duties and has not performed with the normal diligence. Moreover, even if the court would conclude that the agent had breach his obligations, the agent may possibly avoid liability as it can claim that the breach is attributable to the principal (LOAEst Article 101 paragraph (3)). Whether a duty to warn exists can only be determined according to the specifics of the case.

FINLAND: If the principal fails to inform the agent, the omission may reduce or eliminate the agent's liability in cases where the prospective contract (or the performance of the agent otherwise) does not correspond to the (undisclosed) needs of the principal. Further, if the agent suffers losses due to the non-disclosure of the principal, the agent may be entitled to damages (including loss of profit where the mandate contract is valid).

FRANCE: The law is silent on the consequences of a failure to provide information, but it is undoubtedly the case that a refusal to reply to questions raised by the agent would exclude the liability of the agent where the mandate failed or was improperly performed. The agent could, however, remain liable to any third party contractor (see Cass.civ. 1re, 13 November 1997, Bull. civ. 1997 I, no. 308). There is no obligation for the agent to inform the principal of the consequences of the refusal to provide the information requested.

GERMANY: As the agent only has to take into account those interests of the principal that he can be aware of, it lies in the principal's best interest to provide all necessary information to the agent. Should he fail to do so and the contract concluded/arranged does not meet his (hidden) interests, the principal is insofar barred from claiming non-performance by the agent.

GREECE: If the principal does not provide information although he is asked to do so, the agent has the right to deny performance of the mandate and the principal is placed under notice according to CC Article 351 (Georgiadis/Stathopoulos/Karasis III, CC Article 713 no. 19). Furthermore, the principal is not entitled due to his failure to provide information to claim a deviation from the limits set in the mandate (CC Article 717). The agent is not required to warn the principal of such consequences. However, in case of the obligatory remunerated mandate between a lawyer and a principal, good faith (CC Article 288) requires the lawyer to warn his principal of the consequences.

HUNGARY: In the case of failure to provide information, the general rules of obligations apply, especially CC Article 277 paragraphs (4) and (5), which places the parties under an obligation to co-operate in the performance of contractual obligations, including the obligation to inform each other of all important circumstances affecting performance. Co-operation is especially important in the case of agency, as CC Article 477 paragraphs (1) and (2) provide that '[t]he agent shall inform his principal of his activities and the state of affairs upon request or, if necessary, even without a request, particularly if employment of another person has become necessary or if the instructions need to be changed due to the occurrence of new circumstances. The agent shall be entitled to depart from the principal's instructions only if it is essential for the principal's interest and if there is no time to notify the principal in advance. In such a case the principal shall be notified without delay'. Furthermore, according to CC Article 476, '[i]f the principal issues imprudent or incompetent instructions, the agent shall call the principal's attention to the matter. If the principal insists on the instructions despite the warning, he shall be liable for the damages sustained on account of the instructions'.

IRELAND: While there is no express duty to inform placed on principals, it has been held that where a principal fails to answer queries from the agent, the agent will not be liable for any consequences following such failures, or for the reasonable interpretations the agent has made of the instructions from the principal *(Ireland v Livingstone* (1872) LR 5 HL 395).

ITALY: The principal is required to answer requests for information by the agent on the basis of the good faith principle and on the basis of the duty of cooperation between the parties to a contract. If the principal fails to answer such requests he is barred from eventually seeking damages against the agent if the damage could have been prevented, had the principal responded to the agent's requests of information. In general terms, the agent is not required to warn the principal of such consequences. However, if the principal is a consumer, the agent has a more intensive duty to investigate the principal's interests, which would often mean that if the principal neglects to answer to the first request, the agent would ask for the required information again and eventually warn the principal of the consequences of his silence (usually in the form of a 'disclaimer').

MALTA: The general principle is that it is the agent who must keep the principal informed of the progress and causes of the contract, and that he should ask clarifications when needed. Therefore it may be presumed that if the agent asks for information to the principal and the principal fails to give such information, the agent would not be held liable for negligence or damages if the contract is not concluded in the manner the principal would have wanted.

NETHERLANDS: The principal does not have a strict duty to inform the agent. However, he may be obliged to provide the agent with information which is necessary to perform the mandate contract. It seems that if the non-performance of the mandate contract by the agent is due to the principal's failure to provide information, the agent is not liable for this non-performance.

POLAND: If the agent may not carry out the contract because the principal refuses to reveal required information the agent who fails to carry out the service will not be liable for the breach of contract.

PORTUGAL: If the principal does not supply the agent with the necessary information so that the mandate can carry out the mandate, the agent can withhold performance of his duties until the principal discharges his duty (CC Article 1168). Moreover, in such a case the possible liability of the agent vis-à-vis the principal can be reduced or excluded.

SCOTLAND: A delay by the principal in the provision of instructions, or the giving of defective instructions, constitutes a breach of the principal/agent contract, which will result in the principal losing the right to damages from the agent for defective performance *(Mackenzie v Blakeney* (1879) 6 R 1329).

SLOVAKIA: In mandate contract covered by civil law, the agent can ask compensation for damages (e.g. compensation of price when the payment of the price is bound to the achievement of the principal's expected result). He may also always terminate the contract. The agent is not required to warn the principal for such consequences. In commercial relations, the agent may demand the performance of obligation from principal, he is entitled to demand from creditor in default compensation for damages. As for possibility to terminate the contract he may to do so only in instances stipulated by the contract or by the law. In such events we should differ where the principal's default constitutes a fundamental breach of a contractual obligation. If the breach is deemed fundamental according to the definition stipulated in the Comm.C, the agent can terminate the contract provided that after having learned of such breach, he informs the delinquent party without undue delay. He has the possibility finish to contract by repudiation,

SPAIN: The natural consequence of the principal's failure to provide information is that the agent is not liable for any harm suffered by the principal as a result of the principal's own failure to provide information.

Where the mandate is a bilateral contract, and the agent has an economic interest in carrying out the affair and being paid, damages may be appropriate.

SWEDEN: If the principal fails to answer a request for information from the agent and the agent suffers damage due to this fact such failure could amount to a non-performance for which the principal could be liable to pay damages to the agent unless the principal can show that the failure is not due to negligence on his part (HaL Article 34).

Article 2:102: Price

(1) The principal must pay a price if the agent performs the obligations under the mandate contract in the course of a business, unless the principal expected and could reasonably have expected the agent to perform the obligations otherwise than in exchange for a price.

(2) The price is payable when the mandated task has been completed and the agent has given account of that to the principal.

(3) If the parties had agreed on payment of a price for services rendered, the mandate relationship has terminated and the mandated task has not been completed, the price is payable as of the moment the agent has given account of the performance of the obligations under the mandate contract.

(4) When the mandate is for the conclusion of a prospective contract and the principal has concluded the prospective contract directly or another person appointed by the principal has concluded the prospective contract on the principal's behalf, the agent is entitled to the price or a proportionate part of it if the conclusion of the prospective contract can be attributed in full or in part to the agent's performance of the obligations under the mandate contract.

(5) When the mandate is for the conclusion of a prospective contract and the prospective contract is concluded after the mandate relationship has terminated, the principal must pay the price if payment of a price based solely on the conclusion of the prospective contract was agreed and
  (a) the conclusion of the prospective contract is mainly the result of the agent's efforts; and
  (b) the prospective contract is concluded within a reasonable period after the mandate relationship has terminated.

Comments

A. General idea

This Article provides that a professional agent is normally entitled to a price for his services, even if the parties neglected to explicitly regulate the matter. This does not apply, however, if it can be proved that the principal expected the contract to be gratuitous and that it was reasonable in the circumstances to think so. Paragraph (2) further provides that, as a default rule, payment of the price is due only after the mandated task (e.g. the conclusion of a prospective contract) has been completed and the agent has informed the principal thereof and given account in accordance with Article 3:402 paragraph (1) (Accounting to the principal).

Paragraph (3) regulates the payment of the price if the agent has not managed to complete the mandated task during the mandate relationship but the parties have agreed on a payment for services rendered. Such payment is due when the agent has given account to the principal in accordance with Article 3:402 paragraphs (1) and (2) (Accounting to the principal).

Paragraphs (4) and (5) concern the consequences of the right to payment for the agent when, despite the efforts made by the agent in concluding the prospective contract, it is eventually concluded by the principal or another agent appointed by the principal. Under paragraph (4), the prospective contract is concluded during performance of the mandate contract, whereas under paragraph (5) the prospective contract is concluded when the mandate relationship is no longer in force. Paragraph (4) indicates that the agent retains the right to be paid, whether fully or partially, if the conclusion of the prospective contract can be attributed in full or in part to the agent's performance of the obligations under the mandate contract. Under paragraph (5) the agent has to show that the contract was mainly the result of the agent's efforts. In addition, the contract must have been concluded within a reasonable period after the relationship is terminated.

B. Price for professional party

Traditionally, the mandate relationship was considered to be of a gratuitous nature. However, the gratuitous nature is no longer self-evident in modern practice. Especially where professional agents are involved, the performance of the mandate – i.e. the service the agent provides – is normally for a price nowadays. This provision in the first half of paragraph (1) reflects the normal situation in practice: an agent who has entered the mandate contract in a professional capacity is entitled to payment, unless the parties have agreed otherwise.

C. Unless principal may reasonably expect no charge

Paragraph (1), however, also provides an exception to the normal rule. No price will be payable if the principal expected the agent to perform the contract gratuitously and it was indeed reasonable to have such an expectation.

Illustration 1
A hotel in Amsterdam informs its guests that it may arrange a tour to the flower exhibition at the *Keukenhof,* mentioning the ticket price but not indicating any price for its service. Steven, a guest at the hotel, thinks the hotel arranges the ticket for free (just as a service) and was not advised otherwise. Even though the hotel is acting in its professional capacity, it is rather common that these services are offered free of charge,

unless the hotel explicitly mentions the opposite. Under these conditions, Steven could reasonably expect that the hotel would be willing to perform this service gratuitously because it is interested in getting positive reports from guests or has hopes of being able to sell other (paid) services.

D. Calculation of price

If the parties explicitly agree upon a price, they will normally also have determined how the price is to be calculated. If they have neglected to regulate the matter, or if they have not explicitly agreed upon a price, but the agent entered the contract in the performance of his business or profession and is entitled to a price, the question arises how this price is to be calculated. This matter is solved by Article 6:104 PECL (Determination of price). Under the PECL, the principal is then required to pay 'a reasonable price'.

Illustration 2
The hotel offering to arrange a tour to the flower exhibition at the *Keukenhof* indicates that 'a service fee' will be charged without indicating how the service fee is calculated. In this case, under the PECL the hotel could only charge a reasonable fee. This would seem to imply that the hotel can charge its ordinary price for such services, provided that the price is reasonable in the circumstances of the case.

E. When the price is payable

Under Articles 7:102 paragraph (3) PECL (Time of performance), when the parties have not agreed differently, performance of an obligation, and therefore also payment by the principal, is due 'within a reasonable time after the conclusion of the contract'. This does not give the parties much guidance in the case of a mandate relationship, which may – but does not always – imply that the agent is to perform the obligations within a certain period of time. In fact, many mandate relationships are long-term contracts, or their performance by the agent may at least take some time, if it is successful at all. This implies that the normal rule of Article 7:102 paragraph (3) PECL (Time of performance) may not provide a proper answer to the question when payment should be due. Paragraph (2) deals with this particular matter.

In theory, at least the three following alternatives to the rule in Article 7:102 paragraph (3) PECL (Time of performance) are imaginable. Each of these alternatives is accepted in at least one European legal system. First, the price could be due when the agent has performed his main obligations under the mandate contract, i.e. after the prospective contract has been concluded. This is the present rule in most European legal systems. Second, the price could also become due only after the agent has successfully performed his main obligations under the mandate contract and also given an account of that. This has the advantage that it provides a good incentive for the agent to give an account of the way he performed the contract, because he will not get paid otherwise. By requiring him to give an account first, the principal would be enabled to evaluate whether the agent has properly performed his obligations under the contract. This solution is accepted in BELGIUM, FINLAND, and ITALY, and also in SWEDEN if an obligation to give an account exists in the circumstances of the case. A third option, which is accepted in ENGLAND and, with restrictions, also in IRELAND and probably in SCOTLAND, would be that the price becomes due only after the prospective contract has been concluded and the agent proves that he was the effective cause of the conclusion of the prospective contract. This option would imply that the agent is only then entitled to a price if he concluded the prospective contract or at least was involved in its conclusion, and he is able to prove that. This would mean that the agent would not be entitled to payment for his services if the principal himself concludes the contract with the third party (unless the parties agreed that the agent would also then be entitled to payment). There is case law in IRELAND, however, where the principal is nevertheless required to pay the agent in this situation.

Paragraph (2) of this Article follows the rule that is accepted in BELGIUM, FINLAND, ITALY, and SWEDEN. Even though this is the minority view in Europe, the choice for such a rule seems justified because it would best satisfy the justified interests of both parties. In this respect, one should take into account that the agent is in any case required to give an account of the performance of his obligations and to indicate to the principal that his efforts have resulted in the conclusion of the prospective contract. By linking the moment when payment becomes due to the moment when an account is given of the conclusion of the prospective contract, the agent has a clear incentive to give an account as soon as possible. A rapid account thereof minimises the risk that the principal would conclude a similar contract himself and therefore the risk of a future non-performance towards one of the other parties. Moreover, the chosen rule has the benefit of establishing a clear-cut moment for the price becoming due that is clear to both parties because the parties have been in contact with each other. This rule therefore stimulates communication between the parties most optimally.

F. When the price is payable for services rendered in case of termination

If the parties had agreed upon payment of a price for services rendered, the agent is also entitled to payment if the mandate relationship has terminated but the mandated task has not been completed (e.g. a prospective contract is ultimately not concluded). In such a case, the agent has already rendered some services. In that case, paragraph (3) provides that the price is payable when the agent has given account of what has been done in the performance of the obligations under the mandate contract under Article 3:402 paragraph (3) (Accounting to the principal).

This solution is considered justified because it best satisfies the interests of both parties. It provides a good incentive for the agent to give an account of the way the mandate has been carried out, as no fee will be due otherwise. Requiring the agent to give an account first means that the principal is able to evaluate whether the agent has properly performed the obligations under the contract. Moreover, this rule has the benefit of establishing a moment when the price becomes due that is clear to both parties because the parties have been in contact with each other. This rule therefore stimulates communication between the parties.

G. Price when prospective contract is not concluded by agent

When the mandate is for the conclusion of a prospective contract, paragraph (4) deals with whether the agent is entitled to be paid if the prospective contract is concluded by the principal personally or by another agent in contracts in which no exclusivity was granted to the agent. In this situation, the mandate contract may be terminated by the agent under Article 6:105 (Termination by agent for extraordinary and serious reason), as in such a case it will usually become impossible or unreasonably difficult for the agent to (also) conclude the prospective contract. Moreover, the possibility for the principal to conclude the prospective contract himself also constitutes a serious reason for the principal to terminate the mandate contract himself under Article 6:103 (Termination by principal for extraordinary and serious reason). In both of these cases, as the parties had not agreed on exclusivity, the principal was well within his right to conclude the prospective contract, and no damages are due. However, under paragraph (4) of the present Article, the agent may be entitled to payment of the price or a part thereof for the services rendered if and in so far as the services rendered have contributed to the conclusion of the prospective contract.

Illustration 3
Simon mandates Lloyd, an agent, to sell Simon's car. Lloyd negotiates with a third party, but the third party refuses the offer made by Lloyd. The third party then contacts Simon directly and they conclude the sales contract. In this case, as the services of Lloyd have undoubtedly contributed to the conclusion of the sales contract, Simon would be entitled to the price (in full or in part).

Illustration 4
Donovan is charged by Evelyne to purchase a specific painting by Renoir. The painting is being sold at an auction in Paris, whereas both Donovan and Evelyne are located in London. Donovan attends the auction, to be told only during the auction that the painting has already been sold. Upon his return to London, he learns that Evelyne had already bought the painting before Donovan travelled to Paris, but had neglected to inform him thereof. Unless agreed otherwise, Donovan is not entitled to payment for his services under Article 2:102 paragraph (4) (Price) as his services did not contribute to the purchase of the painting. Donovan will be entitled to reimbursement of his travel expenses under Article 2:103 (Expenses incurred by agent). Moreover, the parties may have agreed – either expressly or tacitly – that Donovan would also receive a price if Evelyne bought the painting herself.

H. Price if prospective contract is concluded after termination, but is mainly the result of the efforts of the agent

Paragraph (5) deals with the situation where (a) the mandate is for the conclusion of a prospective contract, (b) the principal's obligation to pay arises only on the conclusion of the prospective contract ('no result, no fee', also called 'no cure, no pay' or contingency fee), (c) the mandate relationship is terminated and (d) the principal or somebody acting on the principal's behalf subsequently concludes the prospective contract. In this situation, the agent retains the right to payment if the contract concluded was mainly the result of the agent's efforts in the performance of the mandate, and if it is concluded within a reasonable time after the mandate relationship is terminated.

In this type of contract, there is a substantial risk that the principal will try to evade the obligation to pay by terminating the mandate relationship just before the principal concludes the prospective contract. To protect the interests of the agent, the principal should in principle be required to pay the price even though the mandate relationship was already terminated before the prospective contract was concluded. On the other hand, it does not seem fair to require the principal, under all circumstances, to pay the full price if the agent did not conclude the prospective contract after all. Therefore, the obligation to pay remains only when certain conditions are fulfilled, i.e. that the conclusion of the contract is *mainly* the result of the agent's efforts and that the contract is concluded within a reasonable period after the mandate relationship has terminated. This is therefore a balanced solution where the interests of both the agent and the principal are safeguarded.

Illustration 5
Frank has commissioned Niels to sell his house on the basis of 'no result, no fee'. Niels places an ad in the local newspaper and on the Internet. Linda sees the ad on the Internet and contacts Niels, who subsequently negotiates the conclusion of the prospective contract with Linda. Before the prospective contract is finally concluded, Frank gives notice of termination of the mandate relationship and then concludes the prospective contract. As the conclusion of the prospective contract here was predominantly caused by the services of Niels, he is entitled to payment, even though the mandate relationship had already terminated.

Illustration 6
Frank has commissioned Niels to sell his house on the basis of 'no cure no fee'. Niels places an ad in the local newspaper and on the Internet. Linda sees the ad on the Internet and contacts Frank, who subsequently terminates the mandate relationship and, after negotiations, concludes the prospective contract with Linda. If Frank and Niels have not agreed otherwise, Niels is not entitled to payment as he did provide some services beneficial to the conclusion of the prospective contract, but his actions were not important enough to have predominantly caused the conclusion of the prospective contract.

Illustration 7
Regina mandates Leo to sell her car. The parties agree that Leo will receive a price for his services only if he succeeds in selling the car on Regina's behalf. Leo negotiates with a third party and comes to an agreement, subject to approval by Regina. Regina does not give the approval, terminates the mandate relationship, and subsequently concludes the sales contract on (almost) the same terms with the third party. In this case, Regina is required to pay Leo the agreed price for his services.

Illustration 8
Regina mandates Leo to sell her car. They agree on a mandate contract with a duration of three months. Leo negotiates with a third party and comes to an agreement, subject to approval by Regina. Regina waits until the three-month period has ended and subsequently concludes the sales contract on (almost) the same terms with the third party. Again, Regina would be required to pay Leo the agreed price for his services.

In all of these cases, it is clear that the principal terminated the contractual relationship (Illustrations 5-7) or waited for the fixed date to expire (Illustration 8) to prevent the agent from concluding the contract with the third party. Under paragraph (5) of this Article, the agent would nevertheless be entitled to payment of the price.

Illustration 9
Regina mandates Leo to sell her car. Leo negotiates with a third party. Regina, not satisfied with the progress Leo makes, terminates the mandate relationship and appoints another agent, Chris. Chris successfully ends the negotiations with the same third party and concludes the sales contract. In this case, Leo's efforts as the first agent contributed to the conclusion of the prospective contract, but they did not mainly result in the conclusion of the contract with the third party: the services of the second agent (Chris) were equally necessary. In this case, the agent is not entitled to payment of the price.

This implies that where the agent performed services that contributed to the conclusion of the prospective contract, but that conclusion is not *mainly* the result of the agent's actions, he will not receive payment. This appears to be a slightly stricter rule than currently exists in most legal systems, where a payment proportionate to the services rendered is due if the former agent shows that the prospective contract was concluded as a result of his efforts.

I. Relation with exclusivity

The situation described in paragraph (4) is to be differentiated from the situation in which the agent was awarded exclusivity but the principal nevertheless concluded the prospective contract personally or had it concluded by another agent. In such a case, the principal is in breach of contract and is liable in damages. If that is the case, the agent would have to be put as nearly as possible into the position that would have prevailed if the principal had respected the exclusivity clause. This would imply that the principal would have to compensate the loss the agent has suffered and the gain of which the agent has been deprived.

In other words, the agent would receive the expectation interest. This would apply even if the conclusion of the contract by the principal cannot be attributed to the agent.

Illustration 10
Mark mandates Dimitri to sell his painting by Monet and awards Dimitri exclusivity in doing so. Mark meets Olivia in a gallery, and she indicates she is interested in purchasing paintings by Monet. After discussing the terms of a sales contract with Olivia, Mark terminates the mandate relationship and subsequently sells the painting directly to Olivia. As the sales contract was concluded after the termination of the mandate relationship, Dimitri is not entitled to payment under paragraph (4). Moreover, as Dimitri had nothing to do with the sale of the painting to Olivia, he is not entitled to the price under paragraph (5) of this Article either. However, by negotiating a contract with Olivia, Mark has breached the agreed exclusivity agreement with Dimitri. As a result, Dimitri is entitled to compensation for breach of contract. The damages that will be awarded to him in fact equal the remuneration he would have received for his services except for expenses saved.

J. Grossly unreasonable prices: No intervention by the court

Another matter regarding the payment of price is whether the court should be allowed to intervene when the (often unilaterally determined) price is unreasonably high. In many legal systems, possibly as a result of the originally fiduciary nature of the services of an agent, the court is awarded the possibility to adjust the price if it is considered to be excessive in relation to the performance of the mandate contract. This is the case in AUSTRIA, BELGIUM, FRANCE, GERMANY, GREECE, HUNGARY, and PORTUGAL. Adjustment of the price is also possible in the Nordic countries on the basis of good faith, and frequently used in business-to-consumer contracts. In other legal systems, such intervention could be seen as an expression of the doctrine of *iustum pretium*, which in most legal systems is not accepted. For that reason, in ENGLAND, IRELAND, ITALY, SCOTLAND, SLOVAKIA, and SPAIN, the courts are generally not allowed to adjust the price for excessiveness. Generally the same holds true for BULGARIA, ESTONIA, THE NETHERLANDS and POLAND. However, in these legal systems it is in theory possible for the court to intervene in the case of unforeseen circumstances, but these powers are used restrictively. In essence, this latter approach is adopted here: there is no general power of the courts to intervene against grossly unreasonable prices, but the court could intervene if the price has become excessive – or if the performance of the agent could become unreasonably burdensome – because of the occurrence of unforeseen circumstances. Yet a specific rule to this extent does not seem to be needed. It should be noted that for such a case, Articles 6:111 PECL (Change of circumstances) may provide relief. Moreover, where the price is determined unilaterally by the agent or a third party, and that price is (grossly) unreasonable, the price will be substituted for a reasonable price under Articles 6:105 PECL (Unilateral determination by a party) or Article 6:106 PECL (Determination by a third person). This means that, in practice, a specific power for the court to adjust the grossly unreasonable price would apply only in specific cases. In the remaining cases, it is thought that the contractual agreement between the parties should prevail.

Illustration 11

Agnetha is a wealthy lady with expensive taste. To upgrade her house, she commissions Bjørn to purchase one of the four versions of 'The Scream' by the painter Edward Munch 'at any cost'. Both parties expect that it will take Bjørn a considerable amount of time and effort before he will be able to buy such a painting. For that reason, they agree that upon the purchase of the painting, Bjørn will be entitled to a price amounting to 10 per cent of the purchase price. However, only a few weeks later a version of 'The Scream' is offered for sale by the private owners, Benny and Annafrid. Bjørn succeeds in buying the painting for a price of € 50 million. Bjørn informs Agnetha of the purchase of the painting, the price and the commission he will charge (€ 5 million). Obviously, Agnetha and Bjørn could – and perhaps should – have anticipated that the purchase of the painting would *not* take as much time as expected. In this respect, the fact that Bjørn was able to purchase the painting after only a few weeks, without spending much effort, could be seen as a change of circumstances. However, the risk of such a change of circumstances would have to be borne by Agnetha, so the price cannot be adjusted under Article 6:111 PECL (Change of circumstances).

K. Relation to the Principles of European Law and the Draft Common Frame of Reference

This Article mirrors that of Article IV.D.– 2:102 DCFR (Price). It builds on the more general rules of Article 6:104 PECL (Determination of price) as regards the calculation of the price and Article 7:102 paragraph (3) PECL (Time of performance) as to the moment when payment becomes due.

Paragraph (5) is worded in a similar manner as Article 2:302 (Entitlement to Commission after the contract) of the Principles of Commercial Agency, Franchise and Distribution Contracts (PEL CAFDC), where the commercial agent under certain conditions is entitled to a commission for contracts concluded after the commercial agency has terminated.

L. Character of the rule

This Article constitutes a default rule from which the parties may derogate.

M. Remedies

If the principal fails to pay the price that is due under this Article, the agent may claim payment under Article 9:101 PECL (Monetary obligations). Alternatively, the agent may claim damages – including interest for late payment – under Articles 9:501 (Right to damages) and 9:508 PECL (Delay in payment of money), or termination of the contract under Articles 9:301 ff PECL (Right to terminate the contract).

Comparative Notes

1. Professional agent entitled to price

In most legal systems, an agent who provides his services on the basis of a mandate contract is entitled to a price if he acts in his professional capacity. In theory, the situation is different in DENMARK and GREECE; in practice, however, the law there follows the general trend.

2. When payment is due

As regards the moment when payment becomes due, in a majority of Member States the agent is entitled to payment when the agent has successfully performed his main obligation under the mandate contract. This is the case in AUSTRIA, BULGARIA, DENMARK, ESTONIA, FRANCE, GERMANY, HUNGARY, MALTA, THE NETHERLANDS, POLAND, PORTUGAL, SLOVAKIA, and SPAIN. An alternative solution is followed in BELGIUM, FINLAND, and ITALY, where payment of the price comes due only when the prospective contract is concluded and the agent gives an account of the way he has performed the mandate contract. The same is true in SWEDEN if an obligation to give an account exists. A more restrictive approach is followed in ENGLAND and IRELAND, and possibly also in SCOTLAND. There, the agent must not only conclude the prospective contract but – in a case of mandate for direct representation where the principal becomes a party to the contract with the third party – also prove that he was the effective cause of the conclusion of that prospective contract. However, where the principal frustrates the conclusion of the contract negotiated by the agent, in IRELAND the court may find an implied term in the contract requiring the principal to pay the agent his remuneration. This case law goes against older English case law.

3. Adjustment of price

In AUSTRIA, BELGIUM, FRANCE, GERMANY, GREECE, HUNGARY, and PORTUGAL, the court is allowed to adjust the price to which the agent is entitled if the court deems the price to be excessive in relation to the performance of the agent. A similar rule is accepted in SWEDEN if the price is unreasonably high considering the circumstances at the time of or occurring after the conclusion of the mandate contract. Adjustment of the price is also possible in DENMARK, FINLAND, and SWEDEN on the basis of good faith, and frequently used in business-to-consumer contracts. In business-to-business relations, the courts have held a restrictive approach. On the other hand, in ENGLAND, IRELAND, ITALY, SCOTLAND, SLOVAKIA, and SPAIN, the courts are generally not allowed to adjust the price for excessiveness, as this would require the court to evaluate whether the value of the respective obligations are more or less equal. Generally the same holds true for BULGARIA, ESTONIA, THE NETHERLANDS, and POLAND. However, in these legal systems it is in theory possible for the court to intervene in the case of unforeseen circumstances, but these powers are used restrictively. Moreover, in IRELAND and SPAIN, specific provisions for the adjustment of the fees of lawyers exist.

4. 'No result, no fee' generally allowed

It should be noted that apart from specific professions, payment on the basis of 'no result, no fee' is generally allowed in all Member States. The principal exception to the admissibility of this agreement is for lawyers, where the possibility of such an agreement is explicitly forbidden in either legislation or deontological rules in BELGIUM, THE NETHERLANDS, POLAND, and PORTUGAL, as well as in BULGARIA in criminal cases. However, a similar statutory ban was considered unconstitutional in GERMANY.

5. Payment if principal concluded prospective contract himself

The Member States differ regarding whether the agent is entitled to payment if the principal has concluded the prospective contract himself. In BELGIUM, BULGARIA, DENMARK, HUNGARY, ITALY, THE NETHERLANDS, SLOVAKIA, and SWEDEN, and probably also in MALTA, the agent is entitled to payment of the full price. In ESTONIA, FINLAND, FRANCE, SPAIN, and probably also in GERMANY, the principal is only required to pay the expenses the agent has incurred during the performance of the mandate contract. However, if it can be established that the conclusion of the prospective contract can be attributed to the services of the agent, he is entitled to payment of the full price in most of these systems. In AUSTRIA, an in-between situation exists, as the agent is entitled to a proportionate part of the price, expenses incurred and losses suffered. Similarly, in ENGLAND, IRELAND, and SCOTLAND, the agent is entitled to damages. Where the agent was appointed as an 'exclusive agent' or the agency is described as a 'sole selling agency', this effectively means that the agent is entitled to payment of the price.

6. Price in case prospective contract is concluded after termination of mandate relationship

If the mandate contract has terminated and subsequently the prospective contract is concluded by the principal or another agent on behalf of the principal, the former agent is in principle not required to pay the price. This is different, however, if the former agent shows that the prospective contract was concluded as a result of his efforts. In that case, the agent may be entitled to full payment or a payment proportionate to the services rendered in ESTONIA, FRANCE, GERMANY, HUNGARY, THE NETHERLANDS, SCOTLAND, SLOVAKIA, and SWEDEN, and possibly also in MALTA. The same is true in the case of commercial agency in BULGARIA. However, no payment is due after termination in ENGLAND and possibly also not in FINLAND.

National Notes

1. Professional agent entitled to price

AUSTRIA: If there is a custom or usage of the particular trade regulating the payment of remuneration, there is a presumption, in the absence of any express or implied agreement to the contrary, that the parties contracted for the payment of the remuneration in accordance with this custom or usage (CC Article 1004; Schwimann/Apathy, Article 1004 Rz 1). Solicitors are to be remunerated for their services (RATG and the subsidiary regulations of CC Article 1002 ff.). The commercial regulations (Comm.C Articles 345, 354, 396 ff.; HVertrG Article 8, 24 ff.) provide similar rules for cases when there are no express contract provisions.

BELGIUM: According to CC Article 1986, a mandate is as a rule non-remunerated, unless the parties agreed expressly or silently on the contrary. A silent clause on remuneration is presumed in favour of a professional agent (Tilleman, p. 103; Wéry, p. 211).

BULGARIA: As a general rule in Bulgarian law of obligations, the mandate is a gratuitous contract. According to OCA Article 28, 'the principal shall pay remuneration to the agent only if it has been negotiated'. As far as the remuneration is concerned, the general mandate rules in force make no difference whether the agent acts in his professional capacity or out of the course of his business – the remuneration is due only if it is explicitly or implicitly stipulated. Special provisions of some of the types of the mandate contract provide for compulsory remuneration, for example CA Article 36 paragraph (1), for the commercial agent CA Article 356 (2), for the commission contract CA Article 361 paragraph (1), for the forwarding contract, BAA Article 36 for a contract between an advocate and a principal. The common feature of all the above-mentioned special mandate contracts is that all agents act in the course of their business. In Bulgarian legal doctrine the mandate contract with agent, acting in his professional capacity, is presumed as a non-gratuitous contract (Меворах/Лиджи/Фархи, III, p. 52).

DENMARK: There are no specific rules providing that the professional agent is entitled to a price for his services if the contract is silent about this, but according to legal theory there may be a presumption that the agent will be remunerated for his services. However, many contracts contain clauses by which the professional agent is entitled to claim a price.

ENGLAND: There is a presumption in a commercial contract that when the principal requests a professional agent to act for him, the agent will be remunerated for his services. It is however a simple presumption and it can therefore be rebutted *(Miller v Beale* (1879) 27 WR 403).

ESTONIA: The rule that the agent who acts as a professional party is entitled to a price for his services is expressly stipulated for the (general) contract for services. 'If the amount of remuneration payable has not been agreed between the parties, remuneration shall be paid if it can be reasonably presumed that the service would only be performed for remuneration, above all if the agent performed the service for the purposes of his professional activities (LOAEst Article 627 paragraph (1)). The same principle applies to the brokerage contract (LOAEst Articles 664-665), contract of agency (LOAEst Article 680 paragraph (1)) and the commissionaire agreement (LOAEst Article 701 paragraph (1)), all of which are non-gratuitous by definition.'

FINLAND: The agent is, unless otherwise agreed, entitled to a reasonable remuneration (Comm.C Article 18:5 and analogous interpretation of the Sale of Goods Act Article 45). The real estate agent is, however, only entitled to the remuneration if the sales contract is executed, unless otherwise agreed between the principal and the agent (REstateA Article 20). The ACRS Article 10 and 11 contain specific rules on remuneration and its amount.

FRANCE: In principle, the mandate is supposed to be a contract without any payment (CC Article 1986), but French case law has decided that where the agent is in business and the contract is silent, he or she is entitled to remuneration (Cass.civ. 1re, 10 February 1981, Bull. civ. 1981 I, no. 50; Cass.civ. 1re, 6 June 1998, Bull. civ. 1998 I, no. 211). This will be determined by the judge, depending on the extent of the services rendered. In certain cases, the statutes do specifically allow a remuneration (e.g. commercial agents: Comm. C Article L.134-5 paragraph (3)), whereas in other cases the statutes will indicate otherwise (e.g. estate agents: Law of 2 January 1970 Article 6).

GERMANY: The professional agent is entitled to a price for his services if the contract keeps silent about this on two separate counts: under the law on contracts for services (CC Article 612 paragraph (1)) and for works (CC Article 632 paragraph (1)), which applies in the framework of CC Article 675. A price is deemed to be agreed upon if, under the circumstances, the service or work can only be expected to be rendered for a price. Under the rules on mandates, no specific provision for the situation addressed exists. However, a dated court decision has relied on an analogous application of CC Article 1835 paragraph (3), thus granting the agent a price if the act(s) performed under the mandate form part of his profession (RGZ 149, 121, 124). This approach is also followed by a number of scholars, but usually under the additional condition that the act performed was not specifically anticipated when the contract of mandate – which in general requires the agent to act gratuitously – was concluded (Seiler, in: Münchener Kommentar zum BGB, 4th. ed., Article 670 no. 21).

GREECE: In case of a mandate relationship, the question as to the price does not arise due to the gratuitous character of the mandate. In case of the obligatory remunerated mandate between the lawyer and the principal, an agreement regarding the remuneration of the lawyer is always required for the validity of the contract (Georgiadis/Stathopoulos/Karasis, CC Article 713 no. 10). In case of intermediation, if the contract keeps silent about the remuneration of a professional broker, CC Article 705 is applicable: 'A remuneration shall be deemed to have been tacitly agreed if the intervention or the indication is in the usual circumstances only made for a remuneration or if the task has been assigned to a professional broker. If the amount of remuneration has not been fixed shall be due a remuneration determined by the rates in force or in the absence of such rates the remuneration which is usual in the locality' (the locality of the conclusion of the contract of brokerage: Georgiadis/Stathopoulos/Karasis, CC Article 705 no. 2; Supreme Court decision no. 710/1986, EEN 1987, 148). A contractual agreement contrary to this rule is permitted (Supreme Court decision no. 1565/1986, NoV 1987, 1044). Regarding intermediation, a person who promises a fee for the procurement of a contract or for information of the opportunity of making a contract is bound to pay the fee only if the contract is concluded in consequence of such procurement or indication. If, in consequence of such procurement or indication, an agreement containing a promise of contract was concluded but the final contract is frustrated, only one half of the fee may be demanded (CC Article 703 paragraph (1)). If the contract is concluded subject to a condition, the fee may not be demanded until the condition is fulfilled (CC Article 704).

HUNGARY: According to CC Article 478, '[t]he principal shall pay an appropriate fee, unless the circumstances, or the relationship between the parties suggest that the agent has assumed the agency without any consideration. The agent shall be entitled to demand remuneration even if his actions brought no results. The principal shall be entitled to reduce the remuneration or refuse to pay it if he is able to prove that success was not achieved in part or in whole for a reason for which the agent is responsible. If the contract is terminated before the agency has been fulfilled, the agent shall be entitled to demand an appropriate fraction of the fee for his activities. Fees shall be payable at the time a contract is extinguished.'

IRELAND: In general, an agent is only entitled to remuneration if that has been agreed with the principal. In a commercial context, it is rare that an agent would agree to act gratuitously. Importantly, the agreement as to remuneration can be express or implied. A right to remuneration will be implied on the same basis that other terms can be implied into contracts. For instance, such a right would probably be implied where the agent is acting in the course of a profession or business (*Miller v Beale* (1879) 27 WR 403), and would more easily be implied where the services have been provided.

ITALY: The general rule is that if the contract keeps silent the agent is entitled to payment. If the agent is a professional the presumption is even stronger.

MALTA: If it is presumed to have been tacitly agreed upon, the agent is entitled to ask for payment. In such a case our law provides that regard be given to the profession of the agent and to other circumstances. This is found in CC Article 1881 paragraph (1): "The principal must repay to the agent the advances and expenses made or incurred by him in carrying out the mandate; and he must pay him the remuneration if promised to him, or if it is presumed to have been tacitly agreed upon, regard being had to the profession of the agent and to other circumstances."

NETHERLANDS: As there is no specific stipulation on the agent's wages in case of mandate relationship, the rules from the general contract for professional services apply. Therefore, according to CC Article 7:405 paragraph (1), if the agent performs the service in the course of his profession, the principal is held to pay wages. However, the contracting parties may agree differently. The contracting parties are allowed to jointly determine the payment of the agent. It will often occur that the exact remuneration is not been specified in the contract. Therefore, if the agent is entitled to payment, but the contracting parties have not specified the exact remuneration, the principal is held liable to pay remuneration as usually charged, or if there is no such measure, fair remuneration (CC Article 7:405 paragraph (2)). If the agent is not a professional party, he cannot make a claim to any remuneration for his services, unless again the opposite follows from the contractual arrangements between the parties.

POLAND: The mandate contract is presumed to be concluded for a remuneration, unless the circumstances of concluding the mandate contract indicate that the service is to be performed without remuneration (CC Article 735 paragraph (1)). The CC makes no distinction between professional and other agents in this respect. An example of circumstances indicating that the service is to be provided without a remuneration may be a custom, cf. Panowicz-Lipska/L. Ogiegło. If the amount of the agent's remuneration has not been specified in the contract the agent is entitled to "usual remuneration paid for similar activities", CC Article 735 (2) provides. The prices must then be appropriate to the services rendered by the agent. The most important factor when it comes to evaluate the remuneration is the amount of time and effort put by the agent into carrying out the mandate, cf. Panowicz-Lipska/L. Ogiegło.

PORTUGAL: In principle, mandate is a unilateral act of the other party conferring agent powers to the agent (CC Article 262). Most often, representation is conferred in a mandate *(mandato)* contract celebrated between the agent and the other party. The mandate is presumed to be gratuitous unless the agent is a professional (CC Article 1158) or in case of commercial mandate (CC Article 232, Comm.C Article 1). The agent bears the burden of proof of being a professional party (STJ 3 December 1974, BMJ 242, 270). If the mandate is remunerated and the parties did not set the price, this is determined according to professional tariffs, market price, uses of commerce or if they do not exist, by equitable decision (CC Article 1158 paragraph (2)).

SCOTLAND: Where the agent is a professional party and the contract is silent on his remuneration, a rebuttable presumption in favour of remuneration exists (Macgregor, paragraph 109). A similar presumption exists where the work involved constitutes the agent's livelihood *(Mackersy's Executors v St Giles Cathedral Managing Board* (1904) 12 SLT 391; *Campbell v Campbell's Exrs* (1910) 47 SLR 837). The court will consider evidence of established custom and trade in order to decide whether remuneration is due, and, if so, how much. An agent who is not a professional person is entitled to remuneration on a *quantum meruit* basis *(Kennedy v Glass* (1890) 17 R 1085). The presumption applicable to professional persons includes inter alia solicitors, who need not stipulate to their principals that remuneration is due. The mere fact of employment is sufficient to allow remuneration at the ordinary rate (Begg, p. 117).

SLOVAKIA: CC Article 730 indicates that the principal shall pay the agent remuneration only when it was agreed or when it is customary in particular with regard to the agent's profession. However, under Com.C. Article 566(2), if the agent's professional activities include making such arrangements, it shall be presumed that some remuneration has been agreed.

SPAIN: The mandate contract is presumed to be gratuitous unless the parties have agreed otherwise (CC Article 1711; confirmed in STS 30 April 1993). The agent has to prove that there is an agreement between the parties, explicit or tacit, as to the remunerated character of the contract (Hernández Gil, p. 453). There is an exception to this rule: if the agent exercises professionally the type of activities which are the object of the mandate contract, then the mandate is presumed to be remunerated (CC Article 1711 paragraph (2)). See also Comm.C Article 277. However, the agent needs to prove that that the activities are indeed those which are exercised in the agent's daily professional activities (STS 7 April 1979; STS 21 February 1995). If there is no price agreed, then it will be established in accordance with professional tariffs, usages, or eventually the determination of the court (Hernández Gil, p. 454).

SWEDEN: According to Comm.C Article 18:5 the agent is entitled to a reasonable price. If the parties have not agreed on a price it follows by analogy from Sale of Goods Act Article 45 that the price shall be reasonable considering the circumstances. In certain categories of agents business practice has developed. Thus, trade agents, commissionaires and real estate agents are entitled to a percentage commission on contracts concluded with a third party, see HaL Article 9, FmL Article 21 and KommL Article 27.

2. When payment is due

AUSTRIA: In the absence of an express agreement, payment of the price is due when the task is fulfilled (Schwimann/Apathy, Article 1004 Rz 5). Rendering of accounts is no precondition. Where the commercial regulations apply, payment of the price is due on results (Comm.C Article 383, 409).

BELGIUM: As a rule the payment of the salary is due at the moment of accounting by the agent, i.e. at the end of the mandate contract. An exception is made for long term contracts for representation or contracts with successive performances. For these contracts, parties can agree on intermediate payments (Tilleman, p. 111; Wéry, p. 214).

BULGARIA: There is no provision in Bulgarian contract law regulating when the stipulated in the mandate contract remuneration is due. The contractual parties can negotiate preconditions and term of this payment. When the mandate contract is silent, the local custom is applicable. In case of absence of a custom, the remuneration is due when the agent has performed his contractual obligation, i.e. he has concluded the prospective contract or performed the judicial act on behalf of the principal (Меворах/Лиджи/Фархи, III, p. 54). Unless otherwise stipulated in the contract, rendering of an account is not a necessary precondition for payment of the remuneration (Supreme Court, Judgment no. 922, 7 October 1993, Civil Case 2050/1993, V). The latter is due even when the agent is only ready to give but has not given the account to the principal yet (Божидар Василев, p. 131). According to the special rule of Article 38 CA the remuneration of the commercial agent is due on monthly payments (Герджиков, Коментар на Търговския закон, I, p. 156). The parties can agree upon a different term of payment, but no later than the end of the month, which follows the three-months-period during each the prospective contract was concluded (CA Article 38).

DENMARK: Unless otherwise expressly agreed upon between the parties, the payment of price and reimbursement will fall due as soon as the agent has fulfilled the contract of representation. A claim for reimbursement will normally be needed to fix the exact amount of the expenses.

ENGLAND: When the agent is entitled to receive commission on the happening of a given result/event he must show that the result/event in question has actually occurred and that he was the effective cause of such a result/event.

ESTONIA: As a general rule the payment of the price for the services is due after the service has been rendered, for the contracts for services that oblige the service provider (the agent) to execute a juridical act, including the mandate in particular, this means that as a general rule the remuneration is payable after the execution of the juridical act, if not agreed otherwise (LOAEst Article 628 paragraph (1) 2nd sentence).

FINLAND: Unless otherwise agreed, the payment is usually due in reasonable time after the fulfilment of the agent's contractual duties and after a demand of the agent. The payment shall not take place until an account is given, if such is required. The agent is usually not entitled to an advance payment. This is, in general, not the case in long-term mandates where periodical payments may take place. The ACRS Article 10 and 11 contain detailed rules concerning the time of payment.

FRANCE: Where the contract is silent, the remuneration is due at the end of the mission, although the Civil Code does not specify the exact moment of this payment. Frequently, the agency contract specifies that remuneration is due only if the mission has been successfully completed. French case law seems to consider that if the agent does not successfully perform the contract, he may not receive any remuneration (despite CC Article 1999(2), which considers that payment may always be due to the agent except where the agent has made a failure – but authors do not agree on this point). However, if the termination of the mandate is caused by reasons that are independent of the parties, the French courts consider that the remuneration normally due may then be limited to the part of the contract which has already been performed or the agent may only receive an indemnity. An indemnity may also be due to the agent when the contract could not be performed because of the principal's and/or a third party's failure.

GERMANY: Payment of the price is due after the service has been rendered (CC Article 614) or the work has been finished and (at least tacitly) accepted by the other party (CC Article 641 paragraph (1)).

GREECE: In case of intermediation, payment of the price is due after the conclusion of the prospective contract as a result of the intervention or indication of the broker.

HUNGARY: In general, according to CC Article 478 paragraph (4), '[f]ees shall be payable at the time a contract is extinguished'. In case of commission agency, '[t]he commission agent shall be entitled to receive a commission only if the sales contract has been performed' (CC Article 511 paragraph (1)).

IRELAND: Case law has addressed some particular questions as to when remuneration is earned/payable (leaving many other questions yet to be addressed). For example, it has been held that where a commission is earned by an agent on bringing about a result, he will only be entitled to payment if he is the effective cause of that result *(Millar, Son & Co v Radford* (1903) 19TLR 575; *Judd v Donegal Tweed Co Ltd* (1935) 69 ILTR 117; *Stokes & Quirke Ltd v Clohessy* [1957] IR 84). Another question which has been addressed by case law is, where an agent is to be remunerated by commission, whether the principal may prevent him earning his commission, for instance, by refusing to perform a contract negotiated, or concluded, by the agent. In the absence of any express provision in the agency agreement, this depends on whether an appropriate term may be implied into the agency contract. For example, in *Cusack v Bothwell* (1943) 77 ILTR 18, an auctioneer was instructed to find a buyer for lands at a certain price. The agent was to receive a commission of 5 per cent. He introduced a buyer but the seller refused to sell and pay the commission. The court awarded the auctioneer a sum equivalent to 5 per cent because he had done what was required of him. This ruling goes against some earlier English case law (see e.g. *Luxor (Eastbourne) Ltd v Cooper* [1941] AC 108 and *French & Co v Leston Shipping Co Ltd* [1922] 1 AC 451) but appears to be supported in more recent case law *(Alpha Trading v Dunshaw-Patten* [1981] QB 290).

ITALY: The agent, unless otherwise agreed by the parties, has a reporting obligation to be performed without delay towards the principal (CC Article 1712 and 1713). In particular, upon conclusion of the mandate the agent shall communicate to the principal the performance of the contract, he shall further report on his activities and render to the principal all and any profits acquired in the performance of the contract. He shall also demonstrate the expenses which he sustained for the performance of the contract. It is only in this moment that the agent has the right to claim the payment of the price and/or reimbursement.

MALTA: Payment of the price is due when the agent has concluded the contract on behalf of the principal.

NETHERLANDS: Payment of the price is due after the service has been performed.

POLAND: Unless the parties have agreed otherwise the payment of the remuneration is due after the service has been rendered by the agent (CC Article 744). However, the agent is entitled to receive some money in advance if a necessity of expenses arises (CC Article 743).

PORTUGAL: The price is due after the execution of the mandate. However, depending upon the uses of trade, a partial initial remuneration may be due to the agent, cf. CC Article 1167 lit (b).

SCOTLAND: It is difficult to identify a general rule on the point at which remuneration becomes due. The issue will probably be determined as a matter of interpretation of the principal/agent contract (Gow, p. 533). If the contract stipulates that the agent's remuneration is dependent on achieving a result, remuneration is payable if the result is achieved and if it is attributable to the agent's efforts. Otherwise, the matter is likely to be governed by general practice in a particular trade. A solicitor can be remunerated before he has achieved a specific result which was the subject of his instructions. Interim fees are possible, subject to obtaining the principal's consent (Paterson, no. 9.04.9). Such fees may debited from the principal's account held with him, but only either with the principal's consent or at least where the principal has been informed (Solicitors

(Scotland) Accounts Rules 2001 rule 6 paragraph (1)(d)). The interim fee must be fair and reasonable in the light of the work carried out to date (Paterson, no. 9.04.4).

SLOVAKIA: Under the Civil Code, payment of the price is due one day after the mandate was performed or the contract was terminated and the agent challenged the principal to pay that. The Comm.C stipulates that the agent is entitled to the remuneration once the activity stipulated in the mandate has been duly carried out, regardless of whether it has led to the expected result or not (unless the mandate contract provides otherwise) and the commission agent is entitled to remuneration when the duties are fulfilled (Comm.C Article 587(2)).

SPAIN: The price is due from the moment the mandate has been performed. There is no need to wait until the agent has given account to the principal of the activities performed (STS 9 July 1991; Hernández Gil, p. 917). This is only an accessory obligation which can be performed later on. Performance does not imply success. The agent has a right to payment even when the performance did not lead to the aim pursued by the principal, unless the agent acted negligently in the performance of the obligations (STS 29 January 2001; Hernández Gil, p. 453). A proportional payment may be justified even in cases where the agent performs partially, because the principal has a partial benefit (Hernández Gil, p. 453).

SWEDEN: Unless otherwise agreed or flowing from accepted practice in a particular line of business, payment is due when the task is fulfilled. In case the agent has a duty to give account of the task the principal is not obliged to pay until such account is given.

3. Adjustment of excessive price by court

AUSTRIA: A court can, in case of avoidance of the contract (on the grounds of error as to the content of the declaration which has been made, laesio enormis, usury, violation of bonos mores), adjust the price (CC Article 1336; CC Article 879 applies for commercial transactions (Krejci, 37 f.)).

BELGIUM: According to established case law, a court can, upon request of one of the parties, set aside the principle of pacta sunt servanda and reduce the salary of the agent when the court considers the salary to be excessive in proportion to the performances (see Cass. 14 October 2002, RW 2003-04, 1297; Cass. 19 September 1985, RW 1985-86, 2638; Cass. 6 March 1980, Pas. 1980, I, 832, concl. Charles, RCJB 1982, 519, note E. Dirix; Tilleman, p. 113-123; Wéry, p. 216). The court must consider the salary excessive in proportion to the performance. There are no further specific conditions (e.g. that the principal abused the inferior position of the agent (Tilleman, p. 114)). In order to decide if the salary is reasonable in proportion to the performances, the court can take into account e.g. the time spent on the execution of the mandate contract, the complexity of the mandate, the liability risk and the expenses made by the agent (Tilleman, p. 114-116).

BULGARIA: General contract law rules are applicable. As a matter of principle in Bulgarian contract law contracts may be amended, terminated, avoided, or revoked only by mutual consent of the parties or on grounds provided by law, cf. OCA Article 20bis(2). The price stipulated in the mandate contract can be adjusted by a court when it has become excessive after the conclusion of the contract as a result of unforeseen circumstances. Then the contract has become excessively burdensome for one of the parties as a result of an unforeseen and unforeseeable change in circumstances that has occurred after the conclusion of the contract. In such situation, to insist on performance according to its terms would not be in conformity with good faith and justice (CA Article 307). If these conditions are not fulfilled, the court is not entitled to adjust the stipulated price (Меворах/Лиджи/Фархи, III, p. 53).

DENMARK: According to Article 36 of the Contract Act (the 'general clause' in contract law) the court can adjust the price and other conditions of the contract: 'An agreement may be amended or set aside wholly or partly if it would be unreasonable or contrary to proper conduct to allow it to stand. The same applies to other legal acts. (…) [R]egard will be had to the circumstances prevailing at the formation of the contract, contents of the contract and subsequent events'. This principle is frequently invoked and widely accepted by the court, especially in consumer cases.

ENGLAND: Technically, the courts cannot at the request of a party adjust the price. In fact, if the right to remuneration arises from an express agreement, the courts will not interfere even if the exact amount of remuneration is left to the principal's discretion *(Kofi Sunkersette Obu v Strauss (A) & Co Ltd* [1951] AC 243) where the contract stipulated that the agent's remuneration was left to the principal's discretion. However, there are some exceptions to this rule of non-interference from the courts. For instance, if the agent performs services at the request of the principal which are outside his duties for which the contract provides express provision, the courts can exceptionally imply that a reasonable remuneration be paid. Moreover, if the contract expressly or impliedly stipulates that a 'reasonable sum' should be paid to the agent, the courts can determine what a 'reasonable sum' should be *(Way v Latilla* [1937] 3 All ER 759). Furthermore, if the contract remains silent, the courts can imply a term following the normal rules of construction. The courts will only imply a term to that effect in the contract if they are satisfied that the parties intended for the agent to be remunerated *(Reeve v Reeve* (1858) 1 F & F280). Payment to be made must be reasonable according to the circumstances (usually on a quantum meruit basis if there is no contract; see however *Withy Robinson (A firm) v Edwards* (1985) 277 EGLR 748; to compare and contrast with *London Commercial and Land Co Ltd v Beazer Lands Ltd* [1990] CLY paragraph 107). The courts can also infer that payment was intended from a trade usage or a custom of the area of the agent (on the conditions for being able to rely on a custom, see *Wilkie v Scottish Aviation Ltd* 1956 SC 198. However, no term can be implied where the term would contradict the express term of a contract *(Kofi Sunkersette Obu v Strauss (A) & Co Ltd,* [1951] AC 243).

ESTONIA: Generally, agreements on the price for the performance of contractual obligations cannot be controlled or adjusted by the courts. The courts have no jurisdiction to rule on the equilibrium of the mutual rights and obligations of the parties and adjust agreements on the contract price, with the general exeption of clausula rebus in LOAEst Article 97. An adjustment rule for the disproportionate brokerage fees under the brokerage contracts (LOAEst Article 666 old) was deleted from the law.

FINLAND: Adjustment of the price is possible in accordance with ContrA Article 36 under the condition that the mandate contract is unfair or its application would lead to an unfair result. In determining what is unfair, the entire content of the contract shall be taken into consideration, as shall the positions of the parties, the positions prevailing at and after the conclusion of the contract, and other factors as well.

FRANCE: A court may adjust the price (Cass.req., 12 December 1911, D.P. 1913, 1, 129), but the principal must demonstrate why the remuneration which was promised is excessive by reference to the service effectively rendered by the agent (Cass.civ. 1re, 24 September 2002, CCC, 2003 no. 3). Such judicial adjustment is not possible after any discharge has been given to the agent or where the remuneration has been agreed on completion of the mandate.

GERMANY: Under brokerage contracts, a court may, upon request of one of the parties, adjust the price according to CC Article 655, but only if the brokerage contract called for the solicitation of a contract for services and the price agreed upon by the parties to the brokerage contract is disproportionately high.

GREECE: In case of a brokerage contract if the agreed remuneration of the broker is disproportionately high it shall be reduced by the Court to the appropriate level at the request of the debtor (CC Article 707). The debtor can either bring an action for the adjustment of the price or raise an objection to the action of the broker demanding payment of the price (Supreme Court decision no. 206/2004, NoV 2004, 1744). The objection for adjustment of the price to the appropriate level can be raised at every stage of the trial because the rule of CC Article 707 is considered to be a rule of *ordre public* (CA Thessaloniki decision no. 2880/2002, Arm 2003, 1423). Criteria for the proportional measure of the remuneration are the work of the broker, the expenses in case that these are not separately paid, the way of intermediation, the time invested and the benefit that the principal has gained (Georgiadis/Stathopoulos/Karasis III, CC Article 707 no. 1; CA Athens decision no. 3790/1985, EllDni 1985, 943; CFI Athens decision no. 16004/1983, EllDni 1984, 1603).

HUNGARY: In general, the price determined by the parties cannot be adjusted by a court. Nevertheless, according to CC Article 201 paragraph (2), '[i]f at the time of the conclusion of the contract the difference between the value of a service and the consideration due, without either party having the intention of bestowing a gift, is grossly unfair the injured party shall be allowed to contest the contract'. CC Article 241 prescribes that '[t]he court may amend a contract when it is injurious to any substantial rightful interest of one of the parties in consequence of a circumstance arising in the long-term relationship of the parties following the conclusion of the contract'.

IRELAND: There is no general provision for an adjustment of the price. There is a specific provision for the adjustment (or taxation) of solicitors fees however.

ITALY: In general terms the determination of the price is subject to party autonomy. However, upon request of the parties, a judge may be called to fix the price in the absence of any specific agreement of the parties. CC Article 1709 provides a hierarchical list of criteria to follow in the determination of the price the agent is entitled to. Unless otherwise agreed by the parties, the price can be determined by reference to the professional fees if the agent acts as a professional, or by reference to usages. In absence of these criteria, the price can be determined by a judge on the basis of his equitable judgment, having regard to the nature, the quantity and the quality of the activity executed by the agent. If the evidence produced by the professional is incomplete and/or insufficient as to the quantum and lacking any tariffs and/or usages, the judge shall determine the compensation on the basis of the kind of activity performed and of the profits thereby achieved by the principal (CC Articles 1709 and 2225; Cass. no. 9829/1995, Arch. civ., 1996, 477).

MALTA: Whilst reiterating the principle that under Maltese law, mandate or mandate is a gratuitous contract, the situation envisaged in the question is not specifically dealt with under Maltese law.

NETHERLANDS: Payment of the agent that is extremely high or low is not against the law. An adjustment of the contractually agreed price is possible only in the case of unforeseen circumstances and only then if the change of circumstances is such that the agent could not have expected the price to remain unaffected by that change and the change should not remain for the account of the principal (CC Article 6:258). This is evaluated very restrictively, effectively leaving little room for the courts to intervene save for very extreme situations.

POLAND: In the case of an extraordinary change of circumstances, the price may be adjusted by the court (CC Article 357). This is a general provision that may be applied to all contracts; there are no specific provisions on adjustment of the remuneration under a mandate contract.

PORTUGAL: Upon request of one of the principal the court can adjust the price if the agent sets an excessive or unjustified fee (CC Article 282) or if the agent takes unjustified advantage of the need, inexperience, imprudence or feebleness of the principal. Though this regime will only apply only in extreme circumstances, in some professions or sectors of trade, professional regulation may provide the principal with an easier chance of adjustment of the fee. E.g. in the case of a dispute between an attorney and a principal, the fee may be adjusted by the court according to the regulations of the Bar.

SCOTLAND: There is no general power vested in a Scottish court to adjust an agent's contractually agreed remuneration. Where the contract is silent, a court can be called upon to assess a reasonable fee or a fee which would be usual in a particular trade or profession (Macgregor, paragraph 109). In the specific case of solicitors, courts are empowered to adjust the fee charged. This process, known as 'taxation,' involves the assessment of a reasonable fee based on the circumstances of the case by an independent auditor attached to the court (Begg, p. 163-177; Paterson, no. 185, footnote 28). The process can be instigated by either solicitor or principal. The auditor has considerable discretion and may increase the account, although this will happen only rarely (Begg, p. 175; *Reeve v Dykes* 7 S 732). The court will not normally interfere with the auditor's taxation except on questions of principle (Begg, p. 176).

SLOVAKIA: There is no possibility to adjust the excessive price by court. If the price was so excessive that it constituted the serious breach of bona mores, there could be the exceptional possibility to declare the contract void.

SPAIN: There is no rule on this point and, in general, no adjustment can be made to the remuneration due under an the agency contract. Exceptions exist only in regulated professions, such as that of a barrister.

SWEDEN: According to Contr.Act Article 36 a court can adjust the price under the condition that the price is found unreasonably high considering circumstances at the time of or occurring after the formation of the contract or due to other circumstances. The rule is accepted by the courts in consumer relations in particular. In business-to-business relations the courts have held a restrictive approach.

4. No result, no fee ('contingency fee') allowed

AUSTRIA: The parties can agree to a price calculated on a 'no result, no fee' basis (Rummel/Strasser, Article 1004 Rz 9; Krejci, Article 879 Rz 209; Griss, Article 383 Rz 13).

BELGIUM: The parties can agree on a 'no result, no fee' price (Paulus & Boes, p. 115; Wéry, p. 213). Only lawyers are forbidden to calculate on a 'no result, no fee' basis.

BULGARIA: Payment on the basis of 'no result, no fee' basis. There is a ban for application of this rule regarding the advocates 'remuneration in criminal cases – Regulation of Minimum Amounts of the Advocates' Fees, Article 17.

DENMARK: The principle of 'no result, no fee' is valid according to Danish law.

ENGLAND: The parties can agree to a clause of 'no result, no fee'. In fact, this is the norm for estate agents since a normal estate agency contract is considered to be unilateral in nature *(Luxor (Eastbourne) Ltd v Cooper* [1941] AC 108, per Lord Russel of Killowen, at p. 124). This means that usually, no task is complete until the agent has performed the task for which he was appointed by the principal.

ESTONIA: The parties can agree to a price calculated on a 'no result, no fee' basis.

FINLAND: In general the parties can agree to a price calculated on a 'no result, no fee' basis. Real estate agents are only entitled to remuneration if the prospective contract is concluded, unless otherwise agreed (REstateA Article 20).

FRANCE: There is complete freedom of contract and the parties can agree on payment on a 'no result, no fee' basis. This is, in fact, the solution imposed on estate agents who are not entitled to any remuneration if the contract envisaged has not been concluded.

GERMANY: There is no rule to the contrary. A specific exception applies to legal services: according to Article 49b(2) of the Federal Act on the Regulation of Attorneys it is illegal to agree on a 'contingency fee'; but even this restriction has most recently been held to be unconstitutional for being excessively broad and not allowing for any exceptions (BVerfG, NJW 2007, 979).

GREECE: In case of intermediation a payment on no result, no fee basis is regulated in CC Articles 703 and 704. According to CC Article 703 paragraph (1), '[a] person who has promised remuneration to somebody for the latter's intervention or for the indication by him of an occasion for the conclusion of a contract shall only be bound to pay the remuneration if the contract was concluded as a result of such intervention or indication. If an agreement containing a promise of contract was concluded but the final contract has been frustrated one half of the remuneration shall only be due.' From that rule it is implied that causality must be proved between the procurement or indication and the conclusion of the contract (Supreme Court decision no. 701/1995, EEN 1996, 601; CA Pireos decision no. 855/1993, EllDni 1994, 1708). According to CC Article 704, '[i]n case of a contract subject to a suspensive condition the remuneration of the broker shall be paid if the condition has been fulfilled. In case of a contract concluded subject to a resolutory condition the remuneration shall be payable upon the conclusion of the contract.'

HUNGARY: Parties are free to agree to a price calculated on a 'no result, no fee' basis (CA Fejér Megyei Bíróság Gf. 40 087/2001/5, in BDT2002. 702). Special rules are established for the commission agency where the agent concludes a contract in his own name but for the account of his principal: according to CC Article 511 paragraph (1), '[t]he commission agent shall be entitled to receive a commission only if the sales contract has been performed'.

IRELAND: In line with the principal of freedom of contract, parties are free to agree as they wish and therefore a price can be calculated on a 'no result, no fee' basis. In some professions, there may be regulatory rules on pricing. For example, in contentious work, solicitors cannot set their fee based on a percentage of damages awarded, though they can work on a 'no foal, no fee' basis.

ITALY: In general terms the issue of payment of a price is subject to party autonomy. However, in some cases special rules apply in favour of the agents (e.g. commercial agents and attorneys at law).

MALTA: Whether or not the parties can agree to a fee based on result is not regulated under Maltese law.

NETHERLANDS: According to HR 23 May 2003, NJ 2003, 518 (Graan Management B.V./PeHa Holding c. s.), in case of mediation contracts, the no result, no fee rule applies (CC Article 7:426). This implies that if the realisation of the contract fails, the agent is not entitled to payment. However, contracting parties may deviate from this rule. Although this reasoning applies to mediation contracts it seems also important to mandate contracts since the payment of the agent in mandate contracts is often related to the realisation of the transaction that is subject to the mandate. The agent is not entitled to wages if the transaction is not accomplished. The wages are usually related to the transaction's 'price'. The 'no result, no fee' agreement is, however, explicitly not allowed for lawyers in their contracts with principals. An experiment by the Dutch Bar Association in cases of personal injury was prevented by intervention of the Minister of Justice in 2005.

POLAND: The parties may agree on a 'no result, no fee' clause on the basis of freedom of contract. Such clauses are forbidden in certain codified ethical rules of legal professions, but those sets of rules are not law.

PORTUGAL: In the framework of the principle of autonomy in contract law, there is no bar to a contingency fee. However, in some circumstances, regulatory law or public order may forbid a contingency fee. This is e.g. the case of representation by an attorney (forbidden by Article 101 Lei 15/2005, 26 January).

SCOTLAND: It is common for principal/agent contracts to provide that agents are only entitled to remuneration where they achieve a specific result (Gow, p. 533). Many estate agent's contracts take this form. Solicitors too commonly enter into so-called 'no result, no fee' agreements. Although this principle tends to be expressed in the context of the solicitor's litigation work, it is clear that it is not limited to litigation (Paterson, no. 9.05.2).

SLOVAKIA: For mandate contracts, 'no result, no fee' is allowed (CC and Comm.C). In the contract for arrangement of the sale of a thing, this is the essential characteristic of the contract type.

SPAIN: The parties can agree on a 'no result, no fee' price (Comm.C Article 272 and Agency Law Article 19).

SWEDEN: Payment on a 'no result, no fee' basis is allowed according to Swedish law.

5. Payment if principal concluded prospective contract himself

AUSTRIA: If the principal concludes the prospective contract of his own motion, the agent is entitled to a proportional part of the price, to his incurred expenses as well as to suffered losses.

BELGIUM: A distinction has to be made. If the only purpose of the clause of irrevocability is to guarantee exclusivity to the agent (more in particular a salary), then the principal is entitled to conclude the prospective contract of his own motion. He only will have to indemnify the agent by paying the price on which they agreed. If the clause of irrevocability is on the contrary a modality to deprive the principal of his right to conclude the prospective contract of his own motion, then the principal must leave the matter entirely to the agent (Foriers, p. 90; Wagemans, p. 193).

BULGARIA: In Bulgarian legal doctrine the conclusion of the prospective contract by the principal himself or by another agent is interpreted as a revocation of the mandate by the principal (Меворах/Лиджи/Фархи, III, p. 176). Such being the case, the agent is entitled to payment of the remuneration agreed upon in the contract (OCA Article 288 paragraph (1)).

DENMARK: A mandate contract does not deprive the principal of the right to conclude the prospective contract himself. This will apply whether the agent is entitled to act in his own name or in the name of his principal. The agent is entitled to the price whether he or the principal concludes the prospective contract. According to the Act Real Estate Agents Act the parties can agree to a clause according to which the agent is entitled to the price even if the principal concludes directly the contract with a third party presented by the agent.

ENGLAND: When an estate agent is granted an exclusivity by being appointed 'sole agent', if the principal then appoints another agent who earns the commission that the first agent should have earned, then the sole agent is entitled to damages *(Milsom v Bechstein* (1898) 14 TLR 159). When the agent is appointed as an 'exclusive agent' or the agency is described as a 'sole selling agency' *(Brodie Marshall & Co (Hotel Division) v Sharer* [1988] 1 EGLR 21), then the principal himself is also prevented from selling the property as the irrevocability then is in the interest of the agent. Should the principal nevertheless do so, he would have to pay the agent the agreed commission *(Snelgrove v Ellringham Colliery Co* (1881) 45 JP 408).

ESTONIA: No general rule exists but the matter would be decided based on a question whether the services of the agent include the mediation or are aimed at achievement of the conclusion of the contract by the agent. In cases where mere mediation is owned the agent would be entitled to a price if the conclusion of the contract (even if achieved through the act of the principal itself) is attributable to the services of the agent. In case of the brokerage contract, this is prescribed by the law as a specific rule (cf. LOAEst Article 661 paragraph (1)).

FINLAND: In general the agent is not entitled to a price for prospective contracts concluded by the principal, unless otherwise agreed. According to ACRS Article 10 the agent shall be entitled to a commission where the transaction has been concluded as a result of his action as well as where the agent has been entrusted with a specific geographical area or group of principals and the transaction has been concluded with party belonging to that area or group of principals.

FRANCE. The agent can claim for the reimbursement of the expenses he made. Regarding his remuneration, it seems not to be due (case law, contrary to CC Article 1992(2); Huet, no 31252).

GERMANY: Under a brokerage contract, the broker is entitled to the full price if the principal has concluded the prospective contract with the third party, as long as the conclusion of the contract was due (but not necessarily exclusively due) to the service rendered by the broker (CC Article 652 paragraph (1)).

GREECE: Consequence of an exclusivity clause is that in case of breach of that contractual obligation the principal is liable for restitution of the damages incurred to the exclusive broker due to violation of the clause of exclusivity (CFI Athens decision no. 4029/1982, EllDni 1984, 848).

HUNGARY: The principal remains always the master of the case, so he can conclude the contract himself. CC Article 478 paragraph (3) establishes that 'If the contract is terminated before the agency has been fulfilled, the agent shall be entitled to demand an appropriate fraction of the fee for his activities.'

IRELAND: In *Murphy, Buckley & Keogh Ltd v Pye (Ire) Ltd* [1971] IR 57, the seller of a factory appointed auctioneers as 'sole agents' in the sale. However, the seller arranged a sale himself without telling the auctioneers. The auctioneers claimed a commission but lost in the High Court. It was held first, that the sole agent had not effected a sale and hence were not entitled to commission. Secondly, it was held that although the auctioneers were the sole agents this did not prevent the seller from effecting a sale himself, merely from appointing any other agents. Hence, where an agent is appointed 'sole agent' to effect a contract, the principal commits a breach if a second agent is appointed; if the second agent then concludes a contract, the first agent would be entitled to damages, equal to the amount of commission of which he is deprived, for breach of that term (see e.g. *Bentall, Horsley and Baldry v Vicary* [1931] 1 KB 253). Moreover, it has been held that where an agent is appointed with 'the sole right to sell', the principal is in breach of contract if he sells in person *(Brodie Marshall & Co v Sharer* [1988] 19 EG 129).

ITALY: CC Article 1748(2), governing commercial agency, states that '[t]he commission is due also for the transactions entered into by the principal with third parties that the agent had previously acquired as principals for transactions of the same kind or pertaining to the area or category or group of principals reserved to the agent, unless otherwise agreed'. Accordingly, even if the contract grants an exclusive right to the agent, the principal keeps the right to conclude the affairs himself in the relevant geographical area; however the agent keeps his right to perceive the full price agreed under the contract without any reduction. See Cass. no. 11197/2001, Contratti, 2001, 1106, with comments by Venezia.

MALTA: If the principal concludes himself the prospected contract, the agent is still entitled to a compensation for the services rendered in order for the transaction to be finalized. This conclusion can be presumed from CA 12 December 1919, *Ciantar et. noe vs Demarco,* whereby the Court held that one must distinguish between brokerage and a compensation due to a person who has, under special authority, helped in the conclusion of a transaction, which compensation is due by the person who requested the relative services in his exclusive interest to conclude the deal. The person entrusted with a service is an agent who has offered his service to who had requested it and is therefore to be compensated. This line of thought was followed in a later judgement, CA (Commercial) 7 March 1932, *Vella Zarb vs Caruana et. noe.* In this case the Court had to decide whether the principal should pay compensation to the agent if the principal has terminated the mandate without a just cause. This situation can be used as an analogy for the situation submitted in the question. The Court held that a paid agent whose mandate has been revoked without a just cause may have a right to be compensated for this revocation. Therefore although Maltese law is silent on the matter whether the agent is still entitled to a price when the principal concludes the contract, from the above it can be presumed that not only would the agent be entitled to the price but he would also have the right to compensation.

NETHERLANDS: According to CC Article 7:411 paragraph (1), the agent may be entitled to fair payment if the contract comes to an end ahead of time. It seems that in the situation that the mandate contract ends because the principal has concluded the prospective contract himself, CC Article 7:411 paragraph (2) applies. According to this article, the agent is entitled to full payment taking in consideration the specific circumstances.

POLAND: The Polish Civil Code contains no provisions regulating this issue.

SCOTLAND: Where the principal has granted 'exclusive rights' to the agent, if the principal subsequently concludes a contract with a third party directly, this could constitute a breach by the principal of the principal/agent contract. The case of the *procuratory in rem suam* also requires special consideration in this context, given the potential for the principal to conclude such a contract on terms which are inconsistent with the agent's interests. There is very little authority on the *procuratory in rem suam.* It is suggested, however, that the principal would not be entitled to conclude such a contract without first obtaining the agent's consent to the same.

SLOVAKIA: Agents are entitled to their remuneration if they have duly performed their activities. The fact that the prospective contract was concluded by the principal himself may not be a ground for refusing to pay the price or the proportional part of it. However, the agent is entitled to the price only if the conclusion of the contract is the result of the agent's effort (see Comm.C Article 651 for the brokerage contract; Comm.C Article 671 for the commercial representation contract).

SPAIN: The conclusion of the prospective contract by the principal is regarded as an implicit revocation by the principal. As a consequence, the contractual relationship terminates from the moment the agent is informed. The effects of the revocation as to the right of payment are not regulated in the civil code, most likely because the typical situation when the civil code was written regarded gratuitous contracts. However, the CC Article 1733 indicates that the principal may revoke the contract at any time. The mandate needs to be performed for the right to payment to arise (Hernández Gil, p. 453). If the principal concludes the contract personally then the principal is not obliged to pay the remuneration but will be obliged to pay the expenses (CC Article 1728), the damages suffered by the agent as a result of the performance of the obligations under the mandate contract (CC Article 1729) and the damages suffered by the agent as a result of the unilateral termination. It seems that parties must have agreed upon the existence of a right of payment to continue even though the contractual relationship has otherwise terminated.

SWEDEN: The agent is entitled to compensation for the work and effort put in to the performance of the mandate contract. This is regardless of whether it is the principal or agent who concludes the prospective contract. A real estate agent is according to FmL Article 21 only entitled to compensation if the conclusion of the contract is due to the efforts of the real estate agent. If the real estate agent has been appointed as an exclusive agent he is entitled to compensation even if the contract was concluded without his efforts.

No answer received: PORTUGAL.

6. Price in case prospective contract concluded after termination of mandate relationship

BULGARIA: Special provisions exist only about the remuneration of a commercial agent in case of conclusion of the prospective contract after termination of his contract with the principal-merchant (CA Article 40). The commercial agent shall be entitled to a compensation upon the termination of the contract with the principal, when the latter continues to enjoy benefits from the principal established by the agent, unless: (a) during one year after the end of the contract the agent does not claim for such compensation; (b) the termination is on account of the agent's fault; (c) the agent has substituted himself with another person in contractual relationship (CA Article 40 paragraphs (1) and (3)). The compensation shall be equal to the agent's annual remuneration, estimated on the ground of his average remuneration for the entire duration of his contract with the principal, but no longer than 5 years (CA Article 40 paragraph (2)).

DENMARK: According to the Danish Act of Real Estate Agents the parties can agree to a clause according to which the agent is entitled to the price even if the principal concludes directly the contract with a third party presented by the agent.

ENGLAND: Unless the contract expressly provides for such a possibility, no commission is payable after termination (Nayler v Yearsley (1860) 2 F & F41). However, more recently, it seems that in case of repeat orders, commission may be payable after termination if, on construction of the contract, it is the intention of the parties (Sellers v London Counties Newspapers [1951] 1 KB 784).

ESTONIA: If the contract is concluded after termination of the mandate agreement, the agent is not entitled to a price except in case of the brokerage agreement, provided that the agent (the broker) can show that the conclusion of the contract was attributable to the information and services rendered by the broker (LOAEst Article 661 paragraph (3)). In case of other agreements under which representation or mediation of an agreement is owned a general rule applies under which the agent is entitled to a price proportionate to the services rendered, if the agreement was terminated prematurely and the termination is attributable to the principal (LOAEst Article 629 paragraph (1)). In cases where the termination is attributable to the agent, the agent is entitled to a proportionate price only if the services rendered prior to termination are of interest to the principal (LOAEst Article 629 paragraph (3)), this would mainly be the case if the principal is able, based on the agent's actions, conclude the intended contract itself after termination of the mandate agreement.

FINLAND: The agent is generally entitled to the agreed fee if the termination is not based on a non-performance of the agent. If a concluded prospective contract or some other action is a prerequisite for the fee, the agent is usually not entitled to remuneration if such contract or other action has not been concluded or taken at the time of termination. The agent is entitled to a compensation for his expenses. REstateA Article 21 contain detailed rules in this respect.

FRANCE: There is no specific dispositions under French law on that topic. The remuneration is not due after termination of the mandate contract if the mandate has not been fulfilled (case law, contrary to CC Article 1999(2); see Huet, no 31252). The situation will be different where the contract is not concluded due to the attitude of the principal and where the agent has sufficiently performed the contract. Thus, an estate agent will be entitled to remuneration if the contract has been entered into between the principal and a third party introduced by the agent (Cass.civ. 1re, 17 November 1993, Bull. civ. 1993 I, no. 323).

GERMANY: Under brokerage contracts (CC Article 652 paragraph (1)), the termination of the contract between principal and broker does not affect the broker's right to demand payment of a price if the prospective contract with a third party is later concluded: The broker is entitled to a price when the contract between principal and third party was concluded due to the services that were rendered by the broker while the brokerage contract was still in force, and the fact that the prospective contract was only concluded after termination of the brokerage contract is of no relevance (BGH, NJW 1966, 2008; Palandt/Sprau, Article 652 no. 47).

HUNGARY: According to CC Article 478 paragraphs (2) to (4), the remuneration of the agent does not depend on the conclusion of the contract. According to CC Article 478 paragraph (2), '(…) [i]f the contract is terminated before the agency has been fulfilled, the agent shall be entitled to demand an appropriate fraction of the fee for his activities. Fees shall be payable at the time a contract is extinguished.'

IRELAND: Remuneration may be payable after termination of the agency contract, depending on the terms of the agreement.

MALTA: In CA (Commercial) 7 March 1932, *Vella Zarb vs Caruana et. noe.,* the Court had to decide whether the principal should pay compensation to the agent if the principal has terminated the mandate without a just cause. The Court held that a paid agent whose mandate has been revoked without a just cause may have a right to be compensated for this revocation.

NETHERLANDS: According to CC Article 7:411 paragraph (1), the agent may be entitled to fair payment if the contract comes to an end ahead of time. According to CC Article 7:411 paragraph (2), the agent is entitled to full payment taking in consideration the specific circumstances. See HR 28 January 2005, NJ 2008, 41 (Van Vulpen/Debetz c.s.).

POLAND: The Polish Civil Code contains no provisions regulating this issue.

SCOTLAND: Where the agency was entered into to achieve a specific purpose, and the principal himself or another agent achieves that purpose, the agency relationship would be brought to an end on the basis that it is now impossible for the agent to achieve the agreed purpose. The agent might remain entitled to payment where the conclusion of the contract which is the purpose of the agency relationship is attributable in part to the agent's efforts, even if the agent is no longer involved at the moment of conclusion (Macgregor, paragraph 112; *Walker, Fraser & Steele v Fraser's Trustees* 1910 SC 222 at 229, per Lord Dundas; *Walker, Donald & Co v Birrell, Stenhouse & Co* (1883) 11 R 369).

SLOVAKIA: The agent is entitled to the price only if the conclusion of the contract is the result of the agent's effort (see Comm.C Article 651 for the brokerage contract; Comm.C Article 671 for the commercial representation contract).

SWEDEN: The agent is entitled to compensation for the work and effort put in to the performance of the Mandate contract. According to KommL Article 27 and HaL Article 10 a commissionaire or a trade agent has a right to compensation *(efterprovision)* even if the prospective contract was concluded after termination of the mandate relationship. This is the case when the prospective contract was concluded due to the efforts of the commissionaire or trade agent.

No answer received: AUSTRIA, BELGIUM, GREECE, ITALY, PORTUGAL, SPAIN.

Article 2:103: Expenses incurred by the agent

(1) When the agent is entitled to a price, the price is presumed to include the reimbursement of the expenses the agent has incurred in the performance of the obligations under the mandate contract.

(2) When the agent is not entitled to a price or when the parties have agreed that the expenses will be paid separately, the principal must reimburse the agent for the expenses the agent has incurred in the performance of the obligations under the mandate contract, when and in so far as the agent acted reasonably when incurring the expenses.

(3) The agent is entitled to reimbursement of expenses under paragraph (2) as from the time when the expenses are incurred and the agent has given account of the expenses.

(4) If the mandate relationship has terminated and the result on which the agent's remuneration is dependent is not achieved, the agent is entitled to reimbursement of reasonable expenses the agent has incurred in the performance of the obligations under the mandate contract. Paragraph (3) applies accordingly.

Comments

A. General idea

In the traditional view of a mandate relationship as a gratuitous service, it is logical that expenses should be reimbursed. However, nowadays mandate relationships are typically remunerated contracts. In paragraph (1) of the present Article, it is presumed that in this case the price agreed by the parties in mandate contracts includes the compensation of the expenses that the agent has to incur in the performance of the mandate. Where the contract is terminated, and as a result the agent loses the right to remuneration for the services rendered, paragraph (4) established his entitlement to a reimbursement of the expenses made. In cases where the parties agree that the expenses are to be paid separately or where there is no price to be paid, paragraph (2) establishes that the principal has to pay only the reasonable expenses, i.e. in so far as the agent acted reasonably when incurring the expenses. Paragraph (3) provides that payment of the compensation becomes due when the expenses are incurred and the agent has given account of that in accordance with Article 3:402 (Accounting to the principal), enabling the principal to question whether the expenses have been made reasonably.

B. Expenses included in the agreed price

Typically, the parties make explicit contractual arrangements as to the reimbursement of expenses. This provision regulates the situation where the contract is for a price and the parties remain silent about the matter of expenses. Paragraph (1) states that the principal – whether a consumer or a business – may reasonably rely on the price encompassing both the profit the agent seeks to gain from performing the contractual obligations and all the costs the agent will incur in carrying out the mandate.

If the default rule did not consider the expenses included in the price, the agent would have no incentive to perform as efficiently as possible, as higher expenses would automatically have to be reimbursed by the principal. If the agent wishes to have the expenses reimbursed separately, this ought to be made clear to the principal by a provision in the contract. The chosen default rule therefore also promotes communication between the parties.

Illustration 1
Donovan is charged by Evelyne to purchase a specific painting by Renoir. The painting is being sold at an auction in Paris, whereas both Donovan and Evelyne are located in London. If Donovan is entitled to a price for his services, it is presumed that the contract price includes a compensation for travel expenses and, if need be, expenses for accommodation.

C. Reasonable expenses only

If expenses are not included in the price – i.e. when on the basis of an express contractual agreement the expenses are to be paid separately or when the mandate is gratuitous – the principal is required to reimburse the agent for the expenses incurred, but only if the agent acted reasonably when incurring those expenses (paragraph (2)) .

Illustration 1 (continued)
If Donovan is not entitled to a price, Evelyne must compensate the expenses Donovan incurred in the performance of his mandate, provided that these expenses are reasonable. Whether it is reasonable for Donovan to travel by plane or train to Paris and book hotel accommodation, and if so, whether he can do so in a 5-star hotel or has to book a 3-star hotel, will depend on the circumstances of the case and on the contract.

D. When expenses payable

If and in so far as the agent is entitled to reimbursement of the expenses, the reimbursement becomes due only when the agent has given an account of the performance of the mandate in accordance with Article 3:402 (Accounting to the principal), as paragraph (3) of the present Article expresses. The reasoning behind this is that the principal need only reimburse the agent for the expenses that were incurred reasonably, and the principal can only evaluate the reasonableness when the agent has provided the means of doing so. The present rule therefore has the advantage that the principal is given an effective instrument to obtain sufficient information to evaluate the reasonableness of the expenses incurred.

E. Expenses still due when no entitlement to price because result not achieved

Where the mandate relationship is terminated before the result is achieved on which payment of remuneration is dependent (typically the conclusion of the prospective contract), the agent is left without payment, unless the parties had agreed upon payment for services rendered. In this respect, the agent is required to reach the envisaged result (typically the conclusion of the prospective contract) or lose the right to payment. This should not mean, however, that the agent then also has to bear the expenses incurred in attempting to carry out the mandate. For that reason, paragraph (4) explicitly provides that the agent is entitled to recovery of the expenses. This provision also prevents an *a contrario* reasoning on the basis of paragraph (1) of the Article.

Illustration 1 (continued)
If Donovan was entitled to a price if he had been able to purchase the painting, but Evelyne revokes his mandate, Donovan loses the chance of remuneration for his services and therefore also the possibility to reclaim the expenses made through the payment of the price. For this reason, under paragraph (4) of this Article, Donovan may claim compensation of the expenses made.

The reimbursement becomes due again when the agent has given an account in accordance with paragraph (3), which implies that the provision of paragraph (2) also applies as to the reasonableness of the expenses incurred. However, given the fact that the agent need not have taken the premature ending of the contract into account when making the expenses, the reasonableness test will need to be applied with some flexibility to safeguard the interests of the agent.

Illustration 1 (continued)
To be able to claim reimbursement of his expenses, Donovan must give an account of those expenses. Only to the extent the expenses were made reasonably is Evelyne required to compensate these costs. However, when determining whether this is the case, it must be borne in mind that had Evelyne not revoked the mandate, Donovan would have been able to bear the costs incurred because they would effectively have been included in the contract price and simply have been deducted from Donovan's expected profit. In this respect, it is of little importance whether Donovan travelled first class or

coach, or stayed in a hotel and, if so, in which price category. As Evelyne determined the revocation of the mandate, she generally has to accept the choices that Donovan made in the performance of his mandate and the costs resulting from these choices. However, Evelyne need not also compensate the expenses incurred because Donovan took his wife with him to spend a lover's weekend in Paris. The additional costs are incurred on a personal basis and are to be borne by Donovan, unless Donovan and Evelyne (implicitly or explicitly) agreed otherwise before these additional costs were incurred.

F. Damage sustained by agent during performance of the mandate contract

Traditionally, a mandate contract is a gratuitous contract. As a result, the general view was not only that any expenses made by the agent in the performance of the contract should be compensated by the principal, but also any damage sustained by the agent as a result of his performance. Such a rule is not self-evident in a situation where the agent receives a price for his services and therefore has the possibility to have the risk of damage covered by insurance and to calculate the price accordingly. In such cases, the agent is usually in a better position to know of the risks involved in the performance of the mandate contract, and therefore to consider whether insurance coverage is needed. However, there are still mandate contracts that are concluded gratuitously. Therefore, the question arises whether for such gratuitous mandate contracts the traditional rule that damage sustained during the performance of the mandate contract is to be compensated by the principal should be kept or whether such a rule should not be included in these Principles.

Where the contract is performed gratuitously, this is actually a friendly turn. Such altruistic behaviour is socially desirable. This implies that the agent should not be withheld from concluding a mandate contract for the mere fear that he may sustain damage without being compensated. Therefore, a gratuitously acting agent should in principle be compensated. As a principle, for gratuitous mandate contracts this is not disputed in any of the Member States. It is also not disputed that the agent is not entitled to damages if the occurrence of the damage can be imputed to him ('if the damage was his own fault'). It is unclear what should happen if the occurrence of the damage can be imputed neither to the agent nor to the principal. In other words: should the principal be liable if the occurrence of damage is caused by *force majeure* or through the act of a third party?

Illustration 2
Alfred is commissioned by Bert to buy a puppy from Bert's neighbour Charlie, a private seller. All of a sudden, another dog bites Alfred in the face; Alfred needs plastic surgery and suffers emotional distress. Of course, Charlie, the owner of the dog, is liable, but he is insolvent. Should the unfortunate Alfred then have a claim against Bert?

In this situation, neither the agent (Alfred) nor the principal (Bert) has done anything wrong. It is also clear that the principal could not have prevented the damage. Under these circumstances, should Alfred have a claim against Bert?

A different question is whether the damage that was sustained should be specific to the performance of the mandate contract and therefore could be seen as an inherent risk to the performance of the mandate contract, or that the manifestation of any danger could trigger the principal's liability. In the case of Illustration 2, Alfred would not have been bitten had he not been at the house where both the puppy and the other dog were present. One may wonder whether the risk of being bitten by a dog is a 'specific risk', at it could also have occurred had Alfred been there as a private person. The absence of a clear link between the performance of the mandate contract and the manifestation of the damage is even stronger in the following case:

Illustration 3
Derek is commissioned to buy a painting at an auction. On his way to the auction, Derek is hurt in an accident by a cyclist, who is guilty of the accident but immediately flees from the scene and cannot be traced.

In this situation, again neither the agent nor the principal has done anything wrong. In this case, the damage sustained is only indirectly related to the performance of the mandate contract: Derek would not have been at the place of the accident had he not been going to the auction, but there is no strong causal link here. Should this mean that the principal need not reimburse Derek for the damage sustained?

In most legal systems, the principal is liable for the damage sustained by the agent in the performance of the mandate contract, unless the principal proves that the agent has acted carelessly or negligently. Typically, it is not relevant whether the principal could have prevented the damage. The same rule also applies in ESTONIA and THE NETHERLANDS if a danger specific to the contract manifests. In these legal systems, no right to compensation exists if the risk of the danger manifesting itself was taken into account when the price was calculated; where the agent acted in the performance of his profession or trade, compensation is due only if the specific risk does not exceed the normal professional risks. By contrast, in DENMARK, FINLAND, HUNGARY, POLAND, and SWEDEN, the principal is not liable if he proves that he (the principal) was not negligent in preventing the damage.

Illustration 2 (continued)
This brief comparative overview indicates that in most legal systems, Alfred would indeed have a claim against Bert.

Illustration 3 (continued)
From the comparative overview, it also follows that Derek is also compensated in most legal systems, but not in DENMARK, FINLAND, HUNGARY, POLAND, and SWEDEN, and also not in ESTONIA and THE NETHERLANDS.

In theory, one could defend five possible rules regarding whether the agent should be entitled to claim damages if he has sustained damage in the performance of the mandate.

1. First, one could argue that when the damage is sustained as a consequence of the performance of the mandate, this damage should be compensated by the principal whether or not he could have prevented the damage. This is in fact a form of strict liability, which is mitigated only if the agent himself was negligent (which the principal will have to prove). This alternative is in accordance with the position taken in most legal systems.

2. The second alternative would be that the principal is liable to compensate the damage sustained by the agent, unless he proves that he could not prevented the damage, i.e. that the occurrence of damage constitutes force majeure.

3. The third alternative, which is in accordance with DUTCH and ESTONIAN law, provides as the main rule that the agent is not entitled to damages, but allows for two exceptions: first, a situation where the risk that has manifested was of such a nature that the agent could not have taken it into account when the agent calculated the price, and second, a situation where no price was agreed upon, i.e. the contract was performed gratuitously.

4. The fourth alternative is that the professional agent is not compensated, but the agent that acted on the basis of a gratuitous contract would be compensated. This alternative starts from the idea that when the agent calculates the price for his services, he is expected to include all the costs, including any insurance premium he needs to pay or any reservation he needs to make to cover unexpected losses. This option is currently defended in DENMARK, FINLAND, HUNGARY, POLAND, and SWEDEN.

5. Finally, the fifth option would be that neither the professional agent nor the agent acting gratuitously would be entitled to compensation. This alternative starts from the basic principle in contract law that each party carries its own costs, unless damage can be attributed to the other party. This solution is currently not accepted in any of the legal systems.

Notwithstanding the fact that such a rule is currently not accepted in any of the Member States, it is this last option that is followed in these Principles: neither in the present Article nor in any other provision of these Principles has a specific provision entitling the agent to damages been included. In other words, it is thought that the agent should not be compensated for damage sustained in the performance of the mandate unless the principal has in fact breached a duty of care owed to the agent. This is thought to be justified, as nowadays most mandate contracts are concluded for a price and the agent should have included a compensation for potential damage or the costs of insurance coverage when calculating the price. This reasoning is, of course, not applicable to gratuitous mandate contracts. However, it was thought that in so far as such contracts involve substantial foreseeable risks for the agent, the parties will normally have made specific arrangements to cover those risks. In so far as this is not the case or an unforeseen risk manifests, it was thought that normally sufficient protection is offered for natural persons through health insurance schemes or public funds. Where this is not the case, the provisions on unforeseen circumstances in Article 6:111 PECL (Change of circumstances) may provide relief.

G. Relation to the Principles of European Law and the Draft Common Frame of Reference

This Article mirrors that of Article IV.D. – 2:103 DCFR (Expenses incurred by agent).

H. Character of the rule

This Article constitutes a default rule from which the parties may derogate.

I. Remedies

If the principal fails to reimburse the expenses the agent is entitled to under this Article, the agent may claim payment under Article 9:101 PECL (Monetary obligations). Alternatively, the agent may claim damages – including interest for late payment – under Articles 9:501 (Right to damages) and 9:508 PECL (Delay in payment of money), or termination of the contract under Articles 9:301 ff PECL (Right to terminate the contract).

Comparative Notes

1. Right to reimbursement of expenses

In all legal systems, the agent is entitled to reimbursement of expenses incurred in the performance of the obligations under the contract if the parties had not agreed upon a price or if it is established that the expenses are not included in the price. In SWEDEN in particular it is held that even though the price is presumed to cover the expenses, the agent can nevertheless claim reimbursement of expenses in addition to the price if it can be shown that the particular expenses were not included in the calculation of the price, especially with regard to unforeseen expenses. In ITALY, MALTA, THE NETHERLANDS, and PORTUGAL, it has been clearly established that the principal is required to pay interest over the expenses to be compensated.

2. Expenses presumed to be included in price

Where the parties had agreed on a price, it is presumed that the expenses are included in the price and therefore cannot be claimed separately in DENMARK, ESTONIA, FINLAND, SWEDEN, and in GERMANY with regard to intermediation contracts. Moreover, in GERMANY, this point of view is argued in legal doctrine for mandate contracts as well, notwithstanding the fact that the text of the Civil Code points in a different direction. The same view is generally accepted in THE NETHERLANDS.

However, in the majority of legal systems, the fact that the parties had agreed upon a price does not stand in the way of the agent claiming expenses separately. This implies that in these countries, expenses are not presumed to have been included in the price. This is the situation in AUSTRIA, BELGIUM, BULGARIA, FRANCE, GREECE, HUNGARY, IRELAND, ITALY, MALTA, POLAND, PORTUGAL, SLOVAKIA, and SPAIN. This is also the case in ENGLAND; however, many professional agents are not usually entitled to expenses in addition to their remuneration.

There is no clear rule in SCOTLAND, though it is generally accepted that a solicitor is entitled to claim both the price and reimbursement of expenses.

3. Reasonable expenses only

In FRANCE, the principal can escape from having to compensate the costs incurred only if he proves that the agent was negligent in incurring the costs, in which case the agent is liable to pay damages towards the principal; these damages will then compensate the amount the principal would have to pay to reimburse the agent.

In most other legal systems, the agent has a duty to act reasonably when incurring expenses. Failure to do so then implies that the principal need not reimburse the agent for these expenses. In PORTUGAL, the test is a double one: the expenses must be reasonable per se, and the agent must have had the conviction that the expenses were necessary. However, the principal bears the burden to prove that the expenses were incurred unreasonably or unnecessarily. The burden of proof is the same in BELGIUM, DENMARK, GREECE, and SLOVAKIA. However, the burden of proof as to whether the expenses have been incurred reasonably rests on the agent in BULGARIA, ESTONIA, FINLAND, and ITALY. Similarly, in GERMANY the agent has to prove the facts based upon which he considered the expenses to be necessary (e.g. a direction the principal gave). In ENGLAND, the agent must prove that he has incurred expenses and that such expenses comply with the conditions defined earlier.

The fact that the agent could have spent less in the performance of the mandate does not stand in the way of his entitlement to claim compensation in full for his expenses in BELGIUM, FRANCE, ITALY, and MALTA.

4. Time when reimbursement of expenses is due and right to advances

Member States differ as to the moment when reimbursement of the expenses is due. In BELGIUM, FIN-LAND, ITALY, THE NETHERLANDS, SLOVAKIA, and SWEDEN, the reimbursement becomes due only when the agent has given an account of the expenses. In AUSTRIA, ENGLAND, ESTONIA, FRANCE, GERMANY, IRELAND, PORTUGAL, and SPAIN, reimbursement of expenses is due immediately when the expenses are incurred. Yet most legal systems that fall in this second category require the agent to prove that the expenses have indeed been incurred, so in fact there is not much difference between these two systems. This may be different in DENMARK, FINLAND, GREECE, MALTA, and POLAND, as in these legal systems the payment of expenses becomes due only when the contract is either performed in full or terminated.

5. Right to advance for expenses

In so far as it is foreseeable that the agent will have to incur expenses in the performance of the contract, he is entitled to an advance thereof in AUSTRIA, BELGIUM, BULGARIA, ESTONIA, GERMANY, GREECE, HUNGARY, ITALY, POLAND, PORTUGAL, SLOVAKIA, and SPAIN, and possibly also in SCOTLAND. No such right (apart from a contractual agreement), however, exists in DENMARK, FINLAND, FRANCE, IRELAND, MALTA and SWEDEN, and probably also not in ENGLAND and THE NETHERLANDS.

6. Compensation of damage sustained

In most legal systems, the agent is entitled to compensation for any damage sustained in the performance of the mandate contract, unless the agent acted negligently and the damage is caused as a result thereof. This is the case in AUSTRIA, BELGIUM, ENGLAND, FRANCE, GERMANY, ITALY, MALTA, PORTUGAL, and SCOTLAND. In these legal systems, the fact that the principal could not have prevented the damage is not relevant. This means that in these legal systems, the principal is, in principle, strictly liable for the occurrence of damage to the agent. The same rule applies in GREECE if the agent was not entitled to a price and did not act in a professional capacity. In ESTONIA and THE NETHERLANDS, the principal is liable for such damage if a danger specific to the contract manifests. In these legal systems, no right to compensation exists if the risk of the danger manifesting itself was taken into account when the price was calculated; where the agent acted in the performance of his profession or trade, compensation is due only if the specific risk does not exceed the normal professional risks.

By contrast, in DENMARK, FINLAND, HUNGARY, and POLAND, the principal is liable only if the occurrence of damage may be attributed to him. This is true also for SWEDEN; however, imputability is presumed, implying that the principal must prove that the damage did not occur as a consequence of his negligence.

National Notes

1. Right to reimbursement of expenses if no price or not included in price

AUSTRIA: The agent is entitled to reimbursement of reasonable (necessary and useful) expenses he made in performance of the contract (CC Article 1014).

BELGIUM: According to CC Article 1999, the agent is entitled to reimbursement of the expenses made in performance of the contract (De Page, p. 423-431; Foriers & Glansdorff, p. 625-626; Tilleman, p. 123-124; Wéry p. 203 ff.). CC Article 1999 states furthermore that if the agent is not in breach, the principal cannot refuse to reimburse the expenses, even if the mandate failed. Neither can the principal reduce the amount of the expenses under the pretext that they could have been lower. As a rule, the principal therefore cannot escape the (integral) reimbursement of the expenses by stating that he could have accomplished the mandate in a cheaper way.

BULGARIA: Even when the remuneration has not been stipulated in a general mandate contract, the principal is obliged, upon a request from the agent, to reimburse the expenses incurred in the course of performance of the contract together with interests (OCA Article 285). Unless otherwise agreed upon in the contract, the commercial agent shall be entitled to reimbursement of usual costs, incurred in the course of his activity (CA Article 39). The principal is obliged to reimburse the commissioner (CA Article 356) and the forwarder (CA Article 361 (2)) for expenses made in the performance of the contract.

DENMARK: According to general acknowledged custom, the agent is entitled to reimbursement of the ordinary expenses incurred in performance of the contract. Normally the claim of reimbursement will be accepted by the court only when the agent has acted reasonably in his effort to perform his duties. If the principal will not pay the expenses, the burden to prove that the agent did not act reasonably lies on the principal.

ENGLAND: In English law, the agent has, generally, a right to be reimbursed for all expenses he may incur in the execution of his authority. In addition, the agent has a right to claim indemnity which covers all liabilities incurred or payments made by the agent whilst performing his duties. The agent's right to indemnity therefore covers all payments which the principal and the agent are liable to make (e.g. *Adams v Morgan & Co* [1924] 1 KB 751). The right of the agent to claim expenses/indemnity varies depending on whether the agency is contractual or not (see generally Bowstead & Reynolds, paragraphs 7.058 and 7.059). When the agency is contractual, unless expressly excluded in the contract, a term – express or implied – will define the conditions of reimbursement of expenses of the agent. The agent cannot claim (a) expenses incurred for an authorised transaction which has not been ratified by the principal; (b) expenses incurred when performing the principal's illegal instructions providing that the agent knows that it is illegal or where the transaction itself is unlawful (e.g. *Re Parker* (1882) 21 Ch D 408, Ex p Mather (1797) 3 Ves 373, *Smith v Lindo* (1858) 5 CBNS 587, *Adamson v Jarvis* (1827) 4 Bing 66); (c) expenses incurred in relation to wagering transactions (Gaming Act 1892, Article 1); or (d) expenses incurred by being negligent, insolvent, by acting in breach of duty or by defaulting (e.g. *Lage v Siemens Bros & Co Ltd* (1932) 42 Ll Rep 252). When the agency is not contractual, the claim of the agent does not cover the full indemnity since it is restitutionary in nature and consequently narrower than for contractual agencies. In such cases, the agent's claim is restricted to the reimbursement of payments for which the principal has the ultimate liability, which were made by the agent under compulsion of law and from which the principal obtains a benefit by the discharge of a liability (*Brook's Wharf & Bull Wharf Ltd v Goodman Bros* [1937] 1 KB 534), Bowstead & Reynolds, paragraph 7.059.

ESTONIA: For the (general) contract for services, the service provider (the agent) is entitled to reimbursement for 'reasonable' expenses unless such expenses are covered by the price (LOAEst Article 628(2)). Where the contract is gratuitous, reimbursement of expenses can therefore always be claimed. Specific rules apply for the contract of agency: an agent may demand reimbursement of reasonable expenses if so agreed upon or if this is usual under the circumstances, regardless of whether the agent has the right to receive an agency fee (LOAEst Article 684).

FINLAND: The agent is, unless otherwise agreed, entitled to a compensation for his reasonable expenses (Comm.C Article 18:5). The burden of proof usually lies on the agent.

FRANCE: The agent is entitled to reimbursement of the expenses (CC Article 1999).

GERMANY: Where the mandate contract is gratuitous, the agent is entitled to reimbursement of the expenses he made in performance of the contract according to CC Article 670.

GREECE: The right of the agent to reimbursement of the expenses he incurred in performance of the contract depends on the internal relationship based on the contract of mandate. According to CC Article 722 a principal shall be bound to reimburse the agent for everything the latter has spent to achieve an orderly performance of the mandate. The parties can deviate from that rule and agree to a restriction or enlargement of the required expenses (CFI Chalkida decision no. 563/2002, NoV 2003, 1271).

HUNGARY: In case of agency, according to CC Article 479 paragraph (1), '[c]osts that arise in connection with the handling of a matter shall be borne by the principal. The agent shall not be obliged to advance any costs'. Contrary to the general rules of agency, in the case of commission agency, '[t]he commission shall include the expenses usually involved with consignment, but it shall not include expenses related to carriage' (CC Article 511 paragraph (2)). Nevertheless, '[t]he commission agent shall be entitled to demand reimbursement for those of his necessary and useful expenses that are not included in the commission; however, he shall only be entitled to demand those of his substantiated expenses otherwise included in the commission only if the sales contract has not been performed due to reasons within the commission agent's control' (CC Article 511 paragraph (3)).

IRELAND: At common law, an agent is entitled to be indemnified against any reasonable expenses and liabilities, necessarily incurred on behalf of the principal in performance of his duties when acting within the scope of his actual authority, or, if his actions are later ratified, or if the agency is one of necessity. Where the agents actions are unauthorised, no right to indemnity arises. Where the agency is contractual the right to indemnity will be an implied term of the contract; where the agency is gratuitous the right will be restitutionary. The right to indemnity does not cover any expenses or liabilities incurred due to the agent's own fault, nor any expenses or liabilities with regard to acts that the agent knew to be unlawful or illegal *(Re Parker* (1882) 21 Ch D 408). The right to indemnity may also cover payments made by an agent even where there was no legal obligation to pay, where there is strong moral and professional pressure to pay *(Rhodes v Fielder, Jones and Harrison* (1919) 89 LJKB 15.

ITALY: The agent is entitled to reimbursement of the expenses he made in performance of the contract (CC Article 1720). The principal has to reimburse any advances on the expenses made by the agent as well as the interests accrued thereupon since the day of payment thereof (e.g. an advance on the final price owed by the principal in his quality as purchaser to the third party).

MALTA: According to CC Article 1881, the agent is entitled to the reimbursement of the advances and expenses incurred whilst carrying out the contract. Such expenses may relate to the costs of carriage, customs duty, costs of unloading, storage expenses etc. In order that such expenses be refunded they must have been necessary for the execution of the mandate. Secondly, the expenses will be refunded only if they were incurred by the agent in good faith. In fact, CC Article 1881(2) states that "If no negligence be imputable to the agent, the principal cannot refuse to make such reimbursement and payment, even though the matter has not been successful; nor can he have the amount of such expenses and advances bona fide incurred or made, reduced, on the ground that they might have been less." From this Article we can infer that the agent is only bound to show that he executed the contract in good faith and that he has used the diligence of a *bonus pater familias.* The agent is thus entitled to be reimbursed for all the expenses although the principal proves that they might have been less. With regard to the reimbursement of expenses, Maltese law also provides that the principal is bound to pay interest to the agent on the sums advanced for the payment of the expenses, from the day of the payment of such sums. CC Article 1883 states that "Interest is due by the principal to the agent on the advances and expenses mentioned in Article 1881 from the day of the payment of such sums."

NETHERLANDS: The reimbursement of expenses of the agent has been established in CC Article 7:406. According to this article, the principal is held to compensate the agent for the expenses that are related to the performance of the service, unless these expenses are included in the agent's wages (CC Article 7:406 paragraph (1)). Often the reimbursement of expenses occurs in case of mandate contracts free of charge.

POLAND: The principal is obliged to pay back all the expenses incurred by the agent regardless of whether the service is provided against a remuneration or not, and the expenses are presumed not to be included in the remuneration (CC Article 742).

PORTUGAL: The agent is entitled to reimbursement, with interest, of the expenses he made in performance of the contract (CC Article 1167).

SCOTLAND: The agent is entitled to be reimbursed his expenses so far as these are properly incurred (Gow, p. 534; *Annan v Marshall* (1887) 25 SLR 94). It is an implied term of the contract entered into between a solicitor and principal to the effect that authorised, or impliedly authorised, outlays incurred in pursuing the principal's case will be reimbursed (Paterson, no. 4.04; Begg, p. 120-1).

SLOVAKIA: Under CC Article 728, unless otherwise agreed, the principal shall provide to agent at the latter's request the appropriate funds for the performance of the mandate in advance and reimburse him subsequently for all necessary and expedient expenses incurred in performing the mandate, even if the result was not attained. After performance of the mandate the agent shall present his account or statement of his costs or expenditure to the principal. The same is true under the provisions of the Commercial Code.

SPAIN: The agent is entitled to reimbursement of expenses (CC Articles 1728 and 1729). The payment of expenses is differentiated in CC Article 1728 from the payment of the price.

SWEDEN: Normally, the price is presumed to cover the expenses, see Hesser, p. 58; Hellner, p. 211. Some-times, however, the agent can claim reimbursement of expenses in addition to the price, see Comm.C Article 18:5, and Tiberg/Dotevall p. 34, in particular with regard to unforeseen expenses which are not included in the price, see Bengtsson, p. 170. If the contract keeps silent, the question of reimbursement of expenses could be determined by reference to accepted practice, when applicable, in a particular line of business and/or the circumstances of the particular case.

2. Expenses presumed to be included in price

AUSTRIA: In the case where the (commercial) agent is entitled to a price and the contract keeps silent about the reimbursement of expenses, the agent may claim both a price and a reimbursement of the ex-penses made (Rummel/Strasser, Article 1014 Rz 3; Straube/Griss, Article 396 HGB Rz 1, 9-14).

BELGIUM: Because the obligation to pay a salary and the obligation to repay the expenses cover both different items, in case of silence of the contract about the reimbursement of expenses, the agent is never-theless entitled to both a price and the reimbursement of expenses.

BULGARIA: Also for non-gratuitous mandate contracts, there is no presumption that the expenses are included in the price and explicit provisions regulate the reimbursement of costs, apart from payment of the remuneration. Such special provisions are, for instance, for the commercial agent CA Article 39, for the commission contract CA Article 356 (2), and for forwarding contracts CA Article 361 (2).

DENMARK: Normally the price agreed upon between the principal and the agent will be presumed to cover the expenses. In other words: the agent is not entitled to claim extra remuneration for the expenses occurred under the performance of the prospective contract.

ENGLAND: In English law, agents have a right, in addition to be remunerated for their services, to claim expenses incurred in the performance of the obligations under the contract. Many professional agents such as auctioneers and estate agents are not usually entitled to expenses in addition to remuneration (Murdoch, 14148, as cited by Bowstead & Reynolds, paragraph 7.061).

ESTONIA: For non-gratuitous contracts LOAEst Article 628(2) stipulates the presumption that the price covers the expenses, which are usually incurred by performance of such contract, and the expenses, which the agent would have incurred even without entering into the contract.

FINLAND: It depends on the circumstances (e.g. nature of the contract, parties, the area of business prac-tice etc.) whether the expenses are included in the price or not. In most cases typical expenses are considered to be included in the price. According to ACRS Article 18, the commercial agent is entitled to a special compensation for costs incurred by measures necessary for the proper execution of the mandate contract. No compensation shall, however, be payable if the costs are incurred as the result of the customary activities of the commercial agent. The regulation in ACRS may, in this respect, have some wider importance throughout analogies.

FRANCE: The law distinguishes clearly between remuneration and reimbursement, which is subject of distinct rules. Where the contract is silent, the provision for remuneration does not include the reimburse-ment of expenses incurred, which are always due (CC Article 1999). For some cases there are specific rules; the remuneration of a real estate agent always includes the expenses he made to fulfil his task.

GERMANY: As CC Article 675 paragraph (1) also makes reference to CC Article 670, this would speak for the expenses not to be covered by the price (to which the agent is always entitled within the sphere of CC Article 675 paragraph (1)). However, some authors point out that CC Article 670 should not be applied when the agent can claim a price (which should be considered to cover expenses), and accordingly argue that – if in doubt – expenses should be construed to be covered by the price under any remunerated contract (Heermann, in: Münchener Kommentar zum BGB, Article 675 no. 20; Palandt/Sprau, Article 675 no. 8).

Under a brokerage contract, the situation is explicitly regulated by CC Article 652 paragraph (2) stipulating that the broker cannot demand reimbursement of expenses unless otherwise agreed.

GREECE: The obligation of the reimbursement of expenses is explicitly regulated in CC Article 722.

HUNGARY: In the case where the agent is entitled to a price and the contract keeps silent about the reimbursement of expenses, CC Article 479 paragraph (1) applies according to which '[c]osts that arise in connection with the handling of a matter shall be borne by the principal. The agent shall not be obliged to advance any costs.' Contrary to the general rules of agency, in the case of commission agency, '[t]he commission shall include the expenses usually involved with consignment, but it shall not include expenses related to carriage' (CC Article 511 paragraph (2)). Nevertheless, '[t]he commission agent shall be entitled to demand reimbursement for those of his necessary and useful expenses that are not included in the commission; however, he shall only be entitled to demand those of his substantiated expenses otherwise included in the commission only if the sales contract has not been performed due to reasons within the interest sphere of the principal' (CC Article 511 paragraph (3)).

IRELAND: An agent's claim to (i) remuneration and (ii) an indemnity for expenses are treated as separate rights, at common law. Therefore, an agent may be entitled to claim both remuneration and an indemnity, separately and cumulatively. However, a contract can provide otherwise. So, for example, it could be agreed that an auctioneer's advertising costs would be included in any commission earned.

ITALY: Unless otherwise specified in the contract, any and all reimbursements are due in addition to the price agreed by the agent and the principal.

MALTA: According to CC Article 1881 paragraph (1), the agent has the right to claim both the price and the reimbursement of the expenses made.

NETHERLANDS: The reimbursement of expenses of the agent is governed by CC Article 7:406. According to this article, the principal is held to compensate the agent for the expenses that are related to the performance of the service, unless these expenses are included in the agent's wages (CC Article 7:406 paragraph (1)). In case of professional mandate contracts, the principal for the most part will not have to compensate for these expenses because they are included in the agent's wages. Often the reimbursement of expenses occurs in case of mandate contracts free of charge. In that case the reimbursement of the agent's expenses have to be fair. It is important to consider that these expenses do not only solely include out of pocket expenses. The agent may also ask reimbursement of the use of his own car.

POLAND: Unless the parties have agreed otherwise the agent has the right to the reimbursement of expenses regardless of whether the service is provided against the remuneration or not. If the parties haven't agreed otherwise the expenses are not included in the price.

PORTUGAL: In case of silence of the contract, the provisions of Article 1167 lit (c) apply, and the agent is due both the price and the expenses incurred.

SCOTLAND. This matter is likely to be governed by custom or practice in the particular commercial context. There appears to be no general rule. In the case of a solicitor, where the contract is silent, there is no presumption that the expenses are included in the price. In other words, the solicitor is entitled to claim both the price and reimbursement of expenses.

SLOVAKIA: CC Article 728 provides that the agent may claim both a price and reimbursement of the expenses made. The same is true in the case of a commercial mandate contract under Comm.C Article 572. However, in the case of a commission agency contract, Comm.C Article 588 indicates that in in case of doubt, it is presumed that the commission also includes compensation for costs and expenses. The principal is bound to reimburse the agent for all expenses that the agent necessarily and purposefully incurred when performing the obligation, unless it follows from the nature of the expenses that they are included in the agent's remuneration (Comm.C Article 572).

SPAIN: The obligation to pay a price or fee and the obligation to reimburse the expenses cover different issues. Therefore in case of silence of the contract about the reimbursement of expenses, the agent is nevertheless entitled to both a price and the reimbursement of expenses (CC Article 1728). The matter is regulated expressly for the commercial commission, Comm.C Articles 277 and 278.

SWEDEN: Normally, the price is presumed to cover the expenses, see Hesser, p. 58; Hellner, p. 211. Sometimes, however, the agent can claim reimbursement of expenses in addition to the price, see Comm.C Article 18:5, and Tiberg/Dotevall, p. 34. A distinction could be made between expenses of a common nature which are to be considered to be included in the price and unforeseen expenses which are not included, see Bengtsson, p. 170. If the contract keeps silent, the question of reimbursement of expenses could be determined by reference to accepted practice, when applicable, in a particular line of business and/or the circumstances of the particular case.

3. Reasonable expenses only

AUSTRIA: The agent has to act reasonably when incurring expenses and bears the burden to prove that he acted reasonably (OGH in SZ 11/239; 29/40; EvBl 1963/309; SZ 7/29). The commercial regulations provide similar rules if there is an express promise (Comm.C Article 396(2) for commission agents, Comm.C Article 440 for forwarders, HVertrG Article 13 for special expenses of commercial agents).

BELGIUM: If expenses were incurred because of a fault of the agent (e.g. superfluous, exaggerated or bad-timed expenses), the court can reduce or refuse these expenses (Tilleman, p. 124; Wéry, p. 206-207, no. 163). CC Article 1999 asserts that only clearly exaggerated expenses can lead to a reduction or a refusal. The legislator wanted to exclude discussions on small economy (De Page, p. 425-426; Tilleman, p. 124). The principal bears the burden of proof (Wéry, p. 206).

BULGARIA: Only necessary expenses justified by the contractual performance have to be reimbursed (Любен Василев, Облигационно право, p. 27). The agent bears the burden of proof regarding the existence and amount of the expenses (Меворах/Лиджи/Фархи, III, p. 159). There are special rules for the commercial agent: if such an agent is a professional agent acting independently in the capacity of a merchant, all underlying expenses connected with the business (e.g. office rent) are on the agent's own account, unless otherwise stipulated. The commercial agent is entitled, however, to reimbursement of usual costs incurred in the course of the activity for performance of the obligations under the contract with the principal (CA Article 39; Герджиков, Коментар на Търговския закон, I, p. 158-159).

DENMARK: Normally the claim of reimbursement will be accepted by the court only when the agent has acted reasonably in his effort to perform his duties. If the principal will not pay the expenses, the burden to prove that the agent did not act reasonably lies on the principal.

ENGLAND: For the agent to be entitled to claim expenses, the agent must have acted reasonably (see *Pettman v Keble* (1850) 9 CB 701), i.e. he must not have acted in breach of his authority, negligently or unlawfully.

ESTONIA: In cases where the agent is entitled to reimbursement of expenses, he bears the burden of proof that he has acted reasonably.

FINLAND: The agent is, unless otherwise agreed, entitled to a compensation for his reasonable expenses (Comm.C Article 18:5). The burden of proof usually lies on the agent.

FRANCE: According to CC Article 1999, even where the principal has proved that the agent could have incurred less expenditure in the performance of the mandate, the expenses must be reimbursed. The only limit is where there has been a breach of the contract or negligence: where the expenses incurred are such that there has been a mismanagement. The agent could then be ordered to indemnify the principal in that respect. Damages will therefore compensate the payment of the excessive expenses. The principal has to prove the existence of such mismanagement.

GERMANY: The agent is entitled to reimbursement of those expenses that he 'could consider to be necessary under the circumstances', CC Article 670. The agent has to prove the facts based upon which he considered the expenses to be necessary (e.g. a direction the principal gave) (Palandt/Sprau, Article 671 no. 7).

GREECE: The agent is obliged, if there is no agreement to the contrary, to incur only the necessary expenses required for the performance of the mandate taking into consideration the aim and the extent of the mandate, the interests of the principal and all the conditions which will lead to the successful performance of the mandate (CC Article 722; Georgiadis/Stathopoulos/Karasis, CC Article 723, no. 4-5). If the agent brings an action for the reimbursement of the expenses, he bears the burden to prove the extent and the necessity of the expenses he incurred in order to achieve an orderly execution of the aim of the mandate. If the principal claims against the action of the agent that the expenses were not necessary he bears the burden to prove such a claim (CA Athens decision no. 8183/1989, EllDni 1991, 210).

HUNGARY: As CC Article 277 paragraph (4) prescribes that '[t]he obligor shall act to perform the contract in the manner that can generally be expected in the given situation, while the obligee shall promote performance in the same manner', only reasonable expenses are to be reimbursed by the principal.

IRELAND: At common law, an agent is entitled to be indemnified against any reasonable expenses and liabilities, necessarily incurred on behalf of the principal in performance of his duties when acting within the scope of his actual authority, or, if his actions are later ratified, or if the agency is one of necessity.

ITALY: The principal is not obliged to reimburse expenses which derive from an irresponsible behaviour of the agent (who thereby acted in breach of contract). On the contrary, the principal cannot refuse to pay reimbursements for the sole reason that the concluded contract turns out to be unsuccessful: the principal's refusal to pay is only justified in case of a negligent conduct of the agent. According to the general rules on evidence, the claimant has to prove the facts he relies upon. Consequently, the onus of proof that the agent acted reasonably and diligently is borne by the agent who seeks reimbursement of his expenses.

NETHERLANDS: Generally, the reimbursement of the agent's expenses have to be fair. This implies that the agent is entitled to reimbursement of expenses if the costs that he made are reasonable regarding the performance of the mandate contract. It is important to consider that these expenses may not only include out of pocket expenses. The agent may also ask reimbursement of the use of his own car.

POLAND: Only reasonable expenses required to properly carry out the mandate contract (CC Article 742).

PORTUGAL: The agent is only to be reimbursed of reasonable expenses he incurred during the execution of the mandate. The criterion is both objective and subjective: the expenses must be per se reasonable, and the agent must have had the conviction that the expenses were necessary. The client would have the burden to prove that these were made unreasonably, after the account given by the agent, under the general rules of contract law.

SCOTLAND: An agent is only entitled to recover expenses which have been properly incurred (Gow, p. 534; *Annan v Marshall* (1887) 25 SLR 94). A solicitor is not entitled to recover expenses which are either unreasonable or manifestly unnecessary unless they have been expressly authorised by the principal (Begg, p. 121).

SLOVAKIA: The agent is entitled to reimbursement of the reasonable expenses. It is relevant whether he acted reasonably, necessarily and purposefully. The agent is required to give a statement of account to the principal. It is, however, the principal who bears the burden to prove that the agent did not act reasonably.

SPAIN: A 'reasonableness' cap to the right to reimbursement is unknown in Spanish law.

SWEDEN: The agent is entitled to reimbursement of the expenses only under the condition that the expenses were necessary when performing the contract or that the agent has reasonably considered the expenses to be necessary, see Bengtsson, p. 170. If the agent ought to have been aware that the expenses were unnecessary he will not be able to claim reimbursement.

4. Time when reimbursement of expenses due

AUSTRIA: In the absence of an express agreement, payment of expenses is due immediately when the expenses are incurred (Rummel/Strasser, Article 1014 Rz 7; OGH in Miet 33/117; Miet 35/10; 36/73; ImmZ 1992, 263; Miet 45/44). Rendering of accounts is no precondition. Where the commercial regulations apply, reimbursement of the expenses is due when the account is rendered (Comm.C Article 384).

BELGIUM: As a rule the payment of the reimbursement of expenses is due at the moment of accounting by the agent, i.e. at the end of the mandate contract. An agent is permitted to ask for an immediate reimbursement, in case of deficiency (Wéry, p. 205).

BULGARIA: Reimbursement of the expenses is due 'under the request' by the agent (OCA Article 285). The principal is obliged to reimburse even when the mandate contract has been terminated as a result of his withdrawal or the performance has become impossible (OCA Article 288).

DENMARK: Unless otherwise expressly agreed upon between the parties, the payment of price and reimbursement will fall due as soon as the agent has fulfilled the contract of representation. A claim for reimbursement will normally be needed to fix the exact amount of the expenses.

ENGLAND: Reimbursement of expenses is due as soon as the agent can prove that he has incurred expenses and that such expenses comply with the conditions defined earlier.

ESTONIA: The reimbursement is due once the expenses have been made (LOAEst Article 113 paragraph (3)).

FINLAND: Unless otherwise agreed, payment is usually due in reasonable time after the fulfilment of the agent's contractual duties and after a demand of the agent. The payment shall not take place until an account is given, if such is required. The agent is usually not entitled to an advance payment. This is, in general, not the case in long-term mandates where periodical payments may take place. The ACRS Article 10 and 11 contain detailed rules concerning the time of payment.

FRANCE: The agent may claim immediate reimbursement of expenses incurred. In effect, the law provides that the principal must pay the agent interest in respect of the sums which have been incurred for the performance of the mandate as soon as such expenses have been incurred (CC Article 2001). It should be noted that since the law is silent on the subject, the indemnification of losses incurred by the agent in performance of the mandate will occur at the end of the mandate.

GERMANY: Reimbursement of expenses is due once the expenses have been made.

GREECE: The reimbursement of expenses (CC Article 722) is due after the performance of the mandate or after the termination of the contract (Georgiadis/Stathopoulos/Karasis, CC Article 722 no. 5).

HUNGARY: CC Article 479 paragraph (1) prescribes that '[c]osts that arise in connection with the handling of a matter shall be borne by the principal. The agent shall not be obliged to advance any costs'. Contrary to the general rules, in case of commission agency, '[t]he commission shall include the expenses usually involved with consignment, but it shall not include expenses related to carriage. The commission agent shall be entitled to demand reimbursement for those of his necessary and useful expenses that are not included in the commission; however, he shall only be entitled to demand those of his substantiated expenses otherwise included in the commission only if the sales contract has not been performed due to reasons within the interest sphere of the principal' (CC Article 511 paragraphs (2) and (3)).

IRELAND: In the absence of express agreement, it seems that the expenses are due as soon as the agent can prove that he has incurred them and that such expenses are lawful and reasonable.

ITALY: The agent, unless otherwise agreed by the parties, has a reporting obligation to be performed without delay towards the principal (CC Articles 1712 and 1713). In particular, upon conclusion of the mandate the agent shall communicate to the principal the performance of the contract, he shall further report on his activities and render to the principal all and any profits acquired in the performance of the contract. He shall also demonstrate the expenses which he sustained for the performance of the contract. It is only in this moment that the agent has the right to claim the payment of the price and/or reimbursement.

MALTA: Reimbursement of expenses is due when the agent has concluded the contract on behalf of the principal.

NETHERLANDS: It seems that the payment of the reimbursement of expenses is due at the moment of accounting by the agent. If the principal fails to pay these expenses, however, the agent may be entitled to interest according to CC Article 6:119 paragraph (1) or, if both parties are professional parties, CC Article 6:119a.

POLAND: The agent is entitled to the recovery of the expenses after the service has been performed.

PORTUGAL: Reimbursement of the expenses is due as of the moment that the agent has incurred in them. Cf. Lima/Varela (1986), p. 726.

SCOTLAND: There is no rule which governs the point at which agents are, in general, entitled to reimbursement of expenses. The issue may be governed by custom and practice in a particular trade. This issue is governed by specific rules in the case of solicitors, who are entitled to interim fees subject to obtaining the prior consent of the client (Paterson, no. 9.04.09). Such fees may be debited from the balance of funds held by the solicitor on the client's account provided again that the client's consent is obtained (Solicitors (Scotland) Accounts Rules 2001 rule 6 paragraph (1)(d); Paterson, no 9.04.4). An interim fee must be fair and reasonable in the light of the work which has been carried out to date (Paterson, no. 9.04.4).

SLOVAKIA: In the case of a mandate contract, in civil relations expenses should be reimbursed after the matter is finished and the account is given. In commercial relations the agent is entitled to the remuneration once the activity stipulated in the mandate has been duly carried out, regardless of whether it has led to the expected result or not. Under a commission agent contract, the reimbursement of expenses is due at the same time as the remuneration.

SPAIN: The agent may claim immediate reimbursement of expenses incurred. CC Article 1728 paragraph (2) provides that the principal must pay the agent interest in respect of the sums which have been incurred for the performance of the mandate as soon as such expenses have been incurred.

SWEDEN: Unless agreed otherwise the payment of the price as well as the expenses are due in arrears, cf. Hellner, p. 225. If the agent has a duty to give an account of the performance, the principal is not obliged to pay until such account is given.

5. Right to advance for expenses

AUSTRIA: The agent is entitled to an advance to cover expenses he will need to make in order to perform the contract (CC Article 1014; Griss, Article 396 Rz 14). The same rule applies to commission agents (Comm. C Article 396(2)) and forwarders (Comm.C Article 409).

BELGIUM: The agent is entitled to an advance (De Page, p. 425; Wéry, p. 206).

BULGARIA: Upon the request from the agent, the principal has to supply him with all means necessary for performance of the mandate (OCA Article 285). In Bulgarian legal doctrine, it is considered that the principal is obliged to give the agent an advance for covering of expenses for the contractual performance. The agent has the right to refuse performance until the payment of the advance (Любен Василев, Облигационно право, p. 27).

DENMARK: The agent is not entitled to an advance to cover expenses he will need to make in order to perform the contract unless this is agreed upon with the principal.

ENGLAND: There does not appear to be any specific case law on this topic. Provided that the principal has agreed to provide the agent with an advance on the reimbursement of expenses, this should be possible.

ESTONIA: LOAEst Article 628 paragraph (4) provides for the (general) contract for services that the service provider (the agent) has the right to demand an advance payment in a 'reasonable amount' of the remuneration and the expenses to be reimbursed before commencing performance of the contract (if the parties have not agreed otherwise).

FINLAND: In general the agent is not entitled to an advance to cover the expenses, if not otherwise agreed.

FRANCE: The agent is not entitled to an advance to cover expenses he will need to make in order to perform the contract. As a result, the agent cannot require any advance. The parties may, of course, provide for this in a specific clause of the contract. It should be recalled that the agent is entitled to immediate repayment of expenses incurred.

GERMANY: The agent is entitled to an advance to cover expenses he will need to make in order to perform the contract (CC Article 669).

GREECE: In case of a mandate contract a principal shall be bound to pay in advance the expenses required for the performance of the mandate (CC Article 721). If the principal refuses to pay in advance he is placed under notice according to CC Article 351: 'A creditor shall be placed under notice if upon being invited by the debtor the creditor has not proceeded with the completion or has not cooperated for the conclusion of an act without which the debtor cannot furnish the performance.'

HUNGARY: According to CC Article 479 paragraph (1), in general, '[c]osts that arise in connection with the handling of a matter shall be borne by the principal. The agent shall not be obliged to advance any costs'. Contrary to the general rules, in the case of commission agency, '[t]he commission shall include the expenses usually involved with consignment, but it shall not include expenses related to carriage' (CC Article 511 paragraph (2)). CC Article 511 paragraph (1) establishes that '[t]he commission agent shall be entitled to receive a commission only if the sales contract has been performed'.

IRELAND: The common law right to be indemnified for expenses operates ex post, so that any claim to cover expenses in advance would have to be provided for in the contract.

ITALY: The principal has to supply the agent with the means necessary to conclude the affair or the prospective contract, unless otherwise agreed (CC Article 1719). This obligation of the principal may also include the obligation to give the agent an advance to cover the expenses that the agent will need to make in order to perform the contract.

MALTA: Maltese law does not envisage that the agent is entitled to an advance for expenses to be made.

NETHERLANDS: Generally, the agent is entitled to wages and reimbursement of expenses made during the performance of the mandate contract. There is no information available on whether the agent is also entitled to an advance.

POLAND: The agent is entitled to receive an advance for future expenses (CC Article 743), however the principal is only obligated to give an advance if the agent asks for such advance.

PORTUGAL: Depending upon the uses of trade, a partial initial remuneration may be due to the agent: cf. CC Article 1167 lit (b). The client must also, in the silence of the contract, supply the agent with all the items that are necessary to the execution of the mandate, such as documents or things (CC Article 1167 lit (a)).

SCOTLAND: There appears to be no specific rule governing the agent's entitlement to an advance to cover payment of expenses. The issue may be governed by custom and practice in a particular trade. In the case of a solicitor, the principal is bound, if required by his solicitor, to supply funds for expenses (Begg, p. 120). There is nothing to prevent such a request being made in advance.

SLOVAKIA: In civil relations, unless otherwise agreed, the principal must pay to the agent presumed expenses at the latter's request (CC Article 728). In commercial relations, if it may be anticipated that substantial expenses would be incurred in arranging a certain matter on the principal's behalf, the agent may request an appropriate advance payment (Comm.C Article 571(2)). According to the rules on the commission agent contract, the agent is not entitled to an advance, but the parties may of course agree otherwise.

SPAIN: The principal is obliged to advance a payment to the agent if the agent asks for this in order to be able to perform the mandate contract. If the principal does not make this advance payment, then the principal will be obliged to reimburse the agent for the costs incurred by the latter to perform the contractual obligations (CC Article 1728 paragraph (1)). The principal does not have to pay the costs if the agent is liable for the non-successful performance of the contract.

SWEDEN: The principal is not obliged to pay any expenses in advance unless the parties have agreed to do so or it follows from the circumstances, see Hellner, p. 224.

6. Compensation of damage sustained

AUSTRIA: The principal is liable for damage sustained by the agent in the performance of the contract CC Article 1014 (Rummel/Strasser, § 1014 Rz 10). It does not matter if the principal could have prevented the damage, if the agent is a professional party or is contractually entitled to a price. The principal is liable for a damage sustained by a forwarder (Article 5 lit b Austrian General Conditions for Forwarders).

BELGIUM: According to CC Article 2000, the principal has a duty to indemnify the losses, on the condition that the agent has not been reproached with imprudence (De Page, p. 423-431; Foriers & Glansdorff, p. 625-626; Tilleman, p. 123-124; Wéry, p. 209). This duty to indemnify applies broadly and includes material damages, as well as physical damages, loss of profit etc (Wéry, p. 209). It makes no difference if the principal could not have prevented the damage: the duty to indemnify includes losses, caused by the agent's fault, as well as losses suffered by coincidence (CA Brussels 1 February 1927, Pas. 1927, II, 165; CA (commercial) Brussels 17 February 1925, T.B.H. 1925, 170; Wéry, p. 209). No distinction is made between a remunerated or a non-remunerated mandate contract (Wéry, p. 209).

DENMARK: Normally the principal will not be liable for damage sustained by the agent in the performance of the contract. A rule contrary to this may prevail if by giving incorrect instructions to the agent the principal has directly or indirectly caused the damage. If the principal could not have prevented the damage, he will not be liable. It makes no difference if the agent is entitled to a price.

ENGLAND: In addition to covering the expenses of the agent, the principal owes the agent an obligation of indemnity, i.e. to indemnify the agent against all losses and damages incurred whilst performing the agency. This right of the agent is quite large since the principal will be liable for the liabilities and the losses that the agent may incur when performing his duties as an agent. The extent of the right for the agent to claim such indemnity is subject to the same restrictions as for expenses. Such an obligation on the principal will however vary if the agency is contractual or not.

ESTONIA: Generally, the principal is liable for damage sustained by the agent in the performance of the contract. However, only specific damage is covered: Article 628 paragraph (5) LOAEst provides that "The principal shall compensate the service provider for damages which are caused upon performance of his duties and which arise from the risks usually involved in the performance of such services or from the instructions of the principal, except in the case where damage is to be covered from the remuneration of the service provider or if the damage was caused by the service provider behaving in a manner which, under the circumstances, could not be deemed to be necessary for performance of the mandate." LOAEst Article

628 paragraph (6) adds that it is presumed that when remuneration is paid to the service provider, it covers the damage specified in Article 628 paragraph (5) LOAEst.

FINLAND: The principal is, in general, liable for damages sustained by the agent in the performance of the contract. The principal is usually not liable for unpreventable damages. It may have some indirect interpretative importance in this respect if the agent is a professional party and/or is contractually entitled to price.

FRANCE: The principal will be required to indemnify the agent for all losses which it may incur in the performance of its mandate (CC Article 2000). This rule will apply even where the principal could not prevent the loss and whether or not the mandate was unremunerated, and whether or not the agent was a professional.

GERMANY: There is no explicit rule, but case law has applied CC Article 670 (dealing with reimbursement of the agent's expenses) and has ruled that the principal has to reimburse the agent for damages incurred (see Palandt/Sprau, Article 670 paragraph 11 with references to case law). The legal construction is highly disputed and discussed in legal writings, although the general result seems to be widely accepted. It is irrelevant whether the principal could have prevented the damage, as the claim under CC Article 670 is not a damage ("fault") claim, but a claim for reimbursement of "expenses". No difference exists between gratuitous and remunerated contracts in this respect, as CC Article 675 paragraph (1) also refers to CC Article 670. However, in one case the BGH (BGH, NJW 1985, p. 269) denied a claim under CC Article 670. In this case, the remunerated *Geschäftsbesorgungsvertrag* between the parties was interpreted as already having covered possible damages through the price charged by the agent.

GREECE: In case of a contract of mandate a principal shall be liable to compensate any loss incurred by the agent without fault on his part in the performance of the mandate (CC Article 723). If the damage caused by the agent are due to his own fault, he is required to restitute those damages and the principal is free from any liability in such a case (CA Athens decision no. 1193/1992, Arm.: 1992, 625). In case of an agent who is a professional party or is contractually entitled to a price such in case of mandate services offered from a lawyer Article 723 does not apply.

HUNGARY: In general, the principal is not liable for damage sustained by the agent in the performance of the contract. To the liability of the principal, the general rules apply, especially CC Article 339 paragraph (1) which establishes that 'A person who causes damage to another person in violation of the law shall be liable for such damage. He shall be relieved of liability if he is able to prove that he has acted in a manner that can generally be expected in the given situation'.

ITALY: According to CC Article 1770 paragraph (2) the principal has to compensate the agent for the damages sustained by him in the performance of the contract, but not for those due to an imprudent/careless activity of the agent. It makes no difference whether or not the agent is a professional party or is contractually entitled to a price, but the standard of care may be evaluated differently.

MALTA: The principal must reimburse the agent for any losses he has sustained due to the contract where no negligence can be imputable to the agent. This is sustained in CC Article 1882 "The principal must also indemnify the agent for the losses he has sustained by reason of the mandate, where no negligence is imputable to him." Thus the agent would lose his right to be indemnified for losses suffered during the execution of the contract only if such losses are imputable to his negligence, that is, the agent would not have reached the required standard of care of a *bonus pater familias*. See also CFI (Civil) 4 November 1957, *Dr. Moore noe. vs Architect Falzon et*. In this case, the court found that an architect engaged in the supervision of construction is bound to check the material that is going to be used for construction and to supervise also the quality of the objects purchased for the construction. Although the architect is, as any other debtor, bound to exercise only the diligence of a *bonus pater familias*, he is also an agent and therefore his responsibility emanates from the object itself for which he has been engaged. As an agent he is bound to perform the contract conferred to him and he must perform it not only in good faith but also with the diligence and ability demanded by the execution of the task undertaken by him. Therefore if the architect offers his services against a price, the judge must be more severe in his assessment. If the architect fails to examine properly the materials used in the construction under his supervision, he is responsible for the damage that is caused by the defective material. Therefore from this it can be seen that when the agent is a professional party, the diligence he must perform in the execution of the contract is more severe, even more so if such performance is against a price.

NETHERLANDS: Under CC Article 7:406 paragraph (2), the principal is required to compensate the damage the agent sustains in the performance of the mandate as a result of the manifestation of a specific risk entailed in the performance of the mandate, provided that its manifestation is not attributable to the agent. If the agent acted in the execution of his trade or profession he is entitled to compensation only in so far as the risk exceeds the normal professional risks. Moreover, if the mandate is performed against a price, the right to compensation arises only if the risks were not taken into account when the price was calculated.

POLAND: In accordance with the general rules of tort liability, the principal is not liable for any damage sustained by the agent unless the principal is responsible for the damage.

PORTUGAL: According to CC Article 1167 lit (d), the principal is liable for damage sustained by the agent, even if the principal did not act with fault. However, if the damage can be attributed to the fault of the agent or of a third party, that liability is excluded: Lima/Varela (1986), p. 726.

SCOTLAND: The institutional writer, Erskine, in his discussion of mandate, confirmed that the mandant (principal) is obliged to replace not only the reasonable expenses of the mandatar (agent) agent, but also the "… damage sustained by him in the execution of the mandate." (Erskine III,3,38). In a modern context the same principle applies to agency rather than gratuitous mandate, and is referred to as the agent's right of relief (see Macgregor, paragraph 123; *Stevenson v Duncan* (1842) 5 D 167). It will not apply where the agent has failed to act in accordance with his instructions, for example, by seeking to defraud the principal *(Robinson v Middleton* (1859) 21 D 1089), and can be limited by a custom of trade *(Robinson v Middleton* (1859) 21 D 1089). There is no indication that the right of relief is affected by any of the three possibilities mentioned in the second sentence of the question.

SWEDEN: The main rule is that the principal can be held liable for damage due to non-performance caused by the principal's negligence. A responsibility is presumed. Thus, the principal is liable to pay damages unless he can show that the non-performance was not due to negligence on his part. Cf. HaL Article 34. No answer received: SPAIN.

Chapter 3:
Performance by the agent
Section 1:
Main obligations of the agent

Article 3:101: Obligation to act in accordance with mandate

At all stages of the mandate relationship the agent must act in accordance with the mandate.

Comments

A. General idea

The agent is performing a service for the principal. The principal determines how the agent is to perform the contractual obligations and, if a prospective contract is to be concluded, what its contents are to be. The agent is required to act in accordance with these instructions and the authority awarded to him. Obviously, this not only means that the agent may not exceed the boundaries of his authority, but also that he is required to do what is necessary to achieve the result.

> *Illustration 1*
> Marij is engaged as a real estate agent to sell Marco's house. In performing her obligations, she must advertise the property, show the house to interested parties and negotiate the sales contract with a potential buyer. However, if Marco has told her not to advertise because he thinks this is a waste of money, Marij is not allowed to advertise the house, even if she paid for these advertisements herself.

B. Authorisation, instruction, and subsequent directions

The mandate granted to the agent, which consists of the authorisation, initial instruction and any subsequent directions of the principal, provides the information pertaining to the performance of the mandate and to the contents of any prospective contract which is to be concluded. This means that the agent undertakes the obligation to act in accordance with the power granted by the principal (authorisation) and within the guidelines given by the principal, both at the time the contract is concluded and subsequently during the performance (instruction and subsequent directions). Such instructions may include, among other things, that the agent is to act in the name of the principal when concluding the prospective contract, but also that he must act in his own name and keep the identity of the principal from the third party.

C. Act in name of principal or in own name

The principal may determine that the agent is to act in his own name or in the name of the principal. In the former case, the mandate is for indirect representation, which implies that the agent himself would be bound by the prospective contract. In the latter case, the mandate is for direct representation, which means that the agent is to disclose the principal's name to the third party and the prospective contract is concluded directly between the principal and the third party. In most cases, the principal will have indicated in which manner the contract is to be performed. If this is not the case, whether the agent is to act in his own name or in the name of the principal may often be deduced from the statements and behaviour of the parties, the usage established between them or the usage in the area of commerce in which the parties operate. If all this still does not provide guidance as to the way the mandate contract is to be performed, then the agent is required to ask for clarification in accordance with Article 4:102 paragraph (2) (Request for a direction).

D. Acting beyond mandate

The present Article requires the agent to act in accordance with his mandate. In principle, the parties may therefore agree that the agent is allowed to overstep the boundaries of his mandate if he perceives this to be in the interest of the principal. Often, however, the parties will rather have provided the agent with a broad mandate to act as he sees fit to achieve the principal's interests. Where the parties have not agreed to such a broad mandate and did not agree that the agent is allowed to overstep the boundaries of his mandate, the agent breaches his contractual obligations toward the principal if he nevertheless oversteps these boundaries, unless the requirements of Article 3:201 (Acting beyond mandate) are fulfilled.

E. Relation to the Principles of European Law and the Draft Common Frame of Reference

This Article mirrors that of Article IV.D. – 3:101 DCFR (Obligation to act in accordance with mandate). What is in accordance with the mandate is to be determined by interpretation of the contract in accordance with Chapter 5 PECL (Interpretation).

F. Character of the rule

This Article constitutes a default rule from which the parties may derogate in the sense that the parties may agree that the agent may under certain conditions exceed the limitations of his mandate. Moreover, the parties may also exclude or restrict the ordinary remedies for breach of the obligations under this Article. It is mandatory, however, in the sense that the parties cannot lawfully agree that the agent may disregard the limits set for the mandate altogether or exclude all remedies for a breach of this obligation. Such a clause would effectively provide the agent with immunity against liability and should be considered contrary to public policy and for that reason void.

G. Remedies

If the agent does not act in accordance with the mandate, the normal remedies for non-performance apply. This is different, however, if the requirements of Article 3:201 paragraph (1) (Acting beyond mandate) are fulfilled, as in such a case paragraph (2) of that Article indicates that the act has the same consequences as an act covered by the mandate. In other words, in such a case, the remedies for non-performance do not apply.

Comparative Notes

1. Act in accordance with mandate

In all legal systems, the agent is under an obligation to obey the instructions provided to him by the principal when awarding him the mandate or afterwards, and therefore shall not exceed his authority. Generally this is considered the logical and essential obligation following from the contract and the nature of the mandate relationship. In BULGARIA, abiding with the instructions and the limits of the authority of the mandate is even considered to be the agent's main obligation. The obligation is derived from the agent's general duty of care in BELGIUM.

2. Liability of agent acting in own name or in name of principal in breach of contract

Where the agent is required under the mandate contract or under a later direction by the principal to conclude the prospective contract in his own name, but he concludes that prospective contract in the name of the principal, the agent is in breach of contract. The same is true if the agent was to act in the name of the principal but acted in his own name. In both cases, in all legal systems the normal remedies for non-performance by the agent apply. In addition, in ENGLAND and IRELAND the principal is not required to pay the contractual price or to compensate the agent for the expenses made in the performance of the contract or at least allowed to reduce these payments. In FRANCE, these payments will be reduced.

National Notes

1. Act in accordance with mandate

BELGIUM: The agent is – in general – under a duty of care (De Page, p. 407). He must act as a bonus pater familias (Paulus & Boes, p. 90; Wéry, p. 148). For specific aspects of the agent's duties, there is a duty to guarantee the result, e.g. the duty to follow imperative instructions of the principal or the prohibition on exceeding the limits of the authority granted.

BULGARIA: The obligation to perform in accordance with the mandate and with the power of attorney (if granted) is the main obligation of the agent, see OCA Article 281 (Любен Василев, Облигационно право, p. 23-25; Меворах/Лиджи/Фархи, III, p. 117).

ENGLAND: It is essential, in every agency relationship, that the agent acts in accordance with the authority he has been given by the principal (express or implied). Cf. Bowstead & Reynolds, paragraph 6.002.

GERMANY: The agent has of course to act in accordance with the mandate and has to exercise due care in doing so (Palandt/Sprau, Article 662 no. 9). Under very narrow circumstances, CC Article 665 entitles the agent to deviate from the mandate if he may assume that the principal would under the given circumstances agree with the deviation and generally only after he informed the principal and waited for his instructions (see Seiler, in: Münchener Kommentar zum BGB, Article 665 no. 9 indicating that CC Article 665 also covers deviations from the mandate contract itself, although this provision only speaks of deviations from 'instructions').

IRELAND: At common law, an agent is obliged to follow the lawful instructions of the principal, which would include acting within the authority/power given. Where an agent exceeds his authority/power, he is in breach of contract.

MALTA: The principle under Maltese law is that once the agent has accepted the contract, he is bound to perform it in accordance with the terms of the contract, cf. CC Article 1873 paragraph (1).

NETHERLANDS: The agent is bound to act in accordance with the mandate and is under the general duty of care incumbent on all service providers (CC Article 7:401).

PORTUGAL: The agent must act according to the instructions given by the other party (CC Article 1178 paragraph (2)).

SLOVAKIA: Under general contract law the agent is required to act in accordance with the mandate.

SPAIN: The agent cannot act beyond the limits established by the principal in the mandate contract (CC Article 1714). The basic obligation of the agent to act within the limits of the mandate comprises: (a) carrying out the legal acts which are the object of the contract; (b) exercising due diligence; (c) acting within the limits established by the principal; and (d) following the instructions of the principal on how to carry out the mandate (Hernández Gil, p. 460-461). The limits within which the agent has to act are not established by the law but by the principal; these limits are to be determined by interpreting the will of the principal (STS 2 February 1976). It is therefore a problem of interpretation of the will of the principal. It is for the agent to interpret what the will of the principal is (STS 30 January 1963), by following the rules on interpretation (the truthful intention of the principal, in light of the nature and finality of the mandate).

SWEDEN: According to Comm.C Article 18:2 the agent has to act in accordance with the power granted to him. Regarding the internal relationship there is no general rule governing the agent's responsibility in case he acts beyond his mandate, see Bengtsson, p. 157. If the agent acts beyond his mandate it is a breach of contract.

No answer received: AUSTRIA, DENMARK, ESTONIA, FINLAND, FRANCE, GREECE, HUNGARY, ITALY, POLAND, SCOTLAND.

2. Liability of agent acting in own name or in name of principal in breach of contract

AUSTRIA: The agent is liable for non-performance if he acts in his own name whereas the contract required him to act in the principal's name (due to a violation of the internal relationship).

BELGIUM: If the agent acts in his own name whereas the contract required him to act in the principal's name, the agent is liable for non-performance of the obligation of loyalty and in particular the transparency requirement (Samoy, p. 306; Wéry, p. 152 and 259). If the principal suffers damage by this non-performance, he can claim damages (e.g. CA Brussels 28 January 1820, Pas. 1820-21, II, 30). When the contract required the agent to act in his own name, then the agent has an obligation to keep the existence and/or identity of the principal secret from the third-party (see for the contract of prête nom: Foriers & Glansdorff, 611; see for the commission contract: CA (commercial) Brussels 1 February 1911, TBH 1911, 201; CA Brussels 17 May 1858,

Pas. 1859, II, 168, B.J. 1859, 406; Foriers & Glansdorff, p. 611; Jassogne, p. 636; Pand. b., v° Commission (contrat de), no. 133; Samoy, p. 191-194; Van der Perre & Lejeune, no. 92; Van Ryn & Heenen, p. 21). This secrecy obligation is a facultative duty to discretion on a contractual base; the obligation relies on the principal's will, accepted by the agent in the mandate contract. When nevertheless the agent acts in the name of the principal, he violates this secrecy obligation. Therefore he risks a contractual liability claim for non-performance (see for the contract of prête nom: Poncet, p. 135; see for the commission contract: Pand. b., v° Commission (contrat de), no. 133; Samoy, p. 192; Van Ryn & Heenen, p. 21 and 22).

BULGARIA: When the agent is authorized and instructed to act in the name of the principal and nevertheless he has performed the mandate contract in his own name, this behaviour in internal relationship is considered a breach of the contract (Меворах/Лиджи/Фархи, III, p. 19). Therefore the agent is obliged to compensate damages caused to the principal by this deviation from the mandate (Любен Василев, Облигационно право, p. 25). Similarly, when the agent acts in the name of the principal, whereas under the mandate he is obliged to act in his own name, in the internal relationship there is a breach of the contract and the agent is liable for damages caused to the principal (Любен Василев, Облигационно право, p. 25). The general rules for non-performance apply, cf. OCA Articles 79-94.

DENMARK: If the agent acts in his own name whereas the contract required him to act in the principal's name, this constitutes a non-performance. The principal will be entitled to claim damages if he proves to have suffered a loss as a consequence of the agent's deviation from the contract. Normally the principal will be entitled to terminate the contract pleading that the agent has failed the fulfilment of the contract in a proper way (lack of trust). The same applies if the agent acts in the name of the principal whereas the contract required him to act in his own name.

ENGLAND: The agent who acts in his own name when he is asked by the principal to act in the principal's name or who acts in the name of the principal when he is asked by the principal to act in his own name is committing a breach of contract and is liable for it towards the principal. This breach is serious and therefore would probably be regarded as repudiatory (albeit that the question seems to have created some controversy amongst academics), allowing the principal to terminate the contract and claim damages. Moreover, the agent would not be entitled to claim remuneration or expenses.

ESTONIA: Any deviation from contractual obligations would lead to a breach. In specific situations, a deviation from the directions of the principal will not amount to a breach of the agent. In case of non-performance by the agent, the principal may choose which remedies to impose (legal remedies for non-performance of an obligation are regulated in the general part of the LOAEst, see LOAEst Articles 100-126). Such remedies include specific performance, damages, price reduction or the right to terminate the contract (if the breach is essential).

FINLAND: If the agent has acted in his own name where the contract required him to act in the principal's name, or vice versa, the agent is liable for non-performance and the principal can claim damages. The principal is entitled to terminate the contract if the non-performance is essential. Price reduction is, in general, possible as well.

FRANCE: The agent who acts in his own name instead of the name of the principal, or vice versa, will incur liability for any failure in the performance of the contract, where loss or damage was incurred by the principal. The principal may decide to unilaterally terminate the mandate (which is always possible, even in the absence of any breach) and the principal may reduce both the remuneration and the repayment of expenses incurred by the agent (CC Article 1999 paragraph (2) a contrario).

GERMANY: If the agent has acted in his own name where he was required to act in the principal's name or vice versa, the agent is liable to the principal because he violated his obligation under the contract. The principal can claim damages under CC Article 280.

GREECE: If the mandate contract includes the explicit requirement that the agent shall act in the principal's name and the agent acts in his own name or vice versa, he may be liable for a defective performance of the mandate (Georgiadis/Stathopoulos/Karasis, CC Article 717 nos. 2-5). According to CC Article 717, '[a] agent may only deviate from the limits set in the mandate if he found himself in the impossibility to notify the principal and it is at the same time obvious that the principal would have allowed the deviation if he had knowledge of the circumstances that prompted such deviation.' The principal can in case of an unjustified deviation of the limits set in the mandate deny the performance and claim damages due to a defective performance of the mandate on the part of the agent (CC Article 714). The principal can also deny the reimbursement of the expenses regarding the defective performance of the mandate (Georgiadis/Stathopoulos/Karasis, CC Article 717 no. 5). On the other hand, the principal has the discretionary power to approve the deviation from the limits of authority set in the mandate (Georgiadis/Stathopoulos/Karasis, CC Article 717 no. 5).

HUNGARY: According to CC Article 277 paragraph (1), '[c]ontracts shall be performed as stipulated, at the place and time set forth and in accordance with the quantity, quality, and range specified therein'. If the agent acts in his own name whereas the contract required him to act in the principal's name, or acted in the principal's name where the contract required him to act in his own name, this constitutes a non-performance of the contract. In case of non-performance, if still possible, the principal can demand a correct repetition of the performance (CC Article 311 lit (a)). Moreover, CC Article 478 paragraph (2) establishes that 'the principal shall be entitled to reduce the remuneration or refuse to pay it if he is able to prove that success was not achieved in part or in whole for a reason for which the agent is responsible.' The agent is liable for damages resulting from non-performance (see CC Articles 310 and 318 paragraph (1)). Moreover, according to CC Article 221 paragraphs (1) and (2), 'A person who transgresses the scope of his authority to represent in good faith or who has concluded a contract in the name of another person without having the right to represent and the person in whose name he has proceeded does not approve his action, such shall pay compensation to the other contracting party for damages incurred in result of the conclusion of the contract.' 'A mala fide false agent shall be liable for full recompense.'

IRELAND: At common law, an agent must obey his principal's lawful instructions. And where the agency is contractual, the agent is liable for breach of contract if he fails to act as instructed. Therefore, where an agent is instructed to act in the principal's name and in fact he acts in his own name, or vice versa, he will be liable for breach of contract. The remedies available following a breach of contract depend on a number of factors including the classification of the term breached and, sometimes, the seriousness of the consequences of the breach. For example, where the term breached is a condition of the contract, the innocent party i.e. the principal can terminate the contract and sue for damages for any resultant loss. Whereas, if the term breached is only a warranty the innocent party i.e. the principal cannot terminate the contract but damages for loss may be sought. Moreover, it seems that where an agent has committed a serious breach of contract he loses his right to remuneration and expenses.

ITALY: In general terms the agent who does not perform the contract of representation correctly is liable for non-performance. Accordingly, if the agent acts in his own name whereas the contract required him to act in the principal's name, or the other way around, he acts in breach of contract and the principal is entitled to exercise the remedies for non-performance.

MALTA: In case of non-performance of the terms of the digital content contracts, e.g. because the agent has acted in his own name where he should have acted in the name of the principal or vice versa, under CC Article 1873 paragraph (1) the principal may claim damages and interest.

NETHERLANDS: If the agent is in breach of contract towards the principal, he has to compensate the principal's damages according to the general CC Article 6:74 paragraph (1).

POLAND: Where the agent has acted in the name of the principal where he should have acted in his own name, or vice versa, the agent is liable for any damages to the principal under the normal rules of contractual liability, cf. CC Article 471.

PORTUGAL: If the agent does not act in accordance with the authority awarded to him, he is liable for non-performance under the general rules of contract law (CC Articles 798 ff.).

SCOTLAND: If an agent acts in his own name where the contract requires him to act in the principal's name, or the other way around, this would constitute a breach of the mandate contract. As a result, the principal would be entitled to claim damages from the agent. If the breach constituted a material breach, the principal would have the right to terminate the mandate contract for non-performance and claim damages. The remedy of price reduction might also be available to the principal. Although at one time this remedy was excluded in Scots law, it is now generally permitted by virtue of the Contract (Scotland) Act 1997, Article 3.

SLOVAKIA: If the agent acts in the name of the client without authorisation, this means that in the internal relationship between the agent and the principal, there is a breach of a contractual obligation. Similarly, if the agent acts in his own name where under the mandate contract he was instructed to act in the name of the client this also constitutes a non-performance by the agent entitling the client to damages for any loss caused.

SPAIN: If an agent acted in the agent's own name, when the contract provided for execution in the principal's name, this would constitute an infringement of contractual duties (CC Article 1718). Probably, also, the principal may claim recovery of the acquired asset as an equitable holder (CC Article 1717 paragraph (3)). The same is true if the agent acts in the principal's name whereas the contract required acting in the agent's own name.

SWEDEN: If the agent acts in his own name whereas the contract required him to act in the principal's name or the other way around, the agent could be held liable for non-performance. If the principal suffers damage due to this non-performance he is entitled to damages. The principal is also entitled to terminate the contract if the non-performance is fundamental.

Article 3:102: Obligation to act in interests of principal

(1) The agent must act in accordance with the interests of the principal, in so far as these have been communicated to the agent or the agent could reasonably be expected to be aware of them.

(2) Where the agent is not sufficiently aware of the principal's interests to enable the agent to properly perform the obligations under the mandate contract, the agent must request information from the principal.

Comments

A. General idea

The purpose of a mandate contract is that the agent acts in the interests and on behalf of the principal by concluding a contract with a third party, by performing another juridical act or by finding a third party with whom the principal can conclude such a contract himself. When the agent accepts the mandate granted by the principal, the agent undertakes the obligation to act in accordance with the mandate (see Article 3:101 (Obligation to act in accordance with mandate)). The agent also takes upon himself the obligation to act in the interests of the principal, as regulated by the present Article. To do so, he will need to know the interests of the principal. In some cases these will be self-evident; in others the agent may have to inquire more specifically. In the latter case, paragraph (2) of this Article requires him to ask the principal for the relevant information.

Illustration 1
Samantha commissions her solicitor to appeal a court decision with which she fundamentally disagrees. In this case, the interests of Samantha are sufficiently clear and no further information is needed for the solicitor to be able to perform his task.

Illustration 2
Simon charges Ruben to buy 'an old-timer car'. As Ruben does not have more information, he will need to ask Simon what the maximum price is for which he may purchase the vintage car and whether there are specific types of old-timers or old-timers of a specific period (e.g. the 1920s or 1950s) that Simon is particularly interested in.

B. Obligation to act in interests of principal

Paragraph (1) of the present Article requires the agent to ensure that he acts in accordance with the principal's interests that he is or should be aware of. These interests include the principal's financial or economic interests, but also any other interests the agent may be aware of.

Illustration 3
Eleanor is asked by Francis, her brother-in-law, to buy 'flowers, preferably roses or something like that', for him to give to his mother-in-law and Eleanor's mother, Georgette. Francis does not know but Eleanor does know that Georgette hates roses but is very fond of tulips. Eleanor is required to buy tulips or other flowers that she knows Georgette likes.

Illustration 4
Tony is charged by Carmela to buy real estate to make a long-term investment. As Tony knows that Carmela intends to use the profits to live from as a sort of old-age pension, he decides to invest in a low-risk apartment building rather than in the more speculative market of offices.

C. Agents obligation to obtain necessary information

An important element of the obligations of the agent is to act in the best interests of the principal. This would seem to imply that the agent should take these interests into account.

The question then arises how the agent should become aware of these interests. Most of the principal's interests are explicitly communicated to the agent either when the mandate contract is concluded or afterwards. Other interests should be known to the agent because they could be inferred from the contract, the authority, the instructions, the subsequent directions of the principal and any other sources of information. In some cases, however, the agent may have to seek further information from the principal about the principal's interests. The agent may, for example, have to ask the principal direct questions pertaining to the content of the prospective contract and the principal's preferences and priorities. For these reasons, the agent may be expected to take active steps to obtain information from the principal to be able to carry out the mandate properly.

Illustration 5
A principal wants to buy a shipment of cocoa beans on the market. As he is too busy to participate on the market himself, he appoints an agent to join in on the bidding on the cocoa beans. The agent is aware that the principal wishes to use the cocoa beans for the production of chocolate bars. As a professional agent active in the purchase and sale of cocoa beans, the agent may be aware of the quality of the beans to be purchased. However, if the principal has not informed him thereof, he will need to inquire where the principal wishes to have the beans stored. Whether he is required to inquire about this before the beans are to be purchased or only when they are (about to be) delivered will depend on the circumstances of the case, in particular of the customs in the relevant branch of industry and trade.

D. Professional insurance required

In most legal systems, there is no general obligation for agents acting in the course of their business to obtain professional insurance coverage. However, an obligation to take out insurance against liability with sufficient coverage exists in all legal systems for many regulated professions – e.g. attorneys and architects – either on the basis of legislation or professional codes of ethics. Such obligatory professional liability insurance may be required in particular where the professional agent performs services involving a direct and particular health, safety or financial risk for the principal or a third person. As such, it is in conformity with Article 23 of the Services Directive (Directive 2006/123/EC of the European Parliament and of the Council of 12 December 2006 on services in the internal market, *OJ* 2006, L 376/36).

E. Relation to other provisions in these Principles

The present Article is of course closely connected with that of Article 3:101 (Obligation to act in accordance with mandate) and that of Article 3:103 (Obligation of skill and care). However, it also is connected with the provisions of Chapter 5 (Conflicts of interests). These provisions require the agent to disclose a possible conflict of interest in two specific cases: when the agent intends to become the third party himself (see Article 5:101 (Self-contracting)); or when he also acts as the agent of the third party (see Article 5:102 (Double mandate)). These two situations may represent the most important cases where a conflict of interest may exist, but certainly are not the only ones.

Illustration 6
Joanna is engaged as a real estate agent to sell Sacha's house. At a certain moment she finds out that her brother is interested in buying the property. As her relationship with the potential buyer may cloud her judgement and her ability to negotiate the best possible price on behalf Sacha, she must disclose her relationship with the potential buyer to Sacha, who may then make an informed decision about whether she trusts Joanna to conclude the prospective contract on her behalf.

F. Relation to the Principles of European Law and the Draft Common Frame of Reference

This Article mirrors that of Article IV.D. – 3:102 DCFR (Obligation to act in interests of principal). What is in accordance with the mandate is to be determined by interpretation of the contract in accordance with Chapter 5 PECL (Interpretation).

Where the agent is in need of specific interests of the principal to properly perform his obligations under the mandate contract, paragraph (2) of this Article indicates that he must request information from the principal. The principal is then required to answer such a request for information under Article 2:101(a) (Obligation to co-operate) of these Principles.

G. Character of the rule

This Article constitutes a default rule from which the parties may derogate in the sense that the parties may agree that the agent need not take into account certain interests of the principal. Moreover, the parties may also exclude or restrict the ordinary remedies for breach of the obligations under this Article. It is mandatory, however, in the sense that the parties cannot lawfully agree that the agent may disregard the principal's interests or exclude all remedies for a breach of this obligation, in which case the agent would be provided with immunity against liability. Such a clause would be contrary to public policy and for that reason would be void.

H. Remedies

If the agent does not act in accordance with this Article, the normal remedies for non-performance apply.

Comparative Notes

1. Act in accordance with interests of principal and obligation to inquire about principal's interests

The agent is required to take the relevant and foreseeable interests of the principal into account when performing his tasks in all legal systems. In a number of legal systems, the obligation of the agent to always take the interests of the principal into account when performing the contract has expressly been accepted. This is the case in DENMARK, ENGLAND, HUNGARY, IRELAND, ITALY, MALTA, THE NETHERLANDS and SWEDEN. In AUSTRIA, ENGLAND, and ITALY, it is even explicitly recognised that in the performance of the mandate contract, the agent is required to let the interests of the principal prevail over the agent's own interests.

If the agent is not aware of the specific interests of the principal but is in need of these interests to properly perform his tasks, he must ask the principal about his specific wishes and needs. In AUSTRIA, ENGLAND, ESTONIA, GERMANY, GREECE, ITALY, MALTA, THE NETHERLANDS, PORTUGAL, and SWEDEN, the agent is under a contractual duty to obtain information from the principal to perform his contractual obligations. The same applies in IRELAND if such a duty follows from the general requirement to act with reasonable care and skill, and in ENGLAND if a direction given by the principal is perceived to be unclear by the agent. In POLAND and SLOVAKIA, an obligation to actively obtain information from the principal is not recognised. Moreover, in DENMARK, ESTONIA, GERMANY, MALTA, THE NETHERLANDS, SLOVAKIA, and SWEDEN, the agent is required to inform or warn the principal and to ask for instructions if, during the performance of the mandate contract, relevant new information is obtained by the agent.

2. Professional insurance required?

In most legal systems, there is no general obligation for agents acting in the course of their business to obtain professional insurance coverage. However, an obligation to purchase insurance with sufficient coverage exists in all legal systems for many regulated professions – e.g. attorneys and architects – either on the basis of legislation or professional codes of ethics.

National Notes

1. Act in accordance with communicated interests of principal

AUSTRIA: An agent owes fiduciary duties to prefer his principal's interests to his own. These duties are based on the contract between principal and agent (CC Article 1009, first sentence, and Article 1013, second sentence; Comm.C Article 384 paragraph (1) and 408; for commercial agents: OGH in ecolex 1992, 317). The commission agent has to make proper efforts to discharge his tasks, e.g. to buy or sell as soon as possible for a good price. The commercial agent is required to take other interests of the principal into account when performing the act, e.g. the duty not to disclose confidential information (Straube/Griss, Article 384 Rz 3 (commission agents); Hügel/Viehböck, p. 204 (commercial agents)).

BELGIUM: There are no specific rules in this field, but it is likely that the obligation of fair dealing in the performance of the agency obligations will require that the agent take account of all the interests of the principal of which the agent was aware.

BULGARIA: The mandate contract establishes a fiduciary internal relationship between the parties. The principal trusts the personal skills, qualifications and features of the agent and expects from the latter to perform the mandate with proper care for his interests (Любен Василев, Облигационно право, p. 20; Голева, Облигационно право, p. 237). Hence, every mandate contract is considered concluded under the implied condition that the agent is obliged to act in accordance with interests of the principal, in the best possible manner under the existing circumstances (Меворах/Лиджи/Фархи, III, p. 120).

DENMARK: If the agent is aware of facts concerning the prospective contract the existence of which are unclear or unknown to the principal, he must contact the principal to make sure that the principal is aware of his position and the possible consequences arising from these facts.

ENGLAND: Since the agent acts on behalf of the principal, he is in a fiduciary position towards the principal. Therefore, as a fiduciary, the agent must always act in the best interest of the principal when performing his duties. Fiduciary duties arise in equity and apply regardless of whether the agent is gratuitous or not. The principal will have communicated his interests to the agent. Failing this, the agent who is not aware of the interests of the principal should ask clarification.

ESTONIA: The law does not prescribe which specific interests the agent must consider. LOAEst Article 621 paragraph (3) merely stipulates that in the case where adherence to the instructions of the principal would be likely to cause unfavourable consequences for the principal, the agent shall comply with the instructions only after he has called the principal's attention to such consequences and if the principal fails to modify the instructions.

FINLAND: The agent is required to take all relevant and foreseeable interests of the principal into account.

FRANCE: There are no specific rules in this field, but it is likely that the obligation of fair dealing in the performance of the agency will require that the agent take account of all the interests of the principal of which he was aware.

GERMANY: When acting under the mandate contract, the agent must take the financial and economic interests of the principal into account. A possible particular expertise of the agent is important in determining this obligation, which may require him to warn or inform the principal.

GREECE: The agent is required to take into account the principal's legal, economic, ethical and social benefit (Georgiadis/Stathopoulos/Karasis, CC Article 713 no. 15).

HUNGARY: According to CC Article 474 paragraph (2), '[a]n agent must fulfil the agency according to the instructions and interests of the principal.' Moreover, CC Article 477 paragraph (1) prescribes that 'The agent shall inform his principal of his activities and the state of affairs upon request or, if necessary, even without a request, particularly if employment of another person has become necessary or if the instructions need to be changed due to the occurrence of new circumstances'. For this reason, the agent has to act in compliance with all the interests of the principal known by him.

IRELAND: Beyond any duties imposed by the contract, the law imposes a variety of duties on an agent, largely with a view to protecting the principal. In general, agents stand in a fiduciary position to their principals and hence quite onerous duties are imposed on agents in this position. Fiduciary duties derive from equity and arise independently of any contract. They are imposed on the fiduciary automatically, as a matter of law, by virtue of the position he holds. Agents are normally subject to fiduciary duties because agents have the power to affect the legal position of their principals in relation to third parties and principals normally place trust and confidence in the agent in the exercise of that power. In the past, fiduciaries of all types tended to be treated similarly. More recently, in England, and arguably in Ireland, there has been a tendency to reduce the force of fiduciary duties between parties in an essentially commercial relationship, such that, the relationship of agency does not necessarily give rise to a fiduciary relationship, or, the scope of the fiduciary duties, although they arise in equity, can be modified by contract (e.g. *Carroll Group Distributors v G & JF Burke* [1990] ILRM 285 at 288, per Murphy J). The core duties of a fiduciary are those of loyalty and fidelity. These core duties have several aspects and an agent's fiduciary duties can be divided into four headings: to avoid conflicts of interest; not to make a secret profit; not to accept a bribe; and to account. Because these duties arise from the fiduciary nature of the relationship, independently of any contract, they may survive the termination of the contract, unless expressly or impliedly excluded by the contract. Where an agent is in breach of his fiduciary duties, a variety of remedies is available: proprietary or personal, at common law or in equity.

ITALY: The agent is required to act in the principal's best interest, so that he has to do all that is possible to satisfy the principal's expectations. This could lead the agent, when performing the contract, to take into account further interests than those directly involved in the affair. However, any interests which are in conflict with those of the principal and may prejudice the satisfaction of his expectations may not be taken into account by the agent unless the principal authorises him to do so.

MALTA: The agent is required to do all that is necessary in order to execute the contract of mandate.

NETHERLANDS: The agent is to observe due care (CC Article 7:401). For instance, the agent is required to obey timely and well considered directions of the principal (CC Article 7:402 paragraph (1)) and keep the principal informed of his activities regarding the performance of the service (CC Article 7:403 paragraph (1)). Furthermore, the agent is accountable to the principal (CC Article 7:403 paragraph (2)).

POLAND: There are no specific rules in the CC provisions on mandate contract other than general duty of every contracting party to act in good faith, with due care and to take into consideration the other parties interests, cf. CC Article 355.

SCOTLAND: The relationship of agent and principal is described as a fiduciary one, characterised by trust and good faith. The agent is therefore subject to far-reaching duties towards his principal (Macgregor, paragraphs 84-101). At its most basic level, this duty would require the agent to act in accordance with the communicated interests of the principal.

SLOVAKIA: In civil relations, there is a general duty to act in accordance with the contract and good faith. In commercial relations, the agent is bound to perform the activity undertaken in accordance with the principal's instructions and interests of which the agent is aware or must be aware and to inform the principal of all circumstances ascertained while arranging the matter and which may result in a change of the principal's arrangements or instructions (Comm.C Article 567 paragraph (2)). The commission agent must protect the principal's known interests, and keep the latter well informed of all circumstances that may lead to a change in the instructions (Comm.C Article 579). The advocate is obliged to protect and assert the principal's rights and interests (Act on Advocacy Article 18).

SPAIN: The agent has to act in the interests of the principal (Hernández Gil, p. 472), in accordance with the will of the principal. The obligation to act in the interests of the principal does not justify deviation from mandatory instructions of the principal. The interests of the principal will govern the performance of the agent as regards the application of the non-mandatory instructions. If the agent uses the power granted by the principal to pursue an interest which contradicts the interests of the principal, this is seen as an abuse of power (STS 5 February 1964; Hernández Gil, p. 465). According to Comm.C Article 255, the agent should ask the principal for guidance, when no special instructions were given. But, if it is not possible to resort to the principal for instructions, the agent should act as if the affair were its own.

SWEDEN: The mandate relationship is considered to be a fiduciary relationship and it follows from general contract law and the duty of loyalty and care that the agent always must act in the best interest of the principal. The parties have a pre-contractual as well as a contractual duty to inform the other party of important issues. Thus, the client has a duty to communicate his interests and needs and the agent must act in accordance with the communicated interests of the principal.

No answer received: PORTUGAL.

2. Agent's obligation to inquire about interests of principal

AUSTRIA: Due to his duty of care the agent is to make proper efforts to discharge his tasks (Rummel/Strasser, Article 1009 Rz 14; OGH in Wbl 1987, 212; RdW 1983, 106), to communicate to the principal all the necessary information and to inquire what the principal's interests and needs are as regards the content of the prospective contract; otherwise he is liable for the damage the principal suffers (Rummel/Strasser, Article 1009 Rz 9, 14 and Article 1012 Rz 18). The professional agent has to meet an even higher standard of care. For example, lawyers are obligated to give detailed information about legal consequences (Rummel/Strasser, Article 1009 Rz 10; OGH in AnwBl 1991, 51; RdW 1990, 340). Commercial agents owe the diligence of a prudent businessman (Comm.C Article 347).

BULGARIA: There is no explicit rule imposing on the agent an obligation to inquire about the interests of the principal. Though, a proper performance of the obligation to act in the best possible manner in accordance with the interests of the principal requires from the agent to make an inquiry about these interests.

DENMARK: If the agent is aware of facts concerning the prospective contract the existence of which is unclear or unknown to the principal, he must inform the principal. The agent may be held responsible for his failure in this respect.

ENGLAND: The principal will usually indicate, in his instructions, what his needs are. Should such instructions be unclear, the agent must seek clarification. Failing to do so, a reasonable interpretation will bind the principal. Moreover, the agent, as a fiduciary, must always act in the best interest of the principal. If the agent, when negotiating a prospective contract on behalf of the principal, is not certain whether such a contract serves the interests of the principal, he should probably voice his concerns. However, if the agent only has authority to negotiate on behalf of the principal, the latter will not be bound by the agent's negotiations until he signs the contract. Should the agent fail to act in the interest of the principal by not checking whether his actions serve the principal's interests, he will be in breach of his fiduciary obligations and liable to the principal.

ESTONIA: The duty to act in the interest of the principal (LOAEst Article 620 paragraph (1)) will require the agent, in most of the cases and in particular where the agent possesses particular expertise, to actively acquire the information that is necessary to establish the interest of his principal in order to comply with the diligence of a good agent (LOAEst Article 620 paragraph (2)). It is the duty of the agent to ascertain what such interests are, in case of doubt the agent could be legally bound to ask for instructions from the principal in order to comply with the obligation to comply with the duty of care the agent is expected to follow.

FINLAND: In general the agent has to pay attention to the interests of the other party. This duty includes an obligation to ensure in a sufficient way that the performance corresponds to the interests of the principal. Should the failure be due to negligence of the agent, the agent is liable for damages the principal suffers.

FRANCE: There is no specific obligation for the agent to inquire about the specific requirements of the principal, but in certain marginal cases, the failure to do so could be considered as negligence or breach of contract, involving the agent's liability (e.g. Cass.civ. 1re, 3 June 1997, no. 95-17111). On the other hand, the professional agent has the duty to inform the principal about the contract which he envisages concluding (e.g. CA Versailles, 11 February 1993, JCP éd. G 1993, IV, 1262).

GERMANY: An obligation to inquire can exist under certain circumstances, in particular where the agent possesses particular expertise. CC Article 666 imposes a (very general) obligation to inform the principal where 'necessary'. If this obligation is breached, it can lead to a claim for damages under CC Article 280 paragraph (1).

GREECE: In case of a contract of mandate the agent is required to inquire about the principal's interests and needs. The agent is specifically required to ask explanations for unclear instructions or to notify the principal about all the circumstances that require a deviation from the instructions (CC Article 717; Georgiadis/Stathopoulos/Karasis, CC Article 717 no. 3). Furthermore, the agent must provide information to the principal about the affairs entrusted to him (CC Article 718). Failure to do so amounts to non-performance and establishes the right to restitution of damages due to such failure (CC Article 714; Georgiadis/Statho-poulos/Karasis, CC Article 718 no. 2).

HUNGARY: According to CC Article 477 paragraph (1), '[t]he agent shall inform his principal of his activities and the state of affairs upon request or, if necessary, even without a request, particularly if employment of another person has become necessary or if the instructions need to be changed due to the occurrence of new circumstances'. Moreover, CC Article 476 prescribes that '[i]f the principal issues imprudent or incompetent instructions, the agent shall call the principal's attention to the matter. If the principal insists on the instructions despite the warning, he shall be liable for the damages sustained on account of the instructions'. In this respect the general rules of obligations also apply, especially CC Article 277 paragraph (4), according to which '[t]he parties shall be under obligation to cooperate in the performance of a contract. The obligor shall act to perform the contract in the manner that can generally be expected in the given situation, while the obligee shall promote performance in the same manner'. The agent is liable for damages resulting from non-performance (CC Article 310). See Supreme Court Pfv. VIII. 22.351/2005, in EBH2006. 1410.

IRELAND: Such a positive duty is not provided for at common law (only three duties are imposed at common law: to obey instructions; to exercise reasonable skill and care; and to perform personally). Further fiduciary duties are imposed by equity. It is important to note that fiduciary duties are imposed on the fiduciary automatically, as a matter of law, by virtue of the position he holds. The core duties of a fiduciary are those of loyalty and fidelity. These core duties have several aspects and an agent's fiduciary duties can be divided into four headings: to avoid conflicts of interest; not to make a secret profit; not to accept a bribe; and to account. It is arguable that in order to obey instruction, and/or to exercise reasonable skill and care, and/or avoid conflicts of interest, an agent might, before and during his performance of the contract, have to inquire about the principal's interests and needs as regards the content of the proposed contract to be negotiated or concluded by the agent. Failure to do so could result in a breach of his duties. I am not aware of any direct case law in this regard.

ITALY: Before and during the agent's performance of the contract, the latter is required to inquire what the principal's interests and needs are, since this is functional to the satisfaction of the principal's interests and therefore to the correct performance of the agent's obligation. A failure in doing so would amount in most cases to a breach of the duty of care and may therefore consist in a breach of contract. Consequently, the principal may claim any damages arising out of the breach and seek termination of the contract, provided that the breach is not irrelevant.

MALTA: It is the agent's duty to request more information with regards to the contract. When the agent fails to do this he would be guilty of negligence, although such negligence may be involuntary. In fact the agent is always bound to be in good faith and to be zealous and diligent. If the agent does not inquire what his principal's interests are, then in this case he was not diligent enough and therefore he will be considered as negligent and therefore liable.

NETHERLANDS: The agent in general is obliged to inform the principal about his activities regarding the fulfilment of the assignment (CC Article 7:403 paragraph (1)). However, there seems no specific obligation of the agent to inquire about the principal's specific needs and wishes.

POLAND: The agent has no duty to inquire about the interests of the principal.

PORTUGAL: An ancillary duty of the agent to provide information and inquire about the interests of the client can according to the circumstances of the case, be deemed to emerge from the general principle of good faith and fair dealing of Articles 227 and 763 paragraph (2) CC. According to Menezes Cordeiro, p. 605, the parties must, during the execution of the contract inform each other of any facts that are related to the contract and to its execution. In STJ 17 June 1998, BMJ 478, 351, the Supreme Court has anchored such a duty of the agent to inform the client on both the general principle of good faith and the duty to give account of Article 1161 lit (d). The breach of such a duty could engage the agent's liability. Furthermore, if the agent is a professional, such a duty could be included in that specific professional's duty of care.

SCOTLAND: The agent is bound to perform in accordance with his instructions (Macgregor, paragraph 84; Gow, p. 530). He is also bound to act in the best interests of his principal (Macgregor, paragraph 97) Such duties are far-reaching, and it is likely that they would extend to requiring the agent to request information from the principal where such information was required for the proper performance by the agent of the mandate contract. Failure to do so would probably constitute a breach of the agent's fiduciary duty for which the principal would be entitled to recover damages.

SLOVAKIA: There is no specific duty to inquire, but it may be considered as implied in the duty of agent to act in accordance with interests of principal and to inform the agent about all of the issues that can influence on the change of the principal's directions (Comm.C paragraph 567(2)).

SPAIN: This duty is expressly provided for in Comm.C Article 255.

SWEDEN: The agent is considered to have a duty to inquire about the principal's interests and needs in order to be able to perform in accordance with the mandate contract. The agent also has a duty to inform the principal of matters and circumstances of which he becomes aware and which are of importance for the performance of the contract, see Ramberg, p. 246-247; J. Hellner, p. 225.

No answer received: BELGIUM

3. Professional insurance required?

AUSTRIA: The canons of professional ethics require the agent to take insurance for professional liability (e.g. Article 3.9 of the Charter of Core Principles of the European Legal Profession and Code of Conduct for European Lawyers).

BELGIUM: The Belgian CC does not contain an obligation to take out insurance for professional liability. The agent is therefore not required to take out insurance for professional liability, unless special rules for certain professions (e.g. the legal profession) apply.

BULGARIA: There are no general rules that impose on the agent an obligation for insurance covering his professional liability. A compulsory insurance 'Professional Liability' is required for advocates, cf. BAA Article 50 paragraph (1).

DENMARK: Normally the agent is not required to take insurance for professional liability. In certain trade and commercial relationships custom may have developed an obligation for the agent to take this kind of insurance. In specific areas (e.g. solicitors and accountants) the taking of insurance will be mandatory.

ENGLAND: There does not seem to be any specific authority on this, but most professional agents will probably be required to take insurance for professional liability (solicitors have to for instance).

ESTONIA: Generally the agent is not required to take insurance for professional liability. However, special conditions apply for some professional agents such as lawyers.

FINLAND: Generally, the agent is not required to take insurance for professional liability. However, real estate agents, insurance brokers and lawyers (only members of the bar) are required to take professional liability insurance.

FRANCE: The Civil Code does not contain an obligation to take insurance for professional liability since the agency is, in principle, not remunerated. On the other hand, certain specific legislations require professional agents to take insurance, e.g. estate agents (Law of 2 July 1970, Article 3-3°), insurance agents (Insurance Code Article L. 530-1), barristers and solicitors (Law of 31 December 1971, Article 27).

GERMANY: The agent is not required to take insurance for professional liability, unless special rules for certain professions (e.g. legal) apply.

GREECE: In case of a mandate contract, the agent is not required to take insurance for professional liability due to the gratuitous character of the mandate. In case of the obligatory remunerated mandate between the lawyer and the principal, the lawyer is not required to take insurance for professional liability.

HUNGARY: The agent is not required to take insurance for professional liability except for some special cases, e.g. attorneys at law (Act XI of 1998 on Attorneys Article 10 paragraph (2)).

IRELAND: An agent per se, is not required to take out professional liability insurance. However, certain professionals are so required. For instance, every solicitor must as a pre-requisite to private practice in the State possess professional liability insurance from an insurer recognised by the Law Society (Solicitors Acts 1954-1994).

ITALY: As a general rule, there is no duty on the agent to take insurance for professional liability. However, depending on the specific professional area of the agent, the taking of insurance is widespread in practice (e.g. lawyers, accountants).

MALTA: If in the normal course of his profession, the agent is required to take insurance for professional liability then he should do so. If in this situation the agent is an architect, he would be required to take insurance for professional liability as this is obligatory for architects according to the Architecture and Civil Engineering Professionals Act Article 11.

NETHERLANDS: Generally, the agent seems not required to take out professional liability insurance. However, in case of professional service providers in general, such as architects, engineers, lawyers, or accountants, several specific laws often include these service providers to be sufficiently insured for their professional liability.

POLAND: Certain professionals are required to have an insurance from civil liability (legal professions, stock brokers).

PORTUGAL: The agent is not generally required to take insurance for professional liability. However, professional regulation may impose such a duty. E.g. in the case of attorneys, Article 99 of Lei 15/2005 of 26 January requires a valid insurance policy with a minimum coverage of €250 000.

SCOTLAND: Whilst agents who are members of distinct professions are, in fact, obliged to carry professional indemnity insurance (for example, solicitors), it is not possible to say that, as a general rule, every agent who is also a member of a profession is similarly obliged to take out such insurance. The answer to this question will vary depending upon the profession in question.

SLOVAKIA: As a general rule, there is no duty on the agent to take insurance for professional liability. However, depending on the specific professional area of the agent, the taking of insurance is widespread in practice (e.g. advocates, accountants).

SPAIN: Professional insurance is not required as a general rule.

SWEDEN: Some categories of agents are required to take insurance for professional liability, such as lawyers, real estate agents and insurance agents. See FmL Articles 5 and 6.

Article 3:103: Obligation of skill and care

(1) The agent has an obligation to perform the obligations under the mandate contract with the care and skill that the principal is entitled to expect under the circumstances.

(2) If the agent professes a higher standard of care and skill the agent has an obligation to exercise that care and skill.

(3) If the agent is, or purports to be, a member of a group of professional agents for which standards exist that have been set by a relevant authority or by that group itself, the agent must exercise the care and skill expressed in these standards.

(4) In determining the care and skill the principal is entitled to expect, regard is to be had, among other things, to:
   (a) the nature, the magnitude, the frequency and the foreseeability of the risks involved in the performance of the obligations;
   (b) whether the obligations are performed by a non-professional or gratuitously;
   (c) the amount of the remuneration for the performance of the obligations; and
   (d) the time reasonably available for the performance of the obligations.

Comments

A. General idea

When performing a mandate contract, the agent needs to take all kinds of decisions to be able to ultimately conclude the prospective contract or to ensure that the principal can conclude that contract. How the agent is to execute these tasks is typically not regulated in all details in the instructions obtained from the principal. Of course, in so far as the instructions and directions are sufficiently clear, the agent will have to base his decisions on these instructions and directions, as indicated in Article 3:101 (Obligation to act in accordance with mandate). Moreover, Article 3:102 (Obligation to act in interests of principal) will also ensure that the agent has some guidance on what is expected of him. Moreover, in so far as this is needed to act in the best interests of the principal, the agent is required to request information from the principal under paragraph (2) of the latter Article. However, there will also be decisions that affect the performance of the mandate contract where the agent can choose between different options that all fall within his mandate and which potentially could all be regarded to be in the interests of the principal. In such a case, neither of these Articles would indicate how the agent is required to act. The present Article provides that in such cases, the agent must act with the care and skill that the principal may expect under the circumstances. The standard of care is also influenced by the way the agent has presented himself and more objective standards, such as a code of professional ethics, applicable to the group of professionals to which the agent belongs or purports to belong.

Illustration 1

A certain law firm specialises in negotiating football players with professional football teams on behalf of professional football players. The firm has a high reputation in the world of football agents and is a founding member of the European Football Agents Associations. The firm must live up to that reputation. Moreover, as a law firm, it must also abide by the code of ethics applicable to lawyers.

B. Determination of standard of care for agents

The default rule is not that the agent guarantees that a result will be achieved (for example, that the prospective contract will be concluded or that a buyer for a property will be found): in the absence of a provision to the contrary in the contract, the obligation is only to perform in accordance with the skill and care that the principal is entitled to expect.

In all legal systems, the agent is required to exercise such care and skill as is needed to safeguard the principal's interests. The legal systems of the Member States more or less agree on the standard of care which is required from the agent, but different terminologies are used. Basically, one could start from the reasonable expectations of the principal, from the care and skill needed for the proper performance of the mandate contract, or from the notion of a 'good housefather'. The agent is expected to exercise the care and skill a normal person would exercise in the same circumstances in BULGARIA, whereas he is expected to exercise the same care as he would for his own affairs in MALTA and SCOTLAND. Generally, a professional agent is required to exercise the care and skill that may be expected from professional agents; therefore, the duty of care is more stringent for such agents. In FINLAND, even more care is expected of a professional agent in a consumer contract. While the duty of care cannot be set aside in FINLAND, it can be limited or even excluded, provided that clear words are used to that extent, in IRELAND.

Paragraph (4) provides an indicative list of factors to be taken into account in determining the standard of skill and care that the principal is entitled to expect from the agent. The fact that no or only a very modest remuneration has been agreed upon may but need not influence the amount of care that may be expected from the agent, as has explicitly been accepted in IRELAND and SCOTLAND with regard to gratuitous mandates.

C. Specific standard of care

Paragraphs (2) and (3) deal with situations in which the agent is obliged, in view of the specific circumstances, to observe a specific standard of skill and care. Paragraph (2) refers to the case in which the agent professes a higher standard of skill and care, whilst paragraph (3) refers to the standard of skill and care expected of agents who belong to a certain group of professional agents. Obviously, the standard of skill and care that may be expected from an agent falling under paragraphs (2) or (3) will also have to be measured against the criteria set out under paragraph (4), taking into account the (purported) higher expertise of such an agent.

D. Relation to the Principles of European Law and the Draft Common Frame of Reference

This Article mirrors that of Article IV.D. – 3:102 DCFR (Obligation of skill and care). What is in accordance with the mandate is to be determined by interpretation of the contract in accordance with Chapter 5 PECL (Interpretation).

This Article sets out general criteria to determine the standard of skill and care expected of an agent. It is worded in almost the same words as the corresponding provision for service contracts in Article 1:107 of the Principles of European Law on Service Contracts (PEL SC) (General Standard of Care for Services).

E. Character of the rule

This Article constitutes a default rule from which the parties may derogate in the sense that the parties may agree to a higher or lower level of care for the agent to exercise in the performance of the mandate contract. Moreover, the parties may also exclude or restrict the ordinary remedies for breach of the obligations under this Article. It is mandatory, however, in the sense that the parties cannot lawfully agree that the agent may exercise full discretion as to the manner in which he performs his obligations, as the agent will always have to maintain a minimum standard of care. A clause limiting the agent's liability even below this minimum would effectively mean that the agent would be provided with immunity against liability. Such a clause should be contrary to public policy and for that reason would be void.

F. Remedies

If the agent does not act in accordance with this Article, the normal remedies for non-performance apply.

Comparative Notes

1. Standard of care for agents

In all legal systems, the agent is required to exercise such care and skill as is needed to safeguard the principal's interests. The agent is expected to exercise the care and skill a normal person would exercise in the same circumstances in BULGARIA, whereas he is expected to exercise the same care as he would for his own affairs in MALTA and SCOTLAND. Generally, a professional agent is required to exercise the care and skill that may be expected from professional agents; therefore, the duty of care is more stringent for such agents. In FINLAND, even more care is expected of a professional agent in a consumer contract. On the other hand, the duty of care may be lower if the agent has acted gratuitously in IRELAND and SCOTLAND. While the duty of care cannot be set aside in FINLAND, in IRELAND it can be limited or even excluded, provided that clear words are used to that extent.

National Notes

1. Standard of care for agents

AUSTRIA: An agent must exhibit such a degree of skill and diligence as is appropriate to the performance of the duties that he has accepted. In carrying out his duties with reasonable care, the agent must act with the care and diligence of a man of ordinary prudence in the line of the employment. Thus he is under a duty of care, not under a duty to guarantee the result expected by the principal. Even if the agent is a professional, he does not guarantee that what he does will have the expected effect. The professional agent only warrants that in performing the task given to him he will exercise the skill generally possessed by his brethren in the profession (CC Article 1299; Schwimann/Apathy, Article 1012 Rz 2.) Solicitors, notaries and tax advisers are liable for blame worthy ignorance of the law (Schwimann/Apathy, Article 1012 Rz 2.). Commercial agents must exhibit the diligence of a prudent businessman (Comm.C Articles 347 and 394, Article 5 HVertrG).

BELGIUM: Beside the exceptional case where the agent does not execute his mandate at all, the agent is – in general – under a duty of care (De Page, p. 407). For specific aspects of the agent's duties, he is nevertheless under a duty to guarantee the result, e.g. the duty to follow imperative instructions of the principal or the prohibition to exceed the limits of his authority. The agent must act as a *bonus pater familias* (Paulus & Boes, p. 90; Wéry, p. 148).

BULGARIA: The agent has to perform his contractual obligation under the mandate contract with the diligence of 'a good householder' (diligentia boni patris familias, cf. OCA Article 281. This is a care that a reasonable person would consider necessary to be taken under the same circumstances (Апостолов, Облигационно право, p. 248). This is the due diligence for both gratuitous and non-gratuitous contracts and it is higher than diligence taken by the agent for his own interests (Любен Василев, Облигационно право, p. 24). The standard of care for the professional agents is even higher and the care of 'a prudent business-man' is required, cf. for the commercial agent CA Article 33 paragraph (1), for the commission agent CA Article 350 paragraph (1), for the forwarding agent CA Article 361 paragraph (1), referring to CA Article 350 (1) (Кацаров, p. 413).

DENMARK: The parties can agree to a 'best-efforts-clause', but normally a clause like this does not involve a duty to guarantee the result expected by the principal.

ENGLAND: Every agent must perform his authority with due care and skill (Bowstead & Reynolds, paragraph 6.015). As long as the agent acts bona fide and in the best interest of the principal, the agent cannot guarantee the result expected of the principal, (unless the agent is *del credere*). The standard of care is determined by reference to what is usual for an agent in his particular line of business or professional position. In *Metropolitan Toronto Pension Plan v Aetna Life Assurance Co of Canada* ((1992) 98 DLR (4th) 582) it was stated that 'if he is an agent following a particular trade or profession (…) he must then show such skill as is usual and requisite in the business for which he receives payment' (Ibid, at 597 per Rosenberg J.). To establish whether or not the agent has met the required standard of care, one usually looks at the terms of the contract and the specific circumstances of a given case. The standard of care of a professional agent is higher than that of a gratuitous agent *(Chaudry v Prabhakar* [1988] 3 All ER 718).

ESTONIA: As a default rule, the agent is under a duty of care (LOAEst Article 620 for the (general) contract for services; the same rule also applies for specific contracts of mandate such as the contract of agency, brokerage agreement and commissionaire agreement). The parties may agree that the agent guarantees the result expected by the principal; in that case, the contract for mandate is a contract for works by type. If the agent is under a duty of care, the standard of care is determined according to LOAEst Article 620 (as a default rule). It distinguishes between the professional and the non-professional service provider. Generally, the service provider (the agent) is obliged to perform his services to the maximum benefit of the principal in the light of and according to his best knowledge and abilities and shall prevent any damage to the property of the principal (subjective standard). The service provider who is acting for the purposes of his economic or professional activities (the professional) is obliged to apply the generally recognised skills of his profession (objective standard).

FINLAND: The agent is under a duty of care during the whole performance. Unless otherwise agreed, he is not under a duty to guarantee the result expected by the principal. The standard of the duty of care varies and cannot be described exclusively. It depends, among other things, on such factors as the area of activity in question, the professional character of the agent's activities, etc. The standard is usually at the highest in consumer agreements. In certain areas of activities the standard has been specified in regulation, e.g. for lawyers, real estate agents (REstateA) and commercial agents (ACRS). The duty of care cannot be set aside.

FRANCE: Depending on the situation, the agent may be liable only to implement suitable means or may be liable for a specific result in terms of the fulfilment of his agency. This will depend on the nature of the conditions affecting the success of the agency. Where the agent is subject to a 'means' obligation, the judge will require reasonable performance of the normally prudent and diligent agent ("good housefather"), without taking account of the specific capacities of the agent himself, but considering whereas he's a professional or not. Where the agent has not reasonably performed the contract, he will be liable to the principal.

GERMANY: The agent is required to exercise due care under the general rule of CC Article 276. Liability thus occurs when he has breached this standard of care intentionally or negligently (CC Article 276 paragraph (1)). A higher standard of care may apply if the agent possesses a particular expertise, and the courts have held such an elevated standard of care to be applicable e.g. when banks or tax consultants acted as agents.

GREECE: In case of a contract of mandate, the agent is obliged to a diligent performance of the mandate. According to CC Article 714, an agent is responsible for any fault, which means that he is also liable for every kind of negligence. The required standard of care is found in CC Article 330: 'A debtor shall be responsible for any default in the performance of his obligation resulting from fraud or negligence imputable to the debtor or to his legal agent. There is negligence when the care required in the carrying out of business was not furnished'. In case of intermediation, good faith requires a diligent performance of the brokerage contract (CC Article 288). The broker is not under a duty to guarantee the result expected by the principal.

HUNGARY: In general, '[a]n agent must fulfil the agency according to the instructions and interests of the principal' (CC Article 474 paragraph (2)). CC Article 478 paragraph (2) establishes that '[t]he agent shall be entitled to demand remuneration even if his actions brought no results'. Contrary to the general rules, in case of commission, '[t]he commission agent shall be responsible to the principal for performance of all of the obligations that are undertaken by his contracting partner in the contract' (CC Article 509 paragraph (2)). CC Article 511 paragraph (1) sets forth that '[t]he commission agent shall be entitled to receive a commission only if the sales contract has been performed'. The general rules of the law of obligations determine the standard of care, especially CC Article 277 paragraph (4): '[t]he obligor shall act to perform the contract in the manner that can generally be expected in the given situation, while the obligee shall promote performance in the same manner.' See Supreme Court Pfv. VIII. 22.351/2005, in EBH2006. 1410; Supreme Court Pfv. V. 21.929/1994, in BH1997. 286; CA Csongrád Megyei Bíróság 1. Gf. 40 118/1997/4, in BDT2000. 128.

IRELAND: As a default rule, all agents are required to act with reasonable care (this is one of the duties which arise at common law). Where the agency is contractual, a term to exercise reasonable care will normally be implied in the contract, at common law. Where services are provided in the course of a business, a term to exercise reasonable care is implied by statute (Sale of Goods and Supply of Services Act 1980, article

39). Where the agency is non-contractual, the duty to exercise reasonable skill and care arises in tort only. Hence, a contractual agent may be subject to concurrent duties in contract and tort unless either is modified or excluded by the contract. It appears that an agent's contractual and tortious duty of care can be limited or excluded by the mandate contract. However, clear words are needed to exclude liability for negligence. The standard of care required is what is reasonable in the circumstances. This will vary depending on the particular facts of the case. In general, the supplier of services, such as agency services, is expected to exercise 'the ordinary skill of an ordinary competent man exercising that particular art'. Where a supplier of a service claims any particular skill, expertise or specialism, that claim may raise the standard of care expected of the service provider. There are various authorities illustrating what is reasonable in a particular trade or profession, in particular circumstances. For example, it has been held that the general duty owed by a solicitor to his client is to show him the degree of care to be expected in the circumstances from a reasonably careful and skilful solicitor *(Roche v Peilow* [1986] ILRM 189 per Henchy J at 196-7). Usually a solicitor will meet this standard if he follows a common practice among the members of his profession *(Daniels v Heskin* [1954] IR 73). But where the common practice has inherent defects, which ought to be obvious to any person giving the matter due consideration, the fact that the practice is shown to have been widely and generally adopted does not make the practice any the less negligent *(O'Donovan v Cork County Council* [1967] IR 173 at 193). The standard of reasonable care may be lower where the agency is gratuitous, though not necessarily *(Chaudrhy v Prabakhar* [1988] 3 All ER 718).

ITALY: As a default rule, the agent has a duty of care towards the principal. He has to act in the principal's account, which implies that he has to act in the principal's best interest, and to satisfy his expectation with respect to the prospective contract. The agent does not have a duty to guarantee a specific result; accordingly, he cannot be considered liable for non-performance when his agent activity turns out to be unsuccessful or when the contract turns out not to be a good affair. The required standard of care is due diligence or reasonable care. Whether or not the agent acted diligently has to be established on a case-to-case basis having regard to the specific circumstances, and depending on whether or not the agent is a professional (in the latter case the standard of care is higher). See Cass. no. 19778/2003, Foro It. Mass., 2003, 19, 4070; Cass. no. 11961/2003, Foro It. Mass., 2003, 20, 4070; Cass. no. 2149/2000, Foro It. Mass., 2000, 9, 4070.

MALTA: An agent under Maltese law must exercise the diligence of a *bonus pater familias.* The standard of reason required is that of a reasonable man, in other words, the standard of care of an honest and diligent person. Therefore under Maltese law the agent would be under a duty of care. In order to establish whether an agent has in fact properly carried out his duty, one is to take into consideration all the circumstances of the case, the nature of the transaction, and the juridical relationship between the parties. Cf. Comm. Court 27 April 1882, *Perini noe. vs Laferla.* Maltese courts have also held that in order to see whether the agent has acted as a bonus pater familias, the only examination should be to see whether the agent has acted as he would have acted if the thing were his own. Cf. CA (Commercial) 11 March 1910, *Vassallo noe. vs Griscti.*

NETHERLANDS: Generally, the agent is to observe due care (CC Article 7:401). For instance, the agent is required to obey timely and well considered directions of the principal regarding the assignment (CC Article 7:402 paragraph (1)) and keep the principal informed of his activities regarding the performance of the service (CC Article 7:403 paragraph (1)). Furthermore, the agent is accountable to the principal regarding the performance of the assignment (CC Article 7:403 paragraph (2)).

POLAND: The agent is required to exercise due care under the general CC Article 355 paragraph (1). A professional agent is expected to act with skill, knowledge and care that may be reasonable expected from professionals, cf. CC Article 355 paragraph (2).

PORTUGAL: The duty of the agent is a duty of care, not a duty to guarantee the result. The standard of care is the diligence of a good *pater familias* according to the specific circumstances of the case, cf. CC Article 487 paragraph (2). In particular, according to CC Article 1161, the agent must execute the mandate according to the instructions of the other party; cf. Lima/Varela (1986), p. 715.

SCOTLAND: The agent's duty of care has been described as similar to that of 'a prudent man in managing his own affairs' (Erskine, III,3,37; Bell, Commentaries, I,516; Bell, Principles, paragraph 221). This contrasts with the lower duty applying to the 'mandatary' (a gratuitous agent) who need only show reasonable care *(Kay v Simpson* (1801) Hume 328; *Grierson v Muir* (1802) Hume 329). The standard is, however, higher in the case of a professional agent, where such an agent must meet the standard of a reasonably careful and competent member of that profession *(Cooke v Falconer's Agents* (1850) 13 D 157, per Lord Fullerton at 172; *Beattie v Furness-Houlder Insurance (Northern) Ltd* 1976 SLT (Notes) 60. In the case of solicitors see Rennie, nos. 3.02 ff.). The agent's duty of care may vary depending upon the particular trade in which he is working, on a prior course of dealing between the parties, or on the circumstances of the case *(Hastie v Campbell* (1857) 19 D 557 per Lord President McNeill at 561, and per Lord Curriehill at 564 and 565; *Alexander Turnbull & Co v Cruikshank and Fairweather* (1905) 7F 101). The conduct of the principal is also relevant to the agent's duty. Delay by the principal or the giving of defective instructions may result in the loss by the principal of his right to sue the agent *(Mackenzie v Blakeney* (1879) 6 R 1329). The principal may also be required to reimburse the agent for any expenses incurred by the agent as a result of the principal's actions *(Dougall v National Bank of Scotland* (1892) 20 R 8). Only agents acting del credere guarantee the result expected by the principal. This is a special type of agency in Scots law which is no longer common (see Bell, Principles, paragraph 286; *Lloyd's Exrs v Wright* (1870) 7 SLR 216).

SLOVAKIA: In civil relations, the standard of care is determined as 'a duty to act according to the agent's ability and knowledge.' In commercial relations, the agent is bound to proceed with professional care when arranging a certain matter on the principal's behalf (Comm.C Article 567 paragraph (1)) and the commission agent is bound to negotiate the principal's affairs with professional care in accordance with the principal's instructions (Comm.C Article 578).

SPAIN: The diligence expected from an agent is the diligence of the *bonus pater familias* (CC Article 1104). The level of diligence is to be determined in each case according to the particular circumstances: the nature of the affair, the skill required by commercial and professional usages, simple rules of prudence, and so on (CC Article 1719 and Comm.C Article 255). The agent typically has an obligation of means (Hernández Gil, p. 472).

SWEDEN: The agent has a general duty of care based on general contract law rules during the performance of his commission. The duty also includes a duty to conclude the task within a reasonable period of time. The duty of care depends on the character of the commission and the mandate contract. One can distinguish a difference between the requirements of the work in its entirety and the responsibility for specific measures. Regarding work in its entirety the principal can only claim non-performance when the work considerably deviates from the standard which can be expected. The requirements for specific measures on the other hand are often high. In particular this concerns measures regulated by law such as observance of time limits or to examine public registers when this is called for. Also, high requirements apply on accuracy as regards information based on facts provided by the agent. If the agent is a professional the duty of care is emphasized. A professional agent is required to timely inform the principal about important issues and also to make sure the principal understands and is able to evaluate the information. He is also required to act in accordance with good business practice when applicable. See Comm.C Article 18:1, KommL Article 7, HaL Article 5.

Section 2:
Consequences of acting beyond mandate

Article 3:201: Acting beyond mandate

(1) The agent may act in a way not covered by the mandate if:
  (a) the agent has reasonable ground for so acting on behalf of the principal;
  (b) the agent does not have a reasonable opportunity to discover the principal's wishes in the particular circumstances; and
  (c) the agent does not know and could not reasonably be expected to know that the act in the particular circumstances is against the principal's wishes.
(2) An act within paragraph (1) has the same consequences as between the agent and the principal as an act covered by the mandate.

Comments

A. General idea

This Article and the next deal with the consequences of the agent's acting outside of his authority in the relation between agent and principal. In this *internal* relationship, the fact that the agent has acted beyond the mandate will normally imply that the agent has failed to perform the contractual obligations towards the principal and will therefore be liable for non-performance, unless this section provides otherwise.

Normally, the agent must act in accordance with the mandate, i.e. the authorisation and instruction given by the principal. If the agent acts outside the boundaries determined by the principal, then the agent is normally liable for non-performance of the contractual obligations. Hence, in the event of new developments, the agent is required to contact the principal and ask for guidance. However, there may be situations in which the agent has to take immediate action to safeguard the interests of the principal but has no time to contact the principal. In such a case, the agent is *allowed* to act beyond the mandate if certain requirements are met. This is the situation regulated in the present Article. Paragraph (1) of this Article sets out when the agent may exceed his authority. Paragraph (2) indicates that when the agent has lawfully exceeded his authority, he is deemed to have had the authority to act and therefore has properly performed his obligations under the mandate contract.

B. Acting beyond mandate allowed?

As the mandate indicates the limits of the agent's authority, an agent who exceeds his authority is normally in breach of his contractual obligations towards the principal. However, there may be cases where it is actually in the best interest of the principal if the agent ignores the limitations in the mandate.

During the performance of a mandate contract, new developments may take place. Some-times, immediate action by the agent may be needed to safeguard the principal's interests, e.g. because an offer made to the agent by the third party expires before the agent is able to contact the principal. In so far as the agent's mandate is broad enough, he will be able to act without such contact, but this is problematic if the agent would have to exceed his power: where the agent exceeds his power without being allowed to do so, he will be liable for non-performance towards the principal. Moreover, if the agent did not agree to the terms of-fered, and the principal afterwards argues that the agent should have accepted the offer and that the agent's mandate was in fact broad enough, the agent may be liable for non-per-formance for *not* – as he perceived it – exceeding his power. Not allowing the agent in certain (emergency) cases to exceed his power may therefore not be in the interests of both the principal and the agent.

Illustration 1
Fiona is charged by Gerald to buy a cottage in Yorkshire on Gerald's behalf for a price not exceeding € 200,000. The asking price is € 203,000. Gerald has made it very clear to Fiona that he has fallen in love with the cottage and that he is keen to buy it. Moreover, as Fiona knows, Gerald can finance a house as long as the sales price does not exceed € 250,000. As both Fiona and Gerald know, the cottage has been on the market for more than a year and the owners have not only received not a single bid, hardly anybody has come to visit the cottage. However, while Fiona is negotiating a sales contract with the owners, out of the blue Hugh makes a bid of € 205,000 for the cottage. The owners inform Fiona, who has to decide on the spot whether she will match that bid. If she does not, the owners make clear that the cottage will be sold to Hugh.

Illustration 2
Samantha is the managing director and sole owner of a small company. For the finan-cial affairs of the company she is advised by Ursula, an independent financial inter-mediary. Ursula is charged with the conclusion of a credit contract for the company. She has received clear instructions from Samantha regarding the terms of the credit contract she is to conclude on behalf of the company. When Samantha is away on holiday for a full month and cannot be reached, the financial situation of the company takes a turn for the worse as a result of the unexpected insolvency of some important debtors. As a consequence, the company is in acute need of liquid assets. Ursula is able to provide the company with the badly needed liquid assets but only by providing the bank with additional securities, whereas the mandate given to her by Samantha does not allow her to agree to such additional securities.

Obviously, where there is time for the agent to contact the principal for instructions, he will have to do so and may be expected to await these instructions. However, in situations like those described in the Illustrations, the agent is basically stuck between a rock and a hard place.

In the case of Illustration 1, if Fiona exceeds her authority and matches Hugh's bid, Gerald may be required to honour the sales contract that Fiona has concluded on his behalf with the owners of the cottage for a price higher than Gerald was willing to pay, and Fiona may be held liable for a breach of her contractual obligations towards Gerald. On the other hand, if Fiona does not exceed her authority, Gerald misses out on the cottage.

Illustration 2 is even more problematic: Samantha has left clear instructions to Ursula, preventing her from agreeing to provide the bank with additional securities. However, the current and acute financial problems of the company can only be solved if Ursula ignores the clear instructions provided by Samantha, and a failure to do so could even mean that the company goes bankrupt.

> The present Article answers whether – and if so, under which conditions – the agent may exceed his authority.

The comparative information indicates that in most legal systems, the agent may indeed be allowed to exceed his authority if he perceives that this is in the best interest of the principal and there is no time to contact the principal or to await his instructions. However, in a number of legal systems (including ENGLAND and FRANCE), the agent is not allowed to exceed his authority even if he believes this to be in the best interest of the principal, and would be liable for breach of contract if he does so anyway. This would seem to imply that under the circumstances of the cases indicated in the Illustrations, in these legal systems Gerald would not become the owner of the cottage, and Ursula would not be able to obtain the credit facilities that Samantha's company is in dire need of. It seems that this rather extreme position cannot be defended.

C. Conditions for acting beyond mandate

In the present Article, the view shared in most legal systems is followed: under certain conditions the agent may exceed his authority if this is in the interest of the principal. Paragraph (1) provides that the agent may act beyond the mandate (without incurring liability for doing so) only when certain cumulative requirements are met. These requirements are intended to protect the principal from acts by an overzealous agent. They limit the agent's discretion to act beyond the mandate to those situations where no reasonable principal could be expected not to agree to grant permission, taking into account all the circumstances that the agent is aware of or could reasonably be expected to be aware of, including the principal's expressed or implied interests.

First, the agent needs to have a reasonable ground for acting beyond the mandate, which means in practice that the agent can do so only if this is necessary to safeguard the principal's interests, e.g. if it is necessary to accept an offer that expires before the agent is able to contact the principal. Second, the agent must not have a reasonable opportunity to discover the principal's wishes in the particular circumstances. Finally the agent must not know that the act in the particular circumstances is against the principal's wishes (or be in a situation where such knowledge could reasonably be expected).

In the situation described in Illustration 2, it is clear that these criteria are met. It is unlikely, however, that a court would find that these criteria are also met in the situation described in

Illustration 1, as it seems that this situation could reasonably have been foreseen by the parties. If the mandate of the agent cannot be interpreted as being broad enough to include the pictured situation under these conditions, it should rather be interpreted as an expression of the principal not to be bound by the sales contract, even if that would mean that the contract would not be concluded.

D. Obligation to act beyond mandate not regulated

If it is accepted that under certain conditions it may be in the best interests of the principal that the agent exceeds his power and such excess is allowed, a further question is whether the agent may also be *required* to do so.

Illustration 2 (continued)
Under the circumstances of the case, Ursula is allowed to conclude the credit contract with the bank and to provide the bank with additional securities. However, as Ursula is aware of Samantha's temper and fears a law suit if she agrees to the terms set by the bank, she hesitates to proceed with the conclusion of the contract. Is Ursula required to set aside her hesitations and conclude the contract in excess of her authority?

It is not difficult to construe that where the agent is allowed to exceed his authority under this Article, he is also required to do so. The reasoning would be the following: if it is apparently in the best interests of the principal that the boundaries indicated in the agent's instructions are not respected, and it is not possible to wait for the principal's approval, it is a matter of some urgency that the agent acts. If this is the case, one could argue that the agent's standard of care not only *allows* the agent to exceed his power, but also *compels* him to do so. Such an obligation is indeed accepted in certain cases in BELGIUM, ESTONIA, and ITALY.

On the other hand, one could also argue that (not only allowing but also) requiring the agent to exceed his power – apart from extreme cases – would unreasonably burden him with the risk of liability. To be safe, the agent would have to evaluate the situation in depth to make the right decision. Not acting when he should have exceeded his authority would mean that he would be liable, whereas acting where he should have respected the limits of his authority equally leads to liability. In this respect it should be noted that especially where matters seem urgent, the agent often does not have all the information needed to make a correct assessment of the situation. For instance, in the case of the situation described in Illustration 2, Ursula may be aware of the acute need for liquid assets, but she may not be aware that another debtor is about to pay its outstanding debts, implying that the necessary liquid assets are likely to be available on time anyway. And even if she is aware of this, can she be sure that this debtor will pay on time?

For these reasons, it is thought that as a general rule the agent should not be required to exceed his authority even if he is authorised to do so, but to leave him a margin of discretion. Obviously, in more extreme cases an obligation to act could follow from the general provisions to act in the interests of the principal under Article 3:102 (Obligation to act in interests of principal) and to exercise due care under Article 3:103 (Obligation of skill and care).

E. Consequences of a permitted excess of mandate

If the agent exceeded his mandate and was allowed to do so under this Article, paragraph (2) of the present Article indicates that the act is seen as an act which falls within the agent's mandate. This implies not only that the agent has not breached his contractual obligations towards the principal, but also that he in turn is entitled to payment of his services under Article 2:102 (Price) or, as the case may be, to reimbursement of his expenses under Article 2:103 (Expenses incurred by the agent).

F. Relation to other provisions in these Principles

There is a close relation between the situations covered by this Article and the ones covered by Article 4:104 (No time to ask or wait for direction) of these Principles: in the situations meant in that Article, the agent is required to ask for direction or even has already requested such direction, but due to external events has to act before a response by the principal is received to properly safeguard the principal's interests. In these cases, the agent may have to go beyond the scope of the original mandate. If the agent then acts in accordance with the criteria indicated by that Article, the conditions set in the present Article are deemed to have been met.

G. Relation to the Principles of European Law and the Draft Common Frame of Reference

This Article mirrors that of Article IV.D. – 3:201 DCFR (Acting beyond mandate). Whether the agent acts in accordance with or in excess of the mandate is to be determined by interpretation of the contract in accordance with Chapter 5 PECL (Interpretation).

This Article does not deal with the *external* consequences of the agent having exceeded the limits of his authority. Whether a contract with a third party has been concluded by the agent by acting beyond the mandate is determined by Chapter 3 PECL (Authority of agents). Where the agent does so act, a prospective contract with the third party may or may not be valid, as there may have been (apparent) authority under Chapter 3 PECL (Authority of agents).

The present Article bears a close resemblance to the situation where a person would be allowed to act on behalf of the principal under the Principles of European Law on Benevolent Intervention (PEL BI). Article 1:101 PEL BI (Intervention to benefit another) indicates the conditions for a benevolent intervener to act on behalf of another person. These conditions are as follows:

(a) the intervener must act with the predominant intention to benefit another,

(b) the intervener must have a reasonable ground for acting,

(c) the intervener may not have had a reasonable opportunity to first discover the other party's wishes and

(d) the intervener could not reasonably be expected to know that the intervention is against the other party's wishes.

If and when these criteria are met, Article 3:106 PEL BI (Authority of intervener to act in the name of the principal) entitles the intervener to conclude legal transactions or perform other juridical acts as a representative for the other party. These criteria and the effect that their fulfilment has on the power of the intervener are the same as the criteria set by this Article for the agent and the consequences on the agent's powers. To put it in different words, this Article starts from the idea that if the agent complies with the criteria which would allow action to be taken as a benevolent intervener – in which case no contractual relationship exists – then the agent is also deemed to be in a situation in which acting beyond the mandate is permissible.

Obviously, the last requirement will cause some difficulty when applied to mandate relationships, as the principal may argue that the agent ought to have known that the intervention is against the principal's wishes, as the mandate granted to the agent itself indicates that the principal does not want the agent to go any further. However, this may not always be true. Especially when unforeseen circumstances manifest themselves, a situation may arise which the parties had not taken into consideration when the power was granted. In such a situation, the agent may need to exceed the mandate to achieve the result as indicated in the mandate contract. If the agent then is not able to first contact the principal and ask for direction, direct action may be needed. The present Article, in the same way as the rules on benevolent intervention, provides for the possibility to do so. A specific provision to this extent is needed here, as the provisions on benevolent intervention arguably do not apply given the exclusions listed in Article 1:103 PEL BI (Exclusions) for persons that are authorised to act under a contractual obligation to the principal.

I. Character of the rule

This Article constitutes a default rule from which the parties may derogate. The parties may therefore exclude the possibility of the agent to act in excess of his mandate. By doing so, they indicate that for any situation where the agent would have to exceed his mandate, the principal does not want him to act without his prior consent even if otherwise the agent could reasonably have believed that the principal would have wanted him to act. In this situation, the requirement set by paragraph (1)(c) of this Article has not been met.

J. Remedies

If the agent is not entitled to exceed his authority under this Article, but nevertheless does so, this constitutes a non-performance of the agent. In principle this will entitle the principal to claim damages under Article 9:501 PECL (Right to damages), or termination of the contract under Articles 9:301 ff PECL (Right to terminate the contract). However, ratification by the principal of the contract concluded by the agent may absolve the agent from liability under the next Article.

Comparative Notes

1. Exceeding mandate allowed in certain circumstances?

In all Member States, the starting point is that the agent is liable for breach of contract if he exceeds the limits of the authority awarded to him.

The agent is not allowed to exceed his authority even if he perceives this to be in the interest of the principal in AUSTRIA, ENGLAND, FRANCE, SCOTLAND, and SLOVAKIA. There is little room for the agent to exceed his authority if he perceives this to be in the interest of his principal in DENMARK. Extraordinarily, in ENGLAND and probably also in SCOTLAND, it seems that the principal could not even ratify that the agent had concluded on his behalf but in excess of his authority.

By contrast, the agent may exceed his authority if this is necessary for the protection of the principal's interests and he may assume that the principal would want him to act accordingly in BELGIUM, BULGARIA, ESTONIA, FINLAND, GERMANY, GREECE, HUNGARY, ITALY, MALTA, THE NETHERLANDS, POLAND, and SWEDEN. The situation is similar in IRELAND under the doctrine of necessity. It should be mentioned, however, that these requirements are nowadays satisfied only rarely, which implies that the doctrine is of limited application today. In SPAIN, although the agent is not allowed to exceed his authority, the matter is solved by considering that if by the agent exceeding his original mandate, the principal is placed in a better position than the one he initially wanted, this is not to be considered as going beyond the limits established by the mandate.

In BULGARIA, ESTONIA, GERMAN, HUNGARY, and SWEDEN, the possibility for the agent to exceed his mandate exists only if it is impossible to first obtain the principal's approval before acting, i.e. the circumstances do not allow for any delay in acting. However, in so far as this is possible, the agent must inform the principal about the need to exceed his original authority and wait for the principal's instructions. It is likely that a similar rule would be adopted in the other legal systems that accept the possibility of an agent to exceed his authority.

In some cases, the agent may even be required to exceed his authority to act in the principal's best interests in BELGIUM, ESTONIA, and ITALY, in particular if following the instructions to the letter would likely cause unfavourable consequences for the principal.

National Notes

1. Exceeding mandate allowed in certain circumstances?

AUSTRIA: The agent is liable for damages if he exceeds the limits of authority (CC Article 1009). His liability amounts to the third party's loss incurred by relying on the validity of a declaration; 'Vertrauensschaden' (Rummel/Rummel/Strasser, Article 1016 Rz 23a). The commercial regulation of Article 8 no. 11 of the 4th EVHGB applies for such a falsus procurator within the scope of commercial transactions (if at least the principal is an entrepreneur). The principal may cure the defective contract by approving subsequently or by accepting the advantages of this contract. The agent is not allowed to exceed his authority even if he perceives this to be in the interest of the principal (Rummel/Rummel/Strasser, Article 1016 Rz 23a).

BELGIUM: CC Article 1989 prescribes that the agent may not exceed the limits of his authority. This is a duty to guarantee the expected results (Wéry, p. 145). If the agent exceeds the limits of authority, he is liable for non-performance. To exceed the limits of authority in itself is nevertheless not sufficient to hold the agent contractually liable. The principal must prove the existence of damage and causality. Often the principal will not suffer any damage, because the principal is not bound by the contract concluded by the agent with the third-party in case of an unauthorised performance (De Page, p. 406-407; Wéry, p. 145). However, the obligation to respect the limits of authority is not absolute. The agent is allowed to perform all acts necessarily related to the entrusted mission, with the exception of acts of disposing. Those acts are considered to be part of his mission (Jassogne, p. 608; Kluyskens, p. 631; Wéry, p. 145). In some cases the agent even has the duty to perform these kind of acts (CFI Brugge 6 July 1874, BJ 1874, 1307; Wéry, p. 145).

BULGARIA: As a general rule in Bulgarian contract law, the agent is obliged to perform within the limits of the mandate as preliminarily determined by the principal mandate. Otherwise, the agent is liable for the damages incurred by the deviation (Любен Василев, Облигационно право, p. 24). Nevertheless, he may exceed these limits under the following two prerequisites: first, when the deviation has become necessary for the protection of the principal's interests, and second, when it is impossible to obtain the principal's consent (OCA Article 282). The agent bears the burden of proof for existence of these conditions (Любен Василев, Облигационно право, p. 24). Special provisions are applicable to the deviation from mandate that has occurred in internal relationship between the commission agent and the principal. In case that the commission agent has bought the goods on a higher price or has sold the goods on a lower price than stipulated, he is obliged to immediately communicate this information to the principal. If the latter does not reject the prospective contract immediately, it is presumed that he has ratified it (cf. CA Article 351 paragraph (2)). The principal is not allowed to reject the prospective contract concluded in deviation from the stipulated buying or selling price in two cases. Firstly, if the agent has declared that the differences between prices will be at his expense (cf. CA Article 351 paragraph (3)). Secondly, although the difference between prices will not be covered by the agent, the latter has succeeded in proving that it was not possible to conclude the prospective contract under the price conditions determined by the principal and by negotiating higher buying or lower selling price, he has prevented the principal from suffering significant damages (cf. CA Article 351 paragraph (4)).

DENMARK: The agent is liable for non-performance if he exceeds the limits of his authority. According to Danish law there is little room for the agent to exceed his authority if he perceives this to be in the interest of his principal.

ENGLAND: The agent will be liable for damages if he exceeds the limits of his authority. This is because one of the first fiduciary duties of the agent is to perform under the terms of his contract and not exceed the authority *(Turpin v Bilton* (1843) 5 Man & G 455). This general rule is very strictly applied by the courts: provided that the instructions are clear and unambiguous, the agent must follow them to the letter or be liable for damages *(Volkers v Midland Doherty Ltd* (1985) 17 DLR (4th) 343). The agent is not entitled or required to exceed the authority even if he perceives such an action to be in the principal's best interest *(Fray v Voules* (1859) 1 E & E839). However, the strictness of the rules can be mitigated. If the authority granted allows him to do so, the agent can exercise a certain discretion (e.g. *Re Newen* [1903] 1 Ch 812).

ESTONIA: As a general rule, the agent is liable for non-performance if he exceeds the limits of his power. However, he is allowed and in certain circumstances even obliged to deviate from the instructions of the principal if he perceives it to be in the best interest of the principal. This is the case if adherence to the instructions would be likely to cause unfavourable consequences for the principal (LOAEst Article 621 paragraph (3)). In such cases, the agent must inform the principal and wait for his further instructions as a rule. The agent is entitled to deviate from the instructions without consulting the principal if the circumstances do not allow for delay (LOAEst Article 621 paragraphs (2) and (3)).

FINLAND: The agent is liable for non-performance if he exceeds his authority. In general, the agent is not entitled to exceed his power, even when it is in the interests of the principal. However, if exceeding the agent's authority is clearly necessary to protect the interests of principal, the agent is, in general, allowed to exceed his authority (Comm.C Article 18:10, Hemmo, Sopimusoikeus I, p. 518-519).

FRANCE: The agent is not authorised to exceed the limits of his authority (CC Article 1989), even if he considers it acting in the interest of the principal and even in case of emergency. He may be liable if he does so anyway. However, the principal may ratify the agent's acts.

GERMANY: The agent may exceed the limits of his power if he perceives this to be in the interest of the principal and if he may assume that the principal would tolerate this step in case he knew of the circumstances. However, the agent is always required to inform the principal about the impending excess and wait for instructions, unless his hesitation might result in danger (CC Article 665).

GREECE: In case of a mandate contract an agent may only deviate from the limits set in the mandate if it is impossible to notify the principal and obvious that the principal would have allowed the deviation if he had knowledge of the circumstances that prompted such deviation (CC Article 717). The agent must prove that these requirements exist. Exceptionally, good faith (CC Article 288) may require the agent to exceed the limits of authority if the principal would have permitted or imposed such a deviation from the limits set in the mandate (Georgiadis/Stathopoulos/Karasis, CC Article 717 no. 4). In case of an unjustified deviation from the limits set in the mandate the principal can claim damages due to a defective performance of the mandate on part of the agent (CC Article 714). However, the principal has the discretionary power to approve the unjustified deviation from the limits of authority set in mandate (Georgiadis/Stathopoulos/Karasis, CC Article 717 no. 5).

HUNGARY: If the agent exceeds the limits of authority, it is a kind of non-performance and the agent is liable for damages resulting from the non-performance. In no case is the agent allowed or required to exceed his powers of representation. CC Article 477 paragraph (2) prescribes that '[t]he agent shall be entitled to depart from the principal's instructions only if it is essential for the principal's interest and if there is no time to notify the principal in advance. In such a case the principal shall be notified without delay'. In the internal relationship, if the agent exceeds the limits of authority without exceeding his powers of representation, it might be considered as a case of impromptu agency according to CC Article 484, which sets forth that '[a] person proceeding in a matter on behalf of another person without being authorised thereto by agency or otherwise shall be obliged to handle the matter as required by the interest and probable intent of the person in whose favour he has intervened'. Concerning powers of representation, CC Article 221 paragraphs (1) and (2) establish that 'A person who transgresses the scope of his authority to represent in good faith or who has concluded a contract in the name of another person without having the right to represent and the person in whose name he has proceeded does not approve his action, such shall pay compensation to the other contracting party for damages incurred in result of the conclusion of the contract.' 'A mala fide false agent shall be liable for full recompense.'

IRELAND: An agent must obey his principal's lawful instructions. Where the agency is contractual, the agent is liable for breach of contract if he fails to act as instructed. Therefore, an agent must follow, but not exceed, the limits of his authority. Where an agent exceeds his authority this can be remedied where the principal later ratifies the agent's conduct (in which case the agent is treated as if he was authorised in the first place). Alternatively, where an agent exceeds his authority this can be remedied under the doctrine of agency of necessity. Under this doctrine a person may have authority to act on behalf of another in certain cases where he is faced with an emergency in which the property or interests of that other person are in imminent jeopardy and it becomes necessary, in order to preserve the property or interests, so to act. Agency

of necessity can operate to extend an agent's authority or to give authority to someone not already an agent. There are four preconditions for agency of necessity to arise:
– it must be shown that the agent could not get instructions from the principal;
– the agent must have acted in the principal's interests and bona fide;
– the agent's actions must be reasonable; and
– there must have been some necessity or emergency which caused the agent to act as he did.

The traditional example of an agent of necessity is the master of a ship who acts in an emergency to save the ship or the cargo *(Hawtayne v Bourne* (1841) 7 M & W595 at 599, per Parke B). Developments in modern communications mean that the first requirement will rarely be satisfied (see *The Choko Star* [1989] 2 Lloyd's Rep 42; and *Surrey Breakdown Ltd v Knight* [1999] RTR 84). Therefore, the doctrine is of limited application today. Where the requirements for creation of agency of necessity are fulfilled, two consequences follow. First, the agent has power to bind the principal to transactions entered into with third parties, and secondly, the relationship of principal and agent is constituted between the principal and the agent even if it did not already exist, so that the agent is entitled to the rights of an agent.

ITALY: As a rule, the agent may not exceed the limits of authority. The acts concluded by the agent exceeding the limits of authority are considered by the law as if they had been concluded by the agent in his own name. Consequently, the agent is directly responsible for these acts towards the third parties, unless the principal ratifies the agent's conduct. Until the said principal's confirmation occurs, the agent is directly liable towards the third parties for the conclusion and execution of the prospective contract. With respect to the internal relationship between the agent and the principal, if the agent exceeds the limits of authority this may or may not constitute a breach of contract depending on the specific circumstances of the case. In some cases this behaviour could satisfy the best interests of the principal, e.g. in case of new circumstances which were unknown and unforeseeable by the principal at the time the authority was granted, provided that these cannot be timely reported to the principal for his instructions, and provided that it can reasonably be held that the principal, had he known of the circumstances, would have granted a wider authority to the agent. The agent is then allowed to exceed the limits of authority and may even be required to exceed them. However, in most cases exceeding the limits of authority amounts to a breach of contract.

MALTA: CC Article 1864 specifically states that "An agent cannot do anything beyond the limits of the mandate." However Maltese law also lists certain acts that the agent may perform although these were not set out in the contract, these are: he may institute legal proceedings; make and prosecute appeals; make proof by reference to the oath of his adversary; take the oath; enforce judgments both on movable and immovable property; make demand for the issue of precautionary acts including those for the issue of which an application or declaration on oath is required; make demand for the personal arrest of the debtor of the principal, where such demand is competent (cf. CC Article 1865). In this respect it must be pointed out that if the agent has given to the party with whom he has contracted in such capacity sufficient information as to his powers, then the agent is not liable for any warranty in respect of what he has done beyond such powers unless he has personally bound himself thereto (cf. CC Article 1879). The main principle under Maltese law with regards to this situation is that if the agent exceeds the limits of his authority, the principal would not be responsible for such actions unless these are ratified by the principal. Such ratification may be express or tacit, cf. CA (Civil) 30 May 1958, *La Rosa noe. vs Galea.* Therefore if, for example, in correspondence held between the principal and the third party who had contracted with the agent, the principal keeps silent or inactive and fails to state to the third party that he (the principal) disapproved of the acts of his agent, the principal is deemed to have tacitly ratified the agent's actions. The principle is that *qui tacet cum loqui potuit et debit consentire videtur* – he who remains silent when he could have and should have talked, is deemed as having consented. In fact, it has also been held that if an agent who exceeds his contract informs his principal of the situation and the latter exhorts him to "do his best" or "do what he can", then this would amount to a ratification by the principal of the agent's actions. Cf. CFI (Civil) 30 October 1936, *Rev. Gauci et. vs Hon. Galizia*. It has also been established by the courts that in order to establish whether an agent has in fact carried out his duty properly, one must take into consideration all the circumstances of the case, the nature of the transaction, and the juridical relationship between the parties. Cf. Comm. Court 27 April 1882, *Perini noe. vs Laferla*. The Court also stated that when the instructions given to the agent are not clear enough or are uncertain, the agent is bound to request clarification of the terms of the contract and should not consider himself authorized to act arbitrarily, unless the situation is so urgent as not to allow time for consultation with the principal. In such a case a distinction should be made between a mandate and a voluntary under-taking of the management of another person's affairs – *negotiorum gestio*. Under Maltese law, when the agent exceeds the limits of his contract, he is only bound to render an account to his principal, and in such a situation he cannot plead that this was due to his own negligence. Cf. CA (Civil Inferior) 19 August 1890, *Azzopardi vs Galdies et.* It has also been held that any agreement entered into by the agent in excess of his contract, does not have any effect with regard to the principal who is a third party to this agreement. This was held in CA (Commercial) 14 May 1923, *Scicluna vs Chircop et.*, whereby the Court stated also that this is based on the principle found in CC Article 1001 whereby "Contracts shall only be operative as between the contracting parties, and shall not be of prejudice or advantage to third parties except in the cases established by law." Thus, these agreements would be inexistent with regard to the principal since he had never con-sented to them. However, our jurisprudence also sustains that the principal would also be bound by the acts which his agent has performed in excess of his contract if the third parties had sufficient reason to believe that these acts were not in excess of the powers granted by the contract, and the contract itself included the power to do such acts. Cf. CA (Civil) 11 March 1935, *Cassar vs Cutajar*.

NETHERLANDS: The agent will be liable for damages if he exceeds the limits of his authority. There is no special rule on the question whether an act of the agent not coverd by the mandate may nevertheless be regarded as covered. It would stand to reason that if the requirements of the rules on *negotiorum gestio* (*zaakwaarneming*, CC Article 6:198-202) are met, and any person would thus be entitled to act on behalf of the principal, so could the agent. CC Article 6:201 would then entitle him also to perform a juridical act on behalf of the principal. Arguably, similar powers may be read into the contract under these circumstances on the basis of good faith and fair dealing (CC Article 6:248).

POLAND: The agent may act contrary to what was agreed if 1) contacting the principal is not possible and 2) taking in consideration the circumstances it is reasonable to believe the principal would have agreed for the contract to be performed differently (CC Article 737). If those conditions are not met then the principal may still approve the contract signed by the agent who exceeded the limits of authority. The agent remains liable for all the damages caused to the principal under the ordinary rules for contractual liability (CC Article 471).

PORTUGAL: In the case the agent would acts ultra vires, outside the scope of his agent powers, the other party is not bound by the juridical act executed by the 'agent' unless he subsequently ratifies it (CC Article 268; RE 27 February 1992, CJ 1992, 1, p. 284). In addition, the agent could be held liable for breach of his duty to carry out the mandate according to the instructions given by the other party. However, according to CC Article 1162, the agent can – or actually is bound by his duty of care to – not carry out his mandate or follow the instructions of the other party if the other party would approve of it, if he would know of certain circumstances that it was impossible to transmit to him in due time. It is argued that the agent must be the intelligent interpreter of the will of the other party, cf. Lima/Varela (1986), p. 718.

SCOTLAND: Generally, an agent who exceeds his authority will be liable to the principal for breach of the mandate contract. There is no general rule which allows the agent to exceed his authority if he perceives this to be in the interests of his principal (Erskine, III,3,35). Indeed, the famous English case of *Keighley Maxsted & Co v Durant* ([1901] AC 240), which held that the principal could not ratify a contract which the agent had purported to enter in excess of his authority, would seem to be inconsistent with this proposition. It is likely that a Scots court would follow this case. A Scottish case reached the opposite conclusion, but is thought to be unsound authority *(Lockhart v Moodie* (1877) 4 R 859, see Gloag, p. 143).

SLOVAKIA: If an agent exceeds his authority, he is himself bound by negotiation, unless the relevant act in law is approved without delay by the principal. Where the principal does not approve the act in law undertaken in excess of a power, the person with whom negotiations took place may demand from the agent either performance of the obligation or compensation for any damage by such negotiation or transaction. Liability for the breach of mandate contract in this case is not specifically regulated, the general rules on liability for damages should be applied.

SPAIN: Spanish law does not generally allow the agent to exceed the limits of the mandate (CC Article 1714 and Comm.C Article 256). The principal is not bound to the third party where those limits are exceeded, whether or not the third party was aware of that (CC Article 1727). However, if the agent acts beyond the mandate but, as a result, the principal has a better position than the one the principal initially wanted, then this is not to be considered as going beyond the limits established by the mandate (CC Article 1715). This refers both to an economic advantage but also to avoiding damage to the patrimony of the principal (Hernández Gil, p. 926).

SWEDEN: The agent is liable for non-performance if he exceeds the limits of authority. If required by circumstances, the agent has a duty to deviate from the limits of authority and act as is necessary considering the circumstances. The agent should seek the principal's instructions prior to such deviation unless the matter is of immediate urgency. See AvtL Article 25, KommL Article 8.

Article 3:202: Consequences of ratification

Where, in circumstances not covered by the preceding Article, an agent has acted beyond the mandate in concluding a contract on behalf of the principal, ratification of that contract by the principal absolves the agent from liability to the principal, unless the principal without undue delay after ratification notifies the agent that the principal reserves remedies for the non-performance by the agent.

Comments

A. General idea

Under the preceding Article, the agent may act beyond the mandate under strict conditions. Where he is not allowed to do so under that Article, the agent may be liable for non-performance of the contractual obligations.

This Article regulates the consequences as to the liability of an agent who acts beyond the mandate if the principal subsequently ratifies the contract concluded by the agent. It indicates that the ratification by the principal implies that the liability of the agent for having acted beyond the mandate is excluded. If the principal nevertheless wants to retain the right to exercise remedies for non-performance, this must be explicitly indicated without undue delay.

B. Consequences of unjustified acting beyond mandate

It may be that the agent has exceeded his power in concluding the prospective contract but perceived his actions to be in the best interest of the principal. Under Article 3:201 (Acting beyond mandate), the agent may exceed the authority awarded to him under strict conditions. If these conditions are met, the agent is deemed to have had the authority to conclude the prospective contract after all.

However, if these conditions are not met, the agent's excess of the mandate power in principle constitutes a non-performance of the mandate contract and may lead to the liability of the agent or the termination of the mandate contract by the principal for non-performance. This is true in particular if the principal by virtue of Article 3:201 paragraph (3) PECL (Express, implied and apparent authority) is bound by the prospective contract on the basis of the *apparent* authority of the agent acting in his name, as in such case the principal is bound by a contract he did not want to conclude. If, on the other hand, the third party may not rely on these provisions and, therefore, the principal is not bound by the contract, the third party may be able to claim damages from the agent for the absence of authority under Article 3:304 paragraph (2) PECL (Requirement of notice). An unjustified excess of authority by the agent therefore opens liability risks towards both the principal and the third party. Moreover, apart from these liability risks, in cases of direct representation, the agent also runs the risk of losing the right to payment: if no contract is validly concluded with the third party, payment has not become due under Article 2:102 paragraph (2) (Price) of these Principles.

If, on the other hand, the principal ratifies the contract concluded on his behalf by the agent, at least the risk of liability towards the third party is taken away: the main consequence of ratification is that with regard to the concluded contract the agent is deemed to have had the required authority to conclude it all along, as set out in Article 3:207 paragraph (2) PECL (Ratification by principal). Moreover, after ratification, the obstacle that the prospective contract needs to have been concluded for the price to become due has been taken away. In several respects, therefore, ratification may have positive consequences for the position of the agent. However, what is not decided is whether the ratification should be interpreted as an approval of the agent's actions as such.

C. Consequences of ratification in internal relationship

One question that arises is what the consequences of the ratification should be as regards the *internal* relationship between the principal and the agent. Should the agent still be liable for non-performance, or should the fact that the principal has ratified the prospective contract mean that the agent is absolved from liability? Or should an in-between position be chosen?

Illustration 1

Anastacia asks Britney to purchase from her regular supplier of cheese and tomatoes, Christina, 1,000 kilos of cheese for a price of € 750, which Anastacia intends to process in the production of pizzas. Britney informs Christina that she is commissioned by Anastacia to purchase 1,000 kilos for a price of € 750. Christina then tells her that if she also buys 1,500 kilos of tomatoes, she will only have to pay the discount price of € 1,250. As Britney knows that this would normally be considered a good deal, she agrees. To keep her relation with her regular supplier smooth, Anastacia ratifies the contract with Christina, even though she intended to buy the tomatoes from another supplier, who offered them at the time for a price of € 450. Does the ratification of the contract by Anastacia mean that Britney no longer can be held liable for exceeding her authority?

In this particular case, even though Britney thought she made a good deal for Anastacia, this was in fact not the case. Nevertheless, Anastacia ratified the contract because she did not wish to endanger her relation with her regular supplier. Should the fact that the contract was ratified mean that Britney can no longer be held liable for the damage of € 50 (i.e. the difference between the price to be paid under the contract and the price to be paid if the contract with the other supplier had been concluded)? Depending on the view taken as regards the consequences of the ratification of the prospective contract, the damage would or would not be recoverable. An in-between position would be that Anastacia would retain the possibility to claim damages if she notifies Britney without undue delay after she ratifies the contract with Christina. If she fails to do so, she automatically loses her right to do so. In this in-between rule, it is assumed that the ratification does indeed indicate that the principal is satisfied with the agent's actions – in which case the principal would not be interested in a possible claim against the agent for exceeding his power and authority – but it is left to the principal to indicate otherwise. In order not to burden the agent with too much uncertainty, the principal would have to notify the agent of his intention to do so without undue delay.

It should be noted that the issue has not attracted much attention in the Member States' legal systems. Statutory provisions dealing with this matter do not exist, whereas case law is very scarce: only an ancient case in France is reported. This seems to indicate that indeed the in-between position – ratification by the principal takes away the liability of the agent, unless the principal notifies the agent that he retains his rights for non-performance by the agent – is probably the position adopted in practice, as is confirmed by most national reports.

In the present Article, this in-between position is codified: it is assumed that the ratification does indeed indicate that the principal tolerates the agent's actions – in which case the principal would not be interested in a possible claim against the agent for acting beyond the mandate – but it is left to the principal to indicate otherwise. The chosen rule may be explained as follows.

The normal case will be that if the principal ratifies the contract, he implicitly recognises that the agent did a good job. However, the Illustration shows that this need not always be the case. For that reason, the principal should be able to retain his claim for non-performance by the agent. On the other hand, the content of the contract concluded by the agent in excess of his power and authority apparently is not such that the principal does not wish to be bound. This indicates that even though the agent was in breach of his contractual obligations towards the principal, the agent's actions were not all that strange or all that contrary to the principal's interests. From this it follows that the agent most likely was acting in good faith and in the belief that his actions were in the best interests of the principal. Under these conditions, he will normally be justified in believing that the principal will agree to his actions, even if he did exceed his power and authority. The in-between solution suggested here by which the agent is in principle absolved from liability unless the principal without undue delay informs him otherwise seems to do justice to the interests of both parties.

D. Retention of remedies

If the principal ratifies the prospective contract even though the agent acted beyond the mandate, the liability of the agent is, in principle, excluded. In order not to burden the agent with too much uncertainty, the principal would have to notify the agent without undue delay of an intention to retain remedies for non-performance. In accordance with Articles 1:303 PECL (Notice), the principal need not adhere to any formal requirements in this respect, as long as it is established that the agent is informed of the retention of remedies.

Illustration 1(continued)
The mere fact that Anastacia wishes to keep her relation with her regular supplier smooth and for that reason ratifies the contract with Christina does not necessarily mean that she was happy with Britney's actions, in particular not when she had previously made her position clear to Britney. In such cases, Anastacia should remain free to claim damages – in this case amounting to the extra price (€ 50) she has had to pay for the tomatoes – or even to terminate the mandate contract for non-performance.

E. Relation to the Principles of European Law and the Draft Common Frame of Reference

This Article mirrors that of Article IV.D. – 3:202 DCFR (Consequences of ratification). It may be seen as an elaboration of the general rule of interpretation of Article II. – 8:201 DCFR (General rules), which indicates that a unilateral juridical act (such as ratification) is to be interpreted in the way in which it could reasonably be expected to be understood by the person to whom it is addressed. Although the declaration of ratification in the first place will be addressed to the third party, it may in addition be interpreted as a tacit statement of the principal absolving the agent of liability save for an express declaration by the principal indicating that he retains his remedies towards the agent.

The Article bears resemblance to the duty to notify under Article III. – 3:107 DCFR (Failure to notify). Under that Article, the creditor of an obligation to supply goods, other assets or services who is of the opinion that the goods, other assets or services delivered by the debtor are not in conformity with the contract, must notify the defect to the debtor within a reasonable time after he has or should have discovered the non-conformity. A failure to do so implies that the creditor may not rely on the non-conformity, i.e. that the creditor loses his remedies for the non-performance. The present Article may be interpreted as indicated when the 'reasonable time' has elapsed: for the purposes of mandate contracts where the agent has exceeded his mandate but the principal has ratified the concluded contract, the 'reasonable time' elapses when the principal does not notify the agent without undue delay after ratification that he wishes to retain his rights towards the agent. This also implies that the principal need not notify the agent of the non-conformity in his performance during the time the principal reasonably needs to make up his mind about whether to ratify the prospective contract.

F. Character of the rule

This Article constitutes a default rule from which the parties may derogate.

G. Remedies

If the principal has ratified the contract concluded on his behalf by the agent who was not authorised to do so, and the principal has not notified the agent of his intention to retain his remedies in accordance with this Article, the principal loses the right to invoke a remedy against the agent.

Comparative Notes

1. Consequences of ratification of prospective contract for liability of agent

Ratification of a contract concluded by the agent in excess of his authority in principle does not have any consequences on the internal relationship between agent and principal in THE NETHERLANDS and SWEDEN. This implies that the agent is still considered to have breached his contractual obligations towards the principal and is therefore liable for damages and subject to termination for non-performance, and may subsequently lose the right to claim a price for the contract concluded in excess of his authority. However, it may be contrary to good faith and fair dealing if the principal ratifies the contract with the third party without indicating to the agent that the principal retains his remedies for the agent's breach of his contractual obligations, and later claims a remedy for non-performance by the agent after all: in such cases the principal may have lost his remedies because of his prior inactivity and the reliance the agent had on the principal's acceptance of his actions.

Where the principal ratifies the prospective contract, this is generally interpreted as an approval of the agent's actions in BULGARIA, FRANCE, GERMANY, IRELAND, and possibly also in SPAIN. In these legal systems, the ratification frees the agent from any claim for non-performance, unless the principal either explicitly or implicitly has reserved his rights towards the agent. In ESTONIA, when the ratification is declared towards the agent, this can be interpreted as a release from liability under the mandate contract.

National Notes

1. Consequences of ratification of prospective contract for liability of agent

BULGARIA: According to OCA Article 42 paragraph (2) a person in his name a contract has been concluded without authorization may ratify it. This is a case of acting beyond the granted authority. In Bulgarian contract law there is no explicit rule for regulation the legal effect of the ratification by the principal of prospective contracts concluded and judicial acts performed beyond the mandate. In Bulgarian legal doctrine, it is considered that the ratification may absolve the agent from liability to the principal, unless the principal, explicitly or implicitly, has reserved remedies for the non-performance by the agent (Меворах/Лиджи/Фархи, III, p. 157).

ESTONIA: The law does not contain a clear provision under what circumstances the ratification of a transaction performed by the agent beyond its powers can release the agent from its liablility towards the principle. This should be determined according to the specifics of the case. It can however be presumed that at least in cases where the the ratification is declared towards the agent this can be interpreted as a release from the liablility under the mandate agreement.

FRANCE: There is no specific provision on that topic; the civil code (Article 1998) just provides that the principal will be engaged by the contract only if he ratifies it. Nothing is said about the consequences of this ratification on the relations between the principal and the agent. But ancient case law considers that the agent won't be liable if the principal ratifies the prospective contract, unless the principal lets the agent know that he retains the possibility to claim damages (Cass.civ., 9 May 1853, D.P. 1853 I, 293).

GERMANY: The consequences of the ratification of the prospective contract are addressed in CC Article 684 as part of the rules on benevolent intervention. Generally, the ratification will absolve the agent from his liability for having acted outside the limits of the mandate contract. It is a different question if the ratification also absolves him from liability that arises not from the fact that he has exceeded his mandate, but from the fact has he has violated another standard of care when doing so – this depends on the interpretation of the ratifying act (Palandt/Sprau, Article 684 no. 42).

IRELAND: Where a principal ratifies the previously unauthorised actions of an agent, the effect is retrospective and it is as if the agent was authorised at all times.

NETHERLANDS: The mere fact that the principal ratifies the previously unauthorised actions of an agent need not imply that in his relations with the agent the principal is satisfied with the agent's performance, as the principal mat well have had other reasons for ratifying the contract that was concluded by the agent in excess of his authority, in particular because the principal may want to secure his relations with the third party. However, it may be contrary to good faith and fair dealing if the principal ratifies the contract with the third party without claiming towards the agent that the agent has breached his contractual obligations, and later claims a remedy for non-performance by the agent after all: in such cases the principal may have lost his remedies because of his prior inactivity and the reliance the agent had on the principal's acceptance of his actions.

POLAND: There are no specific provisions in the Polish CC regulating the consequences for the agent of ratification of the agent's actions by the principal.

SCOTLAND: The principal's ratification of the agent's unauthorised actions binds the former in contract with the third party, with retrospective effect, binding the principal from the moment the agent entered the contract. There appears to be no case where a ratifying principal has also reserved or made a claim against the agent for resultant losses.

SLOVAKIA: Consequences of ratification for the internal relation between principal and agent and his liability to principal are not covered, there are not known any cases dealing with this problem.

SPAIN: Ratification renders the agent's act binding to the principal (CC Article 1259). The law is silent as to whether the ratification also amounts to a waiver of claims based on the agent's non-performance. Probably the rule stated in the present Article should apply.

SWEDEN: According to general contract law rules the principal may ratify the prospective contract if the agent has exceeded his power when concluding it. Ratification does not deprive the principal from his right to hold the agent liable for breach of contract.

No answer received: AUSTRIA, BELGIUM, DENMARK, ENGLAND, FINLAND, GREECE, ITALY, MALTA, PORTUGAL.

Section 3:
Mandate normally not exclusive

Article 3:301: Exclusivity not presumed

The principal is free to conclude, negotiate or facilitate the prospective contract directly or to appoint another agent to do so.

Comments

A. General idea

The present Article starts from the presumption that the principal remains free, despite the mandate contract with an agent, to conclude, negotiate, or facilitate the prospective contract personally or to appoint another agent to do so. The parties may, however, agree otherwise by awarding the agent exclusivity.

B. Exclusivity not presumed

The main rule is that the principal may still conclude the prospective contract himself or have it concluded by other appointed agents. When he does, the mandate contract may be terminated by the agent under Article 6:105 (Termination by the agent for extraordinary and serious reason), as in such a case it will usually become impossible or unreasonably difficult for the agent to (also) conclude the prospective contract. Moreover, the possibility for the principal to conclude the prospective contract himself also constitutes a serious reason for the principal to terminate the mandate contract himself under Article 6:103 (Termination by the principal for extraordinary and serious reason). In each of these cases, as the parties had not agreed on exclusivity, the principal was well within his right to conclude the prospective contract, and no damages are due. However, under Article 2:102 paragraph (4) (Price), the agent may be entitled to payment of the price or a part thereof for the services rendered if and in so far as the services rendered have contributed to the conclusion of the prospective contract.

C. Exclusivity clause

The parties may prevent the principal from retaining that freedom by awarding the agent exclusivity. The question arises whether such clauses should be allowed. An exclusivity clause is only in the interest of the agent and is not needed from the viewpoint of the principal. Exclusivity allows the agent to best safeguard interests other than the price he will receive if the prospective contract is concluded, e.g. the need to establish good working relations with possible third parties or to have a visible presence as a way of advertising. It may, however, be in the best interests of the principal to have more parties involved in trying to affect his legal relations to speed up the conclusion of the prospective contract. An exclusivity clause prevents the principal from asking the help of other agents or from concluding the contract himself. If an exclusivity clause is allowed, the principal in effect can only appoint another agent or conclude the contract himself if he first terminates the mandate relationship with the agent who was awarded exclusivity. This obviously is not in the principal's interests if he wishes to speed up the process of concluding the prospective contract. Allowing exclusivity therefore leads to a possible conflict between the commercial interests of the agent and the interests of the principal.

On the other hand, an exclusivity clause ensures the agent that his efforts in finding a possible candidate with whom to conclude the prospective contract will not be in vain because the principal concludes the prospective contract himself: instead of payment of the price for services already rendered and damages for non-observance of the notice period under Articles 2:102 paragraph (3) (Price) and 6:101 paragraph (6) (Termination by notice in general) of these Principles, if the efforts of the agent in concluding the prospective contract were successful, the agent would be entitled to the full price and therefore to the expected full profit of the contract under Article 2:102 paragraph (4) (Price) of these Principles. An exclusivity clause could therefore be a stimulant for the agent to perform the mandate contract as well as possible. In this respect, exclusivity may also be in the interests of the principal. For these reasons, exclusivity clauses are allowed in principle. However, rules of consumer protection may intervene regarding the agent's possibility to claim exclusivity, especially in so far as this occurs by way of standard contract terms. In such contracts, the agent in practice is able to unilaterally dictate the terms of the contract, so that in most cases a term such as the present – which is exclusively in the interest of the agent – cannot be considered to have been agreed upon by parties with equal bargaining power.

D. Interpretation of exclusivity clause

The present Article provides that the principal is free to conclude the prospective contract himself or by another agent appointed by him. However, the parties may derogate from that default rule and agree otherwise, thus awarding the agent exclusivity. As this exclusivity is primarily in the interest of the agent and the agent is normally a professional party, he may be expected to clearly indicate the scope of the exclusivity clause. Under the general rules of interpretation, where a clause is ambiguous, it is to be interpreted against the party who supplied it (cf. Article 5:103 PECL (Contra proferentem rule)). The question then arises how such an ambiguous term should be interpreted. It can also be difficult to determine whether the term was supplied by the principal or the agent, especially in cases where the parties drafted the mandate contract together.

Illustration 1
Agnetha and Bjørn negotiate the terms of a mandate contract under which Bjørn would be asked to buy one of the four versions of 'The Scream' by the painter Edward Munch. Bjørn is willing to do so, but not if Benny – who is also a reputed agent in this industry – could also be asked to represent Agnetha. Agnetha and Bjørn negotiate a

term in their contract by which Bjørn is awarded 'exclusivity'. They do not indicate whether Agnetha would still be allowed to buy the painting herself. Should Agnetha in this case be free to buy the painting herself without having to pay Bjørn the full price for his services? Or should she be required to pay the full price? In other words: who bears the risk because the meaning of the term 'exclusivity' is not spelled out by the parties?

The default situation is that the principal is free to conclude the prospective contract himself and to appoint other agents to that extent. An exclusivity clause limits the principal's freedom in this respect. Exclusivity is primarily in the interest of the agent. From the normal rules of interpretation, it follows that the agent must prove that the parties intended not only to prevent the principal from appointing other agents but also that the principal is not free to conclude the prospective contract himself. This means that an explicit rule to this extent is not needed. The answer to the Illustration above is therefore that Agnetha is allowed to buy the painting herself without having to pay Bjørn the full price for his services. This is in accordance with the provision of Article 2:102 paragraph (4) (Price) of these Principles, where it is stated that when the principal concludes the contract himself, he is required to pay the agent the price or a proportionate part of it (only) if the conclusion of the prospective contract can be attributed in full or in part to the agent's performance of the obligations under the mandate contract.

E. Consequences of breach of agreed exclusivity

Even when the exclusivity clause is to be interpreted as prohibiting the principal to conclude the prospective contract himself, as such this only means that the principal is not *allowed* to do so. The validity of the contract with the third party (the prospective contract) is not affected if the principal breaches such an exclusivity clause, either by concluding the prospective contract himself or enabling another agent to do so. The conclusion of the prospective contract by the principal or another agent appointed by the principal entitles the agent to terminate the mandate contract under Article 6:105 (Termination by agent for extraordinary and serious reason), as in such a case it will usually become impossible or unreasonably difficult for the agent to (also) conclude the prospective contract, or to revoke a remedy for non-performance under Chapter 8 PECL (Non-performance and remedies in general). Moreover, the principal may then be required to pay the agent the agreed remuneration in part or in full in accordance with Article 2:102 paragraphs (3) or (4) (Price) of these Principles. Moreover, as the principal in such case is in breach of his contractual obligations, he is also liable towards the agent for any damage resulting from the breach of contract.

F. Conclusion of prospective contract by principal in case of irrevocable mandate

As indicated in Comment D, the conclusion of the prospective contract by the principal or another agent appointed by the principal will terminate the mandate relationship if the mandate was solely for the conclusion of a specific contract. That will have the effect of a revocation of the mandate in accordance with Article 1:104 paragraph (2) (Revocation of the mandate). However, in a case where the agent is awarded an irrevocable mandate in accordance with Article 1:105 (Irrevocable mandate), this usually implies that the agent is also awarded exclusivity. This then implies that the principal may no longer conclude the prospective contract personally or by means of another agent.

This may, however, not always be the case.

Illustration 2
The successors of the former owner of a car decide that the car is to be sold for a good price. They mandate two of them to execute their decision independently of each other, agreeing that the car is to be sold for a price of more than € 10,000 and that the first who sells the car will accordingly receive payment of 1 per cent of the sale price, whereas the other will not be rewarded. As one of the successors has a fickle nature and might all of a sudden change his mind, the successors decide to make both mandates irrevocable. In this case, the irrevocability is not combined with exclusivity.

It is therefore necessary to determine whether the parties to the underlying legal relationship, when agreeing on an irrevocable mandate, have intended to grant the agent exclusivity. However, this will normally be the case.

G. Relation to the Principles of European Law and the Draft Common Frame of Reference

This Article mirrors that of Article IV.D. – 3:301 DCFR (Exclusivity not presumed).

H. Character of the rule

This Article constitutes a default rule from which the parties may derogate.

I. Remedies

If the principal has agreed to exclusivity for the agent and subsequently breaches the exclusivity clause by appointing a second agent or, as the case may be, by concluding the prospective contract himself, the agent may be entitled to a remuneration in part or in full in accordance with Article 2:102 paragraphs(3) or (4) (Price) of these Principles, and to damages in accordance with Article 9:501 PECL (Right to damages). When the prospective contract has not yet been concluded, the agent may also require specific performance of the exclusivity clause, thus demanding the principal to terminate the mandate contract with the second agent, or to refrain from concluding the prospective contract himself. Article 9:102 PECL (Non-monetary obligations) applies to such a claim.

Comparative Notes

1. Exclusivity: no other agents to be appointed?

The parties can agree upon an exclusivity clause prohibiting the principal to appoint a second agent in all Member States. There is a presumption of exclusivity in MALTA and, for commercial agents, in BULGARIA, whereas such a clause is typical for distribution contracts in ITALY. In other legal systems an express exclusivity clause is required.

In FINLAND, an exclusivity clause will be invalid if it infringes public interests, e.g. is contrary to competition law. Limitations to the validity of exclusivity clauses may follow from standard terms legislation, in particular with regard to brokerage contracts, in GERMANY and GREECE.

2. Principal entitled to conclude prospective contract himself and consequences of
*   breach of exclusivity clause*

The existence of an exclusivity clause does not deprive the principal from concluding the prospective contract himself in any legal system, unless the parties have agreed otherwise. A failure by the principal to comply with such a clause does not have any effect on the thus concluded contract, but leads to liability of the principal and/or the obligation to pay the agent his remuneration. This is different, however, if the agent was provided an irrevocable mandate and this mandate is considered valid under national law.

National Notes

1. Exclusivity: no other agents to be appointed?

AUSTRIA: The parties to the contract for mandate can validly stipulate that the principal is not allowed to appoint another agent next to the agent with whom the contract for mandate is concluded (CC Article 1011).

BELGIUM: The parties can agree to a clause by which the agent is awarded exclusivity (Wéry, p. 277-278).

BULGARIA: In Bulgarian contract law there is no explicit rule with neither presumption of exclusivity of representation nor prohibition for stipulation of such exclusivity. Hence, the exclusivity clause in the mandate contract is considered to be valid (Мевораx/Лиджи/Фарxи, III, p. 28). For a commercial agent there is a special rule. Once having appointed a commercial agent for a definite region, he principal is not allowed to authorize another one for the same territory, cf. CA Article 46 paragraph (2).

DENMARK: The parties can validly emphasise that the agent is not allowed to appoint another agent next to the agent with whom the mandate contract is concluded. An exclusivity-clause of this character will be respected in practice and in court.

ENGLAND: Exclusivity clauses are possible, especially for estate agents. When an estate agent is granted an exclusivity by being appointed 'sole selling agent', if the principal then appoints another agent who earns the commission that the first agent should have earned, then the sole selling agent is entitled to damages (*Milsom v Bechstein* (1898) 14 TLR 159). A sole selling agent will also prevent the principal from selling or at least claim the commission if the principal sells his property himself (*Snelgrove v Ellringham Colliery Co* (1821) 45 JP 408).

ESTONIA: The parties can agree to a clause by which the agent is awarded exclusivity. If no such explicit agreement exists, LOAEst Article 622 provides (as a presumption) that the service provider (the agent) has to perform in person (this does not exclude 'using the help of the third persons' upon performance).

FINLAND: The agent may, in general, be awarded exclusivity, unless the public interests (e.g. competition law) provide otherwise.

FRANCE: The mandate may be exclusive if there is a specific provision in the mandate contract.

GERMANY: Exclusivity is not presumed, but the parties can validly stipulate that the principal is not allowed to appoint another agent. Case law has applied restrictions in the field of brokerage contracts (CC Article 652) containing an exclusivity clause, which are subjected to control under CC Article 307 paragraph (2) when contained in standard conditions.

GREECE: In case of intermediation the parties can validly agree to a clause by which the broker is awarded exclusivity. According to that clause the conclusion of the contract is limited to the exclusive broker and a conclusion of the same brokerage contract with third parties is prohibited (Georgiadis/Stathopoulos/Karasis, CC Article 703 CC no. 21). Consequence of such a clause is that in case of breach of that contractual obligation the principal is liable for restitution of the damages incurred to the exclusive broker due to violation of the clause of exclusivity (CFI Athens decision no. 4029/1982, EllDni 1984, 848). No specific rules of consumer protection are applicable, but if the principal in a brokerage contract can be considered as a consumer according to Article 1 of the law no. 2251/1994 (Government Gazette A 191/16.11.1994) about consumer protection, the clause of exclusivity may fall under the notion of abusive standard clauses (Article 2).

HUNGARY: The parties to the mandate contract can validly stipulate that the principal is not allowed to appoint another agent next to the agent with whom the mandate contract is concluded, but in this respect CC Article 207 paragraph (3) applies: 'Should a person waive his rights in part or in full, such a statement cannot be broadly construed'. In case of a consumer contract, according to CC Article 207 paragraph (2), '[i]f the contents of a consumer contract cannot be clearly established ..., the interpretation that is more favourable to the consumer shall be authoritative'.

IRELAND: In line with the principal of freedom of contract, and following *Murphy, Buckley & Keogh Ltd v Pye (Ire) Ltd* [1971] IR 57, the parties can validly stipulate that an agent is awarded exclusivity.

ITALY: The parties to a mandate contract may validly stipulate that the principal is not allowed to appoint another agent next to the agent with whom the mandate contract is concluded (i.e. exclusivity clause). Indeed, it is a typical clause in most distribution contracts.

MALTA: Under Maltese law it is presumed that the principal appoints one agent. This can be presumed because the law specifically provides for the situation when the principal appoints more than one agent. Thus, it seems that the principal and the agent may validly stipulate a clause attributing exclusivity.

NETHERLANDS: The principal is allowed to give the agent exclusivity regarding the mandate. In that case, the principal is not allowed to appoint another agent next to the first agent.

POLAND: Exclusivity may be granted to the agent on the basis of freedom of contracts, however it will not be presumed.

PORTUGAL: CC Article 1171 provides that, if the other party appoints another agent to execute the same acts next to the agent with whom the mandate contract was concluded, the previous contract is deemed revoked (revogação tácita), with effect as of the moment that the agent knows of the subsequent appointment. According to Lima/Varela (1986), p. 733, this is only the case if the second appointment is incompatible with the previous mandate contract. Cf. also STJ 7 December 1989, BMJ 392, 444.

SCOTLAND: In Scots law the exclusivity of the agent is not presumed. An express clause to this effect is required in the mandate contract (*Graham v United Turkey Red Co Ltd* (1882) SC 533).

SLOVAKIA: The parties can validly stipulate that the principal is not allowed to appoint another agent. For the commercial representation contract, a specific regulation of the exclusivity clause can be found in Comm.C Article 665 (exclusive commercial representation).

SPAIN: Under Spanish law, any kind of mandate may be agreed as exclusive.

SWEDEN: Exclusivity is not presumed but the parties can agree to an exclusivity clause.

2. Principal entitled to conclude prospective contract himself and consequences of breach of exclusivity clause

AUSTRIA: Apart from the possibility of an irrevocable mandate, the principal is entitled to conclude the prospective contract of his own motion. The mandate contract does not deprive him of the right to conclude the prospective contract himself. It is the same with commercial agents. The employment of an agent on the terms that his commission is payable on results does not deprive the principal of his freedom to take any step which results in the agent being deprived of his opportunity to earn commission, unless there is an express promise or trade custom to the contrary, or unless a promise to the contrary must be implied to give efficiency to the contract or otherwise to effect the intention of the parties. This can be explained on the basis that a person (the principal) is entitled to deal with his property as he chooses and to carry on his business or give up carrying on his business as he wishes. The principal can in fact revoke the granted authority at any time. It is not relevant whether the agent acted in the principal's name or in his own name if the contractual relationship between indirect agent and principal is that of a mandate in terms of CC Article 1002 ff.. If the principal concludes the prospective contract himself, the agent is entitled to a proportional part of the price, to incurred expenses and to suffered losses.

BELGIUM: As the principal can always revoke ad nutum the authority to represent, the principal is entitled to conclude the prospective contract of his own motion. The conclusion of the contract by the principal himself is considered to be a silent revocation (De Page, p. 462). The parties to the mandate contract can validly stipulate that the principal is not allowed to conclude the prospective contract of his own motion, by inserting a clause of irrevocability (De Page, p. 463). If the clause only aims to award the agent an indemnification, the principal can still conclude the prospective contract of his own motion. The clause obliges him only to indemnify the agent, e.g. by paying the agreed salary. If the clause, on the contrary, aims to deprive the principal of his authority to conclude the contract, the principal can no longer conclude the contract himself (De Page, p. 463; Foriers, p. 90; Wagemans, p. 193).

BULGARIA: As a general rule, the authorization of an agent does not mean that the principal himself or other appointed by him person (another agent) is not allowed to conclude the prospective contract or to perform the judicial act the agent is obliged to conclude or perform (Меворах/Лиджи/Фархи, III, p. 28). There is an exception for a commercial agent, see CA Article 46 paragraph (2). The parties are free to stipulate in the mandate contract an exclusive representation and a prohibition for the principal to conclude the prospective contract. If in such case the principal concludes the prospective contract by himself, there is a breach and he is liable for the damages suffered by the agent (Меворах/Лиджи/Фархи, III, p. 28). Apart from this compensation, as the conclusion of the prospective contract under such circumstances is considered to be an implicit revocation of the mandate contract, the agent is entitled to receive stipulated remuneration and reimbursement of expenses incurred, cf. OCA Article 288.

DENMARK: The parties to the mandate contract can validly agree to a clause according to which the principal is not allowed to conclude the prospective contract himself. According to the Real Estate Agents Act the parties can agree to a clause according to which the agent is entitled to the price even if the principal concludes the contract directly with a third party presented by the agent. A mandate contract does not deprive the principal of the right to conclude the prospective contract himself. This will apply whether the agent is entitled to act in his own name or in the name of his principal. Unless otherwise agreed upon, normally the agent is entitled to the price whether he or the principal concludes the prospective contract.

ENGLAND: A distinction must be made between the type of exclusivity which has been granted. When the agent is appointed as a 'sole agent', this does not preclude the principal from negotiating the contract himself *(Bentall, Horsley & Baldry v Vicary* [1931] 1 KB 253). In such a case, the agent will not be entitled to commission if the principal contracts directly with the third party. When the agent is appointed as an 'exclusive agent' or the agency is described as a 'sole selling agency' *(Brodie Marshall & Co (Hotel Division) v Sharer* [1988] 1 EGLR 21), then the principal is prevented from selling the property himself. Should the principal nevertheless do so, he would then be liable for commission to the agent *(Snelgrove v Ellringham Colliery Co* (1881) 45 JP 408).

ESTONIA: As a rule, the contract of mandate will not deprive the principal of his right to conclude the prospective contract himself. The parties may of course agree otherwise. Specific rules apply for commercial agents. LOAEst Article 675 paragraph (2) stipulates that if the principal has nominated an agent for a certain area or for specific principals, it is presumed that the agent has an exclusive right to conclude contracts in that area or with the principals (unless agreed otherwise in writing).

FINLAND: The parties are allowed to agree that the principal is not entitled to conclude a prospective contract. This may also follow from exclusivity of the agent's mandate.

FRANCE: Granting an agency does not, in principle, deprive the principal of the right to enter into the envisaged contract directly and personally, whether the agent is to act in the name of the principal or in his own name. The parties may decide to prevent the principal from entering into the envisaged contract himself, but such prohibition will not affect the validity of the contract entered into. The parties are not only free to provide that the remuneration of the agent will be due (this is a standard clause in contracts with French estate agents), but they may go further by providing for liquidated damages (except where there is a specific legal prohibition: see the Decree of 20 July 1972, Article 76 applicable to estate agents).

GERMANY: Courts have held that it is impossible to grant an authority which excludes conclusion of contracts by the principal (BGHZ 3, 358; BGHZ 20, 364), and the literature agrees (Schramm, in: Münchener Kommentar zum BGB, Article 167 no. 114). Therefore, even in the case of an exclusivity clause, the principal may still conclude the prospective contract himself. If the principal does so, under a brokerage contract the agent is entitled to a price when the contract is concluded due to the service rendered by the broker (CC Article 652 paragraph (1)).

GREECE: In case of a mandate contract the person represented is not deprived of the right to conclude the prospective contract of his own motion (Georgiadis/Stathopoulos/Doris, CC Article 211 no. 11). In this respect it is irrelevant whether the agent is entitled to act in his name or in the name of the principal. If the person represented concludes the contract of his own motion the question whether the agent is entitled to the price depends on the internal relationship on which the mandate is based. In case of a mandate contract that question does not arise at all due to the gratuitous character of mandate. In case of intermediation the principal also has the right to conclude the contract of his own motion without the intervention of the broker (CA Athens decision no. 12896/1988, NoV 1989, 1226). In such a case the broker is not entitled to payment according to CC Article 703 which obliges the principal to pay remuneration only if the contract was concluded as a result of the broker's intervention or indication (Georgiadis/Stathopoulos/Doris, CC Article 703, no. 21). If an irrevocable mandate has been granted it is accepted that the person represented is still entitled to conclude the prospective contract or to execute the prospective other juridical act of his own motion because irrevocability does not mean exclusivity of the authority conferred to the agent (Georgiadis/Stathopoulos/Doris, CC Article 218-221 no. 13).

HUNGARY: If the principal did not expressly renounce his right to conclude the prospective contract of his own motion (without the intervention of the agent), he is entitled to do so. In this respect CC Article 207 (3) applies: 'Should a person waive his rights in part or in full, such a statement cannot be broadly construed'. In case of consumer contract, according to CC Article 207 paragraph (2), '[i]f the contents of a consumer contract cannot be clearly established ..., the interpretation that is more favourable to the consumer shall be authoritative'. In general, according to CC Article 478 paragraph (2), '[t]he agent shall be entitled to demand remuneration even if his actions brought no results' which also means that the salary of the agent is not conditioned to the conclusion of the contract by himself. Paragraph (3) of this same Article establishes that 'If the contract is terminated before the agency has been fulfilled, the agent shall be entitled to demand an appropriate fraction of the fee for his activities.'

IRELAND: Whether the principal is entitled to conclude the prospective contract himself depends on the nature of the mandate contract and, in particular, the terms of the agent's appointment. For example, in *Murphy, Buckley & Keogh Ltd v Pye (Ire) Ltd* [1971] IR 57, the seller of a factory appointed auctioneers as 'sole agents' in the sale. However, the seller arranged a sale himself without telling the auctioneers. The auctioneers claimed a commission but lost in the High Court. It was held that although the auctioneers were the sole agents this did not prevent the seller from effecting a sale himself, merely from appointing any other agents. Hence, where an agent is appointed 'sole agent' to effect a contract, the principal commits a breach if a second agent is appointed; if the second agent then concludes a contract, the first agent would be entitled to damages, equal to the amount of commission of which he is deprived, for breach of that term *(Bentall, Horsley and Baldry v Vicary* [1931] 1 KB 253). Moreover, it has been held that where an agent is appointed with 'the sole right to sell', the principal is in breach of contract if he sells in person *(Brodie Marshall & Co v Sharer* [1988] 19 EG 129).

ITALY: The possibility for the principal to conclude the prospective contract directly is expressly recognised in CC Article 1748 paragraph (2): 'The commission is due also for the transactions entered into by the principal with third parties that the agent had previously acquired as principals for transactions of the same kind or pertaining to the area or category or group of principals reserved to the agent, unless otherwise agreed'. Accordingly, even if the contract grants an exclusive right to the agent, the principal keeps the right to conclude the affairs himself in the relevant geographical area; however the agent keeps his right to receive the full price agreed under the contract without any reduction. Also the fact that the contract is irrevocable does not affect the fact that the principal is entitled to conclude the prospective contract of his own motion. The irrevocability does not imply that the principal renounces his right to act directly to conclude the contract in his interest. This may be inferred from the text of CC Article 1724 which provides that '[t]he appointment of a new mandatory for the same transaction, or the completion of the transaction by the principal, implies a revocation of the mandate and takes effect from the day on which the agent has been notified thereof'.

MALTA: A breach of an exclusivity clause entitles the agent to a compensation for the services rendered in order for the transaction to be finalized and damages. This conclusion can be deduced from CA 12 December 1919, *Ciantar et noe. vs Demarco*. In CA (Commercial) 7 March 1932, *Vella Zarb vs Caruana et. noe,* the Court had to decide whether the principal should pay compensation to the agent if the principal has terminated the mandate without a just cause. The Court held that a paid agent whose mandate has been revoked without a just cause may have a right to be compensated for this revocation.

NETHERLANDS: The contracting parties may agree that the principal is not allowed to take actions against third parties during the mandate contract (CC Article 7:423 paragraph (1)). If the contracting parties have agreed on the exclusion of the principal's authority to act himself, the principal is not entitled to conclude the prospective contract. This provision has been principally established for organisations such as Buma Stemra, that administer the rights of the joined authors. However, the exclusivity stipulation may also apply to patents for instance (H.TK. 1991/92, 17 779, no. 8, p. 10).

POLAND: The principal retains the right to conclude the contract himself even if exclusivity is granted, since one may not limit his own legal capacity to conclude contracts and if the contracts concluded by the principal were to be void it would endanger third parties interests. However breach of exclusivity clause would be a breach of contract and would entitle the agent to a claim for damages.

PORTUGAL: The principal is not prevented from concluding the prospective contract himself, but may be liable to pay compensation for the losses that the agent has incurred (CC Article 1172 lit (b)). Losses covered are only those related to the recuperation of the contractual balance (excluding for instance loss of reputation of the agent). Cf. Lima/Varela (1986), p. 735.

SCOTLAND: In Scots law where the principal has granted authority to an agent to carry out a specific task, but not exclusivity, this does not divest or limit the principal's capacity to carry out that task himself. It makes no difference whether the agent acts in the name of his principal or in his own name. Whether the agent would remain entitled to a price would depend on the factual scenario. If the agent was unaware that the principal had concluded such a contract, and had expended efforts on his own part to conclude a similar contract, for example, for the same goods from another source, the agent ought to be entitled to his fee in the normal way. An agent's fee very often takes the form of commission. If the agent has actually concluded a contract, his commission ought to remain payable even where the principal has already concluded a similar contract himself. If the agent was either made aware by the principal that a contract had already been concluded, or became aware that this was the case, the agent might be prevented from concluding a contract, and thus from earning a fee or commission. Depending upon the terms of the mandate contract this might constitute a breach on the part of the principal, for which the agent could claim damages. Where the agent has been granted exclusivity and the principal concludes the contract himself in breach of this exclusivity, the principal will be liable to the agent in damages. The applicable measure of damages would be the expectation interest, or the net profit which the agent would have expected to gain from proper performance of the contract by him.

SLOVAKIA: The parties can validly stipulate that the principal is not allowed to do so. Such a stipulation would make the principal liable for damages but would not deprive the principal of the possibility to conclude contract with a third party.

SPAIN: The parties may decide to prevent the principal from entering into the envisaged contract personally, both by stipulating an exclusivity clause or by rendering the mandate irrevocable, but such prohibitions will not affect the validity of the contract entered into. Normal remedies for non-performance apply. The principal can always revoke the authority to represent, being therefore entitled to conclude the prospective contract personally. The conclusion of the contract by the principal is considered to be a tacit revocation, cf. Gordillo, p. 1589.

SWEDEN: A mandate contract does not deprive the principal of the right to conclude the prospective contract himself, cf. Adlercreutz, p. 203.

Article 3:302: Subcontracting

(1) **The agent may subcontract or delegate the performance of the obligations under the mandate contract in whole or in part without the principal's consent, unless personal performance is required by the contract.**

(2) **Any subcontractor so engaged by the agent in the performance of the mandate contract must be of adequate competence.**

(3) **In accordance with Article 8:107 PECL (Performance entrusted to another) the agent remains responsible for performance.**

Comments

A. General idea

In principle, the agent may entrust the performance of the agent's obligations under the mandate contract to a third party, unless the parties have agreed that the agent would personally perform the mandate contract. Similarly, the parties may agree that the mandate contract is to be performed by a specific person indicated by the principal. Where the agent subcontracts, paragraph (2) indicates that the agent must ensure that the subagent is competent to carry out the contract. In accordance with general contract law, but different from the current law in many Member States, paragraph (3) determines that the agent remains liable for the proper performance of the mandate contract, whether he has subcontracted or merely delegated the authority to a member of his staff.

B. Subcontracting allowed in principle

Notwithstanding the fact that traditionally the mandate contract was considered to be a personal contract since the personal characteristics of a given agent are important, subcontracting is allowed in all legal systems if the principal consents thereto. In most legal systems, consent need not be given expressly and may be assumed if subcontracting is considered 'normal' in the relevant branch of industry or trade. Moreover, in several legal systems the agent is also considered to be allowed to subcontract if this is necessary to properly protect the principal's interests.

Whereas the traditional approach would seem to imply that the possibility of subcontracting is the exception to the rule – subcontracting is not allowed unless the principal has given his prior consent thereto – the present Article starts from the other side by indicating that subcontracting is allowed in principle unless the parties have agreed otherwise. It is thought that such an approach fits better because nowadays most mandate contracts are remunerated and subcontracting is rather common.

Illustration 1
David asks Eric, an art expert, to bid for him at a painting auction and to purchase a painting for an amount of no more than € 10,000. When the auction takes place, Eric finds himself unavailable to participate in the auction. He mandates Franklin to attend the auction in his place and to bid on behalf of David.

Illustration 2
Simone is the victim of a traffic accident. She engages Timothy, a lawyer, to claim damages from the tortfeasor. As Timothy is not an expert in personal injury cases, he engages Ursula, a specialist in this field, to prepare and submit the lawsuit on behalf of Simone.

In both cases, subcontracting is allowed. This is different in the next case:

Illustration 3
Hans is also the victim of a traffic accident. He engages Christian, a lawyer specialised in personal injury claims, to claim damages from the tortfeasor. Hans has engaged Christian specifically for his expertise in these cases. In this case, personal performance of the mandate contract by Christian is required by the contract.

C. Liability of agent for performance by subcontractor

The legal systems of the Member States differ as regards the extent of the agent's liability in case of a non-performance by the subagent. Whereas it is generally understood that the agent would be liable for the subagent's actions towards the principal if the principal had not consented to the agent subcontracting the mandate to the subagent and if the agent was not allowed to do so on other grounds – in particular, necessity to protect the principal's interests – opinions are divided if the agent was allowed to subcontract. In a slight majority of legal systems, the agent is liable only if he has chosen a subagent who is clearly incapable or insolvent *(culpa in eligendo)*. This approach is also taken in FRANCE, but there the agent may also be liable for insufficient supervision of the performance of the submandate contract by the subagent. In a large minority of legal systems, however, the agent is simply liable for the actions of the subagent, who is then seen as merely an auxiliary of the agent in the latter's performance of the mandate contract. The differences between these approaches is shown in the following Illustration:

Illustration 2 (continued)
Simone is the victim of a traffic accident. She engages Timothy, a lawyer, to claim damages from the tortfeasor. As Timothy is not an expert in personal injury cases, with the consent of Simone he engages Ursula, a specialist in this field, to prepare and submit the lawsuit on behalf of Simone. When preparing the lawsuit, Ursula makes an important mistake, and as a consequence Simone loses the case against the tortfeasor.

In the first approach, Timothy would not be liable for the non-performance by Ursula, as the choice of Ursula as the subagent in itself is a good one. This implies that Simone would have to instigate proceedings directly against Ursula. The legal basis for such proceedings is not unproblematic – in some legal systems it would be based on tort law, and in other systems on a direct claim on the basis of representation in the conclusion of the submandate contract. In the second approach, however, Timothy would be contractually liable for the error made by Ursula. This second approach seems to fit better because the agent is remunerated, whereas a contract mandate was traditionally a gratuitous contract – which justifies a rather restrictive approach to liability for the actions of others. It is this second approach which is adopted in paragraph (3) of this Article. However, a reminiscence of the first approach may be read into paragraph (2), which requires the agent to be diligent in the choice of a subagent. This provision introduces a separate liability of the agent, which may be invoked next to the liability for the actions of the subagent under paragraph (3).

D. No direct claims of principal and subagent

In some of the Member States where the agent is not contractually liable for the actions of the subagent, as a counterbalance a direct claim by the principal against the subagent is accepted, and sometimes also a direct claim of the subagent against the principal for payment of the price and reimbursement of expenses made. As in these Principles the agent is liable for the actions of the subagent towards the principal, and the subagent may direct its claim for the price and expenses to the agent as his contractual counterpart, there is no need for such claims under these Principles.

E. Nomination of designated person performing the mandate

Where the agent is, in principle, allowed to subcontract, he obviously is also allowed to determine which person within his staff will perform the contract. This is different where the principal has concluded the contract with the intention that the contract is to be performed by a specific person, e.g. an employee who is renowned for his specific expertise. In such a case, this specific person is to perform the mandate contract. Of course, this also implies that subcontracting is not allowed in such cases.

Illustration 3 (continued)
Hans is the victim of a traffic accident. He engages Christian, a lawyer specialised in personal injury claims, to claim damages from the tortfeasor. Hans has engaged Christian specifically for his expertise in these cases. In this case, personal performance of the mandate contract by Christian is required by the contract, even if the mandate contract was not concluded by Christian himself but by the law firm that employs him.

Obviously, the principal may nominate the specific person who is to perform the contract before or at the moment of conclusion of the mandate contract. This approach is accepted in all Member States. In this situation, the agent can take this demand of the principal into account when concluding the contract, e.g. by ascertaining whether that person is actually available to perform the mandate contract. Where the person indicated by the principal is not available, the agent can then either refrain from contracting or suggest another person to perform the mandate contract. This is different if the nomination is made after the conclusion of the contract by way of a direction as the contract has already been concluded. Possibly for this reason, in many legal systems the agent is not bound by such a decision of the principal once the contract has been concluded. On the other hand, in other Member States, the agent is bound by such a direction in principle unless there are good reasons why such should not be the case in the circumstances of that case – for instance, because the agent had made it clear in the contract that in accordance with its general policy it would determine who would perform the mandate contract, if the nomination of the specific person would cause additional costs or difficulty for the agent, or if the nomination of the designated person conflicts with the services already carried out in good faith by the original person engaged in the performance of the mandate contract.

The second approach is followed under these Principles, in particular by how the possibility of the principal to give directions is construed in Article 4:101 (Directions given by the principal) of these Principles. According to the first paragraph of this Article, the principal may also indicate the person who is to perform the mandate contract by way of a direction. The agent is then required to follow the direction or to give a warning to the principal that performance by the person indicated in the direction would make the performance of the mandate contract significantly more expensive or that performance would take significantly more time than agreed, or is inconsistent with the purpose of the mandate contract or may otherwise be detrimental to the interests of the principal. Obviously, the agent is required to explain why the direction of the principal may not be in his interests as the warning is meant to enable the principal to make up and, if necessary, to change his mind. Article 4:101 paragraph (4) (Directions given by the principal) of these Principles provides that if the principal does not change the direction after having been warned, the direction is regarded as a change of the contract and the contract must be performed by the person indicated in the direction. If the agent still believes that the direction is not in the principal's interests or that he cannot be required to follow the direction in the circumstances of the case, the agent may then terminate the mandate contract for extraordinary and serious reason under Articles 4:201 paragraph (3) (Changes of the mandate contract) and 6:105 (Termination by agent for extraordinary and serious reason).

Illustration 4
Marco has successfully withdrawn from a distance contract during the withdrawal period. He is entitled to reimbursement of the payments made under the contract. However, the seller refuses to do so. Marco engages the law firm of Bueno Díaz and Associates to instigate legal proceedings against the seller to reclaim the payments made. As long as the law firm has not performed the mandate contract, Marco may determine that the mandate contract is to be performed by a specific attorney employed by the firm. If Marco decides to do so when Bueno Díaz and Associates had already appointed another attorney, and as a consequence additional costs must be incurred because the case must be transferred to the attorney indicated by Marco, he must be warned thereof. If Marco then insists on the transfer of the case to the attorney indicated by him, the law firm is required to comply.

F. Nominated person not personally liable except for tort law

The parties may have agreed – either at the moment of conclusion of the contract or later by way of a direction of the principal which is not followed by termination of the mandate contract by the agent – that a specific person is to perform the mandate contract. This agreement, however, does not bind the nominated person: the agreement of the principal and the agent is relevant in the internal relationship between these parties only. The agreement itself is not binding upon the nominated person. This does not mean that the nominated person is not required to perform the mandate contract in person. Such an obligation, however, then results from the relationship between the agent and that person, e.g. from the labour contract between these parties. Where such a relationship does not exist, the nominated person cannot be required to act on behalf of the principal. Moreover, given the absence of a contractual relationship between the nominated person and the principal, the nominated person cannot be held personally liable if the mandate contract is not properly executed. This is different only if an independent legal ground exists under which the nominated person would be liable, e.g. in the case of an unlawful act committed by the nominated person vis-á-vis the principal.

Illustration 4 (continued)
Marco has engaged the law firm of Bueno Díaz and Associates to instigate legal proceedings against the seller to reclaim the payments made under the distance contract from which he has successfully withdrawn. He has nominated Esli to perform the mandate contract. If Esli does not properly perform the task entrusted to her, the law firm of Bueno Díaz and Associates is liable for the non-performance of the mandate contract, but Esli is not personally liable, unless, for instance, she caused damage to Marco by intentionally breaching confidentiality, in which case she could be personally liable under tort law, more specifically under Articles 1:101 (Basic rule) and 2:205 (Loss upon breach of confidence) of the Principles of European Law on Non-Contractual Liability Arising out of Damage Caused to Another (PEL Liab. Dam.).

G. Assistance and temporary substitution

Even if personal performance of the contract by the agent or the nominated person is agreed upon and therefore subcontracting is not allowed, this need not imply that the agent is required to perform the mandate contract in all aspects in person. In most legal systems it is thought that unless agreed otherwise, the agent may leave the performance of tasks that do not require specific knowledge or trust from the principal's side to be carried out by another person, in particular to another person working within the same organisation, provided that the agent or the nominated person remains responsible for the performance of the mandate contract. Similarly, if this is needed for the proper performance of the contract, the agent or the nominated person may be temporarily substituted.

Illustration 4 (continued)
Marco has nominated Esli to instigate legal proceedings against the seller, who refuses to reimburse him for the payments made under the distance contract from which he has successfully withdrawn. Esli may call in the assistance of Lotte to make photocopies of the documents needed for the preparation of the case, and she may also be replaced by Lotte during periods of illness or holidays, provided that Lotte is competent to replace Esli. Lotte will perform the task entrusted to her under the responsibility of Esli. The agent – be that Esli herself or the law firm that has employed her – remains liable if Lotte does not properly perform the task entrusted to her.

H. Death of the agent or the nominated person

In the case of the death of the agent or the nominated person, a temporary substitution will of course not solve the problems. Under Article 7:102 (Death of the agent) of these Principles, the mandate contract normally is terminated automatically when the agent dies. This is true in particular when personal performance is required under the contract. As the Comments to Article 7:102 (Death of the agent) indicate, this may be different when the mandate contract does not depend on the personal qualities of the agent. In such cases, colleagues or employees can carry out the performance of the obligations. However, such a substitution of the agent must be agreed upon by the parties, either when the original mandate contract was concluded or at a later moment, e.g. by way of a new mandate contract between the principal and the heirs or successors of the deceased agent.

If the principal had nominated a person to perform the mandate contract, the situation is different. The death of that person does not automatically terminate the mandate contract. However, the death of the nominated person may constitute an extraordinary and serious reason for the principal and the agent to terminate the mandate contract under Articles 6:103 (Termination by principal for extraordinary and serious reason) and 6:105 (Termination by agent for extraordinary and serious reason) entitling either the principal or the agent to terminate the mandate contract. This is always the case if at the time the mandate contract was concluded, the parties had intended the contract to be performed by that nominated person, as paragraph (3) of both Articles indicates. Where the principal had decided to nominate a specific person at a later stage by giving a direction, performance by that person will not always constitute such an extraordinary and serious reason: in such a case, there is a substantive chance that other employees of the agent may sufficiently represent the principal's interests instead of the deceased person. This implies that in this case, the circumstances of the case will be decisive in determining whether the mandate contract may be terminated for extraordinary and serious reason.

I. Relation to the Principles of European Law and the Draft Common Frame of Reference

This Article mirrors that of Article IV.D. – 3:302 DCFR (Subcontracting). It regulates the possibility of subcontracting in the same manner as the corresponding provisions in Articles 1:106 paragraphs (1) and (2) of the Principles of European Law on Service Contracts (PEL SC) (Duties of the Service Provider regarding Input).

The Article particularises the rule in Article 8:107 PECL (Performance entrusted to another), which makes performance by a third party possible unless the contract requires personal performance. When a third party is involved in the performance of the contract, the party that entrusts the performance to this third party is still responsible for the performance under that Article. The rules of the present Article do not change this; they merely add an obligation for the agent – to select adequately the subcontractors involved in the performance of the service.

J. Character of the rule

This Article constitutes a default rule from which the parties may derogate, both by determining that the agent is not allowed to subcontract or by determining a restricted scope for liability if the agent does so.

K. Remedies

If the agent does not act in accordance with this Article, the normal remedies for non-performance apply. Moreover, as set out in paragraph (3) of this Article, the agent remains responsible for the performance of the mandate contract by the subagent as if he had performed the mandate contract himself. The principal may still give directions in accordance with Article 4:101 paragraph (1) (Directions given by the principal) of these Principles, which under paragraph (2) of that Article must then be followed by the agent (and by consequence also by the subagent).

Comparative Notes

1. Subcontracting allowed but agent liable for performance by subcontractor

Subcontracting is allowed in all legal systems if the principal consents thereto. In most legal systems, consent need not be given expressly and may be assumed if subcontracting is considered 'normal' in the relevant branch of industry or trade. Moreover, in BULGARIA, ENGLAND, GREECE, ITALY, and POLAND, the agent is also allowed to subcontract without consent of the principal if this is necessary to properly protect the principal's interests. In BULGARIA, the agent who has subcontracted must immediately inform the principal thereof and communicate the identity of the subcontractor to the principal.

The agent remains liable for the performance of the subagent in DENMARK, ENGLAND, FINLAND, GERMANY, HUNGARY (own employees only), ITALY, THE NETHERLANDS, SCOTLAND (unless the principal has agreed to the substitution of agents), SLOVAKIA (commission agency contract), and SWEDEN. The same is true if the principal has not (tacitly or expressly) consented to the agent subcontracting the mandate to a subagent in AUSTRIA, BULGARIA, ESTONIA, FRANCE, GREECE, HUNGARY, SPAIN, and probably also in BELGIUM, MALTA, and PORTUGAL. By contrast, in these legal systems the agent is not liable for the non-performance of the subagent, but may be liable if the agent has clearly chosen an incapable or insolvent person to act as the subagent *(culpa in eligendo)*. In FRANCE, by virtue of case law of the Supreme Court, the agent is expected to supervise the performance of the submandate contract and remains liable for a failure to do so towards the principal. By contrast, in BELGIUM, by concluding the mandate contract with the subagent the agent is thought to have performed the mandate contract and is therefore in principle freed from liability. In SCOTLAND, the same is true if the principal has consented to the substitution of the agents (and not merely to subcontracting).

In AUSTRIA, DENMARK, ENGLAND, FINLAND, GERMANY, HUNGARY, IRELAND, and SCOTLAND, the subagent is not entitled to claim remuneration or reimbursement of expenses for the performance of the submandate contract directly from the principal, but instead must address his claim to the agent (who is the principal in the submandate contract). By contrast, in a case where the agent was allowed to subcontract, the subagent may directly claim payment of the remuneration or reimbursement of expenses from the principal in BELGIUM, ESTONIA, FRANCE, and MALTA and, if both the agent and the subagent acted in the name and on behalf of the principal, also in BULGARIA.

2. Nomination by principal of specific person designated to perform the contract

In all legal systems, the principal can require the agent to have the contract for mandate be carried out by a specific person if the parties agree on this. The principal has to make his wish known to the agent before the conclusion of the contract in AUSTRIA, ENGLAND, ESTONIA, FINLAND, MALTA, THE NETHERLANDS, PORTUGAL, and SCOTLAND. The principal may also make his wish known to the agent by way of a direction in DENMARK, FRANCE, GERMANY, GREECE, ITALY, POLAND, and SLOVAKIA. Such a direction may be refused if it is contrary to the general policy of the agent in DENMARK, or cause additional costs or difficulty for the agent in FRANCE. Similarly, in ITALY, the nomination of the designated person can no longer take place if this conflicts with the services already carried out in good faith by the original agent.

The provision establishing the possibility to nominate a person to perform the mandate contract is highly controversial in THE NETHERLANDS as it could be interpreted as implying that the designated person would be personally liable in case of a breach of the contract, where this designated person is not a contracting party himself and is also not entitled to the payment of the price.

3. Subcontracting if specific person was designated to perform the mandate contract

If the mandate has been given to the agent with a view to performance by a specific person, subcontracting is allowed only with the express consent of the principal in most legal systems. However, if the principal is informed of the submandate and does not protest, his tacit consent is assumed in MALTA

Moreover, the absence of express consent does not mean that the designated person must perform the mandate contract in all aspects in person: in BELGIUM, ESTONIA, FINLAND, GREECE, THE NETHERLANDS, PORTUGAL, and SPAIN, it is thought that unless agreed otherwise, the designated person may leave the performance of tasks that do not require specific knowledge or trust from the principal's side to be carried out by another person, in particular to another person working within the same organisation, provided that the designated person remains in charge of the performance of the mandate contract. In ITALY and THE NETHERLANDS, it is thought that the designation of a specific person to perform the mandate contract does not stand in the way of allowing that person to make use of the aid of his auxiliaries and of allowing temporary substitution in the case of illness or holiday.

National Notes

1. Subcontracting allowed but agent liable for performance by subcontractor

AUSTRIA: An agent cannot, except with the express or implied assent of the principal, delegate his authority, and the principal will not be bound by the act or contract of a sub-agent whose appointment is not thus sanctioned (CC Article 1010; Comm.C Article 384; Straube/Griss, Article 384 Rz 4; Comm.C Article 407; Rummel/Rummel/Strasser, Article 1009 Rz 8 and Article 1010 ABGB; Straube/Griss, Article 384 Rz 4; Krejci, 306 f)). The normal effect of delegation is that the sub-agent is responsible to the agent; there is no privity of contract between a principal and sub-agent merely because delegation has been authorised. The agent remains liable to the principal (for non-performance and compensation) for the sub-agent's breaches of duty when the sub-agent is appointed without the principal's knowledge (Rummel/Rummel/Strasser, Article 1010 Rz 4, 5; Koziol/Welser, p. 364). The agent remains liable to the principal for *culpa in eligendo* (failure for a poor choice of a sub-agent when the sub-agent is appointed with the principal's knowledge (Rummel/ Rummel/Strasser, Article 1010 Rz 4; Schwimann/Apathy, Article 1010 Rz 5)). The sub-agent has no direct claim towards the principal for payment of the price.

BELGIUM: For the majority of the authors, subcontracting is permitted if the mandate contract is silent on the issue, unless the mandate contract is intuitu personae to a high degree (Wéry, p. 182-185). According to CC Article 1994 paragraph (1), in the legal relation between the parties to the original mandate contract (i.e. the original principal and the original agent), a distinction is made depending on whether subcontracting is permitted or forbidden. The permission to subcontract can be express or implied (Foriers & Glansdorff, p. 612-613; Foriers, p. 476 and 478; Van Der Perre & Lejeune, no. 117). If subcontracting is permitted, the original agent obtained authority to subcontract and he can therefore choose between an own performance or a performance by another person. If he chooses to subcontract, he concludes a new mandate contract with the sub-agent to act in the name and on behalf of the original principal. By concluding this new mandate contract, the original agent has fulfilled his mission. He does not guarantee the good performance by the sub-agent towards the original principal, unless in case of *culpa in eligendo* (choice of a clearly incapable or insolvent sub-agent). If subcontracting is forbidden, the original agent has no authority to subcontract. The original agent exceeds the limits of his authority by concluding a new mandate contract and he remains liable for the sub-agent's acts. According to CC Article 1994 paragraph (2), the original principal has in any case a direct claim towards the sub-agent. If subcontracting is permitted, this direct claim is based on the effect of representation. The original agent has granted authority to the sub-agent to act in the name and on behalf of the original principal; not only does the original principal have a direct claim towards the sub-agent, but also the other way around (Claeys, p. 281; De Page, p. 415; Foriers, p. 476; Laurent, p. 494). But there is no direct action in the technical meaning; the rules on (non-)invocability of defences, typical for a direct action, therefore do not apply (Foriers, p. 63). If subcontracting is forbidden, the authority to represent the original principal fails. The original agent has exceeded the limits of his authority by concluding a new mandate contract with the sub-agent. Therefore only the legal relation between both agents shall be effected (Foriers, p. 478). The direct claim of the original principal cannot be based any longer on the effect of representation, but must originate from other rules of the general contract law. Some authors try to explain the direct claim by stating that the sub-agent, by accepting the subcontracting, has become a party to the original mandate contract by unilateral action of the will (Cass. 17 September 1993, Arr. Cass. 1993, 705, Pas. 1993, I, 700, RW 1993-94, 752, RHA 1994, 23, note and TBH 1994, 533, note C. Dieryck; Dirix, 56; Foriers & Glansdorff, 618). For other authors, the sub-agent is liable by accepting the subcontracting without checking the authority to subcontract of the original agent. The direct claim sanctions the prohibition of subcontracting (Dekkers, p. 720). This analysis leads to the conclusion that only the original principal has a direct claim against the sub-agent, but not the other way around (Foriers, p. 478).

BULGARIA: As a general rule in the Bulgarian law of obligations, the mandate contract is considered intuitu personae, cf. Голева, Облигационно право, p. 238; Любен Василев, Облигационно право, p. 24; Supreme Court, Judgment no. 942, 7 April 1978, Civil Case 2668/1977, I. As a consequence, the agent has to personally perform his contractual obligations, cf. OCA Article 283 paragraph (1). Nevertheless, subcontracting of the performance of these obligations is allowed when: (a) the subcontracting has been permitted by the principal; or (b) without a permission, it has become necessary for protection of the principal's interests and without it the principal would have incurred damages, see OCA Article 283 paragraph (2). In the latter case the agent bears the burden of proof about the existence of the required prerequisites for entrusting a performance. Having appointed a subcontractor, the agent is obliged to immediately communicate the subcontracting to the principal (OCA Article 283 paragraph (3)). As far as the liability of the agent in a case of subcontracting is concerned, legal consequences differ depending on whether the agent is entitled to subcontract or not. As he is permitted to entrust a new agent with his contractual obligations, regardless of the permission that has been given by the principal or has become necessary for protection of his interests, the original agent is liable only for culpa in eligendo, namely for the appointment of an unskilled and an incompetent person. When the agent has not been entitled to subcontract, he remains liable for the actions of the subcontractor in the same manner as for his own actions, see OCA Article 283 paragraph (4), Любен Василев, Облигационно право, p. 25. As for the direct claims of the principal towards the subcontractor and vice versa, provided that the subcontracting has been permitted, in Bulgarian legal doctrine a distinction is made between the following hypotheses. First, the agent, acting in the name of and on behalf of the principal, has entrusted the subcontractor with mandate to act in the same way. Second, the agent, acting in the name of and on behalf of the principal, has entrusted the subcontractor with mandate to act in his own name but on behalf of the principal. In these two cases, the principal can claim directly towards the sub-agent and vice versa. Third, the agent, acting in his own name and on behalf of the principal, has entrusted the subcontractor with mandate to act in the name and on behalf of the agent. Furthermore, the agent, acting in his own name and on behalf of the principal, has entrusted the subcontractor with mandate to act in his own name, but on behalf of the agent. In the latter two hypotheses, direct claims between the principal and the subcontractor are not allowed, cf. Меворах/Лиджи/Фархи, III, p. 134-143.

DENMARK: The main rule in Danish law is that a contract according to which the agent has agreed to represent a principal is personal. In certain sectors, e.g. representation by lawyers or real estate agents, practical reasons may validly legitimate that an employee or a staff member of the firm to which the designated agent belongs, takes over the representation. However, the parties can validly stipulate that the agent is not allowed to appoint another agent next to the agent with whom the mandate contract is concluded. An exclusivity clause of this character will be respected in practice and in court. It follows that subcontracting normally will presuppose that the parties in the contract of representation have agreed upon this to be a possibility. If subcontracting is allowed by the contract, but the contract is silent on whether the original agent will remain liable, the original agent will still be liable with respect to the non-performance of the mandate contract. Unless otherwise agreed upon in the contract, the sub-agent will not have a direct claim towards the principal for payment of (a part of) the price, because the principal does not have a contractual relationship with the sub-agent.

ENGLAND: The agency is a personal contract since the personal characteristics of a given agent are important. The general position under the fiduciary obligations is therefore that the agent must not delegate by appointing a sub-agent unless he has express or implied authority to do so. If the agent is a natural person, it is possible for the principal to prevent the agent from sub-delegating his authority to another agent. In fact, in the light of the personal nature of the agency relationship, the agent may not delegate his authority unless he has express or implied authority to do so: *De Bussche v Alt* (1878) 8 Ch D 286. The agent is entitled to delegate where (a) delegation is the usual practice in the trade the agent is involved in *(Solley v Wood* (1852) 16 Beav 370); (b) the act delegated is purely ministerial such as digging a grave or ringing a bell *(St Margaret's Rochester Burial Board v Thompson* (1871) LR 6 CP)) or giving a notice to quit *(Allam & Co Ltd v Europa Poster Services Ltd* ([1968] 1 All ER 826)); (c) the act delegated is strictly necessary *(De Bussche v Alt* (1878) 8 Ch D 286); (d) delegation is necessary due to unforeseen circumstances; (e) at the time of the creation of the agency agreement the principal was aware of the agent's intentions to delegate and the principal did not object. Even when delegation is authorised, the main agent remains liable to the principal for the acts of the sub-agent *(Mackersys v Ramsays, Bonars & Co* (1843) 9 C & F818). To know whether the sub-agent can have a direct claim for commission against the principal raises the question of whether there is privity arising between the principal and the sub-agent. This depends on the precise facts of a given case. In general, just because the agent has authority to delegate, that does not mean that privity is created between the principal and the sub-agent. The rule nowadays is that privity between the sub-agent and the principal requires precise proof *(Calico Printers' Association v Barclays Bank* (1931) 145 LT 51; *De Bussche v Alt* ((1878) 8 Ch D 286, where privity was created between the sub-agent and the principal, is now regarded as an exception; see also *Prentis Donegan & Partners Ltd v Leeds & Leeds Co Inc* ([1998] 2 Lloyd's Rep 326 per Rix J at 334). Because there is only privity between the sub-agent and the principal in an exceptional case, none of the normal consequences of an agency relationship apply: the principal is not liable for remuneration to the sub-agent *(Schmaling v Tomlinson* (1815) 6 Taunt 147). Similarly, the principal cannot recover money from the sub-agent *(Calico Printers Association v Barclays Bank Ltd* (1931) 145 LT 51, CA). Even if there is no direct agency relationship between the sub-agent and the principal, the sub-agent may still owe a duty of care to the principal in tort under the general principles of negligence *(Henderson v Merrett Syndicates Ltd* [1994] 3 WLR 761). Moreover, the sub-agent still owes fiduciary duties to the principal and the former will be liable to the principal if he makes a secret profit from his position *(Powell & Thomas v Evans Jones & Co* [1905] 1 KB 11).

ESTONIA: As a default rule, it is presumed that the agent is obliged to perform his duties in person; nevertheless, the agent is entitled to use the assistance of third parties in performing the contract (LOAEst Article 622). This presumption does not apply if the mandate agreement is not based on the relationship of personal trust or if the agent has no discretion as to the contents of the contract to be concluded or on the choice of the counterparty. If the parties ruled out the possibility to subcontract, the agent will be liable for the acts of the sub-agent as he would be for his own acts and the sub-agent does not have a direct contractual claim towards the principal. In the (rare) cases where the agent is not under a duty of care but guarantees a result, a different rule applies: it is presumed that a contractor is not required to perform the obligations arising from the contract in person (LOAEst Article 635 paragraph (3)).

FINLAND: In general, a contracting party is allowed to subcontract. In case of a mandate contract the authority given is, however, usually not transferable, which restricts the right to subcontract. Subcontracting is possible only when the mandate is not personal (the parties have agreed on subcontracting or the person of the authorized party is left open in the mandate contract). The original agent remains liable in contract towards the principal. The direct claim is generally not applicable (Hemmo, Sopimusoikeus I, p. 498-500, Hemmo, Sopimus ja delikti p. 118, Norros Vastuu sopimusketjussa, p. 103 and passim, Kivimäki/Ylöstalo, p. 348).

FRANCE: CC Article 1994 allows the agent to freely appoint any other person to accomplish all or part of his mandate. No permission is required from the principal, unless the agency agreement was clearly entered into taking account of the personal nature of the agent. The agent is not, however, relieved from his obligations by having recourse to a third party: where he has had no authority to subcontract his obligations, he remains fully liable for the acts of the sub-agent. On the other hand, where the agent has been authorised to subcontract his obligations, the Civil Code will only render him liable towards the principle for a possible inappropriate choice of sub-agent, where the sub-agent is 'unable to perform or insolvent'. However, case law has extended the liability of the agent in the latter case towards the principal by considering that the agent, having been authorised to subcontract, remains subject to an obligation of supervision as regards the sub-agent for the proper performance of the mandate (Cass.civ. 1re, 29 May 1980, Bull. civ. 1980 I, no. 163). As regards the sub-agent, he may act directly against the principal for payment of his remuneration or repayment of expenses (Cass.civ. 1re, 27 December 1960, Bull. civ. 1960 I, no. 573), notwithstanding the fact that CC Article 1994 only provides for a direct right of action of the principal against the sub-agent. This action is possible in all cases, whether the substitution of a sub-agent has been authorised or not.

GERMANY: If the contract is a 'mandate contract' under German law (i.e. gratuitous), 'when in doubt' the agent is not allowed to subcontract (CC Article 664 paragraph (1)), because mandates are often based on a relationship of personal trust between the parties. Under a remunerated contract according to CC Article

675 paragraph (1), it is generally admissible for the agent to have the representation performed through a third person. In this case, the original agent remains liable under the contract (CC Article 664 paragraph (1)), and the sub-agent does not have a direct claim towards the principal for payment of the price, but only a claim towards the agent (being his own contracting partner). It has, however, been held that sub-contracting under remunerated contracts is not possible in situations in which a relationship of personal trust exists (RGZ 78, 310, 313; BGH, NJW 1993, 1705).

GREECE: Unless the contract provides otherwise, an agent shall not be entitled to substitute another for himself in the performance of the mandate, except if he has been forced by the circumstances or if a substitution is usual (CC Article 715). If an agent has proceeded with the substitution without being entitled to do so, the agent shall be responsible for faults of the substitute as for his own faults (CC Article 716 paragraph (1)). If the agent has appointed a substitute while being entitled to do so, the agent shall be liable only for the faulty choice of the substitute and for the instructions he gave to such substitute (CC Article 716 paragraph (2); Supreme Court decision no. 25/1995, EEN 1995, 158). In both cases of substitution, either permitted or not, the principal may directly bring actions against the third party which the agent has against the third party (CC Article 716 paragraph (3)). From that rule it is concluded that the relationship between the principal and the agent is treated as an assignment of claims, in which the principal holds the position of the assignee and the agent the position of the assignor. Due to the gratuitous character of mandate the question whether the sub-agent has a direct claim towards the principal for payment of the price does not arise. However that question does arise in case of obligatory remunerated mandate between the lawyer and the principal. In such case it is accepted that the sub-agent lawyer has a direct claim towards the principal for remuneration only if such a substitution is permitted or is usual according to CC Article 715 (Supreme Court decision no. 296/1983, EEN 1983, 803; CA Patra decision no. 235/1993, Achaiki Nomologia 1994, 110).

HUNGARY: According to CC Article 475 paragraph (1), '[t]he agent shall proceed in person; he shall, however, be entitled to employ other persons if the principal has agreed thereto or if it is implied by the nature of the agency. An agent shall be liable for the persons he employs as if he himself had carried out the matter entrusted to him'. Moreover, CC Article 475 paragraphs (2), (3) and(4) establish that '[t]he agent shall also be entitled to employ other persons if it is required in order to protect the principal from sustaining injury. In such cases, the agent shall not be liable for the persons employed if he is able to prove that he has acted in a manner that can generally be expected in the particular situation in respect of choosing, instructing, and supervising such persons. If the agent has not been authorised to employ other persons, he shall be liable for damages that would not have occurred without the employment of such person. If a person employed by the agent has been selected by the principal, the agent shall not be responsible for this person if he is able to prove that he has acted in a manner that can generally be expected in the particular situation with regard to instructing and supervising the person'. Because of the lack of contract between the sub-agent and the principal, the sub-agent does not have a direct claim towards the principal for payment of the price.

IRELAND: One of the agent's three duties which arises, at common law, is the duty to perform personally. Since an agent is often chosen for his personal qualities the general rule is that he must perform his duties personally and cannot delegate performance *(delegatus non potest delegare)* unless delegation is authorised by the principal. In practice, delegation is quite common. For example, in relation to a company where the authority to act on behalf of the company is vested in the board of directors, the board usually delegates authority to individual directors, who in turn delegate to senior executives, who in turn delegate to junior executives and other employees. Accordingly, a long chain of delegation and authorisation can link the individual acts of a junior employee (such as a shop-assistant) back to the board of directors, thereby legally binding the company. Where delegation is authorised and the agent (A) employs a sub-agent (S), the agency agreement must be construed in order to determine whether the relationship of principal and agent is created between the principal (P) and S. The key is the agent's authority: is A authorised to create privity of contract between P and S? Just because the agent has authority to delegate to S, does not mean that he has authority to create privity of contract between P and S. Generally, where delegation is authorised S will be the agent of A, so that there will be no legal relationship between P and S; A will remain liable to P for performance of his duties *(Lockwood v Abbey* (1845) 14 Sim 437; *Calico Printers' Association v Barclays Bank Ltd* (1931) 145 LT 51). However, A can be authorised to create privity between P and S, as in *De Bussche v Alt* (1878) 8 Ch D 286, where P engaged A to sell a ship in India, China or Japan. A had no offices in Japan and so obtained P's consent to the appointment of a sub-agent, S, who had a presence in Japan. The Court of Appeal found that the delegation was authorised and that A was given express authority to create privity between P and S. In such circumstances, S has a direct contract link with P, and therefore could pursue P directly for the price, for instance.

ITALY: In general terms, the agent may have the contract performed by another party, provided that certain circumstances are met. CC Article 1717 paragraph (1) provides that '[a] agent who, in the performance of the mandate, substitutes others to himself without authorisation or when not necessary for the nature of the task to be performed, is responsible for the activities of such substitute'. It is therefore not forbidden for the agent to grant authority to another (sub)agent to execute the original contract of representation. However, this is only possible if the following conditions are met: firstly, the submandate must not prejudice the principal's interests; secondly, this possibility must not be excluded by the original contract of mandate. In consideration of the specific circumstances of the case and having regard to the specific kind of activity to execute, in some cases it could also be considered necessary for the agent to appoint a subcontractor. See Cass. no. 15000/2004, Foro It. Mass., 2004, 4, 4070; CFI Roma, 20 March 2000, Giur. it., 2001, 104. In spite of the sub-mandate, the original agent remains liable for the execution of the contract vis-à-vis the principal. This means that the original agent shall be liable for breach of contract if the subcontractor fails to perform the mandate as a consequence of defective instructions given to him by the original agent (CC Article 1717 paragraph (3)). As a rule, the sub-agent does not have a direct claim towards the principal for payment of the price. Indeed, the principal may not be considered in breach of contract if he only pays the original agent. See Cass. no. 10263/1991, Foro It. Mass., 1991, 11, 4070.

MALTA: Maltese law follows the principle *delegatus non potest delegare* – that is the agent may not substitute another person for himself unless he has been empowered to do so by the principal, cf. CC Article 1876 paragraph (1). When the agent has been empowered to do so, if however the substitute's name is not chosen by the principal but by the agent, then the agent would be answerable for the substitute if the person he chose was notoriously incompetent or insolvent, cf. CC Article 1876 paragraph (2). When the agent was empowered to appoint a sub-agent, then the sub-agent may claim the price directly from the principal. However when the sub-agent was appointed by the agent, although not empowered to do so, the sub-agent may claim the price from the agent. This can be presumed from a situation where, when the substitute agent is a legal procurator who has been appointed to act as such, the legal procurator may sue the agent for fees and expenses, see CC Article 1876 paragraph (2).

NETHERLANDS: Mandate contracts may include the agent's personal service performance. This has been established in CC Article 7:404. However, the agent may be allowed to delegate (parts of) the performance of the mandate contract to a sub-agent who acts in his own name. Such delegation is allowed if the mandate allows the agent to have others perform the mandate contract under his responsibility (CC Article 7:404). In this situation, the legal act that has been subject of the mandate contract is not performed in name of the agent, nor in name of the principal. If the contracting parties have not made explicit agreement on this delegation in the mandate contract, the mandate's nature is a decisive factor. Furthermore, the reasonableness and fairness are important as well. The agent who delegates (parts of) the mandate to a sub-agent, remains fully liable for the acts of this sub-agent (CC Article 6:76) if the sub-agent fails in complying with the acts that follow from the mandate.

POLAND: Under the contract of mandate the agent may appoint a sub-agent only if a) the mandate contract allows the sub-agent to be appointed b) it is a custom to appoint sub-agents for the task given by the principal, and c) the agent is forced by specific circumstances to use a sub-agent, cf. CC Article 738.

PORTUGAL: Subcontracting in case of a mandate contract *(substabelecimento)* is allowed in two cases (CC Articles 1165 and 264 paragraph (1)): when this is authorised by the client or when the possibility of subcontracting results from the contents of the contract or of the nature of the legal relationship (as is the case of the mandate of an attorney-at-law). Subcontracting does not exclude the first agent from the mandate contract, unless the subcontracting parties indicate otherwise *(substablecimento sem reserva)*: CC Article 264 paragraph (2). The agent is only liable vis-à-vis the client if he was negligent as to the choice of the second agent (CC Article 264 paragraph (3)).

SCOTLAND: In accordance with the maxim *delegatus non potest delegare,* delegation is, as a general rule, excluded *(Robertson v Beatson, McLeod & Co Ltd* 1908 SC 921; *Knox & Robb v Scottish Garden Suburb Co Ltd* 1913 SC 8721 (distinguishing Black v Cornelius (1879) 6 R 581)). This is an application of the general rule of contract law that where a contracting party has been chosen for his particular skill, the choice of that party rules out performance by another party. The general rule is subject to many exceptions (Gow, p. 530). Where the task is one which does not involve any particular skill, delegation may be possible (Stair, I,12,7; Erskine, III,3,34). Delegation is permitted where this is consistent with practice in a particular trade (Erskine, III,3,34; Bell, Commentaries, I,517). Whether the original agent remains liable notwithstanding delegation depends upon whether, in actual fact, sub-contracting has occurred or whether, instead, the new agent has merely been substituted for the old one. The latter is a form of novation, and would require the consent of the principal. If this consent has been properly obtained, the obligations of the original agent would not survive, and he would not remain liable. If the consent of the principal was not obtained, then only sub-contracting would be possible. In this case, the obligations of the original agent would survive and he would remain liable. Where novation rather than sub-contracting has occurred, the principal will have expressly agreed to be liable for the new agent's fees *(Robertson v Beatson, McLeod & Co Ltd* 1908 SC 921 at 928, per Lord McLaren). Where, by contrast, the principal has not consented to the delegation of the work, the original agent will be absolutely liable for the fees of the new agent (Erskine, III,3,34).

SLOVAKIA: General rules for direct representation (CC Article 33a): The agent may grant to another person the authority to act in his place in the name of the principal: a) if he is expressly authorized to do so by the terms of his power of attorney or b) if the agent is a legal entity. The principal shall be directly bound by acts in law undertaken by such substitute agent. In the case of a contract for the procurement of a thing, the agent shall have the right to procure the thing through another person in order to achieve the result. In the case of a commercial relations mandate contract, the agent is bound to arrange an agreed matter personally only if it is stipulated in the mandate contract. If the agent breaches his duty, he is liable for any damages, cf. Comm.C Article 568. Unless the contract provides otherwise, the agent is bound to make use of the other persons to perform his obligation arising from the contract with the principal, if he is unable to perform these obligations himself. If the agent makes use of other persons to perform in his stead, he remains liable for their performance as if he negotiated the arrangement himself. There is a special regulation in the Act on Advocacy.

SPAIN: CC Article 1721 allows the agent to freely appoint any other person to accomplish all or part of the mandate, unless the contract excludes this. Despite the silence of the law, there is probably another restriction where the agency agreement was clearly entered into taking account of the personal condition of the agent. The agent is not, however, relieved from obligations by virtue of sub-contracting to the third party: where there is no authority to subcontract the obligations, the agent remains fully liable for the acts of the sub-agent. On the other hand, where the agent has been authorised to subcontract the obligations, the Civil Code will only render the agent also liable towards the principal for a possible inappropriate choice of sub-agent, where the sub-agent is 'unable to perform or is insolvent'. This note does not deal with the question of a transfer of the agent's whole contractual position to another agent, with the consent of the principal, which is a different question. Where the agent merely delegates parts of his activities, the agent remains responsible and therefore liable.

SWEDEN: According to Swedish law a person representing a client in court is not allowed to subcontract his task without specific consent from the client. The same is considered to apply regarding other commissions based on trust. However, it is to some extent considered allowed to subcontract a minor and limited part of the task without prior explicit consent from the client. In particular, this applies when the agent lacks expert knowledge or if measures are to be performed at a different locality. The agent possesses a greater freedom to perform the task in case of company representation. If the agent has subcontracted the task or a part of it he still remains liable in contract for damage caused by the sub-agent's negligence.

2. Nomination by principal of specific person designated to perform the contract

AUSTRIA: The principal can require the agent to have the contract for mandate be carried out by a specific person, if the parties agree on this. It is just a matter of construction of the contract. The principal has to make his wish known to the agent before the conclusion of the contract.

BELGIUM: The principal may grant the authority to represent to the agent with consideration to performance of the mandate by a specific person.

BULGARIA: The principal of the mandate contract is allowed not only to permit subcontracting, but to also specify third persons who may be appointed by the agent as subcontractors, cf. Меворах/Лиджи/Фархи, III, p. 135. Under the mandate contract between a law firm (the agent) and the client (the principal), the latter is entitled to give his permission for an appointment of the particular advocate from the firm that performs the assigned legal task, see BAA, Article 77 paragraph (2).

DENMARK: If the parties contractually agree upon having the representation carried out by a specific person, this agreement is a valid and for the parties binding disposition. In principle, the wish to have a particular person as an agent may be communicated by means of direction. The principal, however, must be prepared to renegotiate the mandate contract. If the principal's wish does not match the general policy of the agent, e.g. a company, the direction may legally be refused.

ENGLAND: In the light of the personal nature of the agency relationship, the principal is free to nominate a specific person to perform the mandate. The principal can do so provided that he clearly indicates his wish before the mandate contract is created; it is probably not sufficient to communicate such a wish as a direction. This is especially important where the principal appoints an agent who is a legal person.

ESTONIA: The principal can require the agent to have the contract for mandate be carried out by a specific person. This is relevant where the agent is a legal person (if the agent is a natural person, it is presumed that he has to perform in person). In case of a legal person, any employee or any other person acting permanently in the undertaking of that legal person can be nominated to perform the contract. If the principal wants a particular person to perform the contract, he has to make this wish known to the agent before the conclusion of the contract.

FINLAND: The parties can agree that the mandate contract will be carried out by a specific person. Such agreement may also be based on mutual consensus. When this is not agreed (in advance or during the mandate period), the agent in general is not obliged to follow the principal's directions concerning the specific person who will represent him.

FRANCE: The principal can require that the mandate be performed by a specific person and the principal may validly prohibit expressly the agent from subcontracting or, on the contrary, appoint the sub-agent himself (CC Article 1994). In principle, such a possibility would be expressed on conclusion of the agency agreement, but it is probably possible that an agreement could be reached on this at a later stage during performance of the mandate, if clearly expressed and where this decision does not involve any difficulty or additional cost for the agent.

GERMANY: The principal can require the agent to have the mandate contract carried out by a specific person by either (a) demanding the handling of the matter by one specific person when concluding the contract, as in this case the obligation under the contract (CC Article 662) is so defined and thus binding to the agent; or (b) subsequently issuing a direction (CC Article 665), which the agent has to follow – if the direction is unacceptable to him, the agent can always terminate/revoke the contract (CC Article 671 paragraph (1)).

GREECE: The principal can require that the contract for mandate will be carried out by a specific person. It is irrelevant in this respect whether the principal has expressed such a desire before the conclusion of the contract or by means of a direction.

HUNGARY: There is no obstacle to a request of the principal that the mandate contract will be carried out by a specific person. Agency is imbued with *intuitus personae* from the part of the principal towards his agent, as is expressed in CC Article 475 paragraph (1): 'The agent shall proceed in person; he shall, however, be entitled to employ other persons if the principal has agreed thereto or if it is implied by the nature of the agency'. According to CC Article 475 paragraph (4), 'If a person employed by the agent has been selected by the principal, the agent shall not be responsible for this person if he is able to prove that he has acted in a manner that can generally be expected in the particular situation with regard to instructing and supervising the person.'

IRELAND: The principal can nominate a specific person to perform the contract.

ITALY: The principal can indicate a specific person to substitute the agent (or exclude this possibility outright). If the principal has not made his wish known to the agent before the conclusion of the contract he may communicate such wish by means of a direction thereafter, provided that this is not in contrast with the activity already performed in good faith by the original agent. If, on the contrary, the principal authorises the substitution without specifying the person to carry out the contract of representation, the agent is entitled to choose a person and he is liable towards the principal in case of fraudulent or negligent choice *(culpa in eligendo,* CC Article 1710).

MALTA: The principal has the right to ask the agent to have the contract carried out by a specific person. The relationship in this case would be between the principal and the person who carried out the mandate contract. It is however relevant that such a wish be communicated to the agent without delay before the conclusion of the contract.

NETHERLANDS: The principal can require that the mandate is performed by a specific person. If so, this person is obliged to personally perform the activities under the mandate contract. See CC Article 7:404. Given the wording of this article, the designation is probably to be communicated before the contract is concluded. This Article is meant to ensure that in situations where professional service providers work together, for instance in a law firm, the person in whom the principal has put his trust is actually the person who performs the contract, irrespective of the formal legal statute of the contracting party (that being a natural person or the firm as a legal entity). The provision is highly controversial, though, as it could be interpreted as implying that the designated person would be personally liable in case of a breach of the contract, where this designated person is not a contracting party himself and is also not entitled to the payment of the price.

POLAND: The agent is obligated to follow the principal's guidelines both to how and by whom the mandate is to be carried out, cf. CC Article 736.

PORTUGAL: In a case decided by CA Lisbon 26 February 1998, CJ 1998, 1, 133, it was stated that "the mandate to a law firm, unless the client specified otherwise in the contract, extends to all practitioners of that firm".

SCOTLAND: There is nothing to prevent the principal and agent from inserting into the mandate contract a clause to the effect that the contract is to be performed by one specific person. The contract would then become one which would fall within the general class of contracts affected by *delectus personae*. In other words, the choice of that person motivated by his particular skill would rule out performance by another party. It is likely that a specific contractual term, whether written or oral, would be required in order to achieve this result. It could not be communicated by a direction only. This latter view is also supported by the fact that the exceptions to the general prohibition against delegation appear to be larger than the rule itself.

SLOVAKIA: The principal's nomination of a specific person may be agreed at the conclusion of mandate contract, later this wish may be regarded as "direction".

SPAIN: The principal can require the agent to have the mandate carried out by a specific person, if the parties agree on this. It is just a matter of construction of the contract, and it deserves no special mention. However, where the principal not only authorises the agent to subcontract the mandate to a specific subcontractor but also indicates who that subcontractor is to be, the first agent is not responsible for the performance of the second agent.

No answer received: SWEDEN.

3. Subcontracting if specific person was designated to perform the mandate contract

AUSTRIA: If the authority to represent has been granted to the agent with consideration to a specific person, this agent cannot, except with the express consent of the principal, delegate his authority (CC Article 1010; Comm.C Article 384 and 407).

BELGIUM: If the authority to represent has been granted to the agent with consideration to a specific person, this would seem to be a case of implied prohibition to subcontract. Note that subcontracting is not at stake if the mandate contract is executed by an employee of the agent or by an organ of a corporation-agent. Both the employee and the organ identify with the agent (Wéry, p. 179).

BULGARIA: Provided that a specified person was designated by the principal to perform the mandate contract, the agent is not allowed to subcontract the performance to another person. Having done so, the agent has committed a breach of contract and may be held liable for damages caused. The agent is not liable for the actions of the designated by the principal subcontractor, unless after the designation the latter has become notorious incapable to perform (Меворах/Лиджи/Фархи, III, p. 136).

DENMARK: If the contract calls for a specific person to represent the principal, this specific person is not allowed to let another person represent the principal.

ENGLAND: The general rule is that an agent may not delegate his authority unless he has express or implied authority to do so *(De Bussche v Alt* (1878) 8 Ch D 286). If the agent was specifically designated as the person to perform the mandate and, without asking the principal first, delegated the task to another, the agent would be committing a breach.

ESTONIA: The agent, when obliged to perform in person, or the specific person required to perform the contract by the principal is entitled to use the assistance of third parties in performing the contract (LOAEst Article 622). In such case only specific duties and not the mandate as a whole can be transferred.

FINLAND: The agent in general is entitled to have some of the tasks not requiring specific knowledge or trust from the principal's side be carried out by another person inside the same organisation. This requires, however, that the original person remains in charge of the performance of the mandate contract. If the principal and the agent have agreed that all possible actions, whether technical in nature or not, are undertaken by a specific person, the agent is not entitled to pass any of the tasks on to another person.

FRANCE: If the agency agreement has been concluded based on personal qualities of the agent or if it contains an express appointment of a sub-agent by the principal, the agent must comply with the wishes of the principal. The agent would be contractually liable to the principal if he subcontracted all or part of the mandate to a third party not approved by the principal (improper performance of the mandate). In any event, the agent would be liable to the principal for any mismanagement by the sub-agent (vicarious liability, CC Article 1994 paragraph (1)).

GERMANY: If the contract called for performance by the specific person only (a matter of interpretation of the contract), the agent or that specific person may not have the mandate contract carried out by another person under the responsibility of the specific person.

GREECE: The agent or the specific person is entitled to have the contract for mandate carried out by another person under the responsibility of the specific person. In such a case the specific person is responsible for a fault of a person whom he employs as he would be for his own faults (CC Article 334; Georgiadis/Stathopoulos/Karasis, CC Article 715-716 no. 1; Supreme Court decision no. 25/1995, EEN 1995, 158).

HUNGARY: If the authority to represent has been granted to the agent with consideration to a specific person, the agent or that specific person is not entitled to have the mandate contract carried out by another person under the responsibility of the specific person, because CC Article 475 paragraph (1) prescribes that '[t]he agent shall proceed in person; he shall, however, be entitled to employ other persons if the principal has agreed thereto or if it is implied by the nature of the agency. An agent shall be liable for the persons he employs as if he himself had carried out the matter entrusted to him'. CC Article 475 paragraph (3) establishes that '[i]f the agent has not been authorised to employ other persons, he shall be liable for damages that would not have occurred without the employment of such person'. However, according to CC Article 475 paragraph (2), '[t]he agent shall also be entitled to employ other persons if it is required in order to protect the principal from sustaining injury. In such cases, the agent shall not be liable for the persons employed if he is able to prove that he has acted in a manner that can generally be expected in the particular situation in respect of choosing, instructing, and supervising such persons'.

IRELAND: In general, an agent may not delegate his authority unless he has express or implied authority to do so (De Bussche v Alt (1878) 8 Ch D 286).

ITALY: If the authority to represent has been granted to the agent with consideration to a specific person, this usually excludes the possibility for the agent or that specific person to have the mandate contract carried out by another person. However, this also depends on the kind of mandate. If it is reasonable, for instance, that a certain activity be performed by the specific agent with the aid of his auxiliaries, this would not be considered to be contrary to the choice of the principal.

MALTA: If a principal engages a lawyer who in turn engages another lawyer in his stead, the principal's acquiescence of this state of fact known to him is to be considered as a tacit mandate, cf. CFI (Civil) 17 March 1936, Zammit vs Dr. Magri.

NETHERLANDS: The principal can require that the mandate is performed by a specific person. If so, the party concluding the contract with the principal is required to ensure that the mandate is perform by the designated person. According to CC Article 7:404 contracting parties may also agree that another person will perform the mandate activities under the responsibilities of the designated person. This may also follow from custom or from the nature of the contract, e.g. in the case of substitution during illness or holiday. When the possibility of substitution cannot be read into the contract this still normally leaves the possibility for the designated person to make use of assistance by other parties, cf. Tekst & Commentaar/Castermans/ Krans, Comment 2 to CC Article 7:404.

POLAND: There are no specific CC provisions on this subject. However, if the contract is carried out by a different person then previously agreed the agent may be held liable for breach of contract.

PORTUGAL: CC Article 264 paragraph (4) provides that the agent can employ aides and helpers while carrying out the mandate, unless the contract specifies otherwise, or it is not in conformity with the nature of the act.

SCOTLAND: If the mandate contract provided that the tasks were to be carried out by a specific individual, then performance of the tasks by another person as a result of delegation would constitute a breach of the mandate contract. The original agent would be liable to the principal in damages in respect of such breach.

SLOVAKIA: The agent is bound to perform the mandate personally. Where he entrusts another person with the performance of the mandate, he shall be liable as if he performed the mandate himself, however, if the principal permitted the agent to appoint the agent, or if this became really necessary, the agent shall be liable only for the fault with the regard to the choice of his agent. Cf. CC Article 726.

SPAIN: This is a question of construction of the will of the principal. When the 'delegation' only amounts to the appointment of auxiliaries, no problem arises.

No answer received: SWEDEN.

Section 4:
Obligation to inform principal

Article 3:401: Information about progress of performance

During the performance of the obligations under the mandate contract the agent must in so far as is reasonable under the circumstances inform the principal of the existence of, and the progress in, the negotiations or other steps leading to the possible conclusion or facilitation of the prospective contract.

Comments

A. General idea

During performance of the obligations under the mandate contract, the agent must keep the principal informed about the performance. This Article opts to impose on the agent – who is aware of all relevant information and who may be in need of sufficiently detailed instructions – the obligation to actively keep the principal informed rather than requiring the principal – who may not know what to ask or what information the agent would be in need of – to ask for information.

B. Exchange of information

This section includes three Articles that require the agent to provide specific information to the principal. The first of these requires the agent to inform the principal about the manner in which the agent is performing his tasks and the success he has in doing so, whereas the second requires the agent to give an account thereof when the prospective contract has been concluded or when the contract has terminated – either by notice in accordance with Chapter 6 (Termination by notice other than for non-performance) or otherwise in accordance with Chapter 7 (Other grounds for termination) because the principal or the agent has died. Finally, Article 3:403 (Communication of identity of third party) requires the agent under certain conditions to disclose the identity of the party with whom the prospective contract has been concluded. In addition to these requirements, Article 4:102 (Request for a direction) obliges the agent to ask the principal for information or a direction as to the further performance of the mandate contract. Article 2:101 (Obligation to co-operate) requires the principal to answer reasonable requests for information and to give a direction where the contract demands this of him or when the agent has requested a direction. All these Articles intend to facilitate a steady flow of information from the agent to the principal and vice versa. Such a flow of information is necessary for both parties, as the principal needs to be able to make informed decisions on the performance of the mandate contract, whereas the agent is in need of such information to best serve the principal's needs and to ultimately be able to conclude the prospective information and receive the remuneration for his services.

C. Information about progress in performance of mandate contract

That the agent is required to keep the principal informed of the existence of, progress in, or absence of negotiations when the principal specifically asks for such information is not disputed as such in any legal system. Such an obligation usually follows from a specific statutory provision or is derived from the principle of good faith, the general duty of care, or the general duty to give account.

What may be more controversial is the extent of the duty to keep the principal informed. In this respect, two different questions must be answered. First, is the agent required to answer to any request for information? And second, is the agent also required to inform the principal without being asked to do so? This second question may also be phrased as follows: must the agent volunteer information to the principal, or is he only required to answer requests of the principal for information?

Illustration 1
Harry buys a new house and subsequently authorises Sally to sell his old house. Just a few weeks later, the housing market collapses as a result of the credit crunch. Harry, who now has to pay the mortgage interest for two houses, is panicking and rings Sally on a daily basis to inquire about the progress of the sale. Sally has patiently informed him about the lack of such progress for two consecutive weeks and is getting fed up with it. Although his actions are perfectly understandable in his dire personal situation, Harry's demands are clearly excessive. Sally is entitled to inform Harry that he ought not to call her this frequently, and she does not need to answer his every single request for information. However, whenever there is something to report about, Sally will have to contact Harry and inform him of recent developments. From time to time, Sally will also have to inform Harry of the lack of progress and, if need be, discuss with him whether to change their approach to the sale.

Illustration 2
Leo Ltd. is contemplating the purchase of new IT equipment and has engaged the services of Christian to negotiate the contract. After one week, Christian informs his principal that he has received offers from two companies and that he will start negotiations with one of them. Three days later, Christian lets the Ltd. know that he has broken off negotiations with the first seller because that seller was not willing to lower its price to meet the demands that the Ltd. had set in its mandate to Christian. Two weeks later, Christian informs his principal that he has negotiated the terms of the sales contract with the second company and informs him of those terms.

From the first Illustration it becomes clear that the first question must be answered in the negative: though the agent is required in principle to answer requests for information on the basis of his obligation to co-operate under Article 1:202 PECL (Duty to co-operate), the agent is not required to answer the principal's questions where this becomes unreasonably burdensome. This follows more clearly from the corresponding provision in Article III. – 1:104 DCFR (Co-operation), which clearly indicates that the obligation to co-operate exists 'to the extent that this can reasonably be expected for the performance of the debtor's obligation'. There is also a substantive reason not to accept an obligation to keep the principal informed all the time: such a far-reaching obligation would hinder the agent in the performance of his services and could even be counterproductive as the principal might be inclined to intervene with the details of the agent's services and thus slow down the actual fulfilment of the mandate (typically the conclusion of the prospective contract) and the emergence of the agent's right to payment. If the principal insists on being informed where this can no longer be demanded, the agent would not only not be bound by that obligation, but it could even be argued that the principal is acting contrary to good faith and fair dealing and thus violating his obligations under Article 1:201 PECL (Good faith and fair dealing).

D. Volunteer information only in so far as is reasonable

Both Illustrations, however, show that in so far as the agent is aware of information of particular relevance to the principal, he is required to inform the principal thereof without being specifically asked. The reason for that is rather evident: even though the principal is interested in receiving information about the progress of the performance of the contract, he may not always know what information he would have to inquire about. If the agent is under an obligation to volunteer information, the principal would be in a better position to give directions as to the performance of the mandate contract. This enhances the chances that the content of the prospective contract is in accordance with the true needs of the principal. An extensive obligation to keep the principal informed is therefore in accordance with the fact that the agent is a mere instrument for the principal in achieving the conclusion of the prospective contract. Moreover, by accepting an obligation for the agent to volunteer relevant information to the principal instead of allowing the agent to be asked for such information, there is no need to accept an unrestricted right for the principal to ask for information as to the progress of the performance of the mandate contract. Imposing the obligation on the agent to volunteer relevant information thus seems to be more sensible and economic for both parties.

However, the obligation to inform the principal without being asked is restricted to cases where this is reasonable, i.e. where the principal would have a reasonable interest in being informed of developments in the performance of the mandate contract. In this respect, a distinction may be made between Illustration 1 and 2. In the first Illustration, the agent is aware of the dire personal situation, which would seem to justify a more proactive approach even if there were no new developments, whereas in the second case the obligation to inform the principal would only arise in case of new developments – including the need to break off negotiations with the first potential seller – or when the principal inquires about the progress of negotiations.

E. Relation to the Principles of European Law and the Draft Common Frame of Reference

This Article mirrors that of Article IV.D. – 3:401 DCFR (Information about progress of performance). It regulates the extent of the obligation of the agent to co-operate with the principal when the latter is in need of information as to the developments in the performance of the mandate contract. As such it specifies the agent's obligation to co-operate under Article 1:202 PECL (Duty to co-operate).

F. Character of the rule

This Article constitutes a default rule from which the parties may derogate.

G. Remedies

If the agent does not act in accordance with this Article, the normal remedies for non-performance apply.

Comparative Notes

1. Duty to inform about progress of performance

In all legal systems, the agent is required to keep the principal informed of the existence of, progress in, or absence of negotiations, at least when the agent is aware that the principal may be in need of the information. In at least BELGIUM, BULGARIA, and HUNGARY, the agent may have to volunteer information, i.e. to provide the information even without having been asked to do so by the principal. In some legal systems, the duty follows from a specific statutory provision; in other legal systems it is derived from the principle of good faith, the general duty of care, or the general duty to give account. The agent is liable for damage caused by a failure to keep the principal informed of information that the principal is in need of. There is no clarity as to the moment when the information is to be provided. In BELGIUM and GREECE it is thought that the agent must inform the principal as soon as possible, in SCOTLAND at regular intervals, whereas no specific period or term for the performance of duty is indicated in FRANCE and ITALY. In AUSTRIA, BELGIUM, and FINLAND, it is made clear that the duty exists both in the case of a mandate contract for direct representation and in the case of a mandate contract for indirect representation.

National Notes

1. Duty to inform about progress of performance

AUSTRIA: Due to his duty of care the agent has to report the existence of, progress in or absence of negotiations to keep the principal constantly informed; otherwise he is liable for damages (Rummel/Rummel/Strasser, Article 1012 Rz 18; SZ 27/211; Straube/Griss, Article 384 Rz 6). It is not relevant whether the agent acted in the principal's or in his own name, if the contractual relationship between principal and indirect agent is that of a mandate in terms of CC Article 1002.

BELGIUM: Whenever an important event ('un fait majeur') occurs, the agent must take the initiative to inform the principal. In absence of a fait majeur, the principal may ask for information at any time, without an obligation for the agent to inform the principal spontaneously (Wéry, p. 160-162). This duty is part of the general duty to give account and also rests on the indirect agent.

BULGARIA: According to OCA Article 284 paragraph (1), 'the agent is obliged to notify the principal about the performance of the mandate'. It seems that the information has to be supplied not only upon a special request from the principal, but also voluntarily by the agent. It is stated in Bulgarian legal writings that the agent is under the obligation to supply the principal with relevant information at any time during the contractual performance – about the progress of actions taken towards the conclusion and about the conclusion itself of the prospective contract (Голева, Облигационно право, p. 238).

ENGLAND: Following the agent's obligation to use due skill and care when fulfilling his obligation towards the principal, the agent is also under an obligation to keep the principal informed of all relevant information. For instance, an estate agent must notify the principal of all the offers received up until a contract is exchanged with a third party (*Keppel v Wheeler* [1927] 1 KB 577). The contract may stipulate precise times at which the agent must pass relevant information to the principal. If the contract does not expressly stipulate times at which the agent must pass relevant information to the principal, the agent must do so as and when relevant with reasonable dispatch. Failing to do so, the agent will be in breach and may therefore be liable for damages.

ESTONIA: LOAEst Article 624 paragraph (1) provides that the service provider (the agent) shall be obliged to inform the principal of all important facts relating to performance of the contract, in particular of facts which may cause the principal to modify its instructions, and, at the request of the principal, shall provide the principal with information on performance of the contract. That would include information on the progress of negotiations.

FINLAND: The agent is required to inform the principal of the existence of, progress in or absence of negotiations for the conclusion of the prospective contract (Comm.C Article 18:1), irrespective of whether the agent is required to act in his own name or in the name the principal. The intensiveness of such a duty of disclosure is, however, substantially dependent on circumstances. In general, a professional party has wide obligations to provide information and evaluate the interests of the other party (HD 2007:27, HD 2001:128, HD 1999:19, HD 1999:80).

FRANCE: The agent and the commission agent are under a general obligation to provide accounts (CC Article 1993), which, according to French legal academic writing, includes all information concerning the performance or failure of the mandate. No time limit is imposed by law to provide such information. A failure to inform the principal could be considered as a breach of contract by the agent (see Cass civ 1re, 11 July 1983, Bull. civ. 1983 I, no. 202; Cass.com., 5 July 1962, Bull. civ. 1962 III, no. 344). This obligation may only be avoided where the parties expressly or impliedly decide to do so.

GERMANY: CC Article 666 requires the agent on one hand to provide the principal with the 'necessary information' and on the other hand to inform the principal about the general state of affairs (the latter being necessary only upon request of the principal). There is no general rule what these obligations exactly cover; it depends upon the circumstances (Palandt/Sprau, Article 666 no. 2). If the conditions of CC Article 280 paragraph (1) are fulfilled (notably fault by the agent), the principal has a claim for damages if the obligation to inform is breached (Palandt/Sprau, Article 666 no. 1).

GREECE: In case of a gratuitous mandate contract the agent is bound to furnish information to the principal about the affairs entrusted to him (CC Article 718), which includes all necessary information about the conclusion of the prospective contract or of the fulfillment of the task entrusted to the agent. Within how much time is the agent required to inform the principal depends on each case, but it has to be as soon as possible. Consequence of not timely informing the principal is that a claim for restitution of damages due to such failure can be established (Georgiadis/Stathopoulos/Karasis, CC Article 718 no. 2).

HUNGARY: According to CC Article 477 paragraph (1), 'The agent shall inform his principal of his activities and the state of affairs upon request or, if necessary, even without a request, particularly if employment of another person has become necessary or if the instructions need to be changed due to the occurrence of new circumstances.' The agent is required to inform the principal of the existence of, progress in or absence of negotiations for the conclusion of the prospective contract within a reasonable time. In this respect, too, the general rules of obligations apply, especially CC Article 277 paragraph (4) which establishes that '[t]he obligor shall act to perform the contract in the manner that can generally be expected in the given situation, while the obligee shall promote performance in the same manner'; see also CC Article 4 paragraph (4). The agent is liable for damages resulting from defective performance, cf. CC Article 310 and 318 paragraph (1), and Supreme Court Pfv. VIII. 22.351/2005, in EBH2006. 1410; Supreme Court Pfv. IX. 23.468/1997, in BH2001. 175; CA Csongrád Megyei Bíróság 1. Gf. 40 118/1997/4, in BDT2000. 128.

IRELAND: The common law does not comprise detailed rules as to the agent's duties, as are outlined in the black letter rules. Instead the agent's duties are described in more general terms and illustrated by case law. In particular, an agent has three common law duties: (i) to obey instructions; (ii) to exercise reasonable skill and care; and (iii) to perform personally. Further, fiduciary duties are imposed in equity, namely: (i) to avoid conflicts of interest; (ii) not to make a secret profit; (iii) not to accept a bribe; (iv) to account. An express duty to inform the principal about progress does not exist at common law, but would probably come within the agent's duty to exercise reasonable skill and care, and/or his wider fiduciary duties to his principal.

ITALY: The agent is required to inform the principal about the existence of progress in or absence of negotiations. This obligation derives from the general duty to inform the principal about every circumstance which is relevant to the conclusion of the prospective contract. Since the duty to inform is not specifically regulated by the law but derives from the general duty of good faith, no specific term is set for the fulfilment of the information obligation. The timeliness of the information shall be evaluated on the basis of the specific circumstances and in of the principle of good faith. The principal may claim damages against the agent, if any damages arise out of the delay.

MALTA: The agent must keep his principal informed of the progress and causes, which hinder performance. Negligence to inform the principal on matters that could influence his decision would render the agent liable for damages. The personal interests of an agent increase his responsibilities, cf. CA (Civil) 14 December 1925, *Prof. Tonna Barthet noe. vs Izzo*. It may be presumed that if the agent asks for information to the principal and the principal fails to give such information, the agent would not be held liable for negligence or damages if the contract is not concluded in the manner the principal would have wanted.

NETHERLANDS: According to CC Article 7:403 paragraph (1), the agent is held to inform the principal about the progress of the agent's activities regarding the mandate contract. The scope of this duty to inform the principal depends on the specific agreements in the individual mandate contract. If these specific agreements lack, the mandate's nature and the circumstances of the case are important. According to literature, the agent may for the most part do with providing the principal brief information.

POLAND: The agent is obligated to inform the principal about the progress, cf. CC Article 740. In particular, the agent is required to provide the principal all the "necessary" information.

PORTUGAL: Whether or not the agent is required to inform the client of the existence of, progress in or absence of negotiations for the conclusion of the prospective contract depends upon the degree of autonomy of the agent and the specific contractual framework of the mandate contract. The agent is always bound to inform the client upon his express request (CC Article 1161), and he might be, according to the specific circumstances of the case, under a duty to inform under the general principle of good faith.

SCOTLAND: The agent is subject to far-reaching fiduciary duties towards his principal, for example, to act with the same duty of care which would be shown by a reasonable and prudent person in managing their own affairs (Erskine, III,3,37; Bell, Commentaries, I,516; Bell, Principles, paragraph 221), or, if a professional person, to meet the standard of a reasonably careful and competent member of that profession *(Cooke v Falconer's Agents* (1850) 13 D 157, per Lord Fullerton at 172; *Beattie v Furness-Houlder Insurance (Northern) Ltd* 1976 SLT (Notes) 60. Whether these duties to act with skill and care would extend as far as obliging the agent to keep the principal informed of the progress of performance is not clear. Certainly, it is unlikely that the agent would be bound to keep the principal constantly informed. It is suggested that the duty of skill and care may bind the agent to provide the principal with updates on the progress of performance at reasonable intervals.

SLOVAKIA: In civil relations, the agent is obliged to present to the principal all information regarding progress in the performance of the mandate when the principal so requests (CC Article 727). In commercial relations, the agent is required to inform the principal of all circumstances which may result in a change of the agent's management of the matter and the instructions (Comm.C Article 567 paragraph (2)). The commission agent must inform the principal of the negotiations in the manner stipulated in the contract or as requested by the principal (Comm.C Article 579 paragraph (2)).

SPAIN: Giving or providing an account to the principal is an explicit legal duty of the agent, during and after carrying out the affair (CC Article 1720). This also encompass the giving of accurate information.

SWEDEN: The agent is required to inform the client of the existence of and the progress of negotiations for the conclusion of the prospected contract upon the client's request. If the client suffers any damage due to the agent's untimely information and this is due to the agent's negligence the client has a right to damages for non-performance. See Comm.C Article 18:1; KommL Article 7; HaL Article 5; Bengtsson, p. 164.

No answer received: DENMARK.

Article 3:402: Accounting to the principal

(1) The agent must without undue delay inform the principal of the completion of the mandated task.
(2) The agent must give an account to the principal:
  (a) of the manner in which the obligations under the mandate contract have been performed; and
  (b) of money spent or received or expenses incurred by the agent in performing those obligations.
(3) Paragraph (2) applies with appropriate modifications if the mandate relationship is terminated in accordance with Chapters 6 and 7 and the obligations under the mandate contract have not been fully performed.

Comments

A. General idea

The present Article requires the agent to inform the principal of details which are of paramount interest to him. It almost goes without saying that the agent must inform the principal when he has succeeded in concluding the prospective contract. This is all the more important to the principal as he may otherwise conclude a second contract with a third party while perhaps wanting or being able to perform only one. Similarly, when the mandated task is not to conclude a contract but to find a person (e.g. a potential buyer or seller or tenant or employee or employer) with whom the principal may wish to conclude a contract, the principal should be informed promptly when one is found so that the principal will be able to take the matter forward.

Second, the agent is required to inform the principal of how he has performed the mandate contract. This information is meant to enable the principal to assess whether the contract was performed properly and to provide him with sufficient information to start proceedings against the agent for non-performance.

On the other hand, the agent himself has an interest in performing the obligations under this Article, as their performance is a prerequisite for him to be entitled to payment of the price under Article 2:202 paragraphs (2) and (3) (Price) or to reimbursement of expenses under Article 2:103 paragraph (3)) (Expenses incurred by the agent) of these Principles.

B. Information about completion of task without undue delay

The agent must inform the principal 'without undue delay' of the completion of the mandated task (e.g. the conclusion of the prospective contract). This is important especially in cases where the agent is not awarded exclusivity and the principal could also conclude the prospective contract personally.

Illustration 1
Izabela has commissioned Joanna, a real estate agent, with the sale of her pied-à-terre in Amsterdam for a price of € 200,000. She has informed Joanna of the fact that she is aware of the interest of neighbours in the purchase of the house and that she may decide to sell them the house herself. Joanna, who realises that the house is in high demand and that it will be necessary to work fast to obtain a price for services rendered, succeeds in selling the house after only two days of work. If Joanna does not report this success without undue delay, there is a substantial risk that Izabela will sell the house herself as well. In that case, the house would be sold twice, leading to liability for Izabela for non-performance of obligations under either the first or the second sales contract.

The agent need not inform the principal of the conclusion of the prospective contract *immediately* after the conclusion; it suffices if he acts as swiftly as he could reasonably be expected to act.

Illustration 1 (continued)
The buyers of Izabela's house faxed their notice indicating the acceptance of Izabela's final offer to Joanna on Friday afternoon after the real estate agency had closed for the weekend. Unless a form requirement exists and that requirement has not yet been met, the sales contract is concluded once the fax reaches Joanna's office. Although the sales contract was concluded on late Friday afternoon, Joanna cannot be expected to inform Izabela of the conclusion of the sales contract before Monday morning, unless they have agreed otherwise.

The principal as well as the agent has an interest in giving an account of the conclusion of the prospective contract or the completion of the mandated task, because the price only becomes due once the agent has informed the principal in accordance with paragraph (1) of this Article, as Article 2:102 paragraphs (2) and (3) (Price) of these Principles provides.

C. Information about manner of performance

Under the present Article, the agent need not only inform the principal about the completion of the mandated task, but also about the way in which he has performed that task. The principal has a clear interest in being informed thereof as such information is usually the only way in which the principal can ascertain whether the agent's actions were in accordance with his contractual obligations. In other words, the principal depends on this information to be able to substantiate a possible claim for non-performance of the mandate contract. This is particularly relevant if the agent has not been successful in concluding the prospective contract, as in such cases he may otherwise not be willing to volunteer this information.

D. Giving account of money received and spent

Under paragraph (2)(b) of the present Article, the agent is also required to give an account of money spent or received or expenses incurred by the agent in performing his task. This obligation is widely recognised in all legal systems. In so far as the agent is entitled to reimbursement of expenses made under Article 2:103 (Expenses incurred by the agent), the performance of the obligation to give an account of money received and spent is a prerequisite for the agent's entitlement to reimbursement of the expenses, as paragraph (3) of that Article makes clear. However, in accordance with GERMAN case law, the obligation under this Article exists irrespective of whether a claim is made by the agent for reimbursement of expenses. Performance of the obligation is in many cases necessary for the principal to evaluate the agent's performance. Therefore, whether a separate claim for reimbursement of expenses is made or the expenses are to be covered by the price that is to be paid to the agent is of no relevance.

The present Article does not require the agent to periodically produce a statement of account on the amount of money spent, as is the case in DENMARK, or to be able to produce such an account at all times, as is the case in ENGLAND. Although it may certainly be useful to accept a right for the principal to a periodical account of money spent or to inspect the account whenever he wishes, in particular in the case of a long-term mandate contract, a general obligation to this extent seems to go too far. Such an obligation may, of course, follow from express contractual obligations between the parties, but occasionally also from the obligations under Articles 3:102 (Obligation to act in interests of principal) and 3:103 (Obligation of skill and care) of these Principles and Articles 1:201 PECL (Good faith and fair dealing).

E. Giving account if mandate relationship is terminated before tasks have been completed

The obligation to give an account of how the obligations were performed is particularly relevant if the agent has not been successful in completing the tasks – for example, concluding the prospective contract or finding a potential buyer. In such cases, the agent may not volunteer information as to the manner in which the obligations were performed because the agent may not be going to receive payment in any case. This is true in particular where the principal terminated the mandate contract for non-performance by the agent. Paragraph (3) of the present Article requires the agent to nevertheless give an account of the way he has performed the mandate contract and of the money received and spent in its performance. The information thus provided by the agent may of course be used by the principal to justify the termination.

F. Relation to the Principles of European Law and the Draft Common Frame of Reference

This Article mirrors that of Article IV.D. – 3:402 DCFR (Accounting to the principal).

G. Character of the rule

This Article constitutes a default rule from which the parties may derogate.

H. Remedies

If the agent does not act in accordance with this Article, the normal remedies for non-performance apply. Moreover, a failure to give an account of the completion of the mandated task implies that the price will not become due under Article 2:102 paragraphs (2) and (3)

(Price) of these Principles, whereas Article 2:103 paragraph (2) (Expenses incurred by agent) of these Principles prevents the agent's claim for the reimbursement of the expenses from becoming due until the agent has given an account of the money received and spent in the performance of the mandate contract in accordance with paragraph (2)(b) of this Article.

Comparative Notes

1. Duty to inform about completion of task

The agent is required to inform the principal of the conclusion of the prospective contract in all legal systems. He must do so promptly after the conclusion of the contract or at least without undue delay in AUSTRIA, BELGIUM, BULGARIA (commercial agency), DENMARK, GERMANY, GREECE, ITALY, MALTA, THE NETHERLANDS, and PORTUGAL. It seems the agent may have slightly more time to inform the principal in ESTONIA, FINLAND, HUNGARY, and SCOTLAND, where the agent must inform the principal 'within a reasonable period of time'. No set time limits for informing of the conclusion of a prospective contract exist in BULGARIA (civil relations), FRANCE, POLAND, and SWEDEN. In all legal systems, where the agent fails to inform the principal of the conclusion of the prospective contract in a timely manner, the normal remedies for non-performance – in particular, the right to claim damages for any damage sustained as a result of the late performance of this obligation – apply.

2. Duty to give account of performance of obligations under mandate contract

The agent is required to give an account to the principal of how he performed his obligations under the contract for mandate in AUSTRIA, BELGIUM, BULGARIA, DENMARK, ENGLAND, ESTONIA, FINLAND, FRANCE, GERMANY, GREECE, HUNGARY, ITALY, THE NETHERLANDS, POLAND, PORTUGAL, SLOVAKIA, SPAIN, SWEDEN, and may probably be derived from the agent's duty to exercise reasonable skill and care, and/or his wider fiduciary duties to his principal, in IRELAND and SCOTLAND. In MALTA, the obligation probably exists only in the case of direct representation.

3. Duty to give account of money spent or received in performance of obligations under mandate contract

The agent is required to give an account of any money spent or of any money received in the performance of the contract for mandate in all legal systems. In GERMAN case law, it is clarified that the obligation also exists where there is no actual claim for reimbursement.

In MALTA, in the case of a gratuitous mandate contract, the obligation is extinguished when the performance of the agent has been approved by the principal by reimbursing the agent for his expenses, unless the principal proves that the agent acted in bad faith or fraudulently and that he was unaware thereof when he reimbursed the agent for his expenses.

The agent must be able to produce accounts of money received and spent at all times in ENGLAND. When the contract is silent about these matters, the agent is required to periodically produce a statement of account on the amount of money spent in DENMARK.

National Notes

1. Duty to inform about completion of task

AUSTRIA: The agent has to inform the principal of the conclusion of the prospective contract immediately; otherwise he is liable for damages (Rummel/Rummel/Strasser, Article 1012 Rz 18; Comm.C Article 384; Schwimann/Apathy, Article 1009 Rz 4). The agent has the duty to provide to the principal the records of transactions he has effected as agent, which duty is a legal consequence of the relationship between principal and agent. This duty subsists notwithstanding termination of the principal's authority. Commission agents and forwarders have to report the finished performance of the contract immediately (Comm.C Article 384; see also Straube/Griss, Article 384 Rz 6).

BELGIUM: The duty to account (CC Article 1993) obliges the agent to account on the results of his performance (Wéry, p. 162-163). This duty is part of the general duty to give account and also rests on the indirect agent. Account should be given as soon as possible (Wéry, p. 163).

BULGARIA: The agent is under an obligation to communicate to the principal the progress of performance of the mandate, including the conclusion of the prospective contract, cf. OCA Article 284 paragraph (1). There is no a general rule regulating time limits for the performance of this information duty. A commercial agent is required to immediately inform the principal about every concluded prospective contract, see CA Article 33 paragraph (1).

DENMARK: Although there does not seem to be a rule stating that the agent is obliged to give notice to the principal of the conclusion of the prospective contract, it is considered a normal and natural obligation for the agent to inform the principal as soon as the conclusion of the contract has taken place. If the mandate contract orders the agent to inform the principal of the conclusion of the contract, the agent must fulfil this obligation within the agreed time. If no exact time for this information is agreed upon in the mandate contract the custom rule will probably be that the information must be given within a reasonable (short) time after the conclusion of the contract. In case the information is given too late the principal may, in principle, cancel the mandate contract. However, it will not be considered to be good practice on the part of the principal to cancel the mandate contract before having informed the agent that time for giving the information in question has run out.

ENGLAND: Following the agent's obligation to use due skill and care when fulfilling his obligation towards the principal, the agent is also under an obligation to keep the principal informed of all relevant information. A broker, for instance, must inform the principal of any contracts he has entered into on his behalf *(Johnson v Kearley* [1908] 2 KB 514). The contract may stipulate precise times at which the agent must pass relevant information to the principal. If the contract does not expressly stipulate times at which the agent must pass relevant information to the principal, the agent must do so as and when relevant with reasonable dispatch. Failing to do so, the agent will be in breach and may therefore be liable for damages.

ESTONIA: LOAEst Article 624 paragraph (1) provides that the service provider (the agent) is obliged to inform the principal of all important facts relating to performance of the contract and, at the request of the principal, shall provide the principal with information on performance of the contract. That would include information on the progress of negotiations. 'As a general rule, LOAEst Article 82 paragraph (3) provides that if the time for the performance of an obligation is not set and is not determinable from the nature of the obligation, the obligor shall perform the obligation within a reasonable period of time (…) after an obligation has arisen (…), taking into particular account the place, manner and nature of the performance of the obligation.' The consequences of not timely informing the principal would be the same as with any other breach: the principal could choose between the general remedies for non-performance of an obligation provided for in LOAEst Article 101 paragraph (1).

FINLAND: The agent is required to inform the principal within a reasonable time about the conclusion of the prospective contract and more generally about the fulfilment of his tasks (Comm.C Article 18:1). The consequences of not doing so depend on the harm caused to the principal. In general, the principal is entitled to compensation of damages due to negligent omission on the part of the agent.

FRANCE: The agent and the commission agent are under a general obligation to provide accounts, which, according to French legal academic writing, includes all information concerning the performance or failure of the mandate. No time limit is imposed by law to provide such information. A failure to inform the principal could be considered as a breach of contract by the agent (see Cass.civ. 1re, 11 July 1983, Bull. civ. 1983 I, no. 202; Cass.com., 5 Jul 1962, Bull. civ. 1962 III, no. 344).

GERMANY: At duty to inform the principal about the conclusion of the contract, the contracting partner and the content of the contract may arise from CC Article 666, these details constituting 'necessary information' (Seiler, in: Münchener Kommentar zum BGB, Article 666 no. 5). The information has to be given without undue delay, no request from the principal being necessary. A similar obligation is expressly laid down in Comm.C Article 384 paragraph (2) requiring the commission agent to give the principal the 'necessary information, especially prompt notice as to the conclusion of the transaction'.

GREECE: In case of a gratuitous mandate contract an agent is bound to furnish information to the principal about the affairs entrusted to him (CC Article 718), which includes all necessary information about the conclusion of the prospective contract or of the fulfilment of the task entrusted to the agent (including the existence or absence of negotiations). Within how much time the agent is required to inform the principal depends on each case, but it has to be as soon as possible. Consequence of not timely informing the principal is that a claim for restitution of damages due to such failure can be established (Georgiadis/Stathopoulos/Karasis, CC Article 718 CC no. 2).

HUNGARY: According to CC Article 477 paragraph (3), '[t]he agent shall notify the principal as soon as he fulfils his agency'. The agent is required to inform the principal of the conclusion of the prospective contract and more generally of the fulfilment of his task within a reasonable time. In this respect, too, the general rules of obligations apply, especially, CC Article 277 paragraph (4) which establishes that '[t]he obligor shall act to perform the contract in the manner that can generally be expected in the given situation, while the obligee shall promote performance in the same manner' (also see CC Article 4 paragraph (4)). The agent is liable for damages resulting from defective performance (see CC Article 310 and 318 paragraph (1)).

IRELAND: An express duty to inform the principal about the conclusion of the contract does not exist at common law, but would probably come within the agent's duty to exercise reasonable skill and care, and/or his wider fiduciary duties to his principal.

ITALY: According to CC Article 1712 paragraph (1), 'the agent shall without delay give the principal notice that the mandate has been performed'. The ratio of this rule consists in the possibility for the principal to evaluate the activity of the agent (see Cass. no. 2428/2004, Foro It Mass., 2004, 1, 4070). The agent has to inform the principal of the conclusion of the contract 'without delay'. The law does not provide for a specific term within which the agent is required to inform principal about the conclusion of the prospective contract. Accordingly the meaning of 'without delay' shall depend on the particular circumstances of the case and on the usages, if any, in the specific business sector. See Cass. no. 16575/2002, Foro It. Mass., 2002, 15, 4070; Cass. no. 2387/1997, Corriere giur., 1997, 903, with comments by Stella, Contratti, 1997, 559, with comments by Zappata; Cass. no. 693/1982, Foro. It. Mass., 1982, 9, 4070; and Cass. no. 3732/1982, Arch. civ., 1982, 981. If not timely informed of the conclusion of the contract the principal may claim damages against the agent, if any damages arise out of the delay.

MALTA: According to Maltese case-law, an agent must without delay, inform his principal that the contract has been performed, otherwise the agent is guilty of negligence, cf. Comm. Court 30 July 1901, *Balbi vs Hare noe.* The personal interested aims of an agent increase his responsibility, therefore when the agent acts in his own name, the duty to inform the principal that the prospected contract has been finalized is applied more rigorously, cf. CA (Civil) 14 December 1925, *Prof. Tonna Barthet noe. vs Izzo*. A specific time period within which the agent must inform the principal is not specified, however if the agent does not inform the principal without delay, the agent is guilty of negligence.

NETHERLANDS: According to CC Article 7:403 paragraph (1), the agent is held to inform the principal about the progress of the agent's activities regarding the mandate contract. Furthermore, the agent is held to immediately notify the principal of the completion of the contract if the principal is unaware thereof. The scope of this duty to inform the principal depends on the specific agreements in the individual mandate contract. If these specific agreements lack, the mandate's nature and the circumstances of the case are important. According to literature, the agent may for the most part do with providing the principal brief information.

POLAND: The agent is obliged to provide the principal with a report and account after the contract has been concluded (or terminated by either side). There are no specific rules as to when those documents should be provided or whether the agent is liable if he doesn't provide those documents/inform the principal about the conclusion of the contract immediately.

PORTUGAL: According to CC Article 1161 lit (c), the agent must inform the client promptly of the fulfilment of the mandate or the reasons why it was not accomplished. How prompt must the communication be is evaluated on a case to case approach. The consequences of the breach of this duty are the contractual liability of the agent under the provision of Article 762 paragraph (2) and 1161 CC. Cf. RC 16 March 1999, CJ 1999, 2, 21.

SCOTLAND: It is likely that a failure to inform the principal of the conclusion of a contract within a reasonable time would be a breach of the agent's duties of skill and care which would result in the agent's liability to the principal in damages.

SLOVAKIA: In civil relations, the agent is required to inform the principal of the conclusion of the prospected contract as it is the part of his obligation to give a report on a progress of his performance. In commercial relations, informing the principal is the condition for the entitlement to price. After the execution of a certain affair, the agent must provide the principal with a report and the related accounting of the results of the arrangements made (Comm.C Article 584 paragraph (1)).

SPAIN: The agent has a duty to give account to the principal on how the contract has been performed (CC Article 1720 paragraph (2)). There is no specific rule relating to the conclusion of the prospective contract, probably because this is considered to be a self-evident application drawn from the main obligation of the agent.

SWEDEN: The agent is required to inform the principal of the conclusion of the prospected contract as well as more generally of the fulfillment of his task "within a reasonable time" or "without delay", see Comm.C Article 18:1, KommL Article 7; HaL Article 5.

2. Duty to give account of performance of obligations under mandate contract

AUSTRIA: The agent is required to give account to the principal of the manner in which he has performed his obligations under the contract for mandate; otherwise the principal could not realise breaches of contract (Schwimann/Apathy, Article 1012 Rz 5). The agent has the duty to provide to the principal the records of transactions he has effected as agent, which duty is a legal consequence of the relationship between principal and agent. This duty subsists notwithstanding termination of the principal's authority

BELGIUM: A first aspect of the agent's duty to give account (CC Article 1993) is the duty to give account of the way the mandate has been performed (Wéry, p. 160-162). This rule also applies to a commission contract (Cass. 21 June 1968, Arr. Cass. 1968, 1285, Pas. 1968, 1212, RHA 1972, 309; De Page, p. 371; Foriers, p. 68;

Pand. b., v° Commission (contrat de), no. 166; Samoy, 186-188; Van Der Perre & Lejeune, no. 128-129; Van Ryn & Heenen, p. 24), a prête nom-contract (Samoy, p. 95) and a mandatary acting in his own name (De Page, p. 436; Paulus & Boes, p. 134; Samoy, p. 306; Tilleman, p. 277-278; Van Der Perre & Lejeune, no. 166; Wéry, p. 152 and 259).

BULGARIA: Rendering an account of the performance is one of the major obligations of the agent, cf. OCA Article 284 paragraph (2). It consists of: (a) calculation of expenses for performance of the mandate contract; (b) transfer from the agent to the principal of all legal effects of the prospective contract and other judicial acts; (c) the delivery to the principal of all goods and documents, received by the agent in the course of the contractual performance. The content of this obligation differs depending on the type of representation. In case of direct representation, the agent has acted in the name of and on behalf of the principal and all legal effects from the concluded prospective contracts and the other performed judicial acts has occurred directly in legal sphere of the principal. In this case, rendering an account means only giving an account of expenses and delivery of goods and documents. When the agent has acted in his own name and on behalf of the principal, apart from giving an account of expenses and delivery, he is under the obligation to transfer to the principal all rights and obligations under the concluded prospective contracts (Голева, Облигационно право, p. 238; Любен Василев, Облигационно право, p. 26; Хорозов, СП, 1995, p. 3, 38-43).

DENMARK: The agent shall exercise due diligence to inform the principal about the manner in which he has performed the mandate contract.

ENGLAND: As part of his obligation to exercise due skill and care when performing his duties, the agent must keep the principal informed of all the material facts. The agent must do so promptly so that the principal can react accordingly: *Proudfoot v Montefiore* (1867) LR 2 QB 511.

ESTONIA: LOAEst Article 624 paragraph (2) provides that upon performance of his services, the service provider (the agent) shall be obliged to give account to the principal with an overview of the expenditure and revenue relating to performance of the services together with the documentation, which is the basis for the account.

FINLAND: The agent is generally required to give account of the manner in which he has performed his obligations (Comm.C Article 18:1), irrespective of whether the agent has acted in his own name or in the name the principal.

FRANCE: The agent must render an account to the principal in connection with the performance of its duties (CC Article 1993). This obligation may only be avoided where the parties expressly or impliedly decide to do so (e.g. in a family context). The agent must keep the principal informed of the performance of his mandate, the difficulties encountered, the state of advancement of his research and the result of his mandate, whether positive or negative. The commission agent, who acts in his own name and for the account of the principal, is, in principle, subject to the same obligation to account for its mandate (customary rule, except in certain cases; see Collart-Dutilleul & Delebecque, no. 664).

GERMANY: The agent is required to give account to the principal of the manner in which he has performed his obligations (CC Article 666, and Comm.C Article 384 paragraph (2) for commission agents).

GREECE: In case of a gratuitous mandate contract an agent shall be bound to furnish information to the principal about the affairs entrusted to him and to render account to the principal upon termination of the mandate (CC Article 718). The lawyer is also obliged to render account to his principal of the case entrusted to him (CFI Pireos decision no. 607/1985, ArchN 1985, 328).

HUNGARY: According to CC Article 477 paragraph (1), '[t]he agent shall inform his principal of his activities and the state of affairs upon request or, if necessary, even without a request, particularly if employment of another person has become necessary or if the instructions need to be changed due to the occurrence of new circumstances'. Moreover, '[a]t the time the contract is extinguished, the agent shall be obliged to settle his accounts and give the principal everything that has been acquired for the purpose of fulfilling his agency or as a result of doing so, except for what he has lawfully used in the course of his agency' (CC Article 477 paragraph (2)). The obligation of the agent to give account to the principal also covers the manner in which he has performed his obligations under the mandate contract. The agent is liable for damages resulting from defective performance (see CC Articles 310 and 318 paragraph (1)).

IRELAND: An express duty to give account of performance of the mandate contract does not exist at common law, but would probably come within the agent's duty to exercise reasonable skill and care, and/or his wider fiduciary duties to his principal.

ITALY: The agent is required to give account to the principal of the manner in which he has performed his obligations under the mandate contract (CC Article 1713).

MALTA: The general principle in Maltese law is found in CC Article 1875 which states that "The agent, unless expressly exempted by the principal, is bound to render to the latter an account of his management and of everything he has received by virtue of the mandate, even if what he has received was not due to the principal." Such an obligation is laid down not only in the interest of the principal, that is, to ensure that the agent did not derive any profit from the execution of the contract, or from the funds entrusted to him. However this obligation is laid down also in the agent's interest, because it is to the credit of the agent to render an open account of his administration, and to show what is due to him side by side with that which he owes. However, although this is not specifically stated in the law, such an obligation seems to arise only in the situation when the agent acted in the name of the principal. This can be presumed from CC Article 1871, which states that "(1) When the agent has acted in his own name, the principal cannot maintain an action against those with whom the agent has contracted, nor the latter against the principal. (2) In any such case, however, the agent is directly bound towards the person with whom he has contracted as if the matter were his own." In fact as can be seen from this provision, the agent in such a case is directly bound towards the person with whom he contracted and not with the principal. Therefore the obligation to render account to the principal would not apply in this case.

NETHERLANDS: According to CC Article 7:403 paragraph (2), the agent must give account of the way he has fulfilled the contract.

POLAND: The agent is obligated to give an account after carrying out the mandate contract or after the contact is terminated by either side, cf. CC Article 740. The remuneration will be due after an account has been given.

PORTUGAL: The duty to give account applies to all paradigms of representation, as even in indirect representation, though the agent acts in his own name, he acts on account of, and according to the instructions from, a client. The duty to give account includes the report of the circumstances of the execution of the mandate (CC Article 1161 lit (c-d)).

SCOTLAND: The agent's duty of good faith has been expressed as follows. 'An agent is bound to maintain the most entire good faith, and make the fullest disclosure of all facts and circumstances concerning the principal's business' (Bell, Principles, paragraph 222). This fiduciary duty is probably sufficiently wide to oblige the agent to provide the principal with an account of the manner in which he has performed the mandate contract. Failure to do so would result in the agent's liability to the principal in damages. What is clear is that the agent is bound to provide the principal with a record of all transactions entered into by the agent on the principal's behalf (Gow, p. 531).

SLOVAKIA: In both civil and commercial relations, the agent is obliged to give a report. In commercial relations, this is a condition for entitlement to the price. As for the commission agency contract, after execution of a certain affair the agent must provide the principal with a report and the related accounting of the results of the arrangements made. In the report, the agent must name the person with whom the contract was concluded.

SPAIN: Accounting to the principal is an explicit legal duty of the agent, during and after carrying out the affair (CC Article 1720) The accounting should cover the outcome and the economic balance of the service made (CC Article 1720 and Comm.C Article 263).

SWEDEN: The agent is required to give account of the manner in which he has performed his obligations under the mandate contract. This is applicable regardless of whether the agent has acted in his own name or in the name of the principal, see Comm.C Article 18:1, KommL Article 7.

3. Duty to give account of money spent or received in performance of obligations under mandate contract

AUSTRIA: The agent is required to give account of any money spent or of any money received in the performance of the contract for mandate (CC Article 1012, Comm.C Article 384 paragraph (2); Comm.C Article 408 (Straube/Griss, Article 384 Rz 7); HVertrG Article 5).

BELGIUM: The second aspect of the agent's duty to account (CC Article 1993) is the duty to put the accounts, showing all incomings and outgoings (Wéry, p. 163-171).

BULGARIA: Under Bulgarian contract law, rendering an account from the agent means also giving an account of money, spent or received in the course of performance of the mandate contract, cf. OCA Article 284 paragraph (2); Меворах/Лиджи/Фархи, III, p. 126-133.

DENMARK: Whether the agent is required to give account for money spent during the course of the performance of his task depends on the wording of the mandate contract. When the contract is silent about these matters, it is a common (customary) rule that the agent will periodically produce a statement of account on the amount of money spent.

ENGLAND: The agent is under a fiduciary duty to account to the principal of all property and/or money he may have in his possession that he has received from the principal or from a third party for the principal's account and any money he has spent whilst performing the authority. As a fiduciary duty, it is applied strictly by the courts. The agent must keep accurate account of all the transactions he has entered into on behalf of the principal during the life of the agency relationship. It is especially important that the agent keeps account of his own money and the money/property belonging to the principal totally separate. The agent must be able to produce such accounts at all times. In the case of *Gray v Haig* (1854) 20 Beav 219, Romilly MR held that when the agent fails to keep an accurate account of all transactions, the court may feel 'compelled (…) to presume everything unfavourable to him' (Ibid, per Romilly MR at 226). The agent must also be able to produce all records and documents relating to the affairs of the principal and such records must be available even after termination of the relationship *(Yasuda Fire & Marine Insurance Co of Europe Ltd v Orion Marine Insurance Underwriting Agency Ltd* [1995] QB 174). On termination, the agent is required to surrender to the principal all books, accounts, documents etc given to him by the principal or that the agent prepared during the agency relationship. This obligation is subject to the lien that an agent may have over such documents in order to secure forthcoming payment from the principal. This general fiduciary duty to account to the principal is a personal one and arises independently of any contract between the principal and the agent. Fiduciary duties apply to paid and gratuitous agents alike but the standard of care owed by a gratuitous agent may be lower than that of a paid agent *(Chaudry v Prabhakar* [1989] 1 WLR 29).

ESTONIA: LOAEst Article 624 paragraph (2) provides that upon performance of his services, the service provider (the agent) shall be obliged to give account to the principal with an overview of the expenditure and revenue relating to performance of the services together with the documentation, which is the basis for the account.

FINLAND: The agent is generally required to give account of the money spent or received in the performance of the mandate contract (Comm.C Article 18:1).

FRANCE: The agent is required to render an account for all sums received and expended in the performance of its mandate. No specific form is required by statute or by case law, but the agent must in all events record all sums held 'even though he may have received sums which are not due to the principal' (CC Article 1993). The agent should comply with accounting rules, particularly if he or she is a professional agent. Rendering accounts also means returning to the principal all sums which are due to it and any sums that the principal remitted to the agent to perform its mandate, as well as sums received from any third party (Cass.civ. 1re, 8 July 1975, Bull. civ. 1975 I, no. 226). The agent would commit the crime of fraud *(abus de confiance)* if it applied such sums or other property to its own benefit. CC Article 1996 provides also that the agent is liable to pay interest on the sums used for its own purposes and the sums which are due to be remitted to the principal as of the date where the agent has received formal notice to do so.

GERMANY: Under CC Article 666 the agent must give account for all sums received and expended in the performance of its mandate. The form of the accounting is governed by CC Article 259. The obligation to give account also exists where there is no actual claim for reimbursement (BGHZ 109, 260, 266).

GREECE: In case of a gratuitous mandate contract the agent is obliged to give account of any money spent or of any money received during the performance of the mandate (CC Article 718). In case of a failure of the agent to render account to the principal, a claim for damages due to such a failure can be established or the principal can deny to pay back the expenses that the agent has incurred during the performance of the mandate (Georgiadis/Stathopoulos/Karasis, CC Article 719 no. 2). An agent must return to the principal everything the agent had received for or has acquired from the performance of the mandate (CC Article 719). If an agent has used money belonging to the principal for his own benefit, the agent shall owe interest thereon as from the date he commenced the use (CC Article 720).

HUNGARY: CC Article 479 paragraph (2) prescribes that '[a]t the time the contract is extinguished, the agent shall be obliged to settle his accounts and give the principal everything that has been acquired for the purpose of fulfilling his agency or as a result of doing so, except for what he has lawfully used in the course of his agency'. Furthermore, '[u]pon termination of contract the principal shall exonerate the agent from obligations assumed against third persons on the basis of the agency and shall reimburse his necessary and useful expenses' (CC Article 479 paragraph (3)).

IRELAND: A duty to account for monies is part of an agent's fiduciary duties. In this regard, an agent must account to the principal for all property (including monies) of the principal he receives in the course of the agency. He must therefore keep his own monies and property separate from those of the principal, unless mixing is authorised. As part of this duty, an agent must keep complete records of transactions entered on the principal's behalf and make them available for inspection to the principal *(Pearse v Green* (1819) 1 Jac & W 135). A court may make adverse inferences where the agent fails in this regard *(Gray v Haig* (1855) 20 Beav 219). On termination of the agency, the agent must deliver up to the principal all books, accounts and other documents given to him by the principal or created in the course of the agency unless he is entitled to exercise a lien over it *(Gibbon v Pease* [1905] 1 KB 810). Moreover, because the duty to account arises from the fiduciary nature of the relationship, independently of any contract, it survives the termination of the contract, unless expressly or impliedly excluded by the contract *(Yasuda Fire and Marine Insurance Co of Europe Ltd v Orion Marine Insurance Underwriting Agency Ltd* [1995] QB 174).

ITALY: The agent is required to give account of the money spent and/or of the money received in the performance of the mandate contract (CC Articles 1713 and 1714). As a rule, it makes no difference whether or not the mandate contract is for a price and whether or not the agent claims reimbursement of expenses. Of course, if the agent claims reimbursement of expenses he will have a duty to prove the expenses.

MALTA: According to CC Article 1875, the agent is required to give account of any money spent or received in the performance of the contract. In a situation whereby the performance of a agent has already been approved by the principal by way of a reimbursement of the expenses, then the agent is not bound to render an account of his administration unless the principal proves that the agent was guilty of bad faith and fraud and that the principal was unaware of this before approving the agent's performance. Cf. CA (Commercial) 13 October 1862, *Semini vs Caruana*. Maltese courts have constantly held that when a mandate (contract) is not gratuitous, then the agent's responsibility is more rigorously enforced. Therefore in a situation when the contract of mandate is for a price, the agent's obligation to render account is more rigorously applied. With regards to the third part of the question, whether it is relevant or not that the agent claims the reimbursement of expenses, due to the fact that according to Maltese law, the reimbursement of expenses is one of the principal's obligations, such a factor would not influence the agent's obligation to render account. See CC Article 1881.

NETHERLANDS: According to CC Article 7:403 paragraph (2), the agent is held to give account of the money spent and/or the money received during the performance of the mandate contract. According to literature, the principal may make a claim to costs specification and delivery of documentary evidence, which enables him to evaluate the revenues and expenditures.

PORTUGAL: Under CC Article 1161 lit (e), the agent is required to transfer to the client what he has received while carrying out the mandate, in so far as he has not spent it in the performance of the mandate contract.

SCOTLAND: The agent is under a duty to give an account of money spent or received in the performance of the mandate contract, although such accounting may be verbal where this is consistent with the performance of the mandate contract *(Russell v Cleland* (1885) 23 SLR 211). Agents are also obliged to keep their personal funds separate from those of their principal, and to provide the principal with a record of all transactions carried out on the principal's behalf (Macgregor paragraph 88; Gow, p. 531).

SLOVAKIA: In civil relations, the agent is bound to present an account (a statement of costs and expenditure) to the principal; this obligation generally corresponds with the obligation of the principal to reimburse the agent's expenses, but the parties can agree otherwise (CC Article 727). In commercial relations, it is relevant whether the agent claims reimbursement of expenses; if the expenses are included in the price, it is not necessary to give an account. On the other hand, if the agent obtained payment in advance for substantial expenses, the agent will probably give an account of spending. Under the commission agent contract, after the execution of a certain affair, the agent must provide the principal with a report and the related accounting of the results of the arrangements made; this is a condition for entitlement to the commission and the reimbursement of expenses.

SPAIN: Under CC Article 1720, the agent must give an account to the principal of money spent or received or expenses incurred by him in performing the obligations under the mandate contract; see Comm.C Article 263. The agent must give an account to the principal of money spent or received or expenses incurred by him in performing the obligations under the mandate contract. The agent has to provide all relevant documents and bills (Hernández Gil, p. 477). CC Article 1720 is a default rule, therefore parties may agree to exclude the obligation to give account. Moreover, this obligation is only secondary and need not be performed in order for the price to become due.

SWEDEN: After fulfilment of the mandate contract the agent is required to give account of money spent and of money received during the performance of the assignment. See Comm.C Article 18:1, KommL Article 7; HaL Article 5; Hellner, p. 223; Bengtsson, p. 164.

No answer received: POLAND.

Article 3:403: Communication of identity of third party

(1) An agent who concludes the prospective contract with a third party must communicate the name and address of the third party to the principal on the principal's demand.
(2) In the case of a mandate for indirect representation paragraph (1) applies only if the agent has become insolvent.

Comments

A. General idea

The present Article contains a duty for the agent to communicate the name and address of the third party to the principal in a situation where the principal is not aware of that name but needs to know it to exercise his rights towards the third party. However, a distinction is made between mandate contracts for direct representation and for indirect representation. In the former case, the duty applies as soon as the principal demands to know the identity of the third party; in the latter case, the agent is required to disclose the identity of the third party only if he is insolvent, as only then would the principal have a justified interest in knowing the identity of the third party because he may have a direct claim towards this third party under the provisions of the Principles of European Contract Law.

B. Disclosure of identity of third party in case of direct representation

In a case of direct representation, the prospective contract is concluded between the principal and the third party. In this situation the principal is contractually bound to perform towards the third party and is entitled to claim performance by the third party of that party's obligations under the concluded contract. Paragraph (1) of this Article requires the agent to inform the principal of the identity of the third party to enable the principal to do so.

Illustration 1
Victor bought a car from Viola Automobiles Ltd. in the name and on behalf of Severine. As the car is defective, Severine wishes to exercise her remedies under the sales contract. Victor is required to inform her of the name and address of Viola Automobiles Ltd. if and when Severine asks him where he bought the car for her.

C. No general obligation to disclose third partys identity in case of indirect representation

In the case of indirect representation – a situation where the agent has acted on behalf of the principal but not in his name – no contractual ties exist between the principal and the third party. In this case, the principal is aware of the identity of the party who is to perform the obligations under the prospective contract, and towards whom he is required to perform himself, as that party is not the third party but the agent himself. Requiring the agent to disclose the identity of the third party is therefore normally not required to safeguard the principal's interests.

Illustration 2
Victor bought a car from Viola Automobiles Ltd. in his own name but on behalf of Severine. As the car is defective, Severine wishes to exercise her remedies under the sales contract. As she does not have a sales contract with Viola Automobiles Ltd. but with Victor, she will have to exercise her remedies against Victor. It is up to Victor to sue Viola Automobiles Ltd. in turn on the basis of his own sales contract.

Whether the agent (Victor) informed the principal (Severine) in this case of the identity of the third party is irrelevant as regards the legal position of the principal. Therefore, no such obligation arises, for such an obligation is not necessary to protect the principal's interests. The principal's interests are generally safeguarded through the fact that the agent is required to ensure that the principal reaps the benefits of the performance by the third party. A non-performance by the third party towards the agent would therefore translate into a non-performance by the agent towards the principal; similarly, when the agent does not retransfer the results of the third party's performance towards him, this also translates into a non-performance by the agent.

D. Limited obligation to communicate third partys identity in case of indirect representation

There are cases, however, where the normal contractual claims against the agent will not help the principal. This is true in particular where the agent is insolvent and the principal's claim for performance, damages, or restitution on the basis of termination will simply fall within the agent's bankruptcy procedure, often implying that these have little or no monetary value. For these situations, however, Article 3:302 PECL (Intermediary's insolvency or fundamental non-performance to principal) offers the possibility to take over the claims of the agent towards the third party for a non-performance by the third party towards the agent.

Illustration 3
Victor bought a car from Viola Automobiles Ltd. in his own name but on behalf of Severine. As the car is defective, Severine wishes to exercise her remedies under the sales contract. If this claim is justified, Victor in turn may have a claim towards Viola Automobiles Ltd. for non-conformity. If Victor is insolvent, both Severine's claim towards Victor and Victor's claim towards Viola Automobiles Ltd. fall within Victor's bankruptcy procedure. However, under Article 3:302 PECL (Intermediary's insolvency or fundamental non-performance to principal), Severine may take over Victor's rights towards Viola Automobiles Ltd. Yet to effect this right, Victor would have to communicate the name and address of the third party – i.e. of Viola Automobiles Ltd. – to Severine. The present Article requires him to do so.

E. Relation to other provisions in these Principles

Under this Article, the agent may be required to inform the principal of the third party's identity upon the latter's demand. This Article does not exclude the possibility that the agent is required to spontaneously inform the principal thereof, i.e. without the principal having to inquire about the identity of the third party. Such an obligation may follow directly from the mandate contract itself, but also from the operation of the provisions on conflict of interests in Chapter 5 (Conflicts of interests) of these Principles, i.e. where the agent intends to become the third party in accordance with Article 5:101 (Self-contracting) or when he also acts as an agent on behalf of the third party in accordance with Article 5:102 (Double mandate). Moreover, such an obligation may also follow from the agent's obligation to act in the best interest of the principal under Article 3:102 (Obligation to act in interests of principal), as comment E to that Article explains.

F. Relation to the Principles of European Law and the Draft Common Frame of Reference

This Article mirrors that of Article IV.D. – 3:403 DCFR (Communication of identity of third party). It is complementary to the provisions of Article 3:302 PECL (Intermediary's insolvency or fundamental non-performance to principal) in the case of the agent's insolvency in a situation of indirect representation.

G. Character of the rule

Paragraph (1) of this Article constitutes a default rule from which the parties may derogate. However, the provisions of paragraph (2), by its very nature, constitute a mandatory rule which is effective even in the case of bankruptcy of the agent and can be invoked against the trustee charged with the bankruptcy affairs.

H. Remedies

If the agent does not act in accordance with this Article, the normal remedies for non-performance apply.

Comparative Notes

1. Obligation to inform about identity of third party in case of direct representation

In case of a mandate contract for direct representation, the agent is required to inform the principal about the identity of the third party in most legal systems. A possible exception to the rule is POLAND, where the obligation in any case is unregulated.

The existence of the obligation is seen as a logical consequence of the agent's duty of loyalty and duty to give account to the principal in BELGIUM, FRANCE, ITALY, and SLOVAKIA. In ESTONIA, MALTA, and SCOTLAND, this obligation follows – at least in cases of direct representation – from the obligation to inform the principal of all important facts related to the performance of the mandate contract. In ENG-LAND, the obligation follows from the requirement to act in the best interest of the principal, which more generally requires him to pass on to the principal any material information, i.e. information that is impor-tant to the principal. In IRELAND, the obligation to inform the principal thereof at the latter's request would probably be included in the obligation to obey the principal's instructions.

2. Limited obligation to inform about identity of third party in case of indirect representation

In case of a mandate contract for indirect representation, in most legal systems the agent is required to inform the principal about the identity of the third party only in specific cases. This is probably different, however, in FRANCE, MALTA, and POLAND. In ESTONIA, THE NETHERLANDS, and probably also in SWEDEN, the obligation exists only if the knowledge of the identity of a third party would be necessary for the principal to exercise the rights acquired by the agent under the contract with the third party – for in-stance, in the case of bankruptcy of the agent. Similarly, in BELGIUM, the commission-agent, who acts on the basis of a mandate contract for indirect representation, in principle has a right of secrecy as to the third party's identity. However, that right is overruled in exceptional cases, such as the bankruptcy of the com-mission-agent.

National Notes

1. Obligation to inform about identity of third party in case of direct representation

BELGIUM: An obligation to inform the principal about the identity of the third party would seem to be regarded as a logical consequence of the agent's duty of loyalty and duty to give account to the principal (CC Article 1993).

BULGARIA: In view of the fact that the agent is obliged to inform the principal about the performance of the mandate, the first appears to be under the duty to also communicate the personal data of the third party with whom the prospective contract has been concluded.

ENGLAND: The agent must act in the best interest of the principal and must pass onto the principal any material information i.e. information which are important to the principal. This would no doubt include the identity of the third party

ESTONIA: The law does not prescribe a specific duty to inform the principal about the identity of a third party. Such obligation can however, at least in cases of a direct representation be derived from the general obligation of the agent to inform the principal of all important facts related to the performance of the man-date agreement (LOAEst Article 624 paragraph (1)).

FRANCE: There are no specific rule or cases about that point, but it's possible to consider that the duty to give account to the principal (CC Article 1993) is including the duty to inform the principal about identity of the third party, as the principal may be informed about all important points of the contract with the third party.

GERMANY: The general information duty in CC Article 666 requires the agent to inform the principal about the name and address of the party with whom the prospective contract has been concluded (Seiler, in: Münchener Kommentar zum BGB, Article 666 no. 5).

IRELAND: The common law does not comprise detailed rules as to the agent's duties, as are outlined in the black letter rules. Nevertheless, an agent's common law duty to obey instructions would probably include a duty to communicate the identity of any third party on the principal's demand.

ITALY: The agent has to comply with the general duties of good faith and loyalty involving, among the others, the obligation to inform the principal about any element that can be relevant and of interest for the latter. Therefore, if the identity of the third party appears to be of relevance for the principal, the agent shall inform him thereof (see CC Article 1710; Cass. no. 19778/2003, Foro It. Mass., 2003, 19, 4070).

MALTA: The agent would be required to communicate the name and address of the third party to the principal. This is presumed from the agent's duty to inform the principal of all that is taking place during the performance of the contract of mandate. The non-performance of this obligation would render the agent liable of negligence.

NETHERLANDS: The general rule duty of the principal to inform the principal (CC Article 7:403) does not mandatorily imply the obligation of the agent to inform the principal of the identity of the third party. Cf. Tekst & Commentaar/Castermans/Krans, Comment 2 to CC Article 7:403 and Comment 4 to CC Article 7:420. Such an obligation is, however, normally accepted in cases of direct representation as in such case the principal would have to perform the prospective contract towards the third party.

POLAND: A duty to inform about the identity of third party is not regulated in the CC provisions on mandate. The parties may decide to include such a duty in the contract, otherwise the agent is not obligated to do so.

SCOTLAND: There is no specific duty to inform the principal of the identity of the third party. However, it may be included within the agent's fiduciary or good faith duty to disclose to the principal all facts and circumstances concerning the latter's business (Bell, Principles, Article 222).

SLOVAKIA: In the case of a commission agency contract, after execution of a certain affair the agent must provide the principal with a report and the related accounting of the results of the arrangements made. In the report, the agent must name the person with whom the contract was concluded.

SWEDEN: In order for the principal to exercise his rights according to the prospective contract towards the third party, the agent has a duty to inform about the identity of the third party.

No answer received: AUSTRIA, DENMARK, FINLAND, GREECE, HUNGARY, PORTUGAL, SPAIN.

2. Limited obligation to inform about identity of third party in case of indirect representation

BELGIUM: A commission-agent has, as a rule, a right of secrecy as to the third party's identity towards the principal (Samoy, p. 188-190; Van Ryn & Heenen, p. 21). This right of secrecy however is not absolute. According to jurisdiction, in certain exceptional cases, the right of secrecy can be overruled by the principal's legitimate interest to know the third party's identity (CA Gent 18 May 1876, Pas. 1876, II, 372; CA (comm.) Brussels 1 February 1911, TBH 1911, 201; Samoy, p. 189-190). The bankruptcy of the commission-agent is one of these exceptional cases.

BULGARIA: Under Bulgarian contract law, both direct and indirect agent appear to be obliged to communicate to the principal personal data of the third person, who is a party of the concluded prospective contract.

ENGLAND: There is no such thing as indirect representation in English law. The closest notion is that of undisclosed agency. However, even in such a case, the agent must still act for the best interests of the principal, therefore there would still be an obligation on the agent to pass the identity of the third party to the principal if requested.

ESTONIA: In case of indirect representation the duty to inform about identity of a third party can be derived from the general obligation of the agent to inform the principal of all important facts related to the performance of the mandate agreement (LOAEst Article 624 paragraph (1)), such duty requires the agent to disclose information if the principal has justified interest towards the disclosure. In case of indirect representation such interest could only exist if it the knowledge of the identity of a third party would be necessary in order to exercise the rights acquired by the agent under the contract with the third party and against such party for the benefit of the principal, for example in case of the commission agent, where the law (see LOAEst Article 700 paragraphs (1) and 3) provide that the commission agent is liable for the performance of the contract with the third party if it does not disclose the identity of the third party to the principal.

FRANCE: Despite the lack of any specific rule on that point in CC or Comm.C, there's no duty to inform about the identity of the third party in case of indirect representation ("commission" contract), in practice.

GERMANY: According to Comm.C Article 384 paragraphs (2) and (3), a duty to inform the principal about the name and address of the contracting partner also arises in cases of indirect representation, namely for commission agents (BGH, WM 1984, 931).

IRELAND: Where the agency is undisclosed (indirect representation) the same duties apply and hence an agent's common law duty to obey instructions would probably include a duty to communicate the identity of any third party on the principal's demand.

ITALY: In case of indirect representation the agent doesn't act in name of the principal but in its own name. This usually implies that the identity of the third party is less relevant for the principal. Nevertheless, the general duties of the agent are those of good faith and loyalty, so that if – on a case to case basis – it appears that the principal has an interest in knowing the identity of the third party, the agent shall inform the principal thereof.

MALTA: In the case of indirect representation, CC Article 1871 states: "When the agent has acted in his own name, the principal cannot maintain an action against those with whom the agent has contracted, nor the latter against the principal. In any such case, however, the agent is directly bound towards the person with whom he has contracted as if the matter were his own." Thus if the agent has acted in his own name, the third party would be directly related to the agent and not to the principal. From this it follows that the agent probably need not disclose the identity of the third party to the principal.

NETHERLANDS: From CC Article 7:420 paragraph (3) it follows (a contrario) that the general rule duty of the principal to inform the principal does not imply that when the contract is one for indirect representation, the agent is in normal circumstances required to inform the principal about the identity of the third party. Cf. Tekst & Commentaar/Castermans/Krans, Comment 2 to CC Article 7:403 and Comment 4 to CC Article 7:420. Such an obligation exists, however, in the situations mentioned in CC Article 7:420 paragraphs (1) and (2). These situations pertain to cases of indirect representation where the agent that has concluded in contract in his own name with a third party and subsequently does not perform his obligations towards the principal or becomes insolvent, or where the third party does not perform his obligations under the prospective contract towards the agent. In these cases, under CC Article 7:420 the principal may bring about a transfer of the rights of the agent towards the third party by giving a written statement to this extent to both the agent and the third party (the third party may in cases of non-performance of the agent towards the third party or in cases of insolvency of the third party do the same, CC Article 7:421 indicates). In order to be able to exercise these rights, the principal of course needs to be aware of the identity of the third party. CC Article 7:420 paragraph (3) requires the agent to disclose that identity in the cases mentioned.

POLAND: A duty to inform about the identity of third party is not regulated in the CC provisions on mandate. The parties may decide to include such a duty in the contract, otherwise the agent is not obligated to do so.

SLOVAKIA: In commercial relationships, in the case of indirect representation, after the execution of a certain affair, the commission agent must provide the principal with a report in which the agent names the person with whom the contract was concluded.

SPAIN: Whether the agent should or should not give notice of the identity of the third party will depend on the nature of the relationship. There is no specific rule obliging the agent to reveal the third party's identity in Spanish law.

SWEDEN: In case of civil commission the agent has a duty to inform about the identity of the third party. In case of trade commission the agent has no duty to inform about the identity of the third party unless the principal is to take over claims against the third party due to e.g. delay of the third party or the bankruptcy of the agent, see KommL Article 7.

No answer received: AUSTRIA, DENMARK, FINLAND, GREECE, HUNGARY, PORTUGAL, SCOT-LAND.

Chapter 4:
Directions and changes

Section 1:
Directions

Article 4:101: Directions given by the principal

(1) The principal is entitled to give directions to the agent.
(2) The agent must follow directions by the principal.
(3) The agent must warn the principal if the direction:
  (a) has the effect that the performance of the obligations under the mandate contract would become significantly more expensive or take significantly more time than agreed upon in the mandate contract; or
  (b) is inconsistent with the purpose of the mandate contract or may otherwise be detrimental to the interests of the principal.
(4) Unless the principal revokes the direction without undue delay after having been so warned by the agent, the direction is to be regarded as a change of the mandate contract under Article 4:201 (Change of mandate contract).

Comments

A. General idea

This Article indicates that the principal is the 'master of the contract': the principal may give directions to the agent regarding the way the mandate is to be performed (paragraph (1)) and the agent is required to follow directions given by the principal after the contract is concluded, even if he disagrees with them (paragraph (2)). However, if the agent thinks that the direction is detrimental to the interests of the principal, the agent must warn the principal accordingly (paragraph (3)). Paragraph (4) requires the agent to wait to see whether the principal, after having been warned that the given direction may be detrimental, wants to revoke it and issue a new direction or leave the matter to the agent, or will insist on the direction given. If the principal holds the agent to the direction, the agent must in principle accept that. However, in such a case the mandate contract will be changed in accordance with Article 4:201 (Changes of the mandate contract), implying that the agent may claim additional payment and/or time or damages or terminate the contract for extraordinary and serious reason.

B. Principals right to give a direction

Paragraph (1) of this Article sets out that the principal is entitled to give a direction to the agent as to the way in which the mandate is to be performed.

Illustration 1

In exchange for a commission, Andrew is charged by Benjamin to purchase 1,000 kilograms of wheat from a third party. Before Andrew has had a chance to conclude the sales contract, Benjamin informs him that the wheat is to have a certain quality. Benjamin is entitled to give Andrew such a direction even if the direction could make it more difficult for Andrew to perform the mandate contract.

The principal's right to give a direction follows from the nature of a mandate contract, as is already demonstrated by the definition of a mandate contract in Article 1:102 (Definitions), which indicates that the mandate of the agent consists of the authorisation, initial instructions, and subsequent directions of the principal. A direction may be described as the decisions of the principal given during the mandate relationship as to the performance of the obligations under the mandate contract or the contents of the prospective contract. The right for the principal to give a direction is recognized in all legal systems, although express statutory provisions to this extent exist only in a few Member States.

C. Agents obligation to follow a direction

The principal's right to give a direction to the agent would be meaningless, of course, if the agent were not bound by such a direction. Paragraph (2) therefore sets out as a general rule that the agent is required to follow the direction. A failure to do so would mean that the agent had not properly performed his obligations under the mandate contract.

Illustration 1 (continued)

After having received the direction as to the required quality of the wheat, Andrew may purchase only wheat of that quality. If Andrew nevertheless purchases wheat of a different quality, this would in principle constitute a non-performance, unless this action were covered by Article 3:201 (Acting beyond mandate).

The direction thus changes the mandate granted to the agent, and under Article 3:101 (Obligation to act in accordance with mandate), the agent is required to act in accordance with the amended mandate.

It should be noted that the principle underlying paragraph (2) is accepted in all legal systems. However, this does not mean that the agent may blindly follow a direction given to him. First, the agent may not act illegally or immorally by following the direction. Moreover, restrictions to the agent's obligation to follow a direction may follow from the agent's professional autonomy and deontological rules.

Yet there are differences in the strictness of the obligation to follow the direction. In some legal systems, the agent is even required to follow a direction if the direction implies that the result envisaged by the principal may not be achieved. In other legal systems, the obligation to follow the direction exists only if the direction is 'reasonable' and given in good time.

In this Article, the first, more restrictive, approach is taken, but it is to some extent mitigated by the fact that the agent is required under paragraph (3) to warn the principal why following the direction would have detrimental consequences for the principal, either because it will lead to an adjustment of the price or the time for performance or because the envisaged result may be more difficult to achieve. If the principal is warned that the envisaged result may be more difficult to achieve, in most situations he will change the direction. If he does not revoke the direction, the agent cannot be held liable for non-performance if the end result does not meet the principal's expectations: that merely shows that the agent's warning was correct. This would be different only if the agent, on the basis of the obligation to exercise due skill and care, could be required in the given circumstances to terminate the mandate relationship.

D. Obligation to warn in case of possibly bad directions

Paragraph (3) has the effect of imposing on the agent an obligation to warn the principal if a direction may be detrimental to the principal's interests or lead to an adjustment of the price or of the time for performance.

Illustration 2
Alfredo is first authorised as a real estate agent to sell a house owned by Ursula for a price of € 400,000 or more. Later, Ursula changes the limit to € 450,000, which is clearly above the market price. The consequence of this change is that it will take Alfredo far more time to sell the house, and there is a serious risk that it will not be possible to conclude the prospective contract at all. However, as Ursula may not be aware of the consequences of her direction – as she may not know that the asking price is now above the market price – Alfredo must warn her of those consequences.

Such a duty to warn against possibly bad directions is accepted in all legal systems. Similarly, the agent must warn the principal if performance of the mandate contract in accordance with the principal's instructions brings about significant expenses, extra time, etc., and if need be ask for new instructions.

E. Upholding a bad direction leads to change in the contract

If the principal, in spite of having been warned that a direction is unreasonable, does not revoke it within a reasonable time, then paragraph (4) indicates that he is considered to have made a change to the mandate contract. The consequences of such a change are regulated in Article 4:201 (Changes of the mandate contract). These consequences include a proportionate adjustment of the price and time for performance and damages, but also the agent's right to terminate the mandate contract for extraordinary and serious reason.

F. Nomination of designated person performing the mandate

A direction may also consist of the nomination of a specific person to perform the mandate contract. In this case, the agent is required to have the contract performed by that specific person, e.g. an employee who is renowned for his specific expertise.

Illustration 3
Hans is the victim of a traffic accident. He engages the law firm of Lockheart/Gardner to handle his case. Later, he is informed that Alicia Florrick, an associate lawyer at Lockheart/Gardner, specialises in this type of case. Hans orders Lockheart/Gardner to appoint Alicia to the case. Lockheart/Gardner is required to follow this direction.

If the person indicated by the principal is not available, the agent must warn the principal thereof. Similarly, if the nominated person is not competent to perform the task, or if her involvement would cost significantly more time or lead to a higher price, the principal must be warned thereof. As with other directions, paragraph (4) provides that if the principal does not change the direction after having been warned, the direction is regarded as a change of the contract and the contract must be performed by the person indicated in the direction.

G. Revocation without undue delay

Paragraph (4) indicates that the principal may revoke the direction 'without undue delay' after having been warned. This implies that the principal must be given the time needed to determine his reaction to the warning. In the meantime, the agent must await the principal's decision.

Illustration 4
Gabriela requests Susan to buy Peruvian artefacts from the Inca era at an auction in Madrid for € 1,000 apiece. Shortly after Susan arrives in Madrid, Gabriela changes her mind and asks Susan to attend a similar auction in Barcelona. If Gabriela may not know that Susan is already in Madrid, Susan must let her know that by changing the mandate Susan will incur additional costs that are to be compensated by Gabriela. Gabriela must be given some time to make up her mind whether she will insist on Susan attending the Barcelona auction or whether she may attend the auction in Madrid after all. However, if there is no time to contact Gabriela because the auction in Madrid is about to start and Susan has good reasons to assume that Gabriela is not aware of the relevant facts, Susan may be allowed to attend the Madrid auction under Articles 3:202 (Excess of power) and 4:104 (No time to ask or wait for direction).

H. No obligation to give a direction

The present Article does not introduce an obligation for the principal to give a direction. This does not mean that the principal may never be under such an obligation. To the contrary, such an obligation may arise from the contract itself or when the principal is requested by the agent to give a direction (Article 4:102 (Request for a direction). In these cases, the obligation to give a direction follows from Article 2:101 paragraph (2)(b) (Obligation to co-operate). A failure to provide such a direction would then be a non-performance by the principal of his obligations under the contract, requiring the principal to compensate the agent for any damage resulting from the failure to give a direction. Moreover, the remedies of Article 4:103 (Consequences of failure to give a direction) will be available to the agent, entitling the agent to base performance upon the expectations, preferences, and priorities the principal could reasonably expect to have.

I. Relation to the Principles of European Law and the Draft Common Frame of Reference

This Article mirrors that of Article IV.D. – 4:101 DCFR (Directions given by principal).

J. Character of the rule

This Article constitutes a default rule from which the parties may derogate.

K. Remedies

If the agent does not follow a direction of the principal or fails to warn the principal of a risk stemming from the direction, he breaches one of his contractual obligations towards the principal. This entitles the principal to claim damages or to terminate the mandate contract for non-performance.

Comparative Notes

1. Right for principal to give direction

The principal is entitled to give the agent directions as to the performance of the mandate contract in all legal systems, with the possible exception of POLAND if this power was not granted to the principal in the original mandate contract. Express statutory provisions to this extent exist, however, only in ESTONIA, GERMANY, and ITALY. In other legal systems, the principal's right to do so is simply derived from the agent's obligation to obey the principal's instructions.

2. Obligation for agent to follow direction

In all legal systems, again with the possible exception of POLAND, the agent is in principle required to follow the instructions given by the principal, unless this would require the agent to act illegally or if the direction may be considered immoral. Moreover, restrictions to the agent's obligation to follow a direction may follow from the agent's professional autonomy and deontological rules.

In FRANCE, an agent who is not a professional is required to follow the direction even if this could lead to a failure in the performance of the mandate contract; a professional agent, however, is expected to inform the principal of the risks.

In AUSTRIA, THE NETHERLANDS, PORTUGAL, and SWEDEN, the obligation to follow directions applies only to reasonable directions, but the agent is required to inform the principal thereof if he does not want to follow a direction; he must then await new instructions unless there is an imminent danger.

3. Duty to warn for bad direction

When the performance of the mandate contract in accordance with the principal's instructions entails a risk, in particular if by following the direction the agent might not be able to achieve the result envisaged by the principal, the agent must warn the principal thereof in all legal systems. Similarly, the agent must warn the principal if performance of the mandate contract in accordance with the principal's instructions brings about significant expenses, extra time, etc.; the agent must warn the principal thereof and ask for new instructions in BULGARIA, DENMARK, and GREECE. The agent must wait for new instructions unless there is imminent danger in AUSTRIA, ESTONIA, GERMANY, GREECE, and HUNGARY.

4. Revocation of direction

After having received a warning, the principal is obviously entitled to change a direction. More generally, the principal is entitled to revoke a direction in most legal systems. However, under certain conditions this may be different if the agent has already started to perform the contract in DENMARK, POLAND, and SLOVAKIA.

National Notes

1. Right for principal to give direction

AUSTRIA: The principal may give the agent directions. Restrictions to the principal's right to give directions may, however, follow from the professional agent's qualifications, e.g. concerning the solicitor's tactics during legal proceedings (OGH in ZBl 1928/3; Rummel/Rummel/Strasser, Article 1009 Rz 14; Schwimann/ Apathy, Article 1009 Rz 13).

BULGARIA: In the Bulgarian law of obligations, there is no explicit rule granting the principal the right to give directions to the agent. Nevertheless, in Bulgarian legal doctrine the existence of such a right is deemed derived from the counter obligation of the agent to act in accordance with the principal's instructions. These instructions may be given either initially, at the time of conclusion of the mandate contract, or subsequently (Голева, Облигационно право, p. 237; Любен Василев, Облигационно право, p. 24). The subsequent directions are not expected to neither significantly alter the given mandate nor make its performance burdensome for the agent (Меворах/Лиджи/Фархи, III, p. 119).

ENGLAND: Since the agent acts not on his own behalf but on behalf of the principal, the latter will give instructions to the agent. Such instructions must be reasonable.

ESTONIA: The principal is entitled to give instructions to the agent as to the performance of the mandate agreement (LOAEst Article 621 paragraph (1)).

GERMANY: The principal's right to give directions to the representative is expressly laid down in CC Article 665.

IRELAND: There is no such express right at common law but in effect this right exists because an agent must obey his principal's lawful instructions.

ITALY: According to Italian law, the principal is entitled to give the agent instructions and directions to be followed in executing the mandate (CC Article 1711) as the agent acts in principal's account.

NETHERLANDS: According to CC Article 7:402 paragraph (1), the agent is held to obey timely and well considered directions regarind the performance of the contract. This stipulation seems to imply that the principal is allowed to give the agent directions. The parties may exclude the principal's right to do so, cf. Van Neer-Van den Broek, Comment to CC Article 7:402, no. 1.

POLAND: It is not clear whether the agent is bound by the principal's directions given after the mandate contract has been signed, unless the mandate contract provides for such directions.

SCOTLAND: It goes without saying that the principal has a right to provide instructions.

SLOVAKIA: The principal is entitled to give directions to the agent as to the performance of the mandate contract.

SPAIN: There is no provision within the rules on mandate in the CC which states as such that the principal is entitled to give instructions. However, such a right for the principal can be inferred from CC Article 1719, which imposes on the agent the obligation to follow the instructions of the principal.

SWEDEN: The principal has a right as well as a duty to give directions in order for the agent to be able to perform in accordance with the mandate contract.

No answer received: BELGIUM, DENMARK, FINLAND, FRANCE, GREECE, HUNGARY, MALTA, POR-TUGAL.

2. Obligation for agent to follow direction

AUSTRIA: The agent has to comply with reasonable instructions (CC Article 1009; Comm.C Article 385 paragraph (1); Comm.C Article 408; Rummel/Rummel/Strasser, Article 1009 Rz 14; Straube/Griss, Article 385 Rz 1. The agent is required to follow directions by the principal even if these make his task more difficult to fulfill (Rummel/Rummel/Strasser, Article 1009 Rz 14; Schwimann/Apathy, Article 1009 Rz 8). The agent must inform the principal if he does not or will not follow the direction (OGH in EvBl 1959/261; Rummel/Rummel/Strasser, Article 1009 Rz 16; ZAS 1985, 170), especially when the agent, by following the direction, may not achieve the result envisaged by the principal (OGH in EvBl 1959/261; Rummel/Rummel/Strasser, Article 1009 Rz 16; ZAS 1985, 170). He has to wait for the principal's decision and to comply with the new instructions or cancel the contract for mandate (Schwimann/Apathy, Article 1009 Rz 4; Straube/Griss, Article 385 Rz 1). In case of imminent danger he may disregard the directions (Schwimann-Apathy, Article 1009 Rz 13; Straube/Griss, Article 385 Rz 2.). A professional agent's qualifications may set a limit to the principal's authority to give directions, e.g. concerning the solicitor's tactics during legal proceedings (OGH in ZBl 1928/3; Rummel/Rummel/Strasser, Article 1009 Rz 14; Schwimann/Apathy, Article 1009 Rz 13).

BELGIUM: As a part of the agent's general duty to perform the mandate faultless, the agent is required to follow the principal's instructions (Wéry, p. 144). A distinction is made between an imperative and a facultative mandate. In case of an imperative mandate, the principal has given precise instructions on the way the mandate contract has to be performed. Imperative instructions must be followed carefully. As a rule no deviation is permitted. Only unforeseen circumstances can permit the agent or even oblige him to deviate from the instructions (De Page, p. 405; Paulus & Boes, p. 90; Wéry, p. 146). A facultative mandate keeps silent on the way the mandate contract has to be performed. Such a mandate must be performed in the best interests of the principal, taking into account the nature of the act, the circumstances of the case and the customs.

BULGARIA: As a general rule, the agent is obliged to follow the directions of the principal. However, in some cases he is entitled to refuse to comply with the subsequent directions and even to terminate the mandate contract for the reason of disagreement with these directions. For instance, when he has a reasonable ground to disagree with the new instructions or they are too burdensome or even dangerous for him (Голева, Облигационно право, p. 237; Любен Василев, Облигационно право, p. 24; Касабова, ТП, 2006, p. 162). Furthermore, the agent is also allowed to refuse performance of illegal or immoral directions of the principal (Меворах/Лиджи/Фархи, III, p. 22).

DENMARK: In general, the agent must follow each kind of (legal) directions given by the principal on how to perform the contract. This is a consequence of the agent's being 'subordinate' to the principal. If the agent does not want to follow the instruction given by the principal, he must immediately give the principal notice in this respect.

ENGLAND: The agent must always act in the principal's best interest. As a result, the agent is under a general duty to follow the instructions given by the principal. However, the agent is not obliged to follow instructions which would require him to act illegally *(Cohen v Kittell* (1889) 22 QBD 680). Moreover, the agent is under a duty to warn the principal of any risks and dangers inherent to such instructions. The duty of a professional agent to obey instructions can also be limited by rules of conduct of a given profession and cannot be required to perform acts which are contrary to such rules *(Hawkins v Pearse* (1903) 9 Com Cas 87). If the agent fails to perform the terms, he can be liable for damages for breach *(Turpin v Bilton* (1843) 5 Man & G 455). The rule is strict and the agent will be liable for not following the instructions even if the agent thought he was acting in the best interest of the principal *(Volkers v Midland Doherty Ltd* (1985) 17 DLR (4th) 343). However, the rule of strict performance can be limited if an actual implied authority allows the agent some discretion. If there is such an actual implied authority, the agent may have a duty to warn the principal of any risks or dangers which are inherent to the instructions, i.e. that the principal may suffer loss if the agent follows such instructions. The agent may also have a fiduciary obligation to warn the principal *(Clark Boyce v Mouat* [1994] 1 AC 428).

ESTONIA: The principal is entitled to give instructions to the agent as to the performance of the mandate agreement (LOAEst Article 621 paragraph (1)).The agent is generally bound by the instructions of his principal (LOAEst Article 621 paragraph (1)). It will not make a difference if the agent, by following the direction, may not achieve the result envisaged by the principal. However, the principal is not allowed to give specific instructions concerning the manner or conditions of performance of the duties of the agent in the case where the agent is expected to perform his duties based on his specific professional skills or abilities (LOAEst Article 621 paragraph (1)). In that case, the agent is free to decide on the specifics of his performance. In all other cases the agent may deviate from the instructions of the principal only if adherence to the instructions of the principal would be likely to cause unfavourable consequences for the principal (in which case the agent shall comply with the instructions only after he has called the principal's attention to such consequences and if the principal fails to modify the instructions; LOAEst Article 621 paragraph (3)). In all cases where the agent wishes to deviate from the instructions of the principal, he shall inform the principal thereof and wait for his decision, except if a delay would be likely to cause unfavourable consequences for the principal and if it may be presumed under the circumstances that the principal will approve of the deviation.

FINLAND: The agent is usually required to follow the principal's directions (Hemmo, Sopimusoikeus I, p. 519). The agent is not required to follow directions if they are illegal or against good practice (e.g. if the directions are harmful for a third party). In some cases, e.g. where the principal is a consumer and in any practice of lawyers, the agent is not generally entitled to follow unreasonable directions. A lawyer is required, or at least entitled, to withdraw from the mandate contract if the principal continuously gives unlawful or unreasonable directions. The agent should inform the principal if he is not going to follow the directions.

FRANCE: In the case of a mandate contract, the agent is obliged to comply with the instructions given by the principal, whether given at the time of conclusion of the mandate contract or subsequently. If the instructions given by the principal to the agent result in a possible failure of the performance of the mandate, the agent is nonetheless required to follow such instructions, but in the case of a professional agent, the latter will be required, in order to satisfy its duty of advice, to inform the principal about such risks. The sole limit is when the directions given by the principal are contrary to law.

GERMANY: The agent is required to follow directions by the principal (CC Article 665). He must always inform the principal before deviating from directions, unless time does not permit this as 'danger' lies ahead. The agent will only be allowed to ignore directions if he may assume that the principal would tolerate this step if he knew of the circumstances. If the principal (after having been advised and warned) insists on a direction that the agent considers to be inappropriate (or even stupid), the agent has the choice between following it or renouncing the contract. He may not impose his own assessment of the situation upon the principal.

GREECE: In case of a mandate contract, Greek legal theory and court practice distinguish between binding and indicative directions. The agent is obliged to strict compliance with binding directions from the principal, even if the former has doubts about the necessity of those directions or if the performance of the mandate requires the specific knowledge and experience of the agent (CA Athens decision no. 10148/1987, EllDni 1988, 353). With regard to indicative directions, the agent is free to make his own decisions, express his doubts about the necessity of the directions and give advice to the principal. Furthermore the agent is required to deviate from the limits set in the mandate, if such a deviation is required by good faith (Georgiadis/Stathopoulos/Karasis, CC Article 717 no. 4). The duty of the agent to notify the principal about deviation from the limits set in the mandate is regulated in CC Article 717: 'An agent may only deviate from the limits set in the mandate if he found himself in the impossibility to notify the principal and it is at the same time obvious that the principal would have allowed the deviation if he had knowledge of the circumstances that prompted such deviation.' From that rule it is implied that if it is possible for the agent to notify the principal about the intended deviation, the former is required to wait for further directions from the latter for the performance of the mandate. If in contrary it is impossible for the agent to notify the principal about the deviation from the directions, the agent is required after the performance of the mandate to inform the principal about the necessity of the deviation and the impossibility to notify him (CC Article 718); otherwise, the principal may claim damages (CC Article 714; CA Athens decision no. 10148/1987, EllDni 1988, 353). In case of a gratuitous mandate contract, the agent is required to follow the directions given by the principal even if that would make his task more difficult to fulfil and would cause more expenses for the principal, but may be subject to a duty to warn the principal.

HUNGARY: According to CC Article 474 paragraph (2), '[a]n agent must fulfil the agency according to the instructions and interests of the principal'. CC Article 476 establishes that '[i]f the principal issues imprudent or incompetent instructions, the agent shall call the principal's attention to the matter. If the principal insists on the instructions despite the warning, he shall be liable for the damages sustained on account of the instructions'. Moreover, CC Article 477 paragraph (2) establishes that '[t]he agent shall be entitled to depart from the principal's instructions only if it is essential for the principal's interest and if there is no time to notify the principal in advance. In such a case the principal shall be notified without delay' (Supreme Court Pfv. VIII. 20.107/2006, in BH2006. 321) In case of commission agency, CC Article 508 establishes that '[i]f the commission agent concludes a sales contract under better conditions for the principal as defined in the commission mandate contract, the benefit originating therefrom shall be due to the principal. If the commission agent makes a sale for a price below the one specified in the commission mandate contract, he shall reimburse the principal for the difference, unless he is able to prove that the sales contract could not have been concluded at the stipulated price, that by making the sale he saved the principal from losses, and that he was not able to notify the principal in time. If the commission agent substantially departs from the conditions stipulated in the commission mandate contract, the principal shall be entitled to reject the sales contract, unless the commission agent has effected purchase at a higher price than stipulated but agreed to reimburse the difference.'

IRELAND: At common law, an agent must obey his principal's lawful instructions. An agent is therefore not obliged to follow instructions which would require the agent to act illegally.

Moreover, a professional agent may be under a duty to warn the principal of any risks/dangers inherent in the instructions given.

ITALY: As a rule, the agent is required to follow the directions given by the principal. In the cases where a departure from the said directions may be justified (e.g. if the agent, by following the principal's directions, may not achieve the result envisaged by the principal), the agent must inform the principal of his intention and explain the reasons justifying a departure from the principal's instructions. In particular, the agent has to inform the principal of the (new) circumstances that may justify the extinction or an alteration of the contract of representation (CC Article 1710 paragraph (2)). See Cass. no. 12647/1995, Foro it., 1996, I, 544; Cass. no. 2387/1997, Corriere giur., 1997, 903, with comments by Stella, Contratti, 1997, 559, with comments by Zappata.

MALTA: The agent is required to follow the directions that the principal gives him in all situations. This can be presumed from the fact that the agent must inform the principal of the progress of the transactions in concluding the contract. In fact the agent may be found liable for negligence if he does not follow the directions of the principal.

NETHERLANDS: According to CC Article 7:402 paragraph (1), the agent is held to obey timely and well considered directions regarding the performance of the contract. Such an obligation does not exist where following the direction would go against the professional autonomy of the agent, in particular where deontological rules demand the agent to act in a particular way. Cf. Van Neer-Van den Broek, Comment to CC Article 7:402, no. 1-2.

POLAND: The agent should follow the directions of the principal if any directions are given. However, it is not clear whether the agent is bound by the principal's directions given after the mandate contract has been signed, unless the mandate contract provides for such directions. If there are no directions given the agent is free to choose how to best carry out his duty.

PORTUGAL: The general principle is, that the agent must follow the client's instructions while carrying out the mandate (CC Article 1161 lit (a)). However, the agent may disregard or deviate from the instructions insofar as it would be reasonable, from an objective pint of view, that, had the client duly known the specific circumstances and reasons supporting the agent's decision, he would have agreed to that course of action (CC Article 1162). However, in some circumstances, the agent may enjoy some degree of autonomy or discretion as to how should the mandate be carried out. For instance, as regards attorneys-at-law, their autonomy in the relationship with the client is safeguarded by Articles 84 and 92, Lei 15/2005 of 26 January.

SCOTLAND: One of the terms of the mandate contract (whether express or implied by law) will normally be that the principal has the power to give directions as to how the obligations under it are to be carried out. So a distinction has to be drawn between a permissible direction and an impermissible change. Describing gratuitous mandate, Erskine stated that "… the mandatary's (agent's) most fundamental duty is to follow the mandant's (principal's) instructions" (Erskine, III,3,35; Bell, Principles, paragraph 220). Erskine also indicated that an agent was bound obey the principal's instructions even if the agent considers that an alternative course of action would be 'more rational.' (Erskine, III,3,35). In modern agency law, as in gratuitous mandate, the agent's principal duty is to follow his instructions (Macgregor, paragraph 84). It is likely therefore that the agent would not have the right to depart from the principal's instructions simply because he considered that they were unlikely to achieve the desired object of the agency relationship. Failure to follow the principal's instructions would be a breach by the agent rendering the agent liable to the principal in damages. The agent will not, however, be liable to the principal for any losses suffered by the principal as a direct result of the ambiguity of the principal's instructions (Macgregor, paragraph 84; *Ireland v Livingston* (1872) LR 5 HL 395).

SLOVAKIA: The agent is required to follow the principal's directions. For civil relations, CC Article 725 indicates that the agent may diverge from the principal's instructions only if this is required by the latter's interest and if he cannot obtain the principal's consent in time, otherwise he shall be liable for damage. In commercial relations, the same is true. However, in such a case, the agent is not allowed to depart from the principal's instructions, if this is prohibited by the mandate or by the principal, as follows from Comm.C Article 567 paragraph (3). The agent has to inform the principal about all matters that may influence the principal to change his directions (Comm.C Article 567 paragraph (2)).

SPAIN: The agent is obliged to follow the instructions of the principal (CC Article 1719). These can be given at the time the contract is concluded or later on (Hernández Gil, p. 461 and 473). According to STS 26 May 1964, instructions can be mandatory, which means that the agent is compelled to follow them and that he cannot deviate from them even when acting in the interests of the principal would require modifying them, or non-mandatory, which are those which leave very much discretion to the agent to act according to the interests of the principal. However, the agent is not bound to follow instructions when that ought to be regarded as a change in the content of the mandate. In such a case, the agent may terminate the contract (CC Article 1735).

SWEDEN: The agent is required to follow the client's directions but only if they are reasonable. All circumstances of the case should be considered when determining whether directions are reasonable or not. The client's directions must be in accordance with good business practice. Directions contrary to law are considered unreasonable, see Tiberg/Dotevall, p. 117. Where the instructions are to be considered reasonable, the agent is required to follow them even if this makes his task somewhat more difficult.

3. Duty to warn for bad direction

AUSTRIA: The agent must inform the principal if he does not or will not follow the direction (OGH in EvBl 1959/261; Rummel/Rummel/Strasser, Article 1009 Rz 16; ZAS 1985, 170), especially when the agent, by following the direction, may not achieve the result envisaged by the principal (OGH in EvBl 1959/261; Rummel/Rummel/Strasser, Article 1009 Rz 16; ZAS 1985, 170). He has to wait for the principal's decision and to comply with the new instructions or cancel the contract for mandate (Schwimann/Apathy, Article 1009 Rz 4; Straube/Griss, Article 385 Rz 1). The agent is required to follow directions by the principal even if these make his task more difficult to fulfil (Rummel/Rummel/Strasser, Article 1009 Rz 14; Schwimann/Apathy, Article 1009 Rz 8). Where the professional agent does not want to follow a direction on account of his professional responsibility, he is required to warn the principal thereof (Straube/Griss, Article 384 Rz 3).

BELGIUM: When an important event (un fait majeur) intervenes, the agent is obliged to inform the principal in advance to enable the principal to change or revoke his instructions (De Page, p. 405; Paulus & Boes, p. 90; Wéry, p. 146-147). A professional agent may not follow the instructions blindly. When the performance of the mandate according to the principal's instructions entails a risk, the agent has a preliminary duty of advice and information (CFI Mons 9 May 1996, RGAR 1998, n° 12.911; CFI Antwerpen 6 October 1992, RW 1994-95, 885; Herbots et al., TPR 2002, n° 906; Wéry, p. 147).

BULGARIA: In Bulgarian contract law, every mandate contract is considered concluded under the implied condition that the agent is obliged to act in accordance with interests of the principal, in the best possible manner under the existing circumstances (Меворах/Лиджи/Фархи, III, p. 120). Hence, the agent is deemed obliged to warn the principal that the observance of the given directions will not result in concluding of the prospective contract or will bring about significant expenses or extra time, etc., and to ask for new instructions (Меворах/Лиджи/Фархи, III, p. 121). If the principal does not revoke the bad directions, the agent has two options: (a) to continue the contractual performance following these bad directions; (b) to terminate the mandate contract (Голева, Облигационно право, p. 237).

DENMARK: In general, the agent must follow each kind of (legal) direction given by the principal on how to perform the contract. If the principal insists, the agent must at any rate warn the principal of the consequences of his upholding his view. If the task proves to be (essentially) more difficult than initially envisaged by the parties, the agent will normally be entitled to claim a higher price for his representing the principal; the terms of the contract will likely be renegotiated under such circumstances. If no such renegotiation takes place, the agent as a *naturalia negotii* must warn the principal that the costs will be higher if he has to follow the new instructions.

ENGLAND: As mentioned previously, the agent is not obliged to follow instructions which would require the agent to act illegally. Moreover, the agent is under a duty to warn the principal of any risks and dangers inherent to such instructions, especially if the agent can be said to have some discretion due to an actual implied authority. The agent may also have a fiduciary obligation to do so *(Clark Boyce v Mouat* [1994] 1 AC 428). Finally, the obligation of a professional agent to follow instructions may be limited by the professional rules of conduct of the given profession of the agent. If the agent has a personal interest in the task he is asked to perform, the agent is under a fiduciary duty to disclose this personal interest to the principal before performing the authority *(Aberdeen Rly Co v Blaikie Bros* (1854) 1 Macq 461 at 471, HL; *Lucifero v Castell* (1887) 3 TLR 371; *De Bussche v Alt* (1878) 8 Ch D 286).

ESTONIA: The agent is required to follow directions by the principal. In case the agent has another interest in the contract besides the entitlement to the price, the principal may grant him an irrevocable authority to conclude the prospective contract (or another juridical act) in his name (GPCCA Article 126 paragraph (2)). In an internal relationship between the agent and the principal it will most likely be agreed (either explicitly or implicitly) that the agent is not bound by the principal's directions as far as these could interfere with the specific interests of the agent in the prospective contract. The agent must warn the principal if a direction could have an apparent adverse effect to the interests of the principal (LOAEst Article 621 paragraph (3)).

FINLAND: The agent should warn the principal for a bad direction. This is especially the case if the agent is a professional actor, who has wide obligations to provide information and evaluate the interests of the other party (HD 2007:27, HD 2001:128, HD 1999:19, HD 1999:80). If the directions are not withdrawn and they are still within the limits of the agreed mandate, the agent is generally required to follow them, even if it makes the fulfilment of the contract somewhat more difficult. This, however, depends somewhat on the type of the mandate. Unless expressly agreed otherwise or when the circumstances do not show otherwise, the agent is not entitled to an additional price for extra work. The question of price is, however, somewhat unclear and depends highly on circumstances. The agent is usually required to inform the principal that the price will be higher (as described above, this often means that the agreement has to be altered).

FRANCE: The agent is required to comply with the instructions of the principal. Even if the agent has an interest in the performance of the mandate (particularly in the case of the so called 'mandate of common interest'), the agent may not rely on such situation to avoid performance of the mandate in accordance with instructions given by the principal. If the agent considers that he has no interest in following the principal's instructions, he may simply decide to renounce the mandate. If the termination causes loss to the principal, the latter may claim damages from the agent (CC Article 2007), but damages may not be due, however, if continuation of the mandate contract would cause serious loss to the agent. If the principal's instructions might lead to the failure of the mandate, the agent is nonetheless required to follow such instructions, but he has to inform the principal in order to satisfy his duty to give advice as a professional agent. On the basis of a general obligation of fair dealing, which applies to the agent, the latter should inform the principal of any possible additional expense involved by new instructions, and ensure that the parties agree on such additional expenses. The French courts have accepted that the remuneration set out in the mandate contract may be revised if the mandate carried out does not correspond to the remuneration initially envisaged.

GERMANY: The agent may have to warn the principal if a direction is problematic. Existence and scope of such an implied duty depend upon the circumstances of the case, primarily on the particular expertise of the agent. Courts have imposed a duty to warn e.g. on attorneys and banks (see Palandt/Sprau, Article 665 no. 9).

GREECE: In case of a gratuitous mandate contract, the agent is required to follow the directions given by the principal even if that would make his task more difficult to fulfil and would cause more expenses for the principal. However, the agent is required by good faith (CC Article 288) to warn the principal that the expenses will be higher if he follows his directions. If the agent decides not to comply with the directions of the principal the former is obliged to inform the latter of non-compliance with the directions. Due to the gratuitous character of the mandate, the question of the right of the agent to a higher price arises only in the case of agent services offered by a lawyer. In such a case, due to the lawyer's specific knowledge and experience, he is required by good faith (CC Article 288) to warn the principal that he is not obliged to follow the principal's directions and if he does so the price will be higher.

HUNGARY: The contract of agency has been modelled so that the principal remains the master of the affair all the time, whatever happens. According to CC Article 474 paragraph (2), '[a]n agent must fulfil the agency according to the instructions and interests of the principal'. The obligation to follow the directions of the principal does not vary if the agent, by following the direction, may not achieve the result envisaged by the principal (i.e. the conclusion of the prospective contract), but CC Article 476 establishes that '[i]f the principal issues imprudent or incompetent instructions, the agent shall call the principal's attention to the matter. If the principal insists on the instructions despite the warning, he shall be liable for the damages sustained on account of the instructions'. On the other hand, CC Article 478 paragraph (2) prescribes that '[t]he principal shall be entitled to reduce the remuneration or refuse to pay it if he is able to prove that success was not achieved in part or in whole for a reason for which the agent is responsible'. Furthermore, '[t]he agent shall be entitled to depart from the principal's instructions only if it is essential for the principal's interest and if there is no time to notify the principal in advance. In such a case the principal shall be notified without delay' (CC Article 477 paragraph (2); Supreme Court Pfv. VIII. 22.351/2005, in EBH2006. 1410).

IRELAND: A professional agent may be under a duty to warn the principal of any risks/dangers inherent in the instructions given.

ITALY: The fact that the agent has another interest in the contract besides his entitlement to the price does not justify a departure from the principal's guidelines which is detrimental to his interests. The agent has to inform the principal timely about the new and different circumstances that could make his task more difficult to fulfil and, if so agreed, he could be entitled to a higher price (CC Article 1710). The agent, moreover, has to inform the principal timely if he intends not to follow the directions received in order to obtain the principal's authorisation. According to the good faith principle the agent has to warn the principal that the price will be higher if he follows the directions. The agent would otherwise be liable for non-performance because of exceeding the limits of his mandate (CC Article 1711). See CFI Milano, 16 February 1989, Giur.it., 1989, I, 2, 628.

MALTA: It can be presumed that although the agent should follow the directions of the principal and call the witness, however if the agent thinks that this could be counter-productive for his principal he should warn him. In fact the agent should always execute his task with the diligence of a *bonus pater familias*.

NETHERLANDS: If the agent is reasonably not willing to perform the mandate contract according to the principal's directions, he may terminate the contract for an extraordinary and serious reason if the principal nevertheless keeps to the directions given to the agent (CC Article 7:402 paragraph (2)). It would stand to reason that a refusal by the agent to comply with a direction should not only be communicated to the principal, but also explained. On the basis of the reasons stated by the agent the principal can then change his mind. From this, a limited duty to warn may be deduced in case the agent does not want to follow the direction. A more general duty to warn for a bad direction may follow from the agent's general duty of care under CC Article 7:401. This duty of care can in extreme cases even require the agent to terminate the contract if the principal continues to require the agent to follow the bad direction.

POLAND: A duty to warn for a bad direction could be derived from the general duty of taking due care in contractual relations, cf. CC Article 355.

PORTUGAL: The agent must promptly inform the client of any decision not to follow the directions, as well as the reasons why he did not follow them (CC Article 1161 lit (c)).

SCOTLAND: Because there are very few authorities on the *procuratory in rem suam,* the Scottish example of an agency in which the agent has an interest, it is impossible to say whether in agencies of that type the general rule still applies, namely that the agent remains bound to follow his principal's instructions even where the agent thinks that they are unlikely to achieve the desired outcome (Erskine, III,3,35). Given the agent's interest in the outcome, it seems logical that the agent should have the ability to dictate the manner in which the mandate contract is performed. If completion of the agent's tasks have proved more problematic than anticipated by both parties, a higher fee might become payable through re-negotiation of the mandate contract. Whether, in terms of the existing contractual relationship, a higher fee might automatically become payable is an issue which would depend upon the interpretation of the contractual terms in question. A higher fee might, for example, be payable where the contract provides that the agent will be entitled to a 'reasonable' fee, or a fee calculated in accordance with a professional scale.

SLOVAKIA: The requirement of the agent to act in the interest of the principal and the good faith principle should be the ground for the agent's duty to warn principal provided his instructions are bad. If the principal does not change his instructions, agent will be obliged to follow them or to terminate the contract.

SPAIN: The agent must warn the principal if the following of a direction is problematic. As far as this direction has and could not have been contemplated by the parties when agreeing on the price, the agent will be entitled to compensation for additional expenses. However, in no case is the agent entitled to proceed against the principal's upholding of the old instructions (Comm.C Article 256). The agent is not bound to follow instructions when that ought to be regarded as a change in the content of the mandate. Finally, the agent may in such a situation withdraw due to good cause (CC Article 1735).

SWEDEN: The agent is required to follow the principal's directions as long as these are not unreasonable. Hence, the agent has to accept to follow directions even if these make his task somewhat more difficult. The agent is entitled to a higher price (additional price) in case the direction involves additional work or if a rise in price is due to circumstances on behalf of the principal and which the agent could not have foreseen at the time of conclusion of the contract. A duty to warn the principal follows from the main duty to act in the interest of the principal.

4. Revocation of direction

AUSTRIA: The principal is entitled to revoke the direction when informed of the consequences (Rummel/Rummel/Strasser, Article 1009 Rz 14; SZ 4/51; Straube/Griss, Article 384 Rz 3).

BELGIUM: The principal may revoke his instructions (Wéry, p. 161).

BULGARIA: Since the principal is considered as 'the master of the mandate contract', he appears to be entitled to revoke the given directions at any time. There is, however, no explicit rule to this extent.

DENMARK: If the agent has not yet revealed the new instructions towards any third party, the principal is entitled to revoke the direction.

ENGLAND: The principal is free to revoke original directions when informed of the consequences of following them.

ESTONIA: The principal is entitled to revoke the direction when warned by the agent.

FINLAND: The principal is entitled to revoke the directions. Where the principal, after having been warned, insists on the direction, the agent is generally required to follow the direction, even if it makes the fulfilment of the contract somewhat more difficult.

FRANCE: The principal may, having been informed of additional costs, cancel the instructions which he had previously given to the agent. He may also revoke the mandate *ad nutum,* under CC Article 2004.

GERMANY: The principal may at any time revoke the direction, otherwise, there would not be a need for an obligation to warn.

GREECE: In case of a gratuitous mandate contract, apart from an irrevocable grant of directions, the directions that the principal has given to the agent are revocable until the performance of the contract has been completed (Georgiadis/Stathopoulos/Karasis, CC Article 717 no. 4). The same applies in case of intermediation.

HUNGARY: The principal remains always the master of the affair and revoke his direction. CC Article 476 prescribes that '[i]f the principal issues imprudent or incompetent instructions, the agent shall call the principal's attention to the matter. If the principal insists on the instructions despite the warning, he shall be liable for the damages sustained on account of the instructions.'

IRELAND: A principal may revoke any directions.

ITALY: As a rule, the principal is entitled to revoke the directions given to the agent if he is informed of new consequences that have an impact thereupon. According to CC Article 1723, '[t]he principal can revoke the mandate but if it was agreed that the mandate should be irrevocable, he is liable for damages, unless revocation is made for a just cause. A mandate which is given also in the interest of the agent or of third persons is not extinguished by revocation by the principal, unless it is otherwise agreed or unless there is a just cause for such revocation; it is not extinguished by the death or supervening incapacity of the principal'. A just cause for revocation may lie in malicious and negligent behaviour of the agent (CC Article 1218) or the fact that he does not respect the instructions received by the principal (CC Article 1711).

MALTA: The principal may revoke the directions given to the agent when he is informed of the consequences. In fact, the principal may revoke the contract for mandate at any moment in time.

NETHERLANDS: The revocation of a direction may be seen as a new direction, which the agent is required to follow if it is given timely and is sensible. Obviously, where the agent had indicated that he was not willing to follow a previous direction and stated his reason for that, this in itself already indicates that the principal is allowed to revoke that direction, in which case the agent may not terminate the contract on the basis of CC Article 7:402 paragraph (2).

In exceptional cases, the agent's duty of care may even imply that the agent is required to terminate the mandate contract if the principal, after having been warned by the agent, does not revoke the direction. Failure to do so would then amount to a breach of the duty of care and thus lead to liability of the agent.

POLAND: The principal is free to give directions when the contract is concluded, it is not clear whether the principal may give new directions or change given direction after the agent has begun to act.

SCOTLAND: There would be nothing to prevent a principal from deciding to revoke his instructions in response to a warning from the agent that his original instructions are unlikely to achieve the desired outcome.

SLOVAKIA: The possibility to revoke the direction depends on the progress of performance and on the possible effects to the third parties.

SPAIN: Although there is no special rule, it is clear that the instructions to be followed are the ones addressed at the time of the contract as well as new instructions given by the principal.

SWEDEN: The principal may revoke a direction by a new direction unless such new direction is unreasonable. The agent is entitled to a higher price (additional price) in case the new direction involves additional work.

No answer received: PORTUGAL

Article 4:102: Request for a direction

(1) The agent must ask for a direction on obtaining information which requires the principal to make a decision pertaining to the performance of the obligations under the mandate contract or the content of the prospective contract.

(2) The agent must ask for a direction if the mandated task is the conclusion of a prospective contract and the mandate contract does not determine whether the mandate is for direct representation or indirect representation.

Comments

A. General idea

In the ideal situation, the agent is perfectly aware of not only the interests of the principal, but also of the principal's preferences with regard to situations not explicitly regulated in the mandate contract. In such an ideal world, parties would not need to consult when unexpected events take place, as the agent would already know what the principal wants him to do.

However, such an ideal world does not exist. The question then is how to deal with such unexpected events. Should the agent ask for instructions, or should the agent act independently on the basis of the existing instructions, taking into account what he may assume that the principal would want him to do based on the existing instructions and the communicated interests of the principal? In the present Article, the former approach is chosen. It indicates that when the agent becomes aware of relevant information for the performance of the mandate contract, he must inform the principal thereof and ask the principal for a direction as to how to react to this new information. Under paragraph (2), the agent is required to inquire whether he is to ask in his own name or in the name of the principal when the parties have not regulated this matter in their contract, be it in writing or tacitly. This provision emphasises, once again, that the principal is the master of the contract, i.e. the party who ultimately determines how the contract is to be performed.

B. Direction as to performance of obligations or as to contents of prospective contract

This Article regulates the situation where the agent has received specific information, either from the principal or from another source, that requires him to change the way in which the mandate contract is performed. This may be because the information has made clear to the agent that it may not be possible to perform the mandate (typically to conclude the prospective contract) as stated or envisaged by the principal at the time of conclusion of the contract, or that the conclusion of the prospective contract may become significantly more expensive or take significantly more time than agreed upon in the mandate contract. Alternatively, the agent may have found out that the conclusion of the prospective contract could damage other interests of the principal of which the agent knows or could reasonably be expected to know. In all of these cases, the agent would need to inform the principal thereof and ask how to deal with the situation at hand.

Illustration 1
Gabriela requests Susan to buy Peruvian artefacts from the Inca era from a private seller in Madrid. When arriving in Madrid, Susan finds out that the seller has put the artefacts for sale at an auction, which may lead to a substantively higher purchase price. Susan must contact Gabriela, inform her of the new developments, and ask her whether to attend the auction and whether Gabriela wishes to amend the maximum price for which Gabriela may buy the artefacts.

Illustration 2
Freddie is charged by Brian to purchase the Aston Martin DB5 that featured in the 1964 James Bond film *Goldfinger* for the amount of £1.4 million. Before Brian is able to buy the car, he is made aware of serious doubts about the originality of the car. Obviously, he needs to consult with Freddie and ask how to proceed.

Illustration 3
Donovan is charged by Evelyne to purchase a specific painting from a private seller. Donovan and Evelyne have agreed that Donovan is to act in his own name when negotiating the contract with the private seller. If the private seller insists on knowing the identity of the buyer for personal reasons, Donovan is required to inform Evelyne hereof and ask for a direction on how to proceed.

It should be noted that the obligation to request a direction emerges irrespective of whether the danger stems from a defect or inconsistency in the mandate of the agent (be it in the mandate contract itself or a subsequent direction) or from the occurrence of other expected or unexpected events. One such event could be the development of the negotiations with the third party. During such negotiations, it can easily be envisaged that the agent may realise that to conclude the prospective contract, it would be necessary to act beyond the mandate. If there is time to contact the principal, the agent is required to do so in order not to breach the contractual obligations, because on the one hand the agent may not exceed the mandate, but on the other hand he is required to act in the best interests of the principal. Paragraph (1) of this Article indicates what the agent then has to do: ask for a direction.

The principal subsequently is required to give such a direction under Article 2:101 (Obligation to co-operate) paragraph (2)(b). A failure to provide such a direction is then regulated in Article 4:103 (Consequences of failure to give a direction).

The most important situation where the agent is required to ask for a direction is when he receives information (either from the principal or from another source) that leads him to believe that he may not be able to conclude the prospective contract as stated or envisaged by the principal at the time of concluding the contract, or that the conclusion of the prospective contract may become significantly more expensive or take significantly more time than agreed upon in the mandate contract. Of course, the same would apply if the conclusion of the prospective contract could damage other interests of the principal that the agent knows about or could reasonably be expected to know about. In this respect, it would not matter whether the danger stems from a defect or inconsistency in the power (be it in the mandate contract itself or a subsequent direction) or from the occurrence of other expected or unexpected events. One such event could of course be the development of the negotiations with the third party. During such negotiations, it can easily be envisaged that the agent realises that to conclude the prospective contract he would have to exceed his power. If there is time to contact the principal, he is required to do so in order not to breach his contractual obligations, because on the one hand he may not exceed his power, but on the other hand he is required to act in the best interests of the principal. Paragraph (1) of this Article indicates what he then has to do: ask for a direction. The principal subsequently is required to give such a direction under Article 2:101(2)(b) (Obligation to co-operate).

C. Direct or indirect representation

Typically the parties to a mandate contract calling for the conclusion of a contract by the agent for the principal indicate expressly or implicitly whether the agent is to act in the agent's own name or in the name of the principal. If that is the case, the agent will be required to act in this manner, as follows from Article 3:101 (Obligation to act in accordance with mandate). It should be remarked that even if the parties have not expressly indicated how the agent is to act, this may follow from custom or usage. In such a case, the parties will have implicitly chosen to follow the rules dictated by custom or usage.

Illustration 4
Samantha commissions her solicitor to appeal a court decision with which she fundamentally disagrees. Obviously, in this case, the solicitor acts in the name of Samantha.

Illustration 5
A principal wants to buy a shipment of cocoa beans on the market. He engages an agent to join in on the bidding on the cocoa beans. It is customary in this particular market for agents to bid in their own name and not to disclose the identity of their principal. If both the agent and the principal are aware of this trade custom and have not explicitly regulated whether the agent is to act in his own name or in the name of the principal,

they are expected to have tacitly agreed to follow the trade custom, thus requiring the agent to act in his own name.

Illustration 6
Paul has commissioned George to negotiate the purchase of the sculpture 'Peace' by the upcoming artist Richard Starkey, without indicating whether to act in Paul's name or in George's own name. If the mandate contract can't be interpreted as providing an answer to how George is to operate, George is required to ask Paul for a direction on this matter.

Only when the parties have neither expressly nor tacitly indicated whether the agent is to act in the name of the principal or in his own name, or that the agent is allowed to determine that himself, does the question arise as to who should determine this. Should the agent then be free to choose how he wishes to perform the contract, or should the default rule then be that he is to act in the principal's or – oppositely – in his own name? In this Article, a third option is chosen: in such a situation, paragraph (2) indicates that the agent must ask for clarification on this point. However, the provision is to be applied only in the rare case where the parties have neither determined the matter expressly or tacitly.

D. Relation to other provisions of these Principles

Under paragraph (1) of this Article, the agent is required to obtain the necessary information from the principal for him to properly perform his obligations towards the principal. When the principal is so asked, he is required to answer such a request for information in accordance with Article 2:101(a) (Obligation to co-operate). This implies that a failure to give a direction constitutes the non-performance of an obligation by the principal. A failure of the principal to give such a direction is sanctioned under Article 4:103 (Consequences of failure to give a direction).

Where the agent has no time to ask or wait for the answer to a request for information or for another direction, he is both allowed and required to act without having obtained the information or direction. This matter is regulated in Article 4:104 (No time to ask or wait for direction).

E. Relation to the Principles of European Law and the Draft Common Frame of Reference

This Article mirrors that of Article IV.D. – 4:103 DCFR (Request for a direction).

F. Character of the rule

This Article constitutes a default rule from which the parties may derogate. In most cases, paragraph (2) will not be applicable as the parties will have determined whether the agent is to act in his own name or in the name of the principal or will have left it to the agent to determine this.

G. Remedies

If the agent does not ask for a direction when he is required to do so under this Article, he breaches one of his contractual obligations towards the principal and is liable for non-performance in accordance with the normal rules for non-performance. If, on the other hand, the principal does not respond to a request for a direction, the principal breaches his obligations under Article 2:101 (Obligation to co-operate) of these Principles. The remedies for this breach are provided in Article 4:103 (Consequences of failure to give a direction) of these Principles and, in so far as the provisions of that Article do not derogate from this, by the general provisions on remedies in Chapters 8 (Non-performance and remedies in general) and 9 PECL (Particular remedies for non-performance).

Comparative Notes

1. Agent's obligation to ask for direction if needed for performance

With the possible exception of POLAND, an obligation for the agent to ask for instructions is recognised in all legal systems. In most legal systems, the obligation is thought to follow from the agent's obligation to act in the interests of the principal, or the agent's obligation of care towards the principal. In SLOVAKIA and SWEDEN, in particular, an obligation to ask for a direction arises if the direction is needed for the agent to properly perform the mandate contract. More specifically, in BELGIUM, BULGARIA, and HUNGARY, the agent may be required to ask for a direction in the case of important unforeseen events or when it becomes apparent that the prospective contract cannot be concluded or cannot be concluded under the conditions previously set by the principal. In ESTONIA, GERMANY, and SWEDEN, the obligation to ask for a direction arises in particular where an existing direction could have adverse effects on the interests of the principal and the agent wants to derogate from the existing direction. In these cases, the requirement to ask for a direction is closely related to the agent's obligation to warn against the negative effects of an existing direction. In ENGLAND, ESTONIA, IRELAND, and MALTA, a more restrictive approach appears to have been accepted: an obligation to ask for a direction is not generally accepted, but the agent may be under an obligation to ask for clarification where the existing directions or instructions are unclear.

2. Agent's obligation to ask for direction whether to act in own name or in name of principal

The legal systems are divided as to whether the agent is to act in his own name or in the name of the principal if the mandate contract is silent on this matter and the principal has not indicated anything at a later moment. In this situation, the agent is free to act in his own name or in the name of the principal in DENMARK, ESTONIA, GERMANY, GREECE, ITALY, THE NETHERLANDS, and SWEDEN. In BULGARIA, the agent is required to act in his own name. This is also true for a commission agent under commercial law in BELGIUM. By contrast, in FINLAND, HUNGARY, MALTA, POLAND, PORTUGAL, and SPAIN, the agent is required to act in the name of the principal in such a case. This is also true for a civil law mandate relationship in BELGIUM. It appears that the agent is not free to choose how to act and would be required to ask the principal for clarification on this matter in AUSTRIA, ENGLAND, FRANCE, IRE-LAND, SCOTLAND, and SLOVAKIA.

National Notes

1. Agent's obligation to ask for direction if needed for performance

BELGIUM: When an important event (un fait majeur) intervenes, the agent is obliged to inform the principal in advance to enable the principal to change or revoke the instructions (De Page, p. 405; Paulus & Boes, p. 90; Wéry, p. 146-147).

BULGARIA: The agent is obliged to act in accordance with interests of the principal, in the best possible manner under the existing circumstances. Therefore, after he has become aware of the fact that the prospective contract cannot be concluded at all or cannot be concluded under the conditions determined by the principal, he is obliged to ask the principal for further directions, unless there is not enough time for new instructions (Меворах/Лиджи/Фархи, III, p. 120-121).

ENGLAND: there does not seem to be any specific case dealing with this specific example. English law only seems to cover the situations when authority given by the principal is ambiguous. In such a situation, any reasonable interpretation of such authority done in good faith by the agent will be binding on the principal, even if this is not what the principal had intended *(Ireland v Livingston* (1872) LR 5 HL 395). It is suggested that since nowadays it is easier to obtain clarification, if the agent fails to do so, he would be liable (Bowstead, para 3.016). In relation to the specific scenario at hand, considering that the agent is under an obligation to exercise skill and care when performing the mandate, and act for the best interest of the principal, should the agent fail to ask directions when direction was needed, he would no doubt be in breach of such obligations

ENGLAND: there does not seem to be any specific case dealing with this specific example. English law only seems to cover the situations when authority given by the principal is ambiguous. In such a situation, any reasonable interpretation of such authority done in good faith by the agent will be binding on the principal, even if this is not what the principal had intended *(Ireland v Livingston* (1872) LR 5 HL 395). It is suggested that since nowadays it is easier to obtain clarification, if the agent fails to do so, he would be liable (Bowstead, para 3.016). In relation to the specific scenario at hand, considering that the agent is under an obligation to exercise skill and care when performing the mandate, and act for the best interest of the principal, should the agent fail to ask directions when direction was needed, he would no doubt be in breach of such obligations

ENGLAND: There does not seem to be any specific case dealing with this specific example. English law only seems to cover the situations when authority given by the principal is ambiguous. In such a situation, any reasonable interpretation of such authority done in good faith by the agent will be binding on the principal, even if this is not what the principal had intended *(Ireland v Livingston* (1872) LR 5 HL 395). It is suggested that since nowadays it is easier to obtain clarification, if the agent fails to do so, he would be liable (Bowstead & Reynolds, paragraph 3.016). In relation to the specific scenario at hand, considering that the agent is under an obligation to exercise skill and care when performing the mandate, and act for the best interest of the principal, should the agent fail to ask directions when direction was needed, he would no doubt be in breach of such obligations.

ESTONIA: No such specific duty is prescribed by law, as far as the agent is under a duty to act in the best interest of the preipal, cf. LOAEst Article 620 paragraph (2), such duty could require the agent to ask, in specific situations, for directions if the interests of the principal are unclear. The agent is under the duty to warn the principle and ask for directions if an existing direction could have an apparent adverse effect to the interests of the principal, see LOAEst Article 621 paragraph (3).

FRANCE: There is no specific duty for agent to ask for direction, but it may result from his general duty to comply with the mandate contract in accordance to the interest of the principal and without making mistake (CC Article 1992) that if the agent needs some directions, he must ask for them.

GERMANY: CC Article 665 requires the agent to ask for direction when he is contemplating to deviate from the mandate contract or from directions previously received.

HUNGARY: According to CC Article 477 paragraph (1), 'The agent shall inform his principal of his activities and the state of affairs upon request or, if necessary, even without a request, particularly if employment of another person has become necessary or if the instructions need to be changed due to the occurrence of new circumstances'.

IRELAND: The common law does not comprise detailed rules as to the agent's duties, as are outlined in the black letter rules. An express duty to ask for directions does not exist at common law, but would probably come within the agent's duty to exercise reasonable skill and care or the wider fiduciary duties to his principal. Further, an agent is obliged to obey the principal's instruction's and where instructions are ambiguous it has been held that an agent will not be held liable where he acts on a reasonable interpretation of the instructions *(Ireland v Livingstone* (1872) LR 5 HL 395), though an agent should seek clarification, where possible *(Woodhouse AC Israel Cocoa Ltd SA v Nigerian Produce Marketing Co Ltd* [1972] AC 741 at 772 per Lord Salmon; *European Asian Bank AG v Punjab & Sind Bank* [1983] 2 All ER 508 at 517 per Goff LJ).

ITALY: The general principle of diligence applies, according to which the agent shall act in order to achieve the principal's best interests. Accordingly, if the agent is in need of some directions by the principal to identify the interests of the latter, he is obliged to ask for them in order to perform correctly and diligently the mandate.

MALTA: According to Maltese jurisprudence, when the instructions given to the agent are not clear enough or they are uncertain, the agent is bound to request clarification of the terms of the contract and should not consider himself authorized to act arbitrarily.

NETHERLANDS: An express obligation for the agent to ask for a direction when this is needed for the performance of the mandate contract is not regulated in Dutch law, but may follow from the agent's general duty of care towards the principal under CC Article 7:401, given the fact that the agent is required to act in accordance of the principal's best interests. Where needed, the agent will need to inquire about these. An obligation to ask for a direction will certainly not be accepted in so far as the parties had not agreed thereupon and it would fall within the agent's professional discretion and expertise to act independently.

POLAND: There are no statutory provisions in the CC as to the question whether the agent is required to ask for a direction. If no directions are given the agent is free to choose how to best carry out the agreement.

SCOTLAND: There appears to be no particular authority requiring the agent to ask for directions in this particular situation. However, the agent's most fundamental duty is to carry out his undertaking, according to his instructions with the requisite degree of skill and care (Gow, p. 530 and Macgregor, paragraphs 84-87). It is likely that an agent would be found to have breached these duties where he failed to request instructions in a situation where a direction is required.

SLOVAKIA: The agent's duty of care implies an obligation to ask for a direction if it is needed for performance of the mandate contract.

SPAIN: In CC Article 1719 paragraph (2) CC, in the absence of instructions from the principal, the agent is required to continue performance in accordance with the diligence of the good father. This may include the obligation for the agent to require the principal to give instructions. The present Article clearly indicates that it is the principal who decides how to be represented, i.e. by way of direct or indirect representation. The principal may indicate that when the mandate contract is concluded or afterwards by way of a direction, cf. IV.D. – 4:101 (Directions given by principal) paragraph (1). When the principal does not (expressly or tacitly) indicate how the representative is to act, the representative must ask for clarification on this point (paragraph (2)).

SWEDEN: It follows from general contract law rules that the agent has a duty to ask for a direction if needed for the performance of mandate contract. In particular this is the case if the agent feels compelled to deviate from the principal's previous instructions, see KommL Article 8.

No answer received: AUSTRIA, DENMARK, FINLAND, GREECE, PORTUGAL.

2. Agent's obligation to ask for direction whether to act in own name or in name of principal

AUSTRIA: If the contract does not provide otherwise, the agent is not free to decide whether he will act in the principal's name or in his own name.

BELGIUM: In the absence of express instructions, a (civil law) agent is presumed to have been instructed to act in the name of the principal. The principal and the agent are mutually bound to an obligation of loyalty. A first aspect of this obligation of loyalty under Belgian law is the 'transparency requirement'. This requirement obliges the agent to reveal the identity of the principal at the moment of the conclusion of the contract by acting in the name of the principal (Samoy, p. 305-306; Wéry, p. 151). In the absence of express instructions, a (commercial law) commission-agent on the contrary is – according to trade customs – presumed to be instructed to act in his own name (Foriers & Glansdorff, p. 611; Jassogne, p. 636; Samoy, p. 511; Van der Perre & Lejeune, no. 92; Van Ryn & Heenen, p. 21).

BULGARIA: It is not within the discretion of the agent to decide whether to act in his own name or in the name of the principal, unless provided otherwise in the mandate contract. Without having been granted the authority to represent the principal the agent is only allowed to act in his own name. The default rule is that the commission agent and the forwarding agent act always in their own names, cf. CA Article 348 paragraph (1), Article 361 paragraph (1). The authority to act in the name of the principal is granted separately from the conclusion of the mandate contract by means of a unilateral legal act of the principal (power of attorney) (Любен Василев, Гражданско право, p. 368). However, if the agent is granted authority, this is deemed to be an instruction to the agent to act in the name of the principal (Любен Василев, Облигационно право, p. 22). In case of reasonable doubts, the requirement to perform with the care of 'a good householder' imposes on the agent to ask for clarification whether to act in his own name or in the name of the principal.

DENMARK: If the matter has not been regulated by the parties the agent is free to decide whether he will act in the principal's or in his own name.

ENGLAND: There does not appear to be any authority on this issue. Whether the agent is to act in the agent's own name (undisclosed) or in the name of the principal (disclosed) seems a crucial term in the contract, especially from the viewpoint of the principal. Considering the fiduciary nature of an agency relationship, if the principal does not make it clear whether the agent is to disclose the agency or not, it seems that the agent would not be entitled to decide independently whether to disclose the agency or not to third parties. Therefore, he would be required to ask the principal to clarify this. Failing to do that, the agent would probably be found to be in breach of his obligation of due care and skill. If the agent cannot get in touch with the principal, it seems that he should act, as another reasonable agent in a similar trade would do. Since disclosed agency seems more common than undisclosed agency, it would probably be regarded as reasonable for the agent to act in the name of the principal.

ESTONIA: The agent is free to decide whether he will act in the principal's name or in his own name if the parties have not decided the matter in the mandate contract. However, as the agent is under a duty to act in the best interest of the principal (cf. LOAEst Article 620 paragraph (2)), this duty could require him to ask for clarification if no such direction exists and the interests of the principal are unclear.

FINLAND: The agent is not allowed to decide independently whether he acts in his own name or in the principal's name. Unless agreed otherwise, the mandate entitles him to act solely in the principal's name.

FRANCE: There's no specific duty for agent to ask for direction whether to act in own name or in name of principal, but the agent is not free to decide whether he or she will act as agent or as "commission" agent. Then, where there is a difficulty, the agent has every interest in requesting the principal to confirm which type of agency has been agreed, because if there is a dispute, the court will have to decide which of the two types of agency should apply, depending on the terms of the contract and the evidence. If it appears that the agent has made a mistake concerning the type of agency which has been put in place, the agent will be liable for the consequences (CC Article 1992).

GERMANY: If the parties have not regulated whether or not the agent is to act in his own name or in the name of the principal, the agent is free to decide whether he will act in the principal's name or in his own name (Seiler, in: Münchener Kommentar zum BGB, Article 662 no. 19). Apart from special circumstances, there is no duty to ask the principal.

GREECE: In case of a mandate contract, if the contract keeps silent about the authority of the agent to act in the principal's name or in his own name the agent is free to decide on that matter (CA Pireos decision no. 278/1988, NoV 1989, 1451). In case of a contract of commission the nature of that contract requires that the agent shall act in his own name.

HUNGARY: The agent may only act in the principal's name if the principal has authorised him expressly to act so (CC Article 222).

IRELAND: At common law, an agent must obey his principal's lawful instructions. It has been held that where instructions are ambiguous (e.g. where it is not clear from the principal's instructions whether the agent is to act in his own name or in the name of the principal) an agent will not be held liable where he acts on a reasonable interpretation of the instructions *(Ireland v Livingstone* (1872) LR 5 HL 395), though an agent should seek clarification, where possible *(Woodhouse AC Israel Cocoa Ltd SA v Nigerian Produce Marketing Co Ltd* [1972] AC 741 at 772 per Lord Salmon; *European Asian Bank AG v Punjab & Sind Bank* [1983] 2 All ER 508 at 517 per Goff LJ).

ITALY: If the parties have not regulated whether the agent should act in his own name or in name of the principal, and if a solution to the issue cannot be derived from an interpretation of the contract, the agent can decide whether to act in the principal's name or in his own name.

MALTA: Under Maltese law it is presumed that in the contract of mandate the agent is acting in the name of the principal. This can be seen from the definition given to the contract of mandate in CC Article 1856: 'Mandate or procuration is a contract whereby a person gives to another the power to do something for him.'

NETHERLANDS: A duty for the agent to ask for a direction whether to act in his own name or in the name of principal does not exist under Dutch law. If the parties have not decided this matter in their contract and the principal has not given a direction at a later moment, the agent may be assumed to either act in his own name or in the name of the principal. In professional mandate contracts the agent will usually be supposed to act in the agent's own name (HR 11 March 1977, NJ 1977, 521 (Kribbenbijter)).

POLAND: If the contract is silent whether the agent should at in his own name or in the name of the principal the agent should act in the name of the principal, see CC Article 734 paragraph (2).

PORTUGAL: The agent must, unless otherwise stipulated in the contract, act in the name of the principal (CC Article 1178 paragraph (2)).

SCOTLAND: If the principal fails to stipulate whether the agent is to act in the name of the principal or in his own name, the agent is probably not entitled to decide this issue for himself. Making such a fundamental decision without first obtaining the principal's consent would probably breach the duty of good faith which the agent owes to the principal. This may, however, not be the case where a standard practice applies in a particular area of commerce i.e. where, as a general rule, agents may choose to act in their own names without first obtaining instructions from their principals.

SLOVAKIA: If the parties have not decided whether the agent is to act in the agent's own name or in the name of the principal, the agent may not make this decision independently (CC Article 32). In practice, mandate and commision agent contracts in commercial relations are not concluded without clear indication in whose name the agent is obliged to act. If the agent has to effect legal acts in the name of the principal, a written granting of authority is required (Comm.C Article 568).

SPAIN: The agent is not free to decide whether to act as agent or as commissioner in its own name. In any case of doubt, direct representation is compulsory (see CC Article 1725). However, the commercial agent not specially instructed may decide how to act (Comm.C Article 245).

SWEDEN: If the parties have not regulated whether the agent is to act in his own name or in the name of the principal and it does not follow from other circumstances the agent is free to decide the matter. However, if the agent chooses to act in his own name he also runs the risk of being considered a party to the prospected contract as it is presumed that when you act in your own name you also act on your own behalf and account, see Ramberg/Ramberg, p. 50.

Article 4:103: Consequences of failure to give a direction

(1) If the principal fails to give a direction when required to do so under the mandate contract or under paragraph (1) of Article 4:102 (Request for a direction), the agent may, in so far as relevant, resort to any of the remedies under Chapters 8 (Non-performance and remedies in general) and 9 PECL (Particular remedies for non-performance); or

   (a) base performance upon the expectations, preferences and priorities a person in the same situation as the principal may reasonably be expected to have, given the information and directions that have been gathered; and

   (b) claim a proportionate adjustment of the price and of the time allowed or required for the conclusion of the prospective contract.

(2) If the principal fails to give a direction under paragraph (2) of Article 4:102 (Request for a direction), the agent may choose direct representation or indirect representation or may withhold performance under Article 9:201 PECL (Right to Withhold Performance).

(3) The adjusted price that is to be paid under paragraph (1)(b) must be reasonable and is to be determined using the same methods of calculation as were used to establish the original price for the performance of the obligations under the mandate contract.

Comments

A. General idea

This provision sets out the consequences if the principal does not give a direction, even though he is required to do so under the contract or because the agent has asked for a direction in accordance with Article 4:102 (Request for a direction). The remedy for not giving a direction as to whether the agent is to act in his own name or in the name of the principal in accordance with Article 4:102 paragraph (2) (Request for a direction) is given in paragraph (2) of the present Article: the agent is free to choose whether to act in his own name or in the name of the principal or to wait with further performance of the contract until the principal makes his decision.

More important is the situation in which the agent is in need of a direction in order to continue performance. Paragraph (1) indicates that in this situation the agent may continue to perform the contract and base that performance on the expectations, preferences, and priorities of a 'normal' principal in the given circumstances, of course taking into account the information and directions that have been gathered, and that the agent is entitled to an additional price and time for performance of the mandate contract that is the result of the failure of the principal to provide the requested direction. Alternatively, since the principal's failure to provide the direction constitutes the non-performance of an obligation, the agent may invoke a remedy for non-performance.

B. Choice of remedies if direction is needed for further performance

In many cases the agent is in need of instructions on how to perform the mandate contract to continue performance. Where the principal fails to provide such a direction, the question arises which remedies the agent is entitled to. In fact, the agent has the choice between two different approaches. First, he may treat the principal's failure as a non-performance by the latter of his contractual obligations, entitling the agent to the full range of remedies for non-performance, including damages and termination of the contract. However, this approach may not be in the interest of the agent (either), because it would mean that the prospective contract was not concluded and the agent (therefore) would not be entitled to the full price. Paragraph (1) of the present Article offers the agent an alternative by allowing the agent to continue to perform the contract and base his performance on the expectations, preferences, and priorities of a normal principal in the given circumstances, of course taking into account the information and directions that have been gathered. Where performance has become more problematic as a result of the principal's failure to provide the direction, the agent is entitled to an additional price and time for performance of the mandate contract.

Illustration 1
Paul has commissioned George to negotiate the purchase of the sculpture 'Peace' by the upcoming artist Richard Starkey, without indicating clearly what price he is willing to pay for the sculpture. Paul and George agreed that George would have two weeks for performing the mandate contract. After one week, George has found John, the owner of the sculpture, willing to sell it for € 10,000. George informs Paul thereof and asks what he should tell John. Paul remains silent for another week.

What should happen in this particular case? Should George be awarded an extension of time for performance? What happens if Paul finally agrees to the purchase price but then John is no longer willing to sell the sculpture for that price?

Under the present Article:

1. George may claim damages if, as a result of the delay in Paul answering George's request for a direction, the contract can no longer be concluded. Chapter 9, Section 5 PECL (Damages and interest) applies to the claim of damages.
2. George may also terminate the contract for non-performance in so far as the non-performance of the obligation to give the direction amounts to a *fundamental* non-performance under Articles 9:301 paragraph(1) (Right to terminate the contract) and 8:103 PECL (Fundamental non-performance).
3. George may also assume that Paul would agree to the purchase price if a reasonable principal in the circumstances of the case, taking into account the express and implied wishes of Paul as these may be known to George, would agree thereto. This is the solution offered by paragraph (1)(a) of the present Article.
4. George may claim extra time for performance of the mandate contract if, due to Paul's delay in answering his question, the previously agreed time for the conclusion of the sales contract has elapsed. This possibility is offered in paragraph (1)(b) of the present Article.
5. Finally, if John is no longer willing to sell the sculpture for the original purchase price as a result of Paul's delay in providing George with an answer, and George needs to re-negotiate the purchase price, he may claim an extra price for his services, as provided in paragraph (1)(b) of the present Article.

The practical question obviously is whether these alternative remedies may be used simultaneously, e.g. allowing George to buy the painting at the price offered (adapted performance (situation 3) *and* awarding George extra time for performance (situation 4) or an extra price for his further performance (situation 5), or awarding George extra time for performance (situation 4) and claiming damages (situation 1) if Paul's failure to give a direction ultimately leads to a lower remuneration for George's services or a loss of interest because George's entitlement to the price for his services becomes due later. In accordance with the general approach to this matter in Article 8:102 PECL (Cumulation of remedies), the remedies of paragraph (1) of the present Article and the general remedies for non-performance under the Principles of European Contract Law may be cumulated in so far as they are not incompatible with each other. This implies that the said combination of remedies is allowed. However, as a combination of the termination of the mandate contract for non-performance under Articles 9:301 paragraph (1) (Right to terminate the contract) and 8:103 PECL (Fundamental non-performance) and the application of paragraph (1)(a) of the present Article is not possible, these remedies may not be combined.

C. Choice of remedies if direction is needed between direct and indirect representation

The remedy for not giving a direction as to whether the agent is to act in his own name or in the name of the principal as the agent is required to ask under Article 4:102 paragraph (2) (Request for a direction) is given in paragraph (2) of the present Article: the agent is free to choose whether to act in his own name or in the name of the principal or to wait with further performance of the contract until the principal makes his decision. The fact that the agent is allowed to withhold performance until the decision is made indicates that other remedies for non-performance are not available to the agent. However, it should be noted that – as was already explained in the Comments to Article 4:102 (Request for a direction) – in most cases the parties will have agreed (either expressly or tacitly) whether the agent is to act in his own name or in the name of the principal. This implies that the remedy set out in paragraph (2) of the present Article will hardly ever be applied.

Illustration 2
Paul has commissioned George to negotiate the purchase of the sculpture 'Peace' by the upcoming artist Richard Starkey, without indicating whether to act in Paul's name or in George's own name. If the mandate contract can't be interpreted as providing an answer to how George is to operate, George is required to ask Paul for a direction on this matter. If Paul fails to provide an answer to this question, paragraph (2) of the present Article indicates that George is free to act either way, or to wait until Paul finally answers the question.

As George has it within his own hands to continue the conclusion of the mandate contract by either acting in his own name or in the name of the principal in this situation, the failure of the principal to provide the answer to how to act does not justify any other remedy than the ones specified in the present Article. This implies that the provision of paragraph (2) of this Article must be seen as derogating from the provisions in Chapters 8 (Non-performance and remedies in general) and 9 PECL (Particular remedies for non-performance).

D. Relation to Article 4:104 (No time to ask or wait for direction)

It should be noted that the present Article does not apply if the agent has requested a direction, but before receiving the answer is forced to react immediately, e.g. because of the occurrence of an imminent danger. In that situation, Article 4:104 (No time to ask or wait for direction) applies, allowing the agent to directly respond in order to safeguard the principal's interests.

E. Relation to the Principles of European Law and the Draft Common Frame of Reference

This Article mirrors that of Article IV.D. – 4:103 DCFR (Consequences of failure to give a direction).

The present Article provides the remedies for a failure by the principal to give a direction where an obligation to that extent follows from the contract or from a request by the agent for such a direction. The principal's obligation to provide such a direction follows from Article 2:101 (Obligation to co-operate) of these Principles. In Comments B and C of the present Article, the relation between the remedies in this Article and the general remedies in Chapters 8 (Non-performance and remedies in general) and 9 PECL (Particular remedies for non-performance) is explained.

F. Character of the rule

This Article constitutes a default rule from which the parties may derogate, either by excluding or restricting the remedies of this Article or by expanding these.

G. Remedies

The present Article constitutes remedies for a failure of the principal to provide a direction in accordance with the contract or in response to a request for a direction under Article 4:102 (Request for a direction) of these Principles.

Comparative Notes

1. Remedies for failure to give direction

A failure by the principal to give a direction where he is required to do so entitles the agent to the normal remedies for non-performance in BELGIUM, THE NETHERLANDS, SLOVAKIA (commercial contracts), and SWEDEN, and to a claim for specific performance of the obligation to give a direction or to termination by the agent in ITALY. Alternatively, in GERMANY, THE NETHERLANDS, SCOTLAND, and SPAIN, the agent may perform the mandate in accordance with the preferences he may assume the principal to have under the given circumstances. In GERMANY, THE NETHERLANDS, SLOVAKIA, and SPAIN, the agent is entitled to compensation for additional expenses. Such a right is expressly denied in ENGLAND and SCOTLAND. In BULGARIA, the rules on *mora creditoris* apply rather than the remedies for non-performance, as the duty to provide directions is normally not an obligation but a mere duty.

If the principal does not provide clear and unambiguous directions after having been asked for such directions by the agent, the agent is not liable if he follows in good faith what he perceives to be the correct interpretation of the given directions in ENGLAND, ESTONIA, FRANCE, IRELAND, SCOTLAND, and SWEDEN.

2. Remedy for failure to indicate whether to act in own name or in name of principal

If the parties have not indicated whether the agent is to act in his own name or in the name of the principal, the agent is required to ask the principal for a direction on how to act in ESTONIA and IRELAND. In ENGLAND, the agent is required to act in accordance with the customs of the trade or profession he is in. In POLAND, SCOTLAND, and SPAIN, he is required to act in the name of the principal in this case, whereas in BULGARIA, ITALY, and SLOVAKIA, the agent is required to act in his own name. Finally, in GERMANY and THE NETHERLANDS, he is free to determine whether he will act in his own name or in the name of the principal.

National Notes

1. Remedies for failure to give direction

BELGIUM: The law on mandate is silent on this question. General contract law (precontractual duties to inform and the duty to execute the contract in good faith (CC Article 1134 paragraph (3)) can oblige the principal to give directions to the agent, if the directions are necessary to fulfil the mission.

BULGARIA: In the Bulgarian law of obligation there are no specific rules regulating remedies for failure of the principal to give directions. General contract rules are applicable. When the agent, in order to perform his contractual obligations, needs information or directions from the principal, the latter has no actual obligation to give directions, but rather a mere burden *(Тежест, Obliegenheit)* for assistance. Therefore, if the principal does not give the necessary instructions, neither voluntarily nor upon a request, there is no breach of a contractual obligation, but a case of *mora creditoris (Забава на кредитора)*, cf. OCA Article 95 (Голева, Облигационно право, p. 110; Апостолов, Облигационно право, p. 331). If this is the case, the agent can terminate the contract and claim the expenses due to *mora creditoris*, cf. OCA Article 98. See Голева, Облигационно право, p. 111; Кожухаров, Облигационно право, I, p. 352).

ENGLAND: There is no specific rule dealing with this particular matter. When the authority given is ambiguous, any reasonable interpretation by the agent in good faith means that the act is treated as having been authorised and the agent incurs no liability: *Ireland v Livingston* (1872) LR 5 HL 395. In particular, there does not seem to be any specific rule allowing adjustment of the price in the agent's favour.

ESTONIA: There does not exist any specific duty for the principal to give instructions. However, such duty can in specific cases be derived from the general duty to co-operate with the other party in good faith in order to achieve proper performance of the agreement (LOAEst Article 23 paragraph (2)). If the principal fails to provide instructions when bound to do so and this leads to non-performance of the mandate, the agent will be able to avoid liability as the non-performance would be attributable to the principal (LOAEst Article 101 paragraph (3)).

FRANCE: The law is silent, but it is undoubtedly the case that a refusal to reply to questions raised by the agent would exclude the liability of the latter where the mandate failed or was improperly performed. However, the agent could remain liable to any third party contractor, see Cass.civ. 1re, 13 November 1997, Bull. civ. 1997 I, no. 308.

GERMANY: Should the principal fail to give the required directions, CC Article 665 entitles the agent to perform the mandate in accordance with the preferences he may assume the principal to have under the given circumstances. As far as this changed performance of the mandate contract has and could not have been contemplated by the parties when agreeing on the price, the agent will be entitled to compensation for additional expenses (CC Article 670).

IRELAND: An agent is obliged to obey the principal's instruction's and where instructions are ambiguous it has been held that an agent will not be held liable where he acts on a reasonable interpretation of the instructions *(Ireland v Livingstone* (1872) LR 5 HL 395), though an agent should seek clarification, where possible *(Woodhouse AC Israel Cocoa Ltd SA v Nigerian Produce Marketing Co Ltd* [1972] AC 741 at 772 per Lord Salmon; *European Asian Bank AG v Punjab & Sind Bank* [1983] 2 All ER 508 at 517 per Goff LJ).

ITALY: If the principal fails to give directions to the agent, the latter may not be able to perform his obligations. Thus, the failure to give directions by the principal may represent a breach of contract. In this case the agent has two possible remedies: he may request the principal to perform the contract or he may terminate the contract for cause. However, if the agent acts despite the lack of direction by the principal and he profitably carries out an activity, the principal may ratify this latter (see Cass. No. 1137/04, Giust. civ., 2003, I, 1812).

NETHERLANDS: Where the principal is required to give a direction but fails to do so, this may be seen as a non-performance on the part of the principal. The consequences of such a breach have not been explicitly regulated, which implies that the general remedies for non-performance would apply. Where the agent sustains damage as a consequence of the failure of the principal to give a direction, the principal would be required to compensate the agent for that (CC Article 6:74). Similarly, the agent could terminate the mandate contract for non-performance (CC Article 6:265), provided that the principal's non-performance would justify such termination, which, however, seems to be exceptional. Where appropriate, the agent may claim specific performance of the obligation to give a direction (CC Article 3:296). However, each of these remedies are likely to be of use only in rare situations. It seems, moreover, likely that an alternative remedy may be found in interpreting the agent's obligation to exercise due care (CC Article 7:401) in such a way that he is required to base his performance on the interests the principal is likely to have. The application of good faith (CC Article 6:248 paragraph (1)) would seem to point in the same direction.

POLAND: There are no specific provisions in the Polish CC. There is neither a duty to ask for a direction nor a duty to give such directions.

SCOTLAND: If the principal provides defective instructions the agent is not liable to the principal for any losses suffered as a direct result of the ambiguity of the instructions (Macgregor, paragraph 84; *Ireland v Livingston* (1872) LR 5 HL 395. In a situation where he does not possess adequate instructions and the agent is unable to obtain clarification of the same, it is suggested that the agent should proceed on the basis of what a reasonable principal would have instructed. In this way the agent will avoid being liable for any losses suffered by the principal. Scots law contains no specific mechanism allowing an adjustment of the price in the agent's favour in this situation. This might only be possible in situations where, either in terms of the contract or at common law, the agent is entitled to payment of a reasonable fee.

SLOVAKIA: For civil relations, the consequences of the creditor's delay are regulated in CC Article 522 (duty to reimburse the agent's expenses occurred during the time of delay; civil liability for damages). For commercial relations, the general rules on remedies for non-performance apply, cf. Comm.C Articles 344 ff.

SPAIN: If there are no instructions from the principal, the agent is to act in accordance with the diligence of the good father of a family *(bonus pater familias),* cf. CC Article 1719 paragraph (2). If a direction is problematic, the agent must warn the principal thereof. As far as this direction has and could not have been contemplated by the parties when agreeing on the price, the agent will be entitled to compensation for additional expenses. However, in no case is the agent entitled to proceed against the principal's upholding of the old instructions (Comm.C Article 256). The agent is not bound to follow instructions when that ought to be regarded as a change in the content of the mandate. Finally, the agent may in such a situation withdraw due to good cause (CC Article 1735).

SWEDEN: If the principal fails to give a direction when obliged to this constitutes a non-performance. The agent is entitled to damages and termination if the non-performance is fundamental. Furthermore, the agent is not in breach of contract if he acts on or is passive due to failure of the principal's failure to give directions. This follows from general contract law.

No answer received from AUSTRIA, FINLAND, GREECE, HUNGARY, MALTA, PORTUGAL.

2. Remedy for failure to indicate whether to act in own name or in name of principal

BULGARIA: When it is not stipulated in the mandate contract whether the representation is direct or indirect and the principal does not answer the request for more clarity on this matter, the agent can either perform the mandate in the agent's own name or terminate the relationship as he cannot perform his mandate contract properly.

ENGLAND: Whether the agency is to be disclosed or not seems a fundamental aspect of the agency relationship. In the absence of any case law dealing with this specific issue, a possible solution would be that the agent should act according to customs of the trade or profession he is in. If the agent is guilty of a breach, the principal will be entitled to breach of contract and should the breach be regarded as sufficiently serious, the principal will be entitled to terminate the contract and claim damages.

ESTONIA: If the mandate agreement does not provide whether the agent is to act in its own name or not and the interests of the principal are unclear the agent is entitled to ask for instructions from the principal. If no instructions are provided, the agent must act according to the presumed interests of the principal, if the agent exercised due care in identifying such interests (LOAEst Article 620 paragraph (2)) and has acted accordingly it will not be in breach of its duties and has performed the mandate in accordance with the agreement.

FRANCE: The law is silent, but it is undoubtedly the case that a refusal to reply to questions raised by the agent would exclude the liability of the latter where the mandate failed or was improperly performed.

GERMANY: Under German law, it is always up to the agent to choose between acting in his own name or in the name of the principal.

IRELAND: An agent is obliged to obey the principal's instruction's and where instructions are ambiguous (e.g. where it is not clear from the principal's instructions whether the agent is to act in his own name or in the name of the principal) it has been held that an agent will not be held liable where he acts on a reasonable interpretation of the instructions *(Ireland v Livingstone* (1872) LR 5 HL 395), though an agent should seek clarification, where possible *(Woodhouse AC Israel Cocoa Ltd SA v Nigerian Produce Marketing Co Ltd* [1972] AC 741 at 772 per Lord Salmon; *European Asian Bank AG v Punjab & Sind Bank* [1983] 2 All ER 508 at 517 per Goff LJ).

ITALY: Whether not specified, the agent is deemed to act in his own name as the agent power shall be expressly granted by virtue of a proxy in the contract of mandate or with a distinct document.

NETHERLANDS: In the odd case where the principal would not indicate whether the agent is to act in his own name or the name of the principal even though the principal would be required to given a direction to that extent – which is normally not the case under Dutch law – in theory the normal remedies for non-performance would apply. It would seem that in such a case the agent would be free to choose how to execute his mandate under CC Article 6:248 paragraph (1) and CC Article 7:401.

POLAND: Since the representation is presumed to be direct, the principal has no duty to indicate whether the agent should act in his own name or in the name of the principal.

SCOTLAND: Where the principal fails to provide instructions on whether the agent is to act in either the principal's or the agent's own name, it is suggested that the agent would be best advised to act in the principal's name, this being the more common method of acting. It is unlikely that the agent would be entitled to make this decision himself, and he may even be best advised to refuse to act.

SLOVAKIA: If the principal does not grant authority to act in his name, it is presumed that the agent has to act in his own name.

SPAIN: Apart from the right to terminate the mandate contract, the agent has to act in the name of the principal, because this is the default rule.

SWEDEN: The principal has a duty to answer requests for information in order for the agent to be able to perform according to the contract. If the principal fails to do so such failure is considered to be a non-performance for which the principal could be liable to pay damages to the agent in case the agent suffers any damage and the principal cannot show that the failure is not due to negligence on his part, see HaL Articles 7 and 34.

No answer received from AUSTRIA, BELGIUM, FINLAND, GREECE, HUNGARY, PORTUGAL.

Article 4:104: No time to ask or wait for direction

(1) If the agent is required to ask for a direction under Article 4:102 (Request for a direction) but needs to act before being able to contact the principal and to ask for a direction, or needs to act before the direction is given, the agent may base performance upon the expectations, preferences and priorities the principal may reasonably be expected to have, given the information and directions that have been gathered.

(2) In the situation referred to in paragraph (1), the agent may claim a proportionate adjustment of the price and of the time allowed or required for the performance of the obligations under the mandate contract in so far as such an adjustment is reasonable given the circumstances of the case.

Comments

A. General idea

This Article deals with the situation where immediate action is required by the agent to prevent detrimental consequences for the principal. The situation is so urgent that the agent has no time to ask or wait for a direction from the principal. If such is the case, the agent is entitled under this Article to continue performing on the basis of the expectations, preferences, and priorities the principal may reasonably be expected to have, given the information and directions that have been gathered. The agent may subsequently claim a proportionate adjustment of the price and of the time allowed or required for the performance of the obligations under the mandate contract (typically, the conclusion of the prospective contract) in so far as such an adjustment is reasonable given the circumstances of the case.

B. No time to wait: what then?

The agent is required to act in accordance with the interests of the principal. Where he is not sufficiently aware of these interests, he is required to inquire about these interests by putting questions to the principal. The principal is required to answer reasonable requests for information under Article 2:101(a) (Obligation to co-operate). One question that arises is what the consequences should be if the principal – for whatever reason – fails to answer such reasonable requests for information, or the agent does not have enough time to either ask for or wait for an answer to a request for information because the circumstances require him to act immediately to safeguard the principal's interests. In both situations, the present Article entitles the agent to immediate action. As in this situation he cannot be aware of the principal's exact wishes and there is no time to become aware of these wishes, the agent is entitled to proceed and base his performance on the expectations, preferences, and priorities a normal principal would have. In determining how to act, the agent is to be awarded the necessary margin of discretion. If the agent acted in a reasonable manner in the circumstances of the case, he cannot be held liable for non-performance if it turns out later that the principal would have wanted the agent to act differently.

Illustration 1

Donovan is charged by Evelyne to purchase a specific painting from a private seller. Donovan and Evelyne have agreed that Donovan is to act in his own name when negotiating the contract with the private seller. If the private seller insists on knowing the identity of the buyer for personal reasons, Donovan is required to inform Evelyne and ask for a direction on how to proceed. However, if the seller insists on being told the identity of the principal immediately and indicates that he will break off negotiations if Donovan does not disclose Evelyne's identity, Donovan is entitled to decide the matter at that moment. In doing so, he must take into account the communicated wishes and interests of Evelyne, including the reason why she and he had agreed that Donovan would act in his own name: if this is because Evelyne's identity would have to remain undisclosed to the third party, Donovan may not disclose her identity to the seller, whereas this is probably different if the reason for agreeing to indirect representation was merely practical in nature.

Illustration 2

Donovan is charged by Evelyne to purchase a specific painting from a private seller. The sale is to be completed within one week before Evelyne goes on holiday. When Donovan negotiates the contract during that week and tries to inform Evelyne of the result, she can't be reached because she went on holiday earlier than expected. Donovan is entitled to make the decision for her, taking into account her earlier expressed wishes and demands, if the seller insists on either concluding the sales contract or breaking off the negotiations before Evelyne can be contacted.

Illustration 3

Fiona is charged by Gerald to buy on Gerald's behalf a cottage in Yorkshire, which is on the market for € 203,000. Gerald has made it very clear to Fiona that he has fallen in love with the cottage and that he is keen to buy it. Moreover, as Fiona knows, Gerald can finance a house as long as the purchase price does not exceed € 250,000. As both Fiona and Gerald know, the cottage has been on the market for more than a year and the owners have not only received not a single bid, but hardly anybody has come to visit the cottage. For that reason, Gerald has instructed Fiona to buy the cottage for no more than € 200,000. However, while Fiona is negotiating a sales contract with the owners, Hugh makes a bid for the cottage out of the blue for € 205,000. The owners inform Fiona, who has to decide on the spot whether she will match that bid. If she does not, the owners make clear that the cottage will be sold to Hugh. In this situation, as Fiona does not have the time to inform Gerald and ask for a direction, she is entitled to decide the matter on the spot. In doing so, she must take into account why Gerald had originally set a limit to the purchase price. If this was only to indicate that Fiona would have to first come back to Gerald before accepting a higher purchase price but it was clear that Gerald would be willing to accept a higher price if it turned out to be necessary, Fiona could agree to the higher purchase price. If, on the other hand, Gerald had indicated that € 200,000 was in any case the maximum price he would be willing to pay for the cottage, Fiona is not allowed to accept the offer made by the owners.

Illustration 4

Hans is the victim of a traffic accident. He engages the law firm of Lockhart/Gardner to handle his case. Alicia Florrick, the lawyer who is appointed to negotiate a settlement with the lawyer representing the tortfeasor, receives an offer to settle the case that is valid only for the next 24 hours. When Alicia tries to contact Hans, he appears to have left for a short holiday and can't be reached within the time limit set by the tortfeasor's lawyer. In this case, Alicia is allowed to determine the matter as a reasonable principal would, given the information and directions that have been gathered. This implies that if Hans had instructed her to negotiate a settlement 'too good to refuse', Alicia may only accept the settlement if she estimates that the offer meets that criterion. If she has further information about the interpretation of the offer, she needs to take that information into account. For instance, if Hans had previously indicated that he expected to receive at least € 100,000 in damages and such is reasonable in the circumstances of the case, she can't agree to a settlement for less than this amount.

C. Amendment of price and time for performance

It may be that in a case where an unforeseen event takes place which requires the agent's immediate action, the agent must incur additional expenses or efforts that were not taken into account when the original mandate contract was concluded. In this case, it may be fair to adjust the mandate contract by awarding the agent an additional payment and/or additional time for performance of the mandate contract. Paragraph (2) provides for such an adjustment.

D. Relation to other provisions in these Principles

There is a close relation between the situations covered by this Article and the ones covered by Article 3:201 (Acting beyond mandate) of these Principles: in the situations meant here, the agent may have to act beyond the scope of the mandate in order to properly safeguard the interests of the principal. As indicated under Article 3:201 (Acting beyond mandate), the agent is allowed to act beyond the scope of the mandate only when certain conditions, enumerated in that Article, are fulfilled. The conditions would be satisfied in the circumstances envisaged by the present Article.

E. Relation to the Principles of European Law and the Draft Common Frame of Reference

This Article mirrors that of Article IV.D. – 4:104 DCFR (No time to ask or wait for direction).

F. Character of the rule

This Article constitutes a default rule from which the parties may derogate, e.g. by restricting or excluding the possibility for the agent to act without an express direction of the principal.

G. Remedies

If the agent does not ask for a direction when he is required to do so under Article 4:102 (Request for a direction) and the conditions of the present Article have not been met, the agent breaches one of his contractual obligations towards the principal. The remedies for this breach are governed by the general provisions on remedies in Chapters 8 (Non-performance and remedies in general) and 9 PECL (Particular remedies for non-performance).

Comparative Notes

1. Agent's right to act if no time to ask or wait for direction

The agent is required to warn for a direction that he perceives to be defective. Moreover, when needed for the proper performance of the mandate contract, the agent is required to ask for a direction (see the Comparative Notes to Articles 4:101 (Directions given by principal) and 4:102 (Request for a direction)). However, in some situations, there is no time to await the principal's reaction to such a warning or request for a direction. In these cases, the agent is allowed to act without having to wait for instructions and may disregard the existing direction in all legal systems. In exercising his task, the agent is required to act reasonably and in the best interests of the principal in BULGARIA, ENGLAND, FRANCE, THE NETHERLANDS, SPAIN, and SWEDEN. In GERMANY, ITALY, THE NETHERLANDS, and SCOTLAND, the agent would have to base his actions in accordance with the preferences he may assume the principal to have under the given circumstances. The agent bears the burden of proof as to the existence of such circumstances requiring immediate action in BULGARIA.

National Notes

1. Agent's right to act if no time to ask or wait for direction

AUSTRIA: In case of imminent danger the agent may disregard the directions of the principal (Schwimann/Apathy, Article 1009 Rz 13; Straube/Griss, Article 385 Rz 2.).

BULGARIA: As a general rule, the agent is under an obligation to ask the principal for approval and new directions for every deviation from the mandate. Nevertheless, in some cases the agent is entitled to act without such approval or further directions. These are cases when there is not enough time to wait for new instructions, so immediate action is then necessary in order to properly protect the principal's interests and to prevent damages, cf. OCA Article 282. The agent bears the burden of proof for existence of these conditions (Любен Василев, Облигационно право, p. 24). Furthermore, the agent can entrust the performance of the mandate to a third person even without a permission, if such subcontracting has become necessary for protection of the principal's interests and without it immediate undertaking the principal would have incurred damages, see OCA Article 283 paragraph (2).

ENGLAND: There does not seem to be any case law dealing with this particular area. If the agent has no time to ask for direction before acting, provided that he acts reasonably in the circumstances and in the best interest of the principal, there would be little risk of liability for breach of the agency contract the act will probably be binding upon the principal.

FRANCE: There's no specific rule about that point, but according to French legal academic writing, agent has a duty to act with diligence in order to comply with the directions given by principal. From this point of view, agent may take the initiative in making everything is necessary in order to answer to the principal interests (Collart-Dutilleul & Delebecque, no. 645; Pétel, no. 248).

GERMANY: In situations in which postponement of action would result in 'danger' to the principal and his interests, CC Article 665 entitles the agent to perform the mandate in accordance with the preferences he may assume the principal to have under the given circumstances. As far as this changed performance of the mandate contract has and could not have been contemplated by the parties when agreeing on the price, the agent will be entitled to compensation for additional expenses (CC Article 670).

HUNGARY: According to CC Article 477 paragraph (2), 'The agent shall be entitled to depart from the principal's instructions only if it is essential for the principal's interest and if there is no time to notify the principal in advance. In such a case the principal shall be notified without delay' (CC Article 477 paragraph (2); cf. also Supreme Court Pfv. VIII. 22.351/2005, in EBH2006. 1410).

IRELAND: An agent is obliged to obey the principal's instruction's and where instructions are ambiguous it has been held that an agent will not be held liable where he acts on a reasonable interpretation of the instructions (*Ireland v Livingstone* (1872) LR 5 HL 395), though an agent should seek clarification, where possible (*Woodhouse AC Israel Cocoa Ltd SA v Nigerian Produce Marketing Co Ltd* [1972] AC 741 at 772 per Lord Salmon; *European Asian Bank AG v Punjab & Sind Bank* [1983] 2 All ER 508 at 517 per Goff LJ). Moreover, the doctrine of agency of necessity may operate to give an agent power to act in 'emergency situations' where communication with the principal is not possible.

ITALY: According to CC Article 1711, if the agent has no time to ask or wait for the directions of the principal, he shall act in the way he reasonably thinks that the principal would have asked him to act had he given some directions. However, if it appears impossible to ask or wait for directions from the principal because of the agent himself, CC Article 1711 does not apply and the agent shall be liable for the activity eventually carried out not in the principal's interests, see Cass. 12647/1995, Foro It. Mass., 1996, I, 544.

NETHERLANDS: In the situation where in principle the agent is required to ask for a direction, but does not have the time to wait for the direction or to even request a direction in the first place, the agent would have to act in accordance with good faith and fair dealing (CC Article 6:248 paragraph (1)) and exercise the care that may be required of him (CC Article 7:401). This would mean that the agent would be required to act in the best interest of the principal and could not postpone his actions.

MALTA: According to Maltese jurisprudence, when the instructions given to the agent are not clear enough or they are uncertain, the agent is bound to request clarification of the terms of the contract and should not consider himself authorized to act arbitrarily, unless the situation is of such urgency as not to allow any time for consultation with the principal.

POLAND: There is no duty to ask for a direction. However, if directions have given the agent may act contrary to such directions only if there is no possibility to contact the principal and it is reasonable to believe the principal would have changed the direction if he knew about the state of affairs (for example: an unforeseen change in the market price).

SCOTLAND: Where the agent has insufficient time to ask for a direction from the principal, and harm to the principal's interests would follow from inaction or delay, it is suggested that the agent is likely to avoid liability by assuming that the principal's direction would accord with that of a reasonable principal with the known needs and preferences of the actual principal, and acting accordingly. If the agent is a 'general agent', employed to carry out all the principal's business, or all business of a particular kind, the agent is assumed to be authorised to do whatever is necessary to serve the principal's interests (Macgregor, paragraph 55).

SLOVAKIA: This right may be covered by the provisions on the possibility to diverge from principal's directions.

SPAIN: The agent is required to act with the diligence of the good father if the agent does not have access to the instructions of the principal (CC Article 1719 paragraph (2) and Comm.C Article 255. Having no time to call for direction, the agent should act according to the best interest of the principal, assessed in the light of the best knowledge of the agent.

SWEDEN: In cases where the agent is required to ask for a direction but immediate action is required by the agent in order to prevent detrimental consequences for the principal the agent is required to act as the circumstances require, see KommL Article 8. This also follows from general contract law rules and the fact that the agent is contractually obliged to act in the interest of the principal.

No answer received: BELGIUM, DENMARK, ESTONIA, FINLAND, GREECE, PORTUGAL.

Section 2:
Changes of the mandate contract

Article 4:201: Changes of the mandate contract

(1) The mandate contract is changed if the principal:
   (a) significantly changes the mandate of the agent;
   (b) does not revoke a direction without undue delay after having been warned in accordance with paragraph (3) of Article 4:101 (Directions given by the principal).
(2) In the case of a change of the mandate contract under paragraph (1) the agent is entitled:
   (a) to a proportionate adjustment of the price and of the time allowed or required for the performance of the obligations under the mandate contract; or
   (b) to damages in accordance with Article 9:502 PECL (General measure of damages) to put the agent as nearly as possible into the position in which the agent would have been if the mandate contract had not been changed.
(3) In the case of a change of the mandate contract under paragraph (1) the agent may also terminate the mandate relationship by giving notice of termination for an extraordinary and serious reason under Article 6:105 (Termination by the agent for extraordinary and serious reason), unless the change is minor or is to the agent's advantage.
(4) The adjusted price that is to be paid under paragraph (2)(a) must be reasonable and is to be determined using the same methods of calculation as were used to establish the original price for the performance of the obligations under the mandate contract.

Comments

A. General idea

The obligations under a mandate contract are not performed instantaneously. The relationship remains in force for a period of time, definite or indefinite. Obviously, the parties are free to renegotiate the mandate contract, including the price and the time for performance. However, a change of the mandate contract may also follow from a unilateral direction of the principal. As the mandate contract is meant to serve the principal's interests in concluding a contract with a third party, and the needs and interests of the principal with regard to that prospective contract may change, the principal must be allowed to give subsequent directions as to the performance of the obligations or the contents of the prospective contract. By doing so the principal may change the content of the mandate contract. In many cases, the parties will have made their own contractual arrangements to deal with such changes. This Article deals with situations where the parties have not made such agreements.

According to this Article, there is a change to the mandate contract when the principal significantly changes the mandate of the agent or when the principal does not revoke a direction without undue delay after having been warned that the direction was unreasonable. Under these conditions, the actions (or, as regards the revocation of the direction, the lack of action) of the principal may be seen as a material change of the contract. Under the present Article, such a change comes about automatically, but it does have important consequences; a change may have strong implications for the obligations of the agent and can't be without consequences – for instance, regarding the remuneration of the agent. This is particularly the case where the principal extends or limits the power of the agent.

B. Significant change in mandate

A change to the contract occurs when the principal extends or limits the mandate of the agent in a significant way.

Illustration 1
Jacqueline is authorised to sell Harry's house for no less than €400,000. Harry subsequently orders her to sell the house for at least €350,000. As a consequence of this direction, Jacqueline's power is extended. Similarly, if Harry in the future tells her to sell the house for at least €450,000, Jacqueline's power is limited. In both cases, the mandate contract is changed under paragraph (1), which in accordance with paragraph (2) may have consequences for the price and the time for performance.

This is also the case if the principal refuses to revoke without undue delay a direction which the agent has warned will cause the conclusion of the prospective contract to become significantly more expensive or take significantly more time than agreed upon in the mandate contract, or where the principal refuses to revoke a direction which the agent has warned is inconsistent with the purpose of the mandate contract or may otherwise be detrimental to the interests of the principal.

Illustration 2
If Jacqueline first was authorised to sell a house owned by Harry for a price of €400,000, but Harry later authorises her to sell the house only for €450,000, which is above the market price, it will take Jacqueline more time to sell the house and there is a serious risk that she will not be able to conclude the prospective contract. After having been warned of this, if Harry nevertheless holds her to the 'unreasonable' direction, this is regarded as a change of the mandate contract under paragraph (1).

C. Consequences when unreasonable direction is not revoked

Under Article 4:101 (Directions given by the principal), the agent is also required to follow a direction which the agent perceives not to be in the best interest of the principal, though he must warn the principal if the direction may lead the conclusion of the prospective contract to become more expensive or to take more time than agreed upon in the mandate contract, or if the direction may otherwise compromise the interests of the principal. Nevertheless, if the principal does not revoke the direction after having been warned, the agent must follow it. One of the consequences of having to follow such a direction is that it may indeed take the agent more time to actually conclude the prospective contract. This also implies that performing his task becomes less profitable for the agent than was anticipated when the price was calculated. The present Article provides in paragraph (1) that such a direction is perceived to be a change of the mandate contract. Under paragraph (2), this leads to an automatic adjustment of the price and time for performance, whereas under paragraph (3) the agent is entitled to terminate the mandate contract for serious and extraordinary reason.

D. Proportionate adjustment of price and time of performance or damages

When a mandate contract is concluded, both parties agree upon a service to be performed in exchange for a price. The price and the time for performance are based upon the cost, time, and effort the performance of the contract requires from the agent. Therefore, a unilateral complication of the content and magnitude of the agent's obligations cannot be without effect on the time the agent has for the performance of the contract and of the price that he will be entitled to when the prospective contract is concluded. Consequently, paragraph (2)(a) entitles the agent to claim extra time for performance and an adjustment of the price.

Especially when the change consists of a limitation of the awarded power, the agent's interests may be endangered in a different way. The following Illustration may clarify this.

Illustration 3
Freddy commissions Brian, a real estate agent, to sell his house for no less than € 250,000. Brian negotiates with Roger, a well-to-do artist, who seems willing to pay the requested sum. Freddy, however, subsequently limits Brian's power by requiring him to negotiate a sales contract for the price of € 200,000 with John, who is less solvent than Roger but with whom Freddy has a personal relationship.

The limitation of the power awarded to Brian may make it more difficult to conclude a contract, as the only possible candidate is now John. This may require a change of the price for the service. Moreover, if the contract is indeed concluded with John, the sales price will be lower than was originally envisaged. With real estate contracts, it is not unusual for the price of Brian's services to be proportionate to the sales price. The limitation of the power awarded to Brian will therefore directly affect the remuneration to be paid to Brian. In a situation such as this, damages may be a more suitable solution. As the change of the contract cannot be seen as a non-performance of the principal since the principal is entitled to limit the power of the agent, an express provision entitling the agent to damages is required here. Paragraph (2)(b) provides for such an entitlement. Under this provision, the agent could instead choose damages to put the agent as nearly as possible into the position in which the agent would have been if the mandate contract had not been changed.

E. Termination for extraordinary and serious reason

Where the principal severely limits the power but does not completely revoke it, this is regarded as a change of the mandate contract under the present Article. However, the change may give the agent reason to believe that he will not be able to conclude the prospective contract. If that is the case, he has a good reason to fear that his services will be to no avail. As the entitlement to a price comes into being only when the prospective contract is concluded, the agent then has an extraordinary and serious reason ('important reason') to terminate his commitment to the mandate contract. Paragraph (3), in combination with Article 6:105 (Termination by the agent for extraordinary and serious reason), entitles him to indeed terminate the mandate contract. As a result, the difference between the situation where the power is revoked (leading to the automatic termination of the mandate relationship) and that where it is 'merely' limited is not as big as it may seem at first glance.

F. No entitlement to termination if change is minor or to agents advantage

Whereas it seems justified to allow the agent to terminate the mandate relationship for extraordinary and serious reason if the mandate is significantly changed, this is not the case where the change is minor. Nor is there any justification for allowing termination when the change actually *improves* the agent's chances of accomplishing the mandated task – for example, concluding the prospective contract – or is otherwise to the agent's advantage. This is the case when the mandate of the agent is extended. In such a case, the agent should not be able to escape from the mandate contract for the mere reason that the content of the mandate contract has changed. Paragraph (3) therefore provides that the change of the mandate contract in these cases does not constitute an extraordinary and serious reason for termination.

Illustration 1 (continued)
Jacqueline is authorised to sell Harry's house for no less than € 400,000. Harry subsequently orders her to sell the house for € 350,000. If Jacqueline has warned Harry that the price in her view is too low but Harry nevertheless insists on the direction, this will lead to a change of the mandate in accordance with paragraph (1) of this Article. As Harry has extended Jacqueline's power, it has become easier for her to conclude the prospective contract. Such a change is to be considered favourable to the agent, which implies that the agent may not terminate for serious and extraordinary on (just) this basis, even though the change may imply that the price he is to receive for his services may be reduced when this is calculated on the basis of the sales price.

Similarly, even if the change may be to the disadvantage of the agent, this does not justify termination for serious and extraordinary reason by the agent if the change is minor. The court would have to determine whether the change of the mandate contract is to be considered minor. This may also depend on the circumstances of the case.

Illustration 1 (continued)
Jacqueline is authorised to sell Harry's house for no less than € 400,000. Whereas Harry first had not indicated anything as to the date of transfer of the house, by a later direction Harry orders Jacqueline to negotiate that the date of transfer is not earlier than the first of September of this year.

In most situations, such a change will not be seen as a significant change of the mandate of the agent. This may be different, however, if it is clear that the house is not in popular demand, and the direction is given at a time when a bid has finally been made, including the requirement of a transfer of the house by the first of May of this year. The direction may then have severe consequences for the possibility of the agent to conclude any contract with a third party.

G. Relation to other provisions in these Principles

This Article is closely related to Article 4:101 (Directions given by principal). Under paragraph (3) of that Article, the agent is required to warn the principal that the direction has the effect that the performance of the obligations under the mandate contract would become significantly more expensive or take significantly more time than agreed upon in the mandate contract or is inconsistent with the purpose of the mandate contract or may otherwise be detrimental to the interests of the principal. If the principal nevertheless holds the agent to the direction, paragraph (4) of the same Article qualifies the direction as a change of the mandate contract under the present Article.

H. Relation to the Principles of European Law and the Draft Common Frame of Reference

This Article mirrors that of Article IV.D. – 4:201 DCFR (Changes of the mandate contract).

I. Character of the rule

This Article constitutes a default rule from which the parties may derogate, e.g. by regulating the consequences of a change of the mandate contract in the original mandate contract or in a subsequent arrangement.

J. Remedies

This Article provides consequences for a change of the mandate contract, and as such may be seen as containing a remedy for the agent in case a change of the mandate contract occurs. The remedies for non-performance do not apply to changes of the mandate contract in accordance with this Article.

Comparative Notes

1. Unilateral change of mandate contract by principal via direction

Obviously, if the parties included a clause in their contract allowing the principal to unilaterally change the content of the mandate contract, the principal is allowed to do so. Apart from that, the principal is not allowed to unilaterally amend the terms of the mandate contract in BULGARIA, GERMANY, IRELAND, POLAND, SCOTLAND, SLOVAKIA, and probably also not in ENGLAND, but he is in practice allowed to do so in FRANCE, THE NETHERLANDS, and SWEDEN, albeit that the agent is allowed in that case to terminate the mandate contract. Moreover, it is emphasised in GERMANY that in practice, the boundary between unilateral changes of the mandate (which are not allowed unless agreed upon) and permissible directions by the principal is often unclear.

2. Consequences of unilateral change of mandate contract

Where the change of the mandate is within the boundaries agreed previously by the parties, the agent is bound by such a change through a direction in all legal systems. In FINLAND, the agent is in principle not entitled to a higher price if extra work is required as a result of the direction. In DENMARK, FRANCE, and probably also in SPAIN, the agent is entitled to a higher price if the change of the mandate makes the performance of the mandate contract substantively more difficult for the agent and if the agent has properly warned the principal thereof. In IRELAND and probably also in SCOTLAND, an agreement to a higher price is a prerequisite for the change of the mandate to become binding on the agent. In THE NETHERLANDS and SWEDEN, the agent would be entitled to a proportionate adjustment of the price. In GERMANY, a right to a higher price would only emerge if at least an implied agreement for the adjustment of the price exists. In GERMANY and SPAIN, the agent is entitled to be compensated for additional expenses. Moreover, if performance of the mandate contract has become too burdensome for the agent as a result of the change, the agent may terminate the mandate contract by notice in BULGARIA, HUNGARY, SLOVAKIA, and SPAIN. The agent is also allowed to terminate the mandate contract in FRANCE, but is required to pay damages to the principal unless continued performance would cause serious loss to the agent.
Directions that amount to a significant alteration of the mandate and go beyond previously agreed limits for amendment of the mandate are deemed to be a unilateral termination of the old mandate contract by the principal and an offer for the conclusion of a new contract in BULGARIA. In ENGLAND and SCOTLAND, such directions are interpreted as a breach of the contract by the principal and entitle the agent to terminate the contract for non-performance and claim damages.

National Notes

1. Unilateral change of mandate contract by principal via direction

BULGARIA: In Bulgarian contract law, a differentiation is made between a mandate contract and a power of attorney. The mandate contract presupposes mutual consensus of the parties – the agent and the principal, and regulates their internal relationship. The power of attorney is a unilateral act of the principal for authorizing the agent to perform in the principal's name. As a general rule, contracts may be amended, terminated, avoided, or revoked only by mutual consent of the parties or on grounds provided in the law, cf. OCA Article 20bis paragraph (2). Taking the lack of a provision permitting unilateral alteration of the mandate contract into consideration, according to Bulgarian law of obligation the mandate contract can be changed only by mutual consent of the parties. The principal is entitled to give subsequent directions that result in a unilateral change of the mandate contract only (a) when they are within the initially stipulated limits for alteration, and (b) provided that these directions do not change significantly the mandate and do not make its performance too burdensome for the agent (Меворах/Лиджи/Фархи, III, p. 119; Любен Василев, Облигационно право, p. 24).

ENGLAND: Doctrinal writing indicates that 'the principal's control over the agent is based on his powers not to grant authority, to limit the authority and to withdraw and revoke the authority' (Bowstead & Reynolds, paragraph 6.009). However, whether a significant change of power of the agent can be done unilaterally is doubtful: Reynolds states that actual authority of the agent can only be modified by consent of the principal and the agent (Bowstead & Reynolds paragraph 10-002)

FRANCE: The principal can change his directions at any time during the mandate contract, as this contract is concluded for his benefit. But one can consider that if the principal changes the power of the agent (for instance, he asks first the agent to rent his flat and then to sell it), the agent may claim for a higher price, as his services have been deeply modified. The agent is required to comply with the instructions of the principal, even though after having warned the principal, when the principal does not answer to his or her warning. There is no change of the mandate contract in that sense.

GERMANY: Under CC Article 665, the principal may only give directions as long as they stay within the agreed framework of the mandate contract; it is not possible for him to unilaterally change the contract by way of a direction (Seiler, in: Münchener Kommentar zum BGB, Article 665 no. 12). The principal may not unilaterally change the mandate contract – any change, significantly or insignificantly, has to be accepted by the agent (as it might lead to a modification of his rights and obligations under the contract). Should the agent not agree to the proposed change, the principal can revoke the mandate (CC Article 671 paragraph (1)). A direction may, however, clarify the agent's obligations under the mandate, and the line between a mere clarification and a unilateral change (extension) might often be difficult to draw. In case the direction given exceeds the contractual limits, the agent acting under a gratuitous contract (CC Article 662) may either ignore the direction (Seiler, in: Münchener Kommentar zum BGB, Article 665 no. 13), upon which the principal may revoke the mandate according to CC Article 671 paragraph (1), or the agent himself might opt for a unilateral revocation under CC Article 671 paragraph (1).

HUNGARY: The principal remains always the master of the affair and can change his directions at any time (Supreme Court Pfv. VIII. 20.107/2006, in BH2006. 321).

IRELAND: While an agent must follow the principal's lawful instructions, the principal cannot unilaterally alter the terms of the mandate contract. Any variation of the terms must be support by fresh consideration, in the absence of a variation clause in the original contract.

ITALY: If the principal changes unilaterally the content of the mandate contract, the agent shall be entitled to terminate the contract if he does not agree with the changes.

NETHERLANDS: The principal may give the agent directions. These directions should be timely and sound. Furthermore, the principal's right to give directions is limited by the scope of the mandate. The mandate contract may also imply that the principal is not allowed to give further directions. See CC Article 7:402 paragraph (1). From this it follows that in principle, the principal is allowed to unilaterally change the authority of the agent. This is true even if this would amount to a partial or even full termination of the mandate contract, cf. CC Article 7:408 paragraph (1). Moreover, under CC Article 7:402, the principal is allowed to give directions to the agent. The agent who is unwilling to perform the contract according to these directions may end the mandate contract after first having warned the principal thereof.

POLAND: The Polish CC does not allow the principal to change the contract after it has been concluded unless the agent agrees. Similarly, it is not clear whether the agent is bound by the principal's directions given after the mandate contract has been signed, unless the mandate contract provides for such directions. The principal may terminate the contract but not change it. If the agent was ordered to buy a painting for set amount and the principal decides to change this amount the contract should be terminated and a new mandate contract should be concluded unless the agent agrees to carry out the modified contract.

SCOTLAND: As the terms of the mandate contract will be agreed from the point of formation, the principal will not be entitled unilaterally to make significant changes to the mandate contract. Of course, one of the terms of the contract (whether express or implied by law) will normally be that the principal has the power to give directions as to how the obligations under it are to be carried out. So a distinction has to be drawn between a permissible direction and an impermissible change. A direction which would bring about a significant change to the agent's obligations to the agent's detriment would not normally be within the permissible range and would be perceived as an attempted unilateral change of the contract.

SLOVAKIA: There is no special regulation in Slovakian law. It depends on the content of the mandate contract itself, otherwise the provisions of general contract law should be applied. The possibilities to change contract are very restricted, as one party is not able to unilaterally change the contract.

SPAIN: The agent may refuse performance of instructions that imply an imbalance in the contractual position of the parties to the detriment of the agent or instructions that imply a modification of the object of the contract (Hernández Gil, p. 472 and 473). There are no rules as to the adjustment of the price of the service in the light of a direction. However, according to the remission to the commercial usages made by CC Article 1711 paragraph (2) and Comm.C Article 277, an adjustment of the price may be reasonable if the service becomes more onerous.

SWEDEN: The agent is required to follow the principal's directions as long as these are considered to be reasonable. However, if the principal significantly changes the power of the agent such change could amount to an important and valid reason entitling the agent to cancel the contract if it cannot reasonably be expected that the contract shall continue, see Hesser, p. 29; KommL Article 51; HaL Article 26.

No answer received: BELGIUM, DENMARK, ESTONIA, FINLAND, MALTA, PORTUGAL

2. Consequences of unilateral change of mandate contract

BULGARIA: Since there are no specific provisions, the consequences of a unilateral change of the mandate contract are governed by general contract law and contractual stipulations. If the principal alters the mandate contract within the stipulated limits, the parties are free to negotiate adjustment of the price and/or the time for performance. If the principal gives new directions which amount to a significant alteration of the mandate, this is deemed to be a unilateral termination of the old mandate contract by the principal and an offer for the conclusion of a new contract. The agent may reject the offer for a new mandate contract (Мевораx/Лиджи/Фарxи, III, p. 119). In case the principal has not exceeded the stipulated limits for changing, but the mandate contract has become too burdensome for performance, this is considered to be a sufficient reason for termination of the contract by the agent with a unilateral notice of termination, cf. OCA Article 289.

DENMARK: If due to a direction the task proves to be (essentially) more difficult than initially envisaged by the parties, the agent will normally be entitled to claim a higher price for his representing the principal; the terms of the contract will likely be renegotiated under such circumstances. If no such renegotiation takes place, the agent as a *naturalia negotii* must warn the principal that the costs will be higher if he has to follow the new instructions.

ENGLAND: It is thought that if a unilateral change of the mandate amounts to a serious breach by the principal, the agent will be entitled to treat the breach as repudiatory, terminate the relationship and claim damages.

FINLAND: If the directions are not withdrawn and they are still within the limits of the agreed mandate, the agent is generally required to follow them, even if it makes the fulfilment of the contract somewhat more difficult. This, however, depends somewhat on the type of the mandate. Unless expressly agreed otherwise or when the circumstances do not show otherwise, the agent is not entitled to an additional price for extra work. The question of price is, however, somewhat unclear and depends highly on circumstances. The agent is usually required to inform the principal that the price will be higher (as described above, this often means that the agreement has to be altered).

FRANCE: If the agent considers that he has no interest in following the principal's instructions, he may simply decide to renounce the mandate. If the termination causes loss to the principal, the latter may claim damages from the agent (CC Article 2007), but damages may not be due, however, if continuation of the mandate contract would cause serious loss to the agent. On the basis of a general obligation of fair dealing, which applies to the agent, the latter should inform the principal of any possible additional expense involved by new instructions, and ensure that the parties agree on such additional expenses. The French courts have accepted that the remuneration set out in the mandate contract may be revised if the mandate carried out does not correspond to the remuneration initially envisaged. The agent may therefore claim for a proportionate adjustment of the price.

GERMANY: If the direction given by the principal results in a change of the gratuitous mandate contract and the agent chooses to follow the direction, he may claim reimbursement of expenses resulting from the change under CC Article 670. Under remunerated mandate contracts (CC Article 675 paragraph (1)), the applicable law on contracts for works or services will require an (at least implied) agreement between the parties for the price to be adjusted. In case the direction given exceeds the contractual limits, the agent acting under a gratuitous contract (CC Article 662) may either ignore the direction (Seiler, Münchener Kommentar zum BGB, Article 665 no. 13), upon which the principal may revoke the mandate according to CC Article 671 paragraph (1), or the agent himself might opt for a unilateral revocation under CC Article 671 paragraph (1).

HUNGARY: The unilateral change of mandate contract can be a ground of unilateral termination of contract for the other party.

IRELAND: A unilateral change in the term of the mandate contract is not effective unless support by fresh consideration and may constitute a breach of contract, allowing the innocent party to repudiate the contract and sue for any damages.

ITALY: Unilateral changes may alter the original contractual balance. Therefore, as a rule, all changes need to be agreed upon between the contractual parties. If the changes are detrimental for the agent (e.g. require higher expenses/time), the latter may seek a higher compensation. If the principal changes the content of the mandate contract unilaterally, the agent shall be entitled to terminate the contract if he does not agree with the changes.

NETHERLANDS: Where the agent's remuneration is based on a payment for the time spent on the performance of the mandate contract, a change of the mandate will automatically lead to an adjustment of the price if the performance of the mandate contract would become more burdensome. Where the price is based on a fixed price and the agent's mandate would be restricted and this would qualify as a partial termination of the mandate contract, CC Article 7:411 may lead to an adjustment of the price. In so far as the agent's obligations would be broadened as a consequence of a unilateral change of the mandate, CC Article 7:405 paragraph (2) may be applied by analogy as regards the additional work resulting from the change, requiring the principal to pay for the additional work; the amount that the principal would have to pay in addition to the original price is to be calculated in accordance with the normally charged price.

POLAND: The principal may not change the scope of mandate contract by a unilateral act.

SCOTLAND: A unilateral attempt to make a significant change to the mandate contract is likely to amount to a material breach on the principal's part, entitling the agent to rescind from the contract and to claim damages. If the agent did not accept the change and the principal refused to renegotiate but also refused to be bound by the original contract this is likely to amount to a material breach, or anticipatory breach, on the principal's part, entitling the agent to terminate the relationship and claim damages. It could happen that an agent's acceptance of a significant change, without express mention of price, resulted in a new contract with an implied term that payment would be on a *quantum meruit* basis (cf. *Head Wrightson Aluminium Ltd v Aberdeen Harbour Commissioners* 1958 SLT (Notes) 12).

SLOVAKIA: The requirement of the agent to act in the interest of the principal and the good faith principle should be the ground for the agent's duty to warn principal provided his instructions are bad. If the principal does not change his instructions, agent will be obliged to follow them or to terminate the contract.

SPAIN: The agent must warn the principal if the following of a direction is problematic. As far as this direction has and could not have been contemplated by the parties when agreeing on the price, the agent will be entitled to compensation for additional expenses. There are no rules as to the adjustment of the price of the service in the light of a direction. However, according to the remission to the commercial usages made by CC Article 1711 paragraph (2) and Comm.C Article 277, an adjustment of the price may be reasonable if the service becomes more onerous. However, in no case is the agent entitled to proceed against the principal's upholding of the old instructions (Comm.C Article 256). The agent is not bound to follow instructions when that ought to be regarded as a change in the content of the mandate. Finally, the agent may in such a situation terminate due to good cause (CC Articles 1735 and 1736).

SWEDEN: The agent is entitled to a price which is reasonable considering the circumstances. A unilateral change of power could lead to an adjustment of the price and time for performance of the contract.

No answer received: BELGIUM, DENMARK, ESTONIA, MALTA, PORTUGAL.

Chapter 5:
Conflicts of interests

Article 5:101: Self-contracting

(1) The agent may not become the principal's counterparty to the prospective contract.
(2) The agent may nevertheless become the counterparty if:
   (a) this is agreed by the parties in the mandate contract;
   (b) the agent has disclosed an intention to become the counterparty and
      (i) the principal subsequently expresses consent; or
      (ii) the principal does not object to the agent becoming the counterparty after having been requested to indicate consent or a refusal of consent;
   (c) the principal otherwise knew, or could reasonably be expected to have known, of the agent becoming the counterparty and the principal did not object within a reasonable time; or
   (d) the content of the prospective contract is so precisely determined in the mandate contract that there is no risk that the interests of the principal may be disregarded.
(3) If the principal is a consumer, the agent may only become the counterparty if:
   (a) the agent has disclosed that information and the principal has given express consent to the agent becoming the counterparty to the particular prospective contract; or
   (b) the content of the prospective contract is so precisely determined in the mandate contract that there is no risk that the interests of the principal may be disregarded.
(4) The parties may not, to the detriment of the principal, exclude the application of paragraph (3) or derogate from or vary its effects.
(5) If the agent has become the counterparty, the agent is not entitled to a price for services rendered as an agent.

Comments

A. General idea

The present Article starts from the same idea as Article 3:205 PECL (Conflict of interest): the presumption that there is a conflict of interests when the agent in his capacity as the agent of the principal concludes a contract on behalf of the principal with himself or herself in a personal capacity. The agent is therefore not allowed to do so. The main differences between the Articles are not of a substantive nature, but follow from their different focus: whereas Article 3:205 PECL (Conflict of interest) deals with the *external* relationship between the principal and the third party, the present Article deals with the *internal* relationship.

Where the agent is not allowed to act as the third party but has nonetheless done so, the act is not in conformity with the best interests of the principal, and the agent is therefore liable for non-performance. However, there are situations where this may be different. Paragraph (2) deals with this matter. For consumers, a more restrictive approach is taken in paragraph (3). This more restrictive rule is mandatory to protect the consumer's interest (paragraph (4)). Paragraph (5) deals with the consequences as regards the payment of the price.

B. Main rule: agent may not act as third party

One of the main obligations of the agent is to act in accordance with the interests of the principal (Article 3:102 (Obligation to act in interests of principal)). In a situation in which the agent is at the same time the third party to the prospective contract (a situation also known as 'self-contracting' or 'Selbsteintritt'), a conflict of interests may arise.

Illustration 1
Shirley mandates Timothy to sell a precious Ming vase. Timothy is himself interested in the purchase of the vase. Whereas Timothy, as a buyer, will want to pay as little as possible, in his function as Shirley's agent, he is required to achieve as high a sale price as possible. These interests clearly collide.

The prohibition of self-contracting to avoid a conflict between the interests of the principal and those of the agent is the main rule in all systems.

Under these Principles, however, an exception to the main rule is possible when a conflict of interest is deemed or may be assumed not to exist. These cases are regulated in paragraph (2). If the conditions set out there are met, the agent does not breach his contractual obligations towards the principal if he becomes a party to the prospective contract.

This is also the approach in the Member States. In all systems there are situations in which self-contracting is deemed justified because the risk of a conflict of interests is neutralised.

C. Self-contracting if agreed in mandate contract

A first exception to the ban on self-contracting is the situation where the contract itself indicates that the agent is entitled to act as the third party. Consent may be express or implied.

Since the rules which impose a prohibition to self-contracting are default in all regimes, parties are free to agree to allow self-contracting in their agreement.

D. Self-contracting if agent discloses intention to become counterparty

The risk of a conflict of interests is to a large extent minimised if there is full disclosure of the fact that the agent wishes to act as the third party to the prospective contract, as in that case the principal is aware that the agent has potentially conflicting interests. Such a principal will be alerted to look critically into whether the prospective contract is beneficial to him or her. Accordingly, when the agent has disclosed the intention of being the third party and the principal does not object, the principal may be assumed to have given consent. In this situation, there is insufficient reason not to allow the agent to also be the third party to the contract.

Illustration 2
Paul lives in Spain but has an apartment for rent in Amsterdam. Before leaving the Netherlands, he authorised and instructed his friend Charo to find lessees for Paul's apartment, at € 1,000 per month. In the last year the apartment has not been rented because of the crisis in the housing market. Charo indicates to Paul that she would like to rent the apartment herself but that she can only pay € 700. Paul agrees to that.

E. Self-contracting if intention not disclosed

The fact that the agent did *not* disclose the intention of acting as the third party should not prevent the agent from nevertheless acting as the third party if the principal otherwise knew or must have known that the agent would act as the third party. There is no substantial difference between those cases where the agent disclosed the conflict and cases where the principal found out or was informed by another party that the agent would become the counterparty to the prospective contract if in both of these types of cases the principal did not object to that situation.

Illustration 3
Jeremy is the proud owner of a 1964 Corvette. Due to financial reasons, he is forced to sell the car. He knows that Simon is interested in buying the car and tells him the car is for sale for € 20,000. Simon is broke and cannot afford to buy the car. He is willing to try to sell the car on Jeremy's behalf for the required amount, however. Two weeks later, Carmela tells Jeremy that Simon has won the lottery. Given that Jeremy is aware of Simon's interest in the car and that Simon's reason for not buying it has now disappeared, it does not come as a surprise to him that Simon has in fact bought the car when Simon tells him later that week that 'the car was sold for the agreed amount'. If Jeremy does not object to Simon becoming the new owner of the Corvette, he may be assumed to have consented to Simon acting as the third party.

In ENGLAND, IRELAND, and SCOTLAND, emphasis is put on the existence of an obligation for the agent to inform the principal about the risk of a conflict of interests in order for the principal to be able to consent to it. In many other systems, consent of the principal is required, but there is no indication as to the existence of an obligation of disclosure for the agent. Under these regimes, the relevant factor is whether the agent knows or should have been aware of the conflict of interests.

This is also the approach under these Principles. The principal may know about the conflict of interests by other means than the agent's disclosure. If the principal knows or should have known about the risk of a conflict of interest and does not object to it, then self-contracting is allowed.

F. Self-contracting if content of the prospective contract excludes risk of conflict of interests

Where the content of the prospective contract is very clearly determined in the mandate contract, a conflict of interests is excluded. In such cases, the contract offered to the third party is more or less non-negotiable. The agent is then no longer in a position to further his or her own interests to the detriment of the principal because the terms of the prospective contract cannot be altered. If that is the case, there is not much risk that the interests of the principal would be jeopardised.

Illustration 4
Norman instructs Natasja to buy 50 shares of Nelson plc at the current market price. Since Natasja has a holding of shares in that corporation and wishes to dispose of them, she sells the shares to the principal for the current market price. The agent is the seller, but the interests of the principal have not been jeopardised.

G. Self-contracting if principal is consumer

A principal-consumer may not be in a position to clearly evaluate whether the agent's own interests have led to a contract that is sub-optimal. To protect the principal from hasty decisions, or even from giving consent by adhering to standard contract terms, this Article demands that consent must be given expressly, in writing or otherwise.

To properly protect the interests of the consumer and also to protect the trust in professional providers of mandate services, a more restrictive provision is needed when it comes to contracts between a business and a consumer. However, it is not in the interest of the consumer to completely exclude the possibility of the agent becoming the principal's counterparty to the prospective contract. The interests of the principal are sufficiently safeguarded with full disclosure of the identity of the agent and express consent by the principal for the particular transaction (paragraph (3)(a)). This implies that the principal cannot by way of agreeing to standard contract terms be forced to accept the agent becoming the counterparty to the prospective contract.

A conflict of interests is also deemed to be excluded in contracts between a business and a consumer when the content of the prospective contract is so precisely determined in the mandate contract that there is no risk that the interests of the principal may be disregarded (paragraph (3)(b)).

Legislation in the Member States generally does not provide this extra protection to principals who are consumers, though such protection is awarded in THE NETHERLANDS.

H. Validity of prospective contract when agent has wrongfully acted as third party

A contract concluded by the agent in his personal capacity, i.e. as the third party, is valid even if the agent was not allowed to act as the third party and thus violated his obligations under this Article. However, the prospective contract may be avoided in accordance with and under the conditions set out in Article 3:205 PECL (Conflict of interest). On the other hand, the principal may also ratify the contract after having been informed of the conflict of interest under Article 3:207 PECL (Ratification by principal). If such a ratification takes place, not only does the principal lose the right to avoid the contract but normally also the right to claim liability of the agent, as stated in Article 3:202 (Consequences of ratification) of these Principles. This implies that the agent is exempted from liability unless the principal notifies the agent without undue delay after ratification that he reserves the remedies.

I. No price if agent becomes the third party

According to paragraph (5), if the agent becomes party to the prospective contract, then he is not entitled to the price for the services rendered.

This approach deviates from the approach in most legal systems. The agent's entitlement to the price remains even if the agent becomes counterparty to the prospective contract in BELGIUM, ENGLAND, FINLAND, FRANCE, GERMANY, GREECE, HUNGARY, IRELAND, ITALY, THE NETHERLANDS, POLAND, SCOTLAND, SLOVAKIA, SPAIN, and SWEDEN. In BULGARIA, the agent is entitled to half of the price.

Under these Principles, the agent is deemed to have fulfilled his financial interests by becoming counterparty to the contract. The agent is therefore no longer entitled to remuneration. Article 5:101 (Self-contracting) is a default rule, and parties may therefore agree otherwise. If the agent wants to keep his right to the price, then he has to take care that the principal agrees to it in the contract. Where his standard contract terms contain a provision to this extent, such a clause is of course subject to the unfairness test of Article 4:110 PECL (Unfair terms not individually negotiated).

J. Relationship with the Principles of European Law and the Draft Common Frame of Reference

The same rule is in the DCFR, in Article IV.D. – 5:101 (Self-contracting). Under the DCFR, the prospective contract concluded by the agent as a third party may be avoided in accordance with and under the conditions set out in Article II. – 6:109 DCFR (Conflict of interest). The principal may also ratify the contract after having been informed of the conflict of interest under Article II. – 6:111 DCFR (Ratification).

K. Character of the rule

This Article constitutes a default rule from which the parties may derogate if both parties are not consumers. Paragraph 3 states a regime for self-contracting applicable when the principal is a consumer. In such a case, as established in paragraph (4), the rule is mandatory to protect the interests of consumers.

L. Remedies

When the agent was not allowed to act as the third party but has nonetheless done so, the act is not in conformity with the best interests of the principal and the agent is therefore liable for non-performance. The normal remedies for non-performance apply.

Comparative Notes

1. Main rule: self-contracting not allowed

The main rule in all legal systems is that self-contracting in mandate contracts is not allowed so as to prevent conflicting interests. In BULGARIA, the explicit prohibition regards direct mandate. The rules are not mandatory, however. Self-contracting is allowed specifically in BULGARIA, GERMANY, and HUNGARY for commercial commission agents.

2. Conditions under which self-contracting is allowed

The general rule in all systems is that the agent may not become a counterparty in the contract concluded with the principal because of the risk of a conflict of interests. However, in all systems there are situations in which self-contracting is deemed justified. The conditions which are to be met are much varied, but they are all meant to preclude a conflict of interests between agent and principal.

The most frequent grounds within the systems to allow self-contracting are as follows: the contractual agreement of the parties, the principal's consent, and the content of the contract is precisely determined so that a conflict of interests is precluded. Contractual agreement of the parties is mentioned as a ground to allow self-contracting in DENMARK, FINLAND, FRANCE, GERMANY, HUNGARY, IRELAND, ITALY, MALTA, POLAND, PORTUGAL, SPAIN, and SWEDEN. Consent of the principal is mentioned as a ground to justify self-contracting in AUSTRIA, BELGIUM, BULGARIA, DENMARK, ENGLAND, FINLAND, FRANCE, GREECE, and SCOTLAND. Emphasis is placed on the obligation of the agent to disclose fully the risk of a conflict of interests in ENGLAND, IRELAND, and SCOTLAND (if real estate agents). Express consent is required in ITALY. The third most common ground is that the content of the contract is so precisely determined that the risk of conflict of interests is precluded because there is no room for negotiation – for example, if the price is determined by objective criteria. This ground is mentioned in ESTONIA, FINLAND, ITALY, THE NETHERLANDS, and PORTUGAL.

Some systems impose formal requirements: in GREECE, a notarial deed is needed; in MALTA, consent needs to be in writing in the instrument of mandate. Written consent of the principal is also required in THE NETHERLANDS if the principal is a consumer, and in SLOVAKIA for commission agents for the procurement of securities.

There are other requirements that are specific to the systems. In AUSTRIA, self-contracting is also allowed if it is advantageous and without risk for the principal, but the prospective contract's wording needs to be explicit and transparent. Custom is a ground for justification in DENMARK and SWEDEN. In IRELAND, real estate agents must also show that the price was fair and that there has been no abuse of the position of agent. Finally, in SCOTLAND, in the relation between solicitor and client, the solicitor must prove that the transaction was fair and honest when entered into and that there was no undue influence.

3. No price in case of self-contracting

The general rule in almost all regimes is that the agent is entitled to the price. This is indeed the case in BELGIUM, BULGARIA (half of the price), ENGLAND, FINLAND, FRANCE, GERMANY, GREECE, HUNGARY, IRELAND, ITALY, MALTA, THE NETHERLANDS, POLAND, SCOTLAND, SLOVAKIA, SPAIN, and SWEDEN. The countries in which there is no right to the price are AUSTRIA, DENMARK, and FINLAND (only for real estate agents).

National Notes

1. Main rule: self-contracting not allowed

AUSTRIA: The agent must not get into a position where the duty to the principal conflicts or may conflict with the agent's own interests or the interests of another principal. There is special commercial regulation for self-contracting in Comm.C Articles 345, 405 and 412 paragraph (1) (Dullinger, RZ 1986, 204 ff; Article 25 GmbHG; Wünsch; Rummel/Strasser, Article 1009 Rz 21).

BELGIUM: The majority defends a general prohibition of self-contracting: the agent is forbidden to be a party to the prospective contract. This prohibition is based on the risk of a conflict of interests. In case of a breach, the contract is (relatively) null and void (nullité relative, Cass. 18 Mar 2004, RW 2004-05, 303, note A. Smets; Cass. 24 September 1981, Pas. 1982, I, 125; Cass. 7 December 1978, Arr. Cass. 1978-79, 407, Pas. 1979, I, 408; De Page, p. 410-412; Ekelmans, p. 9-10; Foriers & Glansdorff, p. 607-610; Foriers, p. 64-65; Samoy, p. 47-49; Wagemans, p. 177; Wéry, p. 154-158).

BULGARIA: Self-contracting is explicitly banned only in cases of direct representation. OCA Article 38 paragraph (1) forbids the (direct) agent to negotiate in the name of the principal with either himself or another person he represents, unless the principal has given consent.

DENMARK: Legislation rules on self-contracting are inadequately treated. The notion appears in the Factors Act Articles 40-45 governing the extent and terms under which a factor may take the buyer's place in a sales factoring situation and the seller's place in a purchasing situation *(contracting for own account)*. Articles 40-45 take account of the fact that it is difficult to deal honestly with oneself. These rules most likely apply to all kinds of representation governed by Danish law.

ENGLAND: The agent cannot be a party to the prospective contract unless certain conditions are fulfilled.

ESTONIA: Self-contracting is regulated both for the internal relationship between the agent and the principal as well as for the external relationship. For the internal relationship, LOAEst Article 623 paragraph (1) (applicable for the (general) contract for services) provides that in case of entry into a transaction, the agent may be the third party or the principal of the third party to the transaction only if the possibility of a conflict of interests is precluded. This would be the case where the content of the second contract is so precisely determined in the contract for mandate that a conflict of interests between the principal and the agent is excluded. LOAEst Article 623 paragraph (2) further provides that the agent must inform the principal of any direct or indirect interest in the prospective transaction.

FINLAND: There are no general rules on self-contracting in Finland. The agent is usually not entitled to be a party to the prospective contract.

FRANCE: On the basis of a general obligation of fair dealing, which is imposed on the agent (see Pétel, no. 172 s.), and in order to reduce the risk of any misuse of power, the agent may not become a party to the contract negotiated for the principal. The sanction is voidability of the contract; the contract may be avoided by the principal (Cass.civ. 1re, 29 November 1988, Bull. civ. I, no. 341). The rule is not, however, one of mandatory public policy. The principal may authorise the agent to become a party to the contract. In addition, the regulations on stockbroking companies allow them to be parties to the contract in certain cases (Comm.C Article L. 131-7). The prohibition on the agent becoming a party to the contract is not established in a general manner by the Civil Code in the Chapter relating to agency, but has been deduced by the courts from CC Article 1596 relating to the particular case of auction sales. It is applied rigorously, even where the price or consideration for the contract is that envisaged by the principal, and even where the agent acts through an intermediary (Cass.civ. 1re, 12 December 2000, Bull. civ. I, no. 319; Civ. 1re, 29 November 1988, Bull. civ. I, no. 341). The general view is that the prohibition on the agent becoming a party to the contract also applies to the commission agent in commercial matters (Huet, no. 31149).

GERMANY: Under the rules on mandate in Germany (CC Articles 662-674) and *Geschäftsbesorgungsvertrag* (CC Article 675(1)), the contract is decisive, the law being silent on this question. The matter is to some extent decided by the rules on authority (CC Article 181), which generally rule out self-contracting *(Insich-Geschäft)*.

GREECE: According to Article 235 paragraph (1) CC an agent may not execute in the name of the (person) represented a deed with himself or herself personally.

HUNGARY: If the agent has to act in the name of the principal, according to CC Article 221 paragraph (3), '[an] agent shall not proceed if the opposite or otherwise interested party is himself or a person whom he also represents. The agent, if a legal person, shall also be allowed to proceed in a case of conflicting interests with the express consent of the person represented'. In case of commission agency, CC Article 510 paragraph (1) provides that '[t]he commission agent can himself conclude a sales contract with the principal.' In all cases, the general rules of obligations apply, especially CC Article 277(5): '[t]he parties shall be under obligation to inform each other of all important circumstances affecting performance of the contract'.

IRELAND: An agent's fiduciary duties include the duty to avoid conflicts of interest. It has been stated: 'It is a rule of universal application, that no one, having [fiduciary] duties to discharge, shall be allowed to enter into engagements in which he has, or can have, a personal interest conflicting, or which possibly may conflict, with the interests of those whom he is bound to protect.' (Lord Cramworth LC in *Aberdeen Rly Co v Blaikie Bros* [1854] 1 Macq 461 at 471). Where the duty applies, there is a breach if, for instance, an agent instructed to buy property, sells the agent's own property to the principal (e.g. *Armstrong v Jackson* [1917] 2 KB 822); or if an agent instructed to sell property, buys it personally (e.g. *McPherson v Watt* [1877] 3 App Cas 254).

ITALY: As a rule, there is no strict prohibition of self-contracting. Self-dealing is governed by CC Article 1395, which is located among the general rules on contracts: 'a contract which the agent makes with himself, whether acting in his own behalf or as the agent of another party, is voidable, unless specifically authorised by the principal or unless the content of the contract is established in such a way to preclude the possibility of a conflict of interests'.

MALTA: The agent can only be a party to the prospected contract is his own name and only if he is allowed by the principal in the written instrument of mandate.

NETHERLANDS: According to CC Article 7:416 paragraph (1), *Selbsteintritt* is allowed only if the juridical acts to be performed by the agent under the mandate contract have been precisely established, so that the interests of the principal and the agent do not conflict. Where the principal is a consumer, the agent may only act as the third party if the principal has given his written consent thereto. Where such written consent is missing, the consumer may void the prospective contract, cf. CC Article 7:416 paragraph (3).

POLAND: Self-contracting is allowed only if the principal has agreed or if there is no danger to the principal's interests.

SCOTLAND: As a general rule, an agent is under a duty not to get into a position in which the agent's own interests would conflict with those of the principal *(Huntingdon Copper and Sulphur Co Ltd v Henderson* (1877) 4 R 294 at 307, per Lord Mure). Self-contracting is therefore only permitted subject to stringent conditions *(McPherson's Trustees v Watt* (1877) 5 R (HL) 9; Macgregor, paragraph 97).

PORTUGAL: Self-contracting in mandate is regulated by CC Article 261. This Article provides that "the deal closed by an agent with himself, in his own name, or in the representation of a third party is avoidable, unless the client has specifically consented on the closing of that deal, or that by its own nature, the deal excludes the possibility of a conflict of interests". The ratio of this rule is to protect the interests of the client. Cf. Vaz Serra, *RLJ* 91 (1958), p. 213; STJ 21 March 1995, CJ/STJ 1995, 1, 130; RC 11 June 1985, CJ 1985, 3, 92.

SLOVAKIA: According to the general rules relating to Representation, no one may act as an agent for another person if his interests conflict with the interests of the person represented (CC Article 22 paragraph (2)). The commission agent must protect the principal's interests known to him, and keep the latter well informed of all the circumstances that may lead to a change in the principal's instructions (Comm.C Article 579 paragraph (1)).

SPAIN: Self-contracting is not explicitly regulated in a general way for mandate contracts. There are however some specific rules that forbid this type of practice. CC Article 1459 does not allow the agent to buy the principal's goods under the agent's administration. See also Comm.C Article 267. It seems that the legislator did not want to allow this type of situation.

SWEDEN: The main rule is that self-contracting is not allowed. A commissionaire is allowed to be a party to the prospective contract only if this right follows from the contract or from trade custom in a particular line of business. A real estate agent is prohibited to be a party to the prospective contract (KommL Articles 40-45; FmL Article 13).

2. Conditions under which self-contracting is allowed

AUSTRIA: An agent is not allowed to be the third party, except if the principal has consented to it, or if self-contracting is only advantageous for the principal and involves no risks for the principal (OGH in ÖBA 1992, 274; SZ 69/90; ZfRV 1997, 246; NZ 1995, 305; NZ 1997, 95; SZ 69/90; RdW 1998, 548), e.g. when there is a current price for the goods. In all these cases, the agent must conclude the prospective contract by express words, so that it is transparent and not easy to escape from by unilateral action at the agent's discretion (OGH in RdW 1986, 39; ZfRV 1997, 246).

BELGIUM: The agent may be party to the prospective contract with the principal's knowledge and permission.

BULGARIA: In general, self-contracting is only possible with the consent of the principal (OCA Article 38 (1)). CA Article 358 provides an exception for commission agents: they may conclude the prospective contract on their behalf if it concerns the sale of goods or securities at market or commodity exchange price.

DENMARK: Under Danish Legislation self-contracting is allowed by the Factors Act only when both parties have agreed upon it or when it is consistent with *custom*.

ENGLAND: The agent can be a party to the contract as long as the principal has full knowledge of the extent of the agent's interests in the transaction and agrees to the transaction. The agent's duty of disclosure is full and must be very precise so that the principal knows all the possible consequences before giving consent. The burden of proving that the duty has been complied with is on the agent. The agent will not be able to evade the rule of no conflict of interest by dealing with the principal through a third party *(McPherson v Watt* (1877) 3 App Cas 254).

ESTONIA: For the internal relationship, LOAEst Article 623 paragraph (1) (applicable for the (general) contract for services) provides that in case of entry into a transaction, the agent may be the third party or the principal of the third party to the transaction only if the possibility of a conflict of interests is precluded. This would be the case where the content of the second contract is so precisely determined in the contract for mandate that a conflict of interests between the principal and the agent is excluded. LOAEst Article 623 paragraph (2) further provides that the agent must inform the principal of any direct or indirect interest in the prospective transaction.

FINLAND: Self-contracting is allowed if agreed. Self-contracting is also allowed when it is clear that no conflict of interests arises (e.g. when the price of the prospective contract is based merely on an objective valuation). Further, an estate agent is entitled to self-contract if the client is informed in advance (REstateAA Article 8).

FRANCE: The prohibition of self-contracting is not one of mandatory public policy. The principal may authorise the agent to become a party to the contract. In addition, the regulations on stock-broking companies allow them to be parties to the contract in certain cases (Comm.C Article L. 131-7). The prohibition on the agent becoming a party to the contract is not established in a general manner by the Civil Code in the Chapter relating to agency, but has been deduced by the courts from CC Article 1596 relating to the particular case of auction sales. It is applied rigorously, even where the price or consideration for the contract is that envisaged by the principal, and even where the agent acts through an intermediary (Cass.civ. 1re 12 December 2000, Bull. civ. I, no. 319; Cass.civ. 1re 29 November 1988, Bull. civ. I, no. 341). The general view is that the prohibition on the agent becoming a party to the contract also applies to the commission agent in commercial matters (Huet, no. 31149).

GERMANY: Rules on mandate (CC Articles 662-674) and *Geschäftsbesorgungsvertrag* (CC Article 675(1)), the contract is decisive (the law being silent on this question). The matter is to some extent decided by the rules on authority (CC Article 181), which rule out self-contracting *(Insich-Geschäft).* The law on commercial commission agents explicitly allows self-contracting *(Selbsteintritt),* provided that the principal has not otherwise instructed the agent (Comm.C Article 400).

GREECE: The agent is allowed to become third party if it has been authorised (explicitly or tacitly) by the principal or if it constitutes exclusively the performance of an obligation (Georgiadis/Stathopoulos/Doris, Article 235 Greek CC no. 1). A contract with oneself which has not been executed in the form of a notarial deed is invalid (CC Article 235 paragraph (2)). If the agent violates these rules and acts as the third party the concluded contract is void (CA Thessaloniki decision no. 2977/1989, EllDni 1991, 1345).

HUNGARY: According to Article 221 paragraph (3) CC, '[an] agent shall not proceed if the opposite or otherwise interested party is himself or a person whom he also represents. The agent, if a legal person, shall also be allowed to proceed in a case of conflicting interests with the express consent of the person represented'. In case of commission agency, CC Article 510 paragraph (1) provides that '[t]he commission agent can himself conclude a sales contract with the principal.' In all cases, the general rules of obligations apply, especially CC Article 277 paragraph (5): '[t]he parties shall be under obligation to inform each other of all important circumstances affecting performance of the contract'.

IRELAND: Self-contracting is not allowed unless all the circumstances are disclosed to the principal and the principal consents to the transaction *(North & South Trust Co v Berkeley* [1971] 1 WLR 470 at 484-485;

Gibson v Jeyes [1801] 6 Ves 266). Where an agent buys the principal's property or sells the agent's own property to the principal, the agent must also show that the price was fair and that there has been no abuse of the position of agent *(McPherson v Watt* [1877] 3 App Cas 254).

ITALY: As a rule, there is no strict prohibition of self-contracting. Self-dealing is governed by CC Article 1395, which is located among the general rules on contracts: 'a contract which the agent makes with himself, whether acting in his own behalf or as the agent of another party, is voidable, unless specifically authorised by the principal or unless the content of the contract is established in such a way to preclude the possibility of a conflict of interests'.

MALTA: The agent can only be a party to the prospected contract is his own name and only if he is allowed by the principal in the written instrument of mandate.

NETHERLANDS: According to CC Article 7:416 paragraph (1), *Selbsteintritt* is allowed only if the juridical acts to be performed by the agent under the mandate contract have been precisely established, so that the interests of the principal and the agent do not conflict.

POLAND: Self-contracting is allowed only if the principal has agreed or if there is no danger to the principal's interests.

PORTUGAL: The avoidability of a contract in which the agent has become counterparty of the principal is cured by the previous or subsequent consent of the client, which does not need to be express (silence can be enough, according to the circumstances of the case: STJ 3 March 1998, BMJ 475, 610). Lima/Varela (1987) point out some cases where it can be deemed that a conflict of interests does not exist: if an agent has the authority to recover several debts and also recovers his own debt; if an agent has the authority to sell a good for a specific price and buys it for himself and/or a third party; if the good has a fixed price (e.g. A buys a theatre ticket for himself).

SCOTLAND: Agents have, in Scottish law, a fiduciary duty towards their principals. This relationship is characterised by trust and loyalty and has several different aspects. The issue has received much attention from academics in the context of the solicitor-principal relationship. If a solicitor makes a contract on behalf of the principal to which the solicitor is a party, then that contract is voidable at the instance of the principal *(McPherson's Trustees v Watt* (1877) 5 R (HL) 9). The onus rests on the solicitor to show why that contract should not be declared void *(Rigg's Exx v Urquhart* (1902) 10 SLT 503 per Lord Stormonth-Darling at 504). However, the transaction may not be voidable if the solicitor can prove that the transaction was fair and honest when entered into; that there was no undue influence; or that the principal gave fully informed consent to the transaction following disclosure to the principal of all the material facts within the solicitor's knowledge (Paterson, no. 172). In the case of estate agents, this question is governed by both 'soft law' and actual legislation. Several codes of practice exist, most notably the Ombudsman's Code of Practice for Estate Agents and the Estate Agency Affairs Board Code of Conduct. The former contains a general duty to avoid conflicts of interest which '… might not be in the best interests of the principal' (Ombudsman's Code of Practice, rule 9d). An estate agent seeking to buy property owned by a principal or sell property owned by the agent to a principal is under a duty, before negotiations begin, to provide all relevant facts in writing to that principal and as soon as possible to the principal's solicitor (Ombudsman's Code of Practice, rule 9b and 9c; see also the Estate Agency Affairs Board Code of Conduct, Article 4.2). The main piece of legislation relevant to estate agents, the Estate Agents Act 1979, contains a similar obligation (Article 21(1)).

SLOVAKIA: Allowance of self-contracting is explicitly regulated for the commission agent contract on the procurement of securities' sale: the agent may perform his obligation by selling his own security to the principal or by buying the principal's security himself, provided that this has been allowed in (written) contract (Act on Securities and Investment Services (Act 566|2001Coll.), Article 33 paragraph (2)).

SPAIN: Recent decisions of the Tribunal Supremo allow self-contracting in cases in which the principal has given consent or when the possibility of a conflict of interests is excluded (STS 24 September 1994; STS 15 March 1996; STS 12 February 1999; see also Lacruz, p. 15).

SWEDEN: The parties can by contract allow self-contracting. An agent is allowed to be a party to the prospective contract only if this right follows from the contract or from trade custom in a particular line of business. If the agent enters into the prospective contract as a party, the agent is obliged to notify the principal about this fact and the duty to act in the principal's interest remains. See KommL Articles 40-45; Ramberg, p. 254; Tiberg/Dotevall, p. 99).

3. No price in case of self-contracting

AUSTRIA: The agent who acts as third party to the prospective contract is not entitled to a price for services rendered or to reimbursement of expenses made. It is in this respect not relevant whether the agent, before becoming a party to the prospective contract, has entered into failed negotiations with a third party (Rummel/Strasser, Article 1009 Rz 21; Straube/Griss, Article 405 Rz 1).

BELGIUM: According to De Page, self-contracting is no longer a question of representation. There is only the prospective contract, the former object of the contract for representation (De Page, p. 412). Recent authors on the contrary consider the permitted self-contracting as a simple modality to execute the contract for representation. Therefore the rights and duties of the contract for representation (e.g. the principal's duty to pay a salary and to reimburse the expenses) remain (Wéry, p. 158).

BULGARIA: In a case of self-contracting the commission agent is entitled to receive half of the remuneration stipulated in the commission contract (CA Article 358(1)).

DENMARK: Danish law in all probability will not entitle the self-contracting agent to claim a price for services or to claim reimbursement of expenses incurred, even if the agent has conducted failed negotiations with a third party.

ENGLAND: Provided that all the relevant conditions of remuneration are complied with, there is no reason why the self-contracting agent should not be entitled to commission. Such an interpretation seems possible relying on *Wilson v Short* ((1848) 6 Hare 366 and *Robinson v Mollett* (1874) LR 7, HL).

ESTONIA: The LOAEst Article 623 paragraph (3) provides that a transaction entered into by the principal with the service provider (the agent) upon the performance of a contract of services does not restrict the right of the service provider (the agent) to receive remuneration and reimbursement of expenses if the provisions of Article 623 paragraph (1) have been adhered to.

FINLAND: There is no clear general rule on this point. Unless otherwise agreed, the agent is normally entitled to remuneration. However, this depends on the circumstances. An estate agent is not entitled to a price for the performance in a case of self-contracting (REstateAA Article 20).

FRANCE: If the principal authorises the agent to be a party to the contract, it would appear that French case law allows the agent to be entitled to payment in respect to what is due under the mandate. French academic legal writing considers in fact that, in that situation, the initial agency remains in place and a second contract is entered into with the agent who has become a party to the contract (Collart Dutilleul & Delebecque, no. 646). This position would not apply, however, if parties decided to first terminate the agency in order to enable the conclusion of the other contract between them (Huet, no. 31149). The French courts do not require any prior condition such as the failure of the transaction with a third party, and it is simply the wish of the principal to accept that the agent become a party to the contract which will determine the position.

GERMANY: In the case of self-contracting, Comm.C Article 403 nevertheless entitles the commission agent to a price for the services and reimbursement of expenses.

GREECE: If the agent is allowed to be the third party, the answer to the question of entitlement to remuneration or reimbursement of expenses depends on the internal relationship which underlies the mandate. In the case of a gratuitous mandate relationship the agent is not entitled to a price in any event. With regard to the reimbursement of expenses CC Article 722 is applicable: '[a] principal shall be bound to reimburse the agent for everything the latter has spent to achieve an orderly performance of the mandate.'

HUNGARY: If the agent has to act in the name of the principal, according to CC Article 221 paragraph (3), the agent 'shall not proceed if the opposite or otherwise interested party is himself or a person whom he also represents. The agent, if a legal person, shall also be allowed to proceed in a case of conflicting interests with the express consent of the person represented'. Because of this prohibition, the agent cannot be entitled to a price or to reimbursement of expenses. In the case of commission agency, CC Article 510 paragraph (1) provides that '[t]he commission agent can himself conclude a sales contract with the principal'. In this case, paragraph (2) of this same Article establishes that '[t]he commission agent's claim for commission shall not be affected if the sales contract with the principal is concluded by the commission agent himself'. According to CC Article 511 paragraph (2), '[t]he commission shall include the expenses usually involved with consignment, but it shall not include expenses related to carriage'. In all other cases CC Article 478 paragraph (1) applies, according to which '[t]he principal shall pay an appropriate fee, unless the circumstances, or the relationship between the parties suggest that the agent has assumed the agency without any consideration' and the first phrase of CC Article 479 paragraph (1) which establishes that '[c]osts that arise in connection with the handling of a matter shall be borne by the principal'.

IRELAND: Bowstead & Reynolds list a number of circumstances where no remuneration is payable, including where the transaction is unauthorised; in cases of misconduct or breach of duty; and in respect of unlawful transactions. There is no mention, in this litany of circumstances, of where the agent is allowed to be the third party. Moreover, given that self-contracting is permissible and not necessarily in breach of any fiduciary duty, provided there is full disclosure etc., it would appear that remuneration and reimbursement of expenses are due in such circumstances *(Wilson v Short* [1848] 6 Hare 366; *Robinson v Mollett* [1874] LR 7).

ITALY: A self-contracting agent is still entitled to a price for the services provided and reimbursement of expenses incurred.

MALTA: The agent is still entitled to a fee for his services of mandate, provided that he has been allowed by the principal to be a party to the prospected contract.

NETHERLANDS: If self-contracting is allowed, the agent remains entitled to remuneration (CC Article 7:416 paragraph (4)). If it is not allowed, however, the agent usually is deprived of the right to payment. Self-contracting which is not allowed is a breach of contract, but the principal may determine to maintain the mandate contract. In that case, the principal may (partially) postpone payment (CC Article 6:262) or deduct the agent's remuneration from the principal's claim for compensation for the agent's breach of contract (CC Article 6:127).

POLAND: There are no Polish CC provisions that would deprive the agent of the remuneration or limit it in any way in case of self-contracting.

PORTUGAL: Notwithstanding the provision of CC Article 261 and the limits imposed by the principle of good faith and fair dealing (CC Article 227 and 763 paragraph (2)), the agent's rights are otherwise unhindered.

SCOTLAND: If the requirements for self-contracting are adhered to, and the contract is not voidable, then there is no reason why the agent should not be entitled to a price for the services and reimbursement of expenses incurred in the normal fashion.

SLOVAKIA: There is no explicit regulation on this issue, but if the contract is not void, the agent will be entitled to a price.

SPAIN: A self-contracting agent is probably still entitled to a price for the services provided and to reimbursement of expenses incurred.

SWEDEN: An agent is entitled to a price which has to be as favourable to the principal as the prevailing price at the time of the self-contracting notification (KommL Article 42).

Article 5:102: Double mandate

(1) The agent may not act as the agent of both the principal and the principal's counterparty to the prospective contract.

(2) The agent may nevertheless act as the agent of both the principal and the counterparty if:
   (a) this is agreed by the parties in the mandate contract;
   (b) the agent has disclosed an intention to act as the agent of the counterparty and the principal
      (i) subsequently expresses consent; or
      (ii) does not object to the agent acting as the agent of the counterparty after having been requested to indicate consent or a refusal of consent;
   (c) the principal otherwise knew, or could reasonably be expected to have known, of the agent acting as the agent of the counterparty and the principal did not object within a reasonable time; or
   (d) the content of the prospective contract is so precisely determined in the mandate contract that there is no risk that the interests of the principal may be disregarded.

(3) If the principal is a consumer, the agent may only act as the agent of both the principal and of the counterparty if:
   (a) the agent has disclosed that information and the principal has given express consent to the agent acting also as the agent of the counterparty to the particular prospective contract; or
   (b) the content of the prospective contract is so precisely determined in the mandate contract that there is no risk that the interests of the principal may be disregarded.

(4) The parties may not, to the detriment of the principal, exclude the application of paragraph (3) or derogate from or vary its effects.

(5) If and in so far as the agent has acted in accordance with the previous paragraphs, the agent is entitled to the price.

Comments

A. General idea

This rule follows the same rationale as Article 5:101 (Self-contracting): there is presumed to be a conflict of interests when the agent also acts as an agent of the third party. The risk of a conflict of interests generally precludes the agent from properly representing both the principal and the third party to the prospective contract. The general rule is therefore that the agent is not allowed to do so.

However, under these Principles there are exceptions to the general rule. Paragraph (2) deals with this matter. For consumers, a more restrictive approach is taken in paragraph (3). This more restrictive rule is mandatory to protect the consumer's interest (paragraph (4)). Paragraph (5) deals with the consequences as regards the payment of the price.

B. Main rule: double mandate not allowed

As is the case with self-contracting, a conflict of interests may arise between the interests of the principal and those of the agent if the latter represents not only the principal but also the third party with whom the prospective contract is to be concluded. This situation is of special relevance in mandate relationships, in which the agent's main obligation is to act in the interest of the principal. The option chosen is to forbid this practice as a general rule, unless a conflict of interests is excluded.

Illustration 1
Eric instructs Ferdinand to sell Eric's house. Ferdinand is also acting as the agent of another principal, George, who is interested in buying that house. In this situation, Ferdinand has to defend the opposing interests of the two principals, because Eric wants to get the highest price possible whereas George wants to pay as little as possible.

C. Exceptions to general rule if conflict excluded

The rationale of the present Article follows that of Article 5:101 (Self-contracting). By way of exception, a double mandate is allowed when a conflict of interests between the principal and the agent is excluded. This approach protects the interests of the principal since it prevents the agent from advancing the interests of the third party while disregarding those of the principal. The grounds that justify an exemption to the general rule prohibiting double mandate are the same as those that justify self-contracting in Article 5:101, paragraph (2). For example, a double mandate is justified when the principal consents to the double representation, explicitly or implicitly, or when the prospective contract is so precisely defined in the mandate contract that a conflict of interests is excluded.

Illustration 2
Abel instructs his agent Georgio to buy 50 shares of Syntus Corporation at the current market price. Georgio is also acting as the agent of Romualdo, who has a holding of shares in Syntus Corporation and wishes to dispose of them at the current market price. Georgio sells the shares of Romualdo to Abel for the current market price. Georgio is performing in the interests of two principals, but the interests of the principals have not been jeopardised.

D. Double mandate if principal consumer

The Article grants extra protection to the interests of a principal who is a consumer. In such a case, the principal's consent in writing is required if the agent wants to represent the third party. In cases where the consumer is not informed that the agent is acting as the agent of the third party, or is informed in a standard contract term only, the consumer may be caught unaware or even feel betrayed when the party entrusted with the negotiation of a contract appears to have used, or abused, that position by defending the conflicting interests of the other party to the prospective contract.

E. Payment in case of permitted double mandate

The agent should be entitled to payment in cases of permitted double representation. In this situation, the agent has done everything required under the contract, and the services provided have led to the conclusion of the prospective contract. As the agent was allowed to act as the agent of the third party, the interests of the principal were not in jeopardy. Under these conditions, there seems to be no reason why the agent should not receive payment.

Illustration 3
Sylvana authorises Thomas to sell her 1964 Corvette. Thomas is looking for such a car because Vanessa has charged him to buy precisely such a car. Both Sylvana and Vanessa are acting in a private capacity. When Thomas discloses the fact that both Sylvana and Vanessa have mandated him to conclude a contract pertaining to the car, and both expressly agree to Thomas continuing to handle their affairs, not only is a contract concluded between Sylvana and Vanessa, but Thomas has properly performed his mandate contract and is entitled to payment.

F. Validity of prospective contract when agent has wrongfully acted as agent to third party

When the agent, in breach of his obligations under this Article, has acted as an agent to both the principal and the third party, the prospective contract with the third party – who may very well be innocent and unaware of this situation – is concluded nevertheless. However, the prospective contract may be avoided in accordance with and under the conditions set out in Article 3:205 PECL (Conflict of interest).

Illustration 3 (continued)
If Thomas has not disclosed the possible conflict of interest to Sylvana, Sylvana may not only avoid the contract under Article 3:205 PECL (Conflict of interest), but may also hold Thomas liable for breach of his contractual obligations towards her. If Thomas has disclosed the possible conflict of interest to Vanessa, Vanessa may not avoid the contract with Sylvana. However, in this case Vanessa may also hold Thomas liable for any damages sustained as a consequence of the voidance of the contract by Sylvana, as by not disclosing the possible conflict of interest to Sylvana and thus opening up the pos-

sibility for Sylvana to void the contract concluded between her and Vanessa, Thomas has also breached his obligation to act in the best interest of Vanessa as required by Article 3:102 (Obligation to act in interests of principal).

On the other hand, the principal may also ratify the contract after having been informed of the conflict of interest under Article 3:207 PECL (Ratification by principal). If such a ratification takes place, not only does the principal lose the right to avoid the contract but also his right to claim the liability of the agent, in accordance with Article 3:202 (Consequences of ratification) of these Principles. This implies that the agent is exempted from liability unless the principal notifies the agent without undue delay after ratification that he reserves the remedies.

G. Relationship with the Principles of European Law and the Draft Common Frame of Reference

The same rule is in the DCFR, in Article IV.D. – 5:102 (Double mandate). Under the DCFR, the prospective contract concluded by an agent who also acts as the agent of the third party may be avoided in accordance with and under the conditions set out in Article II. – 6:109 DCFR (Conflict of interest). The principal may also ratify the contract after having been informed of the conflict of interest under Article II. – 6:111 DCFR (Ratification).

H. Character of the rule

This Article constitutes a default rule from which the parties may derogate if both parties are not consumers. Paragraph 3 states a regime for self-contracting applicable when the principal is a consumer. In such a case, as established in paragraph (4), the rule is mandatory to protect the interests of consumers.

I. Remedies

If the agent was not allowed to act as the agent of the third party but has nonetheless done so, the act is not in conformity with the best interests of the principal, and the agent is therefore liable for non-performance. The normal remedies for non-performance apply.

Comparative Notes

1. Main rule: double mandate not allowed

Double mandate is not allowed as a main rule in AUSTRIA, BULGARIA, GERMANY, ENGLAND, ESTONIA, FINLAND, GERMANY, GREECE, HUNGARY, ITALY, IRELAND, MALTA, THE NETHERLANDS, PORTUGAL, SCOTLAND, SPAIN, and SWEDEN.

Double mandate is allowed in BELGIUM, FRANCE, and GERMANY. However, in BELGIUM and FRANCE, certain requirements are to be fulfilled. In BELGIUM, part of the doctrine has indicated that both principals are to be informed, and in FRANCE, the double mandate is to be implemented with total transparency. For other specific relationships it is generally accepted that an agent may represent the principal and the third party. This is the case in FRANCE for insurance agents.

2. Double mandate allowed if agreed by or disclosed to principal

The national rules that do not allow double mandate are default rules. Parties can therefore agree that an agent may also be authorised and instructed by the third party to the prospective contract. Moreover, in many legal regimes, there are situations in which double mandate is allowed if certain conditions are fulfilled. These conditions are meant to neutralise the risk of a conflict of interest between both principals. In some systems, the condition to be fulfilled is presented in very general terms: if risk conflict of interests is excluded, double mandate is allowed. This is the case in AUSTRIA (where the agent is of a type known to act for many parties), ESTONIA, THE NETHERLANDS, POLAND, PORTUGAL, SCOTLAND, SLOVAKIA (for advocate-client), and SPAIN. But there are also more specific conditions. The consent of principals, explicit or implicit, is required in BULGARIA, FINLAND, IRELAND (solicitor-clients), ITALY (priority rule, consent of the first principal), MALTA, POLAND, and PORTUGAL. An express or implied term in the contract allows double mandate in IRELAND. Custom is a ground to allow double mandate in SWEDEN. This is similar to AUSTRIA, in which principals are deemed to assent to double mandate if it is known that they typically represent the interests of both parties, e.g. real estate agents. In THE NETHERLANDS, where the principal is a consumer, the agent may only act as the third party's agent if the principal has given his written consent thereto.

3. Right to price if double mandate allowed

An agent has no right to payment in cases of double mandate in BULGARIA, FINLAND, and SLOVAKIA. However, in more legal systems the right to payment remains intact, i.e. in FRANCE, GERMANY, IRELAND, POLAND, SCOTLAND, and SWEDEN. In PORTUGAL, the right to payment depends on the agreement of the agent with the third party. In THE NETHERLANDS, the agent is not entitled to payment from the principal who is a buyer or a lessee if the contract pertains to the sale or lease of immovable property and one of the principals is a consumer.

National Notes

1. Main rule: double mandate not allowed

AUSTRIA: The agent may generally not also act as agent of the third party, as the agent may in case of conflicting interests be in breach of duty to one principal by acting with the intention of furthering the interest of another.

BELGIUM: Serving two principals seems to be allowed (Cass. 18 March 2004, RW 2004-05, 303, note A. Smets (implicit confirmation); Beltjens, no. 53; Ekelmans, p. 16; Samoy, p. 48-49). Some authors require nevertheless that both principals are informed, expressly or tacitly (e.g. through the agent's profession; cf. Wéry, p. 158-159).

BULGARIA: Although there is no explicit prohibition on double mandate, in legal writings it is considered inadmissible for the agent to act on behalf of both parties to the prospective contract simultaneously (Меворах/Лиджи/Фархи, III, 120). This conclusion is deduced from the requirement that the agent acts in accordance with the interests of the principal in the best possible manner under the existing circumstances. There are some special provisions on this matter. First, OCA Article 38 paragraph (1) forbids direct agents from negotiating in the name of the principal with another person also represented by them, unless the principal has given consent. Second, BAA Article 43 paragraph (3) contains special rules for advocates with regard to representation of counterparties. Third, commercial procurators and commercial agents are under a general prohibition of acting in competition with the principal, including representing the principal's competitors (CA Article 29 and Article 44).

DENMARK: According to Article 15 of the Real Estate Agency Act an estate agent is not allowed to represent both the seller and the buyer before the conclusion of the prospective contract has taken place. Article 15 is a mandatory rule for a special situation and cannot without reservation be extended to cover other types of representation.

ENGLAND: Similarly to the duty imposed on the agent to disclose when the agent's own personal interests may conflict with those of the principal, the rule of disclosure prevents the agent from getting into a position where the interests of one principal might conflict with the duty to the other principal in the same transaction. This will arise when a solicitor acts for the vendor and the buyer of a property.

ESTONIA: The conflict of interest provision in the Estonian LOAEst Article 623 paragraph (1) applies both in cases of self-contracting and in cases where the agent (also) acts as an agent to the third party: this is only allowed if the possibility of a conflict of interests is precluded.

FINLAND: There is no regulation in this respect. In the literature, a double mandate is not allowed and a prospective contract between two or more clients represented by the same agent is effective only if expressly accepted by the principal. In case there is no acceptance, the prospective contract is voidable (Hemmo, Sopimusoikeus I, p. 460-464).

FRANCE: The hypothesis of a double mandate is not envisaged by the legislation on agency, but the situation is sometimes regulated by specific legislation (e.g. Article 2 of the Decree of 26 December 1971 concerning notaries, and Article 155 paragraph (1) of the Decree of 27 November 1991, concerning lawyers). The hypothesis is accepted without difficulty for insurance agents (Cass.req., 26 November 1928, S. 1929, 1, 94; CA Paris 8 May 1981, GP. 1981, 2, 801). Academic legal writers cannot agree about this question, and French courts have adopted a prudent position. In general, the double mandate is accepted, provided that it is implemented with complete transparency (see, for example, the case concerning an estate agent: Cass.civ. 1re, 13 May 1998, Bull. civ. I, no. 169, RTD civ. 1998, 927). It may be supposed that in the absence of transparency in the case of the double mandate, the contract entered into with a third party could be avoided at the instance of the principal (contract voidable and not void). This would be on the basis of the failure of performance of the agent to satisfy its obligation of fair dealing (see Malaurie, Aynès & Gautier, no. 566). An action for negligence could also be envisaged against the agent.

GERMANY: Acting as the agent to a third party is considered to be analogous to an 'Insich-Geschäft' (self-contracting); the law on authority (CC Article 181) therefore declares it to be generally inadmissible. The law on brokerage is less strict: CC Article 654 indicates that a double mandate is only inadmissible if it runs contrary to the brokerage contract, thus making it permissible where the contract does not (expressly or impliedly) provide otherwise (BGHZ 61, 17; Palandt/Sprau, Article 654 no. 4).

GREECE: According to the CC Article 235 paragraph (1) an agent may not execute in the name of the person represented a deed in the capacity as agent of a third party except if any such deed had been authorised (explicitly or tacitly) by the person represented or if it constitutes exclusively the performance of an obligation (Georgiadis/Stathopoulos/Doris, Article 235 CC no. 1).

HUNGARY: If the agent has to act in the name of the principal, according to the CC Article 221 paragraph (3), '[a] agent shall not proceed if the opposite or otherwise interested party is himself or a person whom he also represents. The agent, if a legal person, shall also be allowed to proceed in a case of conflicting interests with the express consent of the person represented'. If the agent does not act in the name of the third party, he may act also as an agent to the third party but he has the obligation to inform the principal about this fact (CC Article 277 paragraph (5)).

IRELAND: As part of the fiduciary duty owed to the principal, an agent must not allow personal interests to conflict with those of the principal. English authority provides that this duty may be excluded by an express or implied term of the contract (e.g. *Kelly v Cooper* [1993] AC 205; *Henderson v Merrett* [1995] 2 AC 145). Whether an Irish court would allow such exclusion remains to be seen. The recognition, by English courts, of the ability of parties to contract out of the 'no conflict rule' reflects modern commercial practice. Nevertheless, critics point to the danger of leaving everything to express and implied terms of the contract, thereby denying the importance of fiduciary obligations.

ITALY: As a rule, the agent may act on behalf of two or more principals. However, if the principals have opposing interests which may lead to a conflict of interests the consent of the first principal is required (priority rule). As a consequence, if the agent who acts for a principal intends to act also for a third party, the agent must notify the first principal of this circumstance in order to receive the principal's authorisation. If the authorisation is not granted, the agent should refuse the mandate.

MALTA: The agent may act also as an agent to the third party if this is made clear to both parties and there is no objection from either of them.

NETHERLANDS: Serving two masters is only allowed if there is no conflict of interests between the principal and the third party (CC Article 7:417 paragraph (1). See also CA Leeuwarden 28 December 1994, NJ 1996, 117.

POLAND: Double mandate is allowed only if the principal has agreed or if there is no danger to the principal's interests.

PORTUGAL: CC Article 261 provides that "the deal closed by an agent with himself, in his own name, *or in the representation of a third party* is avoidable, unless the client has specifically consented on the closing of that deal, or that by its own nature, the deal excludes the possibility of a conflict of interests".

SCOTLAND: As a general rule, an agent is under a duty not to get into a position in which the agent's interests would conflict with those of the principal *(Huntingdon Copper and Sulphur Co Ltd v Henderson* (1877) 4 R 294 at 307, per Lord Mure). Acting for two principals may put the agent in breach of this rule. However, double mandate is possible in certain contexts.

SLOVAKIA: the advocate is obliged to refuse to perform legal services for a person if he or she has performed legal services for another person (client) in the same or a related matter and the client's interests conflict with the interests of the person concerned.

SPAIN: The opinion has been put forward that the self-contracting prohibition does not apply when the agent acts both for the principal seller and for the principal who gave a mandate to buy (Castro, p. 391). Yet the question remains doubtful, and, given the silence of the law, every situation may depend upon the possibility of an eventual conflict of interests.

SWEDEN: It is unclear whether double mandate is allowed.

2. Double mandate allowed if agreed by or disclosed to principal

AUSTRIA: Where the agent is of a type known to act for many parties (e.g. an estate agent or a lawyer who draws up a contract) it may be held that the situation is assented to by the principals (CC Article 879) and that there is no breach of duty (Rummel/Strasser, Article 1009 Rz 22; Koziol/Welser, 194; Krejci, 212 (Doppelvertretung)).

BELGIUM: Serving two principals seems to be allowed (Cass. 18 March 2004, RW 2004-05, 303, note A. Smets (implicit confirmation); Beltjens, no. 53; Ekelmans, p. 16; Samoy, p. 48-49). Some authors require nevertheless that both principals are informed, expressly or tacitly (e.g. through the agent's profession; Wéry, p. 158-159).

BULGARIA: Direct agents may act on behalf of the counterparty to the prospective contract if the principal has given consent (OCA Article 38(1)). Advocates may act as an agent of both counterparties if the parties consent and do not have contradictory interests (BAA Article 43 paragraph (3)).

DENMARK: According to Article 15 of the Real Estate Agency Act an estate agent is not allowed to represent both the seller and the buyer before the conclusion of the contract between the parties has taken place. Article 15 is a mandatory rule for a special (although important) situation. The prohibition cannot without reservation be extended to cover other types of representation.

ENGLAND: In a case where a solicitor acts for the vendor and the buyer of a property and there is a high probability that the interests of the respective principals will conflict, the agent can only act providing that informed consent has been obtained from the two principals (*Clark Boyce v Mouat* ([1994] 1 AC 428). Informed consent in this case was held to mean consent given in the knowledge that there is a conflict between the parties and that, as a result, the solicitor may be disabled from disclosing to each party the full knowledge which the solicitor possesses in relation to the transaction or may be disabled from giving advice to one party which conflicts with the interest of the other. The same obligation applies regardless of whether the agent acts gratuitously. For the financial sector, the rules appear to be more stringent, but it seems that it will depend on the size of the corporations involved. For big corporations, there is a risk that one department may act for a principal and another department may work for another principal whose interests will conflict with the first one. In order to avoid this kind of conflict, financial institutions will use what are called 'chinese walls' to ensure that confidential information from one department of a company will not leak to the other. The House of Lords had to consider the efficacy of such Chinese walls in protecting confidential information in the case of *Bolkiah v KPMG* [1999] 2 AC 222 If the same agent acts for two potentially conflicting principals in two separate transactions, there does not seem to be a problem: *Kelly v Cooper* [1993] AC 205). In this case the contract was held to contain an implied term that the agent would be allowed to act for more than one principal at a time whose interests might conflict and that the agent could keep confidential information received whilst acting for competing principals.

ESTONIA: The conflict of interest provision in the Estonian LOAEst Article 623 paragraph (1) applies both in cases of self-contracting and in cases where the agent (also) acts as an agent to the third party: this is only allowed if the possibility of a conflict of interests is precluded.

FINLAND: There is no regulation in this respect. In the literature, a double mandate is not allowed and a prospective contract between two or more clients represented by the same agent is effective only if expressly accepted by the principal. In case there is no acceptance, the prospective contract is found to be voidable (Hemmo, Sopimusoikeus I, p. 460-464). Should the principal agree on double mandate, the agent is, in general, allowed to act for two clients. A disclosure by the agent is not sufficient unless the principal clearly accepts the double mandate.

FRANCE: The hypothesis of a double mandate is not envisaged by the legislation on agency, but the situation is sometimes regulated by specific legislation (e.g. Article 2 of the Decree of 26 December 1971 concerning notaries, and Article 155 paragraph (1) Decree of 27 November 1991, concerning lawyers). The hypothesis is accepted without difficulty for insurance agents (Cass.req., 26 November 1928, S. 1929, 1, 94; CA Paris 8 May 1981, GP 1981, 2, 801). Academic legal writers cannot agree about this question, and French courts have adopted a prudent position. In general, the double mandate is accepted, provided that it is implemented with complete transparency (see, for example, the case concerning an estate agent: Cass.civ. 1re, 13 May 1998, Bull. civ. I, no. 169, RTD civ. 1998, 927). It may be supposed that in the absence of transparency in the case of the double mandate, the contract entered into with a third party could be avoided at the instance of the principal (contract voidable and not void). This would be on the basis of the failure of performance of the agent to satisfy its obligation of fair dealing (see Malaurie, Aynès & Gautier, no. 566). An action for negligence could also be envisaged against the agent.

GERMANY: The parties may agree to deviate from the German CC Article 181 and allow a double mandate. No form requirements apply. CC Article 181 *ad fine* furthermore declares a double mandate to be admissible where the legal act performed by the agent 'consists exclusively in the fulfilment of an obligation', e.g. an already existing legal obligation to execute said act – in this case, no conflict of interest is possible, as the agent merely does what the principal was already obliged to do before the agent got involved.

GREECE: According to the Greek CC Article 235 paragraph (1) an agent may not execute in the name of the person represented a deed in the capacity as agent of a third party except if any such deed had been authorised (explicitly or tacitly) by the person represented or if it constitutes exclusively the performance of an obligation (Georgiadis/Stathopoulos/Doris, Article 235 CC no. 1).

HUNGARY: If the agent has to act in the name of the principal, according to CC Article 221 paragraph (3), '[a] agent shall not proceed if the opposite or otherwise interested party is himself or a person whom he also represents. The agent, if a legal person, shall also be allowed to proceed in a case of conflicting interests with the express consent of the person represented'. If the agent does not act in the name of the third party, he may act also as an agent to the third party but he has the obligation to inform the principal about this fact (CC Article 277 paragraph (5)).

IRELAND: As part of the fiduciary duty owed to the principal, an agent must not allow personal interests to conflict with those of the principal. English authority provides that this duty may be excluded by an express or implied term of the contract (e.g. *Kelly v Cooper* [1993] AC 205; *Henderson v Merrett* [1995] 2 AC 145). Whether an Irish court would allow such exclusion remains to be seen. The majority of cases concern an agent taking up a position of conflict with the principal. Interesting questions have arisen where an agent takes a position where the duty to one principal may conflict with the duty to another principal. In the English case of *Kelly v Cooper* an estate agent, A, acted for two principals, P and X, who owned two adjacent properties. They both instructed A to sell their properties. A showed both properties to T, who agreed to buy X's property. T subsequently made an offer to P to buy his property. P, unaware that T had already agreed to buy X's property, accepted the offer. When P discovered that T had agreed to buy X's property, he argued that had he known that fact he would have been able to negotiate a higher price for his property because it was clear that T wanted both properties. P argued that A was in breach of his fiduciary duties in failing to disclose that T had agreed to buy X's property and in placing himself in a position where his duties to his two principals would conflict. He claimed damages for loss of the chance to negotiate a higher price. The Privy Council held that where an agent acts in pursuance of a contract, the scope of his fiduciary duties is determined by the contract. Since it was well known that estate agents might act for more than one principal, the agency contract in this case contained an implied term that the agent would be permitted to act for more than one principal, whose interests might compete, and to keep confidential information received whilst acting for other principals. On the facts, the contract could not include a term preventing the agent acting for other principals. This decision has wide implications because situations where an agent acts for more than one principal are increasingly common, as with financial advisors and solicitors, especially as firms become larger. In *Clarke Boyce v Mauot* ([1994] 1 AC 428), the Privy Council went a step further when it held that a solicitor was entitled to act for both parties in *the same transaction* even where their interests might conflict, provided the informed consent of both parties was obtained. The recognition, by English courts, of the ability of parties to contract out of the 'no conflict rule' reflects modern commercial practice.

Nevertheless, critics point to the danger of leaving everything to express and implied terms of the contract, thereby denying the importance of fiduciary obligations.

ITALY: As a rule, the agent may act on behalf of two or more principals. However, if the principals have opposing interests which may lead to a conflict of interests the consent of the first principal is required (priority rule). As a consequence, if the agent who acts for a principal intends to act also for a third party, the agent must notify the first principal of this circumstance in order to receive the principal's authorisation. If the authorisation is not granted, the agent should refuse the mandate.

MALTA: The agent may act also as an agent to the third party if this is made clear to both parties and there is no objection from either of them.

NETHERLANDS: Serving two masters is only allowed if there is no conflict of interests between the principal and the third party (CC Article 7:417 paragraph (1)). If the principal acts as a consumer, the principal's written approval is required before the agent is allowed to serve two masters (CC Article 7:417 paragraph (2); Haak/Zwitser, p. 161). If in this case the agent serves two masters without having received the principal's written approval, the agent not only loses his right to payment from the principal whose written consent was required, but is also liable for any damage resulting from his actions towards this principal (CC Article 7:417 paragraph (3)). This provision is mandatory.

POLAND: Double mandate is allowed only if the principal has agreed or if there is no danger to the principal's interests.

PORTUGAL: Article 261 CC provides that "the deal closed by an agent with himself, in his own name, *or in the representation of a third party* is avoidable, unless the client has specifically consented on the closing of that deal, or that by its own nature, the deal excludes the possibility of a conflict of interests".

SCOTLAND: Scottish solicitors are prohibited from acting for two different parties whose interest's conflict (Begg, p. 363; Solicitors (Scotland) Practice Rules 1986, rule 3). Provided however that no conflict arises, there is no bar to acting for two parties. The rules on conflict of interest are complex and are not explored in full here. The issue is governed by both the Code of Conduct for Scottish Solicitors 2002, rule 3 and the Solicitors (Scotland) Practice Rules 1986. The former provides that, in choosing to act for two parties, solicitors must have regard to any possible risk of breaches of confidentiality and impairment of independence arising in the future (Code of conduct for Scottish solicitors 2002, rule 3). A different kind of agent, a 'broker', also has a limited ability to act for two principals. The term 'broker' has been defined as '… a limited agent who is employed in making bargains or contracts between other persons in matters of trade, commerce, and navigation'. (Graham, paragraph 553). It is accepted that a broker may be the agent of both parties (Graham, paragraph 553). The various estate agency codes which regulate the actions of their members all contain provisions on conflicts of interest (Ombudsman's Code of Practice, rule 9a; Estate Agency Affairs Board Code of Conduct, Article 4.1.4 and the National Association of Estate Agents Rules of Conduct, rule 10).

SLOVAKIA: The advocate is obliged to refuse to perform legal services for a person if he or she has performed legal services for another person (client) in the same or a related matter and the client's interests conflict with the interests of the person concerned.

SPAIN: The opinion has been put forward that the self-contracting prohibition does not apply when the agent acts both for the principal seller and for the principal who gave a mandate to buy (Castro, p. 391). Yet the question remains doubtful, and, given the silence of the law, every situation may depend upon the possibility of an eventual conflict of interests.

SWEDEN: The parties can agree on a double mandate. It may also follow from usages. There are cases where a double mandate is allowed. An example is an auctioneer's office which acts as an agent for both the seller and the buyer, both the seller and the buyer paying a commission of a certain percentage of the sales price to the commissionaire (see Håstad, p. 302).

3. Right to price if double mandate allowed

BULGARIA: There are no explicit rules. Legal doctrine considers it unallowable for the agent to receive remuneration from both parties to the prospective contract (Меворах/Лиджи/Фархи, III, 120).

FINLAND: If the prospective contract is valid, the agent is in general entitled to charge a fee and reimbursement of expenses. A real estate agent, however, is entitled to charge only one price if the agent represents both parties to a purchase (REstateA Article 20).

FRANCE: In the case of a transparent double mandate, the agent would normally be entitled to double remuneration and to obtain repayment of all expenses in accordance with the terms of each agency contract entered into. If the double mandate is not transparent, there are cases where the agent would certainly be held to be liable and the damages would be set off against any remuneration and repayment which may be due to the agent. This situation has not, however, been clearly defined by French case law and litigation is exceptional.

GERMANY: If the double mandate was permissible, the agent is entitled to the price. For brokerage contracts, the CC Article 654 explicitly declares that neither price nor reimbursement of expenses may be claimed if the double mandate was contrary to the brokerage contract, thus indicating that in cases of permissible double mandate the broker maintains the right to claim the price.

IRELAND: Given that double mandate may be permissible and not necessarily in breach of any fiduciary duty, provided there is full disclosure etc., it would appear that remuneration and indemnity are payable in such circumstances.

NETHERLANDS: If double mandate is allowed, the agent is entitled to remuneration. However, the agent is not entitled to payment from the principal who is a buyer or a lessee if the contract pertains to the sale or lease of immovable property and one of the principals is a consumer. This provision is mandatory, unless the contract pertains to the lease of only a part of a house and that part can't be used as a self-standing house (i.e. only a room and not the whole house or apartment is let to the lessee), CC Article 7:417 paragraph (4) provides.

POLAND: There are no Polish CC provisions that would deprive the agent of the remuneration or limit it in any way in case of double mandate.

PORTUGAL: The right to payment of the price depends on the contractual framework of the agent-third party internal relation.

SCOTLAND: If acting for both parties is permitted the normal rules on remuneration apply.

SLOVAKIA: In the case of commercial representation, the agent cannot claim entitlement to a commission and agreed compensation for costs if the agent acted, as a commercial agent or as a broker, for the party with whom the principal has concluded the business deal (Comm.C Article 659 paragraph (3); see Comm.C Article 617 paragraph (1) for the brokerage contract).

SPAIN: There are no rules which states that the agent loses his right to payment in situations of double mandate.

SWEDEN: The agent is entitled to a price for the services as well as reimbursement of expenses. This is regardless of whether the double mandate is disclosed or not and it may lead to a double remuneration.

No answer received from AUSTRIA, DENMARK, ESTONIA, HUNGARY, ITALY, MALTA.

Chapter 6:
Termination by notice other than for non-performance

Article 6:101: Termination by notice in general

(1) Either party may terminate the mandate relationship at any time by giving notice to the other.
(2) For the purposes of paragraph (1), a revocation of the mandate of the agent is treated as termination.
(3) Termination of the mandate relationship is not effective if the mandate of the agent is irrevocable under Article 1:105 (Irrevocable mandate).
(4) The effects of termination are governed by the general rules in Chapter 9 Section 3 PECL (Termination of the contract).
(5) When the party giving the notice was justified in terminating the relationship no damages are payable for so doing.
(6) When the party giving the notice was not justified in terminating the relationship, the termination is nevertheless effective but the other party is entitled to damages in accordance with the rules in Chapter 9 Section 5 PECL (Damages and interest).
(7) For the purposes of this Article the party giving the notice is justified in terminating the relationship if that party:
   (a) was entitled to terminate the relationship under the express terms of the contract and observed any requirements laid down in the contract for doing so;
   (b) was entitled to terminate the relationship under Article 9:301 PECL (Right to terminate the contract); or
   (c) was entitled to terminate the relationship under any other Article of the present Chapter and observed any requirements laid down in such Article for doing so.

Comments

A. General idea

This Article provides, first, that a notice of termination by either party has the effect of terminating the mandate relationship (paragraph (1)). In accordance with the general rule on notice in Article 1:303 PECL (Notice), the termination is effective when the notice of termination reaches the other party or when a period indicated in the notice has elapsed if the notice so provides and in so far as this moment is later than when the notice reaches the other party. Paragraph (4) of this Article provides that the effects of termination are governed by the general rules in Chapter 9, Section 3 PECL (Termination of the contract). This means that termination has a prospective effect only, subject to the restitution of certain benefits, but does not affect provisions for the settlement of disputes or other provisions intended to survive the termination of the mandate relationship (Article 9:305 paragraph (2) PECL (Effects of termination in general)).

The notice leads to the termination of the mandate relationship, whether or not the party giving notice had a right to terminate the relationship under the express terms of the contract or under the rule on termination for fundamental non-performance or under any other rule in the present Chapter, such as the rule on termination of a relationship of indefinite duration by giving notice of reasonable length. If there is such a right to terminate, and if the requirements for such termination are observed (i.e. if the termination is justified within the meaning of paragraph (7)) no damages are payable for terminating the relationship (paragraph (5)). However, if there is no right to terminate under the express terms of the contract or under the provisions on fundamental non-performance or the equivalent or under any other rule of this Chapter, the aggrieved party will be entitled to damages (paragraph (6)). This also applies if the requirements for exercising such another right to terminate were not observed – for example, if a reasonable period of notice is required but only an inadequate period of notice is given. As the mandate relationship is ended, the aggrieved party is not entitled to claim specific performance of the obligations under the mandate contract, i.e. cannot force the party wrongfully terminating the mandate relationship to continue performance. However, the aggrieved party can ask for specific performance of obligations relating to the settlement of disputes and other obligations that are intended to survive termination of the mandate relationship (Article 9:305 paragraph (2) PECL (Effects of termination in general)).

According to paragraph (2), a notice of revocation of the mandate of the agent is to be treated as a notice by the principal terminating the mandate relationship.

B. Notice of termination effective

The character of mandate relationships, with their strong foundation in trust and confidence, suggests that the parties should not be compelled to continue the relationship once one of them has shown an intention to terminate it. If, for example, the agent would be obliged to continue performance for a period after giving notice, it might be asked whether the agent would in fact be very active in facilitating, negotiating, or concluding the prospective contract during that period. Similarly, there is a strong argument for not placing the principal in a situation where another person can affect the principal's legal position after a notice of immediate termination of the relationship has been given: once notice has been given, the required strong basis in trust and confidence between the parties is missing. For that reason, a notice of termination leads in any case to the termination of the mandate relationship, whether or not the party has a right to terminate under any other rule.

This is also the approach in all legal systems when the principal is the party who notifies his intention to terminate the mandate contract. However, notice of termination given by the agent is effective unconditionally only in some countries. Other countries set some limits to the effects of a notice of termination by the agent. In these systems the agent is required to continue the relationship in order to take care of urgent matters of the principal and in this manner prevent substantial prejudice to the principal. This is the case in AUSTRIA, ESTONIA, SLOVAKIA, and SPAIN. Moreover, specific statutory periods are provided in

SLOVAKIA, where in commercial relations, notice is effective at the end of the month following the month the notice was delivered to principal.

C. Termination not effective if mandate irrevocable

There is, however, one exception to the rule that the notice of termination is always effective, whether or not the conditions for termination have been met. This is the case where the mandate is irrevocable under Article 1:105 (Irrevocable mandate). If termination of an irrevocable mandate were possible, the consequences of irrevocability could be easily circumvented by giving notice of termination. This is exactly what is not intended in the case of irrevocability. The present paragraph (3) therefore excludes the effectiveness of a notice of termination in the case of an irrevocable mandate. Along the same lines, Article 1:105 paragraph (3) excludes the effectiveness of a notice of revocation of the mandate of the agent which is irrevocable.

However, revocation of an irrevocable mandate and subsequent termination of the contract will still be effective in the cases enumerated under Article 1:105 paragraph (2) (Irrevocable mandate), i.e when there is a fundamental non-performance of the agent or when the principal has an extraordinary and serious reason to terminate.

Illustration 1
(Loss of trust in agent): A bank indicates that it is willing to award a credit contract to a consumer, provided that it is secured by a mortgage on the house of the consumer. In the credit contract, the consumer agrees to give an irrevocable mandate to the bank to establish the mortgage. Before the credit is provided and the mortgage established, the possible collapse of the bank is reported on the front pages of all national newspapers.

In this case, the principal should be able to revoke the mandate for serious and extraordinary reason (Article 1:105 paragraph (2)(a)(iii) (Irrevocable mandate)) if the bank is not yet insolvent, or for non-performance by the bank if it already has become insolvent (Article 1:105 paragraph (2)(a)(i) (Irrevocable mandate)). Since revocation of the mandate implies termination of the mandate contract and vice versa (Articles 1:104 paragraph (2) (Revocation of the mandate) and paragraph (2) of the present Article), the principal can equally terminate the mandate contract for serious and extraordinary reason.

In most countries, parties are limited in their possibilities to revoke or terminate an irrevocable mandate contract. However, in HUNGARY and PORTUGAL, a notice of termination of an irrevocable mandate is always effective.

D. Non-compliance with requirements for termination only relevant to liability in damages

There are some situations where a party to a mandate relationship has a right under other rules to terminate it by notice without being liable to pay damages for so doing. Paragraph (7) of the present Article lists the relevant situations for present purposes. One such situation is where the contract itself confers an express right to terminate, perhaps after giving a reasonable period of notice. Another is where there has been fundamental non-performance (or the equivalent) by the other party of obligations under the contract. See Article 8:103 PECL (Termination). Other situations are provided for in the present Chapter. As far as the principal is concerned, the relevant provisions are Article 6:102 (Termination by principal when relationship is to last for an indefinite period or when mandate is for a particular task), which applies when the mandate relationship is not irrevocable and the mandate contract was concluded for an indefinite period or for a particular task, and Article 6:103 (Termination by principal for extraordinary and serious reason). Under both provisions, notice must be given. Under the first, a notice period of reasonable length must be observed, and under the second there must be an extraordinary and serious reason to terminate the contractual relationship immediately. For the agent, Article 6:104 (Termination by agent when relationship is to last for indefinite period or when it is gratuitous) and Article 6:105 (Termination by agent for extraordinary and serious reason) contain similar provisions. If the requirements of these provisions are observed, paragraph (5) of the present Article clarifies that there is no liability in damages for the party who wants to terminate.

Paragraph (7) of this Article provides that damages for breach of contract are due when the party is not entitled to terminate on the basis of one of the grounds mentioned in this Article, or when the requirements to terminate agreed by the parties are not fulfilled. However, if the requirement that is not fulfilled consists of granting a reasonable period of notice before termination (see Articles 6:102 (Termination by principal when relationship is to last for an indefinite period or when mandate is for a particular task) and 6:104 (Termination by agent when relationship is to last for indefinite period or when it is gratuitous)), and such a period is not observed, only damages for premature performance are due. Termination is in any case effective.

Illustration 2
Marina is a professional photographer. She has emigrated to Spain, but she has authorized an agent in the Netherlands to take care of the public relations of Marina's company in order to find new Dutch clients. The agent fulfils the mandated task on a full-time basis. The parties have not limited the duration of the contract, and they have agreed that Marina is obliged to give notice three months in advance if she wants to terminate the mandate relationship. Business does not go well in Spain, and Marina decides to return to the Netherlands. When she arrives in the Netherlands, she sends an email to the agent to inform him that from that moment on she will take care of the public relations of her company.

In this case, Marina has not respected the agreed period to provide notice of termination. Under these Principles, notice of termination is nevertheless effective, but the agent has a right to damages for premature termination.

E. Revocation of mandate of the agent implies termination of mandate relationship

Revocation of the mandate of the agent leads to the termination of the mandate relationship by the principal. As stated in Article 1:104 paragraph (1) (Revocation of the mandate), the mandate of the agent can be revoked at any time by giving notice to the agent. By revoking the mandate, the principal takes away the core of the content of the mandate relationship, and as a result the whole of the mandate relationship consequently comes to an end. For that reason, paragraph (2) provides expressly that revocation of the mandate of the agent is regarded as termination by notice under paragraph (1).

Vice versa, when the mandate contract has been terminated by the principal, this also amounts to the revocation of the mandate granted to the agent, as stated in Article 1:104 paragraph (2) (Revocation of the mandate).

In almost all legal systems, the revocation of the authority of the agent by the principal amounts to the termination of the relationship. Although in ENGLAND and SCOTLAND the possibility exists for the non-terminating party to accept or refuse 'repudiation', with a refusal implying that the relationship could continue, in practice agents opt in such cases for not continuing the relationship and instead claiming damages. In HUNGARY, revocation of the mandate does not imply in general that the relationship ends.

The fact that the principal is allowed to revoke the mandate and thereby terminate the mandate relationship does not mean that the revocation is always 'free of charge'. As revocation of the mandate is treated as a termination, the rules of Chapter 6 (Termination by notice other than for non-performance) apply. This implies that termination is in any case effective, but the principal may be required to pay damages under paragraph (5) of the present Article. This is the case when (a) the agent has not been guilty of fundamental non-performance, (b) the principal does not have an extraordinary and serious reason to revoke, (c) the principal is not entitled to terminate or revoke under the express terms of the contract, and (d) the principal does not observe a notice period of reasonable length in revoking the mandate of the agent in a contractual relationship of indefinite duration.

Illustration 3
Martha is leaving on a trip around the world. She authorises and instructs her friend Nico to rent Martha's apartment in her name. While she is still abroad, Martha learns from a trustworthy source that Nico has used Martha's house to organise drug parties. Martha then revokes the authority she granted to Nico because she no longer trusts him. Revocation of this authority implies termination of the mandate relationship between Martha and Nico with immediate effect.

Martha has a serious reason to revoke, which means that revocation of the authority and consequently termination of the mandate relationship is justified under the rules in Chapter 6 (Termination by notice other than for non-performance) and there is no ground to claim damages.

F. Calculation of damages

If the principal terminates the mandate relationship without being justified in doing so under paragraph (7) of the present Article, and if damages are consequently payable, the general rules on the calculation of damages come into operation. Under Article 9:502 PECL (General measure of damages), the agent is entitled to be put as nearly as possible into the position in which the agent would have been if the principal's obligations under the mandate contract had been duly performed. In this respect it should be noted that, if the mandate contract has been concluded for an indefinite period or for a particular task, then – unless the parties have validly derogated from Article 6:102 (Termination by the principal when relationship is to last for an indefinite period or when mandate is for a particular task) – the principal may at any time terminate the mandate relationship by giving notice of reasonable length. In that case, the damage sustained by the agent is not the fact that the agent could not conclude the prospective contract, but the fact that the notice period was not observed and, therefore, that the agent lost the chance of being able to conclude the prospective contract in the remaining period in which the mandate contract would have been in force. In these cases, the effect of Article 9:502 PECL (General measure of damages) is to substitute a monetary sum for the reasonable notice period. Damages will be payable instead of a reasonable period of notice. If the contract was concluded for a definite period, the damages would be for the loss of the chance of concluding the prospective contract in the remainder of the period.

G. Restitutionary effects of termination

The restitutionary consequences of termination are dealt with under paragraph (4) of the present Article. The effect of that paragraph is that the general rules in Chapter 9 Section 3 PECL (Termination of the contract) apply. These rules require a party who has received any benefit from the other's performance of the obligations under the contract to return the benefit: Articles 9:307 (Recovery of money paid) and 9:308 PECL (Recovery of property) provide that a benefit that is transferable must be transferred back to the other party. Article 9:309 PECL (Recovery for performance that cannot be returned) adds that if the benefit is not transferable, its value must be paid. As any benefit received by the performance of the agent, in so far as it has already been rendered, normally cannot be transferred, the principal will have to pay the value of any performance which has been received but for which payment was not yet due at the time of termination. Comment B to Article 9:309 PECL (Recovery for performance that cannot be returned) clarifies that the principal should not be required to pay the cost to the agent of having provided its performance if the net benefit is less than those costs, since the principal is only enriched for the amount of the net benefit. On the other hand, if the net benefit is greater that the costs for the agent, the principal should be liable for no more than an appropriate part of the contract price. However, Article 9:305 paragraph (2) PECL (Effects of termination in general) provides that the rights and liabilities that have accrued up to the time of termination are not affected by it. This implies that in so far as payment had already become due, the principal remains required to pay for the performance rendered but is not required to return the monetary value of the performance of the agent.

Whereas the provisions of the PECL are elegant, they do not give much guidance to the parties on the amount that is to be paid by the principal for the performance of the agent. In this respect, one may turn to the DCFR, which provides a method of calculating the payment. If a price is payable under the contract, the basic rule is that the payment due is that proportion of the price which the value of the actual performance (received but for which payment was not due at the time of termination) bears to the value of the promised performance (Article III. – 3:513 paragraph (2) DCFR (Payment of value of benefit)). If a price per hour or day of work by the agent was payable under the contract, the payment due will be calculated by reference to that price. If, however, the price was due only if the prospective contract was concluded, it will usually be difficult to argue that the agent is entitled to any restitutionary payment. The comparison then would be between what was promised (a result) and what was provided (no result). This means that if, in such 'no result, no pay' cases, the agent terminates the relationship without justification before the result is achieved, the agent will receive nothing. If the principal terminates the relationship without justification before the result is achieved, the agent will receive nothing *by way of a restitutionary payment,* but he will be entitled to damages for the loss of the chance of concluding the prospective contract. If the agent had been on the point of concluding the prospective contract, these damages should approach or even equal the amount of the commission which would have been due.

H. Relationship with the Principles of European Law and the Draft Common Frame of Reference

This Article mirrors Article IV.D. – 6:101 DCFR (Termination by notice other than for non-performance).

The provision adds to Article 6:109 PECL (Contract for an indefinite period), which allows either party to terminate a contract for an indefinite period by giving notice of reasonable length. This general provision only provides a solution to contracts for an indefinite period, whereas most mandate contracts are for a particular task or are otherwise for a determined period. Moreover, Article 6:109 PECL (Contract for an indefinite period) does not provide for clear rules on the consequences of wrongful termination, i.e. a notice of termination that does not meet the requirements of that Article. The present Article fills both gaps.

The present Article is closer to the general rule in Article III. – 1:109 paragraph (1) DCFR (Variation or termination by notice). Under that provision, a contractual relationship can be terminated by notice by either party 'where this is provided for by the terms regulating it'. The present Article is an example of such a term. It is a mandatory rule. Parties may not agree on excluding the right to terminate by giving notice. However, some of its paragraphs are default. The parties may include a different term in the mandate contract – for example, one providing that termination by notice will take place only after a period of a prescribed length. Given the nature of a mandate contract, however, such a term would be unusual as it would not be in the interests of the principal.

The consequences for not observing a reasonable notice period are regulated differently under these Principles if compared to the DCFR. Under Article III. – 1:109 paragraph (2) DCFR (Variation or termination by notice), the observance of a reasonable period is a requirement for effective termination. If not observed, the contract continues. Under these Principles, notice is always effective (unless the contract is irrevocable). This solution is in line with the solution chosen as to the termination of commercial agency, franchise, and distribution contracts, which are concluded for an indefinite period, as stated in Article 1:302 (Unilateral ending of a contract for an indefinite period) of the Principles of European Law on Commercial Agency, Franchising and Distribution Contracts and also in Article IV.E. – 2:302 DCFR (Contract for an indefinite period). However, the approach is different as to the available remedies in case of an unjustified termination of a contract concluded for a definite period because the non-terminating party in such a case has the right to ask for continuation of the relationship, whereas in a mandate contract the non-terminating party only has recourse to damages.

I. Character of the rule

Paragraphs 1 to 4 of the present Article have a mandatory character. Paragraphs 5 to 7 are default. Parties may derogate from them.

J. Remedies

If termination by the parties is not justified or the requirements for termination are not observed, the non-terminating party is entitled to claim damages. There is no entitlement, though, to claim specific performance, i.e. the continuation of the relationship.

Comparative Notes

1. Termination by notice

In all countries, parties to a mandate contract can at any time bring the relationship to an end by giving notice. In most countries, notice of termination can also be implicit.

2. Revocation of mandate is considered to be termination

In most legal systems, the revocation of the mandate leads to termination of the relationship. In GERMANY, it is a question that should be answered by way of interpretation. In German law, termination of the contract always leads to the revocation of the mandate, but there is nothing said on whether revocation of the mandate also automatically leads to termination. In HUNGARY, revocation of the mandate does not always lead to termination of the contractual relationship.

3. Notice of termination always brings about termination

A notice of termination by the principal in all legal systems leads to termination of a mandate relationship. The agent has no possibility to claim continuation of the relationship.

In contrast, the effectiveness of a notice of termination by the agent is subject to limitations in some member states. In THE NETHERLANDS, if it is the agent who does not observe the requirements and does not have an extraordinary and serious reason to terminate, the contractual relationship will not terminate. In some systems, the agent is required to continue the relationship in order to take care of urgent matters of the principal and in this manner prevent substantial prejudice to the principal; this is the case in AUSTRIA, ESTONIA, SLOVAKIA, and SPAIN. Specific statutory periods are required in SLOVAKIA: in commercial relations, a notice is effective at the end of the month following the month the notice was delivered to principal.

4. Consequences of termination for payment of the agent

If the principal terminates the mandate relationship, the agent has still the right to partial remuneration in AUSTRIA, BELGIUM, BULGARIA, ENGLAND, ESTONIA, FINLAND, FRANCE, HUNGARY, IRELAND, THE NETHERLANDS, POLAND, SCOTLAND, SLOVAKIA, SPAIN, and SWEDEN.

Payment of expenses incurred by the agent until the moment that the contract is terminated are due in AUSTRIA, BELGIUM, BULGARIA, ENGLAND, ESTONIA, FINLAND, FRANCE, IRELAND, POLAND, SLOVAKIA, SPAIN, and SWEDEN.

In some countries, there is a limitation to the right to remuneration. Such is the case in ENGLAND, where the agent has no right to payment if the agent continues performing the contract after he knew or should have known that the contract had been terminated. In FRANCE, there is no right to remuneration if the non-continuation of the contract is due to *force majeure*. There is no right to remuneration, but only to damages in MALTA.

BULGARIA seems to be the only regime that acknowledges a right for the agent to remuneration due as result of enjoyment of clientele by the principal.

5. No justification to terminate: right to damages for breach

Under all regimes, the party terminating the contract is obliged to compensate the other party for the damage suffered if the terminating party does not observe the requirements (legal or contractual) to terminate.

6. Notice period not observed: right to damages in lieu of notice

The regimes in the reported countries do not refer to the category of damages for premature termination. In some countries, the existence of a period of notice is a question of contractual agreement. This is why non-observance of the agreed period leads to damages for breach of contract in BELGIUM, BULGARIA, ENGLAND, FRANCE, IRELAND, SPAIN, and SWEDEN. Actually, this is the case in every country in which the parties have agreed on observing a notice period for termination and this is not observed.

Damages are due when a reasonable period is not observed in GERMANY, HUNGARY, MALTA, and SWEDEN. However, damages are only described in general terms. In SCOTLAND (despite the system's apparent similarity to ENGLAND), the lack of notice implies that the notice is of no effect. Compensation is due because the non-terminating party normally accepts 'repudiation' by the other party and claims damages.

National Notes

1. Termination by notice

For the National Notes, see the National Notes to Articles 6:102 to 6:105.

2. Revocation of mandate is considered to be termination

AUSTRIA: An agent's authority can be terminated at any time by the express revocation of it by the principal (CC Article 1020). The question of termination of the contractual relationship is the same as that of termination of authority.

BULGARIA: The principal has the right to revoke the mandate at any time by unilateral notice to the agent (OCA Article 288; Любен Василев, Облигационно право I, p. 29). This revocation terminates the contractual relationship (Любен Василев, Облигационно право I, p. 29; Голева, Облигационно право II, p. 239; Меворах/Лиджи/Фархи, III, p. 170) from the moment when the agent gets to know or could have become aware of the revocation (OCA Article 290; Любен Василев, Облигационно право I, p. 30).

ENGLAND: When the principal revokes the agent's authority, this amounts to termination of the agent/principal relationship.

FRANCE: The French Civil Code gives the principal the possibility of terminating the agent's authority *ad nutum*, i.e. at any time, without specific reason and without any right to compensation (art. 2004). The termination may even occur as a result of notice to the agent of the appointment of a new agent for the same transaction (CC Article 2006). The principal does, however, have to inform any possible third party contractors of such revocation in order to give them binding notice (CC Article 2005).

GERMANY: Whether under German law revocation of the authority granted to the agent also results in termination of the mandate relationship is a question of interpretation of the revocation notice. CC Article 168 addresses the reverse situation and stipulates that the authority ends when the underlying legal relationship (e.g. a mandate contract) ends, but no general rule about the effect of a revocation of authority for the mandate relationship exists.

HUNGARY: Even if the revocability of the contract for representation is restricted, the principal can withdraw the powers of representation from the agent at any time during the execution of the contract and is entitled to conclude the prospective contract (or to execute the prospected other juridical act) personally. In general, the revocation of a power of representation is not considered to be termination of the agency relationship.

IRELAND: Since agency is a consensual relationship it can be terminated if either party withdraws consent. Where the principal withdraws consent, the principal is said to 'revoke' the agent's authority. No formality is required for a revocation. Revocation is effective even if in breach of contract. However, while the agency relationship may be effectively terminated, other liabilities may arise. For example, the agent may continue to have apparent authority, thereby binding the principal with third parties. Moreover, revocation before the expiry of a fixed term may give rise to liability for breach of contract (e.g. damages for loss of opportunity to earn commission) on the principal's part, unless justified by a prior breach by the other party. Where an agent is appointed for an indeterminate period the agency can be terminated in accordance with any provision in the agreement for termination by notice. In the absence of any express term, it will normally be implied that the agency can be terminated, by either party, on reasonable notice.

NETHERLANDS: The principal is allowed to revoke the agent's mandate. However, there are restrictions if the mandate is irrevocable according to CC Article 7:422 paragraph (2) (Haak/Zwitser, p. 157; CFI Roermond 11 February 1999, NJ 1999, 607; HR 29 September 1989, NJ 1990, 307).

POLAND: There are no specific provisions on this matter. Since the agent may not carry out agency duties after the revocation it should be considered equal in effect to termination.

SCOTLAND: The entire revocation of the agent's mandate would be equivalent to the termination of the agency relationship. Cf. Macgregor, paragraphs 25 and 183.

SLOVAKIA: The provisions on termination of authority (external level) should be applied to the termination of the agency relationship (internal level); the CC Article 731 implies a strong link between revocation of authority and termination of the mandate relationship. Revocation of power definitely terminates the contractual relationship. The same applies to commercial relations.

SWEDEN: A revocation of power is considered to be a termination of the agent's assignment, provided that the agent knows of the revocation.

No answer received: BELGIUM, MALTA, PORTUGAL, SPAIN.

3. Notice of termination always brings about termination

AUSTRIA: An agent's authority can be terminated at any time by the express revocation of it by the principal (CC Article 1020).

BULGARIA: Unilateral notice of termination from one of the parties to the other one always ends the legal relationship. However, the prerequisites for lawful unilateral ending of the relationship are different for the principal and for the agent. The former, as 'master of the contract', is entitled to give a notice at any time (OCA Article 288), whereas the latter may only end the relationship for a 'serious reason' (OCA Article 289; Любен Василев, Облигационно право I, p. 29-30). Unless agreed otherwise, the commission agent is not allowed to unilaterally end the agency, except if the principal has breached the contract (CA Article 359 paragraph (1)). The commercial agent and the principal are permitted to unilaterally end their relationship on equal terms (CA Article 47 paragraphs (1) and (2)).

ENGLAND: When one party gives notice of termination but fails to comply with a period of notice required by the contract, this usually amounts to a repudiatory breach; normal common law rules of contract apply (*Atlantic Underwriting Agencies Ltd v Compagnia di Assicurazione di Milano SpA* [1979] 2 Lloyd's Rep 240). So, at common law, a repudiation only has the effect of ending the contractual relationship if it is accepted by the other. It is therefore up to the agent to accept the repudiation or not. If the agent does not, the contractual relationship remains alive. However, in practice, it is in the agent's interest to accept the repudiation and end the relationship if the agent wants to claim damages for breach.

FRANCE: The rule entitling the parties to freely terminate the agency is a matter of mandatory public policy. The parties cannot validly agree that the agency will be irrevocable. In practice, there are clauses in contracts entitled 'irrevocabilité', but these would be interpreted as simply giving rise to compensation for the agent (Cass.civ. 1re, 5 February 2002, Bull. civ. 2002 I, no. 40), and would also not prevent the principal from carrying out the transaction personally (Cass.civ. 1re, 16 June 1970 D. 1971, 261).

GERMANY: According to CC Article 671 paragraph (2), a revocation of the mandate by the agent is also valid if it has been declared in violation of the requirements of this provision (Palandt/Sprau, Article 671 no. 3). The principal is, however, entitled to damages.

HUNGARY: According to CC Article 483 paragraphs (1), (2) and (4), 'The principal shall be entitled to abrogate the contract with immediate effect at any time; the principal, however, shall be obliged to uphold the obligations already assumed by the agent. The agent shall also be entitled to abrogate the contract at any time; however, the period of notice must be sufficient for allowing the principal to handle the matter. In the event of the principal's grave breach of contract, abrogation can have immediate effect. Any limitation or exclusion of the right of cancellation shall be null and void; however, the parties shall be entitled to agree on the limitation of the right of cancellation with regard to continuous agencies.' For commission agency, CC Article 512 prescribes that 'Prior to the conclusion of a sales contract, the principal shall be entitled to terminate the contract by notice with immediate effect, and the commission agent by fifteen-days' notice. Any limitation or exclusion of the right of rescission shall be null and void.'

IRELAND: As a general rule, either party may terminate the agency relationship (although such termination may amount to a breach of contract), in accordance with any notice period in the contract, or, if the contract is silent, on reasonable notice. An ineffective termination would usually amount to a repudiation or anticipatory breach.

MALTA: D the only available remedy for the aggrieved party is damages. The contract therefore cannot be continued if one of the parties terminates it unilaterally.ue to the general provision found in CC Article 1887, that the principal may revoke the contract whenever he chooses, it can be presumed that the principal may conclude the prospected contract of his own motion Therefore the reasons for the cancellation (revocation) of the irrevocable grant of authority may be similar to, e.g., the fundamental violation of the agent's duties (for instance, the agent does not perform his duties or performs them unduly, undermines the interests of the principal or performs other acts that causes or may cause the damage to the interests of the principal) or the disappearance of the reason for the irrevocability of the grant of authority.

NETHERLANDS: The principal may in general end the relationship without giving notice of reasonable length at any time according to CC Articles 7:408 paragraph (1) and. 7:422 paragraph (1), a rule that is mandatory (CC, Article 7:422 paragraph (2)), whereas the agent may only do so for extraordinary and serious reason (CC Article 7:402)

POLAND: There is no similar rule in the Polish Civil Code. Parties may only terminate the contractual relationship if entitled to do so.

SCOTLAND: Where the principal's notice of termination is served in circumstances which do not comply with the terms of the agency contract, the notice will have no immediate terminating effect (on the assumption that it is not given for fundamental breach by the agent). By requiring a period of notice the parties would have contracted out of the normal rule that the principal could terminate at any time. However, an ineffective notice of termination would usually amount to a repudiation by the principal (in effect a declaration that the principal no longer wished to be bound by the contract) which would give the agent the option of terminating the relationship and claiming damages. It would usually be in the agent's interest to exercise this option as the relationship would be precarious and unsatisfactory once the principal's notice has been given. The same would apply in reverse if the agent purported to terminate the relationship but did not observe a period of notice required by the contract.

SLOVAKIA: The notice period for the agent's termination in commercial relations must be observed if the parties have not agreed otherwise; the contract is terminated by the end of the notice period. In other cases, the notice has immediate effect; the only limitation may be the obligation of the commercial agent to take preventive measures if needed.

SPAIN: Notice of termination by either party is always effective. However, agents under Spanish law are required to continue performance until the principal can take the measures necessary to adapt to the new situation (CC Article 1737).

SWEDEN: Notice leads to the ending of the contract (with immediate effect or after a notice period).

4. Consequences of termination for payment of the agent

AUSTRIA: If the principal terminates the relationship, the agent is entitled to a proportional part of the remuneration or price, to reimbursement of any expenses incurred and to damages for losses suffered (Rummel/Strasser, Article 1020 Rz 2-8e and 3 1021 Rz 15-26). The common Civil Code rules apply to the termination of a commission business or forwarding (see CC Article 918 ff., 1020, 1022, 1024 and 1447).

BELGIUM: Revocation has effect *ex nunc* and has no retroactive effect. The principal is obliged to reimburse the past expenses and losses of the agent and to pay a salary pro rata (Foriers & Glansdorff, p. 640, Tilleman, p. 304-305; Wéry, p. 215 and 273).

BULGARIA: Unilateral withdrawal of the principal does not deprive the agent of the remuneration agreed upon and reimbursement of expenses (OCA Article 288 paragraph (1)). The commission agent is entitled to receive remuneration and reimbursement of expenses for prospective contracts concluded on behalf of the principal until the end of the contractual relationship (CA Article 360). Unilateral termination by the principal does not eliminate the commercial agent's right to remuneration if the principal continues to enjoy benefits from the clientele established by the agent, except if the termination is due to the agent's fault (CA Article 47 paragraph (3) referring to Article 40).

ENGLAND: Termination does not affect any rights that the agent had accrued before termination, i.e. commission, indemnity, right to sue for breach etc. If termination by the principal amounted to a breach, the agent will still be entitled to sue for this breach and claim damages. Once the agent has received notice of the termination, any act that the agent does afterwards is not binding on the principal and will not give rise to commission, indemnity etc.

ESTONIA: In case of termination by the principal, the agent is entitled to the price for the services rendered until the termination (LOAEst Article 195) and to the costs incurred so far as these are not covered by the price for the services rendered (LOAEst Article 628 paragraph (2)).

FINLAND: If the contract requires specific personal trust (e.g. mandates for legal services), the principal is entitled to cancel the mandate contract at any time without any reason for the termination. In these cases, the agent is usually entitled to charge a fee only for the tasks already fulfilled. Otherwise the right of termination should be considered in light of the type of the mandate and other circumstances. The principal is generally entitled to cancel the mandate contract with a reasonable period of notice, unless the contract is concluded for a definite period of time (ACRS Article 22-23). The REstateAA contains provisions concerning termination of the mandate relationship in cases where the contract has become unreasonably disadvantageous for the principal (Article 6 REstateAA). the agent is generally entitled to the agreed fee if the termination is not based on a non-performance of the agent. If a concluded prospective contract or some other action is a prerequisite for the fee, the agent is not usually entitled to remuneration if such contract or other action has not been concluded or taken at time of termination of the mandate contract. The agent is entitled to compensation for expenses incurred.

FRANCE: If the termination is based on the fact that the mandate can no longer be performed for reasons that are independent of the parties, the French courts consider that the remuneration normally due may then be limited to the Principles of the contract which has already been performed (Cass.com., 21 December 1981, Bull. civ. 1981 IV, no. 450). If the mandate has not been performed for reasons of *force majeure*, it is thought that the remuneration will not be due. In any event, the agent will be entitled to repayment of expenses already incurred. There are, however, several limits to the absence of compensation of the agent in the case of termination of the mandate, e.g. in case of misuse by the principal of the right to freely terminate the agency (Cass.civ. 1re, 2 May 1984, Bull. civ. 1984 I, no. 143), in case of termination of a fixed-term agency (the termination must be based on a proper ground; see Cass.civ. 1re, 28 January 2003, Bull. civ. 2003 I, no. 27) and in case the agency contract provides for compensation in the event of unilateral termination

(Cass.civ. 1re, 6 March 2001, Bull. civ. 2001 I, no. 56). A special category is formed by the agency 'd'intérêt commun' ('of common interest'), which has been distinguished by the courts since the end of the 19th century. In this case, the mandate is freely terminable, but the agent must be compensated for the losses suffered in making specific efforts to develop the business or the custom in performance of the mandate.

HUNGARY: According to CC Article 478 paragraph (4), 'Fees shall be payable at the time a contract is extinguished.'

IRELAND: Termination of the agency does not affect existing liabilities. For instance, an agent is entitled to any commission earned and, to any indemnity due in respect of liabilities incurred, before termination. An agent may also be entitled to commission on contracts performed after termination of the agency where they were entered into prior to termination. Termination without notice will be justified where the other party has been guilty of a serious breach of contract. In other cases, termination without notice, or with less than the full notice required by the agreement, will terminate the agent's authority but may give rise to liability for breach of contract where the agency is contractual. Usually, this will be a claim against the principal by a dismissed agent. An agent is dismissed in breach of contract may claim damages in respect of the loss of the opportunity to earn commission had the contract been performed. As with any claim for breach of contract, the claimant will have to show that the loss is not too remote and will have to mitigate the loss.

MALTA: The agent has to be compensated for the damage suffered if the principal has no good reason to terminate, and if a contract for a definitive period is brought to an end before the day that it expires, cf. Comm. Court 12 November 1934, *Salomone vs Mifsud Speranza et noe*. The agent however has no right to remuneration.

NETHERLANDS: Although the principal may end the agency at any time without giving notice of reasonable length, that does not alter the fact that the agent is entitled to wages according to CC Article 7:411 paragraph (2). Obviously, the individual circumstances should be taken into account.

POLAND: The agent is entitled to receive partial remuneration and compensation for all incurred expenses. The agent is entitled to claim for the loss only if the contract was terminated without 'important reasons' (CC Article 746).

SCOTLAND: Termination by the principal will be without prejudice to the agent's accrued rights in respect of remuneration and/or commission, relief, and damages for breach of contract (Macgregor, paragraph 114; Gow, p. 536). As a general rule, however, the agent is not entitled to commission on orders received after the principal has terminated the agency relationship (Macgregor, paragraph 114; Black, paragraph 518). The principal is also bound to relieve the agent for any losses suffered where revocation prevents the agent from completing unfinished transactions (Macgregor, paragraph 183).

SLOVAKIA: In civil relations, where the mandate has been revoked by the principal, the principal is obliged to compensate the agent for all expenses incurred before revocation, for damages suffered and if any remuneration is due for work that the agent performed, for such work or part thereof. The same probably applies in case of termination by the agent. In commercial relations, the agent is entitled to reimbursement of expenses and to a proportionate part of remuneration for duly rendered services before the day the notice takes effect.

SPAIN: The right to terminate the agency does not make the principal free from the obligation to reimburse incurred expenses or the liability to pay damages for any loss suffered by the early termination (STS 3 March 1998, RJA 1998, 1129). In STS 3 March 1998, RJA 1998, 1129 the Tribunal Supremo held that the principal was not entitled to freely terminate the mandate where a price for the services and a definite time had been agreed.

SWEDEN: Where the principal terminates the relationship, the agent is entitled to payment for work already performed.

No answer received: GERMANY, GREECE, PORTUGAL.

5. No justification to terminate: right to damages for breach

AUSTRIA: If the principal terminates the relationship, the agent is entitled to damages for losses suffered (Rummel/Strasser, Article 1020 Rz 2-8e and 3 Article 1021 Rz 15-26).

BULGARIA: When the agent wants to unilaterally end the mandate contract for a 'serious reason', the agent is obliged to notify the principal in due time; otherwise, he may be held liable for damages incurred by the principal (OCA Article 289).

ESTONIA: The agent may terminate a mandate relationship entered into for an indefinite period only under the condition that the principal can receive the service or enter into the transaction in another manner; otherwise, the agent must compensate the principal for any damage caused by the termination (LOAEst Article 630 paragraph (2)).

FRANCE: Compensation of the agent is due: a) in the case of misuse by the principal of the right to freely terminate the agency (Cass.civ. 1re, 2 May 1984, Bull. civ. 1984 I, no. 143), b) in case of termination of a fixed-term agency (the termination must be based on a proper ground; see Cass.civ. 1re, 28 January 2003, Bull. civ. 2003 I, no. 27) and c) in case the agency contract provides for compensation in the event of unilateral termination (Cass.civ. 1re, 6 March 2001, Bull. civ. 2001 I, no. 56).

MALTA: If termination by the agent is prejudicial to the principal, the principal must be compensated by the agent, except when it is impossible for the agent to continue carrying out the contract without suffering himself considerable prejudice (CC Article 1889 paragraph (2). The agent has to be compensated for the damage suffered if the principal has no good reason to terminate, and if a contract for a definitive period is brought to an end before the day that it expires.

HUNGARY: According to CC Article 483 paragraph (3), 'If the agency is cancelled without substantial grounds, the damages that are caused shall be indemnified, unless the agency is gratuitous and the period of notice is sufficient for allowing the principal to handle the matter.'

SLOVAKIA: In civil relations, where the mandate has been revoked by the principal, the principal is obliged to compensate the agent for all expenses incurred before revocation, for damages suffered and if any remuneration is due for work that the agent performed, for such work or part thereof. The same probably applies in case of termination by the agent. In commercial relations, the agent is entitled to reimbursement of expenses and to a proportionate part of remuneration for duly rendered services before the day the notice takes effect.

SPAIN: The right to terminate the mandate does not make the principal free from the obligation to reimburse incurred expenses or the liability to pay damages for any loss suffered by the early termination (STS 3 March 1998, RJA 1998, 1129). In STS 3 March 1998, RJA 1998, 1129 the Tribunal Supremo held that the principal was not entitled to freely terminate the mandate where a price for the services and a definite time had been agreed.

6. Notice period not observed: right to damages in lieu of notice

BELGIUM: If the contract provides for a notice period and this period is not upheld, the agent may have a right to damages on the basis of breach of contract.

BULGARIA: When the agent wants to unilaterally end the mandate contract for a 'serious reason', the agent is obliged to notify the principal in due time; otherwise, he may be held liable for damages incurred by the principal (OCA Article 289).

ENGLAND: If the principal fails to give the required period of notice, the agent will usually be entitled to treat this as an anticipatory breach, terminate the relationship and claim damages for breach. The same applies if the agent fails to provide notice as agreed.

FRANCE: If a notice period provided for in the contract was not upheld, the agent may have a right to damages on the basis of breach of contract. The same applies in the agent fails to provide notice as agreed.

GERMANY: According to CC Article 671 paragraph (2), the principal is entitled to damages if the agent has revoked the mandate contract in an untimely manner.

HUNGARY: According to CC Article 483 paragraph (3), 'If the agency is cancelled without substantial grounds, the damages that are caused shall be indemnified, unless the agency is gratuitous and the period of notice is sufficient for allowing the principal to handle the matter.' According to the decision of the Supreme Court Nr. 3/2006 on the Uniform Application of Law, CC 483 paragraph (3) applies also to the principal and 'If a remunerated agency is cancelled without substantial grounds with immediate effect, the damages of the agent that are caused shall be indemnified by the principal'. See CA Jász-Nagykun-Szolnok Megyei Bíróság 4. Gf. 16-00-000016/12, in BDT2002. 577.

IRELAND: Failure to observe a notice period or provide reasonable notice is a breach of contract for which damages may be payable.

MALTA: If termination by the agent is prejudicial to the principal, the principal must be compensated by the agent, except when it is impossible for the agent to continue carrying out the contract without suffering himself considerable prejudice (CC Article 1889 paragraph (2)).

NETHERLANDS: If the contractual requirements as to a notice period are not observed by the principal, the agent is entitled to remuneration according to CC Article 7:411; if it is the agent who does not observe the requirements and does not have an extraordinary and serious reason for this, the contractual relationship will not terminate.

SCOTLAND: Where the principal serves notice of termination without cause, but without observing the requirements for an effective notice laid down in the agency contract, the agent will usually be entitled to treat this as a repudiation and will then have the option of terminating the relationship and claiming damages. It should be noted that the failure to observe the notice period would not be itself a non-performance of an obligation. A requirement of a certain period is just that – a requirement and not an obligation – and the sanction for non-compliance is the ineffectiveness of the notice.

SLOVAKIA: The notice period for the agent's termination in commercial relations must be observed

SPAIN: There is no legal period of notice. If parties agree on a reasonable period of notice and this is not observed, damages for breach are due.

SWEDEN: If the parties have agreed upon a notice period and such period is not upheld by a party, this constitutes non-performance for which the other party could claim damages.

No answer received: AUSTRIA, ESTONIA, POLAND, SLOVAKIA.

Article 6:102: Termination by the principal when relationship is to last for indefinite period or when mandate is for a particular task

(1) The principal may terminate the mandate relationship at any time by giving notice of reasonable length if the mandate contract has been concluded for an indefinite period or for a particular task.

(2) Paragraph (1) does not apply if the mandate is irrevocable.

(3) The parties may not, to the detriment of the principal, exclude the application of this Article or derogate from or vary its effects, unless the conditions set out under Article 1:105 (Irrevocable mandate) are met.

Comments

A. General idea

Following the approach in Article 6:109 PECL (Contract for an indefinite period), the present Article provides the principal with a means to terminate a mandate relationship concluded for an indefinite period by giving notice of reasonable length. The Article follows the generally accepted principle that nobody can be contractually bound to another eternally. But these Principles also extend this right of the principal to terminate by notice to those cases in which the contract has been concluded for a particular task. The justification for this solution is that this type of contract may give rise to a relationship where the parties are bound to each other eternally since it is uncertain if and when the envisaged result will be achieved.

B. Termination by notice of reasonable length when contract for an indefinite period

The principal is allowed to bring a mandate relationship entered into for an indefinite period to an end (even in the absence of an extraordinary and serious reason) provided that the principal notifies the decision to terminate a reasonable time in advance to grant the agent some time to adapt to the new situation.

Whether a period is reasonable would have to be determined in light of the relevant circumstances. Comment C to Article 6:109 PECL (Contract for an indefinite period) indicates that these would include the time the contract has lasted, the efforts and investments which the agent has made in performing the contract, the time it may take the agent to obtain another contract, and any relevant usages or practices. Under these Principles, a notice of termination would not be of reasonable length if the principal would be required to observe a longer period for termination than the agent is required to observe.

Illustration 1
Marina is a professional photographer. She has emigrated to Spain but she has authorized an agent in the Netherlands to take care of the public relations of Marina's company in order to find new Dutch clients. The parties have not limited the duration of the contract. Two years later Marina decides to return to the Netherlands. She wants to terminate the relationship with her agent in the Netherlands. Under these Principles, Marina has to give notice of reasonable length to the agent before bringing the relationship to an end.

Illustration 2
Lionel is a professional football player. He has engaged for an indefinite period the services of Orange SA, a professional agency arranging the commercial affairs of their players towards the media. As Lionel is not satisfied with the profit Orange SA obtains on his behalf for his participation in advertisement campaigns, after one year Lionel

decides to terminate the mandate contract, effective from the beginning of the next football season, which starts in three months. In this case, Lionel has observed a reasonable period of notice and need not pay damages for premature termination.

The right of the principal to terminate a mandate contract for an indefinite period is acknowledged under all regimes.

C. Termination by notice of reasonable length when contracting for a particular task

A mandate relationship entered into for a particular task terminates when the particular task is completed (e.g. when the prospective contract is concluded). It is therefore not a contract concluded for an indefinite period but rather one for a definite period, despite the fact that the exact date of expiry is not known exactly. Under Article 6:101 (Termination by notice in general), a principal who terminates a contract for a definite period before the agreed date of expiry (i.e. the specific date or the date when the envisaged result is achieved) is in principle liable in damages, unless there is some other legitimate reason for early termination.

However, under the present Article, a principal is entitled to terminate a mandate relationship entered into for a *particular task* by giving notice of reasonable length and to do so without liability for damages. Although this type of contract could be classified as for a definite period, its specific characteristics are deemed to justify the right to terminate at any time by giving notice. Indeed, since it is uncertain when the envisaged result will be achieved or even whether it will be finally achieved, the parties may be *de facto* linked to the contract for an indefinite period, in particular in the situation where the agent fails to conclude the prospective contract without breaching the obligations under the mandate contract – in which case the mandate relationship cannot be terminated for non-performance either. However, the principal is not allowed under this Article to terminate the contract immediately: it is essential to give notice of reasonable length to the agent to provide some time for adjustment to the new situation.

Illustration 3

Bernard entrusts Julian, an estate agent, with the task of selling Bernard's house without specifying a time within which this is to be done. After a year and a half the house has still not been sold, even though Bernard has twice given the estate agent a direction to reduce the price. By this time, the number of house sales has dropped significantly and it does not appear that the housing market will soon recover. For these reasons, Bernard finally decides not to pursue the attempt to sell the house.

In this situation the principal can terminate the mandate relationship concluded for a particular task, without incurring liability for damages for so doing, by giving a reasonable period of notice.

Whether a period of notice is of reasonable length is to be determined according to the relevant circumstances as stated in Comment C to Article 6:109 PECL (Contract for an indefinite period) and in Comment B to this Article. Under these Principles, if the principal would be required to observe a longer period for termination than the agent is required to observe.

D. No termination if irrevocable mandate

Paragraph (2) of the present Article provides that the principal's right to terminate under paragraph (1) does not apply in the case of an irrevocable mandate. If termination of an irrevocable mandate were possible, the consequences of irrevocability could be easily circumvented by giving notice of termination.

Illustration 3
A group of music composers (the principals) agree that in their common interest an organisation of music composers (the agent) will be mandated to act on their behalf with regard to the exploitation of their intellectual property rights. Parties have agreed on the irrevocability of the mandate granted to the agent. The contract is furthermore concluded for an indefinite period. After two years, one of the principals notifies the agent that he is not interested in continuing with the mandate relationship and he informs the agent that the contract with this principal will come to an end in three months. Termination by notice, even if the notice in itself is of reasonable length, is of no effect because the parties had agreed on the irrevocability of the mandate. This implies that the mandate contract continues to exist and both parties to the contract remain bound by the ensuing obligations.

Contrary to the system in most Member States, the solution chosen under these Principles is to limit the effectiveness of a notice of termination if the contract is irrevocable. In this manner, the legitimate interest of the agent in the irrevocability of the mandate contract is protected.

E. Relationship with the Principles of European Law and the Draft Common Frame of Reference

This Article mirrors that of Article IV.D. – 6:102 DCFR (Termination by principal when relationship is to last for indefinite period or when mandate is for a particular task). Article 1:302 (Unilateral ending of a contract for an indefinite period) of the Principles of European Law on Commercial Agency, Franchising and Distribution Contracts and also in Article IV.E. – 2:302 DCFR (Contract for an indefinite period) include the same rule for the termination of commercial agency, franchising, and distribution contracts concluded for an indefinite period.

F. Character of the rule

This Article constitutes a mandatory rule from which the parties may not derogate to the detriment of the principal.

The principal's right to terminate the mandate relationship for an indefinite period of time or a particular task is mandatory in favour of the principal – whether the principal is a consumer or a business. If the parties could not terminate a mandate relationship entered into for an indefinite period of time, the contract would in fact be concluded for eternity, and this is considered to be contrary to public policy or good morals in many legal systems. Moreover, if the parties could exclude the right to terminate the mandate relationship, this would undoubtedly lead to a stretching of the notion of 'extraordinary and serious reason' under the following Article, thus enabling the principal to escape from the contract, but without even having to observe a notice period of reasonable length. Whereas the public policy argument does not apply to contracts for a particular task, the argument regarding a stretching of the notion of 'extraordinary and serious reason' under the following Article does apply to such contracts. For this reason, the mandatory nature of the present Article also applies to mandate contracts for a particular task. This idea is expressed in paragraph (3). However, in this paragraph an exception to the mandatory character of the rule is established: by agreeing on the irrevocability of the mandate, parties may agree on excluding the possibility to terminate by giving notice of reasonable length. However, such an agreement will only be effective if the conditions of Article 1:105 paragraph (1) (Irrevocable mandate) of these Principles are met and the conditions of paragraph (2) of that Article are not fulfilled.

G. Remedies

If the principal terminates a mandate relationship concluded for an indefinite period or for a particular task but does not grant the agent a reasonable notice period, the agent is entitled to claim damages for premature termination. There is no entitlement, though, to claim specific performance of the notice period, i.e. the continuation of the mandate relationship during the notice period.

Comparative Notes

1. Termination by principal by giving notice of reasonable length

The principal is in all legal regimes allowed to terminate a contract for an indefinite period by giving notice. A reasonable period of notice is not required by law in AUSTRIA, BELGIUM, BULGARIA, DENMARK, FRANCE, ENGLAND, THE NETHERLANDS, POLAND, SCOTLAND, SPAIN, and SWEDEN. In these systems, a period of notice can be agreed in the contract. When not observed, it leads to damages for breach, except in SCOTLAND, where lack of due notice implies that the notice is ineffective. In practice, however, agents there generally choose to accept termination and ask for damages. In ENGLAND, if the parties to a contract for an indefinite duration have not provided for a notice, the courts may imply a reasonable notice.

A period of notice needs to be observed – even if not agreed – in FINLAND, GERMANY (exceptions depending on the type of mandate), IRELAND (implied), ITALY, HUNGARY, PORTUGAL, and SLOVAKIA. Where this period is not respected, damages are due in these legal systems.

A specific notice period is required in ESTONIA. If the contract is entered into for the life of one party or for a period longer than five years, the principal has the right to terminate the contract once five years have passed from the date of conclusion of the contract by giving at least six months' advanced notice (LOAEst Article 630 paragraph (3)).

2. No termination if mandate irrevocable

Notice of termination is effective – even if the mandate is irrevocable – in BULGARIA, ENGLAND, MALTA, and PORTUGAL. Notice of termination concerning an irrevocable mandate is only effective if the agent agrees to it in IRELAND, THE NETHERLANDS, and SCOTLAND. Irrevocable mandates are not accepted in FRANCE, POLAND, and SLOVAKIA, which implies that the termination of the 'irrevocable' mandate is possible but leads to a claim for damages for the agent.

National Notes

1. Termination by principal by giving notice of reasonable length

AUSTRIA: This question is submerged in the principal's general right to terminate. An agent's authority can be terminated at any time by the express revocation of it by the principal (CC Article 1020). The question of termination of the contractual relationship is the same as that of termination of authority.

BELGIUM: According to the Belgian CC Article 2004, a principal can always revoke the authority to represent ad nutum, i.e. without a motive and without a term or amount of notice (De Page, p. 460-462; Foriers & Glansdorff, p. 639; Tilleman, p. 301-305; Wéry, p. 267-273). It is irrelevant whether the contract for representation is non-remunerated (e.g. Cass. 28 June 1993, Pas. 1993, I, 628, and RW 1993-94, 1425, note A. Van Oevelen). As a unilateral juridical act, the revocation does not have to be accepted by the agent to be effective (De Page, p. 462-463; Tilleman, p. 281 and 290-291).

BULGARIA: As a general rule, the principal can revoke the mandate relationship with the agent at any time and without any reason (Bulgarian OCA Article 288 paragraph (1)). This rule is applicable to both gratuitous and non-gratuitous contracts and to contracts for an indefinite or a fixed period (Любен Василев, Облигационно право, p. 29; Голева, Облигационно право II, p. 239). The principal can end the contract either explicitly by a unilateral notice to the agent or implicitly by the conclusion of the prospective contract by the principal himself or another agent (Меворах/Лиджи/Фархи, III, p. 176).

DENMARK: Apart from the special (mandatory) rules of the Commercial Agents and Travellers Act, Danish law contains no specific rules on termination of a contract between a principal and the agent when the contract for representation has been concluded for an indefinite period of time and does not end by the conclusion of the prospective contract. If the parties have not agreed otherwise, the principal is entitled to bring the contract to an end at any time by giving a termination notice to the agent. Under these circumstances the agent is not entitled to claim compensation even if the period of representing the principal had been expected to last for a longer time. The agent may claim compensation for the expenses incurred during the period of the representation.

ENGLAND: Under the general principle of revocation, the principal may revoke the agent's authority by giving notice before the authority has been fully exercised *(Hampden v Walsh* (1876) 1 QBD 189)). This rule of 'unfettered revocation' applies even where the agency is described as irrevocable *(Vynior's case* (1609) 8 Co Rep 81b). In case of an indefinite duration contract, the principal must give notice of the revocation to the agent since the agent's authority does not end until receipt of actual notice of the revocation *(Re Oriental Bank Corpn, ex p Guillemin* (1884) 28 Ch D 634). Once the agent knows about the revocation, any future acts are ineffective and the agent loses the right to future remuneration and indemnity. However, if the notice by the principal is a breach of contract, the agent will be entitled to damages. If the agent is an employee, it may also be possible to claim for compensation for unfair dismissal or for a redundancy payment. For contracts entered into for a particular task, it is accepted that the contract is often unilateral in nature, i.e. that the agent is under no obligation to perform the task and that the principal is bound to pay only when the agent has actually performed the task. In such cases the agent accepts the risk that the principal may withdraw at any time until the agent has performed the required task and therefore bears the risk of not being paid should that occur: *Luxor (Eastbourne) Ltd v Cooper* [1941] AC 108 (estate agency case). Even though this seems to be the normal interpretation of estate agency contracts, this is subject to express or implied terms to the contrary as is clear from *Alpha Trading Ltd v Dunshaw Patten* [1981] QB 290 where a collateral contract was implied to restrict the principal's freedom to withdraw at any time. In the case of a fixed term contract an attempted termination before the expiry of the term constitutes a repudiatory breach, entitling the agent to claim damages (e.g. *Turner v Goldsmith* [1891] 1 QB 544). This is so, unless termination is justified by an earlier breach committed by the other party: *Boston Deep Sea Fishing and Ice Co v Ansell* (1888) 39 Ch D 339, CA.

ESTONIA: The principal may, as far as the internal relationship to the agent is governed by the (general) contract for services terminate the contract at any time, no special cause for termination is needed (LOAEst Article 630 paragraph (1)). If the contract is entered into for the life of one party or for a period longer than five years, the principal has the right to terminate the contract once five years have passed from the date of conclusion of the contract by giving at least six months' advance notice (LOAEst Article 630 paragraph (3)).

FINLAND: If the contract requires specific personal trust (e.g. mandates for legal services), the principal is entitled to cancel the mandate contract at any time without any reason for the termination. In these cases, the agent is usually entitled to charge a fee only for the tasks already fulfilled. Otherwise the right of termination should be considered in light of the type of the mandate and other circumstances. The principal is generally entitled to cancel the mandate contract with a reasonable period of notice, unless the contract is concluded for a definite period of time (ACRS Articles 22-23). The REstateAA contains provisions concerning termination of the mandate relationship in cases where the contract has become unreasonably disadvantageous for the principal (Article 6 REstateAA). The agent is generally entitled to the agreed fee if the termination is not based on a non-performance of the agent. If a concluded prospective contract or some other action is a prerequisite for the fee, the agent is not usually entitled to remuneration if such contract or other action has not been concluded or taken at time of termination of the mandate contract. The agent is entitled to compensation for expenses incurred.

FRANCE: The principal can terminate the contract *ad nutum*, i.e. at any time, without a specific reason and without any liability to pay compensation (CC Article 2004). The termination may even occur as a result of notice to the agent of the appointment of a new agent for the same transaction (CC Article 2006).

GERMANY: A gratuitous mandate relationship may be terminated at any time (CC Article 671 paragraph (1)). Termination of a remunerated relationship *(Geschäftsbesorgungsvertrag)* is governed by the law on contracts for services or contracts for works. The rules on contracts for services allow termination by the principal as well as the agent (CC Article 621). The termination period depends on the time frame according to which the service provider is paid. Contracts for services under which payment is not made after particular time periods can be cancelled at any time. Additionally, either party has the right to terminate irrespective of any termination period where there is an important reason which makes it unacceptable for the party to continue the contract (CC Article 626). Furthermore, termination is possible even without an important reason where the contract calls for services 'of a higher kind which are usually assigned on the basis of particular trust' (CC Article 627 paragraph (1)). This will often be the case where a contract for representation is concluded.

GREECE: In case of a gratuitous mandate relationship the principal is entitled to revoke the mandate at any time. An agreement to the contrary is void, except if the mandate also concerns the interest of the agent or of a third party (CC Article 724). If the revocation takes place before completion of the mandate it results in cancellation of the contract. If it takes place after a part of the mandate has been performed, the revocation concerns only the future performance of the mandate *(ex nunc)*. A contractual agreement of restrictions or requirements for the exercise of the right of revocation can be concluded only if the mandate also concerns the interest of the agent or of a third party. The revocation of the agent results in the cessation of the power to represent the principal. Due to the gratuitous character of the contract of mandate the question regarding the entitlement of the agent to a price does not arise. The principal is only obliged to reimburse the expenses that the agent has incurred prior to the revocation of the mandate. However that question arises in the case of the obligatory remunerated mandate between lawyer and client regulated in Article 170 of the Code of Attorneys (legislative decree no. 3026/1954). If revocation of the mandate was unjustified, the principal should perform all contractual obligations to the lawyer, such as payment of remuneration. If revocation was justified, the principal should only pay remuneration or expenses incurred prior to the revocation of the mandate (Supreme Court decision no. 1/1987, EEN 1987, 783).

HUNGARY: According to CC Article 483 paragraph (1), '[t]he principal shall be entitled to abrogate the contract with immediate effect at any time; the principal, however, shall be obliged to uphold the obligations already assumed by the agent'. CC Article 478 paragraph (3) establishes that '[i]f the contract is terminated before the agency has been fulfilled, the agent shall be entitled to demand an appropriate fraction of the fee for his activities'. It is not relevant in this respect whether the principal is a consumer. In the case of commission agency, according to CC Article 512, '[p]rior to the conclusion of a sales contract, the principal shall be entitled to terminate the contract by notice with immediate effect, and the commission agent by fifteen-days' notice. Any limitation or exclusion of the right of rescission shall be null and void'. Also in this case CC Article 511 paragraph (1) applies, according to which '[t]he commission agent shall be entitled to receive a commission only if the sales contract has been performed'.

IRELAND: Where an agent is appointed for an indeterminate period the agency can be terminated in accordance with any provision in the agreement for termination by notice. In the absence of any express term, it will normally be implied that the agency can be terminated, by either party, on reasonable notice.

ITALY: According to the Italian CC Article 1723 paragraph (1) 'the principal can revoke the mandate, but if it was agreed that the mandate should be irrevocable, he is liable for damages, unless revocation is made for a just cause'. The general principle concerning termination by the principal is that of the free revocability of the authority granted to the agent, while the irrevocable mandate is considered an exception to this general rule. If the agent is entitled to a price, CC Article 1725 provides that 'the revocation of a non-gratuitous mandate given for a specified period of time or for a specified transaction renders the principal liable for damages if the revocation was made before the expiration of the time limit or before the completion of the transaction, unless there is just cause for the revocation'. Accordingly, the principal's freedom to revoke an onerous mandate is subject to the following alternative conditions: reasonable notice or just cause. In the absence thereof the principal must pay damages to the agent.

MALTA: The principal is allowed to terminate and no specific requirements are to be fulfilled: no notice of reasonable length is therefore required, CC Article 1887 paragraph (1). He is however liable in damages if he has no good reason to terminate.

NETHERLANDS: The principal is in general allowed to terminate the relationship at any time without having to give reasonable notice (CC Articles 7:408 paragraph (2) and 7:422). It is only in the exceptional case that parties have agreed a mandate contract that is to be performed in the interest of the agent or of third party that the relationship cannot be ended freely by the principal.

POLAND: The principal is always entitled to revoke the mandate due to 'important reasons'. The contracting parties may not derogate from this rule (CC Article 746 paragraph (3)). The principal's right to terminate the contract on other grounds may be excluded.

PORTUGAL: The principal is liable for the cancellation of a contract concluded for an indefinite period if he did not notify the agent in a reasonable term of notice (CC Article 1172 lit (a-c)). A reasonable term of notice is still considered by the literature to be that provided by CC Article 1368 (old), "the necessary time for the parties to provide for their interests". Cf. Lima/Varela (1986).

SCOTLAND: The principal is entitled to end an agency of unlimited duration at any time (unless the agency is irrevocable). Cf. Stair, I,12,8; Erskine, III,3,40; Gow, p. 536; *Walker v Somerville* (1837) 16 S 217. This is not so where the contract is a fixed term one, where termination by the principal before the expiry of the agreed term will constitute a breach of contract (Black, paragraph 551). The principal's right to terminate may also be excluded as a matter of construction of the agency contract *(Galbraith and Moorhead v Arethusa Ship Co Ltd* (1896) 23 R 1011). Although the authorities are ambiguous on this point, it seems that the principal must communicate the termination to the agent (Erskine, III,3,40). The principal is, nevertheless, bound to relieve the agent of any losses the agent suffers where termination prevents the agent from completing a transaction, and indeed, termination may only be possible once the agent has been so relieved (Erskine, III,3,40). Termination is subject to the agent's other accrued rights such as payment of remuneration or commission, or damages for breach of contract (Gow, p. 536; *Galbraith and Moorhead v Arethusa Ship Co Ltd* (1896) 23 R 1011).

SLOVAKIA: The principal is always entitled to terminate the contractual relationship without any conditions (CC Article 33b). The question of termination of the contract is the same as that of termination of authority. Where the mandate has been terminated by revocation, the principal is obliged to compensate the agent for all expenses incurred before revocation and for the damage suffered and if any remuneration is due for work that the agent performed, for such work or part thereof. In commercial relations, the client may also terminate the mandate partly or fully at any time. Unless the term of notice stipulates otherwise, the notice takes effect as of the day on which the agent has or could have learned about it. The agent is entitled to compensation of expenses and to a proportionate part of the remuneration for duly rendered services before the day when the notice takes effect (Comm.C Article 574).

SPAIN: The principal may terminate the relationship at any time (CC Article 1732). Some legal authors argue that in the case of a remunerated mandate contract termination implies that the principal has to pay damages to the agent, on the basis of the doctrine of abuse of right or the principle of good faith in CC Article 1258 (Hernández Gil, p. 512). However, according to Lete del Río, the principal will have to indemnify the agent if the principal terminates in order to damage the interests of the agent or if the termination is based on unlawful reasons (Lete del Río, p. 413). It is doubtful whether cases of implicit revocation in which the principal concludes the contract personally or by means of another agent are to be regarded as lawful reasons or reason within the limits of the good faith principle. For the case law, see Díaz-Regañón, p. 75 ff).

SWEDEN: When the contract has been concluded for an indefinite period of time, the principal may terminate the contractual relationship at any time without cause and usually with immediate effect. The agent can only claim reasonable compensation for work already performed under the contract (Bengtsson, p. 153; Hesser, p. 30).

2. No termination if mandate is irrevocable

AUSTRIA: Though an agent's authority is normally revocable at any time (CC Article 1020) without prejudice to his right to damages for breach of contract, there is an exception: if the authority is coupled with an interest outside the contract for mandate and the irrevocability is stipulated for contract for a definite period of time, such an authority is irrevocable (Schwimann/Apathy, Article 1020 Rz 7; Straube/Griss, Article 383 Rz 13).

BULGARIA: Even when the mandate contract is said to be irrevocable the principal can unilaterally end it at any time.

ENGLAND: The concept of 'irrevocable agency' is somewhat complicated and very specific. The agent's authority will be irrevocable in two instances: (1) when it is coupled with an interest belonging to the agent, i.e. that 'the authority is given for the purpose of being a security' *(Smart v Sandars* [1848] 5 CB 895, 918 per Wilde CJ) so that security and authority are closely connected with one another, or (2) when a power of attorney is given to secure an interest, or some obligation, to the donee; the consent of the donee is then required for the authority to be revoked (Power of Attorney Act 1971, Article 4).

FRANCE: The rule entitling the parties to freely terminate the mandate or agency is a matter of mandatory public policy and the parties cannot validly agree that the agency is irrevocable. In practice, there are clauses in contracts entitled 'irrevocabilité', but these are interpreted as simply giving rise to compensation for the agent (Cass.civ. 1re, 5 February 2002, Bull. civ. 2002 I, no. 40), and do not prevent the principal from carrying out the transaction himself (Cass.civ. 1re, 16 June 1970, D. 1971, 261).

IRELAND: An agency may be irrevocable where e.g. (i) the agent is given a 'power with an interest', that is, where an agent is given power and a personal interest, as where the principal owes the agent money, and gives authority to sell property and thereby raise funds to pay the debt; or (ii) where a power of attorney is expressed to be 'enduring' or irrevocable under the Powers of Attorney Act, 1996.

MALTA: Due to the general provision found in Article 1887 of the Maltese Civil Code, that the principal may revoke the contract whenever he chooses, it can be presumed that the principal may conclude the prospected contract of his own motion, even when it is irrevocable.

NETHERLANDS: If the mandate deals with performing a legal act in the interest of the agent or a third party, the contracting parties can agree that the principal is not allowed to terminate the relationship (CC Article 7:422 paragraph (2)). In this case, the mandate is irrevocable.

POLAND: Polish law does not recognise irrevocable mandates.

PORTUGAL: An irrevocable grant of authority clause is allowed, but does not preclude the cancellation of the mandate by the principal, it only has liability consequences (Lima/Varela (1986)).

SCOTLAND: Where the agency is, in effect, an irrevocable mandate, or *procuratory in rem suam,* the principal is not entitled to terminate without the consent of the agent (Black, paragraph 551).

SLOVAKIA: Irrevocable mandate is not allowed.

No answer received: BELGIUM, DENMARK, ESTONIA, FINLAND, GERMANY, GREECE, HUNGARY, IRELAND, ITALY, MALTA, SPAIN, SWEDEN.

Article 6:103: Termination by the principal for extraordinary and serious reason

(1) The principal may terminate the mandate relationship by giving notice for extraordinary and serious reason.
(2) No period of notice is required.
(3) For the purposes of this Article, the death or incapacity of the person who, at the time of conclusion of the mandate contract, the parties had intended to perform the agent's obligations under the mandate contract, constitutes an extraordinary and serious reason.
(4) This Article applies with appropriate adaptations if the successors of the principal terminate the mandate relationship in accordance with Article 7:101 (Death of the principal).
(5) The parties may not, to the detriment of the principal or the principal's successors, exclude the application of this Article or derogate from or vary its effects.

Comments

A. General idea

The present Article introduces a right for the principal to immediately terminate a mandate relationship without having to observe a notice period and without having to pay damages. This right can be exercised when there is an extraordinary and serious reason which justifies termination. Termination is by notice by the principal to the agent of the decision to terminate the mandate relationship. Extraordinary and serious reasons to terminate a mandate relationship may arise in very different circumstances. Paragraphs (3) and (4) mention two situations which are classified as extraordinary reasons to terminate.

B. No exhaustive list of extraordinary and serious reasons

This provision refers in paragraphs (3) and (4) to two situations that are to be regarded as extraordinary reasons which justify termination: the death or incapacity of the person who, at the time of conclusion of the mandate contract, the parties had intended to perform the agent's obligations under the mandate contract (paragraph (3)) and, for the successors of the principal, the death of the principal (paragraph (4)). This list does not purport to provide an exhaustive enumeration of the reasons that justify immediate termination. Whether a reason qualifies as 'extraordinary and serious' within the meaning of this Article and justifies immediate termination is to be determined on a case-by-case basis.

C. Loss of confidence and trust in the agent

Termination by the principal for an extraordinary and serious reason may occur when the principal no longer believes that the agent is acting in the principal's best interest and has lost trust in the agent. For instance, this may occur when the agent has breached an implied or explicit obligation of confidentiality. There may also be an extraordinary and serious reason for the principal to terminate if the result to be achieved by the agent has become pointless for the principal.

Illustration 1
Marco concludes a mandate contract in which he entrusts Julka with the task of negotiating the purchase of a major bank. The following week a fraud case involving Julka is reported on the front page of all national newspapers. Whether or not the accusations are true, Julka's business reputation is seriously damaged and Marco does not have sufficient trust in Julka being able, at this time, to properly negotiate with the current owners of the bank. Even though there is no case of non-performance by the agent, under these circumstances Marco cannot be expected to continue allowing Julka to take care of the transaction.

However, there is no provision stating that whenever the principal justifiably loses trust and confidence in the agent, there is a serious and extraordinary reason for termination of the mandate relationship. Such an explicit rule could tempt principals to argue that there was a loss of confidence and trust just to escape having to respect a notice period or, after the fact, to prevent having to pay damages for wrongfully terminating the mandate relationship with immediate effect. It is thought better to leave the matter for the court to decide on the basis of the general provision in paragraph (1).

D. Conclusion of prospective contract by the principal or by another agent

When the principal concludes the prospective contract personally or by means of another agent, this implicitly revokes the agent's mandate to conclude that contract on the principal's behalf. Under Article 6:101 paragraph (2) (Termination by notice in general), revocation of the mandate of the agent is treated as termination.

Under these Principles, if the parties have not agreed on exclusivity, the principal is free to conclude the prospective contract himself or by means of another agent without having to pay damages to the agent. As is explained in Comment B to Article 3:301 (Exclusivity not presumed), this implies that the conclusion of the prospective contract by the principal or by another agent is regarded as a serious and extraordinary reason for the principal to terminate the mandate contract. This means that the contract comes to an end and that the principal does not have to pay damages for terminating the mandate contract or for not observing a reasonable period of notice. However, in this situation the agent may be entitled to payment of the price or a part thereof for the services rendered under Article 2:102 paragraph (4) (Price) if and in so far as the services rendered by the agent have contributed to the conclusion of the prospective contract. The agent would also be entitled to payment if the parties had agreed on payment of a price for services rendered (Article 2:102 paragraph (3)) (Price).

E. No notice period

If there is indeed an extraordinary and serious reason which justifies termination of the contract, termination should take immediate effect. In this specific situation, the party giving notice is not required to observe any other condition than notifying the other party about the decision to terminate. In particular, no notice period needs to be observed, as follows from paragraph (2). It follows from the general rules on notice in Article 1:303 PECL (Notice) that there is no form requirement regarding the notification.

F. Termination also if mandate irrevocable

Article 1:105 (Irrevocable mandate) provides in its paragraph (2) that an irrevocable mandate may nevertheless be revoked in the case of an extraordinary and serious reason. From Article 6:101 paragraph (3) (Termination by notice in general) it follows that in such cases the mandate contract may also be terminated by the principal.

Illustration 2
A group of music composers (the principals) agree that in their common interest an organisation of music composers (the agent) will be mandated to act on their behalf with regard to the exploitation of their intellectual property rights. The parties agree on the irrevocability of the mandate. The contract is concluded for an indefinite period. After two years, it becomes clear that the agent is involved in improper affairs. Because one of the principals is afraid that this may hurt his own career, he terminates the contract by giving notice based on this ground.

Under these Principles, this can be considered an extraordinary and serious reason for the principal to terminate a mandate relationship. This termination has effect even when the parties agreed that the mandate was irrevocable.

G. Death of the principal

Whereas the death of the agent leads to the automatic termination of the mandate contract under Article 7:102 (Death of the agent), Article 7:101 paragraph (1) (Death of the principal) indicates that the death of the principal does not end the mandate relationship. However, under paragraph (2) of that Article, the successors of the principal are given the right to terminate the mandate contract under this Article. As in this case it is not the principal himself but his successors who have the right to terminate the mandate contract, paragraph (4) of the present Article provides that this Article applies with the appropriate modifications to this situation.

H. No provision on automatic termination in case of incapacity of principal or agent

In most Member States, the supervening incapacity of the principal or that of the agent is also regarded as bringing the mandate relationship to an end. The laws on the legal effects of mental incapacity, however, differ from one country to another. Some countries have special regimes for mandates with a view to incapacity or enduring powers of attorney. There are also differences among the Member States as to the moment in which incapacity has an effect on the mandate contract.

The rules on the legal effects of mental incapacity differ greatly from one country to another. Given that the law governing mental incapacity is not covered by these Principles or by the Principles of European Contract Law, it is thought that it is best left to national law whether or not the supervening incapacity of either party to the mandate relationship should lead to the end of the mandate relationship – and what the consequences should be if that happens. However, if incapacity of the principal or of the agent does not lead to the automatic termination of the mandate contract under national law, the agent or the principal, or their legal representatives, may invoke termination of the mandate contract for extraordinary and serious reason under this Article (for the principal in case of incapacity of the agent and for the legal representative of the principal in case of incapacity of the principal) or under Article 6:105 (Termination by the agent for extraordinary and serious reason) (for the agent in case of incapacity of the principal and for the legal representative of the agent in case of incapacity of the agent).

I. No provision on termination in case of bankruptcy

Bankruptcy law in the Member States determines whether or not the mandate relationship ends by the bankruptcy of either the principal or the agent. Given the fact that bankruptcy law is not covered by these Principles or by the Principles of European Contract Law, it is thought that it is best left to national law whether the bankruptcy of either party to the mandate relationship should lead to the end of the mandate relationship – and what the consequences should be if it is so terminated.

J. Relation to termination for non-performance

In many cases where the principal has an extraordinary and serious reason to terminate the contractual relationship, there will also be a fundamental non-performance of obligations by the agent allowing the principal to terminate. Termination of the mandate relationship under the present Article does not as such entitle the principal to damages, whereas this will normally be the case when the principal terminates the contractual relationship for fundamental non-performance.

K. Relationship with the Principles of European Law and the Draft Common Frame of Reference

This Article mirrors that of Article IV.D. – 6:103 DCFR (Termination by the principal for extraordinary and serious reason).

In some cases where there is a serious and extraordinary reason justifying termination, Article 6:111 PECL (Change of circumstances) may be applicable. Under that Article, the parties would be expected to enter into negotiations to adapt the terms of the contract or to terminate the contractual relationship. If negotiations fail, it would be for the judge to decide between adaptation and termination. Under the present Article (and the corresponding provision in Article 6:105 (Termination by the agent for extraordinary and serious reason)), the party who does not want to continue performance can terminate with immediate effect. The party who has an extraordinary and serious reason to terminate is therefore discharged of the burden of trying to negotiate with the other party and of going to court to bring the relationship to an end.

L. Character of the rule

The right to terminate the mandate relationship for extraordinary and serious reason is mandatory, as is expressed in paragraph (4). This cannot reasonably be otherwise if the right to terminate for extraordinary and serious reason is to mean anything in practice, because the parties could effectively exclude its application by way of standard contract terms. This would in fact mean the exclusion of the good faith principle, which underlies the present Article.

Parties may agree, however, that a particular reason which may typically qualify as a serious reason is not to be regarded as such in the frame of their relationship. This may be the case, for example, with the provision in Chapter 7 which establishes that the death of the agent leads to termination of the relationship, or with the right of the principal to revoke the mandate of the agent if the principal himself or another agent concludes the prospective contract. If parties agree on exclusivity, they limit the possibility of the principal to revoke the mandate on the ground that he himself or another agent concludes the prospective contract.

M. Remedies

This Article provides for a remedy in case a serious and extraordinary reason to terminate the mandate contract occurs. As such it does not lead to a remedy for breach of contract itself. However, in a case where the agent arguably has committed a fundamental non-performance, but the principal could have difficulty in proving that the requirements for a remedy for fundamental non-performance have been met, the present Article could serve as an alternative means to bring the mandate contract to an immediate end.

Comparative Notes

1. Termination by principal for extraordinary and serious reason

A notice of termination given by the agent is effective without a serious reason being needed in AUSTRIA, BELGIUM, BULGARIA, ENGLAND, FRANCE, THE NETHERLANDS, SLOVAKIA, SPAIN, and SWEDEN. However, if termination is grounded on a serious reason, the principal is exempted from observing a reasonable notice period in ENGLAND. In contrast, a serious reason is a requirement for termination to be effective in GERMANY.

If the principal terminates for a serious reason, he is exempted from having to pay damages to the agent in ESTONIA, FRANCE, FINLAND, HUNGARY, THE NETHERLANDS, POLAND, SCOTLAND, SPAIN, and SWEDEN.

2. No notice period required

In all countries, if there is a serious breach, no notice of reasonable length is to be observed by the aggrieved party who wants to terminate the relationship.

A reasonable period of notice is not required by law in AUSTRIA, BELGIUM, BULGARIA, DENMARK, FRANCE, ENGLAND, THE NETHERLANDS, POLAND, SCOTLAND, SPAIN, and SWEDEN.

The law requires parties to observe a reasonable notice period before termination in FINLAND, GERMANY, IRELAND (implied), ITALY, HUNGARY, PORTUGAL, and SLOVAKIA. However, in GERMANY, HUNGARY, and SWEDEN, the existence of a serious ground to terminate exempts the principal from having to provide reasonable notice.

3. Specific cases of extraordinary and serious reason

The death of the agent leads to the automatic termination of the mandate relationship in all Member States (cf. notes to Article 7:102 (Death of agent)). In ENGLAND and IRELAND, the frustration of the contract, i.e. impossibility or illegality, is mentioned as a typical case of an extraordinary and serious reason to terminate.

4. Conclusion of prospective contract by the principal or by another agent

The conclusion of the prospective contract by the principal or by another agent is qualified as an implicit revocation of mandate granted to the agent and leads to termination of the mandate relationship in BELGIUM, BULGARIA, ENGLAND, FRANCE, GERMANY, IRELAND, SCOTLAND, and SPAIN. This is not the case in SWEDEN, where the principal still has to notify the agent. In ENGLAND and IRELAND, termination depends on whether the agent has been granted exclusivity.

5. Termination of irrevocable mandate in case of fundamental non-performance

In all countries, a non-performance is a ground for termination, even if the mandate is irrevocable.

A serious reason justifies termination of an irrevocable mandate in AUSTRIA, BELGIUM BULGARIA, ESTONIA, GERMANY, GREECE, HUNGARY, IRELAND, and the NETHERLANDS. In ENGLAND, if it is possible to agree to the irrevocability of the contract for representation and the parties have not provided for the irrevocability to end, this irrevocability will only end once the interest of the agent has been satisfied.

In FRANCE, POLAND, and SLOVAKIA, irrevocable mandates are not allowed, thus termination is always effective.

6. Incapacity of the parties

In most Member States, the incapacity of the principal is regarded as a cause for termination: BELGIUM, FRANCE, GRECECE, HUNGARY, IRELAND, PORTUGAL, and SWEDEN. The same is true for ITALY, unless the mandate was for the conclusion of a contract pertaining to business activities and the business of the principal remains in operation. In SPAIN, the incapacity of the principal also leads to the termination of the mandate relationship, unless the contract indicates otherwise or unless the mandate relationship was precisely concluded for the situation that the principal would later be declared incapable. In this case, the mandate relationship remains in force in accordance with the conditions imposed by the principal.

The contractual relationship does not terminate when the principal is declared incapable in AUSTRIA, THE NETHERLANDS, POLAND, and SLOVAKIA. It follows that in those legal regimes, the mandate relationship continues between the agent and the curator of the principal. In ENGLAND, the mandate relationship terminates unless the Enduring Power of Attorney Act applies.

If the incapacity of the principal terminates the mandate relationship, the relevant moment is the moment when the incapacity is declared by a court or specific body in FRANCE, SLOVAKIA, and SPAIN. In most other systems, the relevant moment is the moment the agent becomes aware of the incapacity. Among these systems, it is possible to differentiate two sub-groups. In a first group of systems, the relationship is deemed to be terminated when the agent knows or ought to have been aware of the incapacity of the principal. This is the regime in BELGIUM, GREECE, HUNGARY, ITALY, and PORTUGAL. In a second group of systems, the relevant moment is when the agent is informed of the incapacity. This is the case in POLAND and SCOTLAND. In this second group, the burden of proof regarding whether the agent was aware of the incapacity seems to lie on the person charged with protecting the interests of the incapacitated principal.

The agent has the obligation to continue performance in order to prevent detriment to the interests of the principal or the principal's successors in AUSTRIA, BELGIUM, DENMARK, FRANCE, GERMANY, GREECE, HUNGARY, IRELAND, ITALY, THE NETHERLANDS, PORTUGAL, SCOTLAND, SLOVAKIA, and SPAIN. In ENGLAND, the agent has to wait for instructions from the successors of the principal. In most countries, the agent seems only to be obliged to continue running the affairs that were already started before the principal was incapacitated. This is the case in BELGIUM, GREECE, ITALY, PORTUGAL, SCOTLAND and SPAIN. In some of these systems, the agent would also be obliged to take urgent measures. This is the case in Italy and the Netherlands. In SLOVAKIA, the agent is only obliged to take urgent measures. In some systems, the obligation to perform these measures is subject to a time limit: the agent has to continue until the curator can take over the responsibility. This is the case in GERMANY, GREECE, and HUNGARY. In THE NETHERLANDS, the time limit is specific: one year.

The agent is entitled to payment in AUSTRIA, DENMARK, FRANCE, GERMANY, GREECE, HUNGARY, IRELAND, ITALY, SCOTLAND, and SLOVAKIA. In THE NETHERLANDS, the agent is entitled to payment if and in so far as this is reasonable in view of the circumstances.

In almost all European legislations, the supervening legal incapacity of the agent implies the termination of the mandate relationship. As far as is known, this is different only in AUSTRIA and SWEDEN.

7. Insolvency of the parties

The insolvency of the agent, similar to death, leads to automatic termination of the mandate contract in most countries. This is indeed the case in AUSTRIA, BELGIUM, DENMARK, ESTONIA, FRANCE, GERMANY, GREECE, IRELAND, ITALY, MALTA, THE NETHERLANDS, POLAND, PORTUGAL, and SPAIN. In some countries, bankruptcy of the agent does not mean automatic termination but may be a ground for the principal to terminate. This is the case in ENGLAND, FINLAND, HUNGARY, SCOTLAND, SLOVAKIA, and SWEDEN. In SCOTLAND, solvency needs to be an implied term of the contract.

Insolvency or bankruptcy of the principal leads to termination of the relationship in AUSTRIA, BELGIUM, BULGARIA, ENGLAND, ESTONIA (except in cases where there is no connexion between contract and bankruptcy), FINLAND, FRANCE, GERMANY, GREECE, HUNGARY, ITALY, MALTA, NETHERLANDS, POLAND, SCOTLAND (with exceptions to protect the interests of the principal), SLOVAKIA, SPAIN, and SWEDEN.

In most systems, termination is effective from the moment the agent knows of the occurrence of the bankruptcy. This is the case in BELGIUM, ESTONIA, FRANCE, GERMANY, GREECE, ITALY, POLAND, SLOVAKIA, and SPAIN. The acts of the agent until that moment are valid. However, these systems are divided as to the relevant moment. In some systems – including GERMANY and SPAIN – it is the moment the proceeding starts; in other systems – including GREECE, POLAND, and SLOVAKIA – it is the declaration of bankruptcy. In AUSTRIA and SLOVAKIA, termination is effective from the moment the bankruptcy occurs because the proceeding has a public character and the principal is presumed to know about it.

National Notes

1. Termination by principal for extraordinary and serious reason

AUSTRIA: An agent's authority can be terminated at any time by the express revocation of it by the principal (CC Article 1020). The question of termination of the contractual relationship is the same as that of termination of authority.

BELGIUM: According to the Belgian CC Article 2004, a principal can always revoke the authority to represent *ad nutum*, i.e. without a motive.

BULGARIA: The principal is entitled to end the mandate contract at any time and without any reason (Bulgarian OCA Article 288 paragraph (1)).

ENGLAND: Following the principle of free revocation, the principal need not have an extraordinary and serious reason to terminate the relationship by notice. If the principal has such reasons, i.e. the agent taking a bribe or the agent being guilty of a serious breach, this would allow the principal to terminate the relationship summarily and therefore with no need to comply with a notice.

ESTONIA: If the contract is concluded for a definite period of time, it may be terminated by each party prior to the expiry of that period only on material grounds (LOAEst Article 631). No notice period is required (LOAEst Article 631).

FINLAND: In general, a contracting party is entitled to terminate the contractual relationship with immediate impact due to an essential breach of contract on the other party's side. Furthermore, ACRS Article 25 contains a provision on ending a mandate contract for 'important reasons', but all such reasons are, according to the list provided in the article, related to disloyal or other such behaviour of the other party.

FRANCE: The French Civil Code gives the principal the possibility of terminating the agency *ad nutum*, i.e. at any time, without specific reason and without any right to compensation (CC Article 2004). However, the non-terminating party has a right to compensation if early termination of a fixed-term agency unless termination is based on a proper ground; see Cass.civ. 1re, 28 January 2003, Bull. civ. 2003 I, no. 27.

GERMANY: Under German law, every contract for a continuing obligation can be revoked when there is an 'important ground' for the revocation – a fundamental principle of German law which was developed by the courts and is now expressly laid down in CC Article 314 paragraph (1). CC Article 626 as part of the law on contracts for service, which may apply to remunerated mandate contracts by virtue of CC Article 675 paragraph (1), provides a special, but quite similar rule.

HUNGARY: According to CC Article 483 paragraph (3), 'If the agency is cancelled without substantial grounds, the damages that are caused shall be indemnified, unless the agency is gratuitous and the period of notice is sufficient for allowing the principal to handle the matter'. This Article has declared to be applicable to termination by the principal according to the decision of the Supreme Court Nr. 3/2006 on the Uniform Application of Law: 'if a remunerated agency is cancelled without substantial grounds with immediate effect, the damages of the agent that are caused shall be indemnified by the principal'. See CA Jász-Nagykun-Szolnok Megyei Bíróság 4. Gf. 16-00-000016/12, in BDT2002. 577.

IRELAND: Where the agency is contractual, breach of a condition of the contract, or of an innominate term where the consequences of the breach are serious, by the agent will enable the principal to terminate the relationship and pursue a remedy in damages. Moreover, where an agent is in breach of fiduciary duties, a variety of remedies is available including termination of the agency, damages in contract or in tort, an account of profits, etc.

NETHERLANDS: The principal is in general allowed to terminate the agency at any time without having to give reasonable notice according to CC Articles 7:408 paragraph (2) and 7:422. The usual effect of the presence of an extraordinary and serious reason is therefore only to prevent the claim for wages the agent is entitled to according to CC Article 7:411.

POLAND: Under Polish law the principal may always terminate the agency if 'important reasons' occur (art. 746 CC).

SCOTLAND: In Scottish law, the principal is entitled to terminate an agency of unlimited duration at any time, and is not required to show an extraordinary and serious reason (Macgregor, paragraph 183; Gow, p. 536). The principal is, of course, entitled to terminate the agency in a case of a material breach on the Principles of the agent. Beyond cases of breach of contract, certain events may act to frustrate, or terminate, the agency relationship, including the termination of the principal's business, and the death, incapacity or bankruptcy of the principal or agent. In cases of death, incapacity or bankruptcy, the agent may remain entitled to act.

SLOVAKIA: The principal is not obliged to respect any notice period. He can always terminate the contract immediately without any reason.

SPAIN: The principal may terminate the mandate relationship at any time without the need to give reasons (CC Article 1733). However, according to the decisions of the Tribunal Supremo, STS 25 November 1993 and STS 3 March 1988, if the principal terminates a relationship concluded for a definite period before the period has expired, damages are to be paid to the agent, unless the principal has a good reason (*justa causa*) to terminate, based on the (lack of) performance of the agent (Hernández Gil, p. 515).

SWEDEN: When the contract has been concluded for an indefinite period of time, the principal may terminate the resulting relationship at any time without cause and unless agreed otherwise may usually terminate with immediate effect. The agent can only claim reasonable compensation for work already performed under the contract (Bengtsson, p. 153; Hesser, p. 30). If the contract was for a definite period of time and the principal terminates the relationship without a valid reason, this constitutes non-performance. The agent has no right to continue performance but is entitled to claim damages (Hellner, p. 215).

No answer received: DENMARK, MALTA.

442

2. *No notice period required*

AUSTRIA: An agent's authority can be terminated at any time by the express revocation of it by the principal (CC Article 1020). The question of termination of the contractual relationship is the same as that of termination of authority.

BELGIUM: According to BELGIAN CC Article 2004, a principal can always revoke the authority to represent *ad nutum,* i.e. without a notice period, unless the parties have agreed upon a notice period in the contract.

BULGARIA: The principal is free to end the mandate relationship without observing any notice period. A requirement for such a period only exists for the principal of a commercial agency contract for an indefinite term (CA Article 47 paragraph (1)).

ENGLAND: If the agent is guilty of a serious breach, the principal will be entitled to terminate the agency immediately.

ESTONIA: No notice period is required in Estonia (LOAEst Article 631).

FRANCE: A notice period is never required for terminating the mandate relationship (except when the parties have agreed to insert a notice period clause in the contract.

GERMANY: Both CC Article 626 paragraph (1) and CC Article 314 paragraph (1) expressly allow for a revocation without observance of a period of notice.

HUNGARY: According to CC Article 483 paragraphs (1) and (2), 'The principal shall be entitled to abrogate the contract with immediate effect at any time; the principal, however, shall be obliged to uphold the obligations already assumed by the agent. The agent shall also be entitled to abrogate the contract at any time; however, the period of notice must be sufficient for allowing the principal to handle the matter. In the event of the principal's grave breach of contract, abrogation can have immediate effect.' In case of commission agency, according to CC Article 512, '[p]rior to the conclusion of a sales contract, the principal shall be entitled to terminate the contract by notice with immediate effect, and the commission agent by fifteen days' notice.

IRELAND: Where the agent has committed a serious breach of contract or breaches fiduciary duties, no notice period is required.

NETHERLANDS: A notice period is not required.

POLAND: Polish law requires no notice period when terminating the mandate relationship, unless the parties have agreed otherwise.

SCOTLAND: Where the principal terminates the agency, whether this is in response to a breach by the agent or not, no period of notice is required (Gow, p. 536).

SLOVAKIA: The principal can always terminate the relationship immediately without any reason.

SPAIN: The principal may terminate the mandate contract at any time.

SWEDEN: If the principal terminates on the basis of a valid reason, no notice period is required.

No answer received: FINLAND, GREECE, ITALY, MALTA, PORTUGAL.

3. *Specific cases of extraordinary and serious reason*

BULGARIA: If the parties have agreed on a particular person to perform the agent's obligation and this person dies or becomes incapable, the principal can end the mandate relationship.

ENGLAND: There would be automatic termination on the occurrence of any event which brought about frustration of the contract (if the contractual obligations become illegal or impossible to perform).

FRANCE: This question does not arise.

GERMANY: Death or incapacity of a 'specific person' without whom the obligations under the mandate relationship cannot be performed would terminate these obligations due to impossibility (CC Article 275 paragraph (1)) and would likely be viewed as an important reason for termination of the contract as a whole.

IRELAND: A contractual agency may be automatically terminated by any event which frustrates the contract. Thus, it will be terminated if performance becomes impossible, for instance, because of the death of either party. Where one of the parties is a company the agency is similarly terminated by the winding up of the company. An agent's bankruptcy will terminate the agency if it makes the agent unfit to continue to act.

NETHERLANDS: Serious reasons are changes in the circumstances that are in all fairness likely to cause the immediate termination of the contract. An example of a serious reason is the situation that the principal has lost faith in the agent (Parl. Gesch. 7, p. 325).

POLAND: The mandate contract does not end in case of death or loss of legal capacity by the principal. It does end in case of death or loss of legal capacity by the agent (art. 748 CC).

SCOTLAND: There appears to be no specific consideration in the authorities of the situation where the specific person who was to perform the obligations under the agency contract dies or becomes incapable (distinguishing this situation from that where the agent as contracting party dies or becomes incapable).

SLOVAKIA: There is no comparable regulation.

SPAIN: A principal has a serious ground to terminate if the agent is in breach. The death or incapacity of the principal or agent are also serious grounds to terminate.

SWEDEN: A valid reason is said to exist if the agent is liable for fundamental non-performance, if it would be unreasonable to demand that the task continues or if another important reason to cancel the agreement exists (KommL Article 51 and HaL Article 26). This may include events of *force majeure* character and also circumstances of a personal nature (e.g. incapacitation of a party).

No answer received: AUSTRIA, BELGIUM, DENMARK, FINLAND, ESTONIA, GREECE, HUNGARY, ITALY, MALTA, PORTUGAL.

4. Conclusion of prospective contract by principal or by another agent

BELGIUM: The classic example of an implied revocation by the principal is the conclusion of the prospective contract by the principal personally (CA Brussels 26 June 1986, Res.Jur.Imm. 1986, no. 6073; Tilleman, p. 294; Wéry, p. 271). The termination may also occur as a result of notice to the agent of the appointment of a new agent for the same transaction (CC Article 2006).

BULGARIA: There is no explicit rule in the sense that the conclusion of the prospective contract by the principal or by another agent, appointed by the principal, is treated as revocation of the mandate. Nevertheless in legal doctrine such behaviour of the principal is interpreted as a case of revocation (Меворах/Лиджи/Фархи, III, 176). This means that the contractual relationship is terminated when the agent gets to know about or could have been aware of either the conclusion of the prospective contract or the authorisation of another agent with the same authority. The contract will keep its legal effect when the principal explicitly states that the previous mandate is not revoked (Меворах/Лиджи/Фархи, III, p. 176).

ENGLAND: The position depends on whether the agent has been granted an exclusivity by the principal or not.

FRANCE: Article 2003 of the French Civil Code, which describes the various situations where an agency will terminate, does not refer to this case. However, it is accepted generally that, on the basis of ordinary rules of contract, the completion of the mandate by the agent or by the principal will result in the termination of the mandate. The termination may even occur as a result of notice to the agent of the appointment of a new agent for the same transaction (CC Article 2006).

GERMANY: While there is no specific provision to this end, general rules of contract law may lead to a mandate relationship ending once the purpose of the mandate has been fulfilled (Palandt/Sprau, Article 671 no. 4). Case law has confirmed this notion at least for the contractual relationship with an executor of a will (BGHZ 41, 23, 25).

IRELAND: It seems likely that, where the mandate is solely for the conclusion of a particular contract, the conclusion of that contract by someone other than the agent would have to result in the termination of the agency (and perhaps also give rise to liability for breach of contract, depending on the terms of the contract).

MALTA: Due to the general provision found in CC Article 1887, that the principal may revoke the contract whenever he chooses, it can be presumed that the principal may conclude the prospected contract of his own motion. If the principal concludes himself the prospected contract, the agent is still entitled to a compensation for the services rendered in order for the transaction to be finalized.

POLAND: There are no specific rules on this matter in the Polish Civil Code.

SCOTLAND: Where the agency was entered into to achieve a specific purpose, and the principal or another agent achieves that purpose, the agency relationship would be brought to an end on the basis that it is now impossible for the agent to achieve the agreed purpose. The agent might remain entitled to payment where the conclusion of the contract which is the purpose of the agency relationship is attributable in part to the agent's efforts, even if the agent is no longer involved at the moment of conclusion (Macgregor, paragraph 112; *Walker, Fraser & Steele v Fraser's Trustees* 1910 SC 222 at 229, per Lord Dundas; *Walker, Donald & Co v Birrell, Stenhouse & Co* (1883) 11 R 369).

SLOVAKIA: The authority as well as the mandate relationship are terminated if the juridical act for which it has been granted is executed (CC Article 33(b) paragraph (1)(a)).

SPAIN: The appointment of a new agent for the same matter amounts to termination of the former mandate (CC Article 1735). It is accepted also that the conclusion of the intended contract by the principal personally brings about the tacit revocation of the previous mandate (Gordillo, p. 1589).

SWEDEN: The conclusion of the prospective contract by the principal or by another agent appointed by the principal would not automatically be treated as a revocation of the mandate of the agent. The principal would still be required to revoke the mandate by notice.

No answer received: AUSTRIA, DENMARK, FINLAND, ESTONIA, GREECE, ITALY, PORTUGAL.

5. Termination of irrevocable mandate in case of fundamental non-performance

AUSTRIA: Even an irrevocable mandate may be terminated in the case of important reasons (loyalty, misrepresentation). The irrevocability is further restricted by case law: revocation is possible when the agent neglects the contractual duties, fails in complying with the duty to represent the interests of the principal or abuses the authority (Rummel/Strasser, Article 1020 Rz 4). An agreement to the contrary is void.

BELGIUM: A clause precluding revocation does not mean that there can be no other grounds to end the contractual relationship. However, much will depend on the interpretation of the relevant clause. A court could interpret a clause excluding revocation as having a broader scope and as also excluding other grounds for ending the relationship (Wéry, p. 278).

BULGARIA: In Bulgarian legal doctrine, the irrevocability of the mandate contract is considered relative (Меворах/Лиджи/Фархи, III, p. 171). Thus, the principal can end the irrevocable contract at any time with or without extraordinary and substantial reasons or terminate it because of a fundamental non-performance but with different legal consequences. Firstly, when the principal revokes, without serious reason, the irrevocable mandate, apart from payment of stipulated remuneration and reimbursement of expenses, the principal can be held liable for damages incurred by the agent (Меворах/Лиджи/Фархи, III, p. 171). On the other hand, in case of a revocation of an irrevocable contract due to extraordinary and serious reasons, under some special rules the principal (client) is obliged to pay the remuneration not in full amount, but only proportionally to the acts performed by the agent (advocate), see BAA, Article 26 paragraph (2). Furthermore, in case of termination as a result of a fundamental non-performance, the principal is not liable for payment of compensation to the agent, but in accordance with general contract law rules is entitled to claim damages from the latter, cf. OCA Article 88 paragraph (1).

DENMARK: A clause excluding the possibility of termination of the contract for fundamental non-performance of the agent may be declared invalid in the situation traditionally called 'breach of basic assumption': 'promise may wholly or partly be set aside with reference to circumstances after its making' (Contract Act Article 36).

ENGLAND: If it is possible to agree to the irrevocability of the contract for representation and the parties have not provided for the irrevocability to end, such irrevocability will only end once the interest of the agent has been satisfied. Note that the rules defined under the Power of Attorney Act 1971 are narrower than the common law rules since it seems possible to revoke the authority under specific circumstances such as death, insanity and bankruptcy as defined by Article 5 paragraph (5).

ESTONIA: The irrevocability of a mandate relationship is restricted in the sense that the relationship may still be terminated on material grounds (LOAEst Article 631). If the contract is entered into for the life of one party or for a period longer than five years, the principal has the right to terminate the relationship once five years have passed from the date of conclusion of the contract by giving at least six months' advance notice (LOAEst Article 630 paragraph (3)). The common understanding in practice is that even although the 'material grounds' justifying the termination may be defined by the contract, the parties cannot exclude termination in cases of fundamental breach.

FRANCE: The parties cannot validly agree that the agency will be irrevocable. In any event, as a matter of general principle, French law does not accept that parties may be subject to perpetual obligations, and CC Article 2003 provides that the agency will terminate by the death, insolvency or incapacity of either party.

GERMANY: Under German law, although CC Article 314 paragraph (1) does not expressly say so, the right to revoke based on an important ground cannot be excluded (Palandt/Heinrichs, Article 314 paragraph (3)).

GREECE: If an irrevocable mandate has been granted it is accepted that such an authority can be nevertheless revoked if serious grounds (breach of contractual obligations, insolvency of the agent) exist (Supreme Court decision no. 1157/1991, EllDni 1992, 841; CA Thessaloniki decision no. 1381/1979, EllDni 1981, 353) or revocation is required on the basis of good faith (Supreme Court decision no. 1108/1984, EEN 1985, 497). Furthermore, the irrevocability ends if the ground that justifies such irrevocability does not exist anymore (Georgiadis/Stathopoulos/Doris, Article 218-221 GCC no. 15).

HUNGARY: According to CC Article 483 paragraph (4), '[a]ny limitation or exclusion of the right of cancellation shall be null and void; however, the parties shall be entitled to agree on the limitation of the right of cancellation with regard to continuous agencies'. Therefore, even in case of a continuous relationship of representation, the revocability of the contract can only be restricted but not excluded. Concerning the powers of representation, CC Article 223 paragraph (2) establishes that '[a] mandate shall be valid until withdrawn, unless otherwise provided; its withdrawal that concerns a bona fide third person shall be operative only if he has been informed thereof. The right of withdrawal cannot be validly waived'. In case of commission agency, CC Article 512 paragraph (2) provides that '[a]ny limitation or exclusion of the right of rescission shall be null and void'.

IRELAND: Under Article 20 of the Power of Attorney Act 1996, where a power of attorney is expressed to be irrevocable and is given to secure (a) a proprietary interest of the donee of the power, or (b) the performance of an obligation owed to the donee, then, so long as the donee has that interest or the obligation remains undischarged, the power shall not be revoked: (i) by the donor without the consent of the donee, or (ii) by the death, incapacity or bankruptcy of the donor or, if the donor is a body corporate, by its winding-up or dissolution.

ITALY: Irrevocability is not restricted in time. The reason thereof lies in the interests of both the agent and the principal's heirs or successors in obtaining performance of the obligations under the contract, i.e. the interest of the agent to a price, if agreed, and the interest of the heirs or successors to the exact execution of the mandate.

NETHERLANDS: The contracting parties may validly agree on an irrevocable mandate in certain cases according to CC Article 7:422 paragraph (2) read in conjunction with CC Article 3:74 paragraphs (1) and (2). The principal cannot then terminate the relationship if the acts in question are in the interest of the agent or a third party (see CFI Roermond 11 February 1999, NJ 1999, 607). However, the judge is allowed to alter such provision because of serious reasons (CC Article 3:74).

POLAND: There is no irrevocable mandate under Polish law; the principal may always terminate the relationship if 'important reasons' occur (e.g. non-performance by the agent or other actions that may lead the principal to lose confidence in the agent).

SCOTLAND: Whether an irrevocable mandate may be revoked because of fundamental non-performance or for serious or extraordinary reasons is an issue which is virtually unexplored. It appears, however, that the Scottish irrevocable mandate, or *procuratory in rem suam,* is absolutely irrevocable, even in cases where serious and extraordinary reasons apply (Black, paragraph 551).

SLOVAKIA: Irrevocable mandate is not allowed.

No answer received: DENMARK, FINLAND, MALTA, PORTUGAL, SPAIN, SWEDEN.

6. Termination in case of incapacity of the agent

AUSTRIA: The contract for mandate does not end if the agent is placed under curatorship, though the agent cannot act for the principal as long as the incapacity renders the agent unable to perform the agency duties (CC Article 1018; CC Article 1018 Rummel/Strasser, no. 5).

BELGIUM: According to the Belgian CC Article 2003 the authority to represent ends by the incapacity of one the parties. The mandate relationship probably ends when the incident occurs or takes effect. According to CC Article 2010, the agent's heirs who are aware of the contract for representation are required to notify the agent's death to the principal and to perform in the meantime all urgent and necessary acts, required in the principal's interest by the circumstances (De Page, p. 454; Wéry, p. 297-298).

DENMARK: The contract for representation will end automatically when the agent is placed under curatorship, becomes bankrupt or is otherwise subjected to rules of insolvency.

ENGLAND: Insanity of the agent automatically terminates the actual authority since the agent is no longer capable to represent the principal.

FINLAND: A curatorship limits the agent's authorisation to those measures the agent is still entitled to take personally.

FRANCE: The incapacity of the agent would effectively involve automatic termination of the mandate or agency (CC Article 2003; for a merger or takeover of the agent, see Cass.civ. 3e, 10 November 1998, Bull. civ. 1998 III, no. 212). The rules above apply unless the agency contract contains a clause to the contrary (e.g. Cass.com., 22 May 1967, JCP 1968, II, 15389). CC Article 2010 indicates that in the event of the death of the agent, the heirs must inform the principal of the event, which raises the presumption that the mandate will terminate at that time. The heirs of the agent must also do whatever is in the interest of the principal for the time being. However, there is no similar rule applicable in the event of incapacity or insolvency of the agent, but it is likely that the mandate will terminate when the principal is informed of the event.

GERMANY: In case of curatorship (if depriving the agent of power to perform juridical acts), this would be considered a case of impossibility of contract performance, thus terminating the agent's obligations (CC Article 275; Palandt/Sprau, Article 673 no. 1). The moment of commencement of curatorship is decisive. According to CC Article 673, the heirs have to continue to perform the obligations under the contract of representation. If this obligation is breached, the heirs are liable for damages according to CC Article 280 paragraph (1) (Palandt/Sprau, Article 673 no. 2).

GREECE: A mandate is dissolved if the agent is being placed under curatorship. In the case of curatorship the contract of mandate ends automatically. Both in case of death and curatorship, the contract ends when the principal becomes aware of the incident by any means (Georgiadis/Stathopoulos/Karasis, Article 726-727 GCC no. 2). If the dissolution of the mandate due to the death or insolvency or curatorship of the agent imperils the interests of the principal the dissolution is suspended temporarily (the agency being continued by the agent's heir or legal agent, if the agent has died) until the principal or the principal's heir or legal agent is able to take care of the principal's affairs (CC Article 727). Failure of the agent or the agent's heir or legal agent to continue temporarily the conduct of the affairs that were entrusted by the principal can establish a claim for damages for any loss caused by such failure. If the agent or the agent's heir or legal agent continues temporarily the conduct of the affairs of the principal there is a right to reimbursement of all expenses incurred.

HUNGARY: If the agent becomes incompetent, the relationship under the contract for representation is terminated (CC Article 481).

IRELAND: A contractual agency may be automatically terminated by any event which frustrates the contract. Thus, it will be terminated if performance becomes impossible, for instance, because of the death of either party. Insanity of the agent also automatically terminates the actual authority since the agent is no longer capable to represent the principal.

ITALY: According to CC Article 1722 paragraph (4), the mandate for representation ends automatically when the agent dies, is placed under curatorship, becomes bankrupt or is otherwise subjected to rules of insolvency law. This happens when the principal is informed of the incident leading to the termination or when the principal becomes anyhow aware of it. According to CC Article 1728 paragraph (2), '[w]hen a mandate is extinguished by the death or supervening incapacity of the agent, if his heirs or the person who represents or assists him have knowledge of the mandate, they shall give prompt notice to the principal and in the meantime shall take the measures which circumstances may require in the interest of the principal'. The heirs or such other persons are required to promptly notify the principal of the agent's death and to take any circumstances which are necessary in the light of the specific circumstances (e.g. urgent activities). They would be liable for failure to take such measures pursuant to CC Article 1728. They do receive payment and/or reimbursement for the expenses they incur in order to take such measures. The mandate ends even if the grant of authority was irrevocable.

MALTA: According to CC Article 1886 lit (b), the contract of mandate is terminated when the agent is placed under curatorship. Although not stated specifically in the law, it is presumed that the contract of mandate ends when the agent/curator inform the principal that he has been placed under curatorship or when the heirs inform the principal that the agent has died, or the contract of mandate is terminated when the declaration of bankruptcy occurs. In the situation when the agent dies, CC Article 1890 states that the agent's heirs must, if they know that he was an agent, give notice thereof to the principal, and attend, in the meantime, to what is required in the interest of the principal, as circumstances may demand.

NETHERLANDS: The mandate relationship ends because of the agent's guardianship order, cf. CC Article 7:422 paragraph (1)(b)).

POLAND: Unless agreed otherwise, the mandate relationship ends on the loss of legal capacity of the agent (Polish CC Article 748).

PORTUGAL: The mandate ends, according to CC Article 1174, by the legal incapacity of the client or the agent. In such a case, the mandate ends, with prospective effects.

SCOTLAND: The incapacity of the agent brings a mandate relationship to an end *(Wink v Mortimer* (1849) 11 D 995; Gow, p. 537).

SLOVAKIA: The relationship under a contract for representation ends automatically when the agent is placed under curatorship (in the latter case the contract ends because a person may not act as an agent for another person if the person himself or herself has no capacity to undertake the relevant juridical acts; CC Article 22 paragraph (2)).

No answer received: BULGARIA, ESTONIA, SPAIN, SWEDEN.

7. Termination in case of incapacity of the principal

AUSTRIA: The mandate survives the principal's incapacity, because the loss of capacity to act (in such a way as to produce legal consequences) is not tantamount to the principal's death (Rummel/Strasser, Article 1020 Rz 28b and Article 1018 Rz 6; OGH in SZ 13/71; 24/244; 26/132; EvBl 1968/60; 1992/76). Previous declarations of intent remain effective, if validly made.

BELGIUM: According to the Belgian CC Article 2003, the authority to represent ends by the incapacity of one of the parties. According to CC Article 2008, the termination of the authority will only be effective at the moment the agent has taken note or ought to have taken note of the termination. Acts concluded without knowledge of the termination are valid. When the principal dies, the agent is bound to continue running affairs (CC Article 1991 paragraph (2)). More precisely, the agent must finish affairs started before the principal's death if any delay in their accomplishment would be harmful (Wéry, p. 301). This provision is strictly interpreted and does not allow the agent to start new affairs (CFI Liège 2 April 1930, Pas. 1930, III, 86; De Page, p. 456). An agent who breaches this duty is liable to the principal or his heirs.

BULGARIA: The mandate relationship is ended *ipso jure* by the legal incapacity of the principal as well as dissolution of the principal legal entity (see OCA Article 287); Любен Василев, Облигационно право, p. 28; Меворах/Лиджи/Фархи, III, p. 163; *Голева,* Облигационно право II, p. 239). Since the rule of OCA Article 287 is not mandatory, the parties can stipulate otherwise. Upon termination of the mandate due to incapacity or dissolution, the heirs, guardian, trustee or the liquidator of the principal are obliged to immediately notify the agent and undertake the necessary steps to protect his or her interests (OCA Article 291).

DENMARK: When the principal is placed under curatorship, a third party with whom the agent concludes a contract does not acquire a better legal position than if the contract had been concluded by the principal personally (cf. Article 22 of the Contract Act).

ESTONIA: The placing of the principal under curatorship has no influence on the contract for services that governs the mandate (and to the authority of the agent in an external relationship).

FINLAND: If the principal is placed under curatorship, the agent is only entitled to take actions which the principal can still undertake personally. The authorisation ends at the time of the placement under the curatorship (ContrA Articles 21-22 and Comm.C Article 18:8).

FRANCE: In principle, the mandate will terminate with the incapacity of the principal (CC Article 2003). The CC does not give any further indication on the exact moment when the mandate will terminate, but Article 2008 provides that all that the agent may have accomplished in ignorance of the incapacity of the

449

principal will be valid. French case law is not, however, very clear on the question of proof of the agent's ignorance of the event. In the event of the death of the principal, the agent is required to complete the mandate if there is an urgent need to do so (CC Article 1991 paragraph (2)), e.g. if the agent was to sell perishable goods. In the event of the principal being declared incapable, the CC does not provide for any similar rule.

GERMANY: The mandate relationship does not normally end automatically when the principal is incapacitated. In cases of doubt, the contract continues to have effect after the principal dies or loses the legal ability to act (CC Article 672). If the contract does cease to have effect, the moment when this happens depends on the interpretation of the contract. The agent is required to continue to carry out the representation if discontinuation of activity would result in danger (CC Article 672).

GREECE: A mandate relationship is dissolved by the placing under curatorship, except if there is an agreement to the contrary (CC Article 726). The relationship ends when the agent becomes aware of the incident by any means, including information received from the heirs in case of death of the principal or from the principal or the curator in case of curatorship (Georgiadis/Stathopoulos/Karasis, Article 726-727 GCC no. 2). In case of curatorship the mandate ends automatically. According to CC Article 727, in the cases provided for in CC Article 726, 'if the dissolution of the mandate imperils the interests of the principal the agent his heir or his legal agent shall be under an obligation to continue the conduct of the affairs that were entrusted to him until such time as the principal or his heir or his curator is in a position to take appropriate steps.' From that rule it is implied that if the dissolution of the mandate due to the death or curatorship of the principal imperils the principal's interests the dissolution of the contract is suspended temporarily until the principal or curator or heir is able to take care of the affairs of the principal. Failure of the agent to continue temporarily the conduct of the affairs can give rise to a claim for damages. An agent who continues temporarily the conduct of the affairs of the principal is entitled to reimbursement of all the expenses incurred for such temporary performance. The contract of mandate cannot be continued between the curator of the principal and the agent.

HUNGARY: According to CC Article 481, '[t]he contract shall be terminated even if the agency has not been fulfilled, if either party dies or, if a legal person, is dissolved, unless the dissolved legal person has a legal successor; the principal becomes partially or fully incompetent or if the agent becomes incompetent'. CC Article 482 establishes that '[i]f the agency is terminated for a reason that is inherent in the person of the principal, termination shall take effect on the date on which the agent credibly acquires knowledge of the cause of termination. In the event of cancellation due to loss of legal competency, the agent shall take such measures as are necessary to protect the interests of the principal even after the cancellation of the contract as long as the principal or its legal successor is unable to attend to the business at hand'. The agent is liable for damages resulting from non-performance (see CC Articles 310 and 318 paragraph (1)). To the remuneration of the agent and to the reimbursement of his expenses, the general rules apply (see CC Articles 478 paragraphs (1) and (2) and 479). The same rules apply for commission agency (CC Article 513 paragraph (2)).

ITALY: According to CC Article 1722 paragraph (4) the relationship under a contract for representation ends on the loss of capacity of the principal; however, if the representation contract is concluded for the conclusion of contracts pertaining to business activities, if the business continues to run, the relationship does not end automatically, without prejudice to the heirs' right to terminate it. The relationship ends when the agent becomes aware of the incapacity. All acts executed by the agent before becoming aware of the event causing the termination are valid and enforceable vis-à-vis the principal or the heirs (CC Article 1729). According to CC Article 1728, the agent has to continue the activity in the principal's or the heirs' account, but only if delaying action would lead to a danger for the represented interests. The agent is then not only required to take specific urgent measures, but to continue the execution of the mandate entirely. In case of failure, the agent is liable for breach of contract. However, it should be stressed that CC Article 1728 is an exception to the general rule stated in CC Article 1722 paragraph (4). An irrevocable representation contract does not end on the loss of capacity of the principal (CC Article 1723 paragraph (2)). Consequently, the agent continues to act on behalf of the principal's heirs and successors.

MALTA: CC Article 1886 states that the contract for mandate is terminated when either the principal or the agent are interdicted or incapacitated. Although not stated specifically in the law, it is presumed that the contract of mandate ends when the agent knows that principal has been placed under curatorship. When the contract of mandate has been terminated due to the fact that the principal has been placed under curatorship the agent is not required to take any particular measures in order to prevent unnecessary harm.

NETHERLANDS: If the mandate contract ends because of the principal's death or guardianship order, the agent is required to do what may be expected in the contracting party's interests, having regard to the specific circumstances (CC Article 7:422 paragraph (3)).

POLAND: The mandate relationship does not end on the principal's loss of legal capacity (declaration of incapacity by the court) (CC Article 747). In case of expiration of the mandate contract after the declaration of incapacity of the principal, the agent should continue to provide services until the principal's successor or incapacitated principal's legal agent decides otherwise (CC Article 747).

PORTUGAL: The mandate ends, according to Article 1174 CC, by the legal incapacity of the principal or the agent. In such a case, the mandate ends, with prospective effects. However, according to Article 1175, if the principal is placed under curatorship, the contract ends when that fact is known by the agent. In addition, it does not end if that would result in detriment to the principal or his inheritors. The successors have a duty to inform the agent of the death or incapacity of the principal and to take the necessary measures (CC Article 1176).

SCOTLAND: Where the issue is mental incapacity of the principal, the matter is now regulated by the Adults with Incapacity (Scotland) Act 2000 (asp 4). The Act makes special provision for 'continuing powers of attorney' which can survive such incapacity but which are subject to special safeguards and regulatory mechanisms. Under Article 18 of the Act an ordinary mandate for representation (power of attorney) has no effect during any period when the principal is mentally incapable of dealing with the matters to which the power relates.

No answer received: ENGLAND, IRELAND, SPAIN, SWEDEN.

8. Termination in case of insolvency or bankruptcy of agent

AUSTRIA: The mandate relationship ends automatically (ipso jure) when the agent becomes bankrupt or is otherwise subjected to rules of insolvency law in so far as the contract for mandate concerns the bankrupt's estate (CC Article 1024; KO Article 26) with the exception of the contract for commission, which is not terminated automatically (HVertrG Article 26, KO Article 26)). If the administrator of the bankrupt's estate insists on the performance of the contract, the principal has a claim for separation and recovery of assets not belonging to the bankrupt's estate (Comm.C Article 383 Straube/Griss) I³, no. 13). If one of the creditors of the commission/commercial agent takes possession of the goods on commission, the principal may bring in an action for recovery of the goods (Comm.C Article 383 Straube/Griss) I³, no. 13). The principal of a commission business is not entitled to exercise the agent's rights towards the third party where the commission agent commits a fundamental non-performance or if prior to the time for performance it is clear that there will be a fundamental non-performance (CC Article 1024 Schwimann/Apathy) V³, no. 1). In case of the agent's bankruptcy or insolvency the contractual relationship ends when the incident leading to the end occurs or takes effect. If it ends for such reason, the agent's heirs are not required to take the necessary measures to prevent unnecessary harm to the interest of the principal. In cases where another person exercised a profession or a business with the agent or in the agent's service and was authorised by the principal in doing so (e.g. another lawyer of the same law firm), such other person is required to take the necessary measures to prevent unnecessary harm to the interest of the principal.

BELGIUM: According to the Belgian CC Article 2003 the authority to represent ends by the apparent insolvency of one the parties, of which bankruptcy is an example. The mandate relationship probably ends when the incident occurs or takes effect.

DENMARK: The contract for representation will end automatically when the agent becomes bankrupt or is otherwise subjected to rules of insolvency.

ENGLAND: Bankruptcy of the agent may end the actual authority, but it is not automatic and will depend upon the terms of the appointment. It may be considered as a frustrating event or a repudiation of the contract depending on the terms in the contract in question *(McCall v Australian Meat Co Ltd* [1870] 19 WR 188; *Hudson v Granger* [1821] 5 B&A).

ESTONIA: As a default rule, it is presumed that the mandate relationship will end in case of bankruptcy, except where there is no connection between the contract and the bankruptcy estate (LOAEst Article 633 paragraph (2)). The contractual relationship will automatically end.

FINLAND: The authorisation does not always end automatically when the agent is declared bankrupt. The bankruptcy estate has, in principle, the right to decide whether the activities of the agent are to be continued. However, the principal is usually entitled to terminate the agency due to the bankruptcy. A commercial agency ends automatically on the date when the bankruptcy application was submitted to a court (ACRS Article 24).

FRANCE: The insolvency of the agent would effectively involve automatic termination of the mandate or agency (CC Article 2003; for a merger or takeover of the agent, see Cass.civ. 3e, 10 November 1998, Bull. civ. 1998 III, no. 212). The rules above apply unless the agency contract contains a clause to the contrary (e.g. Cass.com., 22 May 1967, JCP 1968, II, 15389). CC Article 2010 indicates that in the event of the death of the agent, the heirs must inform the principal of the event, which raises the presumption that the mandate will terminate at that time. The heirs of the agent must also do whatever is in the interest of the principal for the time being. Although there is no similar rule applicable in the event of incapacity or insolvency of the agent, but it is likely that the mandate will terminate when the principal is informed of the event.

GERMANY: Bankruptcy and insolvency of the agent have no effect on the contract (Insolvenzordnung (InsO) Articles 115 and 116 *a contrario;* cf. Häuser, in: Münchener Kommentar zum HGB, Article 383 no. 97; Palandt/Sprau, Article 671 no. 5). According to CC Article 673, the heirs have to continue to perform the obligations under the contract of representation. If this obligation is breached, the heirs are liable for damages according to CC Article 280 paragraph (1) (Palandt/Sprau, Article 673 no. 2).

GREECE: A mandate is dissolved by the agent becoming bankrupt (CC Article 726). If the agent becomes bankrupt or is otherwise subjected to rules of insolvency law, the mandate relationship ends automatically from the time of the publication of the decision which declares the insolvency of the agent, irrespective of whether the principal is informed of it (Georgiadis/Stathopoulos/Karasis, Article 726-727 GCC no. 4). If the dissolution of the mandate due to insolvency imperils the interests of the principal the dissolution is suspended temporarily (the agency being continued by the agent's heir or legal agent, if the agent has died) until the principal or the principal's heir or legal agent is able to take care of the principal's affairs (CC Article 727). Failure of the agent or the agent's heir or legal agent to continue temporarily the conduct of the affairs that were entrusted by the principal can establish a claim for damages for any loss caused by such failure. If the agent or the agent's heir or legal agent continues temporarily the conduct of the affairs of the principal there is a right to reimbursement of all expenses incurred.

HUNGARY: The relationship under the contract for representation does not end automatically when the agent becomes bankrupt or is otherwise subject to rules of insolvency law, but according to Bankruptcy Act

Article 35 paragraph (1), '[a]t the time of the beginning of the liquidation proceedings, all the debts of the economic entity become expired (due)'.

IRELAND: A contractual agency may be automatically terminated by any event, which frustrates the contract. An agent's bankruptcy will terminate the agency if it makes the agent unfit to continue to act. Even an an irrevocable grant of authority terminates on the death of the agent.

ITALY: According to the Italian CC Article 1722 paragraph (4), the mandate for representation ends automatically when the agent becomes bankrupt or is otherwise subjected to rules of insolvency law. This happens when the principal is informed of the incident leading to the termination or when the principal becomes anyhow aware of it.

MALTA: The mandate contract terminates by the declaration of bankruptcy of the principal or of the agent, cf. CC Article 1886 lit (b).

NETHERLANDS: The mandate relationship ends because of the agent's insolvency or the applicability of debt rescheduling to the agent (CC Article 7:422 paragraph (1)(b)).

SCOTLAND: Whether the agent's bankruptcy (sequestration) terminates the mandate relationship is a difficult question, and it may be that this is the case only where the agent's solvency is an implied term of the agency contract (Gow, p. 537-8, relying on English authority: *McCall v Australian Meat Co Ltd* (1870) 19 WR 188; *Hudson v Granger* (1821) 5 B&A).

SLOVAKIA: The relationship under a contract for representation ends automatically when the agent dies or is placed under curatorship (in the latter case the contract ends because a person may not act as an agent for another person if the person himself or herself has no capacity to undertake the relevant juridical acts; CC Article 22(2)) The relationship does not end automatically when the agent becomes bankrupt, but the administrator of the bankruptcy assets may terminate it.

SWEDEN: It is somewhat uncertain whether the mandate relationship ends automatically or not on the bankruptcy of the agent. In case a commissionaire is declared bankrupt, the mandate ends automatically. In other cases, the bankruptcy of the agent may only result in a right for the client to cancel the contract.

No answer received: BULGARIA, POLAND, PORTUGAL, SPAIN.

9. Termination in case of insolvency or bankruptcy of principal

AUSTRIA: The mandate relationship ends automatically when the principal becomes bankrupt or is otherwise subject to rules of insolvency law (Austrian CC Article 1024, KO Article 26), independent of the agent's awareness of the incident. This is so even if the grant of authority was irrevocable (Rummel/Strasser, Article 1020 Rz 8a).

BELGIUM: According to the Belgian CC Article 2003, the authority to represent ends in case of apparent insolvency of one of the parties, e.g. bankruptcy, at the moment the incident occurs or takes effect. Nevertheless, the termination will only be effective when the agent has taken note or ought to have taken note of the termination (CC Article 2008). Acts concluded without knowledge of the termination are valid.

BULGARIA: In Bulgarian private law, only business persons (natural or legal) can be declared bankrupt by virtue of a court judgment in a special civil proceeding (CA Article 607bis). Non-business persons, other than companies, can be declared bankrupt as an exception (CA Articles 609-610). In legal doctrine, it is considered that the mandate relationship terminates when the principal is declared bankrupt, because the principal cannot conclude new contracts (Меворах/Лиджи/Фархи, III, p. 165).

DENMARK: If the principal becomes bankrupt, a third party with whom the agent concludes a contract will not acquire a better legal position than if the contract had been concluded by the principal personally. This follows from Article 23 of the Contract Act, which must be interpreted in connection with Article 29 of the Bankruptcy Act. Article 29 lays down that upon pronouncement of the adjudication the principal (and thus the agent of the principal as well) will lose the right to assign or abandon the principal's property, to accept payments etc. The fact that the debtor (and the agent) upon pronouncement of the adjudication order is barred from disposing as regards the estate does not mean that this applies towards third parties as well. Only after the expiry of the day and night on which publication of the bankruptcy has been made in the official gazette will the debtor's (the agent's) loss of power be effective towards the whole world (cf. Article 30 of the Bankruptcy Act). Until this point in time, the loss of the power to dispose is effective only against a party who knew or ought to have known of the bankruptcy. This means that a third party who has made a contract with the agent of the debtor in the interval between the pronouncement of the order and its publication will prevail in a question with the estate if the third party acted in good faith as regards the announcement of the adjudication order. Thus the contract is treated as if made before the bankruptcy. The rule in Article 30 applies not only to dispositions whereby rights are created against the estate but also to payments to the agent. A party who has made a bona fide payment of a debt to the debtor (the agent) before the publication of the order will thus be discharged as against the bankrupt estate. These rules will apply even if the grant of authority was irrevocable.

ENGLAND: The bankruptcy of the principal automatically terminates the authority. Bankruptcy is treated similarly to death. Upon the principal becoming bankrupt, the property of the principal is vested in the trustee in bankruptcy *(Dawson v Sexton* (1823) 1 LJOS Ch 185)). Because bankruptcy is treated similarly to death, the principal cannot be bound by apparent authority. However, third parties are protected by certain measures (Insolvency Act 1986, Article 284 paragraphs (4) and (5)).

ESTONIA: The contract for services governing the mandate will cease to have effect upon bankruptcy of the principal, except in the case where there is no connection between the contract and the bankruptcy estate (LOAEst Article 632). LOAEst Article 632 paragraph (3) provides that the contract is nevertheless deemed to be in force until such time as the service provider (the agent) becomes aware or ought to become aware of the declaration of the principal as bankrupt. The authorisation of the agent (for the purposes of the external relationship) will also expire (GPCCA Article 125 paragraph (2)). However, third parties in good faith can rely on the authorisation if the grant of the authorisation was communicated to them or if an authorisation document was issued and presented (GPCCA Article 127 paragraph (1)).

FINLAND: The mandate relationship normally ceases to have effect automatically when the principal is declared bankrupt. The ACRS Article 24 proscribes, however, that if the assets of the principal are surrendered into bankruptcy, the representation contract shall be deemed to have expired on the date when the bankruptcy application was submitted to a court.

FRANCE: In the event of insolvency of the principal (or more generally, 'bankruptcy', according to the case law), the general rules are the same as those concerning the case of death or incapacity of the principal. The mandate will be terminated by such event (CC Article 2003) as soon as the agent has become aware of the event, even if the contract includes an irrevocability clause.

GERMANY: In the case of bankruptcy, the mandate relationship terminates (art. 115 paragraph (1) InsO for gratuitous mandate relationships and Article 116 InsO for *Geschäftsbesorgungsverträge).* In principle, the termination occurs when the insolvency proceedings are commenced (InsO Article 115 paragraph (1)). InsO Article 115 paragraph (3), however, contains a rule protecting the agent: as long as the agent was without fault unaware of the commencement of the insolvency proceedings, the mandate/Geschäftsbesorgungsvertrag continues. The mandate relationship also ends when the grant of power was irrevocable, as Article 119 InsO explicitly declares any agreement deviating from Article 103-118 InsO to be null and void.

GREECE: According to CC Article 726 a mandate shall be dissolved by the placing under the bankruptcy of the principal (or liquidation if it concerns a legal person). If the principal becomes bankrupt or is otherwise subjected to rules of insolvency law the mandate ends automatically from the time of the publication of the decision which declares the insolvency of the principal. In this respect it is irrelevant if the agent is informed by the principal or when the agent otherwise becomes aware of the insolvency (Georgiadis/Stathopoulos/ Karasis, Article 726-727 GCC no. 4). In the case of an irrevocable mandate, the mandate ends in case of the insolvency of the principal as it cannot be continued between the trustee in insolvency and the agent (Georgiadis/Stathopoulos/Karasis, Article 726-727 GCC no. 4).

HUNGARY: According to CC Article 481 lit (b), '[t]he contract shall be terminated even if the agency has not been fulfilled, if either party dies or, if a legal person, is dissolved, unless the dissolved legal person has a legal successor', so that the contract for representation does not end automatically when the principal becomes bankrupt or is otherwise subjected to rules of insolvency law. However, according to Article 35 paragraph (1) of the Bankruptcy Act, '[a]t the time of the beginning of the liquidation proceedings, all the debts of the economic entity become expired (due)'. The same rules apply for the commission agency (CC Article 513 paragraph (2)).

IRELAND: The principal's bankruptcy terminates the agency and deprives the agent of authority, although there are a number of rules designed to protect agents and third parties in respect of acts done before they have notice of the bankruptcy (see Bankruptcy Act 1988).

ITALY: The same answers for the case of death of the principal apply to the case of opening of insolvency proceedings involving the principal as the insolvent debtor (see CC Articles 1722, 1723 and 1728 and Insolvency Law Article 78; this last provision clearly states that any contract of mandate ends in case of the insolvency of one of the parties).

MALTA: The contract for mandate ends automatically on the declaration of bankruptcy on the basis of CC Article 1886 lit (b). As the contract terminates by the declaration of bankruptcy, this entails that the contract ends when the declaration occurs.

NETHERLANDS: According to the CC Article 7:422 paragraph (1)(a), the mandate relationship ends in case of the principal's insolvency or the applicability of debt rescheduling to the principal.

POLAND: The mandate relationship ends on the day the bankruptcy is declared by the court (art. 102 of the Bankruptcy Law). The agent may claim damages.

PORTUGAL: There is no provision in the Civil Code on the consequences of the declaration of bankruptcy of the principal. This is due to the existing latitude given to both parties as regards cancellation.

SCOTLAND: Although in general the principal's bankruptcy (sequestration) acts to terminate the agency relationship, this general rule is subject to practical exceptions which aim to facilitate the efficient administration of the principal's assets. The case of *Pollok v Paterson* (10 Dec 1811 FC (369), a case decided by a bench of five judges, suggests that the agent's authority may continue notwithstanding sequestration (the judges relying on Stair, 1.12.6; Erskine, III,3,41). Sequestration will certainly not have this effect in relation to transactions already commenced (Bell, Commentaries, I,525-526). Others have suggested that the principal's sequestration merely 'entitles the agent to decline to act further' (Gow, p. 537, relying on Goudy, p. 368).

SLOVAKIA: The relationship under the contract for representation ends automatically when the principal becomes bankrupt, but not when the principal is otherwise subjected to the rules of insolvency law. The relationship ends when the bankruptcy is declared. It is not relevant whether the agent is actually aware of the declaration of bankruptcy; it is presumed that everyone is because it is promulgated by the court in public and published in the official commercial bulletin.

SPAIN: The commencement of the insolvency proceeding of any of the parties extinguishes the mandate (CC Article 1732 paragraph (3)).

SWEDEN: Bankruptcy of the principal automatically terminates the agency (Hesser, p. 32).

Article 6:104: Termination by the agent when relationship is to last for indefinite period or when it is gratuitous

(1) The agent may terminate the mandate relationship at any time by giving notice of reasonable length if the mandate contract has been concluded for an indefinite period.
(2) The agent may terminate the mandate relationship by giving notice of reasonable length if the agent is to represent the principal otherwise than in exchange for a price.
(3) The parties may not, to the detriment of the agent, exclude the application of paragraph (1) of this Article or derogate from or vary its effects.

Comments

A. General idea

In the normal case, the mandate relationship will terminate when the agent has concluded the mandated task (typically the conclusion of the prospective contract) on behalf of the principal. There may be situations, however, in which the agent no longer wants to continue to carry out the contractual obligations even though the prospective contract or other task has

not been concluded. The present Article enables the agent to terminate the mandate relationship, if the contract is for an indefinite period of time or provides for gratuitous representation, by giving notice of reasonable length.

B. Termination by notice when mandate contract concluded for indefinite period

Following the regime in Article 6:109 PECL (Contract for an indefinite period), the present Article allows the agent, as is the case with the principal, to terminate the mandate contract, if it is for an indefinite period, by giving notice of reasonable length. Agents are not to be compelled to be bound to their principals eternally, but if they want to end a relationship entered into for an indefinite period they do have to give the principal notice of reasonable length. Notification is designed to give the principal enough time to adapt to the new situation, e.g. to find another agent.

Illustration 1
Marina is a professional photographer. She has emigrated to Spain but she has authorized an agent in the Netherlands to take care of the public relations of Marina's company in order to find new Dutch clients. The parties have not limited the duration of the contract. After two years, the agent decides not to continue with this task and sends a brief to Marina to tell her that he will stop with the representation activities as soon as she receives the notification. This notice of termination is effective, but the agent has not observed a reasonable period of notice to grant enough time to Marina to find another agent. Marina therefore has the right to damages for premature termination.

Illustration 2

Lionel is a professional football player. He has engaged for an indefinite period the services of Orange SA, a professional agency arranging the commercial affairs of their players towards the media. When Lionel's star begins to set after five years, Orange SA decides to terminate the mandate contract, effective in three months, i.e. from the beginning of the next football season. In this case, Orange SA has observed a reasonable period of notice and need not pay damages for premature termination.

The legal systems in Europe are divided into two groups. In approximately half of the systems, agents must observe a reasonable notice period to terminate a mandate relationship concluded for an indefinite period. In the other half, a reasonable notice period for the agent to terminate is not required. However, in some of these systems the agent is obliged to continue with the mandated task to prevent substantial harm to the principal. In these Principles, the first approach is chosen to guarantee that the principal is granted a period to adapt to the new circumstances. Article 6:102 paragraph (1) (Termination by the principal when relationship is to last for indefinite period or when mandate is for a particular task) imposes a similar obligation on the principal who wishes to terminate a mandate contract for an indefinite period. Both parties therefore have to observe the same requirements to terminate the mandate contract without having to pay damages.

Whether a period is reasonable would have to be determined in light of the relevant circumstances. Comment C to Article 6:109 PECL (Contract for an indefinite period) indicates that these would include the time the contract has lasted, the time it may take the principal to obtain another contract, and any relevant usages or practices. Under these Principles, a notice period would not be unreasonable per se if the agent would be required to observe a longer period for termination than the principal is required to observe.

C. Termination by notice when agent not entitled to remuneration

Traditionally, the mandate contract was considered to be of a gratuitous nature. This is no longer the case, and the typical contract regulated by these rules will not be gratuitous. Nevertheless, some mandate contracts are still gratuitous.

When the mandate contract is not remunerated, some specific provisions apply. Article 2:103 paragraph (2) (Expenses incurred by the agent) explicitly entitles the agent to the reimbursement of reasonable expenses. Moreover, the non-remunerated nature of the mandate contract influences the care that may be expected of the agent (cf. Article 3:103 paragraph (2)(c) (Obligation of skill and care)). As a general rule, however, the position of an agent acting gratuitously does not differ much from the position of a remunerated agent. This implies that the obligations resulting from the mandate contract may easily become too burdensome for the agent. Even though this latter reason will often also qualify as a serious and extraordinary reason for the agent to terminate, a specific provision was deemed necessary here to emphasize the right of the agent to freely terminate the relationship in these cases. The agent is granted the right to be freed from these obligations by giving notice of the termination of the mandate relationship, provided the period of notice is of reasonable length. This applies even if the gratuitous mandate was for a definite period.

Illustration 3
Martha is leaving on a trip around the world. She authorises and instructs her friend Nico to rent in her name and on her behalf Martha's apartment. As her friend, Nico agrees to provide his services for free. However, finding lessees for Martha's apartment takes a lot of Nico's time and effort. He no longer has the time and the energy to take care of the mandate granted by his friend and therefore seeks to terminate the mandate contract. Under this Article, Nico may terminate the mandate contract at will because the contract is gratuitous. However, he has to notify Martha a reasonable time in advance that he does not want to continue taking care of renting her apartment. In this manner, he allows Martha to find another agent to represent her.

D. Relation to Principles of European Law and to Draft Common Frame of Reference

This Article mirrors Article IV.D. – 6:104 DCFR (Termination by agent when relationship is to last for indefinite period or when it is gratuitous). Article 1:302 (Unilateral ending of a contract for an indefinite period) of the Principles of European Law on Commercial Agency, Franchising and Distribution Contracts and also Article IV.E. – 2:302 DCFR (Contract for an indefinite period) include the same rule for the termination of commercial agency, franchising, and distribution contracts concluded for an indefinite period.

The provision adds to Article 6:109 PECL (Contract for an indefinite period), which allows either party to terminate a contract for an indefinite period by giving notice of reasonable length. This general provision only provides a solution to contracts for an indefinite period, whereas most mandate contracts are for a particular task or are otherwise for a determined period. Moreover, Article 6:109 PECL (Contract for an indefinite period) does not provide clear rules on the consequences of wrongful termination, i.e. a notice of termination that does not meet the requirements of that Article. The present Article fills both gaps.

The present Article is closer to the general rule in Article III. – 1:109 paragraph (1) DCFR (Variation or termination by notice). Under that provision, a contractual relationship can be terminated by notice by either party 'where this is provided for by the terms regulating it'. The present Article is an example of such a term. It is a mandatory rule. Parties may not agree on excluding the right to terminate by giving notice. However, some of its paragraphs are default. The parties may include a different term in the mandate contract – for example, one providing that termination by notice will take place only after a period of a prescribed length. Given the nature of a mandate contract, however, such a term would be unusual as it would not be in the interests of the principal.

The consequences for not observing a reasonable notice period are regulated differently under these Principles compared to the DCFR. Under Article III. – 1:109 paragraph (2) DCFR (Variation or termination by notice), the observance of a reasonable period is a requirement for effective termination. If not observed, the contract continues. Under these Principles, notice is always effective, but wrongful termination may lead to damages under Article 6:101 (Termination by notice in general).

E. Character of the rule

For the reasons explained above in relation to the principal's corresponding right, it is generally regarded as contrary to public policy to bind parties to contracts for eternity. For these reasons the possibility for the agent to terminate a mandate contract that is concluded for an indefinite period of time is mandatory. This is made explicit in paragraph (3). The parties may, however, agree on a provision derogating to the advantage of the agent, e.g. by allowing the agent to terminate without having to observe a notice period or by restricting the notice period to a fixed period. Of course, where a term to this extent is included in standard terms, the term is subject to the unfairness test of Article 4:110 PECL (Unfair terms not individually negotiated). Paragraph (2) regarding the right to terminate the relationship arising from a non-remunerated contract contains a default rule from which the parties may derogate.

F. Remedies

If the agent terminates a mandate relationship concluded for an indefinite period or a gratuitous mandate contract but does not grant the principal a reasonable notice period, the principal is entitled to claim damages for premature termination. There is no entitlement, though, to claim specific performance of the notice period, i.e. the continuation of the mandate relationship during the notice period.

Comparative Notes

1. Termination by agent of mandate relationship entered into for indefinite period

In approximately half of the legal systems, agents must observe a reasonable notice period to terminate a mandate relationship concluded for an indefinite period. This is the case in BULGARIA, GERMANY, FINLAND, GREECE, HUNGARY, IRELAND (implied term), ITALY, THE NETHERLANDS, SCOTLAND, and SLOVAKIA. Specific statutory periods are imposed in BULGARIA if the agent is a commission agent: one month if the mandate contract is terminated after the first year, two months if the mandate contract is terminated after the second year, and three months if the mandate contract has lasted three years or longer. In SLOVAKIA, in commercial relations the notice of termination is effective at the end of the month following the month the notice was delivered to the principal.

The other half do not require a reasonable notice period for the agent to terminate. This is the case in AUSTRIA, BELGIUM, DENMARK, ENGLAND, ESTONIA, FRANCE, SLOVAKIA, SPAIN, and SWEDEN. However, in many of these systems the agent is obliged to continue with the mandated task to prevent causing substantial harm to the principal. This is the regime in AUSTRIA, ESTONIA (for the time a substitute is found), SLOVAKIA, and SPAIN. Continuation is required under these systems unless continuing with the mandated task implies that the agent will suffer substantial damage. This latter factor is relevant in BELGIUM and FRANCE as a ground that exempts the agent from having to pay damages to the principal in case the agent terminates the relationship.

In MALTA, termination by the agent (apart from fundamental non-performance) is allowed only if there is a serious ground to terminate.

2. Termination by agent of mandate relationship entered into for definite period

A contract of mandate concluded for a definite period may be terminated at will by the agent, i.e. without a serious reason for termination, in AUSTRIA, BELGIUM, FRANCE, SLOVAKIA, and SPAIN. In some of these systems, the agent is obliged to continue acting in order to prevent substantial harm to the principal. A serious reason to terminate a mandate contract for a definite period is required in BULGARIA, ESTONIA, GERMANY, GREECE, HUNGARY, ITALY, THE NETHERLANDS, POLAND, and SWEDEN.

Non-performance of the principal is in some countries the only ground which justifies termination of a contract for a definite period before the agreed period has expired. This is the case in DENMARK, FIN-LAND, IRELAND, and SCOTLAND.

3. Termination by agent in case of a gratuitous mandate contract

No difference is made between the regimes for gratuitous and non-gratuitous contracts in BELGIUM, BUL-GARIA, ENGLAND, FRANCE, GERMANY, and SPAIN. In SCOTLAND, the agent may renounce a gratuitous mandate but may be liable in damages for losses to the principal resulting from the timing of the renunciation. In THE NETHERLANDS, an agent not acting in the performance of his business or profession may terminate the gratuitous mandate contract at will, but a party acting in the course of his business or profession may only do so in case of serious reason or if the contract is for an undetermined period of time and does not end by the completion of the task.

National Notes

1. Termination by agent of mandate relationship entered into for indefinite period

AUSTRIA: The agent can cancel the mandate contract concluded for an indefinite period of time at any time under the AUSTRIAN CC Article 1021, but has to carry on urgent business until the principal can make other arrangements (CC Article 1025).

BELGIUM: According to the Belgian CC Article 2007, the agent has the right to cancel the contract for representation. The cancellation can be given *ad nutum*, i.e. without a motive, but the agent must notify the cancellation to the principal. If the cancellation prejudices the principal, the agent must indemnify the principal. Exceptionally, the agent will be exempt from indemnification, if the agent cannot fulfil the mission to represent without harming his or her own position in a significant way (Dekkers, p. 735-736; Delahaye, p. 53-55; Foriers & Glansdorff, p. 642; Paulus & Boes, p. 156-159; Tilleman, p. 285; Wéry, p. 291-296).

BULGARIA: Provided that there is a substantial reason, the agent can end the relationship under a mandate contract concluded for an indefinite period of time with unilateral notice duly sent to the principal (OCA Article 289). If the does not observe these prerequisites, the agent is liable in damages for any loss incurred by the principal. Unless agreed otherwise, the commission agent is entitled to terminate the agency only in case of a breach of contractual obligations by the principal (CA Article 359 paragraph (1)). A contractual relationship entered into for an indefinite term between the commercial agent and the principal may be terminated by either party with a notice period of one month during the first year, of two months during the second year and of three months thereafter (CA Article 47 paragraph (1)).

DENMARK: The agent may at any time cancel the contract for representation where the contract is concluded for an indefinite period of time. In the case of cancellation, the agent is not entitled to claim compensation other than for the expenses incurred during the period of the representation.

ENGLAND: In the case of an indefinite duration contract, similarly to the principal being entitled to unilaterally terminate the relationship at any time, the agent can also renounce the authority at any time. Such a renunciation will be valid even if it is a breach of contract. There is however no case law on the matter and doctrine stipulates that the agent renouncing authority will not terminate the agency until the principal accepts such a renunciation (Bowstead & Reynolds, Article 119, paragraph 10-004, Article 122).

ESTONIA: The agent may terminate a mandate relationship entered into for an indefinite period only under the condition that the principal can receive the service or enter into the transaction in another manner; otherwise, the agent must compensate the principal for any damage caused by the termination (LOAEst Article 630 paragraph (2)).

FINLAND: The agent is, in general, entitled to terminate the mandate relationship on giving a reasonable period of notice. A liability to pay damages may arise in specific circumstances, e.g. if it is evident that the termination is substantially harmful for the principal, or when a reasonable period of notice is not given. A lawyer is not entitled to terminate the relationship with the client, except in specific circumstances. A professional agent has to pay special attention to the interests of the principal, especially when the latter is a consumer.

FRANCE: The agent may terminate the mandate relationship at any time by simply notifying the decision to the principal (CC Article 2007). The agent may, however, have to pay compensation to the principal if such termination causes loss to the principal, unless the agent can demonstrate that the continuation of the agency would have involved substantial losses for the agent. The agency agreement may provide for a notice period or compensation in the form of liquidated damages to be paid to the principal in the event of termination.

GERMANY: A gratuitous mandate relationship may be terminated at any time under the German CC Article 671 paragraph (1). Termination of a remunerated relationship *(Geschäftsbesorgungsvertrag)* is governed by the law on contracts for services or contracts for works. The rules on contracts for services allow termination by the principal as well as the agent (CC Article 621). Either party has the right to terminate irrespective of any termination period where there is an important reason which makes it unacceptable for the party to continue (CC Article 626). Furthermore, termination is possible even without an important reason where the contract calls for services 'of a higher kind which are usually assigned on the basis of particular trust' (art. 627 paragraph (1)). This will often be the case where a contract for representation is concluded.

GREECE: In the case of representation based on a contract of mandate, an agent is entitled to terminate the mandate relationship at any time provided this right has not been renounced. The termination is without effect if there are serious grounds militating against it. If the termination was notified at an inappropriate time (the time is considered to be inappropriate when it is impossible for the principal to take care of the affairs at the time of the termination; see CFI Thessaloniki decision no. 280/1984, EllDni 1985, 758) without serious ground, the agent is liable to compensate the principal for the loss caused (CC Article 725). If the termination was notified at an inappropriate time but with a serious ground, such as the illness of the agent, the latter is not obliged to pay compensation.

HUNGARY: CC Article 483 paragraphs (2) and (3) establishes that '[t]he agent shall also be entitled to abrogate the contract at any time; however, the period of notice must be sufficient for allowing the principal to handle the matter. In the event of the principal's grave breach of contract, abrogation can have immediate effect. If the agency is cancelled without substantial grounds, the damages that are caused shall be indemnified, unless the agency is gratuitous and the period of notice is sufficient for allowing the principal to handle the matter'. In this respect it is not relevant whether the agent is a professional party or whether the principal is a consumer. In the case of commission agency, according to CC Article 512, '[p]rior to the conclusion of a sales contract, the principal shall be entitled to terminate the contract by notice with immediate effect, and the commission agent by fifteen days' notice. Any limitation or exclusion of the right of rescission shall be null and void'. In this respect it is not relevant whether the agent is a professional party or whether the principal is a consumer.

IRELAND: Since agency is a consensual relationship it can be terminated if either party withdraws consent. Where an agent withdraws consent, the agent is said to 'renounce' the agency. No formality is required for a renunciation. Where an agent is appointed for an indefinite period of time the agency can be terminated in accordance with any provision in the agreement for termination by notice. In the absence of any express term, it will normally be implied that the agency can be terminated, by either party, on reasonable notice. What constitutes reasonable notice will depend on the facts of the particular case.

ITALY: The agent may cancel a contract for representation for an indefinite period of time in case of just cause (CC Article 1727). In the absence of just cause the agent may cancel the contract by giving a reasonable notice to the principal. If a reasonable period of notice is not given the agent is liable for damages vis-à-vis the principal. According to CC Article 1727 paragraph (2), '[i]n all cases except those of grave difficulty for the agent, the renunciation must be made in such manner and at such times as will enable the principal to make other arrangements'. In sum, the agent may terminate the relationship either for just cause or at will, but is required to give a reasonable notice and try to mitigate the negative consequences for the principal.

MALTA: Agents are not subject to specific requirements in order to terminate the contract. An agent who is a professional is not allowed to terminate unless he has a good reason. However, it is unclear whether the contract continues if there agent does not have a good reason to terminate the mandate contract.

NETHERLANDS: According to CC Article 7:408 paragraph (2), the agent who has entered into a mandate relationship in the course of a profession, may terminate the relationship by giving notice of reasonable length, if this contract applies for an indefinite period (and does not end because of completion).

POLAND: It is a general rule of Polish contract law that any contractual relationship entered into for an indefinite period of time (including agency) may be terminated by any party (art. 365 CC). This right may be limited but not excluded, since nobody may be forced to remain in a contractual relation forever.

SCOTLAND: Whether the agent is entitled unilaterally to terminate the relationship depends on the terms of the mandate contract. There are no formal requirements. See Macgregor, paragraph 182. In general contract law a contract of indefinite duration may be terminated by reasonable notice on either side (Stair, paragraphs 9.12-9.21).

SLOVAKIA: In Slovakian civil relations, the agent may terminate the mandate relationship without any reason. The agent is nevertheless bound to perform any immediately necessary juridical acts to prevent detriment to the rights of the principal. Acts thus performed have the same legal effects as if the representation had continued, unless such acts conflict with the arrangements made by the principal (CC Article 33b). In commercial relations, the agent may also terminate the relationship, and the termination will take effect at the end of the month following the month the notice was delivered to the principal, unless a later date ensues from the notice (Comm.C Article 575 paragraph (1)). The agent's obligation to perform activities on behalf of the principal expires on the day the notice becomes effective. If the principal may incur damage due to discontinuation of certain activities, the agent must inform the principal of the measures to be taken in order to prevent such damage. If the principal cannot take the measures even by means of other persons, and asks the agent to effect them, the agent is bound to do so.

SPAIN: Under Spanish law, the agent may also terminate the relationship, subject to certain conditions: (1) the agent has to inform the principal (CC Article 1736 paragraph (1)); (2) the agent has to indemnify the principal if the latter suffers damage, unless the agent terminates because continuing with the mandate will cause serious detriment to the agent (e.g. illness of the agent, refusal of the principal to pay an advance or an unfriendly relationship between the parties) (CC Article 1736 paragraph (2)); (3) the agent has to continue performance until the principal can take the measures necessary to adapt to the new situation (CC Article 1737). As is the case for the principal, notice of termination by the agent is effective in any case.

SWEDEN: When the contract is for an indefinite period of time, the agent may terminate the relationship at any time without cause and unless agreed otherwise usually with immediate effect. The principal has no right to compensation.

No answer from PORTUGAL

2. Termination by agent of mandate relationship entered into for definite period

AUSTRIA: The agent can terminate a mandate relationship entered into for a definite period at any time (CC Article 1021), but has to carry on urgent business until the principal can make other arrangements (CC Article 1025) and has to indemnify the principal for losses suffered due to the termination of the relationship before the agreed date (except for unforeseen legal and material obstacles).

BELGIUM: According to Belgian CC Article 2007, the agent has the right to terminate the agency relationship.

BULGARIA: A mandate relationship for a fixed period of time can be ended unilaterally by the agent under the same prerequisites as a relationship entered into for an indefinite period – as long as there is a serious reason for this and a notice has been duly given to the principal – Bulgarian OCA Article 289 (Меворах/Лиджи/Фархи, III, p. 178; *Голева*, Облигационно право II, p. 239). A commercial agency that has been entered into for a definite period may be terminated before its expiration if the party wishing to terminate it compensates the other party for the damage caused – CA Article 47 paragraph (2).

DENMARK: If the contract for representation is concluded for a definite period of time or if the agency would otherwise have ended by the conclusion of the prospective contract, the agent cannot rightfully terminate during the agreed period. The agent may, however, in a case of non-performance of the principal immediately terminate the relationship when the non-performance occurs.

ENGLAND: It seems that when the contract is for a specified period of time, the agent can only renounce the authority if it is because of a breach by the principal: termination by either party of a fixed-term relationship before expiry of the term is a repudiatory breach: *Boston Deep Sea Fishing and Ice Co v Ansell* (1888) 39 Ch D 339, CA. If the contract is for a specific task, as mentioned earlier, since the contract is treated as unilateral in most instances, the agent is under no obligation to perform and is therefore under no obligation to provide the principal with notice.

ESTONIA: Under Estonian law the agent may terminate the mandate relationship that is entered into for a definite period only on material grounds (LOAEst Article 631), i.e. if it becomes evident that, bearing in mind all the circumstances and the interests of both parties, the party wishing to terminate cannot be expected to continue performance until expiry of the term for termination or the term of the agreement or until the services are performed.

FINLAND: It follows from the general principles of contract law that the agent is not entitled to terminate a mandate relationship that has been entered into by a contract concluded for a definite period of time. This does not apply when the principal has been guilty of a fundamental non-performance.

FRANCE: The rules under French law are the same whether the mandate was concluded for a fixed term or an indefinite term, whether or not the mandate has been substantially performed or not. CC Article 2007 makes no distinction. The agent therefore has the right to cease performance of the mandate. The agent will, nonetheless, have to compensate the principal for any loss suffered and the agent's remuneration will be reduced *pro rata temporis* or *pro rata* the work performed. In some cases, the right to remuneration may not arise if the mandate has failed due to the agent's decision.

GERMANY: A mandate relationship under a contract concluded for a definite period of time may be terminated by the agent under the same conditions as one under a contract concluded for an indefinite period of time. However, the conclusion of a contract for a restricted period of time can arguably be construed as the agent's waiver of the right to termination under CC Article 671 paragraph (1). Whether such an interpretation is feasible depends on the circumstances of the particular case. There is no case law on this question.

GREECE: An agent can terminate a mandate relationship under a contract for a definite period on the same conditions as a mandate relationship under a contract for an indefinite period.

HUNGARY: CC Article 483 paragraphs (2) and (3) establishes that '[t]he agent shall also be entitled to abrogate the contract at any time; however, the period of notice must be sufficient for allowing the principal to handle the matter. In the event of the principal's grave breach of contract, abrogation can have immediate effect. If the agency is cancelled without substantial grounds, the damages that are caused shall be indemnified, unless the agency is gratuitous and the period of notice is sufficient for allowing the principal to handle the matter'. In this respect it is not relevant whether the agent is a professional party or whether the principal is a consumer. In the case of commission agency, according to CC Article 512, '[p]rior to the conclusion of a sales contract, the principal shall be entitled to terminate the contract by notice with immediate effect, and the commission agent by fifteen days' notice. Any limitation or exclusion of the right of rescission shall be null and void'. In this respect it is not relevant whether the agent is a professional party or whether the principal is a consumer.

IRELAND: Where the contract is for a specified period of time, the agent may renounce the authority and terminate the relationship but this may constitute a breach of contract unless the principal has already committed a breach of contract which allows the agent to terminate.

ITALY: If the contract for representation is concluded for a definite period of time the agent may terminate the relationship only for just cause. In the absence of just cause the agent is liable to the principal for damages.

NETHERLANDS: The agent may terminate a mandate relationship entered into for a definite period only in case of serious causes (CC Articles 7:408 paragraph (2) and 7:402 paragraph (2)).

POLAND: The agent may terminate the agency relationship at any time. However, if the service was provided against a remuneration, the agent may terminate only in case of 'important reasons'.

SCOTLAND: The agent, like the principal, is entitled to terminate an agency of unlimited duration at any time (Erskine, III,3,10; Gow, p. 536). This rule does not apply in cases of fixed term agency contracts where, in the absence of provision in the contract allowing unilateral early termination, termination by one party prior to the agreed expiry will amount to a breach of contract.

SLOVAKIA: An agent can terminate a mandate relationship for a definite period under the same conditions as one entered into for an indefinite period of time.

SPAIN: The agent may terminate the relationship at any time. However, the agent is liable to compensate the principal's loss, unless the agent may prove a serious reason for the termination (CC Article 1736).

SWEDEN: When the contract is for a definite period of time, the agent may terminate the relationship for a valid cause. The agent cannot be forced to finish the performance. However, the agent will be liable for non-performance if the termination is without cause (Hellner, p. 215).

No answer received from PORTUGAL, MALTA.

3. Termination by agent in case of a gratuitous mandate contract

BELGIUM: No distinction is made between a remunerated or a non-remunerated contract for representation.

BULGARIA: The general rule of the Bulgarian OCA Article 289 concerning unilateral ending of the mandate relationship by the agent is applicable to both gratuitous and non-gratuitous contracts (Меворах/ Лиджи/Фархи, III, p. 178).

ENGLAND: There does not seem to be any rule dealing specifically with this particular question on gratuitous agencies. However, it seems that a gratuitous agent should be entitled to terminate the relationship at any time.

FRANCE: The rules are the same whether the mandate is gratuitous or not; the Civil Code makes no distinction.

GERMANY: For a gratuitous mandate contract, termination is possible at any time. CC Article 671 paragraph (2) provides for an additional condition (applicable to both gratuitous and remunerated contracts): the agent may only terminate in a manner that will allow the principal to make suitable arrangements for the subject matter the agent attended to, unless there is an 'important reason' *(wichtiger Grund)* for the immediate termination. It is not relevant whether the principal is a consumer.

NETHERLANDS: Where the agent has concluded the mandate contract in the course of his business or profession, he may terminate the mandate contract only in case of serious reason or if the contract is for an undetermined period of time and does not end by the completion of the task (CC Article 7:408 paragraph (2)). This would imply that in the case where the agent is not a professional party, termination is allowed. Moreover, it would also imply that if the agent was a professional party who had agreed to perform this particular mandate contract gratuitously, he would not be allowed to terminate, unless the mandate contract was concluded for an undetermined period of time. This provision is, however, not mandatory, implying that the parties may agree that also a professional agent may at will terminate the mandate contract.

POLAND: The agent may terminate the agency relationship at any time. If the service was provided against a remuneration, the agent may terminate only in case of 'important reasons'.

SCOTLAND: In a gratuitous contract of mandate the agent may renounce the contract, but may be liable in damages for losses to the principal resulting from the timing of the renunciation (Stair, paragraphs 9.25; Erskine, III,3,40).

SPAIN: There is no difference made in the CC on this point between non remunerated and remunerated agreements.

No answer received: AUSTRIA, ESTONIA, FINLAND, GREECE, HUNGARY, IRELAND, ITALY, MALTA, SLOVAKIA, SWEDEN.

Article 6:105: Termination by the agent for extraordinary and serious reason

(1) **The agent may terminate the mandate relationship by giving notice for extraordinary and serious reason.**

(2) **No period of notice is required.**

(3) **For the purposes of this Article an extraordinary and serious reason includes:**

    (a) **a change of the mandate contract under Article 4:201 (Changes of the mandate contract);**

(b) the death or incapacity of the principal; and

(c) the death or incapacity of the person who, at the time of conclusion of the mandate contract, the parties had intended to perform the agent's obligations under the mandate contract.

(4) The parties may not, to the detriment of the agent, exclude the application of this Article or derogate from or vary its effects.

Comments

A. General idea

The present Article introduces a right for the agent to immediately terminate a mandate relationship, no matter whether the contract has been concluded for a definite or indefinite period, without having to observe a notice period and without having to pay damages. This applies when the agent can invoke an extraordinary and serious reason which justifies termination.

Extraordinary and serious reasons to terminate a mandate relationship may arise in very different circumstances. Paragraph (3) provides a non-exhaustive list, implying that courts may accept other grounds justifying the immediate termination of the mandate contract.

B. No exhaustive list of extraordinary and serious reasons

Paragraph (3) refers to three situations that are to be regarded as extraordinary reasons which justify termination: (a) a case where the mandate contract is changed under Article 4:201 (Changes of the mandate contract); (b) the death or incapacity of the principal; and (c) the death or incapacity of the designated person to perform the agent's obligations under the mandate contract. This list does not purport to provide an exhaustive enumeration of the reasons that justify immediate termination. Whether a reason qualifies as 'extraordinary and serious' within the meaning of this Article and justifies immediate termination is to be determined on a case-by-case basis.

C. Changes of the mandate

The first listed ground that constitutes an extraordinary and serious reason to terminate is the situation where the mandate contract is changed in accordance with Article 4:201 paragraph (1) (Changes of the mandate contract), i.e. where the principal significantly changes the mandate of the agent or refuses to revoke a direction after having been warned by the agent for the possible detrimental consequences thereof in accordance with Article 4:101 paragraph (3) (Directions given by the principal). In these cases, the change may give the agent reason to believe that he will not be able to conclude the prospective contract and therefore have to perform his services without a good chance of being rewarded for them.

Illustration 1
Alfredo is first authorised as a real estate agent to sell a house owned by Ursula for a price of € 400,000 or more. Later, Ursula changes the limit to € 450,000, which is clearly above the market price. Even though Alfredo has warned Ursula that he will not be able to sell the house for the amended asking price, Ursula insists on it. As Alfredo realises his services will be in vain, he wishes to terminate in accordance with Article 4:201 paragraph (3) (Changes of the mandate contract) and the present Article.

D. Death or incapacity of principal or agent

In most Member States, the supervening incapacity of the principal or that of the agent is also regarded as bringing the mandate relationship to an end. The laws on the legal effects of mental incapacity, however, differ from one country to another. Some countries have special regimes for mandates with a view to incapacity or enduring powers of attorney. There are also differences among the Member States as to the moment in which incapacity has effect on the mandate contract.

The rules on the legal effects of mental incapacity differ greatly from one country to another. Given the fact that the law governing mental incapacity is not covered by these Principles or by the Principles of European Contract Law, it is thought that it is best left to national law whether the supervening incapacity of either party to the mandate relationship should lead to the end of the mandate relationship – and what the consequences should be if that happens. However, if incapacity of the principal or of the agent does not lead to the automatic termination of the mandate contract under national law, the agent or the principal, or their legal representatives, may invoke termination of the mandate contract for extraordinary and serious reason under this Article (for the agent in case of incapacity of the principal and for the legal representative of the agent in case of incapacity of the agent) or under Article 6:103 (Termination by principal for extraordinary and serious reason) (for the principal in case of incapacity of the agent and for the legal representative of the principal in case of incapacity of the principal). Given the more limited possibilities for the agent to terminate, it was thought wise to list this particular situation here for the agent.

E. Death or incapacity of designated person to perform the mandate contract

The agent normally is allowed to determine which person within his staff will perform the contract. This is different if the principal has concluded the contract with the intention that the contract is to be performed by a specific person, e.g. an employee who is renowned for his specific expertise. In such a case, this specific person is to perform the mandate contract. If this designated person subsequently dies or becomes incapacitated, the agent's position becomes problematic, as the contract can't be performed by the designated person. The present Article offers a way out by allowing the agent to terminate the contract for serious and extraordinary reason.

Illustration 2

Hans is the victim of a traffic accident. He engages Christian, a lawyer specialised in personal injury claims, to claim damages from the tortfeasor. Hans has engaged Christian specifically for his expertise in these cases. In this case, personal performance of the mandate contract by Christian is required by the contract, even though the mandate contract is concluded by the law firm that employs him. Christian later becomes incapacitated and is no longer able to perform the mandate contract. The law firm may terminate the mandate contract under paragraph (3)(c) of the present Article.

F. Loss of confidence and trust in the principal

In many cases, the well-founded loss of trust and confidence in the principal will constitute an extraordinary and serious reason for the agent to terminate a mandate relationship. In these cases, the confidence in the other party was necessary for the proper performance of the obligations under the mandate contract. The present Article accordingly introduces a right for the agent to immediately terminate a mandate relationship without having to observe a notice period and without having to pay damages.

However, it does not seem wise to include a general provision stating that whenever the agent justifiably loses trust and confidence in the principal, there is a serious and extraordinary reason for termination of the mandate relationship. Such an explicit rule could tempt agents to argue that there would be a loss of confidence and trust just to escape having to respect a notice period or, after the fact, to avoid having to pay damages for wrongfully terminating the mandate relationship with immediate effect. It is thought better to leave the matter for the court to decide on the basis of the general provision of paragraph (1).

Illustration 3

Marco concludes a mandate contract in which he entrusts Julka with the task of negotiating the purchase of a major bank. The following week a fraud case implicating Marco is reported on the front page of all national newspapers. Whether or not the accusations are true, Marco's business reputation is damaged. As Julka's work as an agent is dependent on an unimpeachable business reputation, she needs to be able to bring the relationship with Marco to an end as soon as possible. Even though there is no case of non-performance by Marco, under these circumstances Julka cannot be expected to continue performance under the mandate contract.

G. No notice period

If there is indeed an extraordinary and serious reason which justifies termination of the contractual relationship, termination should take immediate effect. In this specific situation, the agent should not be required to observe any other condition than notifying the principal about the decision to terminate. In particular, no notice period needs to be observed, as indicated in paragraph (2). There is no form requirement regarding the notification.

Illustration 3 (continuation)
Julka sends a letter to Marco to let him know that she is immediately stopping her performance of the mandated task. Marco claims that he has not been granted a reasonable period to be able to find a new agent. Paragraph (2) of the present Article provides, however, that since there was an extraordinary and serious reason for Julka to terminate the mandate contract, Julka is justified in terminating the contract with immediate effect.

H. No provision on termination in case of bankruptcy

Bankruptcy law determines whether or not the mandate relationship ends by the bankruptcy of either the principal or the agent. Given the fact that bankruptcy law is not covered by these Principles, it is thought that it is best left to national law whether the bankruptcy of either party to the mandate relationship should lead to the end of the mandate relationship – and what the consequences should be if it is so terminated.

I. Relation to Principles of European Law and to Draft Common Frame of Reference

This Article resembles Article IV.D. – 6:105 DCFR (Termination by agent for extraordinary and serious reason).

In some cases where there is a serious and extraordinary reason justifying termination, Article 6:111 PECL (Change of circumstances) may be applicable. Under that Article, the parties would be expected to enter into negotiations to adapt the terms of the contract or to terminate the contractual relationship. If negotiations fail, it would be for the judge to decide between adaptation and termination. This would all take a long time, however, during which there is uncertainty as to the position of the parties. Where the agent can terminate the mandate relationship for an extraordinary and serious reason, this long process and the possible need of an application to the court is avoided.

J. Character of the rule

The right to terminate the mandate relationship for extraordinary and serious reason is mandatory, as is expressed in paragraph (4), for the reasons given in Comment L to Article 6:103 (Termination by the principal for extraordinary and serious reason).

K. Remedies

This Article provides for a remedy in case a serious and extraordinary reason to terminate the mandate contract occurs. As such, it does not lead to a remedy for breach of contract itself. If the agent terminates the contract with immediate effect and an extraordinary and serious reason is deemed absent, this amounts to a breach of contract by the agent. In this case, the principal has recourse to the remedies for non-performance except for specific performance, i.e. continuation of the relationship.

Comparative Notes

1. Termination by agent for extraordinary and serious reason

There is no serious reason required for the agent to terminate a mandate relationship in BELGIUM, ENG-LAND, GREECE, HUNGARY, PORTUGAL (notice period of reasonable length), and SPAIN, and also not in MALTA if agent is not a professional party.

Even though there may be no breach, compensation is still due in BELGIUM, GREECE, HUNGARY, MAL-TA, PORTUGAL, and SPAIN. However, no compensation is due in BELGIUM, GREECE, MALTA, and SPAIN if continuing performance would have meant that the agent would have harmed his position significantly. Similarly, no compensation is due in HUNGARY and SPAIN if the agent has a serious reason for termination, a reasonable notice period has been observed in HUNGARY and PORTUGAL, or in the case of a gratuitous contract in HUNGARY.

A serious reason is required for an agent to be able to terminate in BULGARIA, ESTONIA, THE NETHER-LANDS, POLAND, and SWEDEN, and therefore termination without a serious reason amounts to a breach of contract. In MALTA, a serious reason is needed when the agent is a professional party.

In IRELAND and SCOTLAND, only the non-performance by the principal is a justified ground for termination of a contract concluded for a definite period.

2. No notice period required

In all legal systems with the exception of HUNGARY and PORTUGAL, no notice period is required in the case of an extraordinary and serious reason.

3. Specific cases of extraordinary and serious reason

In none of the reported countries is there an exhaustive list of extraordinary and serious reasons to terminate.

4. Incapacity of the parties

In most Member States – including BELGIUM, FRANCE, GRECECE, HUNGARY, IRELAND, PORTU-GAL, and SWEDEN – the incapacity of the principal is regarded as a cause for termination. The same is true for ITALY, unless the mandate was for the conclusion of a contract pertaining to business activities and the business of the principal remains in operation. In SPAIN, the incapacity of the principal also leads to the termination of the mandate relationship, unless the contract indicates otherwise or unless the mandate relationship was precisely concluded for the situation that the principal would later be declared incapable. In this case, the mandate relationship remains in force in accordance with the conditions imposed by the principal.

The contractual relationship does not terminate when the principal is declared incapable in AUSTRIA, THE NETHERLANDS, POLAND, and SLOVAKIA. It follows that in those legal regimes the mandate relationship continues between the agent and the curator of the principal. In ENGLAND, the mandate relationship terminates unless the Enduring Power of Attorney Act applies.

If the incapacity of the principal terminates the mandate relationship, the relevant moment is the moment when the incapacity is declared by a court or specific body in FRANCE, SLOVAKIA, and SPAIN. In most other systems, the relevant moment is the moment the agent becomes aware of the incapacity. Among these systems, it is possible to differentiate two sub-groups. In a first group of systems, the relationship is deemed to be terminated when the agent knows or ought to have been aware of the incapacity of the principal. This is the regime in BELGIUM, GREECE, HUNGARY, ITALY, and PORTUGAL. In a second group of systems, the relevant moment is when the agent is informed of the incapacity. This is the case in POLAND and SCOTLAND. In this second sub-group, the burden of proof regarding whether the agent was aware of the incapacity seems to lie on the person charged with protecting the interests of the incapacitated principal.

The agent has the obligation to continue performance in order to prevent detriment to the interests of the principal or the principal's successors in AUSTRIA, BELGIUM, DENMARK, FRANCE, GERMANY, GREECE, HUNGARY, IRELAND, ITALY, THE NETHERLANDS, PORTUGAL, SCOTLAND, SLOVAKIA, and SPAIN. In ENGLAND, the agent has to wait for instructions from the successors of the principal. In most countries, the agent seems only to be obliged to continue running the affairs that were already started before the principal was incapacitated. This is the case in BELGIUM, GREECE, ITALY, PORTUGAL, SCOTLAND, and SPAIN. In some of these systems, the agent would also be obliged to take urgent measures. This is the case in ITALY and THE NETHERLANDS. In SLOVAKIA, the agent is only obliged to take urgent measures. In some systems, the obligation to perform these measures is subject to a time limit: the agent has to continue until the curator can take over the responsibility. This is the case in GERMANY, GREECE, and HUNGARY. In THE NETHERLANDS, the time limit is specific: one year.

The agent is entitled to payment in AUSTRIA, DENMARK, FRANCE, GERMANY, GREECE, HUNGARY, IRELAND, ITALY, SCOTLAND, and SLOVAKIA. In THE NETHERLANDS, the agent is entitled to payment if and in so far as this is reasonable in view of the circumstances.

In almost all European legislations, the supervening legal incapacity of the agent implies the termination of the mandate relationship. As far as is known, this is different only in AUSTRIA and SWEDEN.

5. Insolvency of the parties

The insolvency of the agent, similar to death, leads to automatic termination of the mandate contract in most countries. This is indeed the case in AUSTRIA, BELGIUM, DENMARK, ESTONIA, FRANCE, GERMANY, GREECE, IRELAND, ITALY, MALTA, NETHERLANDS, POLAND, PORTUGAL, and SPAIN. In some countries, bankruptcy of the agent does not mean automatic termination but may be a ground for the principal to terminate. This is the case in ENGLAND, FINLAND, HUNGARY, SCOTLAND, SLOVAKIA, and SWEDEN. In SCOTLAND, solvency needs to be an implied term of the contract. Insolvency or bankruptcy of the principal leads to termination of the relationship in AUSTRIA, BELGIUM, BULGARIA, ENGLAND, ESTONIA (except in cases where there is no connexion between contract and bankruptcy), FINLAND, FRANCE, GERMANY, GREECE, HUNGARY, ITALY, MALTA, THE NETHERLANDS, PO-

LAND, SCOTLAND (with exceptions to protect the interests of the principal), SLOVAKIA, SPAIN, and SWEDEN.

In most systems, termination is effective from the moment the agent knows of the occurrence of the bankruptcy. This is the case in BELGIUM, ESTONIA, FRANCE, GERMANY, GREECE, ITALY, POLAND, SLOVAKIA, and SPAIN. The acts of the agent until that moment are valid. These systems are divided as to the relevant moment, however. In some systems – including GERMANY, and SPAIN – it is the moment the proceeding starts; in other systems – including GREECE, POLAND, and SLOVAKIA – it is the declaration of bankruptcy. In AUSTRIA and SLOVAKIA, termination is effective from the moment the bankruptcy occurs because the proceeding has a public character and the principal is presumed to know about it.

6. Mandatory rule

The right for the agent to unilaterally terminate the contract is mandatory in BULGARIA, FRANCE, GERMANY, and SWEDEN.

National Notes

1. Termination by agent for extraordinary and serious reason

AUSTRIA: The agent can cancel the mandate contract concluded for an indefinite and for a definite period of time at any time under the Austrian CC Article 1021, but has to carry on urgent business until the principal can make other arrangements (CC Article 1025). The agent has to indemnify the principal for losses suffered due to the termination of the relationship before the agreed date (except for unforeseen legal and material obstacles).

BELGIUM: According to the Belgian CC Article 2007, the agent has the right to cancel the contract for representation *ad nutum,* i.e. without a motive, by notifying the cancellation to the principal. The Civil Code does not require an extraordinary and serious reason. If the cancellation however prejudices the principal, the agent must indemnify the principal Exceptionally, the agent will be exempt from indemnification, if the agent cannot fulfil the mission to represent without harming the agent's own position in a significant way.

BULGARIA: Whereas the principal is entitled to unilaterally end the mandate relationship without any reason, the agent can only terminate the relationship on the ground of 'a serious reason' (OCA Article 289; Любен Василев, Облигационно право, p. 29-30).

ENGLAND: In the light of the principle of free renunciation of authority mentioned earlier, the agent is free to renounce the authority and need not mention any reason for it. If the principal is guilty of a serious breach, the agent will be entitled to treat the breach as repudiatory and therefore terminate the relationship immediately. Apart from instances of breach of contract, there will be events which will frustrate the contract and therefore will terminate the agency such as death, bankruptcy, insanity etc of the principal.

ESTONIA: Each of the parties is entitled to terminate the mandate relationship for an important reason. No notice period is required (LOAEst Article 631).

GERMANY: Every contract for a continuing obligation can be revoked when there is an 'important ground' for the revocation – a fundamental principle of German law which was developed by the courts and is now expressly laid down in CC Article 314 paragraph (1). CC Article 626 as part of the law on contracts for service, which may apply to remunerated mandate contracts by virtue of CC Article 675 paragraph (1), provides a special, but quite similar rule.

GREECE: Under Greek law, the agent may terminate the mandate at any time by simply notifying this decision to the principal (CC Article 2007). The Civil Code does not require an extraordinary and serious reason in any case. The agent may, however, have to pay compensation to the principal if the termination causes loss to the principal, unless the agent can demonstrate that the continuation of the mandate would have involved 'substantial loss' for the agent. The agency agreement may provide for a notice period and/or compensation in the event of termination.

HUNGARY: CC Article 483 paragraphs (2) and (3) establishes that 'the agent shall also be entitled to abrogate the contract at any time; however, the period of notice must be sufficient for allowing the principal to handle the matter. In the event of the principal's grave breach of contract, abrogation can have immediate effect. If the agency is cancelled without substantial grounds, the damages that are caused shall be indemnified, unless the agency is gratuitous and the period of notice is sufficient for allowing the principal to handle the matter'.

IRELAND: Where the agency is contractual, breach of a condition of the contract by the principal, or of an innominate term where the consequences of the breach are serious, will enable the agent to terminate the relationship and pursue a remedy in damages.

MALTA: The agent may renounce to the contract of mandate by giving notice of his renunciation to the principal, cf. CC Article 1889 paragraph (1). There is no specification with reference to whether the contract of mandate was for a definite or an indefinite time period. There are no specific requirements concerning the right to terminate. Only if termination is prejudicial for the principal, damages are to be paid unless continuing performance will be prejudicial for the agent. In the situation where the agent is a professional party, e.g. if the agent is a legal procurator, he cannot renounce to the mandate without a just cause (CFI (Civil) 14 February 1883, *Busuttil vs Busuttil*. Such a just cause must be personal to the agent such as for example, ill health or the incompatibility of the agent's new job with exercise of his duties as agent, cf. CA (Civil) 16 June 1909, *Portelli vs Neechamel.*

NETHERLANDS: The agent may terminate the agency without giving notice only in case of a serious cause for termination (CC Articles 7:408 paragraph (2) and 7:402 paragraph (2)).

POLAND: The agent may terminate a non-gratuitous mandate relationship only if 'important reasons' arise; otherwise the agent can be held liable for in damages.

PORTUGAL: The agent is always allowed to cancel the contract *(revogação)* (CC Article 1170). He will be liable if he does terminate without granting a reasonable notice period.

SCOTLAND: There is no special rule on termination for extraordinary and serious reason falling short of a material breach of contract (Macgregor, paragraph 183; Gow, p. 535-6). Where the principal is in material breach of the agency contract, the agent is, of course, entitled to terminate for that reason. Beyond cases of breach of contract, certain events may act to frustrate and thus terminate the agency relationship, including the termination of the principal's business, and the death, incapacity or bankruptcy of the principal or agent. In cases of death, incapacity or bankruptcy, the agent may remain entitled to act, as is explored in more detail below.

SLOVAKIA: Slovakian law does not recognise termination for important reasons.

SPAIN: According to CC Articles 1732 and 1736, the agent may terminate the mandate relationship at any time *(renuncia),* irrespective of whether it has been concluded for a definite or indefinite period. Notification is the only condition imposed. There is no other requirement. The only limit to the freedom to exit is the duty to pay damages for loss suffered by the principal when the termination is not supported by a 'just cause' (serious reason). The only sure thing one may say about this expression is that the Code has weakened the exoneration requirements set up by the *rebus sic stantibus rule.*

SWEDEN: When the contract is for an indefinite period of time, the agent may cancel it at any time without cause and unless agreed otherwise usually with immediate effect. When the contract is for a definite period of time, the agent may cancel it for a valid reason. The agent cannot, however, be forced to finish the performance. The agent will be liable for non-performance on terminating without cause and the principal will be entitled to claim damages (Hellner, p. 215).

No answer received: DENMARK, FINLAND, FRANCE, ITALY.

2. No notice period required

AUSTRIA: The agent has the right to terminate the contract at any time, and without any reason.

BELGIUM: The agent has the right to cancel the contract for representation *ad nutum,* i.e. without notice period.

BULGARIA: In order to escape liability for a breach of contract, the agent does not only have to have a serious reason to unilaterally end the relationship, but is also obliged to give a notice of reasonable length (OCA Article 289). Otherwise, the is obliged to compensate the principal for any damage caused.

ENGLAND: If the principal is guilty of a serious breach or other important reasons mentioned above, the agent can terminate the contract immediately.

FRANCE: No notice period is required.

GERMANY: Both CC Article 626 paragraph (1) and CC Article 314 paragraph (1) expressly allow for a revocation without observance of a period of notice.

IRELAND: Where the principal has committed a serious breach of contract, no notice period is required.

MALTA: No reasonable notice period is required.

NETHERLANDS: If there is a serious cause for termination (CC Articles 7:408 paragraph (2) and 7:402 paragraph (2)), the agent does not have to observe a notice period when terminating.

POLAND: The contract ends when the notice of termination reaches the principal.

PORTUGAL: The agent is always allowed to cancel the contract *(revogação)* (CC Article 1170) but he will be liable if he does terminate without granting a reasonable notice period.

SCOTLAND: Where the agent terminates the agency relationship (e.g. in response to a breach by the principal), no specific period of notice is required.

SLOVAKIA: Slovakian law does not recognise termination for important reasons. A notice period is required in commercial relations, but parties may agree otherwise.

SPAIN: In Spanish Law, CC Article 1736 does not require any notice period.

SWEDEN: If the agent terminates the relationship on the basis of a valid reason, no notice period is required (HaL Article 26).

No answer received: DENMARK, ESTONIA, FINLAND, GREECE, HUNGARY, ITALY.

3. Specific cases of extraordinary and serious reason

BULGARIA: If the principal has given directions resulting in a unilateral change of the mandate contract and its performance has become too burdensome for the agent, this is considered a sufficiently serious reason for termination of the relationship by the agent with a unilateral notice of termination (OCA Article 289; Меворах/Лиджи/Фархи, III, p. 119; Любен Василев, Облигационно право, p. 24).

GERMANY: Under German law, the principal is not entitled to change the content of the mandate contract unilaterally, but only as far as the agent agrees – an agreed change can therefore not constitute grounds for termination. The death of the principal generally ('in doubt') does not lead to the termination of the mandate (CC Article 672). Death or incapacity of a 'specific person' without whom the agent's obligations under the mandate relationship cannot be performed would terminate these obligations due to impossibility (CC

Article 275 paragraph (1)), but would not give the *agent* an important reason to terminate the relationship.

NETHERLANDS: CC Article 7:402 paragraph (2) mentions the case where the agent is upon reasonable grounds not willing to carry out the mandate according to the instructions given, as a case of an extraordinary and serious reason for termination by the agent.

POLAND: There are no examples of 'important reasons' in the Polish Civil Code.

SCOTLAND: This question does not arise as termination by a party for extraordinary and serious reasons falling short of material breach is not recognised.

SLOVAKIA: Slovakian law does not recognise termination for important reasons.

SPAIN: In Spanish law, the death, the commencement of insolvency proceedings and the insanity or loss of mental capacity automatically put the mandate to an end, without any required manifestation of will.

SWEDEN: A valid reason is said to exist if the agent is liable for fundamental non-performance, if it would be unreasonable to demand that the task continues or if another important reason to cancel the agreement exists (KommL Article 51 and HaL Article 26). This may include events of *force majeure* character and also circumstances of a personal nature (e.g. incapacitation of a party).

No answer received: AUSTRIA, BELGIUM, DENMARK, ENGLAND, ESTONIA, FINLAND, FRANCE, GREECE, HUNGARY, IRELAND, ITALY, MALTA, PORTUGAL.

4. Incapacity of the parties

See national notes to Article 6:103.

5. Insolvency of the parties

See national notes to Article 6:103.

6. Mandatory rule

BELGIUM: The rule that the agent has the right to cancel the contract for representation ad nutum, is not mandatory (Tilleman, p. 335; Wéry, p. 294). An exception is made by some authors for contracts for an indefinite period (Paulus & Boes, p. 159).

BULGARIA: In Bulgaria legal doctrine, any contractual stipulation that obstructs the agent in exercising the right to unilaterally terminate the mandate relationship is deemed null and void (Меворах/Лиджи/Фархи, III, p. 178). However, a stipulation to that effect may render the agent liable for damages if the agent terminates in breach of it.

FRANCE: The rule is mandatory.

GERMANY: Although CC Article 314 paragraph (1) does not expressly say so, the revocability based on an important ground cannot be excluded (Palandt/Grüneberg, Article 314 no. 3).

SLOVAKIA: The rules on termination are not mandatory, except in the case of a commercial representation contract.

SPAIN: There is discussion about whether the parties can contract out of the agent's right to terminate and further about whether there would be any sense in the principal agreeing to this (Gordillo, p. 1591)

SWEDEN: The rules concerning a right to cancel on the basis of a valid reason are of a mandatory character (KommL Article 51 and HaL Article 26).

No answer received: AUSTRIA, DENMARK, ENGLAND, ESTONIA, FINLAND, GREECE, HUNGARY, IRELAND, ITALY, MALTA, THE NETHERLANDS, PORTUGAL, POLAND, SCOTLAND.

Chapter 7:
Other grounds for termination

Article 7:101: Death of the principal

(1) The death of the principal does not end the mandate relationship.
(2) Both the agent and the successors of the principal may terminate the mandate relationship by giving notice of termination for extraordinary and serious reason under Article 6:103 (Termination by the principal for extraordinary and serious reason) or Article 6:105 (Termination by the agent for extraordinary and serious reason).

Comments

A. General idea

Under the present Article, the mandate relationship does not terminate automatically if the principal dies. The position of the principal is to be taken over by the successors (i.e. the heirs or the executors). This approach presumes that the interest of the principal may very well be the same as those of the successors and that they can continue the relationship.

Illustration 1
Paul lives in Spain but has an apartment for rent in Amsterdam. A real estate agent in the Netherlands takes care of renting Paul's apartment. At the death of Paul, his house is inherited by his daughter Alicia, who also lives in Spain. Since Alicia is interested in continuing to rent her apartment in Amsterdam, the contract continues between her and the real estate agent.

Yet as the interests of the principal may be different from those of the successors, they should be entitled to escape from the mandate relationship without having to observe a notice period. Similarly, as it may become more onerous for the agent to have to deal with the whole of the successors – with possibly conflicting views on the pursuit of their interests – the agent should also be able to escape from the mandate relationship. For these reasons, both the agent and the successors of the principal may give notice of termination of the mandate relationship for extraordinary and serious reasons under Article 6:103 (Termination by the principal for extraordinary and serious reason) or Article 6:105 (Termination by agent for extraordinary and serious reason). On this ground, no period of notice needs to be observed.

Illustration 2
Simone lives in Paris but has an apartment for rent in Seville. A real estate agent in Spain takes care of renting Simone's apartment. Upon Simone's death, her house is

inherited by her daughter Tanja. Tanja decides to live in Seville. For that reason, she wishes to terminate the mandate contract with the real estate agent.

Under the present rule, the contract of mandate continues between the heirs and the real estate agent, unless one of them decides not to continue the mandate relationship and terminates the relationship on the ground of the death of the original principal. Both the heirs and the agent are entitled to terminate the relationship due to the occurrence of a serious reason without observing a reasonable notice period.

The approach chosen in this Article deviates from the solution taken in most Member States, in which the death of the principal leads to the automatic termination of the mandate relationship. A similar rule as accepted in this Article exists in approximately one-third of the Member States. These Principles opt for the latter solution to protect the interests of the heirs of the principal. In this manner, the agent must continue taking care of the mandated task, which will presumably be the most convenient solution for the heirs of the agent and for the agent himself. If this is not the case, both the heirs and the agent have the possibility to bring the mandate relationship to an end without having to observe a notice period.

However, it should be noted that, in practice, the approach taken in these Principles does not deviate much from the regimes in the Member States where the death of the principal leads to the automatic termination of the mandate contract; in a great majority of these legal regimes, and despite the fact that the mandate contract itself has terminated, the agent is still required to continue performing the necessary acts to prevent any harm to the interests of the heirs of the principal.

B. Conclusion of the prospective contract after termination of mandate relationship due to the death of the principal

It should be noted that Article 2:102 paragraph (5) (Price) remains applicable if the prospective contract is concluded after the mandate relationship has terminated by notice for serious and extraordinary reason under Articles 6:103 (Termination by the principal for extraordinary and serious reason) or 6:105 (Termination by the agent for extraordinary and serious reason) because of the death of the principal. Successors of the principal must thus pay the agreed price to the agent if the prospective contract is concluded within a reasonable period after the mandate relationship has terminated and if the prospective contract can be mainly attributed to the agent's efforts.

Illustration 3
Paul lives in Spain but has an apartment for rent in Amsterdam. Paul has decided to stay in Spain for good, and therefore he asks the real estate agent to put the apartment up for sale. The agent will receive a commission once the apartment is sold. Despite the crisis in the housing market, the agent has found a potential buyer for the apartment, Rutger. Rutger has visited the apartment and is negotiating with the bank to get a mortgage. During this period, Paul has a heart attack and dies before the sales contract is

concluded. His daughter Alicia, who inherits the apartment, terminates the mandate relationship with the real estate agent in Amsterdam for extraordinary and serious reason. Two months later Rutger confirms that he has obtained the finances to pay for the purchase of the apartment and subsequently concludes the sales contract with Alicia.

Under Article 2:102 paragraph (5) (Price), Alicia is obliged to pay to the real estate agent the commission that Paul had agreed with the agent because the conclusion of the sales contract takes place within a reasonable time after the mandate relationship was terminated and can be mainly attributed to the efforts of the agent.

C. Relationship with the Principles of European Law and the Draft Common Frame of Reference

This Article mirrors Article IV.D. – 7:102 DCFR (Death of the principal).

D. Character of the rule

This Article constitutes a default rule from which the parties may derogate. This provision therefore permits the parties to create a power of mandate which endures after the principal's death, but also to agree that the mandate contract terminates automatically in the event of the principal's death.

E. Remedies

As this Article does not create any obligations between the parties but merely rights for the agent and the successors of the principal to terminate the contract, there are no remedies related to this Article.

Comparative Notes

1. Death of principal

The death of the principal leads to automatic termination of a mandate relationship in most Member States. This is the situation in AUSTRIA, BELGIUM, BULGARIA, ENGLAND, FRANCE, GREECE, HUNGARY, IRELAND, ITALY, MALTA, THE NETHERLANDS, PORTUGAL, SCOTLAND, SLOVAKIA, and SPAIN. This rule is mandatory in THE NETHERLANDS, unless the mandate contract has been agreed in the interest of the agent or a third party.
The systems in which the death of the principal does not lead to automatic termination are DENMARK, ESTONIA, FINLAND, GERMANY, POLAND (unless parties have agreed on termination), SPAIN (for commercial mandate), and SWEDEN. However, in these systems, the circumstances may indicate that the mandate has become pointless with the death of the principal. In those cases, the mandate terminates.

In most countries, termination is effective from the moment the agent knows or should have known about the principal's death. Acts performed by the agent until that moment are valid in AUSTRIA, BELGIUM, BULGARIA, ESTONIA (in the exceptional cases where the mandate ends), FRANCE, GREECE, HUNGARY, ITALY, MALTA, THE NETHERLANDS, POLAND, PORTUGAL, SCOTLAND, SLOVAKIA, and SPAIN. In AUSTRIA and BULGARIA, there is a specific obligation for the heirs of the principal to inform the agent. Termination is effective at the moment of death, even if the agent does not know about it, in ENGLAND and IRELAND. The acts of the agent after the death of the principal do not bind the principal's heirs, but the heirs may ratify them.

In a great majority of countries, despite the main rule being automatic termination, the agent is still required to continue performing the necessary acts to prevent any harm to the interests of the heirs of the principal. The agent is to be remunerated for that. This is the regime in AUSTRIA, BELGIUM, FRANCE, GREECE, HUNGARY, ITALY, MALTA, THE NETHERLANDS, PORTUGAL, SCOTLAND, and SPAIN. This implies that, in effect, the mandate contract continues to exist in so far as is necessary to protect the interests of the heirs, and the contractual arrangements made by the parties also apply to these post-contractual activities of the agent. In GREECE, PORTUGAL, and SCOTLAND, the contract even terminates only once the agent has performed the necessary acts. In some countries, this obligation of the agent is limited: in FRANCE, only urgent issues need to be handled, e.g. regarding the sale of perishable goods; in MALTA, only performances which began before death need to be continued; in SCOTLAND, only contracts where performance had already started before death continue. Such an obligation is not imposed on the agent in BULGARIA, ENGLAND, or IRELAND. In BULGARIA, the heirs of the principal, and not the agent, are deemed responsible for preventing harm to their interests. In ENGLAND and IRELAND, the agent has to stop acting after the death of the principal, but if he does act, the heirs of the principal are not bound by the acts of the agent unless they ratify the contract.

National Notes

1. Death of principal

AUSTRIA: If the principal dies, the mandate is automatically revoked subject to the statutory regulation of CC Article 1022 (except in case of a *mandatum post mortem*). The mandate relationship ends even if the grant of authority was irrevocable. In many cases this is inconvenient, since the power may have been granted, for example by an elderly person, with this very contingency in mind. The case-law therefore permits a person to create, subject to restrictions, a power of mandate which endures after the principal's death (OGH in JBl 1991, 244; SZ 64/13). In cases where the mandate ends with the principal's death, the agent is required to take the necessary measures to prevent impending unnecessary harm to the interest of the principal or the principal's heirs (CC Article 1002; Rummel/Strasser, Article 1002 Rz 21). The agent is liable for failure to take required measures. The agent is reimbursed for the expenses incurred in order to take such measures. According to Article 35 paragraph (1) ZPO solicitors also have to continue to act for such reason. In commercial relations, the mandate is in doubtful cases not automatically terminated with the entrepreneur's death (Art. 8 Nr. 10 of the 4th EVHGB; Comm.C Article 52 paragraph (3)). The mandate survives the principal's incapacity, because the loss of capacity to act (in such a way as to produce legal consequences) is not tantamount to the principal's death (Rummel/Strasser, Article 1020 Rz 28b and Article 1018 Rz 6; OGH in SZ 13/71; 24/244; 26/132; EvBl 1968/60; 1992/76). Previous declarations of intent remain effective, if validly made.

BELGIUM: According to the Belgian CC Article 2003, the authority to represent ends by the death or the incapacity of one of the parties. According to Article 2008 CC, the termination of the authority will only be effective at the moment the agent has taken note or ought to have taken note of the termination. Acts concluded without knowledge of the termination are valid. When the principal dies, the agent is bound to continue running affairs (CC Article 1991 paragraph (2)). More precisely, the agent must finish affairs started before the principal's death if any delay in their accomplishment would be harmful (Wéry, p. 301). This provision is strictly interpreted and does not allow the agent to start new affairs (CFI Liège 2 April 1930, Pas. 1930, III, 86; De Page, p. 456). An agent who breaches this duty is liable to the principal or his heirs.

BULGARIA: The mandate relationship is ended *ipso jure* by death or legal incapacity of the principal as well as dissolution of the principal legal entity (see OCA Article 287); Любен Василев, Облигационно право, p. 28; Меворах/Лиджи/Фархи, III, 163; Голева, Облигационно право II, p. 239). Since the rule of OCA Article 287 is not mandatory, the parties can stipulate otherwise, including *post mortem* mandate (Меворах/Лиджи/Фархи, III, p. 164). Upon termination of the mandate due to death, incapacity or dissolution, the heirs, guardian, trustee or the liquidator of the principal are obliged to immediately notify the agent and undertake the necessary steps to protect his or her interests (OCA Article 291).

DENMARK: According to Article 21 of the Contracts Act the mandate relationship does not end automatically when the principal dies. Special circumstances, e.g. the agent being instructed to buy personal things for the principal, may lead to termination. Even if such special circumstances are present, a contract concluded by the agent is still effective vis-à-vis the estate of the deceased principal if the third party did not know about the death. When the principal is placed under curatorship, a third party with whom the agent concludes a contract does not acquire a better legal position than if the contract had been concluded by the principal personally (cf. Article 22 of the Contract Act). Under circumstances where the mandate relationship ends, e.g. the death of the principal, the agent is obliged (and entitled) to take the necessary steps to protect the interests of the heirs until the estate of the deceased principal takes over (Article 24 of the Contract Act). An agent who takes such measures can claim a price for the activities and compensation for the expenses incurred. These rules apply even if the contract for representation was irrevocable.

ENGLAND: Following the case of *Wallace v Cook* ((1804) 5 Esp 117), the death of the principal automatically terminates the agent's actual authority, unless the authority is irrevocable. The agent cannot therefore sue for remuneration or indemnity for acts performed after the death of the principal even if the agent was not aware of the principal's death *(Pool v Pool* (1889) 58 LJP 67; *Campanari v Woodburn* (1854) 15 CB 400). Once the agent becomes aware of the death of the principal, the agent must stop acting and wait for new instructions from the estate of the principal. If the agent nonetheless continues to act, the agent will be liable for any losses the actions cause the principal's estate *(Re Overweg, Haas v Durant* [1900] 1 Ch 209). When the agent does an act on behalf of the principal after the latter's death, the estate is not bound by the act *(Blades v Free* (1829) 9 B & C167) but the estate may choose to be bound through ratification of the act. However, the estate is not bound to pay the agent's remuneration unless the estate also ratifies the contract with the agent. In such a case, the estate must however pay a reasonable sum to the agent for services rendered *(Campanari v Woodburn* (1801) 6 Ves 266; *Lunghi v Sinclair* [1966] WAR 172). Insanity of the principal terminates the agent's actual authority and any transaction that the agent performs is void for lack of authority *(Drew v Nunn* (1879) 4 QBD 661)).

ESTONIA: As a default rule, it is presumed that the contract for services, governing the mandate, will not cease to have effect with the death of the principal (LOAEst Article 632 paragraph (1)). In exceptional cases where the mandate relationship expires upon the death of the principal, LOAEst Article 632 paragraph (3) provides that the contract is nevertheless deemed to be in force until such time as the service provider (the agent) becomes aware or ought to become aware of the death of the principal. The placing of the principal under curatorship has no influence on the contract for services that governs the mandate (and to the authority of the agent in an external relationship).

FINLAND: A mandate contract including the right to conclude contracts on behalf of the principal continues to have effect after the principal has died, unless circumstances show otherwise (e.g. the prospective contract is pointless after the death of the principal). In other cases the mandate relationship usually ends when the principal dies, unless otherwise agreed between the agent and the estate of the deceased. If the principal is placed under curatorship, the agent is only entitled to take actions which the principal can still undertake personally. The authorisation ends at the time of the placement under the curatorship (ContrA Articles 21-22 and Comm.C Article 18:8).

FRANCE: In principle, the mandate will terminate with the death or incapacity of the principal (CC Article 2003), even if it includes an irrevocability clause, subject to the existence of any mandate *post mortem*, which is accepted in French law, provided it does not affect mandatory rules of succession. See also the recent law which deals with 'the mandate with posthumous effect' (Law no. 2006-728 of 23 June 2006, Chapter 6). The CC does not give any further indication on the exact moment when the mandate will terminate, but Article 2008 provides that all that the agent may have accomplished in ignorance of the death of the principal will be valid. French case law is not, however, very clear on the question of proof of the agent's ignorance of the event. In the event of the death of the principal, the agent is required to complete the mandate if there is an urgent need to do so (CC Article 1991 paragraph (2)), e.g. if the agent was to sell perishable goods. In the event of the principal being declared incapable, the CC does not provide for any similar rule.

GERMANY: A mandate relationship does not normally end automatically when the principal dies or is incapacitated. In cases of doubt, the contract continues to have effect after the principal dies or loses the legal ability to act (CC Article 672). If the contract does cease to have effect, the moment when this happens depends on the interpretation of the contract. The agent is required to continue to carry out the representation if discontinuation of activity would result in danger (CC Article 672).

GREECE: A mandate relationship is dissolved by the death of the principal or of the agent as well as by the placing under curatorship or the bankruptcy of either, except if there is an agreement to the contrary (CC Article 726). The relationship ends when the agent becomes aware of the incident by any means, including information received from the heirs in case of death of the principal or from the principal or the curator in case of curatorship (Georgiadis/Stathopoulos/Karasis, Article 726-727 GCC no. 2). In case of curatorship the mandate ends automatically. In case of an agreement on continuance after the death of the principal, the prospective contract is concluded in the name of the heirs of the principal who can revoke the power of representation under the same conditions as the principal could have done if alive (Supreme Court decision no. 564/1989, EllDni 1990, 624). If there is no agreement on continuance the principal's heirs are obliged to reimburse the expenses that the agent incurred for the performance of the mandate until the death of the agent (Supreme Court decision no. 57/1995, NoV 1996, 1239). According to CC Article 727, in the cases provided for in CC Article 726, 'if the dissolution of the mandate imperils the interests of the principal the agent his heir or his legal agent shall be under an obligation to continue the conduct of the affairs that were entrusted to him until such time as the principal or his heir or his curator is in a position to take appropriate steps.' From that rule it is implied that if the dissolution of the mandate due to the death or curatorship of the principal imperils the principal's interests the dissolution of the contract is suspended temporarily until the principal or curator or heir is able to take care of the affairs of the principal. Failure of the agent to continue temporarily the conduct of the affairs can give rise to a claim for damages. An agent who continues temporarily the conduct of the affairs of the principal is entitled to reimbursement of all the expenses incurred for such temporary performance. An irrevocable mandate does not end automatically when the principal dies, but continues between the heir of the principal and the agent (Georgiadis/Stathopoulos/Karasis, Article 726-727 GCC no. 2). The contract of mandate cannot be continued between the curator of the principal and the agent.

HUNGARY: According to CC Article 481, '[t]he contract shall be terminated even if the agency has not been fulfilled, if either party dies or, if a legal person is dissolved, unless the dissolved legal person has a legal successor; the principal becomes partially or fully incompetent or if the agent becomes incompetent'. CC Article 482 establishes that '[i]f the agency is terminated for a reason that is inherent in the person of the principal, termination shall take effect on the date on which the agent credibly acquires knowledge of the cause of termination. In the event of cancellation or the principal's death or loss of legal competency, the agent shall take such measures as are necessary to protect the interests of the principal even after the cancellation of the contract as long as the principal or its legal successor is unable to attend to the business at hand'. The agent is liable for damages resulting from non-performance (see CC Articles 310 and 318 paragraph (1)). To the remuneration of the agent and to the reimbursement of his expenses, the general rules apply (see CC Articles 478 paragraphs (1) and (2) and 479). The same rules apply for commission agency (CC Article 513 paragraph (2)).

IRELAND: A contractual agency may be automatically terminated by any event, which frustrates the contract. Thus, it will be terminated if performance becomes impossible, for instance, because of the death of either party. Therefore, the death of the principal automatically terminates the agent's actual authority *(Wallace v Cook* [1804] 5 Esp 117). The agent cannot therefore sue for remuneration or indemnity for acts performed after the death of the principal even if the agent was not aware of the principal's death *(Pool v Pool* [1889] 58 LJP 67). Once the agent becomes aware of the death of the principal, the agent must stop acting as the agent and wait for new instructions from the estate of the principal. An agent who nonetheless continues to act will be liable for any losses the actions cause the principal's estate *(Re Overweg, Haas v Durant* [1900] 1 Ch 209). When the agent does an act on behalf of the principal after the principal's death, the estate is not bound by the act *(Blades v Free* [1829] 9 B & C167) but the estate may choose to ratify such an act. However, the estate is not bound to pay the agent's remuneration unless the estate also ratifies the contract with the agent. An irrevocable grant of authority does terminate on the death of the principal.

ITALY: According to the Italian CC Article 1722 paragraph (4) the relationship under a contract for representation ends on the death or loss of capacity of the principal; however, if the representation contract is concluded for the conclusion of contracts pertaining to business activities, if the business continues to run, the relationship does not end automatically, without prejudice to the heirs' right to terminate it. The relationship ends when the agent becomes aware of the death or incapacity. All acts executed by the agent before becoming aware of the event causing the termination are valid and enforceable vis-à-vis the principal or the heirs (CC Article 1729). Special rules apply for representation in court proceedings: the death of the principal represented in court by the attorney only acquires a judicial meaning (i.e. entailing the interruption of the proceedings) when the attorney gives notice of it in the forms prescribed by the law. According to CC Article 1728, the agent has to continue the activity in the principal's or the heirs' account, but only if delaying action would lead to a danger for the represented interests. The agent is then not only required to take specific urgent measures, but to continue the execution of the mandate entirely. In case of failure, the agent is liable for breach of contract. However, it should be stressed that CC Article 1728 is an exception to the general rule stated in CC Article 1722 paragraph (4). An irrevocable representation contract does not end on the death or loss of capacity of the principal (CC Article 1723 paragraph (2)). Consequently, the agent continues to act on behalf of the principal's heirs and successors.

MALTA: CC Article 1886 states that the contract for mandate is terminated when either the principal or the agent die or are interdicted or incapacitated. Although not stated specifically in the law, it is presumed that the contract of mandate ends when the agent knows that principal has died or has been placed under curatorship. When the contract of mandate has been terminated due to the fact that the principal has been placed under curatorship or because the principal has died, the agent is not required to take any particular measures in order to prevent unnecessary harm. However if the contract is terminated due to the death of the principal, the agent is bound to conclude any matter, which he commenced before the death of the principal, delay of which might be prejudicial to the principal (CC Article 1873 paragraph (2)). When there was an irrevocable grant of authority, the death of the principal does not terminate the contract for mandate.

NETHERLANDS: As mandate contracts have a personal nature, the mandate ends after the death of the principal (CC Article 7:422 paragraph (1)(a)), a provision that is mandatory (CC, Article 7:422 paragraph (2) first sentence). In that case, the mandate ends when the agent has knowledge of the principal's death. However, if the mandate is in the interest of the agent or a third party, the parties may stipulate that the death of the principal does not result in the ending of the mandate (CC Article 7:422 paragraph (2). If the mandate contract ends because of the principal's death or guardianship order, the agent is required to do what may be expected in the contracting party's interests, having regard to the specific circumstances (CC Article 7:422 paragraph (3)).

POLAND: The mandate relationship does not end on the principal's death (CC Article 747) or loss of legal capacity (declaration of incapacity by the court). In case of expiration of the mandate contract after the death or declaration of incapacity of the principal, the agent should continue to provide services until the principal's successor or incapacitated principal's legal agent decides otherwise (CC Article 747).

PORTUGAL: The mandate contract ends, according to CC Article 1174, by the death or legal incapacity of the principal or the agent. In such a case, the mandate ends, with prospective effects. However, according to CC Article 1175, if the principal dies or is placed under curatorship, the contract ends when that fact is known by the agent. In addition, it does not end if that would result in detriment to the principal or his inheritors. The successors have a duty to inform the agent of the death or incapacity of the principal and to take the necessary measures (CC Article 1176).

SCOTLAND: As a general rule, the relationship under a contract of representation is terminated by the death of the principal (Erskine, III,3,40; *Pollok v Paterson* 10 Dec 1811 FC at 376, per Lord Meadowbank; *Kennedy v Kennedy* (1843) 6 D 40; *Lord Advocate v Chung* 1995 SC 32). However, there are many exceptions to this rule. Where the agent continues to act in ignorance of the principal's death, the acting may be ratified by the heirs of the principal (Stair, I,12,6; Erskine, III,3,41). The institutional writers Stair and Erskine indicate that the agent should be encouraged to continue acting until receipt of reliable intelligence of the death of the principal (Stair, I,12,6; Erskine, III,3,41); therefore it seems that the mandate relationship does not end until such reliable intelligence has been received by the agent. Furthermore, it seems that an agent may be entitled to continue to carry out the obligations under the contract for representation if informed of the principal's death at a time when a transaction has been begun but not yet completed (Stair, I,12,6; Erskine, III,3,41). It is thought that the agent would be entitled to carry out all necessary work in order to complete the transaction, and would be entitled to remuneration in the normal manner. Where the issue is mental incapacity of the principal, the matter is now regulated by the Adults with Incapacity (Scotland) Act 2000 (asp 4). The Act makes special provision for 'continuing powers of attorney' which can survive such incapacity but which are subject to special safeguards and regulatory mechanisms. Under Article 18 of the Act an ordinary mandate for representation (power of attorney) has no effect during any period when the principal is mentally incapable of dealing with the matters to which the power relates.

SLOVAKIA: The relationship under a contract of representation terminates by the death of the principal, unless it has been stipulated otherwise in the contract (CC Article 33(b) paragraph (1)). If the principal dies, the agent is nevertheless bound to perform any immediately necessary juridical acts to prevent detriment to the rights of the principal. Acts thus performed have the same legal effects as if the representation had continued, unless such acts conflict with the arrangements made by the principal's legal successors or curators (CC Article 33(b) paragraph (6)). The agent is liable for failure to take such measures. If the agent takes the required measures the agent can claim remuneration (if the contract is remunerated) and expenses from the heirs.

SPAIN: According to CC Article 1732 paragraph (2), the death of the principal terminates the mandate relationship. The agent is however obliged to continue performance if otherwise the interests of the successors of the principal would be in danger (CC Article 1718 paragraph (2)). Performance of the agent without being aware of the death of the principal is valid and effective with regard to third parties who have contracted with the agent in good faith (CC Article 1738). The commercial code establishes a different regime for mandates of a commercial nature. The death of the principal in a mandate regulated in the commercial code does not imply the termination of the relationship, although the successors of the principal have the right to revoke it (Comm.C Article 280).

SWEDEN: According to Comm.C Article 18:8 the mandate relationship should end at the death of the principal. However, this rule is considered to be out-of-date and questionable and according to Contracts Act Article 21 the relationship does not end automatically when the principal dies. Only special circumstances may end it. Such circumstances could be that the contract relates to matters which concern the principal personally and which lose their meaning after the death of the principal (see Adlercreutz, p. 206).

Article 7:102: Death of the agent

(1) The death of the agent ends the mandate relationship.
(2) The expenses and any other payments due at the time of death remain payable.

Comments

A. General idea

According to this provision, the death of the agent brings the mandate relationship to an end. This approach implies that it is by virtue of the personal characteristics of the agent that the principal entrusts the agent with the responsibility to carry out actions on the principal's behalf. Accordingly, the relationship ends if the agent cannot comply with the contractual obligations any longer (paragraph (1).

Illustration 1
Paul lives in Spain but has an apartment for rent in Amsterdam. During the last 10 years, his former neighbour and good friend Charo has acted as his agent in Amsterdam and has taken care to find leasers for Paul's apartment. The death of Charo brings the relationship to an end.

B. Obligation to pay remains

The successors of the deceased agent will take the agent's place as creditor of the payment obligation. The provisions under Article 2:102 paragraph (5) (Price) and Article 2:103 (Expenses incurred by agent) apply. The effect of the former is that the price will often be payable if the prospective contract is concluded within a reasonable period after the mandate relationship has ended due to the death of the agent and the conclusion of the prospective contract can be mainly attributed to the performance of the mandate by the agent.

Illustration 2
Paul lives in Spain but has an apartment for rent in Amsterdam. Paul has decided to stay in Spain for good, and therefore he asks his real estate agent to put the apartment up for sale. The agent will receive a commission if the apartment is sold. Despite the crisis in the housing market, the agent has found a potential buyer, Rutger, for the apartment. Rutger has visited the apartment and is negotiating with the bank to get a mortgage. During this period, the agent has a heart attack and dies before the sales contract is concluded. The mandate contract terminates on this ground. Two months later, Rutger confirms that he has obtained the finances to pay for the purchase of the apartment, and he subsequently concludes the sales contract with Paul. Under these Principles, the promised commission remains payable because the sales contract is concluded within a reasonable period after the automatic termination of the mandate relationship resulting from the agent's death and because its conclusion was the result of the efforts of the agent.

C. Contract may provide otherwise

There may be cases where the mandate relationship does not depend on the personal qualities of the agent and where the fact that the agent dies does not by itself mean that the obligations under the contract can no longer be performed. If the agent dies, colleagues or employees can often carry out the performance of the obligations. In such a case, therefore, an automatic ending of the mandate relationship may not be in the interests of any of the parties involved. In such cases, the parties may agree that the death of the agent will not lead to the automatic termination of the mandate contract.

Illustration 3
Paul lives in Spain but has an apartment for rent in Amsterdam. Before leaving the Netherlands, he authorised Tom, a real estate agent, to take care of the lease of his apartment. As Tom's physical condition has been deteriorating for some time, he has included in his standard terms that in the event of his premature death, the performance of existing mandate contracts are to be taken over by his only heir, Tim, who also works at the real estate company. When Tom dies, Tim takes over the performance of the mandate contract regarding the lease of Paul's apartment.

D. Death of the designated person

When it is not the agent himself who dies, but the person who was to perform the contract on behalf of the agent, a different situation exists. In this situation, the contract was not concluded with the deceased person but with his employer. In this case, chances are even higher that the agent has other staff members available to perform the contract. For this reason, automatic termination of the mandate contract is not in the interest of either party to the mandate contract. However, the parties may decide that termination of the contract is nevertheless in their best interests. If they have not agreed to that, Article 6:103 paragraph (3) (Termination by the principal for extraordinary and serious reason) and Article 6:105 paragraph (3) (Termination by the principal for extraordinary and serious reason) enable either party to terminate the mandate contract with immediate effect for extraordinary and serious reason.

Illustration 4
Paul lives in Spain but has an apartment for rent in Amsterdam. Before leaving the Netherlands, he authorised Tom, an agent working for Rots Vast (a real estate company) to take care of the lease of his apartment. When Tom dies, the company names another employee to take care of Paul's affairs. As the second employee is capable of doing so, Paul decides not to terminate the mandate contract.

Illustration 5
Hans is the victim of a traffic accident. He engages Christian, a lawyer specialised in personal injury claims, to claim damages from the tortfeasor. Hans has engaged Christian specifically for his expertise in these cases. In this case, personal performance of the mandate contract by Christian is required by the contract, even though the mandate contract is concluded by the law firm that employs him. When Christian dies, the law firm appoints Martin, a junior associate with little experience in traffic liability cases. Hans decides to take his business elsewhere. Article 6:103 paragraph (3) (Termination by principal for extraordinary and serious reason) allows him to terminate the mandate contract with immediate effect.

E. Relationship with the Principles of European Law and the Draft Common Frame of Reference

This Article mirrors Article IV.D. – 7:103 DCFR (Death of the agent).

F. Character of the rule

This Article constitutes a default rule from which the parties may derogate. This provision therefore permits the parties to create a power of mandate which endures after the agent's death.

G. Remedies

As this Article does not create any obligations between the parties but merely sets out the consequences of the agent's death, there are no remedies related to this Article.

Comparative Notes

1. Mandate relationship ends automatically on death of agent

Death of the agent leads to the automatic termination of the mandate relationship in all Member States. FRANCE is the only country where this rule is mandatory. In other countries, the parties may dispose otherwise.

The moment of effective termination varies in some countries. In some legal systems, this is the moment of death itself. This is the case in AUSTRIA, BELGIUM, and GERMANY. In other legal systems, the relevant moment is when the principal is aware of the occurrence of the death of the agent. This is the case in ESTONIA, FRANCE, GREECE, ITALY, MALTA, and SPAIN. In these countries, the heirs of the agent are obliged to inform the principal about the occurrence of the cause for termination.

Even though the contract terminates, in some countries, the heirs of the agent are required to continue performing the necessary activities to prevent harm to the principal. This is the case in BELGIUM, GERMANY, GREECE, ITALY, MALTA, THE NETHERLANDS, and SPAIN. In AUSTRIA and THE NETHERLANDS, this obligation is also applicable to colleagues of the agent. These activities are provided in exchange for the agreed remuneration.

2. Termination of mandate relationship in case of death of specific person designated
to perform the mandate contract

This is a question that has not been regulated in many Member States, as explicitly indicated in the reports of BULGARIA, DENMARK, FRANCE, ITALY, MALTA, POLAND, SCOTLAND, SLOVAKIA, and SPAIN. However, in some legal systems it has explicitly been provided that the death of the specific person designated to perform the mandate contract leads to the automatic termination of the mandate contract between principal and agent. This appears to be the case in AUSTRIA, BELGIUM, DENMARK, ENGLAND, FINLAND, FRANCE, IRELAND, THE NETHERLANDS, and SWEDEN. This conclusion is reached in some Member States in view of the personal nature of the relation between principal and the designated person. This is the case in ENGLAND, FRANCE, IRELAND, and SWEDEN. In ESTONIA and HUNGARY, this fact is described as a ground for the principal to terminate.

National Notes

1. Mandate relationship ends automatically on death of agent

AUSTRIA: The mandate relationship ends automatically *(ipso jure)* when the agent dies (Austrian CC Article 1022) or becomes bankrupt or is otherwise subjected to rules of insolvency law in so far as the contract for mandate concerns the bankrupt's estate (CC Article 1024; KO Article 26) with the exception of the contract for commission, which is not terminated automatically (HVertrG Article 26, KO Article 26)). If the administrator of the bankrupt's estate insists on the performance of the contract, the principal has a claim for separation and recovery of assets not belonging to the bankrupt's estate (Comm.C Article 383 Straube/Griss) I³, no. 13). If one of the creditors of the commission/commercial agent takes possession of the goods on commission, the principal may bring in an action for recovery of the goods (Comm.C Article 383 Straube/Griss) I³, no. 13). The principal of a commission business is not entitled to exercise the agent's rights towards the third party where the commission agent commits a fundamental non-performance or if prior to the time for performance it is clear that there will be a fundamental non-performance (CC Article 1024 Schwimann/Apathy) V³, no. 1). The contract for mandate does not end if the agent is placed under curatorship, though the agent cannot act for the principal as long as the incapacity renders the agent unable to perform the agency duties (CC Article 1018; CC Article 1018 Rummel/Strasser) I³, no. 5). In case of the agent's death, bankruptcy or insolvency the contractual relationship ends when the incident leading to the end occurs or takes effect. If it ends for such reason, the agent's heirs are not required to take the necessary measures to prevent unnecessary harm to the interest of the principal. In cases where another person exercised a profession or a business with the agent or in the agent's service and was authorised by the principal in doing so (e.g. another lawyer of the same law firm), such other person is required to take the necessary measures to prevent unnecessary harm to the interest of the principal.

BELGIUM: According to the Belgian CC, in Article 2003, the authority to represent ends by the death, the incapacity or the apparent insolvency of one the parties, of which bankruptcy is an example. The mandate relationship probably ends when the incident occurs or takes effect. According to CC Article 2010, the agent's heirs who are aware of the contract for representation are required to notify the agent's death to the principal and to perform in the meantime all urgent and necessary acts, required in the principal's interest by the circumstances (De Page, p. 454; Wéry, p. 297-298).

DENMARK: The contract for representation will end automatically when the agent dies, is placed under curatorship, becomes bankrupt or is otherwise subjected to rules of insolvency.

ENGLAND: The death of the agent automatically ends the authority. The basis for such a rule is the fact that the agency is a personal contract (Farrow v Wilson [1869] LR 4 CP 744). Should there be joint agents, the death of only one of them is sufficient to end the agency relationship (Adams v Buckland [1705] 2 Vern 514). Because of the personal aspect of the contract, there is no possibility for another agent to come in as a substitute of the original dead agent. Insanity of the agent also automatically terminates the actual authority since the agent is no longer capable to represent the principal. Bankruptcy of the agent may end the actual authority, but it is not automatic and will depend upon the terms of the appointment. It may be considered as a frustrating event or a repudiation of the contract depending on the terms in the contract in question (McCall v Australian Meat Co Ltd [1870] 19 WR 188; Hudson v Granger [1821] 5 B&A). In relation to the agent's cessation of business, the rules are less clear: in Triffit Nurseries v Salads Etcetera Ltd [1999] 1 Lloyd's Rep 697, affd [2000] 2 Lloyd's Rep 74, the Court of Appeal held that the appointment of a receiver did not automatically end the authority of the agent (see Longmore J ([1999] 1 Lloyd's Rep 697 at 700) who stated that 'cessation of busines' was an uncertain concept and therefore could not be added to the list of causes of automatic termination.

ESTONIA: As a default rule, it is presumed that the mandate relationship will end with the death of the agent (LOAEst Article 633 paragraph (1)). The same applies in case of bankruptcy, except where there is no connection between the contract and the bankruptcy estate (LOAEst Article 633 paragraph (2)). The contractual relationship will automatically end. The heirs are obliged to inform the principal of the death of the agent (LOAEst Article 634).

FINLAND: The mandate relationship ends automatically when the agent dies and the estate of the deceased does not generally have any specific personal duties towards the principal. The authorisation does not always end automatically when the agent is declared bankrupt. The bankruptcy estate has, in principle, the right to decide whether the activities of the agent are to be continued. However, the principal is usually entitled to terminate the agency due to the bankruptcy. A commercial agency ends automatically on the date when the bankruptcy application was submitted to a court (ACRS Article 24). A curatorship limits the agent's authorisation to those measures the agent is still entitled to take personally.

FRANCE: The death, insolvency or incapacity of the agent would effectively involve automatic termination of the mandate or agency (CC Article 2003; for a merger or takeover of the agent, see Cass.civ. 3eme, 10 November 1998, Bull. civ. 1998 III, no. 212). The rules above apply unless the agency contract contains a clause to the contrary (e.g. Cass.com., 22 May 1967, JCP 1968, II, 15389). CC Article 2010 indicates that in the event of the death of the agent, the heirs must inform the principal of the event, which raises the presumption that the mandate will terminate at that time. The heirs of the agent must also do whatever is in the interest of the principal for the time being. There is no similar rule applicable in the event of incapacity or insolvency of the agent, but it is likely that the mandate will terminate when the principal is informed of the event.

GERMANY: In case of doubt, the mandate ends when the agent dies (CC Article 673). In case of curatorship (if depriving the agent of power to perform juridical acts), this would be considered a case of impossibility of contract performance, thus terminating the agent's obligations (CC Article 275; Palandt/Sprau, Article 673 no. 1). Bankruptcy and insolvency of the agent have no effect on the contract (InsO Articles 115 and 116 *a contrario;* cf. Häuser, in: Münchener Kommentar zum HGB, Article 383 no. 97; Palandt/Sprau, Article 671 no. 5). The moment of death/commencement of curatorship is decisive. According to CC Article 673, the heirs have to continue to perform the obligations under the contract of representation. If this obligation is breached, the heirs are liable for damages according to CC Article 280 paragraph (1) (Palandt/Sprau, Article 673 no. 2).

GREECE: A mandate is dissolved by the death of the agent (except if there is an agreement to the contrary) as well as by the agent's being placed under curatorship or becoming bankrupt (CC Article 726). In the case of curatorship the contract of mandate ends automatically. Both in case of death and curatorship, the contract ends when the principal becomes aware of the incident by any means (Georgiadis/Stathopoulos/Karasis, Article 726-727 GCC no. 2). If the agent becomes bankrupt or is otherwise subjected to rules of insolvency law, the mandate relationship ends automatically from the time of the publication of the decision which declares the insolvency of the agent, irrespective of whether the principal is informed of it (Georgiadis/Stathopoulos/Karasis, Article 726-727 GCC no. 4). If the dissolution of the mandate due to the death or insolvency or curatorship of the agent imperils the interests of the principal the dissolution is suspended temporarily (the agency being continued by the agent's heir or legal agent, if the agent has died) until the principal or the principal's heir or legal agent is able to take care of the principal's affairs (CC Article 727). Failure of the agent or the agent's heir or legal agent to continue temporarily the conduct of the affairs that were entrusted by the principal can establish a claim for damages for any loss caused by such failure. If the agent or the agent's heir or legal agent continues temporarily the conduct of the affairs of the principal there is a right to reimbursement of all expenses incurred.

HUNGARY: If the agent dies or becomes incompetent, the relationship under the contract for representation is terminated (CC Article 481). It does not end automatically when the agent becomes bankrupt or is otherwise subjected to rules of insolvency law, but according to Bankruptcy Act Article 35 paragraph (1), '[a]t the time of the beginning of the liquidation proceedings, all the debts of the economic entity become expired (due)'.

IRELAND: A contractual agency may be automatically terminated by any event, which frustrates the contract. Thus, it will be terminated if performance becomes impossible, for instance, because of the death of either party. Therefore, the death of the agent automatically ends the contract. This is also supported by the fact that the agency is a personal contract *(Farrow v Wilson* [1869] LR 4 CP 744). Insanity of the agent also automatically terminates the actual authority since the agent is no longer capable to represent the principal. An agent's bankruptcy will terminate the agency if it makes the agent unfit to continue to act. Even an an irrevocable grant of authority terminates on the death of the agent.

ITALY: According to the Italian CC Article 1722 paragraph (4), the mandate for representation ends automatically when the agent dies, is placed under curatorship, becomes bankrupt or is otherwise subjected to rules of insolvency law. This happens when the principal is informed of the incident leading to the termination or when the principal becomes anyhow aware of it. According to CC Article 1728 paragraph (2), '[w]hen a mandate is extinguished by the death or supervening incapacity of the agent, if his heirs or the person who represents or assists him have knowledge of the mandate, they shall give prompt notice to the principal and in the meantime shall take the measures which circumstances may require in the interest of the principal'. The heirs or such other persons are required to promptly notify the principal of the agent's death and to take any circumstances which are necessary in the light of the specific circumstances (e.g. urgent activities). They would be liable for failure to take such measures pursuant to CC Article 1728. They do receive payment and/or reimbursement for the expenses they incur in order to take such measures. The mandate ends even if the grant of authority was irrevocable.

MALTA: A mandate contract terminates by the death, the interdiction or the incapacitation, whether general or special, from entering into contracts, the declaration of bankruptcy, or the *cessio bonorum* either of the principal or of the agent. According to CC Article 1886 lit (b), the contract of mandate is terminated when the agent dies, or is placed under curatorship, or if he becomes bankrupt. Although not stated specifically in the law, it is presumed that the contract of mandate ends when the agent/curator inform the principal that he has been placed under curatorship or when the heirs inform the principal that the agent has died, or the contract of mandate is terminated when the declaration of bankruptcy occurs. In the situation when the agent dies, CC Article 1890 states that the agent's heirs must, if they know that he was an agent, give notice thereof to the principal, and attend, in the meantime, to what is required in the interest of the principal, as circumstances may demand.

NETHERLANDS: A mandate relationship ends because of the agent's death, guardianship order, the agent's insolvency or the applicability of debt rescheduling to the agent (CC Article 7:422 paragraph (1) (b)). If the relationship ends because of the agent's death, the heirs may be obliged to do what may be expected in the contracting party's interests, as far as they have knowledge of the succession and the mandate. Such obligation may apply to those who exercised a profession or business with the agent (CC Article 7:422 paragraph (4)).

POLAND: Unless agreed otherwise, the mandate relationship ends on the death or loss of legal capacity of the agent (Polish CC Article 748).

PORTUGAL: A mandate contract ends, according to CC Article 1174, by the death or legal incapacity of the client or the agent. In such a case, the mandate ends, with prospective effects.

SCOTLAND: The death of the agent terminates the agency relationship (Stair, I,12,6; Erskine, III,3,40; Gow, p. 537). This rule reflects the 'personal' nature of the agency relationship (Stair, I,12,6). The incapacity of the agent has the same effect *(Wink v Mortimer* (1849) 11 D 995; Gow, p. 537). Whether the agent's bankruptcy (sequestration) has a similar effect is a more difficult question, and it may be that this is the case only where the agent's solvency is an implied term of the agency contract (Gow, p. 537-8, relying on English authority: *McCall v Australian Meat Co Ltd* (1870) 19 WR 188; *Hudson v Granger* (1821) 5 B&A).

SLOVAKIA: The relationship under a contract for representation ends automatically when the agent dies or is placed under curatorship (in the latter case the contract ends because a person may not act as an agent for another person if the person himself or herself has no capacity to undertake the relevant juridical acts; CC Article 22 paragraph (2). The relationship does not end automatically when the agent becomes bankrupt, but the administrator of the bankruptcy assets may terminate it.

SPAIN: According to CC Article 1732 paragraph (2), the death of the agent ends the mandate relationship. See also Comm.C Article 280. CC Article 1739 states that in this case the successors of the agent must inform the principal of the death of the agent and must act according to what is needed to protect the interests of the principal. According to Lete del Río, this is not possible if the mandate was concluded in view of the personal characteristics of the agent and the successors cannot act as substitutes in the activity (Lete del Río, p. 415).

SWEDEN: A mandate relationship ends automatically on the death of the agent. The estate of the deceased has no other duty than to provide an account of the work performed by the agent prior to his/her death (Comm.C Article 18:8; Bengtsson, p. 156). It is somewhat uncertain whether the mandate relationship ends automatically or not on the bankruptcy of the agent. In case a commissionaire is declared bankrupt, the mandate ends automatically. In other cases, the bankruptcy of the agent may only result in a right for the client to cancel the contract.

No answer received from BULGARIA.

2. Termination of mandate relationship in case of death of specific person designated to perform the mandate contract

AUSTRIA: The mandate relationship ends automatically when the specific person with consideration to whom the authority to represent the principal had been granted dies (CC Article 1020). When this person is placed under curatorship, the contractual relationship does not automatically end, though the agent cannot act for the principal as long as the incapacity precludes performance of the duties (CC Article 1018; CC Article 1018 Rummel/Strasser I³, no. 5).

BELGIUM: The relationship under a contract for representation ends automatically when the specific person with consideration to whom the authority to represent the principal had been granted dies or is placed under curatorship.

BULGARIA: There is no explicit rule regulating the legal effect on the mandate relationship of the death of the specific person designated to perform the contract. The parties are free to stipulate this in the contract.

DENMARK: This situation has not been resolved in Danish legislation or case law. The relationship will probably end automatically when the specific person dies or is placed under curatorship.

ENGLAND: If a specific person has been appointed to represent the principal, then, given the personal nature of the relationship *(Farrow v Wilson* [1869] LR 4 CP 744), it seems that the same rules as in the case of death, incapacitation or bankruptcy of the agent defined above will apply.

ESTONIA: The mandate relationship will not end automatically when the specific person dies or is incapacitated, however the principal will most likely be able to terminate it on 'material grounds' according to LOAEst Article 631.

FINLAND: If the mandate is of highly personal nature, the relationship usually ends when the specific person dies or is placed under curatorship.

FRANCE: No rule has been established by legislation or case law on this point. One can consider that if the event occurs, the agent would have to carry out the mandate personally or find a replacement since the initial mandate would not be affected by this event (academic opinion: see Mallet-Bricout, no. 180). But if the principal has designated the person whom the principal wishes to carry out the mandate, it is likely that the mandate will be treated as having a personal nature and the death or incapacity of the sub-agent or the specific person will bring the agency to an end. It would obviously be preferable to deal with this specifically in the contract.

GERMANY: Under German law every contract for a continuing obligation can be revoked when there is an 'important ground' for the revocation – a fundamental principle of German law which was developed by the courts and is now expressly laid down in CC Article 314 paragraph (1).

GREECE: In the case of substitution CC Article 726, is analogously applicable (Georgiadis/Stathopoulos/ Karasis, Articles 726-727 GCC no. 6). According to that rule a mandate will be dissolved by the death of the substitute mandatory (except if there is an agreement to the contrary) as well as by the placing under curatorship of such a substitute.

HUNGARY: On the basis of the rule of CC Article 481, the contractual relationship is not terminated if the specific person with consideration to whom the authority to represent the principal had been granted dies or is placed under curatorship (and not one of the parties to the contract). However, the principal is entitled to terminate the relationship with immediate effect at any time (CC Article 483). The same rules apply for the commission agency (CC Article 513 paragraph (2)).

IRELAND: Because of the highly personal nature of an agency contract, the death of the specific person identified to perform the obligations under the contract will terminate the agency.

ITALY: The Italian Civil Code does not contain any specific rules with regard to this matter, but a systematic interpretation of the provisions governing mandate, in light of the fact that in case of sub-representation the original agent remains liable for the performance of the contractual obligations vis-à-vis the principal, leads to the conclusion that the relationship under the contract for representation does not end automatically if the third party dies.

MALTA: There are no specific rules on this issue.

NETHERLANDS: According to CC Article 7:409 paragraph (1), a contract for professional services in general ends on the death of the specific person designated to perform the obligations under it. That person's heirs may be obliged to do what may be expected in the contracting party's interests, as far as they have knowledge of the succession and the mandate. Such obligation may apply to those who exercised a profession or business with the agent (CC Article 7:409 paragraph (2)). There is no such provision that applies specifically to mandate contracts.

POLAND: Polish law does not provide a straight answer to this question. Since the mandate relationship ends on the death of the agent it may be assumed that it also ends on the death of the person who was chosen to perform the obligations under the contract. Additionally, it is a general rule that if contractual obligations can no longer be performed, the contractual relation ends (art. 475 CC).

SCOTLAND: There appears to be no specific consideration in the authorities of this situation, namely where the specific person who was to perform the obligations under the agency contract dies (distinguishing this situation from that where the agent as contracting party dies). It is likely that a court would seek to ascertain whether the 'agent' was in fact the contracting party or the person designated to carry out the work. Only where the specific person was truly the 'agent' would the agency relationship terminate on that person's death. In other situations, the agency relationship would continue. It is likely that the same approach would be adopted in a case of incapacity, i.e. only where the party incapacitated could truly be described as the agent would the relationship terminate.

SLOVAKIA: This issue is not specifically regulated, but on the basis of general provisions on impossibility of performance, it can be argued that when the specifically designated person dies or is placed under curatorship, performance of the contractual obligations is not possible and thus the relationship terminates (CC Article 575). This provision, however, is not applicable to commercial relations; in these cases it is always possible for both parties to terminate the relationship.

SPAIN: Spanish law does not contain any provision as to the present question. But the analogy of the death of the agent is persuasive when the conditions of the dead person were decisive for giving the authority.

SWEDEN: The death of the agent usually ends the mandate relationship. The reason for this is that the mandate contract usually and to a high degree based on personal trust. However, in case the task is assigned to a certain company and the client does not attach great importance to the particular person representing the company, the mandate contract does not end automatically on the death of the person carrying out the tasks. The principal is granted a right to cancel the contract (Bengtsson, p. 156).

No answer received from PORTUGAL

Annexes

Table of Abbreviations

A	Agent
ABA	Austrian Brokerage Act (Maklergesetz)
ABGB	See CC
AC	Law Reports, Appeal Cases (House of Lords) (cited by year, book, and page)
ACRS	Act of Commercial Agents and Salesmen (Finland)
affd	affirmed
AG	Aktiengesellschaft (joint-stock company, plc)
AK	See CC
All ER	All England Law Reports (cited by year, book, and page).
AnwBl.	Österreichisches Anwaltsblatt (cited by year and page)
Arch. civ.	Archivio civile (cited by year and page)
ArchN	Archeion Nomologicas (cited by volume, year, and page)
Arm	Armenopoulos miniaia nomiki epitheorisis (cited by year and page)
Arr. Cass.	Arresten van het Hof van Cassatie (cited by year and number)
Art.	Article(s)
BAA	Bar Association Act (Bulgaria)
B&A	Barnewall and Alderson's Reports, King's Bench (cited by volume and page)
B&C	Barnewall & Cresswell's King's Bench Reports (cited by year, volume and page)
Beav	Beaven's Rolls Court Reports (cited by year, volume and page
BGB	See CC
BGH	Bundesgerichtshof (Federal Supreme Court in civil cases, Germany)
BGHZ	Amtliche Sammlung der Entscheidungen des Bundesgerichtshofes in Zivilsachen (cited by volume and page)
Bing	Bingham's Reports, Common Pleas (cited by year, volume and page)
BMJ	Boletim do Ministério da Justiça (cited by volume, year, and page)
Bull. civ.	Bulletin des arrêts de la Cour de Cassation rendus en matière civile (cited by year, book, and number)
BVerfG	Bundesverfassungsgericht (Federal Constitutional Court, Germany)
CA	Commercial Agency Act (Bulgaria)
CA	Corte d'Appello (Italy); Cour d'Appel (Belgium, France); Court of Appeal (England); Efeteion (Greece); High Court (Ireland) (in its appellate jurisdiction); Gerechtshof (The Netherlands); Megyei birosàg (Hungary); Relação (Portugal)
Camp	Campbell's King's Bench Reports (cited by year, volume and page)
Cass.	Hof van Cassatie/Cour de Cassation (Belgium); Cour de Cassation (France), Corte Suprema di Cassazione (Italy)
Cass.civ.	Cour de cassation, Chambre Civile (France)
Cass.com.	Cour de cassation, Chambre Commerciale et financière (France)
Cass.req.	Cour de cassation, Chambre des Requêtes (abolished) (France)
CB	Common Bench Reports

CBNS	Common Bench Reports, New Series
CC	Civil Code
	Allgemeines Bürgerliches Gesetzbuch (ABGB, Austria), Astikos Kodikas (AK, Greece), Bürgerliches Gesetzbuch (BGB, Germany), Burgerlijk Wetboek (BW, Belgium, The Netherlands), Civil Code (CC, Malta), Code Civil (Cc, Belgium, France, Luxembourg), Codice Civile (Cc, Italy), Código Civil (CC, Portugal, Spain), Kodeks cywilny (KC, Poland), Obcansky zakonik (OZ, Slovakia), Polgári Törvényköny (Ptk, Hungary)
CCC	Contrats, concurrence et consommation
CCP	Code of Civil Procedure
CE	Constitución Española (Constitution, Spain)
cf.	confer
CFI	Court of First Instance, general jurisdiction
Ch	Law Reports, Chancery (cited by year, volume and page)
Ch D	The Law Reports, Chancery Division (cited by year, volume and page; see L.R.)
CJ	Colectânea de Jurisprudência (cited by year, volume and page); Lord Chief Justice (England)
CJ/ST	Colectânea de Jurisprudência, Acórdãos do Supremo Tribunal de Justiça (cited by year, volume, and page)
Comm	Commercial (Court) Comment(s)
Comm.C	Commercial Code
	Código comercial (Portugal); Código de comercio (Spain); Code de commerce (France); Handelsgesetzbuch (Austria, Germany); Wetboek van Koophandel/Code de commerce (Belgium); Handelsbalken (Sweden)
Corriere giur.	Corriere giuridico (cited by year and page)
CP	Common Pleas Cases (cited by year, volume and page; see L.R.)
C & P	Carrington and Payne's Reports
D.	Recueil de jurisprudence Dalloz (cited by year, part, and page)
DL	Decreto legge, decreto ley (Decree-law, Greece, Italy, Portugal)
DLR	Dominion Law Reports (cited by year, volume and page)
DNotZ	Deutsche Notarzeitschrift (cited by year and page)
D.P.	Recueil périodique et critique mensuel Dalloz (cited by year, part, and page)
East	East's Term Reports, King's Bench (cited by year, volume and page)
EC	European Community
ECJ	European Court of Justice (Luxembourg)
ecolex	Fachzeitschrift für Wirtschaftsrecht (cited by year and page)
ed.	edition, editor(s)
EEN	Ephimeris Ellinon Nomikon (cited by volume, year, and page)
e.g.	exempli gratia (for example)
EGLR	Estates Gazette Law Reports (cited by year, volume and page)
EllDni	Elliniki Dikeosini (cited by volume, year, and page)
ER	English Reports (cited by volume and page)
Esp	Espinasse's King's Bench Reports) (cited by year, volume and page)

et al.	et alii (and others)
etc.	et cetera
EvBl	Evidenzblatt der Rechtsmittelentscheidungen (at present included in the Österreichische Juristenzeitung ; (cited by year and page)
EVHGB	Einführungsverordnung zum Handelsgesetzbuch (Introductory Act to the Commercial Code, Austria)
f(f)	following page(s)
F&F	Foster & Finlason's Nisi Prius Reports (cited by year, volume and page)
FC	Fraser's Session Cases, 5th Series
FmL	Swedish Estate Agents Act
Foro it.	Il Foro italiano: raccolta di giurisprudenza civile, commerciale, penale, amministrativa (cited by year, book, and column)
Foro it.Mass.	Massimario del Foro italiano (cited by volume, year, number, and column)
GesRZ	Der Gesellschafter (cited by year and page)
Giur.it.	Giurisprudenza italiana (cited by year, part, and if necessary, section and column)
GmbH	Gesellschaft mit beschränkter Haftung (private company limited by shares)
GmbHG	Gesetz über Gesellschaften mit beschränkter Haftung (Austria)
GPCCA	General Part of the Civil Code Act (Estonia)
HaL	Commercial Agency Act (Sweden)
HD	Redogörelser och meddelanden angående högsta domstolens avgöranden (cited by year, number and page)
HD	Högsta domstolens domar (Supreme Court, Finland)
HGB	See Comm.C
HL	See LR
HR	Hoge Raad (Supreme Court, The Netherlands)
H.TK.	Handelingen Tweede Kamer
HVertrG	Handelsvertretergesetz
i.e.	id est (that is to say)
ILRM	Irish Law Reports Monthly
ILTR	Irish Law Times Reports
ImmZ	Österreichische Immobilien-Zeitung (cited by year and page)
IR	Irish Reports (cited by year and page)
J	Justice
Jac & W	Jacob & Walker's Chancery Reports (cited by year, volume and page)
JBl	Juristische Blätter (cited by year and page)
JCP	Juris-Classeur périodique. La Semaine Juridique
JCP éd. G	Juris-Classeur périodique. La Semaine Juridique, édition générale
JT	Journal des Tribunaux (cited by year and page)

KB	Law Reports. King's Bench Division (cited by year, book and page)
KO	Konkursordnung (Bankruptcy Act, Austria)
KommL	Swedish Act regarding Factors
L	Law; Loi (France); Lag (Finland, Sweden)
LC	Lord Chancellor (UK)
lit.	litera
LJ	Lord Justice (Court of Appeal judge, UK)
	Law Journal Reports, London. Various series: LJOS (Old series); LJP (New Series, Privy Council); LJKB (King's Bench)
Lloyd's Rep	Lloyd's Law Reports (cited by volume, year and page)
LOAEst	Estonian Law of Obligations Act
LR	Law Reports. Publications of the Incorporated Council of Law Reporting
Ltd	Limited (limited company)
Macn&G	Macnaghten & Gordon's Chancery Reports (cited by year, book and page)
Miet	Mietrechtliche Entscheidungen (cited by volume and number)
MR	Master of the Rolls (Member and President of the Court of Appeal, UK)
M & W	Meeson and Welsby's Reports, Exchequer (cited by year, volume and page)
NJ	Nederlandse jurisprudentie (cited by year and number)
NJW	Neue Juristische Wochenschrift (cited by year and page)
	Nieuw Juridisch Weekblad (cited by year and page)
no(s).	number(s); margin number(s)
NZ	Österreichische Notariats-Zeitung (cited by year and page)
ÖBA	Österreichisches Bankarchiv (cited by year and page)
OCA	Obligations and Contracts Act (Nulgaria)
OGH	Oberster Gerichtshof (Supreme Court, Austria)
OJ	Official Journal of the European Communities/European Community/ European Union (cited by issue, number, date and page)
P	Principal
p.	Page(s); paragraph(s)
Pand. B.	Pandectes belges
Parl. Gesch.	Parlementaire geschiedenis
Parl. St. Kamer	Parlamentaire Stukken Kamer
Pas.	Pasicrisie belge; Recueil général de la jurisprudence des cours et tribunaux de Belgique (cited by year, book and page)
PECL	Principles of European Contract Law
PEL	Principles of European Law
PEL Ben.Int.	Principles of European Law – Benevolent Intervention in Another's Affairs
PEL CAFDC	Principles of European Law – Commercial Agency, Franchising and Distribution Contracts
PEL SC	Principles of European Law – Service Contracts

PEL Unj.Enr.	Principles of European Law – Unjustified Enrichment
plc	public limited company
PPr	Polymeles Protodikio (Multi-member first instance court, Greece)
QB	Law Reports, Queen's Bench Division (cited by year, book, and page)
QBD	Queen's Bench Division (cited by year, book and page); see L.R.
R	Rettie's Session Cases
RATG	Rechtsanwaltstarifgesetz (Law on Attorney Fees, Austria)
RCJB	Revue critique de jurisprudence belge (cited by year and page)
RdW	Österreichisches Recht der Wirtschaft (cited by year and page)
REstateAA	Real Estate Agent Act (Finland)
ref.	reference
Res.Jur.Imm.	Res Jura Immobilia (cited by year and number)
RG	Reichsgericht (Supreme Court of the German Reich, Germany)
RGAR	Révue générale des assurances et des responsabilités (cited by year and number)
RGEN	Receuil Général de l'Enregistrement et du Notariat (cited by year and page)
RGZ	Amtliche Sammlung der Entscheidungen des Reichsgerichtes in Zivilsachen (cited by volume and page)
RHA	Rechtspraak van de Haven van Antwerpen (cited by year and page)
RLJ	Revista de Legislação e Jurisprudência (cited by volume, year and page)
RTD civ.	Revue trimestrielle de droit civil; see Rev.trim.dr.civ.
RW	Rechtskundig Weekblad (cited by year and page)
RZ	Österreichische Richterzeitung (cited by year and page)
S	Shaw's Session Cases, First Series
S	Sub-agent
S.	Receuil (Dalloz-) Sirey; see D.
SC	Session Cases. New Series. Cases decided in the Court of Session, and also in the Court of Justiciary (J.C.) and the House of Lords (H.L.) (cited by year and page)
Scot CS	Approved judgment of the Court of Session. Scotland
SI	Statutory Instrument
Sim	Simon's Vice Chancellor's Court (cited by year, volume and page)
SLR	Scottish Law Reporter (1865-1925)
SLT	Scotts Law Times (cited by volume, year and page)
STJ	Supremo Tribunal da Justiça (Supreme Court, Portugal)
STS	Sentencia del Tribunal Supremo (decision of the Supreme Court, Portugal and Spain)
SZ	Entscheidungen des österreichischen Obersten Gerichtshofs in Zivilsachen (cited by volume, number, and page)
TBH	Tijdschrift voor Belgisch handelsrecht/Revue de droit commercial belge (cited by year and page)
TLR	Annual Digest of the Times Law Reports (cited by volume, year and page)
T. not.	Tijdschrift voor notarissen (cited by year and page)
TPR	Tijdschrift voor Privaatrecht (cited by year and page)

v.	versus
Vern	Vernon's Chancery Reports
vol(s)	Volume(s)
WBl	Wirtschaftsrechtliche Blätter (cited by year and page)
WLR	Weekly Law Reports (containing decisions in the House of Lords, the Privy Council, the Supreme Court of Judicature, Assize Courts; cited by year, book and page)
WM	Wertpapier-Mitteilungen, Zeitschrift für Wirtschafts- und Bankrecht (cited by year and page)
WR	Weekly Reporter
X	Other or third party
ZBl.	Zentralblatt für die juristische Praxis (cited by year and page)
ZfRV	Zeitschrift für Rechtsvergleichung (cited by year and page)
ZPO	Zivilprozeßordnung (Code of civil procedure, Austria and Germany)

Table of legislation, cases and literature

Austria

Legislation

4. EVHGB
article 8   Art. 3:201 Note 1; Art. 7:101 Note 1

CC
article 879	Art. 2:102 Note 3; Art. 5:102 Note 2
articles 918 ff	Art. 6:101 Note 4
articles 1002 ff	Art. 1:101 Note 1, 2; Article 1:104 Note 1; Art. 2:102 Note 1; Art. 3:301 Note 1
article 1002	Art. 1:101 Note 2; Art. 3:401 Note 1
article 1004	Art. 1:101 Note 4; Article 2:102 Note 1
article 1006	Art. 1:101 Note 5
article 1009	Art. 3:102 Note 1; Art. 3:201 Note 1; Art. 4:101 Note 2
article 1010	Art. 3:302 Note 1; Art. 3:302 Note 1, 3
article 1011	Art. 3:301 Note 1
article 1013	Art. 3:102 Note 1
article 1014	Art. 2:103 Note 1, 5, 6
article 1018	Art. 6:103 Note 6; Art. 7:102 Note 1
article 1020	Art. 1:105 Note 1; Art. 6:101 Note 2, 3, 4; Art. 6:102 Note 1, 2; Art. 6:103 Note 1, 2
article 1021	Art. 6:104 Note 1, 2; Art. 6:105 Note 1
article 1022	Art. 6:101 Note 4
article 1024	Art. 6:103 Note 7, 9; Art. 7:102 Note 1
article 1025	Art. 6:104 Note 1, 2; Art. 6:105 Note 1
articles 1027-1029	Art. 1:101 Note 1
article 1033	Art. 1:101 Note 1
article 1299	Art. 3:103 Note 1
article 1336	Art. 2:102 Note 3
article 1447	Art. 6:101 Note 4

Comm.C
article 56	Art. 1:101 Note 1
article 345	Art. 2:102 Note 1; Art. 5:101 Note 1
article 347	Art. 3:102 Note 1; Art. 3:103 Note 1
article 354	Art. 2:102 Note 1
articles 373-406	Art. 1:101 Note 5
articles 383 ff	Art. 1:101 Note 1, 2, 5
article 383	Art. 2:102 Note 2

Gesetz über Gesellschaften mit beschränkter Haftung (GmbHG)

Handelsvertretergesetz (HVertrG)

Konkursordung (KO)

Maklergesetz (Austrian Broker Act, ABA)

Rechtsanwaltstarifgesetz (RATG)

Zivilprozessordnung (ZPO)

Case law

OGH, *EvBl* 1992/76	Art. 6:103 Note 7; Art. 7:101 Note 1
OGH, *GesRZ* 1980, 95	Art. 1:101 Note 3
OGH, *ImmZ* 1992, 263	Art. 2:103 Note 4
OGH, *JBl* 1991, 244	Art. 7:101 Note 1
OGH, *Miet* 33/117	Art. 2:103 Note 4
OGH, *Miet* 35/10	Art. 2:103 Note 4
OGH, *Miet* 36/73	Art. 2:103 Note 4
OGH, *Miet* 45/44	Art. 2:103 Note 4
OGH, *NZ* 1995, 305	Art. 5:101 Note 2
OGH, *NZ* 1997, 95	Art. 5:101 Note 2
OGH, *ÖBA* 1992, 274	Art. 5:101 Note 2
OGH, *RdW* 1983, 106	Art. 3:102 Note 1
OGH, *RdW* 1986, 39	Art. 5:101 Note 2
OGH, *RdW* 1990, 340	Art. 3:102 Note 1
OGH, *RdW* 1998, 548	Art. 5:101 Note 2
OGH, *SZ* 7/29	Art. 2:103 Note 3
OGH, *SZ* 11/239	Art. 2:103 Note 3
OGH, *SZ* 13/71	Art. 6:103 Note 7; Art. 7:101 Note 1
OGH, *SZ* 24/244	Art. 6:103 Note 7; Art. 7:101 Note 1
OGH, *SZ* 26/132	Art. 6:103 Note 7; Art. 7:101 Note 1
OGH, *SZ* 27/211	Art. 3:401 Note 1
OGH, *SZ* 29/40	Art. 2:103 Note 3
OGH, *SZ* 69/90	Art. 5:101 Note 2
OGH, *WBl* 1987, 212	Art. 3:102 Note 2
OGH, *ZAS* 1985, 170	Art. 4:101, Note 2, 3
OGH, *ZBl* 1928/3	Art. 4:101 Note 1, 2
OGH, *ZfRV* 1997, 246	Art. 5:101 Note 2

Literature

P. Rummel, *Kommentar zum ABGB,* Wien: Manz, 3rd. edition 2000-2004

M. Schwimann, *Praxiskommentar zum ABGB,* Wien: Manz, 2nd. edition 1997

M. Straube, *Kommentar zum HGB* I, Wien: Manz, 3rd. edition, 2003

H. Klang, *Kommentar zum ABGB,* Wien: Österreichische Staatsdruckerei, 2nd. edition, 150 ff

A. Ehrenzweig, *System des österreichischen allgemeinen Privatrechts, Allgemeiner Teil,* Wien: Manz, 1951

P. Jabornegg, *Kommentar zum HGB,* Wien/New York: Springer, 1997

H. Krejci, 'Unternehmensrecht', in: H. Krejci, K. Schmidt, *Vom HGB zum Unternehmergesetz,* Wien: Manz, 2002

H.F. Hügel, G. Viehböck, 'Handelsvertretervertrag', *ecolex* 1993, 204

H. Krejci, *Handelsrecht,* 2nd. edition, Wien: Manz, 2001

H. Koziol, R. Welser, *Grundriss des bürgerliches Recht, Teil I,* Wien, Manz, 13th. edition, 2006

H. Koziol, R. Welser, *Grundriss des bürgerliches Recht, Teil II,* 12th. edition, 2002

S. Dullinger, 'Die gesetzliche Vertretung Minderjähriger bei Rechtsgeschäften', *RZ* 1986, 202

H. Wünsch, 'Zur Lehre vom Selbstkontrahieren im Gesellschaftsrecht', in: H. Wünsch, *Festschrift für H. Hämmerle,* Graz: Leykam, 1972

P. Csoklich, 'Zur Anspruchsberechtigung im Straßengüterverkehr', *RdW* 1997, 188

H. Koziol, *Österreichisches Haftpflichtrecht, Allgemeiner Teil,* Wien: Manz, 3rd. edition, 1997

Belgium

Legislation

CC

article 1134	Art. 2:101 Note 1; Art. 4:103 Note 1
article 1986	Art. 2:102 Note 1
articles 1984-2007	Art. 1:101 Note 1
article 1988	Art. 1:101 Note 4
article 1989	Art. 3:201 Note 1
article 1991	Art. 6:103 Note 7; Art. 7:101 Note 1
article 1992	Art. 1:101 Note 4
article 1993	Art. 3:402 Note 1, 2, 3; Art. 3:403 Note 1
article 1994	Art. 3:302 Note 1
article 1999	Art. 2:103 Note 1, 3
article 2000	Art. 2:103 Note 6
article 2003	Art. 6:103 Note 6, 7, 8, 9; Art. 7:101 Note 1; Art. 7:102 Note 1
article 2004	Art. 1:104 Note 1; Art. 6:102 Note 1; Art. 6:103 Note 1, 2
article 2005	Art. 1:104 Note 1
article 2006	Art. 1:104 Note 1; Art. 6:103 Note 4
article 2007	Art. 6:104 Note 1, 2; Art. 6:105 Note 1
article 2008	Art. 6:103 Note 7; Art. 7:101 Note 1
article 2010	Art. 6:103 Note 6; Art. 7:102 Note 1

Case law

Cass. 17 April 1848, *Pas.* 1848, I, 387, *B.J.* 1848, 758	Art. 1:101 Note 2
Cass. 21 June 1968, *Arr. Cass.* 1968, 1285, *Pas.* 1968, 1212, *RHA* 1972, 309	Art. 3:401 Note 2
Cass. 7 December 1978, *Arr. Cass.* 1978 79, 407, *Pas.* 1979, I, 408	Art. 5:101 Note 1
Cass. 6 March 1980, *Pas.* 1980, I, 832, *RCJB* 1982, 519	Art. 2:102 Note 3
Cass. 24 September 1981, *Pas.* 1982, I, 125	Art. 5:101 Note 1
Cass. 19 September 1985, *RW* 1985-86, 2638	Art. 2:102 Note 3
Cass. 28 June 1993, *Pas.* 1993, I, 628, *RW* 1993-94, 1425	Art. 6:102 Note 1
Cass. 17 September 1993, *Arr. Cass.* 1993, 705, *Pas.* 1993, I, 700, *RW* 1993-94, 752, *RHA* 1994, 23, *TBH* 1994, 533	Art. 3:302 Note 1
Cass. 14 October 2002, *RW* 2003-04, 1297, *NJW* 2002, 462	Art. 2:102 Note 3
Cass. 18 March 2004, *RW* 2004-05, 303	Art. 5:101 Note 1; Art. 5:102 Note 1
CA (labour) Antwerpen 23 November 1989, *Pas.* 1990, II, 110	Art. 1:101 Note 3

CA Brussels 28 January 1820, *Pas.* 1820-21, II, 30	Art. 1:101 Note 2;
	Art. 3:101 Note 2
CA Brussels 17 May 1858, *Pas.* 1859, II, 168, *B.J.* 1859, 406	Art. 3:101 Note 2
CA Brussels 26 June 1986, *Res.Jur.Imm.* 1986, no. 6073	Art. 1:104 Note 2;
	Art. 6:102 Note 4
CA Brussels 1 February 1927, *Pas.* 1927, II, 165	Art. 2:102 Note 6
CA Brussels 22 February 1927, *Pas.* 1928, II, 153	Art. 1:101 Note 2
CA Brussels 10 December 1958, *J.T.* 1959, 225	Art. 1:101 Note 2
CA (commercial) Brussels 1 February 1911, *TBH* 1911, 201	Art. 3:403 Note 1
CA (commercial) Brussels 17 February 1925, *TBH* 1925, 170	Art. 2:102 Note 6
CA (commercial) Brussels 1 February 1911, *TBH* 1911, 201	Art. 3:101 Note 2
CA Gent 18 May 1876, *Pas.* 1876, II, 372	Art. 3:403 Note 2
CA Liège 18 June 1981, *RGEN* 1982, 286	Art. 1:101 Note 3
CA Mons 22 January 1990, *Pas.* 1990, II, 145	Art. 1:101 Note 3
CFI Antwerpen 6 October 1992, *RW* 1994-95, 885	Art. 4:101 Note 3
CFI Brugge 6 July 1874, *B.J.* 1874, 1307	Art. 3:201 Note 1
CFI Liège 2 April 1930, *Pas.* 1930, III, 86	Art. 6:103 Note 7;
	Art. 7:101 Note 1
CFI Mons 9 May 1996, *RGAR* 1998, n° 12.911	Art. 4:101 Note 3

Literature

G. Beltjens, *Encyclopédie du droit commercial belge, volume I,* Namen: Jacques Godenne, 1899; *volume III,* Brussel: Bruylant, 1914

I. Claeys, *Samenhangende overeenkomsten en aansprakelijkheid. De quasi-immuniteit van de uitvoeringsagent herbekeken,* Antwerpen: Intersentia, 2003

E. Dirix, *Obligatoire verhoudingen tussen contractanten en derden,* Antwerpen: Kluwer, 1984

F. Deckers, 'Le mandat', in: *Répertoire notarial,* Brussel: Larcier, 1979

R. Dekkers, *Handboek van burgerlijk recht,* II, Brussel: Bruylant, 1957, 720

Th. Delahaye, Résiliation et résolution unilatérales en droit commercial belge, Brussel: Bruylant, 1984

L. Delwaide and J. Blockx, 'Kroniek van zeerecht (1976-1988)', *TBH* 1989, p. 1038

E. Dirix, *Obligatoire verhoudingen tussen contractanten en derden,* Antwerpen: Kluwer, 1984

E. Dirix, 'De rechtsverhouding tussen principaal, commissionair en derde', in E. Dirix, W. Pintens, P. Senaeve and S. Stijns (eds.), *Liber Amicorum Jacques Herbots,* Antwerpen: Kluwer, 2002

M. Ekelmans, 'Conflits d'intérêts. Contrats d'intermédiaires', in: *Les conflits d'intérêts,* Brussel: Bruylant, 1997

P.-A. Foriers, F. Glansdorff, *Contrats spéciaux,* Brussel: Presses Universitaires de Bruxelles, 2000, volumes I and III

P.-A. Foriers, 'Observations sur l'article 1994 du Code civil et l'action directe née de la substitution', *RCJB* 1981, 476 and 478

P.-A. Foriers, 'Le droit commun des intermédiaires commerciaux: courtiers, commissionnaires, agents', in: B. Glansdorff (ed.), *Les intermédiaires commerciaux,* Brussel: Editions du Jeune Barreau de Bruxelles, 1990

L. Fredericq, *Handboek van Belgisch Handelsrecht,* IV parts, Brussel: Bruylant, 1976-1981

W. Van Gerven, *Bewindsbevoegdheid,* Brussel: Bruylant, 1962, 175

J. H. Herbots, S. Stijns, E. DeGroote, W. Lauwers, I. Samoy, "Overzicht van rechtspraak (1995-1998): Bijzondere Overeenkomsten", *TPR* 2002, 57-923

C. Jassogne (ed.), *Traité pratique de droit commercial,* II, Brussel: Story-Scientia, 1992, 636

A. Kluyskens, *Beginselen van burgerlijk recht,* IV, *De contracten,* Antwerpen: Standaard, 1952

F. Laurent, *Principes de droit civil français,* 33 parts, Brussel: Bruylant, 1878

Pandectes belges, Inventaire général du droit belge à la fin du XIX siècle, Brussel: Larcier, 1886-1910

C. Paulus, R. Boes, 'Lastgeving', in: *Algemene Praktische Rechtsverzameling,* Gent: Story-Scientia, 1978

I. Samoy, *Middellijke vertegenwoordiging,* Antwerpen: Intersentia, 2005

B. Tilleman, 'Lastgeving', in: *Algemene Praktische Rechtsverzameling,* Deurne: Kluwer, 1997

H. de Page, *Traité élémentaire de droit civil belge,* V, Brussel: Bruylant, 1975

A. Poncet, *Du prête-nom,* Paris: A. Chevalier-Maresco & Cie éditeurs, 1901

L. Simont, 'Le problème de la représentation dans le contrat de commission sur marchandises', *TBH* 1956, p. 133

M.E. Storme, 'Hoever reikt de regel van de onherroepelijkheid van een lastgeving van gemeenschappelijk belang in het bijzonder bij enkele toepassingen in de notariële praktijk', *T. Not.* 1996, p. 7-19

V. Van Der Perre, A. Lejeune, 'Droit commercial, I, De la commission', in: *Les Novelles,* Brussel: Picard, 1931

J. Van Ryn, J. Heenen, *Principes de droit commercial,* Brussel: Bruylant, 4 parts, 1957-1988

M. Wagemans, 'Le mandat, la commission, le courtage et la filialisation', in: *La distribution commerciale dans tous ses états,* Brussel: Edition du Jeune Barreau de Bruxelles, 1997

P. Wéry, 'Droit des contrats, Le mandat', in: *Répertoire Notarial,* Brussel: Larcier, 2000

Bulgaria

Legislation

Bar Association Act (BAA)

article 26	Art. 6:103 Note 5
article 36	Art. 1:202 Note 1
article 43	Art. 5:102 Note 1, 2
article 50	Art. 3:102 Note 3
article 77	Art. 3:302 Note 2

Commercial Agency Act (CA)

articles 21-25	Art. 1:101 Note 5
article 21	Art. 1:101 Note 5
article 22	Art. 1:101 Note 5
articles 26-31	Art. 1:101 Note 5
article 26	Art. 1:101 Note 5
article 29	Art. 5:102 Note 1
articles 32-48	Art. 1:101 Note 4, 5
article 32	Art. 1:101 Note 5
article 33	Art. 3:103 Note 1; Art. 3:402 Note 1

article 36	Art. 1:202 Note 1
article 38	Art. 1:202 Note 2
article 39	Art. 1:203 Note 1, 2, 3
article 40	Art. 1:202 Note 6; Art. 6:101 Note 4
article 42	
article 44	Art. 5:102 Note 1
article 46	Art. 3:301 Note 1, 2
article 47	Art. 6:101 Note 3, 4; Art. 6:103 Note 1; Art. 6:104 Note 1, 2
article 307	Art. 1:202 Note 3
articles 348-360	Art. 1:101 Note 2, 4
article 348	Art. 1:101 Note 4; Art. 4:102 Note 2
article 350	Art. 3:103 Note 1; Art. 3:103 Note 1
article 351	Art. 3:201 Note 1
article 356	Art. 1:202 Note 1; Art. 1:203 Note 1, 2
article 358	Art. 5:101 Note 2, 3
article 359	Art. 6:101 Note 3; Art. 6:104 Note 1
article 360	Art. 6:101 Note 4
articles 361-366	Art. 1:101 Note 4
article 361	Art. 1:101 Note 4; Art. 1:202 Note 1; Art. 1:203 Note 1, 2; Art. 3:103 Note 1; Art. 4:102 Note 2
article 607bis	Art. 6:103 Note 9
articles 609-610	Art. 6:103 Note 9

Obligations and Contracts Act (OCA)

article 20bis	Art. 1:202 Note 3; Art. 4:201 Note 1
article 28	Art. 1:202 Note 1
articles 36-43	Art. 1:101 Note 1, 5
article 38	Art. 5:101 Note 1, 2; Art. 5:102 Note 1, 2
article 41	Art. 1:105 Note 1
article 42	Art. 3:202 Note 1
article 63	
article 72	Art. 1:103 Note 2
articles 60-62	Art. 1:102 Note 2
articles 79-94	Art. 3:101 Note 2
article 88	Art. 6:103 Note 5
article 95	Art. 2:101 Note 2; Art. 4:103 Note 1
article 98	Art. 2:101 Note 2; Art. 4:103 Note 1
articles 280-292	Art. 1:101 Note 1, 2, 3, 4, 5; Art. 2:101 Note 1
article 280	Art. 1:101 Note 1
article 281	Art. 3:101 Note 1; Art. 3:103 Note 1
article 282	Art. 3:201 Note 1; Art. 4:104 Note 1
article 283	Art. 3:302 Note 1; Art. 4:104 Note 1
article 284	Art. 3:401 Note 1; Art. 3:402 Note 1, 2, 3
article 285	Art. 1:203 Note 1, 4, 5
article 286	Art. 1:101 Note 4
article 287	Art. 1:103 Note 1, 2; Art. 6:103 Note 7; Art. 7:101 Note 1

article 288	Art. 1:104 Note 1; Art. 1:105 Note 1; Art. 1:202 Note 5; Art. 3:301 Note 2; Art. 6:101 Note 3, 4; Art. 6:102 Note 1; Art. 6:103 Note 1
article 289	Art. 4:201 Note 1; Art. 6:101 Note 3, 5, 6; Art. 6:104 Note 1, 2, 3; Art. 6:105 Note 1, 2, 3
article 290	Art. 1:104 Note 1; Art. 6:101 Note 2
article 291	Art. 6:103 Note 7; Art. 7:101 Note 1

Regulation of Minimum Amounts of the Advocates' Fees

article 17	Art. 1:202 Note 4

Case law

Supreme Court, Judgment no. 942, 7 April 1978, Civil Case 2668/1977, I	Art. 3:302 Note 1
Supreme Court, Judgment No.922, 7 October 1993, Civil Case 2050/1993, V	Art. 1:202 Note 2
Supreme Court, Judgment No. 31, 4 April 1995, Civil Case 2453/1993, V	Art. 1:101 Note 1
Supreme Court, Judgment No. 1511, 6 October 1995, Civil Case 2551/1994, V	Art. 1:101 Note 1
Supreme Court, Judgment No.209, 4 July 1999	Art. 2:101 Note 2

Literature

Божидар Василев, Облигационно право – специална част. Отделни видове договори.,
(1st ed., София 1992)

Любен Василев, Облигационно право. Отделни видове облигационни отношения,
(1st ed., София 1954)

Любен Василев, Гражданско право – обща част, (2nd ed., Варна 1993)

Огнян Герджиков, Коментар на Търговския закон. Книга първа. (1st ed., София 1991)

Поля Голева, Търговско право. Книга първа. (1st ed., София 2001)

Константин Кацаров, Систематичен курс по българско търговско право, (4th ed., София 1990)

Поля Голева, Облигационно право (2nd ed., София 2004)

Иван Апостолов, Облигационно право: част първа. Общо учение за облигацията.
(2nd ed., София 1990)

Александър Кожухаров Облигационно право: общо учение за облигационното отношение.
Книга първа. (2nd ed., София 1992)

Георги Хорозов, Правна характеристика, предмет и значение на отчетните операции при
косвеното представителство, Съвременно право (СП), 1995, 3, p. 37 47

Георги Хорозов, Придобиване на права от свое име за чужда сметка – терминологични и
тълкувателни въпроси, Съвременно право (СП), 1996, 6, p. 26-33

Стоян Ставру, Косвеното представителство, Търговско право (ТП), 2006, p. 325-343

Любен Диков, Неотменимост на пълномощието, Юридически архив (ЮА) 1931, I, p. 1-32

Камелия Касабова, Новото във фигурата на търговския представител след поредната
законодателна интервенция в Търговския закон, Търговско право (ТП), 2006, p. 159-170

Denmark

Legislation

Bankruptcy Act
article 29   Art. 6:103 Note 9
article 30   Art. 6:103 Note 9

Commercial Agents
and Travellers Act   Art. 1:101 Note 1, 4; Art. 6:102 Note 1

Contracts Act
part II   Art. 1:101 Note 1, 3
article 21   Art. 7:101 Note 1
article 22ʼ   Art. 6:103 Note 7; Art. 7:101 Note 1
article 23   Art. 6:103 Note 9
article 24   Art. 7:101 Note 1
article 36   Art. 2:102 Note 3; Art. 6:103 Note 5

Factors Act   Art. 1:101 Note 4; Art. 5:101 Note 2
article 40-45   Art. 5:101 Note 1

Real Estate Agents Act   Art. 2:102 Note 5; Art. 3:301 Note 1
article 15   Art. 5:102 Note 1, 2

England

Legislation

Gaming Act 1892
article 1   Art. 2:103 Note 1

Insolvency Act 1986,
article 284   Art. 6:103 Note 9

Power of Attorney Act 1971
article 4   Art. 1:105 Note 1; Art. 6:102 Note 2
article 5   Art. 6:103 Note 5

Case law
Aberdeen Rly Co v Blaikie Bros (1854) 1 Macq 461   Art. 4:101 Note 3
Adams v Buckland [1705] 2 Vern 514   Art. 7:102 Note 1

Turpin v Bilton (1843) 5 Man & G 455 — Art. 2:101 Note 1; Art. 3:201 Note 1; Art. 4:101 Note 2

Triffit Nurseries v Salads Etcetera Ltd [1999]
1 Lloyd's Rep 697, affd [2000] 2 Lloyd's Rep 74 — Art. 7:102 Note 1

Turner v Goldsmith [1891] 1 QB 544)

UK Mutual Steamship Assurance Association v Nevill (1887) 19 QBD 110 — Art. 1:101 Note 2

Vynior's case (1609) 8 Co Rep 81b — Art. 6:102 Note 1

Volkers v Midland Doherty Ltd (1985) 17 DLR (4th) 343 — Art. 3:201 Note 1; Art. 4:101 Note 2

Wallace v Cook ((1804) 5 Esp 117 — Art. 7:101 Note 1

Way v Latilla [1937] 3 All ER 759 — Art. 2:102 Note 3

White v Jones [1995] 2 AC 207 — Art. 2:101 Note 1

Wilkie v Scottish Aviation Ltd 1956 SC 198 — Art. 2:102 Note 3

Wilson v Short ((1848) 6 Hare 366 — Art. 5:101 Note 3

Withy Robinson (A firm) v Edwards (1985) 277 EGLR 748 — Art. 2:102 Note 3

Woodhouse AC Israel Cocoa Ltd SA v Nigerian
Produce Marketing Co Ltd ([1972] AC 741 — Art. 2:101 Note 1

Yasuda Fire & Marine Insurance Co of Europe Ltd
v Orion Marine Insurance Underwriting Agency Ltd [1995] QB 174 — Art. 3:402 Note 3

Literature

F.M.B. Reynolds, M. Graziadei, W. Bowstead, *Bowstead & Reynolds on agency*,
   London: Sweet & Maxwell, 18th. ed. 2006

Estonia

Legislation

General Part of the Civil Code Act (GPCCA)

article 115–131	Art. 1:101 Note 5
article 125	Art. 6:102 Note 9
article 126	Art. 1:104 Note 1; Art. 4:101 Note 3
article 127	Art. 6:102 Note 9

Law of Obligations Act Estonia (LOAEst)

article 1	Art. 1:101 Note 3
article 23	Art. 4:103 Note 1

Finland

Legislation

Act of Commercial Agents and Salesmen (ACRS)	Art. 1:101 Note 1, 5, 6; Art. 3:103 Note 1
article 8	Art. 2:101 Note 1
article 10	Art. 2:102 Note 1, 2, 5; Art. 2:103 Note 4
article 11	Art. 2:102 Note 1, 2; Art. 2:103 Note 4
article 18	Art. 2:103 Note 2
articles 22-23	Art. 6:101 Note 4; Art. 6:102 Note 1; Art. 6:103 Note 1
article 24	Art. 6:103 Note 8, 9; Art. 7:102 Note 1
article 25	Art. 6:103 Note 1
Attorneys Act	Art. 1:101 Note 1
Code of Judicial Procedure	
Chapter 15	Art. 1:101 Note 1
Comm.C	
Chapter 18	Art. 1:101 Note 1
article 18:1	Art. 3:401 Note 1; Art. 3:402 Note 1, 2, 3
article 18:5	Art. 2:102 Note 1; Art. 2:103 Note 1; Art. 2:103 Note 3
article 18:8	Art. 6:103 Note 7; Art. 7:101 Note 1
article 18:10	Art. 3:201 Note 1
Consumer Protection Act	Art. 1:101 Note 1
Contracts Act	
Chapter 2	Art. 1:101 Note 1
articles 21-22	Art. 6:103 Note 7; Art. 7:101 Note 1
article 36	Art. 2:102 Note 3
Insurance Agent Act (IAAI)	Art. 1:101 Note 1, 6
Real Estate Agent Act (REstateAA)	Art. 1:101 Note 1, 6; Art. 3:103 Note 1
article 6	Art. 6:101 Note 4; Art. 6:102 Note 1
article 8	Art. 5:101 Note 2
article 20	Art. 2:102 Note 1, 4; Art. 5:101 Note 3; Art. 5:103 Note 3
article 21	Art. 2:102 Note 6
Sale of Goods Act	Art. 1:101 Note 1
article 45	Art. 2:102 Note 1

Case law

HD 1999:19	Art. 3:401 Note 1; Art. 4:103 Note 3
HD 1999:80	Art. 3:401 Note 1; Art. 4:103 Note 3
HD 2001:128	Art. 3:401 Note 1; Art. 4:103 Note 3
HD 2007:27	Art. 3:401 Note 1; Art. 4:103 Note 3

Literature

M. Hemmo, *Sopimusoikeus* I, Helsinki: Talentum, second edition, 2003

M. Hemmo, *Sopimus ja delikti,* 1998

O. Norros, *Vastuu sopimusketjussa,* dissertation Helsinki, 2007

T. M. Kivimäki, M. Ylöstalo, P. E. von Bonsdorff, *Lärobok i Finlands civilrätt,*
   Vammala: Juridiska Studentfakultetens Expedition, 1961

France

Legislation

CC

article 1596	Art. 5:101 Note 1, 2
articles 1779-1799	Art. 1:101 Note 6
articles 1984-2007	Art. 1:101 Note 1, 4
article 1986	Art. 1:101 Note 4
article 1987	Art. 1:101 Note 5
article 1988	Art. 1:101 Note 5
article 1989	Art. 3:201 Note 1
article 1991	Art. 6:103 Note 7; Art. 7:101 Note 1
article 1992	Art. 1:101 Note 4; Art. 4:102 Note 1, 2
article 1993	Art. 3:401 Note 1; Art. 3:402 Note 2, 3; Art. 3:403 Note 1
article 1994	Art. 3:302 Note 1, 2, 3, 4
article 1998	Art. 3:201 Note 2
article 1999	Art. 2:102 Note 2, 5, 6; Art. 2:103 Note 1, 2, 3; Art. 3:101 Note 2
article 2000	Art. 2:103 Note 6
article 2001	Art. 2:103 Note 4
article 2003	Art. 1:103 Note 1; Art. 1:104 Note 2; Art. 6:103 Note 4, 5, 6, 7, 8, 9; Art. 7:101 Note 1; Art. 7:102 Note 1
article 2004	Art. 1:104 Note 1; Art. 4:101 Note 4; Art. 6:101 Note 1; Art. 6:102 Note 1; Art. 6:103 Note 1
article 2005	Art. 1:104 Note 1; Art. 6:101 Note 1
article 2006	Art. 1:104 Note 1, 2; Art. 6:101 Note 1; Art. 6:102 Note 1; Art. 6:103 Note 4
article 2007	Art. 4:101 Note 3; Art. 4:201 Note 2; Art. 6:104 Note 1, 2
article 2008	Art. 6:103 Note 7; Art. 7:101 Note 1
article 2010	Art. 6:103 Note 6, 8; Art. 7:102 Note 1

Comm.C

article L. 131-7	Art. 5:101 Note 1, 2
articles L. 132-1 ff	Art. 1:101 Note 2
articles L. 134-1 ff	Art. 1:101 Note 1
article L. 134-1	Art. 1:101 Note 6
article L.134-4	Art. 2:101 Note 1
article L.134-5	Art. 2:102 Note 1

Insurance Code

articles L. 520-1 ff	Art. 1:101 Note 1
article L. 530-1	Art. 3:102 Note 3

Law of 2 January 1970

article 5	Art. 1:101 Note 6
article 6	Art. 2:102 Note 1

Law of 2 July 1970

	Art. 1:101 Note 1
article 3-3°	Art. 3:102 Note 3

Law of 31 December 1971

	Art. 1:101 Note 1
article 27	Art. 3:102 Note 3

Law of 25 June 1991

article 1	Art. 1:101 Note 6

Law no. 2006-728 of 23 June 2006

Chapter 6	Art. 7:101 Note 1

Decree of 20 July 1972

article 76	Art. 3:301 Note 2

Decree of 26 December 1971

article 2	Art. 5:102 Note 1, 2

Decree of 27 November 1991

article 155	Art. 5:102 Note 1, 2

Case law

Cass.req., 12 December 1911, D.P. 1913, 1, 129	Art. 2:102 Note 3
Cass.req., 26 November 1928, S. 1929, 1, 94	Art. 5:102 Note 1, 2
Cass.civ., 9 May 1853, D.P. 1853 I, 293	Art. 3:202 Note 1
Cass.civ. 1re, 27 December 1960, Bull. civ. 1960 I, no. 573	Art. 3:302 Note 1
Cass.civ. 1re, 16 June 1970, D. 1971, 261	Art. 1:105 Note 1;
	Art. 6:101 Note 1;
	Art. 6:102 Note 2

Cass.civ. 1re, 8 July 1975, Bull. civ. 1975 I, no. 226	Art. 3:402 Note 3
Cass.civ. 1re, 29 May 1980, Bull. civ. 1980 I, no. 163	Art. 3:302 Note 1
Cass.civ. 1re, 10 February 1981, Bull. civ. 1981 I, no. 50	Art. 2:102 Note 1
Cass.civ. 1re, 11 July 1983, Bull. civ. 1983 I, no. 202	Art. 3:401 Note 1; Art. 3:402 Note 1
Cass.civ. 1re, 2 May 1984, Bull. civ. 1984 I, no. 143	Art. 6:101 Note 4, 5
Cass.civ. 1re, 29 November 1988, Bull. civ. I, no. 341	Art. 5:101 Note 1, 2
Cass.civ. 1re, 17 November 1993, Bull. civ. 1993 I, no. 323	Art. 2:102 Note 6
Cass.civ. 1re, 3 June 1997, no. 95-17111	Art. 3:102 Note 2
Cass.civ. 1re, 13 November 1997, Bull. civ. 1997 I, no. 308	Art. 2:101 Note 2; Art. 4:103 Note 1
Cass.civ. 1re, 13 May 1998, Bull. civ. I, no. 169, RTD civ. 1998, 927	Art. 5:102 Note 1, 2
Cass.civ. 1re, 6 June 1998, Bull. civ. 1998 I, no. 211	Art. 2:102 Note 1
Cass.civ. 1re, 12 December 2000, Bull. civ. I, no. 319	Art. 5:101 Note 1, 2
Cass.civ. 1re, 6 March 2001, Bull. civ. 2001 I, no. 56	Art. 6:101 Note 4, 5
Cass.civ. 1re, 5 February 2002, Bull. civ. 2002 I, no. 40	Art. 1:105 Note 1; Art. 6:101 Note 2; Art. 6:102 Note 2
Cass.civ. 1re, 24 September 2002, CCC, 2003 no. 3	Art. 2:102 Note 3
Cass.civ. 1re, 28 January 2003, Bull. civ. 2003 I, no. 27	Art. 6:101 Note 4, 5; Art. 6:103 Note 1
Cass.civ. 3e, 8 February 1978, Bull. civ. 1978 III, no. 74	Art. 1:101 Note 3
Cass.civ. 3e, 28 February 1984, JCP éd. G 1984, IV, 146	Art. 1:104 Note 1
Cass.civ. 3e, 10 November 1998, Bull. civ. 1998 III, no. 212	Art. 6:103 Note 6, 8; Art. 7:102 Note 1
Cass.com., 5 July 1962, Bull. civ. 1962 III, no. 344	Art. 3:401 Note 1; Art. 3:402 Note 1
Cass.com., 22 May 1967, JCP 1968, II, 15389	Art. 1:101 Note 6; Art. 6:103 Note 6, 8; Art. 7:102 Note 1
Cass.com., 21 December 1981, Bull. civ. 1981 IV, no. 450	Art. 6:101 Note 4
Cass.com., 22 May 1991, RTD civ. 1992 p. 86	Art. 1:101 Note 6
CA Paris 8 May 1981, GP 1981, 2, 801	Art. 5:102 Note 1, 2
CA Versailles, 11 February 1993, JCP éd. G 1993, IV, 1262	Art. 3:102 Note 2

Literature

A. Bénabent, *Droit civil, Les contrats spéciaux civils et commerciaux,*
    Paris: Domat-Montchrestien, 7th ed. 2006

F. Collart-Dutilleul, Ph. Delebecque, *Droit civil, Contrats civils et commerciaux,*
    Paris: Précis Dalloz, 7th ed. 2004

J. Huet, Traité de droit civil, *Les principaux contrats spéciaux,* Paris: LGDJ, 2nd ed. 2001

Ph. Malaurie, L. Aynès, P.-Y. Gautier, *Droit civil, Les contrats spéciaux,* Paris: Defrénois, 3rd ed. 2007

B. Mallet-Bricout, *La substitution de mandataire,* Paris: Panthéon-Assas, 2000

Ph. Pétel, *Les obligations du mandataire,* Paris: Litec, Bibl. droit privé n° 20, 1988

Germany

Legislation

CC

article 168	Art. 1:105 Note 1; Art. 6:101 Note 2
article 181	Art. 5:101 Note 1, 2; Art. 5:102 Note 1, 2
article 259	Art. 3:402 Note 3
article 275	Art. 6:103 Note 3, 6; Art. 6:105 Note 3; Art. 7:102 Note 1
article 276	Art. 3:103 Note 1
article 280	Art. 1:101 Note 5; Art. 3:101 Note 2; Art. 3:102 Note 2;
	Art. 3:401 Note 1; Art. 6:103 Note 6; Art. 7:102 Note 1
article 307	Art. 3:301 Note 1
article 314	Art. 6:103 Note 1, 2, 5; Art. 6:105 Note 1, 2, 6; Art. 7:102 Note 2
articles 611 ff,	
article 612	Art. 2:102 Note 1
article 614	Art. 2:102 Note 2
article 621	Art. 1:104 Note 1; Art. 6:102 Note 1; Art. 6:104 Note 1
article 625	Art. 1:103 Note 3
article 626	Art. 1:104 Note 1; Art. 6:102 Note 1; Art. 6:103 Note 1, 2;
	Art. 6:104 Note 1; Art. 6:105 Note 1, 2
article 627	Art. 1:104 Note 1; Art. 6:102 Note 1; Art. 6:104 Note 1
articles 631 ff	Art. 1:101 Note 1
article 632	Art. 2:102 Note 1
article 641	Art. 2:102 Note 2
articles 652-655	Art. 1:101 Note 6
article 652	Art. 2:102 Note 5, 6; Art. 2:103 Note 2; Art. 3:301 Note 1, 2
article 654	Art. 5:102 Note 1, 3
article 655	Art. 2:102 Note 3
articles 655a-656	Art. 1:101 Note 6
articles 662-674	Art. 1:101 Note 1; Art. 5:101 Note 1
article 662	Art. 1:101 Note 1, 4, 5; Art. 3:302 Note 2; Art. 4:201 Note 1, 2
articles 663-674	Art. 1:101 Note 1, 4
article 663	Art. 1:101 Note 1
article 664	Art. 1:101 Note 4; Art. 3:302 Note 1
articles 665-670	Art. 1:101 Note 1
article 665	Art. 3:101 Note 1; Art. 3:201 Note 1; Art. 3:302 Note 2;
	Art. 4:101 Note 1, 2; Art. 4:102 Note 1; Art. 4:103 Note 1;
	Art. 4:104 Note 1; Art. 4:201 Note 1
article 666	Art. 3:102 Note 2; Art. 3:401 Note 1; Art. 3:402 Note 1, 2, 3;
	Art. 3:403 Note 1
article 669	Art. 2:103 Note 5
article 670	Art. 2:103 Note 1, 2, 3, 6; Art. 4:103 Note 1; Art. 4:104 Note 1
article 671	Art. 1:101 Note 1, 4; Art. 1:104 Note 1; Art. 3:302 Note 2;
	Art. 4:201 Note 1, 2; Art. 6:101 Note 3, 6; Art. 6:102 Note 1;
	Art. 6:104 Note 1, 2, 3; Art. 6:105 Note 1

articles 672-674	Art. 1:101 Note 1
article 672	Art. 6:103 Note 7; Art. 6:105 Note 3; Art. 7:101 Note 1
article 673	Art. 6:103 Note 6, 8; Art. 7:102 Note 1; Art. 7:102 Note 1
article 675	Art. 1:101 Note 1, 4; Art. 1:103 Note 3; Art. 1:104 Note 1; Art. 2:102 Note 1; Art. 2:103 Note 2, 6; Art. 3:302 Note 1; Art. 4:201 Note 2; Art. 5:101 Note 1, 2; Art. 6:103 Note 1
articles 675a-676h	Art. 1:101 Note 1
article 684	Art. 3:202 Note 1
article 1835	Art. 2:102 Note 1

Comm.C

articles 93-104	Art. 1:101 Note 6
article 93	Art. 1:101 Note 6
articles 383-406	Art. 1:101 Note 2
article 383	Art. 1:101 Note 2
article 384	Art. 3:402 Note 1, 2; Art. 3:403 Note 2
article 400	Art. 5:101 Note 2
article 403	Art. 5:101 Note 3

Federal Act on the Regulation of Attorneys

article 49b	Art. 2:102 Note 4

Insolvenzordnung

articles 103-118	Art. 6:103 Note 9
article 115	Art. 6:103 Note 8, 9; Art. 7:102 Note 1
article 116	Art. 6:103 Note 8, 9; Art. 7:102 Note 1
article 119	Art. 6:103 Note 9

Case law

BVerfG 12 December 2006, NJW 2007, 979	Art. 2:102 Note 4
RG 2 March 1912, RGZ 78, 310	Art. 3:302 Note 1
RG 25 October 1935, RGZ 149, 121	Art. 2:102 Note 1
BGH 10 November 1951, BGHZ 3, 358	Art. 3:301 Note 2
BGH 14 May 1956, BGHZ 20, 364	Art. 3:301 Note 2
BGH 22 January 1964, BGHZ 41, 23	Art. 1:104 Note 2; Art. 6:103 Note 4
BGH 22 June 1966, NJW 1966, 2008	Art. 2:102 Note 6
BGH 13 May 1971, WM 1971, 956	Art. 1:105 Note 1
BGH 18 March 1973, BGHZ 61, 17	Art. 5:102 Note 1
BGH 22 March 1984, WM 1984, 930	Art. 3:403 Note 2
BGH 30 November 1989, BGHZ 109, 260	Art. 3:402 Note 3
BGH 17 December 1992, NJW 1993, 1705	Art. 3:302 Note 1

521

Literature

O. Palandt, *Bürgerliches Gesetzbuch,* München: Beck, 66th ed., 2007

K. Rebmann, F.J. Säcker, R. Rixecker (eds.), *Münchener Kommentar zum Bürgerlichen Gesetzbuch,* München: Beck, 4th ed., 2005

K. Schmidt (ed.), *Münchener Kommentar zum Handelsgesetzbuch,* München: Beck, 2004

Greece

Legislation

CC

article 722	Art. 2:103 Note 1, 2, 3, 4; Art. 5:101 Note 3
article 723	Art. 2:103 Note 6
article 724	Art. 1:105 Note 1; Art. 6:102 Note 1
article 725	Art. 6:104 Note 1
article 726	Art. 6:103 Note 7, 8, 9; Art. 7:101 Note 1; Art. 7:102 Note 2
article 727	Art. 6:103 Note 5, 6, 7, 8; Art. 7:101 Note 1
article 2007	Art. 6:105 Note 1

Code of Attorneys,
legislative decree nr. 3026/1954   Art. 1:101 Note 4

article 170   Art. 6:102 Note 1

Law no. 2251/1994

article 1	Art. 3:301 Note 1
article 2	Art. 3:301 Note 1

Case law

Supreme Court decision no. 58/1975, NoV 1975, 879	Art. 1:101 Note 5
Supreme Court decision no. 197/1983, EEN 1983, 714	Art. 1:105 Note 1
Supreme Court decision no. 296/1983, EEN 1983, 803	Art. 3:302 Note 1
Supreme Court decision no. 1108/1984, EEN 1985, 497	Art. 6:103 Note 5
Supreme Court decision no. 710/1986, EEN 1987, 148	Art. 2:102 Note 1
Supreme Court decision no. 1565/1986, NoV 1987, 1044	Art. 2:102 Note 1
Supreme Court decision no. 1/1987, EEN 1987, 783	Art. 6:102 Note 1
Supreme Court decision no. 752/1987, NoV, 1426	Art. 1:101 Note 1, 2
Supreme Court decision no. 564/1989, EllDni 1990, 624	Art. 7:101 Note 1
Supreme Court decision no. 1157/1991, EllDni 1992, 841	Art. 6:102 Note 5
Supreme Court decision no. 25/1995, EEN 1995, 158	Art. 3:302 Note 3
Supreme Court decision no. 57/1995, NoV 1996, 1239	Art. 7:101 Note 1
Supreme Court decision no. 701/1995, EEN 1996, 601	Art. 2:102 Note 4
Supreme Court decision no. 752/2003, NoV 2004, 238	
Supreme Court decision no. 206/2004, NoV 2004, 1744	Art. 2:102 Note 3
CA Athens decision no. 3790/1985, EllDni 1985, 943	Art. 2:102 Note 3
CA Athens decision no. 10148/1987, EllDni 1988, 353	Art. 4:101 Note 2
CA Athens decision no. 12756/1987, EllDni 1989, 1195	
CA Athens decision no. 12896/1988, NoV 1989, 1226	Art. 3:301 Note 2
CA Athens decision no. 8183/1989, EllDni 1991, 210	Art. 2:103 Note 1
CA Athens decision no. 9826/1989, EllDni 1991, 1631	Art. 1:101 Note 1, 2
CA Athens decision no. 1193/1992, Arm.: 1992, 625	Art. 2:103 Note 6
CA Patra decision no. 235/1993, Achaiki Nomologia 1994, 110	Art. 3:302 Note 1
CA Pireos decision nr. 278/1988, NoV 1989, 1451	Art. 4:102 Note 2
CA Pireos decision no. 855/1993, EllDni 1994, 1708	Art. 2:102 Note 4
CA Thessaloniki decision no. 1381/1979, EllDni 1981, 353	Art. 6:103 Note 5
CA Thessaloniki decision no. 2977/1989, EllDni 1991, 1345	Art. 5:101 Note 2
CA Thessaloniki decision no. 2880/2002, Arm 2003, 1423	Art. 2:102 Note 3

CFI Athens decision no. 4029/1982, EllDni 1984, 848	Art. 2:102 Note 5;
	Art. 3:301 Note 1
CFI Athens decision no. 16004/1983, EllDni 1984, 1603	Art. 2:102 Note 3
CFI Chalkida decision no. 563/2002, NoV 2003, 1271	Art. 2:103 Note 1
CFI Pireos decision no. 607/1985, ArchN 1985, 328	Art. 3:402 Note 2
CFI Thessaloniki decision no. 280/1984, EllDni 1985, 758	Art. 6:103 Note 5;
	Art. 6:104 Note 1

Literature

A. Georgiadis, M. Stathopoulos (ed.), Civil Code Commentary, Volumes I-X, Athens, 2nd ed. 1978-2007
K.D. Kerameus, P.J. Kozyris (eds.), *Introduction to Greek law,* Deventer/Boston: Kluwer 2nd ed., 1993
V. Vathrakokilis, *Detailed interpretation & jurisprudence of the Civil Code, volume I,*
    Athens/Komotini: Sakkoulas Publishers, 1989

Hungary

Legislation

Act XXII of 1992 on the
Code of Labour   Art. 1:101 Note 1

Act XI of 1998 on Attorneys
article 10   Art. 3:102 Note 3

Bankruptcy Act
article 35   Art. 6:103 Note 8, 9; Art. 7:102 Note 1

CC

article 4	Art. 3:401 Note 1; Art. 3:402 Note 1
article 201	Art. 2:102 Note 3
article 205	Art. 2:101 Note 1
article 207	Art. 3:301 Note 1, 2
articles 219-225	Art. 1:101 Note 1
article 221	Art. 3:101 Note 2; Art. 3:201 Note 1; Art. 5:101 Note 1, 2, 3;
	Art. 5:102 Note 1, 2
article 222	Art. 4:102 Note 2; Art. 6:103 Note 5
article 223	Art. 1:105 Note 1
article 241	Art. 2:102 Note 3
article 277	Art. 2:101 Note 1, 2; Art. 2:103 Note 3; Art. 3:101 Note 2;
	Art. 3:102 Note 2; Art. 3:103 Note 1; Art. 3:401 Note 1;
	Art. 3:402 Note 1; Art. 5:101 Note 1, 2; Art. 5:102 Note 1, 2

Case law

Ireland

Legislation

Case law

Aberdeen Rly Co v Blaikie Bros [1854] 1 Macq 461	Art. 5:101 Note 1
Alpha Trading v Dunshaw-Patten [1981] QB 290	Art. 2:102 Note 2
Armstrong v Jackson [1917] 2 KB 822	Art. 5:101 Note 1
Bentall, Horsley and Baldry v Vicary [1931] 1 KB 253	Art. 2:102 Note 5; Art. 3:301 Note 2
Blackburn v Scholes [1810] 2 Camp 341	Art. 1:103 Note 1
Blades v Free [1829] 9 B & C167	Art. 7:101 Note 1
Brodie Marshall & Co v Sharer [1988] 19 EG 129	Art. 2:102 Note 5; Art. 3:301 Note 2
Calico Printers' Association v Barclays Bank Ltd (1931) 145 LT 51	Art. 3:302 Note 1
Carroll Group Distributors v G & JF Burke [1990] ILRM 285	Art. 3:102 Note 1
Chaudrhy v Prabakhar [1988] 3 All ER 718	Art. 1:101 Note 4; Art. 3:103 Note 1
Clarke Boyce v Mauot ([1994] 1 AC 428	Art. 5:102 Note 2
Cusack v Bothwell (1943) 77 ILTR 18	Art. 2:102 Note 2
Daniels v Heskin [1954] IR 73	Art. 3:103 Note 1
De Bussche v Alt (1878) 8 Ch D 286	Art. 3:302 Note 1, 3
European Asian Bank AG v Punjab & Sind Bank [1983] 2 All ER 508	Art. 2:101 Note 1; Art. 4:102 Note 1, 2; Art. 4:103 Note 1, 2; Art. 4:104 Note 1
Farrow v Wilson [1869] LR 4 CP 744	Art. 7:102 Note 1
French & Co v Leston Shipping Co Ltd [1922] 1 AC 451	Art. 2:102 Note 2
Gibbon v Pease [1905] 1 KB 810	Art. 3:402 Note 3
Gibson v Jeyes [1801] 6 Ves 266	Art. 5:101 Note 2
Gray v Haig (1855) 20 Beav 219	Art. 3:402 Note 3
Hawtayne v Bourne (1841) 7 M & W595	Art. 3:201 Note 1
Henderson v Merrett [1995] 2 AC 145	Art. 5:102 Note 1, 2
Ireland v Livingstone (1872) LR 5 HL 395	Art. 2:101 Note 1, 2; Art. 4:102 Note 1, 2; Art. 4:103 Note 1, 2; Art. 4:104 Note 1
Judd v Donegal Tweed Co Ltd (1935) 69 ILTR 117	Art. 2:102 Note 2
Keighley Maxsted & Co v Durant [1901] AC 240	Art. 1:101 Note 2
Kelly v Cooper [1993] AC 205	Art. 5:102 Note 1, 2
Lockwood v Abbey (1845) 14 Sim 437	Art. 3:302 Note 1
Luxor (Eastbourne) Ltd v Cooper [1941] AC 108	Art. 2:102 Note 2
McPherson v Watt [1877] 3 App Cas 254	Art. 5:101 Note 1, 2
Millar, Son & Co v Radford (1903) 19TLR 575	Art. 2:102 Note 2
Miller v Beale (1879) 27 WR 403	Art. 2:102 Note 1
Murphy, Buckley & Keogh Ltd v Pye (Ire) Ltd [1971] IR 57	Art. 2:102 Note 5; Art. 3:301 Note 1, 2
North & South Trust Co v Berkeley [1971] 1 WLR 470	Art. 5:101 Note 2
O'Donovan v Cork County Council [1967] IR 173	Art. 3:103 Note 1
Pearse v Green (1819) 1 Jac & W 135	Art. 3:402 Note 3

Pool v Pool [1889] 58 LJP 67	Art. 7:101 Note 1
Re Overweg, Haas v Durant [1900] 1 Ch 209	Art. 7:101 Note 1
Re Parker (1882) 21 Ch D 408	Art. 2:103 Note 1
Rhodes v Fielder, Jones and Harrison (1919) 89 LJKB 15	Art. 2:103 Note 1
Robinson v Mollett [1874] LR 7	Art. 5:101 Note 3
Roche v Peilow [1986] ILRM 189	Art. 3:103 Note 1
Said v Butt [1920] 3 KB 497	Art. 1:101 Note 2
Stokes & Quirke Ltd v Clohessy [1957] IR 84	Art. 2:102 Note 2
Surrey Breakdown Ltd v Knight [1999] RTR 84	Art. 3:201 Note 1
The Choko Star [1989] 2 Lloyd's Rep 42	Art. 3:201 Note 1
Wallace v Cook [1804] 5 Esp 117	Art. 7:101 Note 1
Wilson v Short [1848] 6 Hare 366	Art. 5:101 Note 3
Woodhouse AC Israel Cocoa Ltd SA v Nigerian Produce Marketing Co Ltd [1972] AC 741	Art. 2:101 Note 1; Art. 4:102 Note 1, 2; Art. 4:103 Note 1, 2; Art. 4:104 Note 1
Yasuda Fire and Marine Insurance Co of Europe Ltd v Orion Marine Insurance Underwriting Agency Ltd [1995] QB 174	Art. 3:402 Note 3

Literature

F.M.B. Reynolds, M. Graziadei, W. Bowstead, Bowstead & Reynolds on agency, London: Sweet & Maxwell, 18th. ed. 2006

Italy

Legislation

CC

article 1175	Art. 2:101 Note 1
article 1218	Art. 1:105 Note 1; Art. 4:101 Note 4
article 1337	Art. 2:101 Note 1
article 1338	Art. 2:101 Note 1
articles 1388 ff	Art. 1:101 Note 1
article 1392	Art. 1:101 Note 3
article 1395	Art. 5:101 Note 1, 2
articles 1703 ff	Art. 1:101 Note 1
article 1705	Art. 1:101 Note 2
article 1707	Art. 1:101 Note 2
article 1708	Art. 1:101 Note 5
article 1709	Art. 1:101 Note 4; Art. 2:102 Note 3

Code of Civil Produre (CCP)

Insolvency Law

Case law

Literature

M. Stolfi, Della mediazione, Comm. Scialoja-Branca, Bologna/Roma, 1996/1967

Malta

Legislation

Architecture and Civil Engineering Professionals Act

CC

article 1887	Art. 1:104 Note 1, 2; Art. 6:101 Note 3; Art. 6:102 Note 1, 4
article 1889	Art. 6:101 Note 5, 6; Art. 6:105 Note 1
article 1890	Art. 6:102 Note 6; Art. 7:102 Note 1

Case law

Comm. Court 27 April 1882, Perini noe. vs Laferla	Art. 3:103 Note 1; Art. 3:201 Note 1
Comm. Court 30 July 1901, Balbi vs Hare noe.	Art. 3:402 Note 1
Comm. Court 12 November 1934, Salomone vs Mifsud Speranza et noe.	Art. 1:104 Note 1; Art. 6:101 Note 4
CA, Salvatore Debono vs. Giuseppe Farrugia et.	Art. 1:101 Note 1
CA 12 December 1919, Ciantar et. noe vs Demarco	Art. 2:102 Note 5; Art. 3:301 Note 2
CA (Civil) 29 October 1869, Messina vs Mamo et.	Art. 1:105 Note 1
CA (Civil) 16 June 1909, Portelli vs Neechamel	Art. 6:105 Note 1
CA (Civil) 14 December 1925, Prof. Tonna Barthet noe. vs Izzo	Art. 3:401 Note 1
CA (Civil) 11 March 1935, Cassar vs Cutajar	Art. 3:201 Note 1
CA (Civil) 30 May 1958, La Rosa noe. vs Galea	Art. 3:201 Note 1
CA (Civil Inferior) 19 August 1890, Azzopardi vs Galdies et.	Art. 3:201 Note 1
CA (Commercial) 13 October 1862, Semini vs Caruana	Art. 3:402 Note 3
CA (Commercial) 11 March 1910, Vassallo noe. vs Griscti	Art. 3:103 Note 1
CA (Commercial) 14 May 1923, Scicluna vs Chircop et.	Art. 3:201 Note 1
CA (Commercial) 7 March 1932, Vella Zarb vs Caruana et. noe.	Art. 2:102 Note 5, 6; Art. 3:301 Note 2
CA (Commercial) 8 June 1936, Anastasi et. vs. Guillamier et.	Art. 1:104 Note 1
CFI (Civil) 14 February 1883, Busuttil vs Busuttil	Art. 6:105 Note 1
CFI (Civil) 17 March 1936, Zammit vs Dr. Magri	Art. 3:302 Note 3
CFI (Civil) 30 October 1936, Rev. Gauci et. vs Hon. Galizia	Art. 3:201 Note 1
CFI (Civil) 4 November 1957, Dr. Moore noe. vs Architect Falzon et.	Art. 2:103 Note 6

Literature

G. Baudry-Lacantinerie, *Traité de droit civil,* Paris, 1905

The Netherlands

Legislation

CC

article 3:74	Art. 6:103 Note 5
article 3:296	Art. 4:103 Note 1
article 6:74	Art. 3:101 Note 2; Art. 4:103 Note 1

article 6:76	Art. 3:302 Note 1; Art. 4:103 Note 1
article 6:119	Art. 2:103 Note 4
article 6:119a	Art. 2:103 Note 4
article 6:127	Art. 5:101 Note 3
articles 6:198-202	Art. 3:201 Note 1
article 6:201	Art. 3:201 Note 1
article 6:248	Art. 3:201 Note 1; Art. 4:103 Note 1, 2; Art. 4:104 Note 1
article 6:258	Art. 2:102 Note 3
article 6:262	Art. 5:101 Note 3
article 6:265	Art. 4:103 Note 1
articles 7:400-413	Art. 1:101 Note 1, 3
article 7:401	Art. 3:101 Note 1; Art. 3:102 Note 1; Art. 3:103 Note 1; Art. 4:101 Note 3; Art. 4:102 Note 1; Art. 4:103 Note 1, 2; Art. 4:104 Note 1
article 7:402	Art. 3:102 Note 1; Art. 3:103 Note 1; Art. 4:101 Note 1, 2, 3, 4; Art. 4:201 Note 1; Art. 6:101 Note 3; Art. 6:104 Note 2; Art. 6:105 Note 1,2, 3
article 7:403	Art. 3:102 Note 1, 2; Art. 3:103 Note 1; Art. 3:401 Note 1; Art. 3:402 Note 1, 2, 3; Art. 3:403 Note 1
article 7:404	Art. 3:302 Note 1, 2, 3
article 7:405	Art. 1:101 Note 4; Art. 2:102 Note 1; Art. 4:201 Note 2
article 7:406	Art. 2:103 Note 1, 2, 6
article 7:408	Art. 1:103 Note 1; Art. 1:104 Note 1; Art. 4:201 Note 1; Art. 6:101 Note 3; Art. 6:102 Note 1; Art. 6:103 Note 1; Art. 6:104 Note 1, 2, 3; Art. 6:105 Note 1, 2
article 7:409	Art. 7:102 Note 2
article 7:411	Art. 1:103 Note 1; Art. 2:102 Note 5, 6; Art. 4:201 Note 2; Art. 6:101 Note 4, 6; Art. 6:103 Note 1
articles 7:414-424	Art. 1:101 Note 1
article 7:414	Art. 1:101 Note 1
article 7:416	Art. 5:101 Note 1, 2, 3
article 7:417	Art. 5:102 Note 1, 2, 3
article 7:420	Art. 3:403 Note 2
article 7:421	Art. 3:403 Note 2
article 7:422	Art. 1:104 Note 1; Art. 6:101 Note 2, 3, Art. 6.102 Note 1, 2, Art. 6:103 Note 1, 5, 6, 7, 8, 9; Art. 7:101 Note 1; Art. 7:102 Note 1
article 7:423	Art. 1:105 Note 1; Art. 3:301 Note 2
articles 425-427	Art. 1:101 Note 6
article 7:426	Art. 2:102 Note 4

Case law

HR 11 March 1977, NJ 1977, 521 (Kribbenbijter)	Art. 4:102 Note 2
HR 17 November 1978, NJ 1979, 96 (Slavenburg's Bank/Jurgens)	Art. 1:104 Note 1
HR 29 September 1989, NJ 1990, 307	Art. 6:101 Note 2

HR 23 May 2003, NJ 2003, 518 (Graan Management B.V./
PeHa Holding c.s.)   Art. 2:102 Note 4
HR 28 January 2005, NJ 2008, 41 (Van Vulpen/Debetz c.s.)   Art. 2:102 Note 5
CA Leeuwarden 28 December 1994, NJ 1996, 117   Art. 5:102 Note 1
CFI's-Hertogenbosch 3 July 1987, NJ 1988, 550 (GIM/Lucas c.s.)   Art. 1:101 Note 5;
                                                           Art. 1:104 Note 1
CFI Roermond 11 February 1999, NJ 1999, 607   Art. 6:101 Note 2;
                                                           Art. 6:103 Note 5

Literature

K.F. Haak, R. Zwitser, *Opdracht aan hulppersonen. Over logistieke dienstverlening in het vervoer,*
    Kluwer: Deventer, tweede druk 2003
S.C.J.J. Kortmann, *mr C. Asser's, Handleiding tot de beoefening van het Nederlands burgerlijk recht;*
    Vertegenwoordiging en rechtspersoon, Asser-serie deel 2-I, Deventer: Kluwer, 8th ed. 2004
J.M.H.P. van Neer-Van den Broek, Opdracht, in: A.P.A. de Klerk-Leenen, B. Wessels (ed.),
    Bijzondere overeenkomsten, Losbladige uitgave (Groene Serie), Deventer: Kluwer, Titel 7.7 BW
J.H. Nieuwenhuis et al. (ed.), *Tekst & Commentaar Vermogensrecht* Deventer: Kluwer, 7th ed. 2007
W.H.M. Reehuis, E.E. Slob (red.), *Parlementaire geschiedenis van het Nieuwe Burgerlijk Wetboek, Invoering*
    Boeken 3, 5 en 6, Boek 7, Bijzondere overeenkomsten, Titels 1, 7, 9 en 14, Deventer: Kluwer, 1991

Poland

Legislation

Bankruptcy Law
article 102   Art. 6:103 Note 9

CC
articles 95-109   Art. 1:101 Note 1, 3
article 352   Art. 2:102 Note 3
article 355   Art. 3:102 Note 1; Art. 3:103 Note 1; Art. 4:101 Note 3
article 365   Art. 6:104 Note 1
article 471   Art. 3:201 Note 1
article 475   Art. 7:102 Note 2
articles 734-750   Art. 1:101 Note 1
article 734   Art. 1:101 Note 1; Art. 4:102 Note 2
article 735   Art. 2:102 Note 1
article 736   Art. 3:302 Note 2
article 737   Art. 3:201 Note 1
article 738   Art. 3:302 Note 1
article 740   Art. 3:401 Note 1; Art. 3:402 Note 2
article 741   Art. 3:101 Note 2

article 742	Art. 2:103 Note 1, 3
article 743	Art. 2:102 Note 2; Art. 2:103 Note 5
article 744	Art. 2:102 Note 2
article 746	Art. 1:105 Note 1; Art. 6:101 Note 4; Art. 6:102 Note 1; Art. 6:103 Note 1
article 747	Art. 6:103 Note 7; Art. 7:101 Note 1
article 748	Art. 6:103 Note 3, 6; Art. 7:102 Note 1
article 750	Art. 1:101 Note 3, 5

Literature

J. Panowicz-Lipska (ed.), *System Prawa Prywatnego. Prawo zobowiązań – część szczegółowa,*
   Tom 8, Warszawa, 2004

Portugal

Legislation

CC

article 227	Art. 3:102 Note 2; Art. 5:101 Note 2
article 232	Art. 1:101 Note 4; Art. 2:102 Note 1
articles 258-269	Art. 1:101 Note 1
article 258	Art. 1:101 Note 3
article 261	Art. 5:101 Note 1, 2; Art. 5:102 Note 1
article 262	Art. 1:101 Note 1, 5; Art. 2:102 Note 1
article 264	Art. 3:302 Note 1, 3
article 265	Art. 1:104 Note 1; Art. 1:105 Note 1
article 268	Art. 3:201 Note 1
article 282	Art. 2:102 Note 3
article 487	Art. 3:103 Note 1
article 763	Art. 3:102 Note 2; Art. 5:101 Note 2
articles 798 ff	Art. 3:101 Note 2
articles 1157 ff	Art. 1:101 Note 1
article 1158	Art. 1:101 Note 4; Art. 2:102 Note 1
article 1159	Art. 1:101 Note 5
article 1161	Art. 3:102 Note 2; Art. 3:103 Note 1; Art. 3:401 Note 1; Art. 3:402 Note 1; Art. 4:101 Note 2, 3
article 1162	Art. 3:201 Note 1; Art. 3:402 Note 1, 2, 3; Art. 4:101 Note 2
article 1165	Art. 3:302 Note 1
article 1167	Art. 2:101 Note 1; Art. 2:102 Note 2; Art. 2:103 Note 1, 2, 5, 6
article 1168	Art. 2:101 Note 2
article 1170	Art. 1:104 Note 1; Art. 1:105 Note 1 Art. 6:105 Note 1, 2
article 1171	Art. 1:104 Note 1; Art. 3:301 Note 1, 2
article 1172	Art. 1:104 Note 1; Art. 3:301 Note 2; Art. 6:102 Note 1

article 1173	Art. 6:103 Note 6, 7
article 1174	Art. 6:103 Note 7; Art. 7:101 Note 1
	Art. 7:102 Note 1
article 1175	Art. 6:103 Note 7; Art. 7:101 Note 1
article 1176	Art. 6:103 Note 7; Art. 7:101 Note 1
article 1178	Art. 3:101 Note 1; Art. 4:102 Note 2
articles 1180-1182	Art. 1:101 Note 2
article 1368 (old)	Art. 6:102 Note 1

Comm.C

article 1	Art. 1:101 Note 4; Art. 2:102 Note 1
articles 266 ff	Art. 1:101 Note 2

Code of Civil Procedure

articles 35 ff	Art. 1:101 Note 3

DL no. 77/99, 16 March 1999   Art. 1:101 Note 6

Lei 15/2005, 26 January 2005

article 84	Art. 4:101 Note 2
article 92	Art. 4:101 Note 2
article 99	Art. 3:102 Note 3
article 101	Art. 2:102 Note 4

Case law

STJ 3 December 1974, BMJ 242, 270	Art. 2:102 Note 1
STJ 7 December 1989, BMJ 392, 444	Art. 1:104 Note 1;
	Art. 3:301 Note 1
STJ 17 June 1998, BMJ 478, 351	Art. 3:102 Note 2
STJ 21 March 1995, CJ/STJ 1995, 1, 130	Art. 5:101 Note 1
STJ 3 March 1998, BMJ 475, 610	Art. 5:101 Note 2
CA Lisbon 26 February 1998, CJ 1998, 1, 133	Art. 3:302 Note 2
RC 11 June 1985, CJ 1985, 3, 92	Art. 5:101 Note 1
RC 16 March 1999, CJ 1999, 2, 21	Art. 3:401 Note 1
RE 27 February 1992, CJ 1992, 1, p. 284	Art. 3:201 Note 1

Literature

A. Menezes Cordeiro, *Da Boa Fé no Direito Civil*, dissertation Lisbon: Almedina, 1984

C.A. Mota Pinto, *Teoria Geral do Direito Civil*, Coimbra: Coimbra Editora, 3rd ed., 1994

M. Pires de Lima, J. De Matos Antunes Varela, *Código Civil Anotado, vol. I* (art. 1-761), Coimbra: Coimbra Editora, 4th ed., 1987

M. Pires de Lima, J. De Matos Antunes Varela, *Código Civil Anotado, vol. II* (art. 762-1250), Coimbra: Coimbra Editora, 3rd ed., 1986

A. Vaz Serra, 'Contrato Consigo Mesmo', *Revista de Legislação e Jurisprudência* 91 (1958), p. 228-231

Scotland

Legislation

Adults with Incapacity (Scotland) Act 2000 (asp 4)

Article 18   Art. 6:103 Note 7; Art. 7:101 Note 1

Code of Conduct for Scottish Solicitors 2002

rule 3   Art. 5:102 Note 2

Commercial Agents (Council Directive) Regulations 1993 (SI 1993/3053)

regulation 4   Art. 2:101 Note 1

Contract (Scotland) Act 1997

article 3   Art. 3:101 Note 2

Estate Agents Act 1979

article 21   Article 5:101 Note 2

Estate Agency Affairs Board Code of Conduct

article 4.1.4   Art. 5:102 Note 2
article 4.2   Art. 5:101 Note 2

National Association of Estate Agents Rules of Conduct

rule 10   Art. 5:102 Note 2

Ombudsman's Code of Practice for Estate Agents

rule 9a   Art. 5:102 Note 2
rule 9b   Art. 5:101 Note 2
rule 9c   Art. 5:101 Note 2
rule 9d   Art. 5:101 Note 2

Solicitors (Scotland) Accounts Rules 2001

rule 6   Art. 2:102 Note 2; Art. 2:103 Note 4

Solicitors (Scotland) Practice Rules 1986

rule 3   Art. 5:102 Note 2

Case law

Alexander Turnbull & Co v Cruikshank and
Fairweather (1905) 7F 101   Art. 3:103 Note 1
Annan v Marshall (1887) 25 SLR 94   Art. 2:103 Note 1, 3
Beattie v Furness-Houlder Insurance (Northern) Ltd 1976 SLT (Notes) 60   Art. 3:103 Note 1;
                                                                  Art. 3:401 Note 1
Black v Cornelius (1879) 6 R 581   Art. 3:302 Note 1

Walker, Donald & Co v Birrell, Stenhouse & Co (1883) 11 R 369)	Art. 1:104 Note 2;
	Art. 6:103 Note 4
Walker, Fraser & Steele v Fraser's Trustees 1910 SC 222	Art. 1:101 Note 6;
	Art. 1:104 Note 2;
	Art. 2:102 Note 6;
	Art. 6:103 Note 4
Walker v Somerville (1837) 16 S 217	Art. 6:102 Note 2
Wink v Mortimer (1849) 11 D 995	Art. 6:103 Note 6;
	Art. 7:102 Note 1

Literature

J. Henderson Begg, Treatise on the law relating to law agents: including the law of costs as between agent and client; with an appendix of relative statutes, acts of sederunt, and all the tables of fees, etc., Edinburgh: Bell & Bradfute, 1873

G.J. Bell, *Commentaries on the Law of Scotland and on the principles of Mercantile Jurisprudence,* 7th ed. edited by J. McLaren, 1870, reprinted with an introduction by R. Black, Edinburgh: Butterworths, 1990 (quoted as: Bell, Commentaries)

G.J. Bell, *Principles of the law of Scotland,* 10th ed. edited by W. Guthrie, 1899, reprinted with an introduction by W.M. Gordon, Edinburgh: Butterworths, 1989 (quoted as: Bell, Principles)

A.C. Black, 'Principal and Agent', in: Green's Encyclopaedia of the Law of Scotland, 2nd ed., volume 9, edited by J. Chisholm, Edinburgh: W. Green & Sons, 1913

J. Dalrymple, 1st Viscount of Stair, *The Institutions of the Law of Scotland,* 10th ed. edited by D.M. Walker, Edinburgh: Butterworths, 1981 (quoted as: Stair)

J. Erskine of Carnock, *An Institute of the Law of Scotland,* 5th ed. edited by J.B. Nicholson, 1871, reprinted with an introduction by W.W. McBryde, Edinburgh, 1989 (quoted as: Erskine)

W.M. Gloag, *The Law of Contract: a Treatise on the Principles of Contract in the Law of Scotland,* 2nd ed., Edinburgh: W. Green & Son, 1929

Goudy, A Treatise on the law of Bankruptcy in Scotland, 4th ed. edited by T.A. Fyfe, Edinburgh: T.&T. Clark, 1914

J.J. Gow, *The Mercantile and Industrial Law of Scotland,* Edinburgh: W. Green, 1964

A. Graham Murray Dunedin, 1st viscount, J.L. Wark, A.C. Black, *Encyclopaedia of the laws of Scotland,* Edinburgh: W. Green & Son, 1926 (quoted as: Graham)

Macgregor: see Broun Smith

A. Paterson, B. Ritchie, *Law, Practice and Conduct for Solicitors,* Edinburgh. Thomson Green, 2006

R. Rennie, Solicitors' Negligence, Edinburgh: Butterworths/Law Society of Scotland, 1997

Th. Broun Smith et al. (ed.), *The Laws of Scotland: Stair Memorial Encyclopaedia Reissue, Agency and Mandate,* Edinburgh: Butterworths and the Law Society of Scotland, 2002 (quoted as: Macgregor)

Th. Broun Smith, *Short Commentary on the law of Scotland,* Edinburgh: W. Green, 1962

Stair: see Dalrymple

Slovak Republic

Legislation

Act on Advocacy   Art. 1:101 Note 1; Art. 3:302 Note 1
article 18   Art. 3:102 Note 1

Act on Securities and Investment Services
article 33   Art. 5:101 Note 2

CC
article 22   Art. 1:101 Note 1; Art. 5:101 Note 1; Art. 6:102 Note 6;
                                          Art. 7:102 Note 1
article 32   Art. 4:102 Note 2
article 33a   Art. 3:302 Note 1
article 33b   Art. 1:103 Note 1; Art. 1:104 Note 1, 2; Art. 1:105 Note 1;
                                          Art. 6:102 Note 1; Art. 6:104 Note 1; Art. 7:101 Note 1
article 522   Art. 4:103 Note 1
article 575   Art. 7:102 Note 2
article 578   Art. 1:103 Note 2
articles 724-732   Art. 1:101 Note 1
article 725   Art. 4:101 Note 2
article 726   Art. 3:302 Note 1
article 727   Art. 3:401 Note 1; Art. 3:402 Note 3
article 728   Art. 2:103 Note 2, 5
article 730   Art. 2:102 Note 1
article 731   Art. 6:101 Note 2
article 732   Art. 1:104 Note 1
articles 733-736   Art. 1:101 Note 1, 2
articles 737-741   Art. 1:101 Note 2
article 774-77   Art. 1:101 Note 6

Comm.C
articles 344 ff   Art. 4:103 Note 1
articles 566-576   Art. 1:101 Note 1
article 566   Art. 2:102 Note 1
article 567   Art. 3:102 Note 1, 2; Art. 3:103 Note 1; Art. 3:401 Note 1;
                                          Art. 4:101 Note 2
article 568   Art. 2:101 Note 1; Art. 3:302 Note 1; Art. 4:102 Note 2
article 571   Art. 2:103 Note 5
article 572   Art. 2:103 Note 2
article 574   Art. 6:102 Note 1, 4
article 575   Art. 6:104 Note 1
articles 577-590   Art. 1:101 Note 2
article 578   Art. 3:103 Note 1
article 579   Art. 3:102 Note 1; Art. 3:401 Note 1; Art. 5:101 Note 1

article 584	Art. 3:402 Note 1
article 587	Art. 2:102 Note 2
article 588	Art. 2:103 Note 2
article 647	Art. 5:102 Note 3
article 651	Art. 2:102 Note 5, 6
articles 652- 672	Art. 1:101 Note 6
article 659	Art. 5:102 Note 3
article 665	Art. 3:301 Note 1
article 671	Art. 2:102 Note 5, 6

Case law

Supreme Court decision, No. 72/2004, legal decisions book 5, 16, 5 Cdo 65/03   Art. 1:101 Note 1

Spain

Legislation

Agency Law

article 19	Art. 2:102 Note 4
article 24	Art. 1:103 Note 2, 3

CC

article 1104	Art. 3:103 Note 1
article 1258	Art. 2:101 Note 1; Art. 6:102 Note 1
article 1259	Art. 3:202 Note 1
article 1459	Art. 5:101 Note 1
articles 1709-1739	Art. 1:101 Note 1
article 1709	Art. 1:101 Note 1, 3
article 1711	Art. 1:101 Note 4; Art. 2:102 Note 1; Art. 4:201 Note 1, 2
article 1712	Art. 1101 Note 5
article 1713	Art. 1101 Note 5
article 1714	Art. 3:101 Note 1; Art. 3:201 Note 1
article 1715	Art. 3:201 Note 1
article 1717	Art. 1:101 Note 1, 2; Art. 3:101 Note 2
article 1718	Art. 3:101 Note 2; Art. 7:101 Note 1
article 1719	Art. 3:103 Note 1; Art. 4:101 Note 1, 2; Art. 4:102 Note 1; Art. 4:103 Note 1; Art. 4:104 Note 1
article 1720	Art. 3:401 Note 1; Art. 3:402 Note 1, 2, 3
article 1721	Art. 3:302 Note 1
article 1725	Art. 4:102 Note 2
article 1726	Art. 1:101 Note 4
article 1727	Art. 3:201 Note 1

STS 20 July 1995	Art. 1:105 Note 1
STS 15 March 1996	Art. 5:101 Note 2
STS 3 March 1998, RJA 1998, 1129	Art. 1:104 Note 1; Art. 6:101 Note 4, 5
STS 30 January 1999, RJA 1999, 331	Art. 1:105 Note 1
STS 12 February 1999	Art. 5:101 Note 2
STS 29 January 2001	Art. 2:102 Not 2
STS 3 September 2007, RJ 2007/4709	Art. 1:105 Note 1

Literature

F. de Castro, 'El autocontrato en el Derecho privado español', *RGLJ* 1927, p. 334 ff

C. Díaz-Regañón García-Alcalá, *La resolución unilateral del contrato de servicios,* Granada: Comares, 2000 (quoted as: Díaz-Regañón)

L. Díez-Picazo, *La representación en el derecho privado,* Madrid: Civitas, 1979 (quoted as: Díez-Picazo)

A. Gordillo Cañas, *Comentario al Código Civil,* Tomo IIMadrid: Ministerio de Justicia, 1993 (quoted as: Gordillo)

F. Hernández Gil, *Comentario al Código Civil,* Libro IV. Obligaciones y Contratos, Tomo 8, Barcelona: Bosch, 2006 (quoted as: Hernández Gil)

J.L. Lacruz Berdejo et al., *Elementos de Derecho Civil vol. II, Derecho de Obligaciones, parte 2, Contratos y cuasicontratos, Delitos y cuasidelitos,* nueva édicion, 2nd ed., Barcelona 2002 (quoted as: Lacruz)

C. Lasarte Alvarez, *Principios de Derecho civil, Contratos, Tomo III, Contratos* 7th ed., Madrid: Marcial Pons, 2003 (quoted as: Lasarte)

J.M. Lete del Río, *Derecho de Obligaciones, volume III, Contratos en particular,* 4h ed., Madrid: tecnos, 2003 (quoted as: Lete del Río)

I. Sierra Gil de la Cuesta et al., *Comentarios del Código Civil,* Barcelona: Bosch, 2006 (quoted as: Sierra Gil de la Cuesta)

Sweden

Legislation

Comm.C

Chapter 18	Art. 1:101 Note 1, 6
article 18:1	Art. 3:103 Note 1; Art. 3:401 Note 1; Art. 3:402 Note 1, 2, 3
article 18:2	Art. 3:101 Note 1
article 18:5	Art. 2:102 Note 1; Art. 2:103 Note 1, 2
article 18:8	Art. 7:101 Note 1; Art. 7:102 Note 1

Literature

A. Adlercreutz, *Avtalsrätt 1*, 9th ed., Lund: Juristförlaget, 1989

B. Bengtsson, *Särskilda avtalstyper1*, 2nd. ed., Stockholm: Norstedt, 1976

K. Grönfors, *Avtalslagen*, 3rd ed., Göteborg, 1995

J. Hellner, *Speciell avtalsrätt II, 1 häftet, Särskilda avtal*, 4th. ed., Stockholm, 2005

J. Hesser, *Immateriella uppdragsavtal*, Stockholm/Lund: Studentlitteratur, 2006

T. Håstad, *Den nya köprätten*, 3rd. ed., Uppsala: Iustus, 1994

C. Ramberg, *Kontraktstyper*, Solna/Stockholm: Norstedts Juridik AB, 2005

C. Ramberg, J. Ramberg, *Allmän avtalsrätt*, 6th ed., Stockholm, 2003

H. Tiberg, R. Dotevall, *Mellanmansrätt*, 9th ed., Göteborg, 2003

Index

(references to Article and then to the relevant Comments; references to Articles in **bold** indicate where the entry is discussed more extensively)